Criminology and the Administration of Criminal Justice

CRIMINOLOGY AND THE ADMINISTRATION OF CRIMINAL JUSTICE

A Bibliography

Leon Radzinowicz and Roger Hood

Mansell 1976

Mansell Information/Publishing Limited
3 Bloomsbury Place London WC1A 2QA England

International Standard Book Number: 0 7201 0522 6

Text set in 9/10pt Monotype Bembo,
printed by letterpress and bound in Great Britain at
The Pitman Press, Bath

British Library Cataloguing in Publication Data
Radzinowicz, Sir Leon
Criminology and the administration of criminal justice: a bibliography.
Index
ISBN 0-7201-0522-6
1. *Title* 2. *Hood, Roger Grahame*
016.364 Z5118.C9
Crime and criminals—Bibliography
Corrections—Bibliography

Contents

Introduction

This bibliography is not the product of conscious design but of our attempts to keep abreast of the spate of criminological literature over the last ten years. It began in 1964 as a modest reading list to meet our teaching requirements in Cambridge and at Columbia Law School. We found it so useful that each summer since then we have set aside time to compare notes, to review the literature and to extend our collection both in the number of items and in the variety of subjects it covers. We have, in other words, never aimed to produce a definitive bibliography with an exhaustive list of publications. Our aim has been more practical, namely to select those most central to our own teaching and research concerns. Yet, while we recognize that any selection is inevitably somewhat arbitrary, we do feel confident that the books, articles, reports and other materials we have listed include those most essential for both students and research workers. Indeed, we venture to believe that if this bibliography has any merit it lies in the element of personal selection and evaluation upon which it is grounded. It has proved an invaluable basis for our work. We shall continue to update and modify it as criminological studies move forward in the hope that it can be of similar practical use to others.

Our title is *Criminology and the Administration of Criminal Justice*. We do not claim that it covers the whole of criminology nor the whole of criminal justice. Nevertheless—as can be seen from the table of contents—we have ranged widely over the field. Our focus on criminology has been predominantly sociological rather than psychiatric and our interest in criminal justice and penology more concerned with issues of policy and the results of research than with day-to-day practical matters. We have not attempted systematically to cover our subjects historically as our interest has here been primarily in crime and its control in the contemporary setting. The references, therefore, relate in the main to the literature of the last twenty years, although here and there we have included a few earlier items which are essential to an understanding of current ideas and developments.

We ceased our search of the literature in August 1974, in order to prepare this bibliography for publication, in the hope that it could be ready in 1975; but it has taken us much longer. We have therefore added to the main body of the material a further selection, bringing the bibliography virtually up to February 1976. We have seized this opportunity to include a few items which earlier slipped through the net or were not available. All these additions form our first *Supplement*, which is to be found at the end of the volume. In due course we plan to make further supplements available.

As it stands now, the bibliography comprehends the following subjects: the state of crime and its interpretation; all the major sociological explanations; the different categories of crime and criminals, including gangs, professional and white collar crime, drugs, drunkenness and some forms of behaviour where the borders of criminality are unclear—abortion, homosexuality, pornography; civil disorder and problems of its control; violence in its cultural and individual aspects; the police—their organization, relations with the community and the exercise of their powers; penal sanctions, their scope, aims and the problems of values inherent in their implementation; mentally abnormal and sex offenders; sentencing practice and ideas for reform; the courts and young offenders; the effectiveness of punishments, including general deterrence; the prison community and standards of penal practice; new ideas for dealing with offenders; parole; the status of prisoners and of offenders in the community; prevention programmes and the prediction of potential delinquency; crime commissions and their recommendations; and last, some international comparative references.

Our search has been mainly concentrated on English language publications. It should also be noted that in some sections, where the subjects spill over into the wider fields of law and the social sciences, we felt it essential to limit ourselves to the references most central to criminology and the administration of justice, and in particular to empirical studies. This applies especially to our lists on the treatment of the mentally ill, plea-bargaining and bail-preventive detention. A few other subjects have not yet been developed as thoroughly as others. They are the newest to be added to the bibliography and deal with abortion, homosexuality, pornography, jury decisions and the background of judges and magistrates. Here we have merely provided the basic points of departure, but a list of specialist bibliographies has been added so that these and other subjects can be followed up in more detail.

We have also been selective in another way. Although we cannot claim to have read every item, almost all have been in our hands. We have therefore been able to select pertinent passages and to draw attention to summaries where these seemed sufficient. Books, articles and reports which deal with a variety of themes have been classified under each relevant heading. As a number of subjects are interrelated, cross-references are provided to those sections of the bibliography where other material may be found.

Under each heading the references have been placed in chronological order to enable the user quickly to see the most recent literature. But we venture to think that this system might also have another use. It shows clearly how, at different periods, themes have emerged to be of central concern to scholars only to recede into the background as new ideas and topics have come to the fore. There are many examples. The bibliography illustrates how the major interests of sociologists have changed over the last fifteen years. Subcultures, gangs and anomie were the subjects of innumerable papers from the late fifties to the late-sixties. Since then attention has focused on deviance, labelling and social interaction—and now new perspectives are being developed. Similarly, the literature on drugs mirrors the enormous concern generated by what appeared as a new social problem in the sixties and the literature on civil disorders flared up and died down in response to the riots themselves. The interest in yet other subjects reflects changing ideological preoccupations and concerns as can be seen in the decline of contributions on prediction and the recent surge of publications on prisoners' rights.

Another advantage of the chronological order is that it will enable the user of the bibliography to add his own items as he goes on to make his own searches and reviews of the literature. To facilitate this we have left a blank space at the end of each section, and similarly in the *Supplement*.

A few other more technical points need to be mentioned. We have used standard abbreviations for journal titles; government publications in the United Kingdom and the United States are simply cited as published in London or Washington, D.C. rather than repeating after each reference Her Majesty's Stationery Office and the United States Government Printing Office; notes and comments published in American law journals are cited under the title of the journal rather than the student author. A list of the major textbooks and 'readers' (anthologies of articles) is also provided. There is a single index of authors to serve the bibliography and its supplement.

We are especially grateful to Mr. Martin Wright and Miss Rosina Perry who as librarians of the Radzinowicz Library at the Cambridge Institute of Criminology have given us so much help over the years and to the staff of the Bodleian Law Library in Oxford. We are indebted to Mrs. Margaret Thompson, Miss Emma Jansen and Mrs. Wendy Shurgold who have done so much to put the lists in good order and to our publishers who have been extremely patient.

Leon Radzinowicz   *Roger Hood*

Periodical abbreviations

The titles of periodicals have been frequently abbreviated, but in a form which should be easily intelligible. The standard abbreviations used are:

Acad.	Academy
Admin.	Administration
Amer.	American
Anthrop	Anthropology
Arch.	Archive
Assn.	Association
Aust.	Australian
Biosoc.	Biosocial
Brit.	British
Bull.	Bulletin
Calif.	California(n)
Camb.	Cambridge
Can.	Canadian
Contemp.	Contemporary
Crim.	Criminal
Criminol.	Criminology, Criminologica
Ct.	Court
Delinq.	Delinquency
Econ.	Economy, Economic
Ed.	Education
Fed.	Federal
Gen.	General
Govt.	Government
Hosp.	Hospital
Internat.	International(e)
J.	Journal
Lit.	Literature
Nat.	National
N.Y.	New York
N.Z.	New Zealand
Penn.	Pennsylvania
Penol.	Penology
Per.	Personality
Pol.	Police, Political
Prev.	Prevention
Prob.	Probation
Psychiat.	Psychiatry, Psychiatric(a)
Psychol.	Psychology
Quart.	Quarterly
Res.	Research
Rev.	Review
Sci.	Science
Scient.	Scientifica
Soc.	Social, Society
Sociol.	Sociological
Stud.	Studies
Univ.	University
Wk.	Work

1 Dimensions of crime and the problem of measurement

1 Criminal statistics and the amount of crime

[*See also Section 3 for references on various types of crime, Section 4 on violence and 5 on civil disorders and lawlessness.*]

SELLIN, T., 1951
The significance of records of crime.
Law Quart. Rev., **67,** 489–504.

SHANNON, L.W., 1954
The spatial distribution of criminal offences by states.
J. Crim. Law, Criminol. & Pol. Sci., **45,** 246–73.

BEATTIE, R.H., 1960
Criminal statistics in the United States.
J. Crim. Law, Criminol. & Pol. Sci., **51,** 49–65.

COUNCIL OF EUROPE, 1960
Juvenile delinquency in post-war Europe.
Strasbourg.

MONAHAN, T.P., 1960
On the incidence of delinquency.
Social Forces, **39,** 66–72.

TAPPAN, P.W., 1960
Crime, justice and correction.
New York: McGraw Hill, 35–64.

GIBBENS, T.C.N., 1961
Trends in juvenile delinquency.
Geneva: World Health Organization.

MCCLINTOCK, F.H., AND GIBSON, E., 1961
Robbery in London.
London: Macmillan, 1–29.

SELLIN, T., 1962
Crime and delinquency in the United States: an overall view.
Annals Amer. Acad. Pol. & Soc. Sci., **339,** 11–23.

MCCLINTOCK, F.H., 1963
Crimes of violence.
London: Macmillan, 1–57.

ROBISON, S.M., 1963
Juvenile delinquency, its nature and control.
New York: Holt, Rinehart and Winston, 13–27, 45–54.

LUNDEN, W.A., 1964
Statistics on delinquents and delinquency.
Springfield, Ill.: C.C. Thomas, 15–56.

SELLIN, T., AND WOLFGANG, M.E., 1964
The measurement of delinquency.
New York: John Wiley & Sons, 1–86.

LITTLE, A., 1965
The increase in crime 1952–62: an empirical analysis of adolescent offenders.
Brit. J. Criminol., **5,** 77–82.

LITTLE, A., 1965
The 'prevalence' of recorded delinquency and recidivism in England and Wales.
Amer. Sociol. Rev., **30,** 260–3.

MORRIS, A. (ED), 1965
What are the sources of knowledge about crime in the U.S.A.?
Correctional Research, Bull. No. 15. United Prison Assn. of Mass.

CUTLER, S., AND REISS, A.J. JR., 1966
Crimes against public and quasi-public organizations in Boston, Chicago and Washington, D.C.
A document submitted to the President's Commission on Law Enforcement and Administration of Justice, Washington, D.C. Mimeo.

QUINNEY, R., 1966
Structural characteristics, population areas, and crime rates in the United States.
J. Crim. Law, Criminol. & Pol. Sci., **57,** 45–52.

CHRISTENSEN, R., 1967
Projected percentage of U.S. population with criminal arrest and conviction records, in *Task force report, science and technology.*
Washington, D.C.: President's Commission

on Law Enforcement and Administration of Justice, 216–28.

Christiansen, K.O., 1967
Report on the post-war trends of crime in selected European countries.
A document submitted to the President's Commission on Law Enforcement and Administration of Justice, Washington, D.C., Mimeo.

Ferdinand, T.N., 1967
The criminal patterns of Boston since 1849.
Amer. J. Sociol., **73,** 84–99.

Reckless, W.C., and Kay, B.A., 1967
The female offender. A document submitted to the President's Commission on Law Enforcement and Administration of Justice, Washington, D.C., Mimeo, 1–12.

Reiss, A.J.Jr., 1967
Measurement of the nature and amount of crime, in Field Surveys III:
Studies in crime and law enforcement in major metropolitan areas, Vol. 2., (1).
Washington, D.C.: President's Commission on Law Enforcement and Administration of Justice, 12–77.

Sellin, T., 1967
Systems of reporting 'crimes known to the police' in selected foreign countries.
A document submitted to the President's Commission on Law Enforcement and Administration of Justice, Washington, D.C., Mimeo.

United States of America, 1967
The challenge of crime in a free society.
Report of the President's Commission on Law Enforcement and Administration of Justice, Washington, D.C., 1–4, 17–32, 55–7.

United States Of America, 1967
Task force report, crime and its impact—an assessment.
Washington, D.C.,: President's Commission on Law Enforcement and Administration of Justice, 1–77.

United States of America, 1967
Homicide in the United States, 1950–1964.
Washington, D.C., Department of Health, Education and Welfare.

Wolfgang, M.E., 1967
Crimes of violence.
A document submitted to the President's Commission on Law Enforcement and Administration of Justice, Washington, D.C., Mimeo, 1–83.

Johnson, E.H., 1968
Crime, correction, and society.
Homewood, Ill.: Dorsey Press, 28–48.

McClintock, F.H., and Avison, N.H., 1968.
Crime in England and Wales.
London: Heinemann, 16–63.

Sagi, P.C., and Wellford, C.F., 1968
Age composition and patterns of change in criminal statistics.
J. Crim. Law. Criminol. & Pol. Sci., **59,** 29–36.

California, State of, 1969
Bank robberies. California compared with other states 1931–1968.
Sacramento: Department of Justice. Mimeo.

Graham, F.P., 1969
A contemporary history of American crime, in H.D. Graham and T.R. Gurr (eds.), *Violence in America: historical and comparative perspectives,* Vol. 2.
A report to the National Commission on the Causes and Prevention of Violence.
Washington, D.C., 371–85.

Normandeau, A., 1969
Trends in robbery as reflected by different indexes, in T. Sellin and M.E. Wolfgang (eds.), *Delinquency, selected studies.*
New York: John Wiley & Sons, 150–7.

Schur, E.M., 1969
Our criminal society.
Englewood Cliffs, N.J.: Prentice-Hall, 23–54.

United States Senate, 1969
Crime in the national capital.
Hearings before the Committee on the District of Columbia. United States Senate. 91st Session. Part 1. A program design for regional law enforcement, crime prevention and criminal justice planning in the Washington Metropolitan area, Washington, D.C., 5–18, 120–30.

Arnott, A.J.E., and Duncan, J.A., 1970
The Scottish criminal.
Edinburgh University Press, 7–34.

CHILTON, R., AND SPIELBERGER, A., 1970
Is delinquency increasing? Age structure and the crime rate.
Social Forces, **49,** 487–93.

CONNOR, W.D. 1970
Juvenile delinquency in the U.S.S.R.: some quantitative and qualitative indicators.
Amer. Sociol. Rev., **35,** 283–97.

HEIDENSOHN, F., 1970
Sex, crime and society.
J. Biosoc. Sci., Supplement 2, 129–36.

HOOD, R. AND SPARKS, R., 1970
Key issues in criminology.
London: Weidenfeld and Nicolson, 11–79.

KELLY, D.H., AND WINSLOW, R.W., 1970
Seriousness of delinquent behaviour: an alternative perspective.
Brit. J. Criminol., **10,** 124–35.

KNUDTEN, R.D., 1970
Crime in a complex society.
Homewood, Ill.: Dorsey Press, 9–39, 58–86.

KUTSCHINSKY, B., 1970
Towards an explanation of the decrease in registered sex crimes in Copenhagen.
Technical report of the Commission on Obscenity and Pornography, **VII,** Washington, D.C., 263–310.

MARTIN, J.P., 1970
Could crime cost less?
Science J., 53–7.

NATIONAL OPINION POLLS, MARKET RESEARCH LIMITED, 1970
Report on attitudes towards crime, violence, and permissiveness in society.
76/86 Strand, London. Mimeo. 1–12, 25–9.

NORMANDEAU, A., 1970
A comparative study of the weighted crime indices for eight countries.
Internat. Crim. Police Rev., No. 234, 15–18.

ROBERT, P., AND BOMBET, J-P., WITH SAUDINOS, D., 1970
Le cout du crime en France.
Annales Internat. de Crim., **9,** 599–679.

BLOCK, R., AND ZIMRING, F.E., 1971
Homicide in Chicago, 1967–1970.
Univ. of Chicago, Center for Studies in Criminal Justice, Mimeo.

BOGGS, S.L., 1971
Formal and informal crime control: an exploratory study of urban, suburban and rural orientations.
Sociol. Quart., **12,** 319–27.

CONKLIN, J.E., 1971
Criminal environment and support for the law.
Law & Society Rev., special police issue, **6,** 247–65.

FURSTENBERG, F.F.JR., 1971
Public reaction to crime in the streets.
Amer. Scholar, **40,** 601–10.

GOULD, L.C., 1971
Crime and its impact in an affluent society, in J.D. Douglas (ed.), *Crime and justice in American society.*
New York: Bobbs-Merrill Co., 81–118.

NEW YORK, CITY OF, 1971
Criminal justice plan for 1971.
Criminal Justice Coordinating Council, Executive Committee, 4–28.

SMALL BUSINESS CHAMBER OF COMMERCE OF THE CITY OF NEW YORK, INC., 1971
A survey of crime, its impact on business, and the economy of central Harlem, New York.

TURK, A.T., 1971
The mythology of crime in America.
Criminology, **8,** 397–411.

WOLF, P., 1971
Crime and development. An international comparison of crime rates.
Scandinavian Studies in Criminology, **3.**
Oslo: Universitetsforlaget, 107–20.

CHILTON, R.J., AND SPIELBERGER, A., 1972
Increases in crime: the utility of alternative measures.
J. Crim. Law, Criminol. & Pol. Sci., **63,** 68–74.

CHRISTIANSEN, K.O., AND JENSEN, S.G., 1972
Crime in Denmark—a statistical history.
J. Crim. Law, Criminol. & Pol. Sci., **63,** 82–92.

COATES, J.F., 1972
The future of crime in the United States from now to the year 2000.
Policy Sciences, **3,** 27–45.

CONKLIN, J.E., 1972
Robbery and the Criminal justice system.
Philadelphia: J.B. Lippincott Co., 1–58.

DURANT, M., THOMAS, M., AND WILLCOCK, H.D., 1972
Crime, criminals and the law.
London: Office of Population Censuses and Surveys, Social Survey Division, 116–39, 232–53.

GATRELL, V.A.C., AND HADDEN, T.B., 1972
Criminal statistics and their interpretation, in E.A. Wrigley (ed.), *Nineteenth century society: essays in the use of quantitative methods in the study of social data,*
Cambridge Univ. Press, 336–96.

GIBBONS, D.C., JONES, J.F., AND GARABEDIAN, P.G., 1972
Gauging public opinion about the crime problem.
Crime & Delinq., **18,** 134–46.

POVEDA, T.G., 1972
The fear of crime in a small town.
Crime & Delinq., **18,** 147–53.

SCHLOSS, B., AND GIESBRECHT, N.A., 1972
Murder in Canada: a report on capital and non-capital murder statistics 1961–1970.
Research report of the Centre of Criminology, Univ. of Toronto.

BARNETT, A., AND KLEITMAN, D.J., 1973
Urban violence and risk to the individual.
J. Res. Crime & Delinq., **10,** 111–16.

BLOCK, M.K., AND LONG, G.J., 1973
Subjective probability of victimization and crime levels: an econometric approach.
Criminology, **11,** 87–93.

CLINARD, M.B., AND ABBOTT, D.J., 1973
Crime in developing countries.
New York: John Wiley & Sons, 1–76.

CONKLIN, J.E., AND BITTNER, E., 1973
Burglary in a suburb.
Criminology, **11,** 206–32.

CRIMINAL LAW BULLETIN, 1973
City crime: report of Council on Municipal Performance. **9,** 563–611.

HSU, M., 1973
Cultural and sexual differences on the judgment of criminal offenses: a replication study of the measurement of delinquency.
J. Crim. Law & Criminol., **64,** 348–53.

ROSHIER, B., 1973
The selection of crime news by the press, in S. Cohen and J. Young (eds.), *The manufacture of news.*
London: Constable, 28–39.

SCARR, H.A., 1973
Patterns of Burglary.
L.E.A.A., National Institute of Law Enforcement and Criminal Justice, U.S. Department of Justice, Washington, D.C.

UNITED KINGDOM, 1973.
Shoplifting and thefts by shop staff.
Report of a working party on internal shop security. London: Home Office.

UNITED STATES OF AMERICA, 1973
A national strategy to reduce crime.
Report of the National Advisory Commission on Criminal Justice Standards and Goals, Washington, D.C.

UNITED STATES OF AMERICA, 1973
Uniform crime reports.
Annually. Washington, D.C. Federal Bureau of Investigation.

WELLFORD, C.F., 1973
Age composition and the increase in recorded crime.
Criminology, **11,** 61–70.

WILSON, P.R., AND BROWN, J.W., 1973
Crime and the community.
Univ. of Queensland Press, 1–29, 91–108.

BERMAN, N.J., AND ALLEN, H.E., 1974
Criminal victimisation in a small town, U.S.A.
Internat. J. Criminol. & Penol., **2,** 391–7.

COUNCIL OF EUROPE, 1974
Methods of forecasting trends in criminality.
Strasbourg.

HINDELANG, M.J., 1974
The uniform crime reports revisited.
J. Crim Justice, **2,** 1–17.

MCCLINTOCK, F.H., 1974
Facts and myths about the state of crime, in R.G. Hood (ed.), *Crime, criminology and public policy: essays in honour of Sir Leon Radzinowicz.*
London: Heinemann, 33–46.

ROSSI, P.H., WAITE, E., BOSE, C.E., AND BERK, R.E., 1974
The seriousness of crimes: normative structure and individual differences.
Amer. Sociol. Rev., **39,** 224–37.

SELOSSE, J., 1974
Statistical aspects of violent crime, in *Violence in society. Collected studies in criminological research*, **11.**
Strasbourg: Council of Europe, 8–60.

UNITED KINGDOM, 1974
Criminal Statistics, England & Wales, annually.
London: Home Office, Cmnd. 5677.

2 Criminal statistics: limitations and possible improvements

SELLIN, T., 1951
The significance of records of crime.
Law Quart. Rev., **67,** 489–504.

ANCEL, M., 1952
Observations on the international comparison of criminal statistics.
Internat. Rev. Crim. Policy, **1,** 41–8.

BEATTIE, R.H., 1955
Problems of criminal statistics in the United States.
J. Crim. Law, Criminol. & Pol. Sci., **46,** 178–86.

CRESSEY, D.R., 1957
The state of criminal statistics.
Nat. Prob. and Parole Assn. J., **3,** 230–41.

KITSUSE, J.I., AND CICOUREL, A.V., 1963
A note on the uses of official statistics.
Social Problems, **11,** 131–39.

SELLIN, T., AND WOLFGANG, M.E., 1963
Constructing an index of delinquency—a manual.
Philadelphia: Center of Criminological Research, Univ. of Pennsylvania.

WILKINS, L.T., 1963
The measurement of crime.
Brit. J. Criminol., **3,** 317–41.

SELLIN, T., 1964
Standardisation of criminal statistics.
Strasbourg: Council of Europe, DPC/CORC (64) 6.

SELLIN, T., AND WOLFGANG, M.E., 1964
The measurement of delinquency.
New York: John Wiley & Sons, 1–333.

ARNOLD, W.R., 1965
Continuities in research: scaling delinquent behavior.
Social Problems, **13,** 59–66.

MARTIN, R.I., AND KLEIN, M.W., 1965
A comparative analysis of four measures of delinquency seriousness.
(Univ. of Southern Calif., Youth Studies Center.) Paper presented at the annual meeting of the Pacific Sociological Assn., Salt Lake City, April 1965.

PITTMAN, D.J., AND HANDY, W. F., 1965
Uniform crime reporting: suggested improvements, in A.W. Gouldner and S.M. Miller (eds.), *Applied sociology. Opportunities and problems.*
New York, Free Press, 180–8.

WILKINS, L.T., 1965
New thinking in criminal statistics.
J. Crim. Law, Criminol. & Pol. Sci., **56,** 277–84.

LEJINS, P.P., 1966
Uniform crime reports.
Michigan Law Rev., **64,** 1011–30.

NORMANDEAU, A., 1966
The measurement of delinquency in Montreal.
J. Crim. Law, Criminol. & Pol. Sci., **57,** 172–7.

ROBISON, S.M., 1966
A critical review of the uniform crime reports.
Michigan Law Rev., **64,** 1031–54.

ROSE, G.N.G., 1966
Concerning the measurement of delinquency.
Brit. J. Criminol., **6,** 414–21.

AKMAN, D.D., FIGLIO, R., AND NORMANDEAU, A., 1967
Concerning the measurement of delinquency—a rejoinder and beyond.
Brit. J. Criminol., **7,** 442–9.

DOUGLAS, J., 1967
The social meanings of suicide.
Princeton, N.J.: Princeton Univ. Press.

UNITED KINGDOM, 1967
Report of the Departmental Committee on Criminal Statistics.
London: Home Office, Cmnd. 3448.

WHEELER, S., 1967
Criminal statistics: a reformulation of the problem.
J. Crim. Law, Criminol. & Pol. Sci., **58,** 317–24.

WOLFGANG, M.E., 1967
International criminal statistics: a proposal.
J. Crim. Law, Criminol. & Pol. Sci., **58,** 65–9.

BEATTIE, R.H., 1968
A state bureau of criminal statistics, in M.E. Wolfgang (ed.), *Crime and culture, essays in honour of Thorsten Sellin.*
New York: John Wiley & Sons, 169–86.

ROSE, G.N.G., 1969
Crime statistics—uses and abuses.
London: Institute for the Study and Treatment of Delinquency.

CHRISTIANSEN, K.O., KUTSCHINSKY, B., AND KARPATSCHOF, B., 1970
Method of using an index of crime of the kind devised by Sellin and Wolfgang in *The index of crime—some further studies. Collected studies in criminological research,* **7.**
Strasbourg: Council of Europe 11–29.

GOLD, M. 1970
Delinquent behavior in an American city.
Belmont, Calif.: Brooks/Cole Publishing Co., 1–34.

LOPEZ-REY, M., 1970
Crime: an analytical appraisal.
London: Routledge & Kegan Paul, 1–51.

ROSE, G.N.G., 1970
The merits of an index of crime of the kind devised by Sellin and Wolfgang in *The index of crime—some further studies. Collected studies in criminological research,* **7.**
Strasbourg: Council of Europe, 33–52.

WARD, P., 1970
'Careers in crime': the F.B.I. story.
J. Res. Crime & Delinq., **7,** 207–18.

WOLFGANG, M.E., 1970
On devising a crime index, in *The index of crime—some further studies. Collected studies in criminological research,* **7.**
Strasbourg: Council of Europe, 55–77.

ROSE, G.N.G., 1971
The classification of theft and malicious damage. *Crim. Law. Rev.*, 1971, 76–86, 162–71.

WALKER, N., 1971
Crime, courts and figures: an introduction to criminal statistics.
Harmondsworth: Penguin Books.

ZEISEL, H., 1971
The future of law enforcement statistics, a summary view, in *Federal statistics.*
Report of the U.S. President's Commission on Federal Statistics, Vol. II. Washington, D.C.

DOLESCHAL, E., AND WILKINS, L., 1972
Criminal statistics.
Center for Studies in Crime and Delinquency. Rockville, Maryland: National Institute for Mental Health.

KAMISAR, Y., 1972
How to use, abuse—and fight back with—crime statistics.
Oklahoma Law Rev., **25,** 239–58.

AMERICAN CRIMINAL LAW REVIEW, 1973
Criminal statistics—can they be trusted? **11,** 1045–86.

HINDESS, B., 1973
The use of official statistics in sociology.
London: Macmillan, 14–27.

WILSON, P.R., AND BROWN, J.W., 1973
Crime and the community.
Univ. of Queensland Press, 74–90.

ZEISEL, H., 1973
The F.B.I.'s biased sampling.
Bulletin of the Atomic Scientists, Jan., 38–42.

EDWARDS, B., 1974
Sources of social statistics.
London: Heinemann, 224–70.

PEASE, K., IRESON, J., AND THORPE, J., 1974
Additivity assumptions in the measurement of delinquency.
Brit. J. Criminol., **14**, 256–63.

3 The dark figure: hidden crime, its nature and extent

POLLAK, O., 1950
The criminality of women.
Philadelphia: Univ. of Penn. Press, 1–7, 16–43.

SHORT, J.F., AND NYE, F.I., 1957
Reported behavior as a criterion of deviant behavior.
Social Problems, **5**, 207–13.

SHORT, J.F., AND NYE, F.I., 1958
Extent of unrecorded juvenile delinquency: tentative conclusions.
J. Crim. Law, Criminol. & Pol. Sci., **49**, 296–302.

DENTLER, R.A., AND MONROE, L.J., 1961
Social correlates of early adolescent theft.
Amer. Sociol. Rev., **26**, 733–43.

MARTIN, J.P., 1962
Offenders as employees.
London: Macmillan, 17–18, 21, 114–19, 125–6.

ERICKSON, M.L., AND EMPEY, L.T., 1963
Courts records, undetected delinquency and decision making.
J. Crim. Law, Criminol. & Pol. Sci., **54**, 456–69.

CAMERON, M.O., 1964
The booster and the snitch: department store shoplifting.
Glencoe Ill.: Free Press, 61–9.

OSBOROUGH, N., 1964
Immunity for the English supermarket shoplifter.
Amer. J. Comparative Law, **13**, 291–9.

SELLIN, T., AND WOLFGANG, M.E., 1964
The measurement of delinquency.
New York: John Wiley & Sons, 1–86.

CHRISTIE, N., ANDENAES, J., AND SKIRBEKK, S., 1965
A study of self-reported crime.
Scandinavian Studies in Criminology, **1.**
London: Tavistock, 86–116.

ELMHORN, K., 1965
Study in self-reported delinquency among schoolchildren in Stockholm.
Scandinavian Studies in Criminology, **1.**
London: Tavistock, 117–46.

VAZ, E.W., 1965
Middle-class adolescents: self-reported delinquency and youth culture activities.
Can. Rev. Sociol. & Anthropol., **2**, 52–70.

DICKENS, B.M., 1966
Abortion and the law.
London: MacGibbon & Kee, 73–89.

EMPEY, L.T., AND ERICKSON, M.L., 1966
Hidden delinquency and social status.
Social Forces, **44**, 546–54.

GOLD, M., 1966
Undetected delinquent behavior.
J. Res. Crime & Delinq., **3**, 27–46.

VOSS, H.L., 1966
Socio-economic status and reported delinquent behavior.
Social Problems, **13**, 314–24.

BIDERMAN, A.D., 1967
Surveys of population samples for estimating crime incidence
Annals Amer. Acad. Pol. & Soc. Sci., **374**, 16–33.

BIDERMAN, A.D., AND REISS, A.J.JR., 1967
On exploring the 'dark figure' of crime.
Annals Amer. Acad. Pol. & Soc. Sci., **374**, 1–15.

BIDERMAN, A.D., ET AL, 1967
Field Surveys I: *Report on a pilot study in the District of Columbia on victimization and attitudes toward law enforcement.*
Washington, D.C.: President's Commission on Law Enforcement and Administration of Justice, 26–118, 119–76.

ENNIS, P.H., 1967
Field Surveys II: *Criminal victimization in the United States: a report of a national survey.*
Washington, D.C.: President's Commission on Law Enforcement and Administration of Justice, 1–109.

GRIFFIN, R.K., 1967
10,212 shoplifting apprehensions. A statistical report.
Security World, **6,** 33–8.

LUNDEN, W.A., SATTERLEE, J.L., AND CONNELL, L.D., 1967
Shoplifting among college students—a survey.
College Store J., Feb./Mar., 69–80.

REISS, A.J. JR., 1967
Measurement of the nature and amount of crime, in Field Surveys III: *Studies in crime and law enforcement in major metropolitan areas*, Vol. 1, Section 1.
Washington, D.C.: President's Commission on Law Enforcement and Administration of Justice, 77–102, 143–71.

BELSON, W.A., 1968
Extent of stealing by London boys and some of its origins.
Advancement of Science, **25,** No. 124, and Reprint Series No. 39, Survey Research Centre, London School of Economics.

ACTOR, S., 1969
Shoplifting: far greater than we know?
Security World, **6,** 12–13.

CHAMBLISS, W.J., AND NAGASAWA, R.H., 1969
On the validity of official statistics. A comparative study of white, black and Japanese high-school boys.
J. Res. Crime & Delinq., **6,** 71–7.

DICKENS, B.M., 1969
Shops, shoplifting and law enforcement.
Crim. Law. Rev. 1969, 464–72.

GOULD, L.C., 1969
Who defines delinquency: a comparison of self-reported and officially reported indices of delinquency for three racial groups.
Social Problems, **16,** 325–36.

HOTSON, B.E., 1969
Thefts from pre-payment meters.
A Cropwood Fellowship study, Univ. of Cambridge, Institute of Criminology. Mimeo.

INSTITUTE FOR LOCAL SELF GOVERNMENT, 1969
Criminal victimization in Maricopa County.
Berkeley, Calif., 1–81.

SOMERVILLE, J.G., 1969
A study of the preventive aspect of police work with juveniles.
Crim. Law. Rev., 1969, 407–14, 472–84.

STARK, J., 1969
The battered child—does Britain need a reporting law?
Public Law, 1969, 48–63.

VAZ, E.W., 1969
Delinquency and the youth culture: upper and middle-class boys.
J. Crim. Law, Criminol. & Pol. Sci., **60,** 33–46.

COURTIS, M.C., 1970
Attitudes to crime and the police in Toronto: a report on some survey findings.
Centre of Criminology, Univ. of Toronto, 5–34.

CROSBY, R., AND SNYDER, D., 1970
Crime victimization in the black community: results of the *Black Buyer II Survey*.
Research document RD-030. Bethesda, Md: Resource Management Corporation.

MCCLINTOCK, F.H., 1970
The dark figure, in *Collected studies in criminological research*, **5.**
Strasbourg: Council of Europe, 9–34.

BOX, S., 1971
Deviance, reality and society.
London: Holt, Rinehart & Winston, 58–97.

ERICKSON, M.L., 1971
The group context of delinquent behavior.
Social Problems, **19,** 114–29.

FOONER, M., 1971
Money and economic factors in crime and delinquency.
Criminology, **8,** 311–32.

ERICKSON, M.L., 1972
The changing relationship between official and self-reported measures of delinquency: an exploratory-predictive study.
J. Crim. Law, Criminol. & Pol. Sci., **63,** 388–95.

FINKELSTEIN, I., AND OLIVIERI, A., 1972
Report on 'victimless crime' in New York state.
New York Law Forum, **18,** 77–120.

HARTMANN, D.P., GELFAND, D.M., PAGE, B., AND WALDER, P., 1972
Rates of bystander observation and reporting of contrived shoplifting incidents.
Criminology, **10,** 247–67.

HINDELANG, M.J., 1972
The relationship of self-reported delinquency to scales of the CPI and MMPI.
J. Crim. Law, Criminol. & Pol. Sci., **63,** 75–81.

INCIARDI, J.A., AND CHAMBERS, C.D., 1972
Unreported criminal involvement of narcotic addicts.
J. Drug Issues, Spring, 57–64.

WILLIAMS, J.R., AND GOLD, M., 1972
From delinquent behavior to official delinquency.
Social Problems, **20,** 209–29.

ZIMRING, F.E., 1972
Of doctors, deterrence and the dark figure of crime—a note on abortion in Hawaii.
Univ. Chicago Law Rev., **39,** 699–721.

FARRINGTON, D.P., 1973
Self-reports of deviant behavior: predictive and stable?
J. Crim. Law & Criminol., **64,** 99–110.

WEST, D.J., AND FARRINGTON, D.P., 1973
Who becomes delinquent?
London: Heinemann, 151–67.

AROMAA, K., 1974
Victimisation to violence: a Gallup Survey.
Internat. J. Criminol. & Penol., **2,** 333–46.

BERAN, N.J., AND ALLEN, H.E., 1974
Criminal victimisation in a small town, U.S.A.
Internat. J. Criminol. & Penol., **2,** 391–7.

BLACKMORE, J., 1974
The relationship between self-reported delinquency and official convictions amongst adolescent boys.
Brit. J. Criminol., **14,** 172–6.

BLOCK, R., 1974
Why notify the police: the victim's decision to notify the police of an assault.
Criminology, **11,** 555–69.

FEYERHERM, W.H., AND HINDELANG, M.J., 1974
On the victimization of juveniles: some preliminary results.
J. Res. Crime & Delinq., **11,** 40–50.

GREVE, V., 1974
Our non-deviant criminals.
Scandinavian Studies in Criminology, **5,** London: Martin Robertson, 99–106.

HAUGE, R., AND WOLF, P., 1974
Criminal violence in three Scandinavian countries.
Scandinavian Studies in Criminology, **5,** 25–33.

HEPWORTH, M., AND FEATHERSTONE, M., 1974
Persons believed missing, in P. Rock and M. McIntosh (eds.), *Deviance and social control.*
London: Tavistock, 163–207.

MARS, G., 1974
Dock pilferage, in P. Rock and M. McIntosh (eds.), *Deviance and social control.*
London: Tavistock, 209–28.

UNITED STATES OF AMERICA, 1974
Crime in eight American cities.
Advance report. L.E.A.A., National Institute of Law Enforcement and Criminal Justice, U.S. Dept. of Justice, Washington, D.C.

UNITED STATES OF AMERICA, 1974
Crimes and victims, a report on the Dayton–San Jose pilot survey of victimization.
L.E.A.A., National Institute of Law Enforcement and Criminal Justice, U.S. Dept. of Justice, Washington, D.C., 1–40.

UNITED STATES OF AMERICA, 1974
Crime in the nation's five largest cities.
Advance report. L.E.A.A., National Institute of Law Enforcement and Criminal Justice, U.S. Dept. of Justice, Washington, D.C.

4 Police and court discretion: their impact on criminal statistics

[*See also Section* 2 (7) *for references on labelling; Section* 4(4) *for references on police discretion to prosecute; and Section* 12(2) *for references on diversion from the criminal justice system.*]

VAN VECHTEN, C.C., 1942
Differential criminal case morality in selected jurisdictions.
Amer. Sociol. Rev., **7,** 833–9.

INSTITUTE OF PUBLIC ADMINISTRATION, 1952
Crime records in police management: New York City, New York.

UNIVERSITY OF PENNSYLVANIA LAW REVIEW, 1952
Philadelphia police practice and the law of arrest. **100,** 1182–216.

NEWMAN, D.J., 1956
Pleading guilty for consideration: a study of bargain justice.
J. Crim. Law, Criminol. & Pol. Sci., **46,** 780–90.

KEPHART, W.M., 1957
Racial factors and urban law enforcement.
Philadelphia: Univ. of Penn. Press, 57–70, 85–95, 105–7.

BREITEL, C.D., 1960
Controls of criminal law enforcement.
Univ. Chicago Law Rev., **27,** 427–35.

GOLDSTEIN, J., 1960
Police discretion not to invoke the criminal process: low visibility decisions in the administration of justice.
Yale Law J., **69,** 545–94.

BARRETT, E.L., 1962
Police practices and the law.
Calif. Law Rev., **50,** 11–55.

FERRACUTI, F., HERNANDEZ, R.P., AND WOLFGANG, M.E., 1962
A study of police errors in crime classification.
J. Crim. Law, Criminol. & Pol. Sci., **53,** 113–19.

GOLDMAN, N., 1963
The differential selection of juvenile offenders for court appearance.
Nat. Council on Crime and Delinquency.

MCCLINTOCK, F.H., 1963
Crimes of violence.
London: Macmillan, 58–74.

BONFIELD, A.E., 1964
The abrogation of penal statutes by non-enforcement.
Iowa Law Rev., **49,** 389–440.

PILIAVIN, I., AND BRIAR, S., 1964
Police encounters with juveniles.
Amer. J. Sociol., **70,** 206–14.

UNIVERSITY OF PENNSYLVANIA LAW REVIEW, 1964
Guilty plea bargaining: compromises by prosecutors to secure guilty pleas.
112, 865–908.

LA FAVE, W.R., 1965
Arrest: the decision to take a suspect into custody.
Boston: Little, Brown & Co., 63–143.

NEWMAN, D.J., 1965
The effect of accommodations in justice administration on criminal statistics, in A.W. Gouldner and S.M. Miller (eds.), *Applied sociology. Opportunities and problems.*
New York: Free Press, 163–79.

LOHMAN, J.D., AND MISNER, G.E., 1966
Field Surveys IV: *The police and the community*, Vol. 1.
Washington, D.C.: President's Commission

on Law Enforcement and Administration of Justice, 108–31.

SKOLNICK, J.H., 1966
Justice without trial: law enforcement in democratic society.
New York: John Wiley & Sons, 164–83.

MCEACHERN, A.W., AND BAUZER, R., 1967
Factors related to disposition in juvenile police contacts, in M.W. Klein (ed.), *Juvenile gangs in context.*
Englewood Cliffs, N.J.: Prentice-Hall, 148–60.

PARNAS, R.I., 1967
Police response to domestic disturbances.
Wisconsin Law Rev., 1967, 914–60.

UNITED STATES OF AMERICA, 1967
Field Surveys V: *A national survey of police and community relations.*
Washington, D.C.: President's Commission on Law Enforcement and Administration of Justice, 363–72.

TERRY, R.M., 1967
Discrimination in the handling of juvenile offenders by social-control agencies.
J. Res. Crime & Delinq., **4,** 218–30.

TERRY, R.M., 1967
The screening of juvenile offenders.
J. Crim. Law, Criminol. & Pol. Sci., **58,** 173–81.

TIFFANY, L.P., MCINTYRE, D.M.JR., AND ROTENBERG, D.L., 1967
Detection of crime.
Boston: Little, Brown & Co., 18–43, 216–30.

WERTHMAN, C., AND PILIAVIN, I., 1967
Gang members and the police, in D.J. Bordua (ed.), *The Police.*
New York: John Wiley & Sons, 56–98.

ALSCHULER, A.W., 1968
The prosecutor's role in plea bargaining.
Univ. Chicago Law Rev., **36,** 50–112.

AMERICAN LAW INSTITUTE, 1968
A model code of pre-arraignment procedure.
Part II. The factual background of in-custody investigation provisions of a model code.
Philadelphia, Pa.: American Law Institute, 101–69.

CARTER, R.M., 1968
Middle class delinquency. An experiment in community control.
A report to the President's Committee on juvenile delinquency and youth development on the Contra Costa County Demonstration Project.
Univ. of Calif., School of Criminology, Mimeo, 19–24.

CHAPMAN, D., 1968
Sociology and the stereotype of the criminal.
London: Tavistock, 97–152.

CICOUREL, A.V., 1968
The social organization of juvenile justice.
New York: John Wiley & Sons, 203–73.

UNIVERSITY OF PENNSYLVANIA LAW REVIEW, 1968
Police discretion and the judgment that a crime has been committed—rape in Philadelphia, **117,** 277–322.

WILSON, J.Q., 1968
The police and the delinquent in two cities, in S. Wheeler (ed.), *Controlling delinquents.*
New York: John Wiley & Sons, 9–30.

AMERICAN LAW INSTITUTE, 1969
Article 3. *Arrest.* A model code of pre-arraignment procedure.
Philadelphia, Pa.: American Law Institute.

DAVIS, K.C., 1969
Discretionary justice: a preliminary enquiry.
Baton Rouge: Louisiana State University Press, 80–96.

HOHENSTEIN, W.H., 1969
Factors in influencing the police disposition of juvenile offenders, in T. Sellin and M.E. Wolfgang (eds.), *Delinquency: selected studies.*
New York: John Wiley & Sons, 138–49.

MILLER, F.W., 1969
Prosecution. The decision to charge a suspect with a crime.
Boston: Little, Brown & Co.

AMERICAN LAW INSTITUTE, 1970
Part II. *Search and seizure.* Tentative draft No. 3. A model code of pre-arraignment procedure.
Philadelphia, Pa.: American Law Institute.

BLACK, D.J., 1970
Production of crime rates.
Amer. Sociol. Rev., **35,** 733–48.

BLACK, D.J., AND REISS, A.J.JR., 1970
Police control of juveniles.
Amer. Sociol. Rev., **35,** 63–77.

FERDINAND, T.N., AND LUCHTERHAND, E.G., 1970
Inter-city youth, the police, the juvenile court and justice.
Social Problems, **17,** 510–27.

GOLD, M., 1970
Delinquent behavior in an American city.
Belmont, Calif.: Brooks/Cole Publishing Co., 100–13.

GREEN, E., 1970
Race, social status and criminal arrest.
Amer. Sociol. Rev., **35,** 476–90.

PARNAS, R.I., 1970
Judicial response to intra-family violence.
Minnesota Law Rev., **54,** 585–644.

ROSE, G., AND HAMILTON, R.A., 1970
Effects of a juvenile liaison scheme.
Brit. J. Criminol., **10,** 2–20.

STEER, D., 1970
Police cautions—a study in the exercise of police discretion.
Oxford: Basil Blackwell.

BLACK, D.J., 1971
The social organization of arrest.
Stanford Law Rev., **23,** 1087–1111.

BOX, S., 1971
Deviance, reality and society.
London: Holt, Rinehart & Winston, 166–217.

CHAMBLISS, W.J., AND SEIDMAN, R.B., 1971
Law, order, and power.
Reading, Mass.: Addison-Wesley Publishing Co., 322–48.

CORNELL LAW REVIEW, 1971
Discrimination on the basis of arrest records.
56, 470–88.

DAVIS, S.M., 1971
Justice for the juvenile: the decision to arrest and due process.
Duke Law J., 1971, 913–37.

DOUGLAS, J.D., 1971
American social order.
New York: Free Press, 79–132.

FAHEY, R.P., 1971
The enforcement of the Illinois felony marijuana law in Chicago.
Washington Univ. Law Quart., 1971, 281–307.

GRUPP, S.E., 1971
Prior criminal record and adult marihuana arrest dispositions.
J. Crim. Law, Criminol. & Pol. Sci., **62,** 74–9.

LAAKSO, S.A., 1971
Arrests for drunkenness—two capital cities compared.
Scandinavian Studies in criminology, **3.**
Oslo: Universitetsforlaget, 89–105.

LOW, C., 1971
The battering parent, the community, and the law.
Applied Soc. Stud., **3,** 65–80.

MINNESOTA LAW REVIEW, 1971
The merchant, the shoplifter and the law.
55, 825–69.

PARNAS, R.I., 1971
Police discretion and diversion of incidents of intra-family violence.
Law & Contemp. Problems, **36,** 539–65.

TAYLOR, M., 1971
Study of the juvenile liaison scheme in West Ham 1961 *to* 1965.
London: Home Office Research Studies **8.**

TIEGER, J.H., 1971
Police discretion and discriminatory enforcement.
Duke Law J., 1971, 717–50.

WEINER, N. L., AND WILLIE, C.V., 1971
Decisions by juvenile officers.
Amer. J. Sociol., **77,** 199–210.

COFFEE, J.C., 1972
Privacy versus *parens patriae:* the role of police records in the sentencing and surveillance of juveniles.
Cornell Law Rev., **57,** 571–620.

CONKLIN, J.E., 1972
Robbery and the criminal justice system.
Philadelphia: J.B. Lippincott Co., 123–50.

FERDINAND, T.N., 1972
Politics, the police, and arresting policies in Salem, Massachusetts, since the Civil War.
Social Problems, **19**, 572–88.

HYMAN, M.M., HELRICH, A.R., AND BESSON, G., 1972
Ascertaining police bias in arrests for drunken driving.
Quart. J. of Studies on Alcohol, **33**, 148–59.

RABIN, R.L., 1972
Agency criminal referrals in the federal system: an empirical study of prosecutorial discretion.
Stanford Law Rev., **24**, 1036–91.

SULLIVAN, D.C., AND SIEGEL, L.J., 1972
How police use information to make decisions.
Crime & Delinq., **18**, 253–62.

WILCOX, A.F., 1972
The decision to prosecute.
London: Butterworths.

WILCOX, A.F., 1972
The use of discretion in enforcing the law.
Medico-Legal J., **40**, Part 1, 3–17.

WILLIAMS, J.R., AND GOLD, M., 1972
From delinquent behavior to official delinquency.
Social Problems, **20**, 209–29.

BOTTOMLEY, A.K., 1973
Decisions in the penal process.
London: Martin Robertson, 35–83.

DOLAN, T.J., 1973
The case for double jeopardy: Black and poor.
Internat. J. Criminol. & Penol., **1**, 129–50.

GLESENER, A., 1973
Le classement sans suite et l'opportunité des poursuites.
Revue de Droit Pénal et de Criminologie, **4**, 353–62.

HAWKINS, P.O., 1973
Who called the cops?: decisions to report criminal victimisation.
Law & Soc. Rev., **7**, 427–44.

PARNAS, R.I., 1973
Prosecutorial and judicial handling of family violence.
Crim. Law Bull., **9**, 733–69.

WALKER, N., 1973
Caution? *Police J.*, **45**, 293–307.

COHEN, L., AND STARK, R., 1974
Discriminatory labeling and the five-finger discount. An empirical analysis of differential shoplifting dispositions.
J. Res. Crime & Delinq., **11**, 25–39.

HINDELANG, M.J., 1974
Decisions of shoplifting victims to invoke the criminal justice process.
Social Problems, **21**, 580–93.

ZIMRING, F.E., 1974
Measuring the impact of pretrial diversion from the criminal justice system.
Univ. Chicago Law Rev., **41**, 224–41.

2 Crime in its social setting

1 Economic conditions

[*See also Section* 15(1*a*) *for references on poverty.*]

BONGER, W.A., 1916
Criminality and economic conditions.
London: Heinemann, 247–90. 377–81.

RADZINOWICZ, L., 1937
Variability of the sex ratio in criminality.
Sociol. Rev., **29,** 1–27.

SELLIN, T., 1937
Research memorandum on crime in the depression.
New York: Social Science Research Council, Bulletin No. 27.

RADZINOWICZ, L., 1939
A note on methods of establishing the connection between economic conditions and crime.
Sociol. Rev., **31,** 260–80.

RADZINOWICZ, L., 1941
The influence of economic conditions on crime.
Sociol. Rev., **33,** 139–53.

VOLD, G.B., 1958
Theoretical criminology.
New York: Oxford Univ. Press, 159–82.

GLASER, D., AND RICE, K., 1959
Crime, age and employment,
Amer. Sociol. Rev., **24,** 679–86.

WOOTTON, B., 1959
Social science and social pathology.
London: Allen & Unwin, 107–13.

STREET, D., AND LEGGETT, J.C., 1962
Economic deprivation and extremism: a study of unemployed Negroes.
Amer. J. Sociol., **67,** 53–7.

QUINNEY, R., 1965
Suicide, homicide, and economic development.
Social Forces, **43,** 401–6.

FLEISHER, B.M., 1966
The effect of income on delinquency.
Amer. Econ. Rev., **56,** 118–37.

GIBBS, J.P., 1966
Crime, unemployment and status integration.
Brit. J. Criminol., **6,** 49–58.

MEISSNER, H.H., 1966
Poverty in the affluent society.
New York: Harper & Row, 91–132.

MILLER, S.W., AND REIN, M., 1966
Poverty, inequality, and policy, in H.S. Becker (ed.), *Social problems: a modern approach.*
New York: John Wiley & Sons, 426–516.

TOBIAS, J.J., 1967
Crime and industrial society in the nineteenth century.
London: Batsford (Penguin books edition, 1972), 179–231.

BECKER, G.S., 1968
Crime and punishment: an economic approach.
J. Political Economy, **76,** 169–217.

ALIX, E.K., 1969
The functional interdependence of crime and community social structure.
J. Crim. Law, Criminol. & Pol. Sci., **60,** 332–39.

GOULD, L. C., 1969
The changing structure of property crime in an affluent society.
Social Forces, **48,** 50–9.

HOVLAND, C.I., AND SEARS, R.R., 1969
Minor studies of aggression: correlations of lynchings with economic indices, in A.D. Grimshaw (ed.), *Racial violence in the United States.*
Chicago: Aldine Publishing Co., 344–49.

MINTZ, A., 1969
A re-examination of correlations between lynchings and economic indices, in A.D. Grimshaw (ed.), *Racial violence in the United States.*
Chicago: Aldine Publishing Co., 349–53.

WEST, D.J., 1969
Present conduct and future delinquency.
London: Heinemann, 67–70.

RADZINOWICZ, L., 1971
Economic pressures, in L. Radzinowicz and M.E. Wolfgang (eds.), *Crime and justice,* Vol. 1. *The criminal in society.*
New York: Basic Books, 420–42.

TAYLOR, L., AND WALTON, P., 1971
Industrial sabotage: motives and meanings, in S. Cohen (ed.), *Images of deviance.*
Harmondsworth: Penguin Books, 219–45.

AMSEL, H.G., 1972
Money and crime. For a reorientation of criminological research.
Internat. Crim. Police Rev., **255,** 54–60.

GATRELL, V.A.C., AND HADDEN, T.B., 1972
Criminal statistics and their interpretation in E.A. Wrigley (ed.), *Nineteenth century society: essays in the use of quantative methods in the study of social data.*
Cambridge Univ. Press, 336–96.

HIRST, P.Q., 1972
Marx and Engels on crime, law and morality.
Economy and Society, **1,** 28–56.

AMSEL, H.G., 1973
Money and criminality: a reorientation of criminological research.
Internat. J. Criminol. & Penol., **1,** 179–87.

CLINARD, M.B., AND ABBOTT, D.J., 1973
Crime in developing countries.
New York: John Wiley & Sons, 172–92.

EHRLICH, I., 1973
Participation in illegitimate activities: a theoretical and empirical investigation,
J. Political Economy, **81,** 521–65.

GORDON, D.M., 1973
Capitalism, class, and crime in America.
Crime & Delinq., **19,** 163–86.

ROTTENBERG, S. (ED.), 1973
The economics of crime and punishment.
Washington, D.C.: American Enterprise Institute for Public Policy Research, 11–62.

SJOQUIST, D.L., 1973
Property crime and economic behavior: some empirical results.
Amer. Econ. Rev., **63,** 439–546.

SULLIVAN, R.F., 1973
The economics of crime: an introduction to the literature.
Crime & Delinq., **19,** 138–49.

TAYLOR, I., WALTON, P., AND YOUNG, J., 1973
The new criminology: for a social theory of deviance.
London: Routledge & Kegan Paul, 209–36.

BUCHHOLZ, E., HARTMANN, R., LEKSCHAS, J., AND STILLER, G., 1974
Socialist criminology: theoretical and methodological foundations.
Lexington, Mass., Saxon House, 27–183.

LEES, D., AND CHIPLIN, B., 1975
Does crime pay?
Lloyds Bank Review, No. 116, 30–39.

TAYLOR, I., WALTON, P., AND YOUNG, J. (EDS.), 1975
Critical criminology.
London: Routledge & Kegan Paul.

2 Crime and social class

[*See also Sections* 1(3) *and* 1(4) *for references on the dark figure and police discretion in relation to the social class of official and hidden delinquents.*]

RADZINOWICZ, L. (ED.), 1957
Sexual offences. (Extract relating to occupation and social status of offenders in Britain).
London: Macmillan, 124–7.

WOOTTON, B., 1959
Social science and social pathology.
London: Allen & Unwin, 100–7.

ENGLAND, R.W., 1960
A theory of middle class juvenile delinquency.
J. Crim. Law, Criminol. & Pol. Sci., **50,**
535–40.

BOHLKE, R.H., 1961
Social mobility, stratification inconsistency and middle class delinquency.
Social Problems, **8,** 351–63.

McCLINTOCK, F.H., AND GIBSON, E., 1961
Robbery in London. (Extract relating to occupation and social status of offenders in Britain.)
London: Macmillan, 55–7.

DENTLER, R.A., AND MONROE, L.J., 1961
Social correlates of early adolescent theft.
Amer. Social. Rev., **26,** 733–43.

CLARK, J.P., AND WENNINGER, E.P., 1962
Socio-economic class and areas as correlates of illegal behavior among juveniles.
Amer. Sociol. Rev., **27,** 826–34.

TRASLER, G., 1962
The explanation of criminality.
London: Routledge & Kegan Paul, 64–83.

WOLF, P., 1962
Crime and social class in Denmark.
Brit. J. Criminol., **3,** 5–17.

McCLINTOCK, F.H., 1963
Crimes of violence. (Extract relating to occupation and social status of offenders in Britain.)
London: Macmillan, 131–3.

WEST, D.J., 1963
The habitual prisoner. (Extract relating to occupation and social status of offenders in Britain.)
London: Macmillan, 16 and 117 (Table 8).

STERNE, R.S., 1964
Delinquent conduct and broken homes.
New Haven: College & Univ. Press.

FANNIN, L.F., AND CLINARD, M.B., 1965
Differences in the conception of self as a male among lower and middle class delinquents.
Social Problems, **13,** 205–14.

MANNHEIM, H., 1965
Comparative criminology: a text book. Vol. 2.
London: Routledge & Kegan Paul, 444–68.

ROBISON, S.M., 1965
Abstract of *Career patterns project: a study of the youthful delinquent behavior of men who are respectable members of society*
Washington, D.C.: U.S. Public Health Service, Mimeo.

VAZ, E.W., 1965
Middle-class adolescents: self-reported delinquency and youth culture activities.
Can. Rev. Sociol. & Anthropol., **2,** 52–70.

WESTIE, F.R., AND TURK, A.T., 1965
A strategy for research on social class and delinquency.
J. Crim. Law, Criminol. & Pol. Sci., **56,**
454–62.

CONGER, J.J., AND MILLER, W.C., ET AL., 1966
Personality, social class, and delinquency.
New York: John Wiley & Sons, 182–220.

DOUGLAS, J.W.B., ROSS, J.M., HAMMOND, W.A., AND MULLIGAN, D.G., 1966
Delinquency and social class.
Brit. J. Criminol., **6,** 294–302.

EMPEY, L.T., AND ERICKSON, M.L., 1966
Hidden delinquency and social status.
Social Forces, **44,** 546–54.

SHANLEY, F.J., LEEVER, D.W., AND RICE, R.E., 1966
The aggressive middle-class delinquent.
J. Crim. Law, Criminol. & Pol. Sci., **47,**
145–52.

VOSS, H.L., 1966
Socio-economic status and reported delinquent behavior.
Social Problems, **13,** 314–24.

POLK, K., 1967
Urban social areas and delinquency.
Social Problems, **14,** 320–25.

SHANLEY, F.J., 1967
Middle-class delinquency as a social problem.
Sociol. & Social Research, **51,** 185–97.

TOBIAS, J.J., 1967
Crime and industrial society in the nineteenth century.

London: Batsford (Penguin books edition, 1972), 59–87. 108–33.

Willie, C.V., 1967
The relative contribution of family status and economic status to juvenile delinquency.
Social Problems, **14,** 326–35.

Chapman, D., 1968
Sociology and the stereotype of the criminal.
London: Tavistock, 54–96.

Glueck, S., and Glueck, E., 1968
Delinquents and nondelinquents in perspective.
Cambridge, Mass.: Harvard Univ. Press, 11–16, 99–106.

Newson, J. and Newson, E., 1968
Four year's old in an urban community.
London: Geo Allen & Unwin, 107–41.

McDonald, L., 1969
Social class and delinquency.
London: Faber & Faber, 62–98.

Vaz, E.W., 1969
Delinquency and the youth culture: upper and middle-class boys.
J. Crim. Law, Criminol. & Pol. Sci., **60,** 33–46.

Gibbons, D.C., 1970
Delinquent behavior.
Englewood Cliffs, N.J.: Prentice-Hall, 102–71.

Gold, M., 1970
Delinquent behavior in an American city.
Belmont, Calif.: Brooks/Cole Publishing Co., 59–81.

Hewitt, J.P., 1970
Social stratification and deviant behavior.
New York: Random House.

Miller, J.G., 1970
Research and theory in middle-class delinquency.
J. Brit. Criminol., **10,** 33–51.

Tobias, J.J., 1970
The affluent surburban male delinquent,
Crime & Delinq., **16,** 273–79.

Box, S., and Ford, J., 1971
The facts don't fit: on the relationship between social class and criminal behavior.
Sociol. Rev., **19,** 31–52.

Bytheway, W.R., and May, D.R., 1971
On fitting the 'facts' of social class and criminal behavior: a rejoinder to Box and Ford.
Sociol. Rev., **19,** 585–607.

Poston, R.W., 1971
The gang and the establishment.
New York: Harper & Row.

Vaz, E.W., 1971
Explorations in the institutionalization of juvenile delinquency.
J. Crim. Law, Criminol. & Pol. Sci., **62,** 396–406.

Wolfgang, M.E., Figlio, R.M., and Sellin, T., 1972
Delinquency in a birth cohort.
Chicago: Univ. of Chicago Press, 53–64, 244–55.

Chevalier, L., 1973
Labouring classes and dangerous classes in Paris during the first half of the nineteenth century.
London: Routledge & Kegan Paul.

Erickson, M.L., 1973
Group violations, socioeconomic staus and official delinquency.
Social Forces, **52,** 41–52.

Gordon, D.M., 1973
Capitalism, class, and crime in America.
Crime & Delinq., **19,** 163–86.

Trasler, G., 1973
Criminal behavior, in H.J. Eysenck (ed.), *Handbook of Abnormal Psychology.*
London: Pitmans, 67–96.

Erlanger, H.S., 1974
Social class and corporal punishment in childrearing: a reassessment.
Amer. Sociol. Rev., **39,** 68–85.

Power, M.J., Ash, P.M., Soenberg, E., and Sirey, E.C., 1974
Delinquency and the family.
Brit. J. Social Wk., **4,**(1), 13–38.

3 Social disorganization and the ecological school

KOBRIN, S., 1951
The conflict of values in delinquency areas.
Amer. Sociol. Rev., **16**, 653–61.

JEPHCOTT, A.P., AND CARTER, M.P., 1954
The social background of delinquency.
Univ. of Nottingham, Mimeo. 1–14, 275–303

LANDER, B., 1954
Towards an understanding of juvenile delinquency.
New York: Columbia Univ. Press.

MAYS, J.B., 1954
Growing up in the city.
Liverpool Univ. Press.

TOBY, J., 1957
The differential impact of family disorganisation.
Amer. Sociol. Rev., **22**, 505–12.

MORRIS, T.P., 1958
The criminal area.
London: Routledge & Kegan Paul.

COHEN, A.K., 1960
The study of social disorganisation and deviant behavior, in R.L. Merton, L. Broom and L.S. Cottrell (eds.), *Sociology today.*
New York: Basic Books, 461–84.

SCARPITTI, F.R., ET AL., 1960
The 'good' boy in a high delinquency area: four years later.
Amer. Sociol. Rev., **25**, 555–8.

SCHNITT, C.F., 1960
Urban crime areas.
Amer. Sociol. Rev., **25**, 527–42, 655–78.

YINGER, J.M., 1960
Contraculture and subculture.
Amer. Sociol. Rev., **25**, 625–35.

MAYS, J.B., 1963
Delinquency areas—a re-assessment.
Brit. J. Criminol., **3**, 216–30.

GLASER, D., 1965
Social disorganisation and delinquent subcultures, in H.C. Quay (ed.), *Juvenile delinquency research and theory.*
Princeton: D. Van Nostrand Co., 27–62.

DOWNES, D.M., 1966
The delinquent solution.
London: Routledge & Kegan Paul, 100–94.

TOBIAS, J.J., 1967
Crime and industrial society in the nineteenth century.
London: Batsford (Penguin books edition, 1972), 134–75.

WALLIS, C.P., AND MALIPHANT, R., 1967
Delinquent areas in the county of London: ecological factors.
Brit. J. Criminol., **7**, 250–84.

WILKS, J.A., 1967
Ecological correlates of crime and delinquency, in *Task force report, crime and its impact—an assessment.*
Washington, D.C.: President's Commission on Law Enforcement and Administration of Justice, 138–156.

LANE, R., 1969
Urbanization and criminal violence in the 19th century: Massachusetts as a test case, in H.D. Graham and T.R. Gurr (eds.), *Violence in America: historical and comparative perspectives.* Vol. 2.
A report to the National Commission on the Causes and Prevention of Violence.
Washington, D.C., 359–70.

MATZA, D., 1969
Becoming deviant.
Englewood Cliffs, N.J.: Prentice-Hall, 3–85.

SHAW, C.R., AND MCKAY, H.D., 1969
Juvenile delinquency and urban areas.
Univ. Chicago Press, rev. ed.

WEST, D.J., 1969
Present conduct and future delinquency.
London: Heinemann, 135–49.

GIGGS, J.A., 1970
Socially disorganised areas in Barry: a multivariate analysis, in H. Carter and W.K.D. Davies (eds.), *Urban essays: studies in the geography of Wales.*
London: Longman, 101–43.

2 Crime in its social setting

LAMBERT, J.R., 1970
Crime, police and race relations.
London: Oxford Univ. Press, 91–130.

BALDWIN, J., 1972
Delinquent schools in Tower Hamlets.
A critique.
Brit. J. Criminol., **12**, 399–403.

BROWN, M.J., MCCULLOCH, J.W., AND HISCOX, J., 1972
Criminal offences in an urban area and their associated social variables, *Brit. J. Criminol.*, **12**, 250–68.

POWER, M.J., BENN, R.T., AND MORRIS, J.N., 1972.
Neighbourhood, school and juveniles before the courts.
Brit. J. Criminol., **12**, 111–32.

ARMSTRONG, G., AND WILSON, M., 1973
Delinquency and some aspects of housing, C. Ward (ed.), *Vandalism.*
London: Architectural Press, 64–84.

CHEVALIER, L., 1973
Labouring classes and dangerous classes in Paris during the first half of the nineteenth century.
London: Routledge & Kegan Paul, 271–355.

CLINARD, M.B., AND ABBOTT, D.J., 1973
Crime in developing countries.
New York: John Wiley & Sons, 77–171.

EDWARDS, A., 1973
Sex and area variations in delinquency rates in an English city.
Brit. J. Criminol., **13**, 121–37.

PALMER, S., 1973
High social integration as a source of deviance.
Brit. J. Sociol., **24**, 93–100.

MCVICAR, J., 1974
McVicar, by himself (edited by G. Rees).
London: Hutchinson, 145–204.

TOBIAS, J.J., 1974
A statistical study of a nineteenth-century criminal area.
Brit. J. Criminol., **14**, 221–35.

4 Differential association

CRESSEY, D.R., 1953
Other people's money.
Glencoe, Ill.: Free Press.

GLASER, D., 1956
Criminality theories and behavioral images.
Amer. J. Sociol., **61**, 433–43.

GLUECK, S., 1956
Theory and fact in criminology: a criticism of differential association.
Brit. J. Delinq., **7**, 92–109.

VOLD, G.B., 1958
Theoretical criminology.
New York: Oxford Univ. Press, 183–202.

COHEN, A.K., 1959
The study of social disorganization and deviant behavior, in R.K. Merton, L.R. Broom and L.S. Cottrell (eds.), *Sociology today.*
New York: Basic Books, 461–84.

CRESSEY, D.R., 1960
Epidemology and individual conduct.
Pacific Soc. Rev., **3**, 47–58.

CRESSEY, D.R., 1960
The theory of differential association: an introduction.
Social Problems, **8**, 4–5.

GLASER, D., 1960
Differential association and criminological prediction.
Social Problems, **8**, 6–14.

SHORT, J.F., 1960
Differential association as a hypothesis: problems of empirical testing.
Social Problems, **8**, 14–25.

CRESSEY, D.R., 1962
Role theory, differential association and compulsive crime, in A.M. Rose (ed.), *Human behaviour and social processes.*
London: Routledge & Kegan Paul, 443–67.

GLASER, D., 1962
The differential-association theory of crime, in A.M. Rose (ed.), *Human behavior and social processes.*
London: Routledge & Kegan Paul, 430–31, 432–37.

CRESSEY, D.R., 1964
Delinquency, crime and differential association.
The Hague: Nijhoff.

FARARO, T.J., AND SUNSHINE, M.H., 1964
A study of a biased friendship net.
Syracuse, N.Y.: Syracuse Univ. Youth Development Center.

WILLETT, T.C., 1964
Criminal on the road—a study of serious motoring offences and those who commit them.
London: Tavistock, 313–16.

HARTUNG, F.E., 1965
Crime, law and society.
Wayne State Univ. Press, 15–88, 125–66.

BURGESS, R.L., AND AKERS, R.L., 1966
A differential association-reinforcement theory of criminal behavior.
Social Problems, **14**, 128–47.

GLUECK, S. AND GLUECK, E., 1968
Delinquents and nondelinquents in perspective.
Harvard Univ. Press, 29–39, 107–21, 169–76.

SHAW, C.R., AND MCKAY, H.D., 1969
Juvenile delinquency and urban areas.
Univ. Chicago Press. Rev. ed.

VOSS, H.L., 1969
Differential association and containment theory: a theoretical convergence.
Social Forces, **47**, 381–91.

GIBBONS, D.C., 1971
Observations on the study of crime causation.
Amer. J. Sociol., **77**, 262–78.

CLARK, R.E., 1972
Reference group theory and delinquency.
New York: Behavioral Publications.

JENSEN, G.F., 1972
Parents, peers and delinquent action: a test of the differential association perspective.
Amer. J. Sociol., **78**, 562–75.

TEC, N., 1972
The peer group and marijuana use.
Crime & Delinq., **18**, 298–309.

ADAMS, R., 1973
Differential association and learning principles revisited.
Social Problems, **20**, 458–70.

AKERS, R.L., 1973
Deviant behavior: a social learning approach.
Belmont, Calif.: Wadsworth Publishing Co., 33–61.

SCHUESSLER, K. F., (ED.), 1973
Edwin H. Sutherland: on analysing crime.
Univ. Chicago Press, 5–43.

SEVERY, L.J., 1973
Exposure to deviance committed by valued peer group and family members.
J. Res. Crime & Delinq., **10**,(1), 35–46.

ADAMS, R., 1974
The adequacy of differential association theory.
J. Res. Crime & Delinq., **11**, 1–8.

ERLANGER, H.S., 1974
Social class and corporal punishment in childrearing: a reassessment.
Amer. Sociol. Rev., **39**, 68–85.

HINDELANG, M.J., 1974
Moral evaluations of illegal behaviors.
Social Problems, **21**, 370–84.

SUTHERLAND, E.H., AND CRESSEY, D.R., 1974
Principles of criminology (9th ed.). Philadelphia & New York: J.B. Lippincott Co., 71–93.

5 Frustrations in opportunity and anomie

[*See also Section* 3(2) *for references relating to study of gangs.*]

(*a*) *Theories and concepts*

DURKHEIM, E., 1893
The division of labour in society.
Glencoe, Ill.: Free Press, 1933, 353–73.

DURKHEIM, E., 1897
Suicide.
London: Routledge & Kegan Paul 1952, 241–76.

BELL, D., 1953
Crime, an American way of life.
Antioch Rev., 1953, 131–54.

COHEN, A.K., 1955
Delinquent boys: the culture of the gang.
Glencoe, Ill.: Free Press.

MERTON, R.K., 1956
The social-cultural environment and anomie, in H.L. Witmer and R. Kotinsky (eds.), *New Perspectives for research on juvenile delinquency.*
Washington, D.C., 24–32, and discussion, 32–50.

MERTON, R.K., 1957
Social theory and social structure.
Glencoe, Ill.: Free Press, 131–94.

KITSUSE, J.I. AND DIETRICK, D.C., 1959
Delinquent boys: a critique.
Amer. Sociol. Rev., **24,** 208–15.

BOHANNAN, P. (ED.), 1960
African homicide and suicide.
New York: Princeton Univ. Press, xiii–xix, 3–29.

CLOWARD, R.A., AND OHLIN, L.E., 1960
Delinquency and opportunity: a theory of delinquent gangs.
Glencoe, Ill.: Free Press.

YINGER, J.M., 1960
Contraculture and subculture.
Amer. Sociol. Rev., **25,** 625–35.

CLINARD, M.B., 1964
The theoretical implications of anomie and deviant behavior, in M.B. Clinard (ed.), *Anomie and deviant behavior.*
New York: Free Press, 1–56.

MATZA, D., 1964
Delinquency and drift.
New York: John Wiley & Sons, 1–68.

MERTON, R.K., 1964
Anomie, anomia, and social interaction: contexts of deviant behavior, in M.B. Clinard (ed.), *Anomie and deviant behavior.*
New York: Free Press, 213–43.

MIZRUCHI, H., 1964
Success and opportunity: class values and anomie in American life.
Glencoe, Ill.: Free Press.

SHORT, J.F., 1964
Gang delinquency and anomie, in M.B. Clinard (ed.), *Anomie and deviant behavior.*
New York: Free Press, 98–127.

COHEN, A.K., 1965
The sociology of the deviant act: anomie theory and beyond.
Amer. Sociol. Rev., **30,** 5–14.

GLASER, D., 1965
Social disorganisation and delinquent subcultures, in H.C. Quay (ed.), *Juvenile delinquency research and theory.*
Princeton: D.Van Nostrand Co., 27–62.

SHORT, J.F., AND STRODTBECK, F.L., 1965
Group process and gang delinquency.
Univ. Chicago Press.

CHAMBLISS, W.J., AND STEELE, M.F., 1966
Status integration and suicide: an assessment.
Amer. Sociol. Rev., **31,** 524–32.

POWELL, E.H., 1966
Crime as a function of anomie,
J. Crim. Law, Criminol. & Pol. Sci., **57,** 161–71.

ROSE, G., 1966
Anomie and deviation—a conceptual framework for empirical studies.
Brit. J. Sociol., **17,** 29–45.

HARGREAVES, D., 1967
Social relations in a secondary school.
London: Routledge & Kegan Paul, 159–92.

HIRSCHI, T., 1969
Causes of Delinquency.
Berkeley: Univ. California Press, 3–34, 225–32.

POWELL, E.H., 1970
The design of discord: Studies of anomie.
New York: Oxford Univ. Press, 105–32.

BUFFALO, M.D., AND RODGERS, J.W., 1971
Behavioral norms, moral norms, and attachment problems of deviance and conformity.
Social Problems, **19**, 101–13.

EMPEY, L., LUBECK, S.G., WITH LA PORTE, R.L., 1971
Explaining delinquency: construction, test and reformulation of a sociological theory.
Lexington, Mass.: Heath Lexington Books, 33–84.

COHEN, H., 1972
The anomia of success and the anomia of failure: a study of similarities in opposites.
Brit. J. Sociol., **23**, 329–43.

PLASEK, W., 1974
Marxist and American sociological conceptions of alienation: implications for social problems theory.
Social Problems, **21**, 316–28.

5. Frustrations in opportunity and anomie

[*See also Section* 3(2) *for references relating to studies of gangs.*]

(*b*) *Empirical studies*

HENRY, A.F., AND SHORT, J.F., 1954
Suicide and homicide.
New York: Free Press, 13–65.

CLARK, J.P., AND WENNINGER, E.P., 1962
Socio-economic class and areas as correlates of illegal behavior among juveniles.
Amer. Sociol. Rev., **27**, 826–34.

KARACKI, L., AND TOBY, J., 1962
The uncommitted adolescent: candidate for gang socialization.
Sociol. Inquiry, **32**, 203–15.

CLARK, J.P., AND WENNINGER, E.P., 1963
Goal orientations and illegal behavior among juveniles.
Social Forces, **42**, 49–59.

GOLD, M., 1963
Status forces in delinquent boys.
Ann Arbor, Michigan: Institute for Social Research, 151–73.

REISS, A.J., AND RHODES, A.L., 1963
Status deprivation and delinquent behavior.
Sociol. Quart., **4**, 135–49.

MORRIS, R.R., 1964
Female delinquency and relational problems.
Social Forces, **43**, 82–9.

SHORT, J.F., 1964
Gang delinquency and anomie, in M.B. Clinard (ed.), *Anomie and deviant behavior.*
New York: Free Press, 98–127.

SPERGEL, I., 1964
Racketville, slumtown, haulburg: an exploratory study of delinquent subcultures.
Univ. Chicago Press, 29–92.

STINCHCOMBE, A.L., 1964
Rebellion in a high school.
Chicago: Quadrangle Books.

CERVANTES, L.F., 1965
The dropout: causes and cures.
Ann Arbour: Univ. Michigan Press, 118–74.

LANDIS, J.R., AND SCARPITTI, F.R., 1965
Perceptions regarding value orientation and legitimate opportunity: delinquents and non-delinquents.
Social Forces, **44,** 83–91.

ROACH, J.L., AND GURSSLIN, O.R., 1965
The lower class, status frustration and social disorganization.
Social Forces, **43,** 501–10.

SHORT, J.F., AND STRODTBECK, F.L., 1965
Group process and gang delinquency.
Univ. Chicago Press.

SPILLER, B., 1965
Delinquency and middle class goals.
J. Crim. Law, Criminol. & Pol. Sci., **56,** 463–78.

ELLIOTT, D.S., 1966
Delinquency, school attendance and dropout.
Social Problems, **13,** 307–14.

HARGREAVES, D., 1967
Social relations in a secondary school.
London: Routledge & Kegan Paul, 159–92.

IGA, M., AND O'HARA, K., 1967
Suicide attempts of Japanese youth and Durkheim's concept of anomie: an interpretation.
Human Organization, **26,** 59–68.

RIVERA, R.J., AND SHORT, J.F.JR. 1967
Occupational goals: a comparative analysis, in M.W. Klein (ed.), *Juvenile gangs in context.*
Englewood Cliffs, N.J.: Prentice-Hall, 70–90.

SUGARMAN, B., 1967
Involvement in youth culture, academic achievement and conformity in school: an empirical study of London schoolboys.
Brit. J. Sociol., **18,** 151–64.

UNITED STATES OF AMERICA, 1967
The challenge of crime in a free society.
Report of the President's Commission on Law Enforcement and Administration of Justice.
Washington, D.C., 5–6, 56–77.

UNITED STATES OF AMERICA, 1967
Task force report: juvenile delinquency and youth crime.
Washington, D.C.: President's Commission on Law Enforcement and Administration of Justice, 41–56, 114–18, 132–44, 145–54, 222–58, 305–16.

ROSENTHAL, R., AND JACOBSEN, L., 1968
Pygmalion in the classroom: teacher expectation and pupils' intellectual development.
New York: Holt, Rinehart & Winston, 174–82.

UNITED STATES OF AMERICA, 1968
Report of the National Advisory Commission on civil disorders.
Washington, D.C., (and New York: Bantam Books), Chapter 7.

DORN, D.S., 1969
A partial test of the delinquency continuum typology: contracultures and subcultures.
Social Forces, **47,** 305–14.

HIRSCHI, T., 1969
Causes of Delinquency.
Berkeley: Univ. California Press.

RHODES, A.L., AND REISS, A.J., 1969
Apathy, truancy and delinquency as adaptations to school failure.
Social Forces, **48,** 12–22.

GOLD, M., 1970
Delinquent behavior in an American city.
Belmont, Calif.: Brooks/Cole Publishing Co., 114–32.

HEWITT, J.P., 1970
Social stratification and deviant behavior.
New York: Random House.

HOOD, R.G., AND SPARKS, R.F., 1970
Key issues in criminology.
London: Weidenfeld & Nicolson, 80–109.

BENJAMIN, R., 1971
Délinquance juvénile et société anomique.
Paris: Centre National de la Recherche Scientifique.

EMPEY, L., LUBECK, S.G., WITH LA PORTE, R.L., 1971
Explaining delinquency: construction, test, and reformulation of a sociology theory.
Lexington, Mass.: Heath Lexington Books, 33–84.

ENGSTAD, P., AND HACKLER, J.C., 1971
The impact of alienation on delinquency rates.
Canad. J. Corrections, **13**, 147–54

PHILLIPSON, C.M., 1971
Juvenile delinquency and the school in W.G. Carson and P. Wiles (eds.), *Crime and delinquency in Britain.*
London: Martin Robertson, 236–58.

POLK, K., AND PINK, W., 1971
Youth culture and the school: a replication.
Brit. J. Sociol., **22**, 160–71.

VAZ, E.W., 1971
Explorations in the institutionalization of juvenile delinquency,
J. Crim. Law, Criminol. & Pol. Sci., **62**, 396–406.

GOLD, M., AND MANN, D., 1972
Delinquency as defense.
Amer. J. Orthopsychiatry, **42**, 463–79.

POLK, K., AND SCHAFER, W.E. (EDS.), 1972
School and delinquency.
Englewood Cliffs, N.J.: Prentice-Hall.

POWER, M.J., BENN, R.T., AND MORRIS, J.N., 1972
Neighbourhood, school and juveniles before the courts.
Brit. J. Criminol., **12**, 111–32.

RITTERBAND, P., AND SILBERSTEIN, R., 1973
Group disorders in the public schools.
Amer. Sociol. Rev., **38**, 461–67.

HINDELANG, M.J., 1974
Moral evaluations of illegal behaviors.
Social Problems, **21**, 370–84.

6 Racial and cultural schisms

[*See also Section* 5(1) *for references relating to racial clashes in civil disorders.*]

SELLIN, T., 1938
Culture conflict and crime.
New York: Social Science Research Council, Bulletin No. 41.

VON HENTIG, H., 1940
The criminality of the Negro.
J. Crim. Law, Criminol. & Pol. Sci., **30**, 662–80.

JOHNSON, G.B., 1941
The negro and crime.
Annals Amer. Acad. Pol. & Soc. Sci., **271**, 93–104.

VAN VECHTEN, C.C., 1941
The criminality of the foreign born.
J. Crim. Law, Criminol. & Pol. Sci., **32**, 139–47.

MOSES, E.R., 1947
Differentials in crime rates between Negroes and whites based on comparisons of four socio-economically equated areas.
Amer. Sociol. Rev., **12**, 411–20.

GARFINKEL, H., 1949
Research note on inter- and intra-racial homicides.
Social Forces, **27**, 369–81.

VOLD, G.B., 1958
Theoretical criminology.
New York: Oxford Univ. Press, 203–20.

SHOHAM, S., 1962
The application of the 'culture-conflict' hypothesis to the criminality of immigrants in Israel.

J. Crim. Law, Criminol. & Pol. Sci., **53**, 207–41.

GLAZER, N., AND MOYNIHAN, D.P., 1963
Beyond the melting pot.
Cambridge, Mass.: Harvard Univ. Press.

PETTIGREW, T.F., 1964
A profile of the Negro American.
Princeton, N.J.: D. Van Nostrand Co., 27–55, 136–56.

SEGAL, B.E., 1964
Racial group membership and juvenile delinquency.
Social Forces, **43**, 70–81.

WILLIE, C.V., AND GERSHENOVITZ, A., 1964
Juvenile delinquency in racially mixed areas.
Amer. Sociol. Rev., **29**, 740–4.

WOLFGANG, M.E., 1964
Crime and race.
New York: Institute of Human Relations Press.

CALIFORNIA, STATE OF, 1965
Violence in the city: an end or a beginning?
Los Angeles: Report of the Governor's Commission on Los Angeles Riots.

LIEBERSON, S., AND SILVERMAN, A.R., 1965
The precipitants and underlying conditions of race riots.
Amer. Sociol. Rev., **30**, 887–98.

LOHMAN, J., 1965
Violence in the streets: its context and meaning.
Notre Dame Lawyer, **40**, 517–33.

MANNHEIM, H., 1965
Comparative criminology: a text book, Vol. 2.
London: Routledge & Kegan Paul, 562–72.

SIMPSON, G.E., AND YINGER, J.M., 1965
Racial and cultural minorities.
New York: Harper & Row (3rd ed.).

TAEUBER, K.E., AND TAEUBER, A.F., 1965
Negroes in cities: residential segregation and neighbourhood change.
Chicago: Aldine Publishing Co.

HIMES, J.S., 1966
The functions of racial conflict.
Social Forces, **45**, 1–10.

LIEBOW, E., 1966
Tally's Corner, Washington, D.C.: a study of Negro street corner men.
New York: Little, Brown & Co.

LOHMAN, J.D., AND MISNER, G.E., 1966
Field Surveys IV: *The police and the community.* Vol. 1.
Washington, D.C.: President's Commission on Law Enforcement and Administration of Justice, 120–31.

MILLER, H.P., 1966
Poverty and the Negro, in L. Fishman (ed.), *Poverty amid affluence.*
Yale Univ. Press.

PARSONS, T., AND CLARK, K.B., (EDS.), 1966
The Negro American.
New York: Houghton Miffin Co.

SHOHAM, S., SHOHAM, N., AND ABD-EL-RAZEK, A., 1966
Immigration ethnicity and ecology as related to juvenile delinquency in Israel.
Brit. J. Criminol., **6**, 391–409.

BIDERMAN, A.D., ET AL. 1967
Field Surveys I: *Report on a pilot study in the district of Columbia on victimization and attitudes toward law enforcement.*
Washington, D.C.: President's Commision on Law Enforcement and Administration of Justice, 135–51.

BLACK, D.J., AND REISS, A.J., JR., 1967
Patterns of behavior in police and citizen transactions, in Field Surveys III: *Studies in crime and law enforcement in major metropolitan areas.* Vol. 2.
Washington, D.C.: President's Commission on Law Enforcement and Administration of Justice, 41–67, 133–39.

BOTTOMS, A.E., 1967
Delinquency among immigrants.
Race, **8**, 357–83.

BULLOUGH, B., 1967
Alienation in the ghetto.
Amer. J. Sociol., **72**, 469–78.

DEFLEUR, L.B., 1967
A cross-cultural comparison of juvenile offenders and offenses: Cordoba, Argentina, and the United States.
Social Problems, **14**, 483–92.

DUNCAN, O.D., 1967
Discrimination against Negroes.
Annals Amer. Acad. Pol. & Sci. Soc., **371**, 85–103.

ENNIS, P.H., 1967
Field Surveys II: *Criminal victimization in the United States: a report of a national survey.*
Washington, D.C.: President's Commission on Law Enforcement and Administration of Justice, 52–79.

LOHMAN, J.D., AND MISNER, G.E., 1967
Field Surveys IV: *The The police and the community*, Vol. 2.
Washington, D.C.: President's Commission on Law Enforcement and Administration of Justice, 159–67.

OVERBY, A.W. JR., 1967
Discrimination against minority groups in the administration of justice.
A document submitted to the President's Commission on Law Enforcement and Administration of Justice. Washington, D.C. Mimeo.

REISS, A.J. JR., 1967
Measurement of the nature and amount of crime, in Field Surveys III: *Studies in crime and law enforcement in major metropolitan areas.*
Vol. 1(1).
Washington, D.C.: President's Commission on Law Enforcement and Administration of Justice, 131–42.

SPERGEL, I., 1967
Deviant patterns and opportunities of pre-adolescent Negro boys in three Chicago neighborhoods, in M.W. Klein (ed.), *Juvenile gangs in context.*
Englewood Cliffs, N.J.: Prentice-Hall, 38–54.

UNITED STATES OF AMERICA, 1967
Field Survey V: *A national survey of police and community relations.*
Washington, D.C.: President's Commission on Law Enforcement and Administration of Justice, 363–72.

UNITED STATES OF AMERICA, 1967
The challenge of crime in a free society.
Report of the President's Commission on Law Enforcement and Administration of Justice.
Washington, D.C.: 44–5, 56–66.

BAGLEY, C., 1968
Migration, race and mental health.
Race, **9**, 345–56.

FERRACUTI, F., 1968
European migration and crime, in M.E. Wolfgang (ed.), *Crime and culture: essays in honor of Thorsten Sellin.*
New York: John Wiley & Sons, 189–289.

GRINDSTAFF, C.F., 1968
The Negro, urbanization, and relative deprivation in the deep south.
Social Problems, **15**, 342–52.

LANDAU, S.F., AND DRAPKIN, S.I., 1968
Ethnic patterns of criminal homicide in Israel.
Final report.
Hebrew Univ. Jerusalem, Mimeo.

SHOHAM, S., 1968
Culture conflict as a frame of reference for research in criminology and social deviation, in M.E. Wolfgang (ed.), *Crime and culture: essays in honor of Thorsten Sellin.*
New York: John Wiley & Sons, 55–82.

STEPHENSON, R.M., AND SCARPITTI, F.R., 1968
Negro-white differentials and delinquency.
J. Res. Crime & Delinq., **5**, 122–33.

SUTTLES, G.D., 1968
The social order of the slum: ethnicity and territory in the inner city.
Univ. Chicago Press, 195–220.

UNITED STATES OF AMERICA, 1968
Report of the National Advisory Commission on civil disorders.
Washington D.C., (and New York: Bantam Books), Chapter 8.

CHAMBLISS, W.J., AND NAGASAWA, R.H., 1969
On the validity of official statistics—a comparative study of white, black and Japanese high school boys.
J. Res. Crime & Delinq., **6**, 71–7.

MASOTTI, L.H., SEMINATORE, K.F., HADDEN, J.K., AND CORSI, J.R., 1969
A time to burn? An evaluation of the present crisis in race relations.
Chicago: Rand McNally & Co.

NETO, V., AND PALMER, T., 1969
Patterns of conflict among higher maturity urban Negro delinquents.

Community Treatment Project Report Series. California Youth Authority, Sacramento. Mimeo, 30–4.

ROSEN, L., 1969
Matriarchy and lower class negro male delinquency.
Social Problems, **17**, 175–89.

BLACK, D.J., AND REISS, A.J., 1970
Police control of juveniles.
Amer. Sociol., Rev., **35**, 63–77.

FORSLUND, M.A., 1970
A comparison of Negro and white crime rates.
J. Crim. Law, Crim. & Pol. Sci., **61**, 214–17.

GREEN, E., 1970
Race, social status and criminal arrest.
Amer. Sociol. Rev., **35**, 476–90.

JOHN, A., 1970
Race in the inner city: a report from Handsworth, Birmingham.
London: Runnymede Trust, 12–19.

LAMBERT, J., 1970
Crime, police and race relations.
London: Oxford Univ. Press, 209–91.

ROBERT, P., BISMUTH, P., AND LAMBERT, T., 1970
La criminalité des migrants en France.
Annales Internat. de Criminol., **9**, 567–97.

AMIR, M., 1971
Criminality among Jews: an overview.
Issues in Criminol., **6**, (2), 1–39.

CROSS, H.J., AND TRACY, J.J., 1971
Personality factors in delinquent boys: differences between blacks and whites.
J. Res. Crime & Delinq., **8**, 10–22.

RIBORDY, F.X., 1971
Conflit de culture et criminalité des migrants Italiens.
Canad. J. Corrections, **13**, 24–42.

RUDOFF, A., 1971
The incarcerated Mexican-American delinquent.
J. Crim. Law, Criminol. & Pol. Sci., **62**, 224–38.

FRANCIS, R.D., 1972
Migration and crime, in D. Chappell and P. Wilson (eds.), *The Australian criminal justice system.*
Sydney: Butterworths, 201–22.

FRANCIS, R.D., 1972
Migrant imprisonment rates in N.S.W. since Federation.
Aust. & N.Z. J. of Criminol., **5**, 206–19.

MUDD, J.E., 1972
Indian juveniles and legislative delinquency in Montana.
Montana Law Rev., **33**, 233–54.

REASONS, C.E., AND KUYKENDALL, J.L., 1972
Race, crime and justice.
California: Goodyear Publishing Co.

SOCIETY, 1973
Special supplement on race, sex, and gangs, articles by W.J. Chambliss, *et al.*
Society, **11**(1), 24–50.

MCCULLOCH, J.W., SMITH, N.J., AND BATTA, I.D., 1974
A comparative study of adult crime amongst Asians and their host population.
Probation J., **21**,(1) 16–21.

SCHULMAN, G.I., 1974
Race, sex and violence: a laboratory test of the sexual threat of the black male hypothesis.
Amer. J. Sociol., **79**, 1260–77.

SILVERMAN, I.J., AND DINITZ, S., 1974
Compulsive masculinity and delinquency: an empirical investigation.
Criminology, **11**, 498–515.

SUTHERLAND, E.H., AND CRESSEY, D.R., 1974
Principles of Criminology (9th ed.).
Philadelphia & New York: J.B. Lippincott Co., 132–51.

7 Deviance: social functions, labelling and interaction

[*See also Section* 1(4) *for references on police discretion to prosecute. Section* 7(1) *for references relating to aims of penal sanctions. Section* 10(1) *for references on the general preventive effects of penal sanctions.*]

DURKHEIM, E., 1895
The rules of sociological method.
Glencoe, Ill.: Free Press, 1958 ed., 65–73.

DURKHEIM, E., 1950
Professional ethnics and civic morals.
London: Routledge & Kegan Paul, 1957, 110–20.

TANNENBAUM, F., 1951
Crime and the community.
Columbia Univ. Press, 3–22 (1st ed. 1938).

VAN BEMMELEN, J.M., 1952
The constancy of crime.
Brit. J. Delinq., **2,** 208–28.

GARFINKEL, H., 1956
Conditions of successful degradation ceremonies.
Amer. J. Sociol., **61,** 420–24.

SYKES, G., AND MATZA, D., 1957
Techniques of neutralisation: a theory of delinquency.
Amer. Sociol. Rev., **22,** 664–70.

DENTLER, R.A., AND ERIKSON, K.T., 1959
The functions of deviance in groups.
Social Problems, **7,** 98–107.

JEFFERY, C.R., 1960
The historical development of criminology, in H. Mannheim (ed.), *Pioneers in criminology.*
London: Stevens, 364–94.

ROSS, H.L., 1960–61
Traffic law violation: a folk crime.
Social Problems, **8,** 231–41.

GOULDNER, A.W., 1961
Anti-minotaur: the myth of a value-free sociology.
Social Problems, **9,** 199–213.

KITSUSE, J.I., 1961
Societal reaction to deviant behavior: problems of theory and method.
Social Problems. **9,** 247–56.

MATZA, D., 1961
Subterranean traditions of youth.
Annals Amer. Acad. Pol. & Soc. Sci., **338,** 102–18.

MATZA, D., AND SYKES, G.M., 1961
Juvenile delinquency and subterranean values.
Amer. Sociol. Rev., **26,** 712–19.

DEUTSCHER, I., 1962
Some relevant directions for research in juvenile delinquency in A.M. Rose (ed.), *Human behavior and social processes.*
London: Routledge & Kegan Paul, 468–81.

BECKER, H.S., 1963
Outsiders. Studies in the sociology of deviance.
Glencoe, Ill.: Free Press, 1–18.

GOFFMAN, E., 1963
Stigma.
Englewood Cliffs, N.J.: Prentice-Hall.

ERIKSON, K.T., 1964
Notes on the sociology of deviance, in H.S. Becker (ed.), *The other side: perspectives on deviance.*
Glencoe, Ill.: Free Press, 9–21.

KITSUSE, J.I., 1964
Societal reaction to deviant behavior, problems of theory and method, in H.S. Becker (ed.), *The other side: perspectives on deviance.*
Glencoe, Ill.: Free Press, 87–102.

TAFT, D.R., AND ENGLAND, R.W., 1964
Criminology.
New York: Macmillan, 271–9.

WILKINS, L.T., 1964
Social deviance: social policy, action and research.
London: Tavistock Publications, 45–103.

BEERMAN, R., 1965
The further development of the anti-parasite law.
Brit. J. Criminol., **5,** 207–11.

QUINNEY, R., 1965
Is criminal behaviour deviant behaviour?
Brit. J. Criminol., **5**, 132–42.

SCHUR, E.M., 1965
Crimes without victims.
Englewood Cliffs, N.J.: Prentice-Hall, 1–10.

SIMMONS, J.L., AND CHAMBERS, H., 1965
Public stereotypes of deviants.
Social Problems, **13**, 223–32.

SUDNOW, D., 1965
Normal crimes: sociological features of the penal code in a public defender office.
Social Problems, **12**, 255–76.

COHEN, A., 1966
Deviance and control.
Englewood Cliffs, N.J.: Prentice-Hall.

COSER, L.A., 1966
Some social functions of violence.
Annals Amer. Acad. Pol. & Soc. Sci., **364**, 8–18.

ERIKSON, K.T., 1966
Wayward puritans.
New York: John Wiley & Sons.

GIBBS, J.P., 1966
Concepts of deviant behavior: the old and the new.
Pacific Soc. Rev., **9** (12), 9–14.

TOBY, J., 1966
Violence and the masculine ideal: some qualitative data.
Annals Amer. Acad. Pol. & Soc. Sci., **364**, 19–27.

BECKER, H., 1967
Whose side are we on?
Social Problems, **14**, 239–47.

BORDUA, D.J., 1967
Recent trends: deviant behavior and social control.
Annals Amer. Acad. Pol. & Soc. Sci., **369**, 149–63.

COHEN, S., 1967
Mods, rockers and the rest: community reactions to juvenile delinquency.
Howard J. Penol. & Crime Prev., **12**, 121–30.

AKERS, R.L., 1968
Problems in the sociology of deviance: social definitions and behavior.
Social Forces, **46**, 455–65.

CAVAN, R.S., AND CAVAN, J.T., 1968
Delinquency and crime: Cross-cultural perspectives.
New York: J.B. Lippincott Co.,

CHAPMAN, D., 1968
Sociology and the stereotype of the criminal.
London: Tavistock.

CICOUREL, A.V., 1968
The social organization of juvenile justice.
New York: John Wiley & Sons.

COHEN, A., 1968
Deviant behavior, in *International encyclopaedia of the social sciences.* Vol. 4, 148–55.

HEIDENSOHN, F., 1968
The deviance of women: a critique and an enquiry.
Brit. J. Sociol., **19**, 160–75.

HOROWITZ, I.L., AND LIEBOWITZ, M., 1968
Social deviance and political marginality: towards a redefinition of the relationship between sociology and politics.
Social Problems, **15**, 280–96.

EMERSON, R.M., 1969
Judging delinquents: context and process in juvenile court.
Chicago: Aldine Publishing Co., 83–171.

MATZA, D., 1969
Becoming deviant.
Englewood Cliffs, N.J.: Prentice-Hall.

SCHUR, E.M., 1969
Reactions to deviance: a critical assessment.
Amer. J. Sociol., **75**, 309–22.

SIMMONS, J.L., 1969
Deviants.
Glendessary Press.

TURK, A.T., 1969
Criminality and legal order.
Chicago: Rand McNally.

BECKER, H.S., 1970
Sociological work.
London: Allen Lane, Penguin Press, 123–34, 329–39, 341–49.

DENZIN, N.K., 1970
Rules of conduct and the study of deviant behavior; some notes on the social

relationship, in J.D. Douglas (ed.), *Deviance and respectability.* New York: Basic Books, 120–59.

DOUGLAS, J.D., (ED.), 1970
Deviance and respectability: The social construction of moral meaning.
New York: Basic Books, 3–30.

DUSTER, T., 1970
The legislation of morality: law, drugs, and moral judgment.
New York: Free Press, 103–29.

ENGQUIST, V., AND COLES, F., 1970
'Political' criminals in America: O'Hare (1923); Cantine and Rainer (1950).
Issues in Criminol., **5,** 209–20.

HORNING, D.N.M., 1970
Blue-collar thefts: conceptions of property, attitudes toward pilfering, and work group norms in a modern industrial plan, in E.O. Smigel and H.L. Ross (eds.), *Crimes against Bureaucracy.*
New York: Van Nostrand Reinhold Company, 46–64.

KIESLER, C.A., AND KIESLER, S.B., 1970
Conformity.
Reading, Mass.: Addison-Wesley Publishing Co.

NATIONAL OPINION POLLS. MARKET RESEARCH LIMITED, 1970
Report on attitudes towards crime, violence, and permissiveness in society.
76/86 Strand, London, W.C.2. Mimeo. 1–12, 25–9.

QUINNEY, R., 1970
The social reality of crime.
Boston: Little, Brown & Co., 3–97, 277–317.

ROTHMAN, D.J., 1970
Conceptions of deviancy in Jacksonian America.
Prison J., **50**(1), 22–32.

SCHWENDINGER, H. AND SCHWENDINGER, J., 1970
Defenders of order or guardians of human rights?
Issues in Criminol., **5,** 123–57.

SMIGEL, E.O., 1970
Public attitudes toward 'chiseling' with reference to unemployment compensation, in E.O. Smigel and H.L. Ross (eds.), *Crimes against bureaucracy.*
New York: Van Nostrand Reinhold Company, 29–45.

SMIGEL, E.O., 1970
Public attitudes toward stealing as related to the size of the victim organisation, in E.O. Smigel and H.L. Ross (eds.), *Crimes against bureaucracy.*
New York: Van Nostrand Reinhold Company, 15–28.

TAPP, J.L., AND LEVINE, F.J., 1970
Persuasion to virtue: a preliminary statement.
Law & Society Rev., **4,** 565–82.

TAYLOR, I., AND WALTON, P., 1970
Values in deviancy theory and society.
Brit. J. Sociol., **21,** 326–74.

BELL, R.R., 1971
Social deviance—a substantive analysis.
Homewood, Ill.: Dorsey Press, 1–35.

BOX, S., 1971
Deviance, reality and society.
London: Holt, Rinehart & Winston Ltd.

BOYDELL, C.L., AND GRINDSTAFF, C.F., 1971
Public attitudes toward legal sanctions for drug and abortion offences.
Can. J. Criminol. & Corrections, **13,** 209–32.

CONNOR, W.D., 1971
Deviant behavior in capitalist society—the Soviet image.
J. Crim. Law, Criminol. & Pol. Sci., **61,** 554–64.

DOWNES, D., AND ROCK, P., 1971
Social reaction to deviance and its effects on crime and criminal careers.
Brit. J. Sociol., **22,** 351–64.

FURSTENBERG, F.F. JR., 1971
Public reaction to crime in the streets.
Amer. Scholar, **40,** 601–10.

JEFFERY, C.R., 1971
Crime prevention through environmental design.
Beverly Hills, Calif.: Sage Publications, 17–36.

MARTIN, J.P., AND WEBSTER, D., 1971
The social consequence of conviction.
London: Heinemann, 57–73, 202–22.

PHILLIPSON, M., 1971
Sociological aspects of crime and delinquency.
London: Routledge & Kegan Paul.

SCHAFER, S., 1971
The concept of the political criminal.
J. Crim. Law, Criminol. & Pol. Sci., **62,** 380–87.

SCHUR, E.M., 1971
Labeling deviant behavior: its sociological implications.
New York: Harper & Row.

STEBBINS, R.A., 1971
Commitment to deviance: the non-professional criminal in the community.
Westport, Conn.: Greenwood Publishing Corp., 74–184.

TAYLOR, I.R., 1971
Soccer consciousness and soccer hooliganism, in S. Cohen (ed.), *Images of deviance.*
Harmondsworth: Penguin Books, 134–64.

TAYLOR, L., 1971
Deviance and society.
London: Michael Joseph, 29–94.

TORNUDD, P., 1971
The futility of searching for causes of crime.
Scandinavian Studies in criminology, **3.**
Oslo: Universitetsforlaget, 23–33.

YOUNG, J., 1971
The Drugtakers.
London: Paladin.

YOUNG, J., 1971
The role of the police as amplifiers of deviancy, negotiators of reality and translators of fantasy: some consequences of our present system of drug control as seen in Notting Hill in S. Cohen (ed.), *Images of deviance.*
Harmondsworth: Penguin Books.

BOCK, F.W., 1972
Reflections on the role of ideology in the definition of crime.
Saint Louis Univ. Law J., **16,** 557–85.

CICOUREL, A.V., 1972
Delinquency and the attribution of responsibility, in R.A. Scott and J.D. Douglas (eds.), *Theoretical perspectives on deviance.*
New York: Basic Books, 142–57.

COHEN, S., 1972
Folk devils and moral panics.
London: MacGibbon & Kee, 9–26, 49–143, 191–204.

CONNOR, W.D., 1972
Deviance in Soviet society. Crime, delinquency, and alcoholism.
New York: Columbia Univ. Press, 236–68.

CONNOR, W.D., 1972
The manufacture of deviance: the case of the Soviet purge, 1936–1938.
Amer. Sociol. Rev., **37,** 403–13.

DESSAUR, C.I., 1972
The perception of deviance and its treatment, in *Deviance and social reaction*, Report No. 3. Proceedings of the Third International Colloquium of the International Penal and Penitentiary Foundation (5-9 June 1972) Vienna.

DOUGLAS, J.D., 1972
The experience of the absurd and the problem of social order, in R.A. Scott and J.D. Douglas (eds.), *Theoretical perspectives on deviance.*
New York: Basic Books, Inc., 189–214.

DOUGLAS, J.D. (ED.), 1972
Research on deviance.
New York: Random House.

FERRACUTI, F., AND NEWMAN, G., 1972
Clinical and psychological perceptions of deviance in *Perception of deviance and criminality.* Collected studies in criminological research, 9.
Strasbourg: Council of Europe, 103–28.

FOSTER, J.D., DINITZ, S., AND RECKLESS, W.C., 1972
Perceptions of stigma following public intervention for delinquent behavior.
Social Problems, **20,** 202–9.

GIBBS, J.P., 1972
Issues in defining deviant behavior, in R.A. Scott and J.D. Douglas (eds.), *Theoretical perspectives in deviance.*
New York: Basic Books, 39–68.

GLASER, D., 1972
Social Deviance.
Chicago: Markham.

KUTSCHINSKY, B., 1972
Sociological aspects of deviance and criminality (A survey of empirical research) in *Perception of deviance and criminality.* Collected studies in criminological research, **9.**
Strasbourg: Council of Europe, 9–99.

LEMERT, E.M., 1972
Human deviance, social problems, and social control.
Englewood Cliffs, N.J.: Prentice-Hall, 3–92. (2nd ed.).

LIAZOS, A., 1972
The poverty of the sociology of deviance: nuts, sluts and preverts.
Social Problems, **20,** 103–20.

LOEBER, D.A., 1972
Nonconformity in the law of socialist states.
South Carolina Law Rev., **24,** 27–36.

PAWLIK, K., 1972
Deviance, crime, and social reactions, in *Deviance and social reaction,* Report No. 2.
Proceedings of the Third International Colloquium of the International Penal and Penitentiary Foundation (5–9 June 1972) Vienna.

SCOTT, R.A., 1972
A proposed framework for analyzing deviance as a property of social order, in R.A. Scott and J.D. Douglas (eds.), *Theoretical perspectives on deviance.*
New York: Basic Books, 9–35.

SCULL, A., 1972
Social control and the amplification of deviance, in R.A. Scott and J.D. Douglas (eds.), *Theoretical perspectives on deviance.*
New York: Basic Books, 282–314.

SEIBEL, H.D., 1972
Social deviance in comparative persepctive, in R.A. Scott and J.D. Douglas (eds.), *Theoretical perspectives on deviance.*
New York: Basic Books, 251–81.

TAYLOR, L., 1972
The significance and interpretation of replies to motivational questions: the case of sex offenders.
Sociology, **6,** 23–39.

THORSELL, B.A., AND KLEMKE, L.W., 1972
The labelling process: reinforcement and deterrent?
Law & Society Rev., **6,** 393–403.

TURNER, R.H., 1972
Deviance avowal as neutralization of commitment.
Social Problems, **19,** 308–21.

VERIN, J., 1972
The jurist and deviance, in *Deviance and social reaction,* Report No. 1.
Proceedings of the Third International Colloquium of the International Penal and Penitentiary Foundation (5–9 June 1972) Vienna.

VERSELE, S.C., 1972
Legal aspects of the perception of deviance and criminality in *Perception of deviance and criminality.* Collected studies in criminological research, **9.**
Strasbourg: Council of Europe, 131–57.

WARREN, C.A.B., AND JOHNSON, J.M., 1972
A critique of labeling theory from the phenomenological perspective, in R.A. Scott and J.D. Douglas (eds.), *Theoretical perspectives on deviance.*
New York: Basic Books, 69–92.

WEBB, S.D., 1972
Crime and the division of labor: testing a Durkheimian Model.
Amer. J. Sociol., **78,** 643–56.

BLUMSTEIN, A., AND COHEN, J., 1973
A theory of the stability of punishment.
J. Crim. Law & Criminol., **64,** 198–207.

CHAPMAN, D., 1973
The stereotype of the criminal and the social consequences.
Internat. J. Criminol. and Penol., **1,** 15–30.

COHEN, S., 1973
Protest, unrest and delinquency: convergences in labels and behaviour.
Internat. J. Criminol. & Penol., **1,** 117–28.

COHEN, S., 1973
Campaigning against vandalism, in C. Ward (ed.), *Vandalism.*
London: Architectural Press, 215–57.

FISHER, G.E., AND ERICKSON, M.L., 1973
On assessing the effects of official reactions to juvenile delinquency.
J. Res. Crime & Delinq., **10,** 177–94.

HIRSCHI, T., 1973
Procedural rules and the study of deviant behavior.
Social Problems, **21,** 159–73.

HOEFNAGELS, G.P., 1973
The other side of criminology: an inversion of the concept of crime.
Deventer, Holland: Kluwer, 15–107.

KUTSCHINSKY, B., 1973
'The legal consciousness': a survey of research on knowledge and opinion about law in A. Podgorecki *et al., Knowledge and opinion about law.*
London: Martin Robertson, 101–38.

MILLER, W.B., 1973
Ideology and criminal justice policy: some current issues.
J. Crim. Law & Criminol., **64,** 141–62.

PLUMB, J.H., 1973
In the light of history.
Boston: Houghton Mifflin, 125–34.

QUINNEY, R., 1973
Crime control in capitalist society: a critical philosophy of legal order.
Issues in Criminol., **8,** 75–99.

REASONS, C.E., 1973
The politicizing of crime, the criminal and the criminologist.
J. Crim. Law & Criminol., **64,** 471–77.

ROBERTSON, R., AND TAYLOR, L., 1973
Deviance, crime and socio-legal control: comparative perspectives.
London: Martin Robertson.

ROCK, P., 1973
Phenomenalism and essentialism in the sociology of deviancy.
Sociology, **7,** 17–29.

ROCK, P., 1973
Deviant behaviour.
London: Hutchinson.

ROSHIER, B., 1973
The selection of crime news by the press, in S. Cohen and J. Young (eds.), *The manufacture of news: social problems, deviance and the mass media.*
London: Constable, 28–39.

SCHUR, E.M., 1973
Radical nonintervention: rethinking the delinquency problem.
Englewood Cliffs, N.J.: Prentice-Hall, 117–50.

SCHWARTZ, M., AND STRYKER, S., 1973
Deviance, selves and others.
Social Forces, **52,** 146–47.

SHOEMAKER, D.J., SOUTH, D.R., AND LOWE, J., 1973
Facial stereotypes of deviants and judgments of guilt or innocence.
Social Forces, **51,** 427–33.

STEFFENSMEIER, D.J., AND TERRY, R.M., 1973
Deviance and respectability: an observational study of reactions to shoplifting.
Social Forces, **51,** 417–26.

TAYLOR, I., WALTON, P., AND YOUNG, J., 1973
The new criminology: for a social theory of deviance.
London: Routledge & Kegan Paul.

ALLEN, F.A., 1974
The crimes of politics, political dimensions of criminal justice.
Cambridge, Mass.: Harvard Univ. Press.

BECKER, H.S., 1974
Labelling theory reconsidered, in P. Rock and M. McIntosh (eds.), *Deviance and social control.*
London: Tavistock, 41–66.

BOSHIER, R., AND JOHNSON, D., 1974
Does conviction affect employment opportunities?
Brit. J. Criminol., **14,** 264–68.

BUCHHOLZ, E., HARTMANN, R., LEKSCHAS, J., AND STILLER, G., 1974
Socialist criminology: theoretical and methodological foundations.
Lexington, Mass.: Saxon House, 27–136.

CARSON, W.G., 1974
The sociology of crime and the emergence of criminal laws, in P. Rock and M. McIntosh (eds.), *Deviance and social control.*
London: Tavistock, 67–90.

COHEN, A., 1974
The elasticity of evil.
Oxford: Basil Blackwell.

COHEN, S., 1974
Criminology and the sociology of deviance in Britain, in P. Rock and M. McIntosh (eds.), *Deviance and social control.*
London: Tavistock, 1–40.

GIBBS, L.E., 1974
The effects of juvenile legal procedures on juvenile offenders' self-attitudes.
J. Research Crime & Delinq., **11,** 51–5.

HALL, S., 1974
Deviance, politics, and the media, in P. Rock and M. McIntosh (eds.), *Deviance and social control.*
London: Tavistock, 261–305.

HEPWORTH, M., AND FEATHERSTONE, M., 1974
'Persons believed missing', in P. Rock and M. McIntosh (eds.), *Deviance and social control.*
London: Tavistock, 163–207.

LEMERT, E.M., 1974
Beyond Mead: the societal reaction to deviance.
Social Problems, **21,** 457–68.

MÄKËLA, K., 1974
The societal tasks of the penal system.
Scandinavian Studies in Criminology, **5.**
London: Martin Robertson, 47–65.

MARS, G., 1974
Dock pilferage, in P. Rock and M. McIntosh (eds.), *Deviance and social control.*
London: Tavistock, 209–28.

MILGRAM, S., 1974
Obedience to authority, an experimental view.
London: Tavistock.

PHILLIPSON, M., AND ROCHE, M., 1974
Phenomenology, sociology, and the study of deviance, in P. Rock and M. McIntosh (eds.), *Deviance and social control.*
London: Tavistock, 125–62.

ROBERTSON, R., AND TAYLOR, L., 1974
Problems in the comparative analysis of deviance, in P. Rock and M. McIntosh (eds.), *Deviance and social control.*
London: Tavistock, 91–123.

ROCK, P., 1974
The sociology of deviancy and conceptions of moral order.
Brit. J. Criminol., **14,** 139–49.

ROSSI, P.H., WAITE, E., BOSE, C.E., AND BERK, R.E., 1974
The seriousness of crimes: normative structure and individual differences.
Amer. Sociol. Rev., **39,** 224–37.

SCHEFF, T.J., 1974
The labelling theory of mental illness.
Amer. Sociol. Rev., **39,** 444–52.

WALKER, N.D., 1974
Lost causes in criminology, in R.G. Hood (ed.), *Crime, criminology and public policy, essays in honour of Sir Leon Radzinowicz.*
London: Heinemann.

WALLER, I., 1974
Men released from prison.
Univ. of Toronto Press, 105–22.

YOUNG, J., 1974
Mass media, drugs, and deviance, in P. Rock and M. McIntosh (eds.), *Deviance and social control.*
London: Tavistock, 229–59.

TAYLOR, I., WALTON, P., AND YOUNG, J., 1975
Critical criminology in Britain: review and prospects, in I. Taylor, P. Walton and J. Young (eds.), *Critical criminology.*
London: Routledge & Kegan Paul, 6–62.

3 Some categories of crime and criminals

1 Problems of classification

FERRI, E., 1917
Criminal sociology.
Boston, Mass.: Little, Brown & Co., 125–67.

HEWITT, L.E., AND JENKINS, R.L., 1936
Fundamental patterns of maladjustment.
Springfield Ill.: State Printer, 33–57.

LINDESMITH, A.R., AND DUNHAM, H.W., 1941
Some principles of criminal typology.
Social Forces, **19**, 307–14.

FRIEDLANDER, K., 1947
The psycho-analytic approach to juvenile delinquency.
London: Routledge & Kegan Paul, 183–7.

GIBBONS, D.C., AND GARRITY, D.L., 1959
Some suggestions for the development of etiological and treatment theory in criminology.
Social Forces, **38**, 51–8.

WOOTTON, B., 1959
Social science and social pathology.
London: Allen & Unwin, 301–8.

AMERICAN LAW INSTITUTE
Model Penal Code.
Proposed official draft (May 4, 1962). Article 6, 91; Tentative draft No. 2 (May 3, 1954). Article 6, 10–11.

GIBBONS, D.C., AND GARRITY, D.L., 1962
Definition and analysis of certain criminal types.
J. Crim. Law, Criminol. & Pol. Sci., **53**, 27–35.

KINCH, J.W., 1962
Continuities in the study of delinquent types.
J. Crim. Law, Criminol. & Pol. Sci., **53**, 323–8.

ROEBUCK, J.B., AND JOHNSON, R., 1962
The jack of all trades offender.
Crime & Delinq., **8**, 172–81.

BECKER, H.S., 1963
Outsiders. Studies in the sociology of deviance.
Glencoe, Ill.: Free Press, 19–39.

GIBBENS, T.C.N., 1963
Psychiatric studies of borstal lads.
London: Oxford Univ. Press, 31–7, 83–94.

ROEBUCK, J.B., 1963
A criticism of Gibbons' and Garrity's criminal typology.
J. Crim. Law, Criminol. & Pol. Sci., **54**, 476–8.

NEW YORK, STATE OF, 1964
Proposed New York Penal Law, Article 15.
New York State Commission on Revision of Penal Law, 22–4, 252–7.

WILLETT, T.C., 1964
Criminal on the road: a study of serious motoring offences and those who commit them.
London: Tavistock, 171–238.

GIBBONS, D.C., 1965
Changing the lawbreaker.
New York: Prentice-Hall, 1–128.

GLUECK, S., AND GLUECK, E., 1965
Varieties of delinquent types.
Brit. J. Criminol., **5**, 236–48, 388–45.

MORRIS, A., 1965
The comprehensive classification of adult offenders.
J. Crim. Law, Criminol. & Pol. Sci., **56**, 197–202.

SIMMONS, J.L., AND CHAMBERS, H.C., 1965
Public stereotypes of deviants.
Social Problems, **13**, 223–32.

SUDNOW, D., 1965
Normal crimes: sociological features of the penal code in a public defender office.
Social Problems, **12**, 255–76.

FERDINAND, T.N., 1966
Typologies of delinquency: a critical analysis.
New York: Random House.

ROONEY, E.A., AND GIBBONS, D.C., 1966
Social reaction to 'crimes without victims'.
Social Problems, **13**, 400–10.

NAHRENDORF, R.O., 1967
Typologies of crime and delinquency: Classification or methodology?
Sociologia Internationalis, **5**, 15–33.

ROEBUCK, J.B., 1967
Criminal typology.
Springfield, Ill.: C. C. Thomas.

STEER, D.J., AND CARR-HILL, R.A., 1967
The motoring offender—who is he?
Crim. Law Rev., 1967, 214–24.

WARREN, M.Q., 1967
Classification of offenders as an aid to efficient management and effective treatment. A document submitted to the President's Commission on Law Enforcement and Administration of Justice, Washington, D.C. Mimeo.

COUNCIL OF EUROPE, 1968
Criminological aspects of road traffic offences.
Collected Studies in Criminological Research, **2.**
Strasbourg: Council of Europe.

WILLETT, T.C., 1968
Research concerning the characteristics of motoring offenders, in *Criminological aspects of road traffic offences.* Collected Studies in Criminological Research, **2.**
Strasbourg: Council of Europe, 23–44.

TOCH, H., 1969
Violent men: an enquiry into the psychology of violence.
Chicago: Aldine Publishing Co., 133–82.

TURK, A.T., 1969
Criminality and legal order.
Chicago: Rand McNally, 108–71.

BUIKHUISEN, W., AND JONGMAN, R.W., 1970
A legalistic classification of juvenile delinquents.
Brit. J. Criminol., **10**, 109–23.

GLUECK, S., AND GLUECK, E., 1970
Toward a typology of juvenile offenders.
New York: Grune & Stratton, 1–23.

GOLD, M., 1970
Delinquent behavior in an American city.
Belmont, Calif.: Brooks/Cole Publishing Co., 35–58.

HOOD, R., AND SPARKS, R., 1970
Key issues in criminology.
London: Weidenfeld & Nicolson, 110–40.

PALMER, T.B., 1971
Patterns of adjustment among delinquent adolescent conformists.
Community Treatment Project Report Series, California Youth Authority, Sacramento. Mimeo.

WARREN, M.Q., 1971
Classification of offenders as an aid to efficient management and effective treatment.
J. Crim. Law, Criminol. & Pol. Sci., **62,** 239–58.

BLUMENTHAL, M.D., KAHN, R.L., ANDREWS, F.M., AND HEAD, K.B., 1972
Justifying violence: attitudes of American men.
Ann Arbor, Michigan: Institute for Social Research, Univ. of Michigan, 179–210.

BOTTOMS, A.E., 1973
Methodological aspects of classification in criminology, in *Methodological aspects of classification in criminology*, Collected Studies in Criminological Research, **10.**
Strasbourg: Council of Europe, 27–76.

CLINARD, M.B., AND QUINNEY, R., 1973
Criminal behavior systems: a typology (2nd ed).
New York: Holt, Rinehart & Winston.

OPP, K.D., 1973
Problems of classification in criminology, in *Methodological aspects of classification in criminology.* Collected Studies in Criminological Research, **10.**
Strasbourg: Council of Europe, 9–23.

SMITH, J.C., AND HOGAN, B., 1973
Criminal law. (3rd ed.),
London: Butterworths, 17–27.

WILLETT, T.C., 1973
Drivers after sentence.
London: Heinemann, 30–76.

2 Delinquent subcultures and youth gangs

[See also Section 2(5) for references on studies of frustrations in opportunity perceived by gang members.]

ASBURY, H., 1927
The gangs of New York.
New York: Alfred A. Knopf.

REDL, F., 1945
The psychology of gang formation and the treatment of juvenile delinquents.
Psychoanalytic Study of the Child, **1,** 366–77.

WATTENBERG, W., AND BALISTRIERI, J.J., 1950
Gang membership and juvenile misconduct.
Amer. Sociol. Rev., **15,** 744–52.

COHEN, A.K., 1955
Delinquent boys: the culture of the gang.
Glencoe, Ill.: Free Press.

WHYTE, W.F., 1955
Street corner society.
Univ. of Chicago Press (2nd ed.).

SCOTT, P., 1956
Gangs and delinquent groups in London.
Brit. J. Delinq., **7,** 8–21.

FINESTONE, H., 1957
Cats, kicks and colour.
Social Problems, **5,** 3–13.

WILMER, D.W. ET AL., 1957
Heroin use and street gangs.
J. Crim. Law, Criminol. & Pol. Sci., **48,** 399–409.

BLOCH, H.A., AND NIEDERHOFFER, A., 1958
The gang: a study in adolescent behavior.
New York: Philosophical Library.

COHEN, A.K., AND SHORT, J.F., 1958
Research in delinquent sub-cultures.
J. Social Issues, **14,** 20–36.

MILLER, W.B., 1958
Lower class cultures as a generating milieu of gang delinquency.
J. Social Issues, **14,** 5–19.

SALISBURY, H.E., 1958
The shook-up generation.
London: Michael Joseph.

KITSUSE, J.I., AND DIETRICK, D.C., 1959
Delinquent boys: a critique.
Amer. Sociol. Rev., **24,** 208–15.

CLOWARD, R.A., AND OHLIN, L.E., 1960
Delinquency and opportunity: a theory of delinquent gangs.
Glencoe, Ill.: Free Press.

NEW YORK CITY YOUTH BOARD, 1960
Reaching the teen-age addict: a study of street club work with a group of adolescent users.
New York: Council of Social and Athletic Clubs.

SHORT, J.F., 1960
The sociocultural context of delinquency.
Crime & Delinq., **6,** 365–75.

THRASHER, F.M., 1960
The gang.
Univ. of Chicago Press, reprint.

YINGER, J.M., 1960
Contraculture and subculture.
Amer. Sociol. Rev., **25,** 625–35.

BORDUA, D.J., 1961
Delinquent subcultures: sociological interpretations of gang delinquency.
Annals Amer. Acad. Pol. & Soc. Sci., **338,** 120–36.

FYVEL, T.R., 1961
The insecure offenders, rebellious youth in the welfare state.
London: Chatto & Windus. (Published also under the title, *Troublemakers: rebellious youth in an affluent society.*
New York: Schocken Books.)

KARACKI, L., AND TOBY, J., 1962
The uncommitted adolescent: candidate for gang socialization.
Sociol. Inquiry, **32,** 203–15.

VAZ, E.W., 1962
Juvenile gang delinquency in Paris.
Social. Problems, **10,** 23–31.

YABLONSKY, L., 1962
The violent gang.
New York: Macmillan.

RICE, R.E., AND CHRISTENSEN, R.B., 1963
The juvenile gang . . . its structure, function, and treatment as perceived by the gang leader.
Los Angeles County Probation Department Research Office Report no. 24, Mimeo.

CHEIN, I. *et. al*, 1964
Narcotics, delinquency and social policy.
New York: Basic Books, 177–92.

GERRARD, N.L., 1964
The core member of the gang.
Brit. J. Criminol., **4**, 361–71.

KLEIN, M.W., 1964
Internal structures and age distributions in four delinquent Negro gangs.
Univ. of Southern Calif., Youth Studies Center. Presented at the annual meetings of the Calif. State Psychological Association, Los Angeles, December 1964, Mimeo.

MYERHOFF, H.L., AND MYERHOFF, B.G., 1964
Field observations of middle class gangs.
Social Forces, **42**, 328–36.

ROBIN, G.D., 1964
Gang member delinquency; its extent, sequence and typology.
J. Crim. Law, Criminol. & Pol. Sci., **55**, 59–69.

SHORT, J.F., 1964
Gang delinquency and anomie, in M.B. Clinard (ed.), *Anomie and deviant behavior.*
New York: Free Press, 98–127.

SPERGEL, I., 1964
Racketville, slumtown, haulberg: an exploratory study of delinquent subcultures.
Univ. of Chicago Press, 29–92.

GEIS, G., 1965
Juvenile gangs.
President's Committee on Juvenile Delinquency and Youth Crimes, Washington, D.C. Mimeo.

KLEIN, M.W., 1965
Judgmental factors in specification of the structure of natural groups.
Univ. of Southern Calif., Youth Studies Center. Paper presented at the annual meetings of the Western Psychological Association, Honolulu, June 17, 1965, Mimeo.

SHORT, J.F., AND RIVERA, R., 1965
Perceived opportunities, gang membership, and delinquency.
Amer. Sociol. Rev., **30**, 56–67.

SHORT, J.F., AND STRODTBECK, F.L., 1965
Group process and gang delinquency.
Univ. of Chicago Press.

SPILLER, B., 1965
Delinquency and middle class goals.
J. Crim. Law, Criminol. & Pol. Sci., **56**, 463–78.

SVERI, K., 1965
Group activity.
Scandinavian Studies in Criminology, **1**.
London: Tavistock, 173–85.

BUIKHUISEN, W., 1966
Research on teenage riots.
Sociologia Neerlandica, **4**, 1–22.

DAVIDMAN, H., AND PREBLE, E., 1966
Schizophrenia among adolescent street gang leaders, in P.H. Hock and J. Zubin (eds.), *Psychopathology of Schizophrenia.*
New York: Grune and Stratton, 372–83.

DOWNES, D.M., 1966
The delinquent solution: a study in subcultural theory.
London: Routledge & Kegan Paul, 177–81, 195–254.

GANNON, T.M., 1966
Emergence of the 'defensive' gang.
Fed. Probation, **30**, (4), 44–8.

JANSYN, L.R., JR., 1966
Solidarity and delinquency in a street corner group.
Amer. Sociol. Rev., **31**, 600–14.

MILLER, W.B., 1966
Violent crimes in city gangs.
Annals Amer. Acad. Pol. & Soc. Sci., **364**, 96–112.

HARGREAVES, D.H., 1967
Social relations in a secondary school
London: Routledge & Kegan Paul, 108–39.

JOURNAL OF RESEARCH IN CRIME & DELINQUENCY, 1967
Special number on gangs, **4**, 1–183.

KLEIN, M.W. (ED.), 1967
Juvenile gangs in context: theory, research and action.
Englewood Cliffs, N.J.: Prentice-Hall.

LERMAN, P., 1967
Gangs, networks, and subcultural delinquency
Amer. J. Sociol., **73**, 63–72.

LOHMAN, J.D., and MISNER, G.E., 1967
Field Surveys IV: *The police and the community*, Vol. 1. Washington, D.C.: President's Commission on Law Enforcement and Administration of Justice, 108–19.

LOHMAN, J.D., AND MISNER, G.E., 1967
Field Surveys IV: *The police and the community*, Vol. 2.
Washington, D.C.: President's Commission on Law Enforcement and Administration of Justice, 137–88.

MILLER, W.B., 1967
Theft behavior in city gangs, in M.W. Klein (ed.), *Juvenile gangs in context.*
Englewood Cliffs, N.J.: Prentice-Hall, 25–37.

MONOD, J., 1967
Juvenile gangs in Paris: towards a structural analysis.
J. Res. Crime & Delinq., **4**, 142–65.

SHERIF, M., AND SHERIF, C.W., 1967
Group processes and collective interaction in delinquent activities.
J. Res. Crime & Delinq., **4**, 43–62.

SPERGEL, I., 1967
Deviant patterns and opportunities of pre-adolescent Negro boys in three Chicago neighborhoods, in M.W. Klein (ed.), *Juvenile gangs in context.*
Englewood Cliffs, N.J.: Prentice-Hall, 38–54.

UNITED STATES OF AMERICA, 1967
Task force report: the police.
Washington, D.C.: President's Commission on Law Enforcement and Administration of Justice, 178–81.

UNITED STATES OF AMERICA, 1967
The challenge of crime in a free society.
Report of the President's Commission on Law Enforcement and Administration of Justice, Washington, D.C., 58–79.

WERTHMAN, C., AND PILIAVIN, I., 1967
Gang members and the police, in D.J. Bordua (ed.), *The Police.*
New York: John Wiley & Sons, 56–98.

WOLFGANG, M.E., 1967
The culture of youth, in *Task force report: juvenile delinquency and youth crime.*
Washington, D.C.: President's Commission on Law Enforcement and Administration of Justice, 145–54.

LERMAN, P., 1968
Individual values, peer values, and subcultural delinquency.
Amer. Sociol. Rev., **33**, 219–35.

SHORT, J.F. (ED.), 1968
Gang delinquency and delinquent subcultures.
New York: Harper & Row.

SUTTLES, G.D., 1968
The social order of the slum: ethnicity and territory in the inner city.
Univ. of Chicago Press, 195–220.

COHEN, B., 1969
The delinquency of gangs and spontaneous groups, in T. Sellin and M.E. Wolfgang (eds.), *Delinquency: selected studies.*
New York: John Wiley & Sons, 61–111.

DUNPHY, D.C., 1969
Cliques, crowds & gangs—group life of Sydney adolescents.
Melbourne, Aust.: F.W. Cheshire Publ., 70–107.

HARDMAN, D.G., 1969
Small town gangs.
J. Crim. Law, Criminol. & Pol. Sci., **60**, 173–81.

KEISER, R.L., 1969
The vice lords: warriors of the streets.
New York: Holt, Rinehart and Winston.

KLEIN, M.W., 1969
Violence in American juvenile gangs, in D.J. Mulvihill, M.M. Tumin and L.A. Curtis (eds.), *Crimes of Violence*, **13.**
Staff report to the National Commission on the Causes and Prevention of Violence, Washington, D.C., Appendix 31, 1427–1460.

PETERSON, V.W., 1969
A report on Chicago crime for 1968.
Chicago: Chicago Crime Commission, 133–58.

GOLD, M., 1970
Delinquent behavior in an American city.
Belmont, Calif.: Brooks/Cole Publishing Co., 82–99.

HOOD, R., AND SPARKS, R., 1970
Key issues in criminology.
London: Weidenfeld and Nicolson, 80–109.

MILLER, W.B., 1970
White gangs, in J.F. Short, Jr., (ed.), *Modern criminals.*
Chicago: Aldine Publishing Co., 45–85.

ROCK, P., AND COHEN, S., 1970
The teddy boys, in V. Bogdanor and R. Skidelsky (eds.), *The age of affluence* 1951–1964.
London: Macmillan, 288–318.

SPERGEL, I.A., 1970
Politics, policies, and the gang problem, in P. Herman (ed.), *Delinquency and social policy.*
New York: Praeger, 390–406.

ERICKSON, M.L., 1971
The group context of delinquent behavior.
Social Problems, **19,** 114–29.

HINDELANG, M.J., 1971
The social versus solitary nature of delinquent involvements.
Brit. J. Criminol., **11,** 167–75.

KENNEDY, J., 1971
The football hooligan.
Social Work Today, **2**(10), 4–7.

KLEIN, M.W., 1971
Street gangs and street workers.
Englewood Cliffs, N.J.: Prentice-Hall.

POSTON, R.W., 1971
The gang and the establishment.
New York: Harper & Row.

TAYLOR, I., 1971
Social work and the soccer hooligan.
Social Work Today, **2**(12), 25–7.

COHEN, S., 1972
Folk devils and moral panics.
London: MacGibbon & Kee.

DANIEL, S., AND MCGUIRE, P., 1972
The Paint House, words from an East End gang.
Harmondsworth: Penguin Books.

KREUZER, A., 1972
An example of group juvenile delinquency: the 'rockers'.
Internat. Crim. Police Rev., **254,** 2–8.

ARMSTRONG, G., AND WILSON, M., 1973
Delinquency and some aspects of housing, in C. Ward (ed.), *Vandalism.*
London: Architectural Press, 64–84.

DAWLEY, D., 1973
A nation of lords: the autobiography of the vice lords.
New York: Anchor Books.

ERICKSON, M.L., 1973
Group violations and official delinquency: the group hazard hypothesis.
Criminology, **11,** 127–60.

ERICKSON, M.L., 1973
Group violations, socioeconomic status and official delinquency.
Social Forces, **52,** 41–52.

PATRICK, J., 1973
A Glasgow gang observed.
London: Eyre Methuen.

REUTERMAN, N.A., LOVE, M.J., AND FIEDLER, F., 1973
A partial evaluation of Bloch and Niederhoffer's theory of gang delinquency.
Criminology, **4,** 415–25.

HOROWITZ, R., AND SCHWARTZ, G., 1974
Honor, normative ambiguity and gang violence.
Amer. Sociol. Rev., **39,** 238–51.

JACOBS, J.B., 1974
Street gangs behind bars.
Social Problems, **21,** 395–409.

KRISBERG, B., 1974
Gang youth and hustling: the psychology of survival.
Issues in Criminol., **9,** 115–31.

PARKER, H.J., 1974
View from the boys: a sociology of down-town adolescents.
Newton Abbott: David and Charles.

3 Professional and organized crime

TRAIN, A., 1912
Imported crime: the story of the Camorra in America.
McClure's, **39**, 82–94.

CLARKE, D.H., 1929
In the reign of Rothstein.
New York: Vanguard Press.

MERRIAM, C.E., 1929
The police, crime and politics.
Annals Amer. Acad. Pol. & Soc. Sci., **146**, 114–20.

FIASCHETTI, M., 1930
You gotta be rough.
New York: Doubleday, Doran & Co.

SHAW, C.R., 1931
The natural history of a delinquent career.
Univ. Chicago Press.

TAFT, D.R., 1936
Nationality and crime.
Amer. Sociol. Rev., **1**, 724–36.

COXE, J.E., 1937
The New Orleans Mafia incident.
Louisiana Historical Quart., **20**, 1067–1110.

SUTHERLAND, E.H., 1937
The professional thief.
Univ. Chicago Press.

KENDALL, J.S., 1939
Blood on the banquette.
Louisiana Historical Quart., **22**, 819–56.

MAURER, D.W., 1940
The big con.
Indianapolis: Bobbs-Merrill Co.

THOMPSON, C., AND ALLEN, R., 1940
Gang rule in New York.
New York: Dial Press.

SHAW, C.R., 1945
The jack roller.
Univ. Chicago Press.

CROUSE, R., 1947
The murder of Arnold Rothstein, in M. Crane (ed.), *Sins of New York.*
New York: Boni & Gaer.

JOHNSON, M., 1950
Crime on the labour front.
New York: McGraw-Hill.

KEFAUVER, E., 1951
Crime in America.
New York: Doubleday & Co.

BARES, J.E., 1954
The abortion mill, an institutional study.
J. Crim. Law, Criminol. & Pol. Sci., **45**, 157–67.

FEDER, S., AND JOESTEN, J., 1954
The Luciano story.
New York: David McKay Co.

MCKITRICK, E., 1957
The study of corruption.
Political Science Quart., **72**, 502–14.

PETERSON, V.W., 1959
Rackets in America.
J. Crim. Law, Criminol. & Pol. Sci., **49**, 583–9.

THORNTON, R.Y., 1959
Organised crime in the field of prostitution.
J. Crim. Law, Criminol. & Pol. Sci., **46**, 775–9.

KENNEDY, R.F., 1960
The enemy within.
New York: Harper Bros.

DAVIS, K., 1961
Prostitution, in R.K. Merton and R.A. Nisbet (eds.), *Contemporary social problems.*
New York: Harcourt, Brace & World, 262–88.

CAVAN, R.S., 1962
Criminology.
New York: Crowell Co., 96–158.

CRIME AND DELINQUENCY, 1962
Special issue on organised crime, **8**, 321–407.

JOHNSON, E. JR., 1962–1963
Organised crime: challenge to the American legal system: I. Organised crime: the nature of its threat, the reason for its survival.
J. Crim. Law, Criminol. & Pol. Sci., **53**, 399–425;
II. The legal weapons: their actual and potential usefulness in law enforcement.
Ibid., **54**, (1963) 1–29.

TYLER, G., 1962
Organised crime in America, a book of readings.
Univ. Michigan Press.

ANNALS OF THE AMERICAN ACADEMY OF POLITICAL AND SOCIAL SCIENCE, 1963
Special issue on combating organised crime, **347,** 1–112.

WEST, D.J., 1963
The habitual prisoner.
London: Macmillan, 100–4.

LEMERT, E.M., 1964
The behavior of the systematic check forger, in H.S. Becker (ed.), *The other side: perspectives on deviance.*
Glencoe, Ill.: Free Press, 211–24.

LEWIS, N., 1964
The honoured society: the Mafia conspiracy observed.
London: Collins.

MACK, J., 1964
Full time miscreants, delinquent neighbourhoods and criminal networks.
Brit. J. Sociol., **15,** 38–53.

MAURER, D.W., 1964
Whiz mob.
New Haven: College and Univ. Press.

TAFT, D.R., AND ENGLAND, R.W., 1964
Criminology.
New York: Macmillan & Co., 182–99.

ANDERSON, R.A., 1965
From Mafia to Cosa Nostra.
Amer. J. Sociol., **71,** 302–10.

IRWIN, J., AND YABLONSKY, L., 1965
The new criminal: a view of the contemporary offender.
Brit. J. Criminol., **5,** 183–90.

UNITED STATES OF AMERICA, SENATE, 1965
Organized crime and illicit traffic in narcotics.
Report of the committee on government operations (March 4, 1965), 89th Congress, 1st Session, Senate, Report no 72.
Washington, D.C.

PANTALEONE, M., 1966
The Mafia and politics.
London: Chatto & Windus.

SOWLE, C.R., 1966
Organized crime and the professional criminal.
New York: Harper & Row.

ANDREOLI, P.D., 1967
Organized crime enterprises—legal, in S.A. Yefsky (ed.), *Law enforcement science and technology.*
Washington, D.C.: Thompson Book Co., 21–7.

BLAKEY, G.R., 1967
Organized crime and corruption practices, in S.A. Yefsky (ed.), *Law enforcement science and technology.*
Washington, D.C.: Thompson Book Co., 15–20.

BLAKEY, G.R., 1967
Aspects of the evidence gathering process in organised crime cases: a preliminary analysis, in *Task force report: organised crime.*
Washington, D.C.: President's Commission on Law Enforcement and Administration of Justice, 80–113.

BROWN, W.P., 1967
The police and corruption.
A document submitted to the President's Commission on Law Enforcement and Administration of Justice, Washington, D.C.
Mimeo., 27–44.

CRESSEY, D.R., 1967
The function and structure of criminal syndicates, in *Task force report: organised crime.*
Washington, D.C.: President's Commission on Law Enforcement and Administration of Justice, 25–60.

DUFFY, W.J., 1967
Organized crime—illegal activities, in S.A. Yefsky (ed.), *Law enforcement science and technology.*
Washington, D.C.: Thompson Book Co., 29–32.

EMRICH, R.L., 1967
Cultural and anthropological analysis of causes and threat of organized crime, in S.A. Yefsky (ed.), *Law enforcement science and technology.*
Washington, D.C.: Thompson Book Co., 41–6.

GARDINER, J.A., AND OLSON, D., 1967
Wincanton: the politics of corruption, in *Task force report: organised crime.*
Washington, D.C.: President's Commission on Law Enforcement and Administration of Justice, 61–79.

HERMAN, R.D., 1967
Gambling.
New York: Harper & Row, 169–243.

LEMERT, E.M., 1967
Human deviance, social problems, and social control.
Englewood Cliffs, N.J.: Prentice-Hall, 99–134.

POLSKY, N., 1967
Hustlers, beats and others.
Chicago: Aldine Press, 13–116.

SALERNO, R.F., 1967
Syndicate personnel structure, in S.A. Yefsky (ed.), *Law enforcement science and technology.*
Washington, D.C.: Thompson Book Co., 9–14.

SCHELLING, T.C., 1967
Economics and the underworld of crime, in S.A. Yefsky (ed.), *Law enforcement science and technology.*
Washington, D.C.: Thompson Book Co., 33–40.

SCHELLING, T.C., 1967
Economic analyses and organised crime, in *Task force report: organised crime.*
Washington, D.C.: President's Commission on Law Enforcement and Administration of Justice, 114–26.

UNITED STATES OF AMERICA, 1967
Task force report: crime and its impact—an assessment.
Washington, D.C.: President's Commission on Law Enforcement and Administration of Justice, 96–101.

UNITED STATES OF AMERICA, 1967
Challenge of crime in a free society.
Report of the President's Commission on Law Enforcement and Administration of Justice, Washington, D.C. 187–209.

UNITED STATES OF AMERICA, 1967
Task force report: organised crime.
Washington, D.C.: President's Commission on Law Enforcement and Administration of Justice, 1–24.

CAMP, G.M., 1968
Nothing to lose: a study of bank robbery in America.
Ann Arbor, Mich.: University Microfilms, 75–128.

HAWKINS, G.J., 1968
God and the Mafia.
Public Interest, **14,** 32–4.

LANDESCO, J., 1968
Organized Crime in Chicago.
Univ. Chicago Press, 169–89, 277–86.

MACK SMITH, D., 1968
A History of Sicily: Medieval Sicily 800–1713.
London: Chatto & Windus, 146–51.

MACK SMITH, D., 1968
A History of Sicily: Modern Sicily after 1713.
London: Chatto & Windus, 294–304, 490–504.

NELLI, H.S., 1968
Italians and crime in Chicago: the formative years, 1890–1920.
Amer. J. Sociol., **74,** 373–91.

SMITH, D.C.JR., 1968
Co-operative action in organized crime control.
J. Crim. Law, Criminol. & Pol. Sci., **59,** 491–98.

CROMSTOCK, A., 1969
Frauds exposed.
Montclair, N.J.: Patterson Smith.

CRESSEY, D.R., 1969
Theft of the nation.
New York: Harper & Row.

FURSTENBERG, M.H., 1969
Violence and organized crime, in D.J. Mulvihill, M.M. Tumin and L.A. Curtis (eds.), *Crimes of violence*, **13.**
A staff report to the National Commission on the causes and prevention of violence.
Washington, D.C. Appendix 18, 911–39.

JACKSON, B., 1969
A thief's primer.
New York: Macmillan Co., 15–183.

PETERSON, V.W., 1969
A report on Chicago Crime for 1968.
Chicago: Chicago Crime Commission, 54–133.

AMERICAN CRIMINAL LAW QUARTERLY, 1970
The American Bar Association's impact on the Organized Crime Control Act of 1970, 8–162.

ASSOCIATION OF THE BAR OF THE CITY OF NEW YORK, 1970
The proposed organised crime control Act of 1969 (*s*.30).
Reports of Committees of the Association of the Bar concerned with Federal Legislation, Vol. 9 Bulletin no. 1, July 1970, 1–49.

COLUMBIA JOURNAL OF LAW AND SOCIAL PROBLEMS, 1970
The strike force: organized law enforcement v. organized crime, **6,** 496.

GARDINER, J.A., 1970
The politics of corruption: organized crime in an American city.
New York: Russell Sage Foundation.

HOWSON, G., 1970
Thief-taker general: the rise and fall of Jonathan Wild.
London: Hutchinson.

LACEY, F.B., 1970
Organized crime: the problem and some suggested approaches.
Seton Hall Law Rev., **2,** 11–18.

McCLELLAN, J.L., 1970
The organized crime control act (s.30) or its critics: which threatens civil liberties?
Notre Dame Lawyer, **46,** 55–200.

NEW YORK, STATE OF, 1970
Organized crime. *Report of the New York State Joint Legislative Committee on Crime, Its Causes, Control & Effect on Society.*
Legislative document (1970) No. 6, 44–55.

WILSON, W., 1970
The threat of organized crime: highlighting the challenging new frontiers in criminal law.
Notre Dame Lawyer, **46,** 41–54.

ALBINI, J.L., 1971
The American mafia—genesis of a legend.
New York: Meredith Corporation.

ANDERSON, A., 1971
Organized crime: the need for research.
Univ. Florida Law Rev., **24,** 42–57.

CHAMBLISS, W.J., 1971
Vice, corruption, bureaucracy and power.
Wisconsin Law Rev., 1971, 1150–73.

CHAMBLISS, W.J., AND SEIDMAN, R.B., 1971
Law, order and power.
Reading, Mass.: Addison-Wesley Publishing Co., 484–501.

HALLER, M.H., Winter 1971–72.
Organised crime in urban society: Chicago in the twentieth century.
J. Social History, **5,** 210–34.

HINDELANG, M.J., 1971
Bookies and bookmaking: a descriptive analysis.
Crime & Delinq., **17,** 245–55.

IANNI, F.A.J., 1971
Formal and social organization in an organized crime 'family': a case study.
Univ. Florida Law Rev., **24,** 31–41.

JOURNAL OF PUBLIC LAW, 1971
Symposium on organised crime, **20,** 1971, 33–165.

KELTON, J.R., AND UNKOVIC, C.M., 1971
Characteristics of organised criminal groups.
Can. J. Corrections, **13,** 68–78.

KOBLER, J., 1971
Capone.
New York: G.P. Putnam's Sons.

McINTOSH, M., 1971
Changes in the organization of thieving, in S. Cohen (ed.), *Images of deviance.*
Harmondsworth: Penguin Books, 98–133.

SMITH, D.C. JR., 1971
Some thing that may be more important to understand about organized crime than Cosa Nostra.
Univ. Florida Law Rev., **24,** 1–30.

TALESE, G., 1971
Honor thy father.
London: Souvenir Press Ltd.

WINICK, C., AND KINSIE, P.M., 1971
The lively commerce: Prostitution in the United States.
Chicago: Quadrangle Books.

ALBANY LAW REVIEW, 1972
The problem of categorising and controlling organised crime. **36,** 330–68.

CRESSEY, D.R., 1972
Criminal organization.
London: Heinemann Educational Books.

DICKINSON LAW REVIEW, 1972
Pennsylvania crime commission . . . heroes or heavies? **77,** 1972, 47–72.

FORDHAM, P., 1972
Inside the under-world.
London: Geo. Allen & Unwin, Ltd.

IANNI, F.A.J., 1972
Authority, power and respect—the interplay of control systems in an organized crime 'family'.
Paper presented at conference on The Economics of Crime and Punishment, July, 1972, Washington, D.C.

IANNI, F.A.J., AND REUSS-IANNI, E., 1972
A family business, kinship and social control in organised crime.
London: Routledge & Kegan Paul.

KING, H., 1972
Box man, a professional thief's journey.
New York: Harper & Row.

LASSWELL, H.D., AND MCKENNA, J.B., 1972?
The impact of organised crime on an inter city community.
New York: Policy Sciences Center.

MACK, J.A., 1972
The able criminal.
Brit. J. Criminol., **12,** 44–54.

NORMANDEAU, A., 1972
Violence and robbery: a case study.
Acta Criminol., **5,** 11–106.

PEARSON, J., 1972
The profession of violence: the rise and fall of the Kray twins.
London: Weidenfeld & Nicolson.

UNITED STATES OF AMERICA. SENATE, 1972
An analysis of criminal redistribution systems and their economic impact on small business.
Washington, D.C.: Staff report prepared for the Select Committee on Small Business, 92nd Congress, 2nd Session.

UNITED STATES OF AMERICA, 1972
Cargo theft and organised crime: a deskbook for management and law enforcement.
Washington, D.C.: L.E.A.A., Department of Justice and Dept. of Transportation.

CONKLIN, J.E. (ED.), 1973
The crime establishment: organised crime and American society.
Englewood Cliffs, N.J.: Prentice-Hall.

CONKLIN, J.E., AND BITTNER, E., 1973
Burglary in a suburb.
Criminology, **11,** 206–32.

COOK, F.J., 1973
Organised crime: the strange reluctance, in P. Watters and S. Gillers (eds.), *Investigating the FBI.*
New York: Doubleday & Co., 140–66.

DICKINSON LAW REVIEW, 1973
The Pennsylvania attack on racketeers in legitimate enterprises, **78,** 176–94.

LETKEMANN, P., 1973
Crime as work.
Englewood Cliffs, N.J.: Prentice-Hall.

MCINTOSH, M., 1973
The growth of racketeering.
Economy & Society, **2,** 35–69.

MACK, J.A., 1973
The 'organised' and 'professional' labels criticised.
Internat. J. Criminol. & Penol., **1**(2), 103–16.

ROSENBLEET, C., AND PARIENTE, B.J., 1973
The prostitution of the criminal law.
Amer. Crim. Law Rev., **11,** 373–427.

ROTTENBERG, S. (ED.), 1973
The economics of crime and punishment, Part III.
Washington, D.C.: American Enterprise Institute for Public Policy Research, 119–78.

SHOVER, N., 1973
The social organization of burglary.
Social Problems, **20,** 499–514.

SNODGRASS, J., 1973
The criminologist and his criminal: the case of Edwin H. Sutherland and Broadway Jones.
Issues in Criminol., **8,** 1–17.

UNITED STATES OF AMERICA. HOUSE OF REPRESENTATIVES, 1973
Organized criminal influence in horseracing.
Report by the Select Committee on Crime, 93rd Congress, 1st Session, Union Calendar No. 154, House Report No. 93–326.
Washington, D.C.

VAN HAECHT, A., 1973
La prostituée: statut et image.
Bruxelles: l'Université de Bruxelles.

YEAGER, M.G., 1973
The gangster as white collar criminal: organized crime and stolen securities.
Issues in Criminol., **8,** 49–73.

BLOK, A., 1974
The Mafia of a Sicilian village 1860–1960, *a study of violent peasant entrepreneurs.*
Oxford: Basil Blackwell.

CHAPPELL, D., AND WALSH, M., 1974
Receiving stolen property: the need for systematic inquiry into the fencing process.
Criminology, **11,** 484–97.

IANNI, F.A.J., 1974
Black Mafia, ethnic succession in organised crime.
New York: Simon & Schuster.

KLEIN, J.F., 1974
Professional theft: the utility of a concept.
Can. J. Criminol. & Corrections, **16,** 133–44.

OZENNE, T., 1974
The economics of bank robbery.
Journal Legal Studies, **3,** 19–51.

SUTHERLAND, E.H., AND CRESSEY, D.R., 1974
Criminology.
Philadelphia: Lippincott (9th ed.), 261–77, 281–91.

VASSALLI, G., 1974
An Italian enquiry concerning the Mafia, in R.G. Hood (ed.), *Crime, criminology and public policy: essays in honour of Sir Leon Radzinowicz.*
London: Heinemann.

MACK, J.R., 1975
The crime industry.
Lexington, Mass.: Saxon House.

4 Drug abuse

(a) *Sources, forms and incidence*

LAW AND CONTEMPORARY PROBLEMS, 1957
Special issue on narcotics, **22,** 9–33, 69–85, 113–37.

ROEBUCK, J.B., 1962
The Negro drug addict as an offender type.
J. Crim. Law, Criminol. & Pol. Sci., **53,** 36–43.

CHEIN, I., GERARD, D.L., LEE, R.S., AND ROSENFELT, E., 1964
Narcotics, delinquency and social policy—the road to H.
New York: Basic Books.

BEWLEY, T., 1965
Heroin addiction in the U.K.
Brit. Med. J., **2,** 1284–86.

HARMS, E. (ED.), 1965
Drug addiction in youth.
International series of monographs on child psychiatry, **3.**
New York: Pergamon Press.

IRWIN, J., AND YABLONSKY, L., 1965
The new criminal: a view of the contemporary offender.
Brit. J. Criminol., **5,** 183–90.

MESSINGER, E., AND ZITRIN, A., 1965
A statistical study of criminal drug addicts.
Crime & Delinq., **11**, 283–92.

O'DONNELL, J.A., 1965
Narcotic addiction and crime.
Social Problems, **13**, 374–85.

RETTERSTÖL, N., AND SUND, A., 1965
Drug addiction and habituation.
Oslo: Universitetsforlaget.

WILKINS, L.T., 1965
A behavioral theory of drug taking.
Howard J., **11**(4), 6–17.

WILNER, D.M., AND KASSEBAUM, G.G. (EDS.), 1965
Narcotics.
New York: McGraw-Hill.

ABELES, H., PLEW, R., LAUDEUTSCHER, I., AND ROSENTHAL, H.M., 1966
Multiple drug addiction in New York City in a selected population group.
Public Health Reports, **81**, 685–90.

BECKER, H.S., 1966
Marihuana: a sociological overview, in D. Solomon (ed.), *The marihuana papers.*
Indianapolis: Bobbs-Merrill Co., 33–65.

GRIFFITH, J., 1966
A study of illicit amphetamine drug traffic in Oklahoma City.
Amer. J. Psychiat., **123**, 560–69.

LEARY, T., 1966
The politics, ethics, and meaning of marijuana, in D. Solomon (ed.), *The marihuana papers.*
Indianapolis: Bobbs-Merrill Co., 82–99.

MASTERS, R.E.L., AND HOUSTON, J., 1966
The varieties of psychedelic experience.
New York: Holt, Rinehart and Winston.

MATTICK, H.W., 1966
The epidemiology of drug addiction and reflections on the problem and policy in the U.S.
Illinois Medical J., Oct. 1966, 436–47.

O'DONNELL, J.A., AND BALL, J.C. (EDS.), 1966
Narcotic addiction.
New York: Harper & Row.

CHAYET, N.L., 1967
Social and legal aspects of LSD usage, in R.C. DeBold and R.C. Leaf (eds.), *LSD, man & society.*
Middletown, Conn.: Wesleyan Univ. Press, 91–124.

FIDDLE, S., 1967
Portraits from a shooting gallery, life styles from the drug addict world.
New York: Harper & Row, 3–54.

INSTITUTE FOR THE STUDY OF CRIME AND DELINQUENCY (California), 1967
A follow-up study of the juvenile drug offender.
31–4.

LAURIE, P., 1967
Drugs—medical, psychological and social facts.
Harmondsworth: Penguin Books.

O'DONNELL, J.A., 1967
The rise and decline of a subculture.
Social Problems, **15**, 73–84.

ROEBUCK, J.B., 1967
Criminal typology.
Springfield, Ill.: C.C. Thomas, 118–35.

SEABERG, G.P., 1967
The drug abuse problems and some proposals.
J. Crim. Law, Criminol. & Pol. Sci., **58**, 349–75.

UNITED KINGDOM, 1967
Drug addiction.
London: Office of Health Economics.

UNITED STATES OF AMERICA, 1967
Task force report: narcotics and drug abuse.
Washington, D.C.: President's Commission on Law Enforcement and Administration of Justice.

UNITED STATES OF AMERICA, 1967
The challenge of crime in a free society.
Report of the President's Commission on Law Enforcement and Administration of Justice, Washington, D.C., 211–31, 302–3.

BECKER, H.S., 1968
History, culture, and subjective experience: an exploration of the social bases of drug-induced experiences, in H.S. Becker, *et al.* (eds.), *Institutions and the person.*
Chicago: Aldine Publ. Co., 272–92.

KAVALER, F., ET AL., 1968
A commentary and annotated bibliography

on the relationship between narcotics addiction and criminology, in *Municipal Reference Library Notes*, New York, **42,** 45–63.

LEWIS, A., 1968
A review of the international clinical literature in *Cannabis*. Report by the Advisory Committee on Drug Dependence.
London: Home Office.

UNITED KINGDOM, 1968
Cannabis. Report by the Advisory Committee on Drug Dependence.
London: Home Office.

BEWLEY, T.H., 1969
Drug dependence—recent changes in England and Sweden, in J.R. Wittenborn, H. Brill, J.P. Smith and S.A. Wittenborn (eds.), *Drugs and youth: proceedings of the Rutgers symposium on drug abuse*.
Springfield, Ill.: C.C. Thomas, 105–22.

BLUM, R.H., 1969
Drugs and violence, in D.J. Mulvihill, M.M. Tumin and L.A. Curtis (eds.), *Crimes of violence*. **13.**
A staff report to the National Commission on the Causes and Prevention of Violence.
Washington, D.C. Appendix 32, 1461–1532.

BLUM, R.H., 1969
Normal drug use, in R.H. Blum *et al.*, *Society and drugs*.
San Francisco: Jossey-Bass Inc., 245–75, 293–320.

CORRECTIONAL ASSOCIATION OF NEW YORK, 1969
Report of New York State Council on drug addiction.

GLASER, D., INCIARDI, J., AND BABST, D., 1969
Later heroin use by adolescent marihuana and heroin users, and by non-drug using adolescent offenders.
New York State Narcotic Addiction Control Commission.

GOODE, E., 1919
Multiple drug use among marijuana smokers.
Social problems, **17,** 48–64.

GRINSPOON, L., 1969
Marijuana. *Scientific American*, **221,** 17–25.

HILL, R.B., ET AL., 1969
The prevalence of drugs among 10–20 year old boys who live in a two-block area of New York City.
Bureau of Applied Social Research, Columbia Univ.

JAMES, I.P., 1969
Delinquency and heroin addiction in Britain.
Brit. J. Criminol., **9,** 108–24.

WEIL, A.T., ZINBERG, N.E., AND NELSEN, J.M., 1969
Clinical and psychological effects of marijuana in man.
Internat. J. Addict., **4,** 427–51.

BECKER, H.S., 1970
Sociological work: method and substance.
London: Allen Lane, Penguin Press, 307–27.

DABIS, J.M., AND MILTE, K.L., 1970
Drug use in Australia—a survey.
Aust. & N.Z.J. of Criminol., **3,** 131–41.

GOODE, E., 1970
The marijuana smokers.
New York: Basic Books, 27–49, 122–242.

HAWKS, D.V., 1970
The epidemiology of drug dependence in the United Kingdom.
Bulletin on Narcotics, **22,** (1), 15–24.

HORMAN, R.E., AND FOX, A.M. (EDS.), 1970
Drug awareness.
New York: Avon Books.

NEW ZEALAND, 1970
Drug dependency and drug abuse in New Zealand.
New Zealand Board of Health Report Series Vol. 14, 23–94.

STIMSON, G.V., AND OGBORNE, A.C., 1970
A survey of a representative sample of addicts prescribed heroin at London clinics.
Bulletin on Narcotics, **22**(4), 13–22.

TINKLENBERG, J.R., AND STILLMAN, R.C., 1970
Drug use and violence, in D.N. Daniels, M.F. Gilula and F.M. Ochberg (eds.), *Violence and the struggle for existence*.
Boston: Little, Brown & Co., 327–65.

UNITED STATES OF AMERICA, SENATE, 1970
Staff study on drug abuse in the Washington area 1970.
Washington, D.C.

ZINBERG, N.E., AND WEIL, A.T., 1970
A comparison of marijuana users and non-users.
Nature, **226**, 119–23.

AMERICAN JOURNAL OF PSYCHIATRY, 1971
Special section on marijuana. Marijuana and health: a report to the Congress, **128**, 189–219.

BEAN, P., 1971
Social aspects of drug abuse: a study of London drug offenders.
J. Crim. Law, Criminol. & Pol. Sci., **62**, 80–6.

BLUM, R.H., 1971
To wear a nostradamus hat: drugs and America.
J. Social Issues, **27**, 89–106.

BOYDELL, C.L., AND GRINDSTAFF, C.F., 1971
Public attitudes toward legal sanctions for drug and abortion offences.
Canad. J. Corrections, **13**, 209–32.

GRINSPOON, L., 1971
Marihuana reconsidered.
Cambridge, Mass.: Harvard Univ. Press.

JAMES, I.P., 1971
The changing patterns of narcotic addiction in Britain, 1959–1969.
Internat. J. Adict., **6**, 119–34.

NEWITT, J., SINGER, M., AND KAHN, H., 1971
Some speculations on U.S. drug use.
J. Social Issues, **27**, 107–22.

SARGENT, M.J., 1971
A cross-cultural study of attitudes and behaviour towards alcohol and drugs.
Brit. J. Sociol., **22**, 83–96.

SCOTT, P.D., AND BUCKELL, M., 1971
Delinquency and amphetamines.
Brit. J. Psychiat., **119**, 179–82.

SMART, R.G., 1971
Illicit drug use in Canada: a review of current epidemiology with clues for prevention.
Internat. J. Addict., **6**, 383–405.

WILLIS, J., 1971
Delinquency and drug dependence in the United Kingdom and the United States.
Brit. J. Addict., **66**, 235–48.

YOUNG, J., 1971
The role of the police as amplifiers of deviancy, negotiators of reality and translators of fantasy: some consequences of our present system of drug control as seen in Notting Hill, in S. Cohen (ed.), *Images of deviance.*
Harmondsworth: Penguin Books, 27–61.

YOUNG, J., 1971
The drugtakers: the social meaning of drug use.
London: Paladin.

ZACUNE, J., 1971
A comparison of Canadian narcotic addicts in Great Britain and in Canada.
Bulletin on Narcotics, **23**(4), 41–9.

ZACUNE, J., AND HENSMAN, C., 1971
Drugs, alcohol and tobacco in Britain.
London: Heinemann Medical Books, 25–41, 55–63, 95–140, 157–207.

BULLETIN ON NARCOTICS, 1972
Drug abuse and criminality, **24**(4), 35–46 and **25**(1), 49–61.

CANADA, 1972
Cannabis. A report of a Commission of Inquiry into the non-medical use of drugs.
Ottowa: Information Canada.

COHEN, H., 1972
Multiple drug use considered in the light of the stepping-stone hypothesis.
Internat. J. Addict., **7**, 27–55.

GOODE, E., 1972
Drugs in Society.
New York: Knopf.

GRUPP, S.E., 1972
Multiple drug use in a sample of experienced marijuana smokers.
Internat. J. Addict., **7**, 481–91.

HINDMARCH, I., 1972
The patterns of drug abuse among school children.
Bulletin on Narcotics, **24**(3), 23–6.

INCIARDI, J.A., AND CHAMBERS, C.D., 1972
Unreported criminal involvement of narcotic addicts.
J. Drug Issues, Spring, 57–64.

KOZEL, N.J., DUPONT, R.L., AND BROWN, B.S., 1972
Narcotics and crime: a study of narcotic involvement in an offender population.
Internat. J. Addict., **7,** 443–50.

NEW YORK, STATE OF, 1972
Report of the New York State Commission on the quality, cost and financing of elementary and secondary education.
(Chairman M. Fleischmann), Vol. 2, sections 10.6–10.10.

ROUSE, B.A., AND EWING, J.A., 1972
Marijuana and other drug use by graduate and professional students.
Amer. J. Psychiat., **129,** 415–20.

STANTON, M.D., 1972
Drug use in Vietnam.
Arch. Gen. Psychiat., **26,** 279–86.

STIMSON, G.V., 1972
Patterns of behaviour of heroin addicts.
Internat. J. Addict., **7,** 671–91.

SWATOS, W.H., 1972
Opiate addiction in the late nineteenth century: a study of the social problem, using medical journals of the period.
Internat. J. Addict., **7,** 739–53.

TEC, N., 1972
Differential involvement with marijuana and it sociocultural context: a study of suburban youths.
Internat. J. Addict., **7,** 655–69.

TEC, N., 1972
The peer group and marijuana use.
Crime & Delinq., **18,** 298–309.

UNITED NATIONS ECONOMIC AND SOCIAL COUNCIL, 1972
Drug abuse and criminality.
Note by the Secretary-General, First session, Item 7 of the provisional agenda. Committee on Crime Prevention and Control, E/AC.57/4 8–17 May 1972.

UNITED STATES OF AMERICA, 1972
Marihuana: signal of misunderstanding.
First Report of the National Commission on Marihuana and Drug Abuse.
Washington. D.C.

UNITED STATES OF AMERICA, 1972
Appendix to Marihuana: signal of misunderstanding.
The Technical Papers of the First Report of the National Commission on Marihuana and Drug Abuse.
Washington, D.C. Vol. 1, 249–477, 600–608, Vol. 2, 855–902, 942–68.

WINSLOW, J., 1972
Drug use in Denmark.
Internat. J. Addict., **7,** 305–19.

BARNES, G.G., AND NOBLE, P., 1973
Deprivation and drug addiction: a study of a vulnerable sub-group.
Brit. J. Social Wk., **2,** 299–311.

BRYDENSHOLT, H.H., AND PALMER, J., 1973
Drugs in Denmark.
Drugs and Society, **2**(6), 11–16.

CANADA, 1973
Final Report of the Commission of Inquiry into the non-medical use of drugs (Le Dain, Commission). Ottowa: Information Canada, 23–44, 277–458, 669–764.

FRIEDMAN, C.J., AND FRIEDMAN, A.S., 1973
Drug abuse and delinquency, in *Patterns and consequences of drug use*, Vol. 1 of the *Appendix* to Drug Use in America: problem in perspective.
The Technical Papers of the Second Report of the National Commission on Marihuana and Drug Abuse.
Washington, D.C., 398–448.

GORDON, A.M., 1973
Patterns of delinquency in drug addiction.
Brit. J. Psychiat., **122,** 205–10.

JACOBY, J.E., WEINER, N.A., THORNBERRY, T.P., AND WOLFGANG, M.E., 1973
Drug use and criminality in a birth cohort, in *Patterns and consequences of drug use*, Vol. 1 of the *Appendix* to Drug use in America: problem in perspective. The Technical Papers of the Second Report of the National Commission on Marihuana and Drug Abuse.
Washington, D.C., 300–43.

JOHNSON, B.D., 1973
Marihuana users and drug subcultures.
New York: John Wiley & Sons.

NAHAS, G.G., 1973
Clinical pharmacology of Cannabis sativa with special reference to delta-9-THC.
Bulletin on Narcotics, **25**(1), 9–39.

STIMSON, G.V., 1973
Heroin and behaviour: diversity among addicts attending London clinics.
Shannon: Irish Univ. Press, 170–206.

SWEZEY, R.W., 1973
Estimating drug-crime relationships.
Internat. J. Addict., **8,** 701–21.

TINKLENBERG, J., 1973
Drugs and crime, in *Patterns and consequences of drug use*, Vol. 1 of the *Appendix* to Drug use in America: problem in perspective. The Technical Papers of the Second Report of the National Commission on Marihuana and Drug Abuse.
Washington, D.C., 240–99.

UNITED STATES OF AMERICA, 1973
Drug use in America: problem in perspective.
Second Report of the National Commission on Marihuana and Drug Abuse,.
Washington, D.C., 1–174.

WORLD HEALTH ORGANISATION, 1973
Youth and drugs.
Report of a WHO study group, Technical Report Series, No. 516. Geneva: W.H.O.

WORLD HEALTH ORGANIZATION, 1973
WHO expert committee on drug dependence.
Nineteenth Report. Technical Report Series, No. 526. Geneva: W.H.O.

YOUNG, J., 1973
The myth of the drug taker in the mass media, in S. Cohen and J. Young (eds.), *The manufacture of news: social problems, deviance and the mass media.*
London: Constable, 314–22.

BROWN, J.W., GLASER, D., WAXER, E., AND GEIS, G., 1974
Turning off: cessation of marijuana use after college.
Social Problems, **21,** 527–38.

COUNCIL OF EUROPE, 1974
Penal aspects of drug abuse.
Strasbourg: European Committee on Crime Problems, 9–67, 148–67.

CUSHMAN, P., 1974
Relationship between narcotic addiction and crime.
Fed. Probation, **38**(3), 38–43.

HESS, A., VAN DER VAART, J., RICKEY, B., AND ROSE, J., 1974
Nature and trends of drug use and abuse.
Crim. Law. Bullletin, **10,** 637–60.

MOTT, J., AND TAYLOR, M., 1974
Delinquency amongst opiate users.
London: Home Office Research Studies, **23.**

YOUNG, J., 1974
Mass media, drugs, and deviance, in P. Rock and M. McIntosh (eds.), *Deviance and social control.*
London: Tavistock, 229–59.

4 Drug abuse

(*b*) *Legal and treatment aspects*

LAW AND CONTEMPORARY PROBLEMS, 1957
Special issue on narcotics, **22,** 9–33, 69–85, 113–37.

NEW YORK CITY YOUTH BOARD, 1960
Reaching the teen-age addict: a study of street club work with a group of adolescent users.
New York: Council of Social and Athletic Clubs.

AMERICAN BAR ASSOCIATION AND THE AMERICAN MEDICAL ASSOCIATION ON NARCOTIC DRUGS, 1961
Drug addiction: crime or disease?
Bloomington: Indiana Univ. Press.

GEIS, G., 1963
Narcotic treatment programs in California.
Paper presented at the conference

'Perspectives on Narcotic Addiction', Chatham, Mass., 9–11 Sept. 1963. Mimeo.

SCHUR, E.M., 1963
Narcotic addiction in Britain and America—the impact of public policy.
Bloomington: Indiana Univ. Press.

CHEIN, I., GERARD, D.L., LEE, R.S., AND AND ROSENFELT, E., 1964
Narcotics, delinquency and social policy—the road to H.
New York: Basic Books.

DISKIND, M.H., AND KLONSKY, G., 1964
Recent development in the treatment of paroled offenders addicted to narcotic drugs.
Albany: New York State Division of Parole.

LINDESMITH, A.R., 1965
The addict and the law.
Bloomington: Indiana Univ. Press.

RICE, J., AND COHEN, L., 1965
Narcotic drug addiction: one year's experiences at Pilgrim State Hospital.
Psychiatric Quart., **39,** 457–65.

SCHUR, E.M., 1965
Crimes without victims: deviant behavior and public policy.
Englewood Cliffs, N.J.: Prentice Hall, 120–80.

WILNER, D.M., AND KASSEBAUM, G.G., (EDS.), 1965
Narcotics.
New York: McGraw-Hill.

YABLONSKY, L., 1965
The tunnel back. Synanon,
New York: Macmillan, 3–74.

AUSUBEL, D.P., 1966
The Dole-Nyswander treatment of heroin addiction (critical commentary).
J. Amer. Med. Assn., **195,** 949–50.

DI SUVERO, H.M., 1966
Drug offenses and the new penal law.
Brooklyn Law Rev., **32,** 287–302.

INSTITUTE ON NEW DEVELOPMENTS IN THE REHABILITATION OF THE NARCOTIC ADDICT, 1966
Rehabilitating the narcotic addict.
New York: Arno Press.

LINDESMITH, A.R., 1966
The marihuana problem: myth or reality?, in D. Solomon (ed.), *The marihuana papers.*
Indianapolis: Bobbs-Merill Co., 18–32.

MATTICK, H.W., 1966
The epidemiology of drug addiction and reflections on the problem and policy in the U.S.
Illinois Medical Journal., Oct. 1966, 436–47

O'DONNELL, J.A., AND BALL, J.C. (EDS.), 1966
Narcotic addiction. New York: Harper & Row.

RICHMAN, A., 1966
Follow up of criminal narcotic addicts.
Can. Psych. Assn. J., **11,** 107–15.

SKOLNICK, J.H., 1966
Justice without trial: law enforcement in democratic society.
New York: John Wiley & Sons, 117–29, 139–63.

UNGERLEIDER, J.T., FISHER, D.D., AND FULLER, M., 1966
The dangers of LSD. Analysis of seven months' experience in a University Hospital's Psychiatric Service.
J. Amer. Med. Assn., Aug 8, 1966, **197** (6), 109–12.

VAILLANT, G.E., 1966
Twelve-year follow-up of New York narcotic addicts:
I. Relation of treatment to outcome.
Amer. J. Psychiat., **122,** 727–37;
II. The natural history of a chronic disease.
New England J. Medicine, 8 Dec. 1966, 1282–88;
III. Some social and psychiatric characteristics.
Arch. Gen. Psychiat., **15,** 599–609.
IV. Some characteristics and determinants of abstinence.
Amer. J. Psychiat., **123,** 573–85.

VAILLANT, G.E., AND RASOR, R.W., 1966
The role of compulsory supervision in the treatment of addiction.
Fed. Probation, **30**(2), 53–9.

ARONOWITZ, D.S., 1967
Civil commitment of narcotic addicts.
Columbia Law Rev., **67,** 405–29.

BLUMER, H., ET AL., 1967
The world of youthful drug use. ADD center project final report.
Univ. of Calif.: School of Criminology. Mimeo.

CHAYET, N.L., 1967
Social and legal aspects of LSD usage, in R.C. DeBold and R.C. Leaf (eds.), *LSD, man & society.*
Middletown, Conn.: Wesleyan Univ. Press, 91–124.

ELDRIDGE, W.B., 1967
Narcotics and the law. A critique of the American experiment in narcotic drug control. (2nd ed.).
Univ. Chicago Press.

LAURENCE, D.R., 1967
Drug control.
Medico-Legal J., **35,** 56–70.

LITTOE, A.D., 1967
Drug abuse and law enforcement.
A document submitted to the President's Commission on Law Enforcement and Administration of Justice, Washington, D.C. Mimeo.

SEABERG, G.P., 1967
The drug abuse problems and some proposals.
J. Crim. Law., Criminol. & Pol. Sci., **58,** 349–75.

TIFFANY, L.P., MCINTYRE, D.JR., AND ROTENBERG, D.L., 1967
Detection of crime.
Boston: Little, Brown & Co., 250–64.

UNITED STATES OF AMERICA, 1967
The challenge of crime in a free society.
Report of the President's Commission on Law Enforcement and Administration of Justice, Washington, D.C. 211–31, 302–3.

UNITED STATES OF AMERICA, 1967
Task force report: narcotics and drug abuse.
Washington, D.C.: President's Commission on Law Enforcement and Administration of Justice.

YALE LAW JOURNAL, 1967
Civil commitment of narcotic addicts, **76,** 1160–89.

CALIFORNIA, STATE OF, 1968
Follow-up study of 1960 *adult drug offenders.*
Sacramento: California Bureau of Criminal Statistics, Department of Justice, 1–2.

COLUMBIA LAW REVIEW, 1968
Hallucinogens, **68,** 521–60.

DOLE, V.P., NYSWANDER, M.E., AND WARNER, A., 1968
Successful treatment of 750 criminal addicts.
J. Amer. Medical Assn., **206,** 2708–11.

KAVALER, F. ET AL., 1968
A commentary and annotated bibliography on the relationship between narcotics addiction and criminology, in *Municipal Reference Library Notes.*
New York, **42,** 45–63.

LINDESMITH, A.R., 1968
Addiction and opiates.
Chicago: Aldine Publishing Co., 207–41.

UNITED KINGDOM, 1968
The rehabilitation of drug addicts.
Report of the Advisory Committee on Drug Dependence.
London: Home Office.

UNITED KINGDOM, 1968
Cannabis.
Report by the Advisory Committee on Drug Dependence.
London: Home Office.

BAUMGARTNER, K.C., 1969
The effects of drugs on criminal responsibility, specific intent, and mental competency.
Amer. Crim. Law Quart., **8,** 118–27.

BRILL, L., AND LIEBERMAN, L., 1969
Authority and addiction.
Boston: Little, Brown & Co.

BROOKS, A.D., 1969
Marijuana and the constitution: individual liberties and puritan virtues, in J.R. Wittenborn, H. Brill, J.P. Smith and S.A. Wittenborn (eds.), *Drugs and youth: proceedings of the Rutgers symposium on drug abuse.*
Springfield, Ill.: C.C. Thomas, 280–98.

CORRECTIONAL ASSOCIATION OF NEW YORK, 1969
Report of New York State Council on drug addiction.

ROBITSCHER, J., 1969
The right of society to protect its members, in J.R. Wittenborn, H. Brill, J.P. Smith and

S.A. Wittenborn (eds.), *Drugs and youth: proceedings of the Rutgers symposium on drug abuse.*
Springfield, Ill.: C.C. Thomas, 299–311.

ROSENTHAL, M.P., 1969
Marijuana: some alternatives, in J.R. Wittenborn, H. Brill, J.P. Smith and S.A. Wittenborn (eds.), *Drugs and youth: proceedings of the Rutgers symposium on drug abuse.*
Springfield, Ill.: C.C. Thomas, 260–79.

STANFORD LAW REVIEW, 1969
Possession of marijuana in San Mateo County: some social costs of criminalisation.
Stanford Law Rev., **22,** 101–28.

TAURO, G.J., 1969
Marijuana and relevant problems—1969.
Amer. Crim. Law Quart., **7,** 174–94.

BONNIE, R.J., AND WHITEBREAD, II, C.H., 1970
The forbidden fruit and the tree of knowledge: an inquiry into the legal history of American marijuana prohibition.
Virginia Law Rev., **56,** 971–1204.

CONNELL, P.H., 1970
Treatment of narcotic and non-narcotic drug dependence: the need for research, in R.V. Phillipson (ed.), *Modern trends in drug dependence and alcoholism.*
London: Butterworths, 22–48.

DAVIS, W.N., 1970
The treatment of drug addiction: some comparative observations.
Brit. J. Addict., **65,** 227–35.

DEEDES, W., 1970
The drugs epidemic.
London: Tom Stacey, 82–143.

DUSTER, T., 1970
The legislation of morality: law, drugs and moral judgment.
New York: Free Press, 153–215.

FARKAS, G.M., PETERSEN, D.M., AND BARR, N.I., 1970
New developments in the federal bureau of prisons addict treatment program.
Fed. Probation. **34**(4), 52–9.

GLATT, M.M., 1970
Psychotherapy of drug dependence: some theoretical considerations.
Brit. J. Addict., **65,** 51–62.

HIRSCHFELDT, F., 1970
Drug addiction and drug abuse in Sweden.
Swedish Information Service.

KAPLAN, J., 1970
Marijuana—the new prohibition.
New York: World Publishing Co.

KRAMER, J.C., 1970
The state versus the addict: uncivil commitment.
Boston Univ. Law Rev., **50,** 1–22.

MUNNS, J.G., GEIS, G., AND BULLINGTON, B., 1970
Ex-addict streetworkers in a Mexican-American community.
Crime & Delinq., **16,** 409–16.

NEW ZEALAND, 1970
Drug dependency and drug abuse in New Zealand.
New Zealand Board of Health Report Series, **14,** 23–94.

ROBERTS, C.F.JR., 1970
A final evaluation of the narcotic control program for youth authority parolees.
Research report No. 58, State of California, Dept. of the Youth Authority, 69–83.

ST JOHN'S LAW REVIEW, 1970
Note, heroin, marijuana and crime: a socio-legal analysis. **45,** 119–78.

SOLURSH, L.P., AND SOLURSH, M.J., 1970
Illusinogenic drugs. Their effects on criminal responsibility.
Toronto: Canadian Mental Health Association.

TOLL, A-M., 1970
Case study on the attitudes of drug addicts to treatment.
Brit. J. Addict., **65,** 139–58.

UNITED STATES OF AMERICA, 1970
National Commission on Reform of Federal Criminal Laws, *Working Papers*, **2.**
Washington, D.C., 1059–65.

WALDORF, D., 1970
Life without heroin—social adjustment

during long-term periods of voluntary abstention.
Social Problems, **18**, 228–43.

White, A., Jackson, C., Taylor, B., and Wilde, E., 1970
Prescription for drugs.
London: Conservative Political Centre.

Connor, T., and Kremen, E., 1971
Methadone maintenance—is it enough?
Brit. J. Addict., **66**, 53–70.

Cuskey, W.R., 1971
Methadone use in the outpatient treatment of narcotic addicts.
Bulletin on Narcotics, **23**(3), 23–30.

Du Pont, R.L., 1971
How corrections can beat the high cost of heroin addiction.
Fed. Probation, **35**(2), 43–50.

Fahey, R.P., 1971
The enforcement of the Illinois Felony Marijuana Law in Chicago.
Washington Univ. Law Quart., 1971, 281–307.

Georgetown Law Journal, 1971
Police perjury in narcotics 'dropsy' cases: a new credibility gap. **60**, 507–23.

Grinspoon, L., 1971
Marihuana reconsidered.
Cambridge, Mass.: Harvard Univ. Press.

Grupp, S.E., 1971
Prior criminal record and adult marihuana arrest dispositions.
J. Crim. Law, Criminol. & Pol. Sci., **62**, 74–9.

Halpern, W.I., and Gordon, A., 1971
Drugs and the youthful police informer.
Amer. J. Psychiat., **128**, 649–51.

Iowa Law Review, 1971
Punishment of narcotic addicts for possession: a cruel but usual punishment, **56**, 578–97.

Kaplan, J., 1971
The role of the law in drug control.
Duke Law J., 1971, 1065–104.

Kittrie, N.N., 1971
Marijuana—the right to truth.
South Carolina Law Rev., **23**, 361–76.

Kittrie, N.N., 1971
The right to be different.
Baltimore, Md.: Johns Hopkins Press, 210–60.

Mahon, T.A., 1971
An exploratory study of hospitalized narcotic addicts in Great Britain.
Acta Psychiatrica Scandinavica. Supplementun 227; Munksgaard, Copenhagen, 8–66.

Miller, M.G., 1971
Social policy and drug dependence.
Brit. J. Addict., **66**, 271–88.

Schofield, M., 1971
The strange case of pot.
Harmondsworth: Penguin Books, 63–194.

Vera Institute of Justice, 1971
Heroin research and rehabilitation program.
New York: Vera Institute of Justice.

Warder, J., and Ross, C., 1971
Alcoholism and its treatment in Scotland: a critical view.
Brit. J. Addict., **66**, 110–22.

Whitford, W.C., 1971
The physician, the law and the drug abuser.
Univ. Pennsylvania Law Rev., **119**, 933–69.

Young, J., 1971
The drugtakers: the social meaning of drug use.
London: Paladin.

Young, J., 1971
The role of the police as amplifiers of deviancy, negotiators of reality and translators of fantasy: some consequences of our present system of drug control as seen in Notting Hill, in S. Cohen (ed.), *Images of deviance.*
Harmondsworth: Penguin Books, 27–61.

Zacune, J., and Hensman, C., 1971
Drugs, alcohol and tobacco in Britain.
London: Heinemann Medical Books, 25–41, 55–63, 95–140, 157–207.

Bassiouni, M.C., 1972
The International Narcotics control system: a proposal.
St John's Law Rev., **46**, 713–763.

Bellassai, J.P., and Segal, P.N., 1972
Addict diversion: an alternative approach for the Criminal Justice system.
Georgetown Law J., **60**, 667–710.

BLUM, R.H., AND ASSOCIATES, 1972
The dream sellers, perspective on drug dealers.
San Francisco: Jossey-Bass, Publishers,
18–58, 183–200, 213–45, 290–348.

BRADSHAW, S., 1972
Drug misuse and the law.
Basingstoke: Macmillan.

CANADA, 1972
Cannabis.
A report of a Commission of Inquiry into
the non-medical use of drugs.
Ottowa: Information Canada.

CANADA, 1972
Treatment.
A report of the Commission of Inquiry into
the non-medical use of drugs.
Ottowa: Information Canada.

DU PONT, R.L., 1972
Heroin addiction treatment and crime
reduction.
Amer. J. of Psych., **128,** 856–60.

ERSKINE, H., 1972
Alcohol and the criminal justice system:
challenge and response.
LEAA, National Institute of Law
Enforcement and Criminal Justice, U.S.
Department of Justice, Washington, D.C.

GEIS, G., 1972
Not the law's business?
Crime and delinquency issues.
Rockville, Md.: N.I.M.H., 105–72.

GLANCY, J.E.McA., 1972
The treatment of narcotic dependence in the
United Kingdom.
Bulletin on Narcotics, **24**(4), 1–9.

GOODE, E., 1972
Drugs in society.
New York: Knopf.

INTERNATIONAL NARCOTICS CONTROL
BOARD, 1972
Report of the International Narcotics
Control Board on its work in 1971.
Bulletin on Narcotics, **24**(2), 29–33.

PACIFIC LAW JOURNAL, 1972
Drug rehabilitation: is a drug court the
answer? **3,** 595–632.

TEFF, H., 1972
Drugs and the law: the development of
control.
Modern Law Rev., **35,** 225–41.

UNITED STATES OF AMERICA, 1972
Marihuana: signal of misunderstanding.
First report of the National Commission on
Marihuana and Drug Abuse.
Washington, D.C.

UNITED STATES OF AMERICA, 1972
Appendix to Marihuana: signal of
misunderstanding.
The Technical Papers of the First Report of
the National Commission on Marihuana and
Drug Abuse.
Washington, D.C. Vol. 1, 481–599, Vol. 2,
611–852, 903–41, 1123–97.

BLUM, R.H., AND ASSOCIATES, 1973
Drug dealers—taking action.
San Francisco: Jossey-Bass, Publishers.

CANADA, 1973
Final report of the Commission of Inquiry into
the non-medical use of drugs (Le Dain,
Commission).
Ottowa: Information Canada, 12–22,
47–178, 559–627, 915–68.

CARD, R., 1973
Drugs and the law in Britain.
St. Louis Univ. Law J., **17,** 301–24.

DENARDIS, R.F., AND ISRAEL, S.M., 1973
The irrationality of a law enforcement
approach to opiate narcotics.
J. Urban Law, **50,** 631–80.

DOCTOR, R.M., AND SIEVEKING, N.A., 1973
The irrationality of a law enforcement
approach to opiate narcotics.
J. Urban Law, **50,** 631–80.

DOCTOR, R.M., AND SIEVEKING, N.A.,
1973
A comparison of attitudes among heroin
addicts, policemen, marijuana users and
non drug users about the drug addict.
Internat. J. Addict., **8,** 691–99.

DOLAN, A.K., 1973
The impact of methadone maintenance on
civil and criminal liability.
Southern Calif. Law Rev., **46,** 713–53.

DOLE, V.P., AND NYSWANDER, M.E., 1973
Rehabilitation of the street addict, in C.D. Chambers and L. Brill (eds.), *Methadone: experiences and issues.*
New York: Behavioral Publications, 67–74.

DOLE, V.P., NYSWANDER, M.E., AND WARNER, A., 1973
Successful treatment of 750 criminal addicts, in C.D. Chambers and L. Brill (eds.), *Methadone experiences and issues.*
New York: Behavioral Publications, 75–85.

GREENSTEIN, H.M., AND DIBIANCO, P.E., 1973
Marijuana laws—crime against humanity.
Notre Dame Lawyer, **48,** 314–39.

JOSEPH, H., 1973
A probation department treats heroin addicts.
Fed. Probation, **37**(1), 35–9.

KOCH, J.V., AND GRUPP, S.E., 1973
Police and illicit drug markets: some economic considerations.
Brit. J. Addict., **68,** 351–62.

McNAMARA, R.M., AND STARR, J.R., 1973
Confidentiality of narcotic addict treatment records: a legal and statistical analysis.
Columbia Law Rev., **73,** 1579–612.

MIKKELSEN, M., 1973
Drug law enforcement.
Internat. Crim. Police Rev., No. 271, 259–71.

MOFFET A.D., SOLOWAY, I.H., AND GLICK, M.X., 1973
Post-treatment behavior following ambulatory detoxification, in C.D. Chambers and L. Brill (eds.), *Methadone: experiences and issues.*
New York: Behavioral Publications, 215–27.

NEW YORK, STATE OF, 1973
Interim report of the New York State Commission of investigation concerning the operations of special narcotics parts of the Supreme Court.
270 Broadway, New York, N.Y. 10007.

QUINN, T.M., AND MCLAUGHLIN, G.T., 1973
The evolution of Federal Drug Control Legislation.
Catholic Univ. Law Rev., **22,** 586–627.

QUINN, T.M., AND MCLAUGHLIN, G.T., 1973
The evolution and present status of New York Drug Control Legislation.
Buffalo Law Rev., **22,** 705–36.

SIMMONS, L.R.S., AND GOLD, M.B., 1973
The myth of international control: American foreign policy and the heroin traffic.
Internat. J. Addict., **8,** 779–800.

SIMONS, B., AND MANSFIELD, M., 1973
The misuse of drugs act.
Drugs and Society, **2**(10), 5–10.

SOUTHERN CALIFORNIA LAW REVIEW, 1973
Drug control of school children: the child's right to choose.
Southern California Law Rev., **46,** 585–616.

UNITED STATES OF AMERICA, 1973
Drug use in America: problem in perspective.
Second Report of the National Commission on Marihuana and Drug Abuse, Washington, D.C., 175–412.

UNITED STATES OF AMERICA, 1973
The legal system and drug control, Vol. 3 of the *Appendix* to Drug use in America: problem in perspective. The Technical Papers of the Second Report of the National Commission on Marihuana and Drug Abuse. Washington D.C.

UNITED STATES OF AMERICA, 1973
Treatment and Rehabilitation, Vol. 4 of the *Appendix* to Drugs use in America: problem in perspective. The Technical Papers of the Second Report of the National Commission on Marihuana and Drug Abuse. Washington, D.C.

VILLANOVA LAW REVIEW, 1973
Contemporary problems of drug abuse: a national symposium for law and medical students. **18,** 787–954.

WORLD HEALTH ORGANIZATION, 1973
WHO expert committee on drug dependence, Nineteenth Report.
Technical Report Series No 526. Geneva: W.H.O.

BEAN, P., 1974
The social control of drugs.
London: Martin Robertson.

CHRISTIANSON, S., 1974
Heroin paraphernalia: a breakdown of a fix.
Crim. Law Bulletin, **10,** 493–515.

COUNCIL OF EUROPE, 1974
Penal aspects of drug abuse.
Strasbourg: European Committee on Crime Problems, 69–145, 168–264.

CUSHMAN, P., 1974
Relationship between narcotic addiction and crime.
Fed. Probation, **38**(3), 38–43.

D'ORBAN, P.T., 1974
Court sentences in female narcotic addicts.
Brit. J. Addict., **69,** 167–71.

HESS, A., VAN DER VAART, J., RICKEY, B., and ROSE, J., 1974
Nature and trends of drug use and abuse.
Crim. Law Bulletin, **10,** 637–60.

STANFORD LAW REVIEW, 1974
Diversion of drug offenders in California.
26, 923–44.

UCLA LAW REVIEW, 1974
Marijuana possession and the California constitutional prohibition of cruel and unusual punishment. **21,** 1136–71.

5 Drunkenness

(*a*) *Sources, forms and incidence*

ASCHAFFENBURG, G., 1913
Crime and its repression.
Boston: Little, Brown & Co., 69–88.

BANAY, R.S., 1942
Alcoholism and crime.
Quart. J. Stud. Alcohol., **2,** 686–716.

SUTHERLAND, E.H., SCHROEDER, H.G., AND TORDELLA, C.L., 1950
Personality traits and the alcoholics: a critique of existing studies.
Quart. J. Stud. Alcohol., **11,** 547–61.

VERKKO, V., 1951
Homicides and suicides in Finland and their dependence on national character.
Copenhagen: G.E.C. Gads Forlag, 77–86.

SELIGER, R.V., 1953
Alcohol and crime.
J. Crim. Law, Criminol. & Pol. Sci., **44,** 438–41.

DEUTSCHER, I., 1954
The petty offender: a sociological alien.
J. Crim. Law, Criminol. & Pol. Sci., **44,** 592–5.

SHUPE, Ll.M., 1954
Alcohol and crime: a study of the urine alcohol concentration found in 882 persons arrested during or immediately after the the commission of a felony.
J. Crim. Law, Criminol. & Pol. Sci., **44,** 661–64.

DEUTSCHER, I., 1955
The petty offender: society's orphan.
Fed. Probation, **19**(2), 12–18.

KRAUWEEL, H.J., 1955
Drinking and criminality in the Netherlands.
Quart. J. Stud. Alcohol., **16,** 290–94.

WATTENBURG, W.W., AND MOIR, J.B., 1956
A study of teen-agers arrested for drunkenness.
Quart. J. Stud. Alcohol., **17,** 426–36.

WOLFGANG, M.E., AND STROHM, R.B., 1956
The relationship between alcohol and criminal homicides.
Quart. J. Stud. Alcohol., **17,** 411–25.

ANNALS OF THE AMERICAN ACADEMY OF POLITICAL AND SOCIAL SCIENCE, 1958
Issue on understanding alcoholism, **315,** 1–11, 22–30, 40–7, 48–72, 99–116.

GLATT, M.M., 1958
Alcoholism and juvenile delinquency.
Brit. J. Delinq., **9**, 84–93.

NOYES, A.P., AND KOLB, L.C., 1958
Modern clinical psychiatry.
Philadelphia: W.B. Saunders, 191–211.

WOLFGANG, M.E., 1958
Patterns in criminal homicide.
Philadelphia: Univ. of Penn. Press, 134–67.

ZWERLING, I., AND ROSENBAUM, M., 1959
Alcoholic addiction and personality (nonpsychotic conditions), in S. Arieti (ed.), *American handbook of psychiatry*, Vol. 1.
New York: Basic Books, 623–44.

JELLINEK, E.M., 1960
The disease concept of alcoholism.
Newhaven: Hillhouse Press.

MCCORD, W., AND MCCORD, J., 1960
Origins of alcoholism.
London: Tavistock, 1–44, 97–142.

ROONEY, J.F., 1961
Group processes among skid row winos.
Quart. J. Stud. Alcohol., **22**, 444–60.

CHAFETZ, M.E., AND DEMONE, H.W., 1962
Alcoholism and society.
London: Oxford Univ. Press.

PITTMAN, D.J., AND SNYDER, C.R. (EDS.), 1962
Society, culture, and drinking patterns.
New York: John Wiley & Sons, 305–600.

BOGUE, D.J., 1963
Skid row in American cities.
Chicago: Community and Family Study Center, Univ. Chicago.

INTERNATIONAL CONFERENCE ON ALCOHOL AND ROAD TRAFFIC, 1963
Alcohol and road traffic.
Proceedings of the third international conference (Sept. 3–7, 1962).
London: B.M.A. House, 14–37, 54–60, 90–107.

JONES, H., 1963
Alcoholic addiction: a psycho-social approach to abnormal drinking.
New York: Humanities Press.

CALIFORNIA, STATE OF, 1960 & 1964
Criminal offenders and drinking involvement. A preliminary analysis, 1960; Part II, 1964.
Alcoholism and California, Publications 3 & 10, Dept. of Health Division of Alcoholic Rehabilitation.

HAVARD, J.D.J., 1964
Road accidents and the drinking driver.
New Scientist, No. 398, 2 July 1964, 23–6.

HOPKINSON, B.R., AND WIDDOWSON, G.M., 1964
Relation of alcohol to road accidents.
Brit. Med. J., **2**, 1569–70.

GLATT, M.M., 1965
Crime, alcohol and alcoholism.
Howard J., **11**, 274–84.

KESSEL, N., AND WALTON, H., 1965
Alcoholism.
Harmondsworth: Penguin Books.

WALLACE, S.E., 1965
Skid Row as a way of life.
Totawa, N.J.: Bedminster Press.

COSPER, R.L., 1966
Drinking and driving in a community setting, in *Alcohol and traffic safety.*
Proceedings of the fourth international conference on alcohol and traffic safety (Dec. 6–10, 1965).
Bloomington: Indiana, 105–11.

GLASER, D., AND O'LEARY, V., 1966
The alcoholic offender.
Washington, D.C.: U.S. Dept. of Health, Education, & Welfare.

UNITED STATES OF AMERICA, 1966
Report of the President's Commission on Crime in the District of Columbia.
Washington, D.C., 474–529.

BAHR, H.M., 1967
The gradual disappearance of Skid Row.
Social Problems, **15**, 41–5.

ROEBUCK, J.B., 1967
Criminal typology.
Springfield, Ill.: C.C. Thomas, 155–71.

UNITED STATES OF AMERICA, 1967
The challenge of crime in a free society.
Report of the President's Commission on Law Enforcement and Administration of Justice, Washington, D.C., 233–43.

UNITED STATES OF AMERICA, 1967
Task force report: drunkenness.
Washington, D.C.: President's Commission on Law Enforcement and Administration of Justice.

HYMAN, M.M., 1968
The social characteristics of persons arrested for driving while intoxicated.
Quart. J. Stud. Alcohol., Suppl. No. 4, 138–77.

MACANDREW, C., AND EDGERTON, R.B., 1969
Drunken comportment. A social explanation.
London: Thomas Nelson and Sons, 1–36, 165–73.

RUBINGTON, E., 1969
Types of alcoholic offenders.
Fed. Probation, **33** (1), 28–35.

WILLIAMS, G.P., 1970
The four faces of drunkenness in England and Wales 1968–1970.
Royston, Herts.: Priory Press Ltd.

BLUMBERG, L.U., SHIPLEY, T.E., JR., AND MOOR, J.O. JR., 1971
The Skid Row man and the Skid Row status community. With perspectives on their future.
Quart. J. Stud. Alcohol., **32,** 909–41.

DOLESCHAL, E., 1971
Victimless crime.
Crime & Delinq. Lit., **3,** 254–69.

HINDERER, H., 1971
Uber die Aufgaben der Bekämpfung des Alkoholismus nach der Strafgesetzgebung der Deutschen Demokratischen Republik.
Brit. J. Addict., **66**(1), 9–17.

LAAKSO, S.A., 1971
Arrests for drunkenness—two capital cities compared.
Scandinavian Studies in Criminology, **3,**
Oslo: Universitetsforlaget, 89–105.

SARGENT, M.J., 1971
A cross-cultural study of attitudes and behaviour towards alcohol and drugs.
Brit. J. Sociol., **22,** 83–96.

WHITLOCK, F.A., 1971
Death on the road: a study in social violence.
London: Tavistock, 66–80

ZACUNE, J., AND HENSMAN, C., 1971
Drugs, alcohol and tobacco in Britain.
London: Heinemann Medical Books, 3–24, 45–53, 67–93, 143–55, 169–207.

CONNOR, W.D., 1972
Deviance in Soviet society: crime, delinquency, and alcoholism.
New York: Columbia Univ. Press, 35–79.

WALLER, J., 1972
Factors associated with alcohol and responsibility for fatal highway crashes.
Quart. J. Stud. Alcohol., **33,** 160–70.

BACON, S.D., 1973
Highway crashes, alcohol problems, and programs for social controls, in P.G. Bourne and R. Fox (eds.), *Alcoholism: progress in research and treatment.*
New York: Academic Press, 311–35.

BAHR, H.M., AND CAPLOW, T., 1973
Old men drunk and sober.
New York: N.Y. Univ. Press.

RUBINGTON, E., 1973
Alcohol problems and social control.
Columbus, Ohio: Charles E. Merill Publishing Co.

THUM, D., WECHSLER, H., AND DEMONE, H.W. JR., 1973
Alcohol levels of Emergency Service patients injured in fights and assaults.
Criminology, **4,** 487–97.

TINKLENBERG, J.R., 1973
Alcohol and violence, in P.G. Bourne and R. Fox (eds.), *Alcoholism: progress in research and treatment.*
New York: Academic Press, 195–210.

5 Drunkenness

(*b*) *Legal and treatment aspects*

DEUTSCHER, I., 1954
The petty offender: a sociological alien.
J. Crim. Law, Criminol. & Pol. Sci., **44,** 592–95.

DEUTSCHER, I., 1955
The petty offender: society's orphan.
Fed. Probation, **19**(2), 12–18.

MYERSON, D.J., 1956
The 'Skid Row' problem. Further observations on a group of alcoholic patients, with emphasis on inter-personal relations and the therapeutic approach.
New England J. Medicine, **254,** 1168–73.

PITTMAN, D.J., AND GORDON, C.W., 1958
Revolving door; a study of the chronic police case inebriate.
Glencoe, Ill.: Free Press.

JELLINEK, E.M., 1960
The disease concept of alcoholism.
Newhaven: Hillhouse Press.

CHAFETZ, M.E., AND DEMONE, H.W., 1962
Alcoholism and society
New York: Oxford Univ. Press.

AARON, J.E., AND SHAFTER, A.J. (EDS.), 1963
The police officer and alcoholism.
Springfield, Ill.: C.C. Thomas.

EDWARDS, G., 1965
The chronic drunkenness offender: a therapeutic alternative to repeated imprisonment.
Univ. of London, Institute of Psychiatry. Mimeo.

VALLANCE, M., 1965
Alcoholism. A two-year follow-up study of patients admitted to the psychiatric department of a general hospital.
Brit. J. Psychiat., **111,** 348–56.

BRITISH MEDICAL JOURNAL, 1966
Correspondence on compulsion in the treatment of alcoholics. **1,** 291, 358, 480, 677, 735.

GLASER, D., AND O'LEARY, V., 1966
The alcoholic offender.
Washington, D.C.: U.S. Dept of Health, Education & Welfare.

MULLAN, H., AND SANGIULIANO, I., 1966
Alcoholism: group psychotherapy and rehabilitation.
Springfield, Ill.: C.C. Thomas, 1–92.

MYERSON, D.J., AND MAYER, J., 1966
Origins, treatment and destiny of Skid-Row alcoholic men.
New England J. Medicine, **275,** 419–25.

UNITED STATES OF AMERICA, 1966
Report of the President's Commission on Crime in the District of Columbia...
Washington, D.C., 474–529.

BITTNER, E., 1967
The police on Skid-Row: a study of peace keeping.
Amer. Sociol. Rev., **32,** 699–715.

UNITED STATES OF AMERICA, 1967
Task force report: drunkenness.
Washington, D.C.: President's Commission on Law Enforcement and Administration of Justice.

UNITED STATES OF AMERICA, 1967
The challenge of crime in a free society.
Report of the President's Commission on Law Enforcement and Administration of Justice, Washington, D.C., 233–43.

GATH, D., HENSMAN, C., HAWKER, A., KELLY, M., AND EDWARDS, G., 1968
The drunk in court: survey of drunkenness offenders from two London courts.
Brit. Med. J., **4,** 808–11.

MERRILL, R.A., 1968
Drunkenness and reform of the criminal law.
Virginia Law Rev., **54,** 1135–64.

RUTGERS LAW REVIEW, 1968
Probation for the chronic alcoholic: the appropriateness of an abstinence condition. **22,** 787–816.

GREENAWALT, K., 1969
'Uncontrollable' actions and the eighth

amendment: implications of Powell v. Texas.
Columbia Law Rev., **69,** 927–79.

Cook, T., and Pollak, B., 1970
In place of skid row. The first three years of the Rathcoole experiment, May 1966–May 1969.
London: The National Association for the Care and Resettlement of Offenders. Reprint. No. 4.

Criminal Justice Coordinating Council & Vera Institute of Justice, 1970
In lieu of arrest—the Manhattan Bowery Project—treatment for homeless alcoholics,
New York.

Edwards, G., 1970
The status of alcoholism as a disease, in R.V. Phillipson (ed.), *Modern trends in drug dependence and alcoholism.*
London: Butterworths, 140–63.

Fingarette, H., 1970
The perils of Powell: in search of factual foundation for the 'disease concept of alcoholism'.
Harvard Law Rev., **83,** 793–812.

Hollister, B.C., 1970
Alcoholics and public drunkenness—the emerging retreat from punishment.
Crime & Delinq., **16,** 238–54.

Nimmer, R., 1970
The public drunk: formalizing the police role as a social help agency.
Georgetown Law J., **58,** 1089–116.

Stewart, E.I., and Malfetti, J.L., 1970
Rehabilitation of the drunken driver: a corrective course in Phoenix, Arizona, for persons convicted of driving under the influence of alcohol.
New York: Teachers College Press, 1–24.

Sweden, 1970
Summary of Swedish DWI report: driving under the influence of alcohol.
Stockholm.

Wilkinson, R., 1970
The prevention of drinking problems: alcohol control and cultural influences.
New York: Oxford Univ. Press, 24–48, 175–90.

Wiseman, J.P., 1970
Stations of the lost. The treatment of skid row alcoholics.
Englewood Cliffs, N.J.: Prentice-Hall.

Goodwin, D.W., Crane, J.B., and Guze, S.B., 1971
Felons who drink. An 8-year follow-up.
Quart. J. Stud. Alcohol, **32,** 136–47.

Grad, F.P., Goldberg, A.L., and Shapiro, B.A., 1971
Alcoholism and the law.
Dobbs Ferry, N.Y.: Oceana Publications.

Kittrie, N.N., 1971
The right to be different.
Baltimore, Md.: Johns Hopkins Press, 261–96.

Nimmer, R.T., 1971
Two million unnecessary arrests: removing a social service concern from the criminal justice system.
Chicago: Amer. Bar Foundation, 1–34, 142–54.

United Kingdom, 1971
Habitual drunken offenders.
London: Home Office.

Zacune, J., and Hensman, C., 1971
Drugs, alcohol and Tobacco in Britain.
London: Heinemann Medical Books, 3–24, 45–53, 67–93, 143–55, 169–207.

Connor, W.D., 1972
Deviance in Soviet society. Crime delinquency and alcoholism.
New York: Columbia Univ. Press, 35–79.

Grad, F.P., 1973
Legal aspects of alcoholism, in P.G. Bourne and R. Fox (eds.), *Alcoholism: progress in research and treatment.*
New York: Academic Press, 385–410.

Leach, B., 1973
Does alcoholics anonymous really work? in P.G. Bourne and R. Fox (eds.), *Alcoholism: progress in research and treatment.*
New York: Academic Press, 245–84.

NEW SOUTH WALES, 1973
City drunks—a possible new direction.
Statistical report 7, Department of the Attorney General and of Justice, N.S.W. Bureau of Crime Statistics and Research.

RUBINGTON, E., 1973
Alcohol problems and social control.
Columbus, Ohio: Charles E. Merill Publishing Co.

WEIS, C.W., 1973
Diversion of the public inebriate from the Criminal Justice system, L.E.A.A., National Institute of Law Enforcement and Criminal Justice, U.S. Dept. of Justice, Washington, D.C.

WILLEMS, P.J.A., LETEMENDIA, F.J.J., AND ARROYAVE, F., 1973
A two-year follow up study comparing short with long stay in-patient treatment of alcoholics.
Brit. J. Psychiat., **122,** 637–48.

HERSHON, H.O., COOK, T., AND FOLDES, P.A., 1974
What shall we do with the drunkenness offender?
Brit. J. Psychiat., **124,** 327–35.

VIANO, E.C., 1974
From dispute settlement to rules creation: the impact of a court decision on the treatment of chronic alcoholics.
Internat. J. Criminol. & Penol., **2,** 275–88.

6 White collar crime

(*a*) *Empirical studies*

EVANS, D.M., 1859
Facts, failures and frauds: revelations, financial, mercantile, criminal.
London: Groombridge & Sons.

CAMPBELL, A.C., 1902
Insurance and crime: a consideration of the effects upon society of the abuses of insurance together with certain historical instances of such abuses.
New York: Knickerbocker Press, 301–25.

NEW YORK, CITY OF, 1945
Black market area; a case study of black market operations in New York State.
Submitted by the Mayor to Members of Congress, New York, June 28.

HENDERSON, L., 1946
How black is our market?
Atlantic Monthly, **178,** 46–53.

CASSEDY, J.E., 1949
False advertisement of food, drugs and cosemetics.
Food, Drugs and Cosmetics Law Quart., **4,** 353.

SUTHERLAND, E.H., 1949
White collar crime.
New York: Holt, Rinehart and Winston, 17–213.

HARTUNG, F.E., 1950
White collar offenses in the wholesale meat industry in Detroit.
Amer. J. Sociol., **56,** 23–34.

CLINARD, M.B., 1952
The black market: a study of white collar crime.
New York: Rinehart & Co

CRESSEY, D.R., 1953
Other people's money.
Glencoe, Ill.: Free Press.

LANE, R.E., 1953
Why businessmen violate the law.
J. Crim. Law, Criminol. & Pol. Sci., **44,** 151–65.

SUTHERLAND, E.H., 1956
Crime of corporations, in K. Schuessler (ed.), *Edwin H. Sutherland on analysing crime.*
Chicago Univ. Press, 1973, 78–96.

BALL, H.V., 1960
Social structure and rent-control violations.
Amer. J. Sociol., **65,** 598–604.

BAUMHART, R.C., 1961
How ethical are businessmen?
Harvard Business Rev., **39,** 6–19, 156–76.

FAULKS, N., 1961
Investigation into the affairs of H. Jasper & Co., Ltd.
London: Board of Trade.

GALBRAITH, J.K., 1961
Kreuger, genius and swindler.
London: Andre Deutsch.

ROSS, H.L., 1961
Traffic law violation: a folk crime.
Social Problems, **8,** 231–41.

SMITH, R.A., 1961
The incredible electrical conspiracy.
Fortune, **63** (April 1961), 132–7 and (May 1961), 161–4ff.

FULLER, J.G., 1962
The gentleman conspirators.
New York: Grove Press, 7–11.

HERLING, J., 1962
The great price conspiracy.
Washington, D.C.: Robert B. Luce, 1–12.

MARTIN, J.P., 1962
Offenders as employees.
London: Macmillan, 109–19.

LANGER, E., 1963
Growing old in America: frauds, quackery, swindle the aged and compound their trouble.
Science, **140,** 470–2.

QUINNEY, R., 1963
Occupational structure and criminal behavior: prescription violations by retail pharmacists.
Social Problems, **11,** 170–85.

DYNES, R.R., CLARKE, A.C., DINITZ, S., AND ISHINO, I., 1964
Social problems. Dissensus and deviation in an industrial society.
New York: Oxford Univ. Press, 565–81.

LEVENS, G.E., 1964
101 British white-collar criminals.
New Society, no. 78, 6–8.

MANNHEIM, H., 1965
Comparative criminology. Vol. 2.
London: Routledge & Kegan Paul, 484–98.

MILLER, N.C., 1965
The great salad oil swindle.
London: Victor Gollancz.

REICHSTEIN, K.J., 1965
Ambulance chasing: a case study of deviation and control within the legal profession.
Social Problems, **13,** 6–17.

SPENCER, J.C., 1965
White collar crime, in T. Grygier, H. Jones and J.C. Spencer (eds.), *Criminology in transition. essays in honour of Hermann Mannheim.*
London: Tavistock, 251–66.

CARLIN, J.E., 1966
Lawyers' ethics. A survey of the New York City Bar.
New York: Russell Sage Foundation, 3–10, 66–83, 119–32, 165–82.

COHEN, S.S., 1966
Morality and the American tax system.
George Washington Law Rev., **35,** 839.

DUKE, H.K., 1966
Insurance ethics—from the inside looking out.
Annals Amer. Acad. Pol & Soc. Sci., **363,** 102–7.

GRETHER, E.T., 1966
Sharp practice in merchandising and advertising.
Annals Amer. Acad. Pol. & Soc. Sci., **363,** 108–16.

MILLER, A.S., 1966
Business morality: some unanswered (and perhaps unanswerable) questions.
Annals Amer. Acad. Pol. & Soc. Sci., **363,** 95–101.

UNITED STATES OF AMERICA, 1966
Home maintenance and repair.
Consumer Issues.
Washington, D.C.: President's Committee on Consumer Interests, 41–77.

GEIS, G., 1967
The heavy electrical equipment antitrust cases of 1961, in M.B. Clinard and

R. Quinney (eds.), *Criminal behavior systems.* New York: Holt, Rinehart & Winston, 139–50.

United States of America, 1967
Task force report: crime and its impact—an assessment.
Washington, D.C.: President's Commission on Law Enforcement and Administration of Justice, 102–9.

United States of America, Congress, 1967
The economic cost of white collar crime.
Congressional Record, February 1967, H 986.

Alatas, S.H., 1968
The sociology of corruption.
Singapore: Donald Moore Press Ltd.

The Banker, 1968
Embezzling by computer. **118,** 1135–9.

Roberts, K., 1968
Antitrust problems in the newspaper industry.
Harvard Law Rev., **82,** 319–66.

Robin, G.D., 1969
Employees as offenders.
J. Res. Crime & Delinq., **6,** 17–33.

Schur, E.M., 1969
Our criminal society. The social and legal sources of crime in America.
Englewood Cliffs, N.J.: Prentice-Hall, 158–90.

Cunningham, J.P., 1970
Undertakings under the Restrictive Trade Practices Acts.
Law Quart. Rev., **86,** 239–63.

Groves, H.M., 1970
An empirical study of income-tax compliance, in E.O. Smigel and H.L. Ross (eds.), *Crimes against bureaucracy.*
New York: Van Nostrand Reinhold Co., 86–96.

Heidenheimer, A.J., (ed.), 1970
Political corruption: readings in comparative analysis.
New York: Holt, Rinehart & Winston, 3–64.

Horning, D.N.M., 1970
Blue-collar thefts: conceptions of property, attitudes toward pilfering, and work group norms in a modern industrial plant, in E.O. Smigel and H.L. Ross (eds.), *Crimes against bureaucracy.*
New York: Van Nostrand Reinhold Co., 46–64.

Leonard, W.N., and Weber, M.G., 1970
Automakers and dealers, a study in criminogenic market forces.
Law and Society Rev., **4,** 407–24.

Markovits, R.S., 1970
Tie-ins, reciprocity, and the leverage theory.
Yale Law J., **80,** 195–315.

Smigel, E.O., 1970
Public attitudes toward 'chiseling' with reference to unemployment compensation, in E.O. Smigel and H.L. Ross (eds.), *Crimes against bureaucracy.*
New York: Van Nostrand Reinhold Co., 29–45.

Turner, J.S., 1970
The chemical feast. The Ralph Nader Study Group Report on Food Protection and the Food and Drug Administration.
New York: Grossman.

Fordham Law Review, 1971
Secret Swiss bank accounts: uses, abuses, and attempts at control, **39,** 500–14.

Hills, S.L., 1971
Crime, power, and morality: the criminal-law process in the United States.
Scranton, Pa.: Chandler Publishing Company, 145–202.

Mintz, M., and Cohen, J.S., 1971
America Inc.: who owns and operates the United States.
New York: Dial Press.

Raw, C., Page, B., and Hodgson, G., 1971
Do you sincerely want to be rich?—Bernard Cornfeld and IOS: an international swindle.
London: Andre Deutsch.

Geis, G., and Edelhertz, H., 1973
Criminal law and consumer fraud: a sociological view.
Amer. Crim. Law Rev., **11,** 989–1010.

Mars, G., 1974
Dock pilferage, in P. Rock and M. McIntosh (eds.), *Deviance and social control.*
London: Tavistock, 209–28.

6 White collar crime

(*b*) *The concept challenged*

SUTHERLAND, E.H., 1940–1956
'White collar criminality' (1940), 'Is "white collar crime" crime?' (1945) and 'Crime of corporations' (1956), in K. Schuessler (ed.), *Edwin H. Sutherland on analysing crime.*
Univ. Chicago Press, 1973, 46–61, 62–77, 78–96.

SUTHERLAND, E.H., 1941
Crime in business.
Annals Amer. Acad. Pol. & Soc. Sci., **217,** 112–18.

TAPPAN, P.W., 1947
Who is the criminal?
Amer. Sociol. Rev., **12,** 96–103.

SUTHERLAND, E.H., 1949
White collar crime.
New York: Holt, Rinehart & Winston, 217–66.

SUTHERLAND, E.H., 1949
The white collar criminal, in V.C. Branham and S.B. Kutash (eds.), *Encyclopedia of criminology.*
New York: Philosophical Library, 511–15.

BURGESS, E.W., 1950
Comment on Hartung—white collar offences in the wholesale meat industry in Detroit.
Amer. J. Sociol., **56,** 32–4.

CLINARD, M.B., 1951
Sociologists and American criminology.
J. Crim. Law, Criminol. & Pol. Sci., **41,** 562–6.

AUBERT, V., 1952
White collar crime and social structure.
Amer. J. Sociol., **58,** 263–71.

VOLD, G.B., 1958
Theoretical criminology.
New York: Oxford Univ. Press, 243–61.

GLUECK, S., 1956
Theory and fact in criminology.
Brit. J. Delinq., **7,** 92–8.

CALDWELL, R.G., 1958
A re-examination of the concept of white collar crime.
Fed. Probation, **22**(1), 30–6.

NEWMAN, D.J., 1958
White collar crime.
Law & Contemp. Problems, **23,** 735–53.

BARNES, H.E., AND TEETERS, N.K., 1959
New horizons in criminology.
Englewood Cliffs, N.J.: Prentice-Hall, 38–49.

TAPPAN, P.W., 1960
Crime, justice and correction.
New York: McGraw-Hill, 1–34.

BLOCH, H.A., AND GEIS, G., 1962
Man, crime and society, the forms of criminal behavior.
New York: Random House, 379–404.

QUINNEY, R., 1964
The study of white collar crime: toward a re-orientation in theory and research.
J. Crim. Law, Criminol. & Pol. Sci., **55,** 208–14.

MANNHEIM, H., 1965
Comparative criminology. Vol. 2.
London: Routledge & Kegan Paul, 469–82.

SPENCER, J.C., 1965
White collar crime, in T. Grygier, H. Jones and J.C. Spencer (eds.), *Criminology in transition: essays in honour of Hermann Mannheim.*
London: Tavistock, 233–51.

GEIS, G., 1968
White collar criminal: the offender in business and the professions.
New York: Atherton Press, 1–19.

BECKER, H.S., 1971
Sociological work: method and substance.
London: Allen Lane Penguin Press, 329–39.

SEYMOUR, W.N., JR., 1973
Social and ethical considerations in assessing white collar crime.
Amer. Crim. Law Rev., **11,** 821–34.

6 White collar crime

(*c*) *Attempts at control*

SWISS BANK CORPORATION, n.d.
The truth about Swiss banking.
15 Nassau St., New York, N.Y. 10005.

HARTUNG, F.E., 1953
Common and discrete values.
J. Soc. Psychology, **38,** 3–23.

SMIGEL, E.O., 1956
Public attitudes toward stealing as related to the size of the victim organization.
Amer. Sociol. Rev., **21,** 320–27.

NEWMAN, D.J., 1957
Public attitudes toward a form of white collar crime.
Social Problems, **4,** 228–32.

DERSHOWITZ, A.J., 1961
Increasing community control over corporate crime—a problem in the law of sanctions.
Yale Law Rev., **71,** 289–306.

WATKINS, M.W., 1961
Electrical equipment antitrust cases—their implications for government and business.
Univ. Chicago Law Rev., **29,** 97–110.

GEORGIA LAW JOURNAL, 1962
Indemnification of the corporate official for fines and expenses resulting from criminal antitrust litigation, **50,** 566–85.

SCHWARTZ, R.D., AND SKOLNICK, J.H., 1962
Two studies of legal stigma. *Social Problems*, **10,** 133–42, and letter from H.L. Ross and reply, 390–2.

WRIGHT, R.L., 1962
Sentencing the income tax violator, statement of the basic problem delivered before the Institute for the Fifth Circuit, **30,**
Federal Rules Decisions, 185, 302, 304–5.

KADISH, S.H., 1963
Some observations on the use of criminal sanctions in enforcing economic regulations.
Univ. Chicago Law Rev., **30,** 423–49.

SPIVACK, G.B., 1963
Antitrust enforcement, a primer.
Connecticut Bar J., **37,** 375, 382.

AMERICAN CRIMINAL LAW QUARTERLY (REVIEW), 1964
The defence of the white collar accused: a symposium. **3,** 124–45.

WRIGHT, R.L., 1964
Jail sentences in antitrust cases, **37.**
Federal Rules Decisions, 183–84.

BALL, H.V., AND FRIEDMAN, L.M., 1965
The use of criminal sanctions in the enforcement of economic legislation: a sociological view.
Stanford Law Rev., **17,** 197–223.

BEERMAN, R., 1965
The further development of the anti-parasite laws.
Brit. J. Crim., **5,** 307–11.

CLABAULT, J.M., AND BURTON, J.F., 1966
Sherman Act Indictments 1955–1965. *A legal and economic analysis.*
New York: Federal Legal Publ., 36–7.

COLUMBIA JOURNAL OF LAW AND SOCIAL PROBLEMS, 1966
Antitrust criminal sanctions, **3**(2), 5–9.

DIXON, P.R., 1966
Federal-State co-operation to combat unfair trade practices.
State Govt., **39,** 37–41.

HARVARD LAW REVIEW, 1966
Nolo pleas in antitrust cases, **79,** 1475–88.

HUNTER, A., 1966
Competition and the law.
London: Geo. Allen & Unwin, 79–84, 161–88.

UNIVERSITY OF PENNSYLVANIA LAW REVIEW, 1966
Translating sympathy for deceived consumers into effective programs for protection, **114,** 395–450.

DAVIDS, L., 1967
Penology and corporate crime.
J. Crim. Law, Criminol. & Pol. Sci., **58,** 524–31.

HADDEN, T., 1967
The origins and the development of conspiracy to defraud.
Amer. J. Legal History, **11,** 25–40.

HARVARD LAW REVIEW, 1967
Developments in the law—deceptive advertising, **80,** 105–163.

HARVARD LAW REVIEW, 1967
Liability insurance for corporate executives, **80,** 648–69.

UNITED STATES OF AMERICA, 1967
Task force report: crime and its impact— an assessment.
Washington, D.C.: President's Commission on Law Enforcement and Administration of Justice, 109–15.

HADDEN, T., 1968
The control of company fraud.
Planning, **34,** (503). London: P.E.P.

CARSON, W.G., 1970
White collar crime and the enforcement of factory legislation.
Brit. J. Criminol., **10,** 387–98.

ROBIN, G.D., 1970
The Corporate and Judicial disposition of employee thieves, in E.O. Smigel and H.L. Ross (eds.), *Crimes against bureaucracy.*
New York: Van Nostrand Reinhold Co., 119–42.

TURNER, J.S., 1970
The chemical feast, the Ralph Nadar Study Group Report on Food protection and the Food Drug Administration.
New York: Grossman.

UNITED STATES OF AMERICA, 1970
The nature, impact and prosecution of white collar crime.
L.E.A.A. National Institute of Law Enforcement and Criminal Justice, U.S. Dept. of Justice, Washington, D.C.

BUXBAUM, R.M., 1971
Public participation in the enforcement of the antitrust laws.
California Law Rev., **59,** 113–44.

DELANCEY, W.J., LIEBMANN, C.W., AND MADDOCK, C.S., 1971
Economic crimes—the proposed new federal criminal code.
The Business Lawyer, **27,** 177–93.

FISSE, B., 1971
The use of publicity as a criminal sanction against business corporations.
Melbourne Univ. Law Rev., **8,** 107–50.

FORDHAM LAW REVIEW, 1971
Secret Swiss bank accounts: uses, abuses, and attempts at control. **39,** 500–14.

HARVARD LAW REVIEW, 1971
'Corrective advertising' orders of the Federal Trade Commission. **85,** 477–506.

HILLS, S.L., 1971
Crime, power, and morality: the criminal-law process in the United States.
Scranton, Pa.: Chandler Publishing Company, 145–202.

KWAN, Q.Y., RAJESWARAN, P., PARKER, B.P., AND AMIR, M., 1971
The role of criminalistics in white-collar crimes.
J. Crim. Law, Criminol. & Pol. Sci., **62,** 437–49.

MATHEWS, A.F., 1971
Criminal prosecutions under the Federal Securities Law and related statutes: the nature and development of SEC criminal cases.
Geo. Washington Law Rev., **39,** 901–70.

POSNER, R.A., 1971
A program for the antitrust division.
Univ. Chicago Law Rev., **38,** 500–36.

ALBANY LAW REVIEW, 1972
The criminal responsibility of corporate officials for pollution of the environment, **37,** 61–96.

COLUMBIA LAW REVIEW, 1972
Corrective advertising—the new response to consumer deception, **72,** 415–31.

GEIS, G., 1972
Criminal penalties for corporate criminals.
Crim. Law Bull., **8,** 377–92.

HANDLER, M., 1972
Twenty-five years of antitrust.
The Record of the association of the Bar of the city of New York, **27,** 653–715.

JUSTICE, 1972
Insider trading.
Report under the chairmanship of William Goodhart. London.

KAISER, G., 1972
Strategien und prozesse strafrechtlichen sozialkontrolle.
Frankfurt am Main: Athenaum Verlag, 100–23.

APEX CHARITABLE TRUST, 1973
The employment future of the ex-offender, a report of the work of the white collar offender and sexual offender project.
London: Apex Charitable Trust.

BREIT, W., AND ELZINGA, K.G., 1973
Antitrust penalties and attitudes towards risk: an economic analysis.
Harvard Law Rev., **86**, 693–735.

DAWIDOFF, D.J., 1973
The power of the securities and exchange commission to require stock exchanges to discipline members.
Fordham Law Rev., **41**, 549–68.

GLENN, M.K., 1973
The crime of 'pollution': the role of federal water pollution criminal sanctions.
Amer. Crim. Law Rev., **11**, 835–82.

MATHEWS, A.F., AND SULLIVAN, W.P., 1973
Criminal liability for violations of Federal Securities laws: the National Commission's proposed federal criminal code, S.1, and S.1400.
Amer. Crim. Law Rev., **11**, 883–958.

OGREN, R.W., 1973
The ineffectiveness of the criminal sanction in fraud and corruption cases: losing the battle against white collar crime.
Amer. Crim. Law Rev., **11**, 959–88.

CARSON, W.G., 1974
Symbolic and instrumental dimensions of early factory legislation, in R.G. Hood (ed.), *Crime, criminology and public policy: essays in honour of Sir Leon Radzinowicz.*
London: Heinemann.

UNITED STATES OF AMERICA, 1974
A handbook on white collar crime.
Washington, D.C.: Chamber of Commerce of the United States.

7 Abortion: criminological and legal aspects: a preliminary list

[*See also Section* 6(1) *on scope of penal sanctions.*]

GEBHARD, P.H., POMEROY, W.B., MARTIN, C.E., AND CHRISTENSON, C.V., 1958
Pregnancy, birth and abortion.
New York: Harper & Row.

WILLIAMS, G., 1958
The sanctity of life and the criminal law.
London: Faber, 139–223.

LADER, L., 1966
Abortion,
New York: Bobbs-Merrill Co.

HARTER, C.L., AND BEASLEY, J.D., 1967
A survey concerning induced abortions in New Orleans.
Amer. J. Public Health, **57**, 1937–47.

POTTS, M., 1967
Legal abortion in Eastern Europe.
Eugenics Rev., **59**, 232–50.

ROEMER, R., 1967
Abortion law: the approaches of different nations.
Amer. J. Public Health, **57**, 1906–22.

TIETZE, C., 1967
Abortion in Europe.
Amer. J. Public Health, **57**, 1923–32.

FREDERIKSEN, H., AND BRACKETT, J.W., 1968
Demographic effects of abortion.
Public Health Reports, **83**, 999–1010.

POTTS, M., 1968
A guide to the Abortion Act 1967.
Wheathampstead, Herts.: Abortion Law Reform Association.

ADDISON, P.H., 1969
The impact of the Abortion Act 1967 in Great Britain.
Medico-Legal J., **38**, 15–21.

LEE, N.H., 1969
The search for an abortionist.
Chicago: Univ. Chicago Press.

SMITHURST, B.A., 1969
The Abortion Act, 1967, of the United Kingdom—an unsatisfactory law.
Med. J. Australia, **2**, 863–65.

BRITISH COUNCIL OF CHURCHES, 1970
The Abortion Act 1967–69. *A factual review.*
London: Witney Press.

BRITISH MEDICAL JOURNAL, 1970
The Abortion Act (1967).
Findings of an inquiry into the first year's working of the Act conducted by the Royal College of Obstetricians and Gynaecologists, **2**, 529–35.

BROWN, B.F., 1970
Natural Law Institute 1970: abortion recent statutes and the crime of abortion.
Loyola Law Rev., **16**, 275–88.

BYRN, R.M., 1970
Abortion-on-demand: whose morality?
Notre Dame Lawyer, **46**, 5–40.

CALLAHAN, D., 1970
Abortion: law choice and morality.
New York: Macmillan.

DIGGORY, P., PEEL, J., AND POTTS, M., 1970
Preliminary assessment of the 1967 Abortion Act in practice.
The Lancet, **1**, 287–91.

FINNIS, J.M., 1970
Three schemes of regulation, in J.T. Noonan Jr. (ed.), *The morality of abortion.*
Cambridge, Mass.: Harvard Univ. Press, 172–214.

GRÜNFELD, B., AND STRØM, A., 1970
Legal abortions in Norway.
World Medical J., **17**, 87,

HALL, R.E. (ED.), 1970
Abortion in a changing world. 2 volumes.
The proceedings of an International Conference convened in Hot Springs, Virginia, November 17–20, 1968, by the Association for the Study of Abortion.
New York: Columbia Univ. Press.

KENEALY, W.J., 1970
Abortion: a human problem.
Loyola Law Rev., **16**, 289–94.

LOUISELL, D.W., AND NOONAN, J.T., 1970
Constitutional balance, in J.T. Noonan (ed.), *The morality of abortion.*
Cambridge, Mass.: Harvard Univ. Press, 220–60.

NATIONAL OPINION POLLS, MARKET RESEARCH LTD., 1970
Survey on abortion.
Report of a survey carried out by National Opinion Polls Ltd. for the Abortion Law Reform Association.
London: NOP/4051.

NATIONAL OPINION POLLS, MARKET RESEARCH LTD., 1970
Survey of general practitioners.
Report on a survey conducted by National Opinion Polls Ltd. for Abortion Law Reform Association.
London: NOP/4052.

NATIONAL OPINION POLLS, MARKET RESEARCH LTD., 1970
Report on attitudes towards crime, violence, and permissiveness in society.
London. Mimeo. 60–63.

ÖHRBERG, K., 1970
Legal abortion in Sweden.
World Med. J., **4**, 85–6.

ROSSI, A.S., 1970
Abortion laws and their victims, in J.F. Short Jr. (ed.), *Modern criminals.*
Chicago: Aldine Publishing Co., 117–32.

SALZMAN, L., 1970
Abortion: a moral or medical problem?
Loyola Law Rev., **16,** 295–98.

SIMMS, M., 1970
Abortion law reform: how the controversy changed.
Crim. Law Rev., 1970, 567–80.

UNIVERSITY OF SYDNEY. FACULTY OF LAW, 1970
Seminar: Abortion.
Proceedings of the Institute of Criminology, No. 1.

WINTON, R., 1970
Medical practice and abortion law in Australia.
World Medical J., **17,** 88.

BELL, R.R., 1971
Social deviance—a substantive analysis.
Homewood, Ill.: Dorsey Press, 117–43.

BOYDELL, C.L., AND GRINDSTAFF, C.F., 1971
Public attitudes toward legal sanctions for drug and abortion offences.
Canad. J. Corrections, **13,** 209–32.

FINNIS, J.M., 1971
The Abortion Act: what has changed?
Crim. Law Rev., 1971, 3–12.

INGRAM, I.M., 1971
Abortion games: an inquiry into the working of the act.
The Lancet, **11,** 969–70.

MEANS, C.C., 1971
The Phoenix of abortional freedom: is a penumbral or ninth-amendment right about to rise from the nineteenth-century legislative ashes of a fourteenth-century common law liberty?
New York Law Forum, **17,** 335–410.

MOORE, E.C., 1971
Abortion and public policy: what are the issues?
New York Law Forum, **17,** 411–36.

NORTH CAROLINA LAW REVIEW, 1971
Abortion laws: a constitutional right to abortion, **49,** 487–502.

PACIFIC LAW JOURNAL, 1971
California's 1967 therapeutic abortion act: abridging a fundamental right to abortion, **2,** 186–205.

PACIFIC LAW JOURNAL, 1971
Is the intentional killing of an unborn child homicide? California's law to punish the wilful killing of a fetus. **2,** 170–85.

SIMMS, M., 1971
The Abortion Act: a reply.
Crim. Law Rev., 1971, 86–8.

SIMMS, M., 1971
The Abortion Act after three years.
Political Quart., **42,** 269–86.

SIMMS, M., 1971
Abortion and the facts.
World Medicine, Jan. 27, 1971, 51–6.

WORLD HEALTH ORGANIZATION, 1971
Abortion laws: a survey of current world legislation.
Geneva: W.H.O.

BALL, D.W., 1972
Self and identity in the context of deviance: the case of criminal abortion, in R.A. Scott and J.D. Douglas (eds.), *Theoretical perspectives on deviance.*
New York: Basic Books, 158–86.

BRITISH JOURNAL OF PSYCHIATRY, 1972
The Royal College of Psychiatrists' memorandum on the abortion act in practice, **120,** 449–51.

CASE WESTERN RESERVE LAW REVIEW, 1972
Symposium: abortion and the law. **23,** 705–895.

DUIN, V.N., 1972
New York's abortion reform law: unanswered questions.
Albany Law Rev., **37,** 22–60.

GEIS, G., 1972
Not the law's business?
Crime and delinquency issues.
Rockville, Md.: N.I.M.H., 53–104.

HART, H.L.A., 1972
Abortion law reform: the English experience.
Melbourne Univ. Law Rev., **8,** 388–411.

UNIVERSITY OF ILLINOIS LAW FORUM, 1972
A survey of the present statutory and case law on abortion: the contradictions and the problems, 1972, 177–98.

WILSON, P.R., 1972
Abortion law reform: some political administrative and law enforcement questions, in D. Chappell and P. Wilson (eds.), *The Australian criminal justice system.*
Sydney: Butterworths, 169–78.

ZIMRING, F.E., 1972
Of doctors, deterrence and the dark figure of crime—a note on abortion in Hawaii.
Univ. Chicago Law Rev., **39,** 699–721.

DAVID, H.P., 1973
Abortion trends in European socialist countries and in the United States.
Amer. J. Orthopsychiat., **43,** 376–83.

SARVIS, B., AND RODMAN, H., 1973
The abortion controversy.
New York: Columbia Univ. Press, 15–69.

SIMMS, M., 1973
How do we judge the Abortion Act?
Reflections on the Lane Committee and the 1967 Abortion Act.
Public Health, **87,** 155–64.

KOHL, M., 1974
The morality of killing: sanctity of life, abortion and euthanasia.
London: Peter Owen.

SIMMS, M., 1974
Abortion law and medical freedom.
Brit. J. Criminol., **14,** 118–31.

SOCIETY FOR THE PROTECTION OF UNBORN CHILDREN, 1974
Comments on the Lane Committee on the working of the Abortion Act.
London.

UNITED KINGDOM, 1974
Report of the committee on the working of the abortion act (Chairman Mrs Justice Lane)
Vol. 1.
London: HMSO, Cmnd. 5579, 4–10, 153–79, 190–200.

8 Homosexuality: criminological and legal aspects: a preliminary list

[*See also Section* 6(1) *on scope of penal sanctions; Section* 11(1) *for references on homosexuality in penal institutions.*]

MCINTOSH, M., 1968
The homosexual role.
Social Problems, **16,** 182–92.

CATHOLIC UNIVERSITY OF AMERICA LAW REVIEW, 1969
Federal employment of homosexuals: narrowing the efficiency standard, **19,** 267–75.

DEISHER, R.W., EISNER, V., AND SULZBACHER, S.I., 1969
The young male prostitute.
Pediatrics, **43,** 936–41.

NETHERLANDS, 1969
Withdrawal of article 248 BIS of the Penal code (Draft law to abolish the existing penal provision concerning homosexual offences with minors).
Translation, London: Albany Trust.

HUMPHREYS, L., 1970
Tearoom trade.
London: Gerald Duckworth & Co.

HYDE, H.M., 1970
The other love: an historical and contemporary survey of homosexuality in Britain.
London: Heinemann.

NATIONAL OPINION POLLS, MARKET RESEARCH LTD., 1970
Report on attitudes towards crime, violence, and permissiveness in society.
London, Mimeo, 68–70.

WARD, D.A., AND KASSEBAUM, G.G., 1970
Lesbian liaisons in J.H. Gagnon and W. Simon (eds.), *The sexual scene.*
Chicago: Aldine Publishing Co., 125–36.

West, D.J., 1970
Aspects of homosexuality.
J. Biosoc. Sci., Supplement, **2,** 43–50.

Williams, C.J., and Weinberg, M.S., 1970
Being discovered: a study of homosexuals in the military.
Social Problems, **18,** 217–27.

Bell, R.R., 1971
Social deviance—a substantive analysis.
Homewood, Ill.: Dorsey Press, 248–305

Driscoll, J.P., 1971
Transsexuals.
Trans-action, **8,** 28–68.

Horenstain, N.G., 1971
Homosexuals and the teaching profession.
Cleveland State Law Rev., **20,** 125–33.

Humphreys, L., 1971
New styles in homosexual manliness.
Trans-action, **8,** 38–66.

Johnson, E., 1971
The homosexual in prison.
Soc. Theory & Practice, **1,** 83–95.

New York Law Forum, 1971
Homosexuality and the law—an overview, **17,** 273–303.

Pittman, D.J., 1971
The male house of prostitution.
Trans-action, **8,** 21–7.

Geis, G., 1972
Not the law's business?
Crime and delinquency issues.
Rockville, Md.: N.I.M.H., 15–52.

Humphreys, L., 1972
Out of the closets: the sociology of homosexual liberation.
Englewood Cliffs, N.J.: Prentice-Hall.

Parker, W., 1972
The homosexual in American society today, The homophile Gay Liberation Movement.
Crim. Law Bull., **8,** 692–99.

Barnett, W., 1973
Sexual freedom and the constitution: an inquiry into the constitutionality of repressive sex laws.
Albuquerque: Univ. Mexico Press.

Feldman, P., 1973
Abnormal sexual behaviour—males, in H.J. Eysenck (ed.), *Handbook of abnormal psychology.*
London: Pitmans, 131–70.

Pearce, F., 1973
How to be immoral and ill, pathetic and dangerous, all at the same time: mass media and the homosexual, in S. Cohen and J. Young (eds.), *The manufacture of news: social problems, deviance and the mass media.*
London: Constable, 284–301.

Yale Law Journal, 1973
The legality of homosexual marriage, **82,** 573–89.

Weinberg, M.S., and Williams, C.T. (1974)
Male homosexuals: their problems and adaptations.
London: Oxford Univ. Press.

Plummer, K., 1975
Sexual stigma: an interactionist account.
London: Routledge & Kegan Paul, 93–202.

West, D.J., 1975
Homosexuality.
London: Gerald Duckworth & Co. (3rd ed.).

9 Pornography: criminological and legal aspects: a preliminary list

[*See also Section* 6(1) *on scope of penal sanctions.*]

ARTS COUNCIL OF GREAT BRITAIN, 1969
The obscenity laws.
A report by the working party.
London: Andre Deutsch.

CORRECTIONAL ASSOCIATION OF NEW YORK, 1969
Report on pornography.
Mimeo.

CHURCH OF ENGLAND, BOARD FOR SOCIAL RESPONSIBILITY, 1970
Obscene publications law and practice.
London: The Church Information Office.

COMMITTEE ON FEDERAL LEGISLATION, 1970
Legislation to bar sexually oriented materials from the mails and interstate commerce.
The Record, **25,** 156–69.

EICH, W.F., 1970
From Ulysses to Portnoy: a pornography primer.
Marquette Law Rev., **53,** 155–71.

HUGHES, D.A., (ED.), 1970
Perspectives on pornography.
New York: St. Martin's Press.

KUTSCHINSKY, B., 1970
Studies on pornography and sex crimes in Denmark.
A report to the US Presidential Commission on Obscenity & Pornography.
Copenhagen: New Social Science Monographs.

MESHER, J., 1970
A new approach to the control of obscenity.
Mod. Law Rev., **33,** 289–301.

UNITED STATES OF AMERICA, 1970
Report of the Commission on obscenity and pornography.
Washington, D.C., (and New York: Bantam Books).

UNITED STATES OF AMERICA, 1970
National Commission on Reform of Federal Criminal Laws.
Working Papers, **2,**
Washington, D.C., 1203–45.

ZELLICK, G., 1970
Violence as pornography.
Crim. Law Rev., 1970, 188–200.

BARNETT, W., 1971
Corruption of morals—the underlying issue of the pornography commission report.
Law & Social Order, 1971, 189–243.

BELL, R.R., 1971
Social deviance—a substantive analysis.
Homewood, Ill.: Dorsey Press, 144–70.

BEN-VENISTE, R., 1971
Pornography and sex crime: the Danish experience.
Technical Report of the Commission on Obscenity and Pornography, **VII.**
Washington, D.C., 245–61.

BONNIWELL, B.L., 1971
The social control of pornography and sexual behaviour.
Annals Amer. Acad. Pol. & Soc. Sci., **397,** 97–104.

CLOR, H.M., 1971
Obscenity and public morality: censorship in a liberal society.
Chicago: Univ. Chicago Press.

COOK, R.F., AND FOSEN, R.H., 1971
Pornography and the sex offender: patterns of exposure and immediate arousal effects of pornographic stimuli. *Technical Report of the Commission on Obscenity and Pornography*, **VII.**
Washington, D.C., 149–62.

DAVIS, K.E., AND BRAUCHT, G.N., 1971
Exposure to pornography, character, and sexual deviance: a retrospective survey.
Technical Report of the Commission on Obscenity and Pornography, **VII.**
Washington, D.C., 173–243.

GOLDSTEIN, M.J., KANT, H.S., JUDD, L.L., RICE, C.J., AND GREEN, R., 1971
Exposure to pornography and sexual behavior in deviant and normal groups.
Technical Report of the Commission on Obscenity and Pornography, **VII.**
Washington, D.C., 1–89.

JOHNSON, W.T., KUPPERSTEIN, L.R., AND PETERS, J.J., 1971
Sex offenders' experience with erotica.
Technical Report of the Commission on Obscenity and Pornography, **VII.**
Washington, D.C., 163–71.

KANT, H.S., 1971
Exposure to pornography and sexual behavior in deviant and normal groups.
Corrective & Social Psychiatry, **17**,(2), 5–17.

KUPPERSTEIN, L.R., AND WILSON, W.C., 1971
Erotica and antisocial behavior: an analysis of selected social indicator statistics.
Technical Report of the Commission on Obscenity and Pornography, **VII.**
Washington, D.C., 311–23.

KUTSCHINSKY, B., 1971
Pornography in Denmark. Pieces of a jigsaw puzzle collected around New Year 1970.
Technical Report of the Commission on Obscenity and Pornography, **IV.**
Washington, D.C., 263–88.

KUTSCHINSKY, B., 1971
Towards an explanation of the decrease in registered sex crimes in Copenhagen.
Technical Report of the Commission on Obscenity and Pornography, **VII.**
Washington, D.C., 263–310.

KUTSCHINSKY, B., 1971
The effect of pornography: a pilot experiment on perception, behavior, and attitudes.
Technical Report of the Commission on Obscenity and Pornography, **VIII.**
Washington, D.C., 133–69.

TEETER, D.L., AND PEMBER, D.R., 1971
Obscenity, 1971: the rejuvenation of state power and the return to Roth.
Villanova Law Rev., **17**, 211–45.

WALKER, C.E., 1971.
Erotic stimuli and the aggressive sexual offender.
Technical Report of the Commission on Obscenity and Pornography, **VII.**
Washington, D.C., 91–147.

WILSON, W. C., 1971.
Facts versus fears: why should we worry about pornography?
Annals Amer. Acad. Pol. & Soc. Sci., **397**, 105–17.

ZELLICK, G., 1971
Films and the law of obscenity.
Crim. Law Rev., 1971, 126–50.

ZURCHER, L.A. JR., KIRKPATRICK, R.G., CUSHING, R.G., AND BOWMAN, C.K., 1971
The anti-pornography campaign: a symbolic crusade.
Social Problems, **19**, 217–38.

LONGFORD, LORD, 1972
Pornography: the Longford Report.
London: Coronet Books.

ROGGE, O.J., 1972
The obscenity terms of the court.
Villanova Law Rev., **17**, 393–462.

SCHNALL, M., 1972
The United States Supreme Court: definitions of obscenity.
Crime & Delinq., **18**, 59–67.

ZELLICK, G., 1972
Offensive advertisements in the mail.
Crim. Law Rev., 1972, 724–43.

GOLDSTEIN, M.J., AND KANT, H.S., 1973
Pornography and sexual deviance.
Berkeley: Univ. California Press.

KUTSCHINSKY, B., 1973
Eroticism without censorship, sociological investigation on the production and consumption of pornographic literature in Denmark.
Internat. J. Criminol. & Penol., **1**, 271–25.

KUTSCHINSKY, B., 1973
The effect of easy availability of pornography on the incidence of sex crimes: the Danish experience.
J. Soc. Issues, **29**, 163–81.

UCLA LAW REVIEW, 1973
New prosecutorial techniques and continued judicial vagueness: an argument for abandoning obscenity as a legal concept.
21, 181–241.

FAHRINGER, H.P., AND BROWN, M.J., 1974
The rise and fall of Roth—a critique of the recent Supreme Court obscenity decisions.
Crim. Law Bulletin, **10**, 785–826.

FINER, J.J., AND GRANT, P.H., 1974
Regulation and prohibition of sensual performances under non-obscenity statutes.
Crim. Law Bulletin, **10**, 717–36.

4 Violence against the person

1 Historical, cultural and biological influences

[*See also Section 5 for references on civil disorder and lawlessness.*]

DOLLARD, J., MILLER, N.E., DOOB, L.W., MOWRER, O.H., AND SEARS, R.R., 1939
Frustration and aggression.
New Haven, Conn.: Yale Univ. Press, 110–41.

HENRY, A.F., AND SHORT, J.F., 1954
Suicide and homicide: some economic, sociological and psychological aspects of aggression.
Glencoe, Ill.: Free Press, 45–65, 82–97, 101–19.

GOLD, M., 1958
Suicide, homicide, and the socialization of aggression.
Amer. J. Sociol., **63,** 651–61.

SCOTT, J.P., 1958
Aggression.
Chicago: Univ. Chicago Press.

CLARK, L.D., 1962
A comparative view of aggressive behavior.
Amer. J. Psychiat., **119,** 336–41.

YATES, A.B., 1962
Frustration and conflict.
London: Methuen, 174–203.

LORENZ, K., 1963
On aggression.
London: Methuen.

MEAD, M., 1963
Violence in the perspective of culture history, in J.H. Masserman (ed.), *Violence and war with clinical studies.*
Science and Psychoanalysis, **VI.**
New York: Grune & Stratton, 92–105.

LORENZ, K., 1964
Ritualized fighting, in J.D. Carthy and F.J. Ebling (eds.), *The natural history of aggression.*
London: Academic Press, 39–50.

WALTER, E.V., 1964
Violence and the process of terror.
Amer. Sociol. Rev., **29,** 248–57.

GOLDIN, G.D., 1965
Violence: the integration of psychiatric and sociological concepts.
Notre Dame Lawyer, **40,** 508–16.

GRIMSHAW, A.D., 1965
Changing patterns of racial violence in the United States.
Notre Dame Lawyer, **40,** 534–48.

LOHMAN, J., 1965
Violence in the streets: its context and meaning.
Notre Dame Lawyer, **40,** 517–26.

STRINGFELLOW, W., 1965
The violence of despair.
Notre Dame Lawyer, **40,** 527–33.

WILKINS, R., 1965
The riots of 1964: the causes of racial violence.
Notre Dame Lawyer, **40,** 552–7.

ARDREY, R., 1966
The territorial imperative.
New York: Athenaeum Press.

COSER, L.A., 1966
Some social functions of violence.
Annals Amer. Acad. Pol. & Soc. Sci., **364,** 8–18.

DAVIS, D.B., 1966
Violence in American literature.
Annals Amer. Acad. Pol. & Soc. Sci., **364,** 28–36.

LARSEN, O.N., 1966
Controversies about the mass communication of violence.
Annals Amer. Acad. Pol. & Soc. Sci., **364,** 37–49.

TAFT, P., 1966
Violence in American labor disputes.

Annals Amer. Acad. Pol. & Soc. Sci., **364,** 127–40.

Berkowitz, L., 1967
Experiments on automatism and intent in human aggression, in C.D. Clement and D.B. Lindsley (eds.), *Aggression and defense: neural mechanisms and social patterns.*
(Brain function, **5**) UCLA forum in medical sciences no. 7.
Berkeley: Univ. Calif. Press, 243–66.

Columbia Law Review, 1967
Exclusion of children from violent movies.
67, 1149–68.

Wolfgang, M.E., and Ferracuti, F., 1967
The subculture of violence: towards an integrated theory in criminology.
London: Tavistock, 140–63.

Ashley Montagu, M.F. (ed.), 1968
Man and aggression.
New York: Oxford Univ. Press.

Benenson, M.K., 1968
A controlled look at gun controls.
New York Law Forum, **14,** 718–48.

Burton, L., 1968
Vulnerable children. Three studies of children in conflict: accident involved children, sexually assaulted children and children with asthma.
London: Routledge & Kegan Paul, 87–169.

Camp, G.M., 1968
Nothing to lose: a study of bank robbery in America.
Ann Arbor, Mich.: University Microfilms, 75–128.

Halloran, J.D., 1968
The influence of films on individuals and groups, in *The cinema and the protection of youth.*
European Committee on Crime Problems.
Strasbourg: Council of Europe, 105–34.

Krug, A.S., 1968
Does firearms registration work? A statistical analysis of New York City crime data.
Riverside, Conn.: National Shooting Sports Foundation.

Larsen, O.N. (ed.), 1966
Violence and the mass media.
New York: Harper & Row.

Lintoff, A.W., 1968
Violence in republican Rome.
Oxford: Clarendon Press, 67–88, 175–208.

Russell, C., and Russell, W.M.S., 1968
Violence, monkeys and man.
London: Macmillan & Co., 146–52.

Arendt, H., 1969
On violence.
London: Allen Lane, Penguin Press.

Blum, R.H., 1969
Drugs and violence, in D.J. Mulvihill, M.M. Tumin and L.A. Curtis (eds.), *Crimes of violence*, **13.** A staff report to the National Commission on the Causes and Prevention of Violence, Washington, D.C.

Bohannan, P., 1969
Cross-cultural comparison of aggression and violence, in D.J. Mulvihill, M.M. Tumin and L.A. Curtis (eds.), *Crimes of violence*, **13.**
A staff report to the National Commission on the Causes and Prevention of Violence.
Washington, D.C. Appendix 25, 1189–1239

Chodorkoff, B., and Baxter, S., 1969
Psychiatric and psychoanalytic theories of violence, in D.J. Mulvihill, M.M. Tumin L.A. Curtis (eds.), *Crimes of violence*, **13.**
A staff report to the National Commission on the Causes and Prevention of Violence.
Washington, D.C. Appendix 23, 1117–62.

Cutler, J.E., 1969
Lynch-law: an investigation into the history of lynching in the United States.
Montclair, N.J.: Patterson Smith.

Furstenberg, M.H., 1969
Violence and organized crime, in D.J. Mulvihill, M.M. Tumin and L.A. Curtis (eds.), *Crimes of violence*, **13.**
A staff report to the National Commission on the Causes and Prevention of Violence.
Washington, D.C., Appendix 18, 911–39.

Goode, W., 1969
Violence among inmates, in D.J. Mulvihill, M.M. Tumin and L.A. Curtis (eds.), *Crimes of violence*, **13.**
A staff report to the National Commission on the Causes and Prevention of Violence.
Washington, D.C., Appendix 19, 941–77.

Graham, H.D., and Gurr, T.R. (eds.), 1969
Violence in America: historical and comparative Perspectives, Vols. 1 and 2.

A report to the National Commission on the Causes and Prevention of Violence. Washington, D.C.

GRIMSHAW, A.D., 1969
Violence: a sociological perspective.
George Washington Law Rev., **37,** 816–34.

HALLER, M.H., 1969
Theories of criminal violence and their impact on the criminal justice system, in D.J. Mulvihill, M.M. Tumin and L.A. Curtis (eds.), *Crimes of violence*, **13.**
A staff report to the National Commission on the Causes and Prevention of Violence.
Washington, D.C. Appendix 28, 1327–57.

HOBSBAWM, E.J., 1969
Bandits.
London: Weidenfeld & Nicolson, 13–33, 72–93, 109–15.

KIRKHAM, J.F. ET AL., 1969
Political assassinations.
Report of Task Force 1 to the National Commission on the Causes and Prevention of Violence. Ch. 4 (Political violence in the United States).
Washington, D.C.

KLAUSNER, S.Z., 1969
Invocation and constraint of religious zealotry, in D.J. Mulvihill, M.M. Tumin and L.A. Curtis (eds.), *Crimes of violence*, **13.**
A staff report to the National Commission on the Causes and Prevention of Violence.
Washington, D.C. Appendix 27, 1291–1325.

KLEIN, M.W., 1969
Violence in American juvenile gangs, in D.J. Mulvihill, M.M. Tumin and L.A. Curtis (eds.), *Crimes of violence*, **13,** Washington, D.C. Appendix 31, 1427–60.

LONDON, P., 1969
Behaviour control, in D.J. Mulvihill, M.M. Tumin and L.A. Curtis (eds.), *Crimes of violence*, **13.**A.
A staff report to the National Commission on the Causes and Prevention of Violence.
Washington, D.C. Appendix 29, 1359–75.

MCCLEARN, G.E., 1969
Biological bases of social behavior with specific reference to violent behavior, in D.J. Mulvihill, M.M. Tumin and L.A. Curtis (eds.), *Crimes of violence*, **13.**
A staff report to the National Commission on the Causes and Prevention of Violence.
Washington, D.C. Appendix 20, 979–1016.

MEGARGEE, E.I., 1969
A critical review of theories of violence, in D.J. Mulvihill, M.M. Tumin and L.A. Curtis (eds.), *Crimes of violence*, **13.**
A staff report to the National Commission on the Causes and Prevention of Violence.
Washington, D.C. Appendix 22, 1037–1115.

MULVIHILL, D.J., AND TUMIN, M.M., 1969
Crimes of violence, **II.**
A staff report submitted to the National Commission on the Causes and Prevention of Violence.
Washington, D.C.

MULVIHILL, D.J., AND TUMIN, M.M., 1969
Crimes of violence, **12.**
A staff report submitted to the National Commission on the Causes and Prevention of Violence.
Washington, D.C.

NEWTON, G.D., AND ZIMRING, F.E., 1969
Firearms and violence in American life.
A report to the National Commission on the Causes and Prevention of Violence.
Washington, D.C., 1–22.

NIEBURG, H.L., 1969
Political violence: the behavioral process.
New York: St Martin's Press, 19–45.

RAPER, A.F., 1969
The tragedy of lynching.
Montclair, N.J.: Patterson Smith.

ROSE, T., 1969
How violence occurs: a theory and review of the literature, in T. Rose (ed.), *Violence in America: a historical and contemporary reader.*
New York: Random House, 26–53.

ROSENBERG, B., AND SILVERSTEIN, H., 1969
The varieties of delinquent experience.
Waltham, Mass.: Blaisdell Publishing Co., 77–95.

SHRAG, C.C., 1969
Critical analysis of sociological theories, in D.J. Mulvihill, M.M. Tumin and L.A. Curtis (eds.), *Crimes of violence*, **13.**
A staff report to the National Commission on the Causes and Prevention of Violence,
Washington, D.C. Appendix 26, 1241–89.

UNITED STATES OF AMERICA, 1969
Dimensions of violence in television drama.
Mass Media Task Force of the National Commission on the Causes and Prevention of Violence.
Philadelphia, Penn.: Univ. Pennsylvania, Annenberg School of Communications.

WALLER, J.A., 1969
Accidents and violent behaviour: are they related? in D.J. Mulvihill, M.M. Tumin and L.A. Curtis (eds.), *Crimes of violence*, **13.**
A staff report to the National Commission on the Causes and Prevention of Violence.
Washington, D.C. Appendix 33, 1525–58.

WALTER, E.V., 1969
Terror and resistance, a study of political violence.
New York: Oxford Univ. Press.

WARD, D.A., JACKSON, M., AND WARD, R.E., 1969
Crimes of violence by women, in D.J. Mulvihill, M.M. Tumin and L.A. Curtis (eds.), *Crimes of violence*, **13.**
A staff report to the National Commission on the Causes and Prevention of Violence.
Washington, D.C., Appendix 17, 843–909.

WEST, D.J. (ED.), 1969
Criminological implications of chromosome abnormalities.
University of Cambridge, Institute of Criminology, 9–31.

BOELKINS, R.C., AND HEISER, J.F., 1970
Biological bases of aggression, in D.N. Daniels, M.F. Gilula and F.M. Ochberg eds.), *Violence and the struggle for existence.*
Boston: Little, Brown & Co., 15–52.

FEIERABEND, I.K., AND NESVOLD, B., WITH FEIERABEND, R.L., 1970
Political coerciveness and turmoil, a cross-national inquiry.
Law and Society Rev., **5,** 93–118.

GIL, D.G., 1970
Violence against children. Physical child abuse in the United States.
Cambridge, Mass.: Harvard University Press.

HALLORAN, J.D., BROWN, R.L., AND CHANEY, D.C., 1970
Television and delinquency.
(Television Research Committee, working paper no. 3.)
Leicester Univ. Press, 123–34, 170–81.

HOFSTADTER, R., AND WALLACE, M. (EDS.), 1970
American violence: a documentary history.
New York: Alfred A. Knopf.

ILFELD, F.W., 1970
Environmental theories of violence, in D.N. Daniels, M.F. Gilula and F.M. Ochberg (eds.), *Violence and the struggle for existence.*
Boston: Little, Brown & Co., 79–95.

KAUFMANN, H., 1970
Aggression and altruism—a psychological analysis.
New York: Holt, Rinehart & Winston.

KRUG, A.S., 1970
Firearms registration, costs vs. benefits. A survey of state law enforcement agencies on firearms registration.
Riverside, Conn.: National Shooting Sports Foundation.

LEIDEN, C., 1970
Assassination in the Middle East, in J.F. Short Jr. (ed.), *Modern criminals.*
Chicago: Aldine Publishing Co., 133–42.

NATIONAL OPINION POLLS, MARKET RESEARCH LTD., 1970
Report on attitudes towards crime, violence, and permissiveness in society, 25–38.
London. Mimeo.

NICHOLAS, H.G., 1970
Violence in American society.
London: Oxford Univ. Press.

OBERSCHALL, A., 1970
Group violence, some hypotheses and empirical uniformities.
Law & Society Rev., **5,** 61–91.

PALMER, S., 1970
Aggression in fifty-eight non-literate societies: an exploratory analysis.
Annales Internat. de Criminol., **9,** 57–69.

SARBIN, T.R., AND MILLER, J.E., 1970
Demonism revisited: the XYY chromosomal anomaly.
Issues in Criminol., **5,** 195–207.

SIEGEL, A.E., 1970
Violence in the mass media, in D.N. Daniels,

M.F. Gilula and F.M. Ochberg (eds.), *Violence and the struggle for existence.* Boston: Little, Brown & Co., 193–239.

Solomon, G.F., 1970
Psychodynamic aspects of aggression, hostility, and violence, in D.N. Daniels, M.F. Gilula and F.M. Ochberg (eds.) *Violence and the struggle for existence.* Boston: Little, Brown & Co., 53–78.

Walker, N., Hammond, W., Steer, D., and Carr-Hill, R., 1970
The violent offender—reality or illusion?
Oxford: Basil Blackwell.

Weatherhead, A.D., and Robinson, B.M., 1970
Firearms in crime.
A Home Office Statistical Division report on indictable offences involving firearms in England and Wales.
London: H.M.S.O.

Berkowitz, L., 1971
The contagion of violence: an S-R mediational anlaysis of some effects of observed aggression, in W.J. Arnold and M.M. Page (eds.), *Nebraska symposium on motivation* 1970.
Lincoln: Univ. Nebraska Press, 95–135.

Cohen, S., 1971
Directions for research on adolescent group violence and vandalism.
Brit. J. Criminol., **11,** 319–40.

Etzioni, A., 1971
Violence, in R.K. Merton and R. Nisbet (eds.), *Contemporary social problems.*
3rd ed. New York: Harcourt Brace Jovanovich, 709–41.

Feshbach, S., and Singer, R.D., 1971
Television and aggression.
San Francisco: Jossey-Bass.

Fox, R.G., 1971
The XYY offender: a modern myth?
J. Crim. Law, Criminol. & Pol. Sci., **62,** 59–73.

Gastil, R.D., 1971
Homicide and a regional culture of violence.
Amer. Sociol. Rev., **36,** 412–27.

Grimshaw, A.D., 1971
Review of: D. Walker (1971), *Rights in Conflict.*
Amer. Sociol. Rev., **36,** 716–27.

International Social Science Journal, 1971
Special issue on understanding aggression, **23,** 7–110.

Menninger, W.W., 1971
The psychiatrist and the violence commission
Amer. J. Psychiat., **128,** 431–74.

Sheppard, C., 1971
The violent offender: let's examine the taboo.
Fed. Probation, **35**(4), 12–19.

Trebat, T.J., 1971
Internal violence and the international system: the experience in Latin America.
Notre Dame Lawyer, **46,** 308–48.

Blumenthal, M.D., Kahn, R.L., Andrews, F.M., and Mead, K.B., 1972
Justifying violence: attitudes of American men.
Ann Arbor, Mich.: Institute for Social Research, Univ. Michigan.

Council of Europe, 1972
Report on the control of the sale and possession of firearms in order to combat violence.
Strasbourg: Consultative Assembly.

Dicks, H.V., 1972
Licensed mass murder. A socio-psychological study of some SS killers.
Chatto & Heinemann, Sussex Univ. Press.

Eron, L.D., Huesmann, L.R., Lefkowitz, M.M., and Walder, L.O., 1972
Does television violence cause aggression?
Amer. Psychologist, **27,** 253–63.

Thomas, M.P., 1972
Child abuse and neglect Part I: historical overview, legal matrix, and social perspectives.
North Carolina Law Rev., **50,** 293–349.

Turner, C.W., and Berkowitz, L., 1972
Identification with film aggressor (covert role taking) and reactions to film violence.
J. Per. & Soc. Psychol., **21,** 256–64.

Wenk, E.A., Robison, J.O., and Smith, G.W., 1972
Can violence be predicted?
Crime & Delinq., **18,** 393–402.

Adamek, R.J., and Lewis, J.M., 1973
Social control violence and radicalization:

the Kent State Case.
Social Forces, **51**, 342–47.

Ball-Rokeach, S.J., 1973
Values and violence: a test of the subculture of violence thesis.
Amer. Sociol. Rev., **38**, 736–49.

Cohen, S., 1973
Protest, unrest and delinquency: convergences in labels and behaviour,
Internat. J. Criminol. & Penol., **1**, 117–28.

Connor, W.D., 1973
Criminal homicide, U.S.S.R./U.S.A.: reflections on Soviet data in a comparative framework.
J. Crim. Law & Criminol., **64**, 111–17.

Denton, F.H., and Phillips, W., 1973
Some patterns in the history of violence, in T. Maple and D.W. Matheson (eds.), *Aggression, hostility and violence.*
New York: Holt, Rinehart & Winston, 114–32.

Gunn, J., 1973
Violence in human society.
Newton Abbot: David & Charles.

Kelman, H.C., 1973
Violence without moral restraint: reflections on the dehumanization of victims and victimizers.
J. Social Issues, **29**, 25–61.

Kniveton, B.H., and Stephenson, G.M., 1973
An examination of individual susceptibility to the influence of aggressive film models.
Brit. J. Psychiat., **122**, 53–56.

Liefbert, R.M., Neale, J.M., and Davidson, E.S., 1973
The early window: effects of television on children and youth.
New York: Pergamon Press, 23–88, 146–56.

Loohi, A.Q., and Tilly, C., 1973
Urbanization, crime and collective violence in 19th-century France.
Amer. J. Sociol., **79**, 296–318.

Maple, T., and Matheson, D.W., 1973
Aggression, hostility and violence: nature or nurture?
New York: Holt, Rinehart & Winston.

Olweus, D.,
Personality and aggression, in J.K. Cole and D.D. Jensen (eds.), *Nebraska, symposium on motivation* 1972.
Lincoln: Univ. Nebraska Press, 261–321.

Berkowitz, L., Parke, R.O., Leyens, J. P., and West, S.G., 1974
Reactions of juvenile delinquents to 'justified' and 'less justified' movie violence.
J. Research Crime & Delinq., **11**, 16–24.

Curtis, L.A., 1974
Victim precipitation and violent crime.
Social Problems, **21**, 594–605.

Hauge, R., and Wolf, P., 1974
Criminal violence in three Scandinavian countries.
Scandinavian Studies in Criminology, **5**.
London: Martin Robertson, 25–33.

Lenke, L., 1974
Criminal policy and public opinion towards crimes of violence, in *Violence in Society. Collected Studies in Criminological Research* **11**,
Council of Europe, Strasbourg, 61–123.

Schafer, S., 1974
The political criminal: the problem of morality and crime.
New Jersey: Free Press.

Schulman, G.I., 1974
Race, sex, and violence: a laboratory test of the sexual threat of the black male hypothesis.
Amer. J. Sociol., **79**, 1260–77.

2 Individual acts

Hentig, H. von, 1948
The criminal and his victim.
New Haven: Yale Univ. Press, 383–450.

McDermaid, G., and Winkler, E., 1960
Psychiatric study of homicide cases.
J. Clinical & Experimental Psychopathology, **XI**, 93–156.

LEWIS, N.D.C., AND YARNELL, H., 1951
Pathological firesetting (pyromania).
New York: Coolidge Foundation, 27–45, 86–134.

BENDER, L., 1953
Aggression, hostility and anxiety in children.
Springfield, Ill.: C.C. Thomas.

MORRIS, A., 1955
Homicide: an approach to the problem of crime.
Boston Univ. Press.

GIBBENS, T.C.N., AND WALKER, A., 1956
Violent cruelty to children.
Brit. J. Delinq., **6,** 260–77.

WOLFGANG, M.E.,, AND STROHM, R.B. 1956
The relationship between alcohol and criminal homicide.
Quart. J. Studies on Alcohol, **17,** 411–25.

CLINARD, M.B., AND WADE, A.L., 1958
Towards the delineation of vandalism as sub-type of juvenile delinquency.
J. Crim. Law, Criminol. & Pol. Sci., **48,** 493–9.

GIBBENS, T.C.N., 1958
Sane and insane homicide.
J. Crim. Law, Criminol. & Pol. Sci., **49,** 110–15.

WOLFGANG, M.E., 1958
Patterns in criminal homicide.
Philadelphia: Univ. Pennsylvania Press, 31–64, 134–99, 203–65.

GOULD, J., 1959
The psychiatry of major crime, in G.W.T.H. Fleming and A. Walk (eds.), *Recent progress in psychiatry*, **3.**
London: J. & A. Churchill, 303–51.

WHEELER, S., 1960
Sex offenses.
Law & Contemp. Problems, **25,** 258–78.

GIBSON, E., AND KLEIN, S., 1961
Murder.
London: Home Office studies in the causes of delinquency and the treatment of offenders, **4.**

MCCLINTOCK, F.H., AND GIBSON, E., 1961
Robbery in London.
London: Macmillan, 13–29, 46–72, 96–106.

BLOCH, H.A., AND GEIS, G., 1962
Man, crime, and society: the forms of criminal behavior.
New York: Random House, 253–81.

FITCH, J.H., 1962
Men convicted of sexual offences against children.
Brit. J. Criminol., **3,** 18–37.

ROEBUCK, J.B., AND JOHNSON, R., 1962
The Negro drinker and assaulter as a criminal type. *Crime & Delinq.*, **8,** 21–33.

YABLONSKY, L., 1962
The violent gang.
New York: Macmillan Co., 3–25, 146–69.

MCCLINTOCK, F.H., 1963
Crimes against the person.
Lecture to the Manchester Statistical Society.
Manchester: Norbury, Lockwood & Co.

MCCLINTOCK, F.H., 1963
Crimes of violence.
London: Macmillan, 24–57, 97–136, 167–77.

MCCORD, J., MCCORD, W., AND HOWARD, A., 1963
Family interaction as antecedent to the direction of male aggressiveness.
J. Abnormal & Social Psychology, **66,** 239–42.

BANDURA, A., AND WALTERS, R.H., 1964
Social learning and personality development.
New York: Holt, Rinehart & Winston, 109–37.

HILL, D., 1964
Aggression and mental illness, in J.D. Carthy and F.J. Ebling (eds.), *The natural history of aggression.*
London: Academic Press, 91–9.

KLOPPER, A., 1964
Physiological background to aggression, in J.D. Carthy and F.J. Ebling (eds.), *The natural history of aggression.*
London: Academic Press, 65–76.

MORRIS, T.P.M., AND BLOM-COOPER, L., 1964
A calendar of murder: summary of cases of homicide in England and Wales in 1961 and 1962.
London: Michael Joseph, 171–268.

PITTMAN, D.J., AND HANDY, W., 1964
Patterns in criminal aggravated assault.
J. Crim. Law, Criminol. & Pol. Sci., **55**, 462–70.

STÜRUP, G.K., 1964
The psychology of murderers.
J. Irish Med. Assoc., **54**(319), 27–32.

GEBHARD, P.H., GAGNON, J.H., POMEROY, W.B., AND CHRISTENSON, C.V., 1965
Sex offenders.
New York: Harper & Row, 133–206.

KNOTT, J.R., 1965
Electroencephalograms in psychopathic personality and in murderers, in W.P. Wilson (ed.), *Applications of electroencephalography in psychiatry.*
Durham, N.C.: Duke Univ. Press, 19–29.

POKORNY, A.D., 1965
A comparison of homicides in two cities.
J. Crim. Law, Criminol. & Pol. Sci., **56**, 479–87.

POKORNY, A.D., 1965
Human violence: a comparison of homicides, aggravated assault, suicide and attempted suicide.
J. Crim. Law, Criminol. & Pol. Sci., **56**, 488–97.

SMITH, S., 1965
The adolescent murderer.
Arch. Gen. Psychiat., **13**, 310–19.

WEST, D.J., 1965
Murder followed by suicide.
London: Heinemann, 27–91, 131–50.

BEATTIE, R.H., AND KENNEY, J.P., 1966
Aggressive crimes.
Annals Amer. Acad. Pol. & Soc. Sci., **364**, 73–85.

GLASER, D., KENEFICK, D., AND O'LEARY, V., 1966
The violent offender.
Washington, D.C.: U.S. Dept of Health, Education and Welfare, 3–32.

MCKERRACHER, D.W., AND DACRE, A.J.I., 1966
A study of arsonists in a special security hospital.
Brit. J. Psychiat., **112**, 1151–4.

MCKNIGHT, C.K., MOHR, J.W., QUINSEY, R.E., AND EROCHKO, J., 1966
Mental illness and homicide.
Canad. Psychiatric Association J., **11**, 91–8.

MILLER, W.B., 1966
Violent crimes in city gangs.
Annals Amer. Acad. Pol. & Soc. Sci., **364**, 96–112.

MOWAT, R.R., 1966
Morbid jealousy and murder: a psychiatric study of morbidly jealous murderers at Broadmoor.
London: Tavistock, 43–68.

SHANLEY, F.J., WELTY LEFEVER, D., AND RICE, R.E., 1966
The aggressive middle-class delinquent.
J. Crim. Law, Criminol. & Pol. Sci., **57**, 145–52.

SPENCER, C., 1966
A typology of violent offenders.
Calif. Dept. of Corrections, Research Report No. 23, Sacramento, 1–25.

AMIR, M., 1967
Patterns of forcible rape, in M.B. Clinard and R. Quinney (eds.), *Criminal behavior systems: a typology.*
New York: Holt, Rinehart & Winston, 60–75.

ELMER, E., 1967
Children in jeopardy: a study of abused minors and their families.
Univ. Pittsburgh Press.

ESSELSTYN, T.C., 1967
The violent offender and corrections.
A document submitted to the President's Commission on Law Enforcement and Administration of Justice, Washington, D.C.

MCCAGHY, C.H., 1967
Child molesters: a study of their careers as deviants, in M.B. Clinard and R. Quinney (eds.), *Criminal behavior systems: a typology.*
New York: Holt, Rinehart & Winston, 75–88.

MYERS, S.A., 1967
The child slayer.
Arch. Gen. Psychiat., **17**, 211–13.

ROEBUCK, J.B., 1967
Criminal typology.
Springfield, Ill.: C.C. Thomas, 106–17, 155–71.

United States of America, 1967
Homicide in the United States 1950–1964,
National Center for Health Statistics,
Series 20, No. 6.
Washington, D.C.: Department of Health, Education and Welfare.

Walker, N., Hammond, W., and Steer, D., 1967
Repeated violence.
Crim. Law Rev., 1967, 465–72.

Wolfgang, M.E., 1967
Crimes of violence.
A document submitted to the President's Commission on Law Enforcement and Administration of Justice, Washington, D.C., 1–175, 208–16.

Wolfgang, M.E. (ed.), 1967
Studies in homicide.
New York: Harper & Row.

Wolfgang, M.E., and Ferracuti, F., 1967
The subculture of violence: towards an integrated theory in criminology.
London: Tavistock, 186–284.

Blackburn, R., 1968
Personality in relation to extreme aggression in psychiatric offenders.
Brit. J. Psychiat., **114,** 821–28.

Cole, K.E., Fisher, G., and Cole, S.S., 1968
Women who kill.
Arch. Gen. Psychiat., **19,** 1–8.

Helfer, R.E., and Kempe, C.H. (eds.), 1968
The battered child.
Chicago: Univ. Chicago Press.

MacDonald, J.M., 1968
Homicidal threats.
Springfield, Ill.: C.C. Thomas, 3–51.

Radzinowicz, L., 1968
The dangerous offender.
Police J., **41,** 414–31.

Rao, S.V., 1968
Murder (a pilot study of urban patterns with particular reference to the city of Delhi).
Faridabad: Government of India Press.

Voss, H.L., and Hepburn, J.R., 1968
Patterns in criminal homicide in Chicago.
J. Crim. Law, Criminol. & Pol. Sci., **59,** 499–508.

West, D.J., 1968
A note on murders in Manhattan.
Medicine, Science and the Law, **8,** 249–55.

Bennie, E.H., and Sclare, A.B., 1969
The battered child syndrome.
Amer. J. Psychiat., **125,** 975–79.

Gibson, E., and Klein, S., 1969
Murder, 1957–1968.
London: Home Office Research Studies, **3.**

Hobsbawm, E.J., 1969
Bandits.
London: Weidenfeld & Nicolson, 13–33, 72–93, 109–15.

Hurley, W., and Monahan, T.M., 1969
Arson: the criminal and the crime.
Brit. J. Criminol., **9,** 4–21.

Nelson, L.S., 1969
Violence in the prison.
Proceedings of the Ninety-Ninth Annual Congress of Correction of the American Correctional Association, Washington, D.C. 65–8.

Newton, G.D., and Zimring, F.E., 1969
Firearms and violence in American life.
A report to the National Commission on the Causes and Prevention of Violence, Washington, D.C., 39–53.

Resnick, P.J., 1969
Child murder by parents: a psychiatric review of filicide.
Amer. J. Psychiat., **126,** 325–34.

Skinner, A.E., and Castle, R.L. 1969
78 battered children: a retrospective study.
London: Battered Child Research Dept., N.S.P.C.C.

Toch, H., 1969
Violent men: an inquiry into the psychology of violence.
Chicago, Ill.: Aldine Publishing Co., 133–82.

United States of America, 1969
D.J. Mulvihill, M.M. Tumin, and L.A. Curtis (eds.), *Crimes of Violence*, **11, 12 & 13.**
Staff reports by the Task Force on Individual Acts of Violence to the National Commission on the Causes and Prevention of Violence, Washington, D.C.

WALBEEHM, T.B., 1969
'De brokkenmaker'. (The accident-prone driver with a compendium in English). Koninklijke Nederlandsche Toeristenbond ANWB., 232–71.

BRITTAIN, R.P., 1970
The sadistic murderer.
Med. Sci. and Law, **10,** 198–207.

CAMERON, J.M., 1970
The battered baby.
Brit. J. Hosp. Med., 1970, 769–77.

EKBLOM, B., 1970
Acts of violence by patients in mental hospitals.
Uppsala: Svenska Bokforlaget, 110–25.

GIBBENS, T., 1970
Hooliganism and vandalism.
Medico-Legal J., **38,** 122–34.

GIL, D.G., 1970
Violence against children: physical child abuse in the United States.
Cambridge, Mass.: Harvard Univ. Press.

GULEVICH, G.D., AND BOURNE, P.G., 1970
Mental illness and violence, in D.N. Daniels, M.F. Gilula and F.M. Ochberg (eds.), *Violence and the struggle for existence.*
Boston: Little, Brown & Co., 309–26.

INSTITUTE FOR THE STUDY AND TREATMENT OF DELINQUENCY, SCOTTISH BRANCH, 1970
The carrying of offensive weapons (Glasgow Working Party).
Brit J. Criminol., **10,** 255–69.

OTTENHOF, R., 1970
Les aspects du vol dans les grands magasins.
Annales Internat. de Criminol., **9,** 455–564.

SOLOMON, G.F., 1970
Case studies of violence, in D.N. Daniels, M.F. Gilula and F.M. Ochberg (eds.).
Violence and the struggle for existence.
Boston: Little, Brown & Co., 367–88.

TINKLENBERG, J.R., AND STILLMAN, R.C., 1970
Drug use and violence, in D.N. Daniels, M.F. Gilula and F.M. Ochberg (eds.).
Violence and the struggle for existence.
Boston: Little, Brown & Co., 327–65.

WALDO, G.P., 1970
The 'criminality level' of incarcerated murderers and non-murderers.
J. Crim. Law, Criminol. & Pol. Sci., **61,** 60–70.

WALKER, N., HAMMOND, W., STEER, D., AND CARR-HILL, R., 1970
The violent offender—reality or illusion?
Oxford: Basil Blackwell.

WEATHERHEAD, A.D. AND ROBINSON, B.M., 1970
Firearms in crime.
A Home Office Statistical Division report on indirectable offences involving firearms in England and Wales.
London: H.M.S.O.

WOLFGANG, M.E., 1970
Youth and violence.
Washington, D.C.: U.S. Department of Health, Education and Welfare.

BAILEY, S.E., 1971
Disruption in urban public secondary schools.
Washington, D.C.: National Association of Secondary School Principals.

BLACKBURN, R., 1971
Personality types among abnormal homicides.
Brit. J. Criminol., **11,** 14–31.

ELLIS, D.P., WEINER, P., AND MILLER, L., III, 1971
Does the trigger pull the finger? An experimental test of weapons as aggression-eliciting stimuli.
Sociometry, **34,** 453–65.

FARRINGTON, D.P., AND WEST, D.J., 1971
A comparison between early delinquents and young aggressives.
Brit. J. Criminol., **11,** 341–58.

GREENLAND, C., 1971
Violence and dangerous behaviour associated with mental illness: prospects for prevention.
Canad. J. Corrections, **13,** 331–39.

JOURNAL OF MARRIAGE AND THE FAMILY, 1971
Special issue on violence and the family, **33,** 624–731.

ROOTH, F.G., 1971
Indecent exposure and exhibitionism.
Brit. J. Hosp. Med., **5,** 521–33.

SHAW, L., AND SICHEL, H., 1971
Accident proneness—research in the occurrence,

causation, and prevention of road accidents.
Oxford: Pergamon Press, 217–36, 335–71.

TENNANT, T.G., MCQUAID, A., LOUGHNANE, T. ET AL., 1971
Female arsonists.
Brit. J. Psychiat., **119**, 497–502.

TRACY, R.G., FRIEL, C.M., KERPER, H.B., AND KILLINGER, G.G., 1971
A study of the relationship between military service in the armed forces and criminality.
A Criminal Justice Monograph, **III**, (1).
Huntsville, Texas: Institute of Contemporary Corrections and the Behavioral Sciences, 1–28, 60–3.

WHITLOCK, F.A., 1971
Death on the road: a study in social violence.
London: Tavistock.

BERLIN, A., 1972
Treatment for the violent offender.
Crime & Delinq. Lit., **4**, 101–15.

COHEN, S., 1972
Folk devils and moral panics.
London: MacGibbon & Kee, 144–76.

CONKLIN, J.E., 1972
Robbery and the criminal justice system.
Philadelphia: J.B. Lippincott Co., 99–122.

EDLAND, J.F., 1972
Suicide by automobile.
Albany Law Rev., **36**, 536–42.

GREENWOOD, C., 1972
Firearms control.
London: Routledge & Kegan Paul, 99–193.

HODGENS, E.J., MCFADYEN, I.H., FAILLA, R.J., AND DALY, F.M., 1972
The offence of rape in Victoria.
Aust. & N.Z. J. Criminol., **5**, 225–40.

HUNT, M., 1972
The Mugging.
New York: Athenium Publishers.

NEW YORK, STATE OF, 1972
Report of the Select Committee on Child Abuse.
New York: Legislative Assembly.

NORMANDEAU, A., 1972
Violence and robbery: a case study.
Acta Criminol., **5**, 11–106.

PEARSON, J., 1972
The profession of violence. The rise and fall of the Kray twins.
London: Weidenfeld & Nicolson.

SCHLOSS, B., AND GIESBRECHT, N.A., 1972
Murder in Canada: a report on capital and non-capital murder statistics 1961–1970.
Research report of the Centre of Criminology, Univ. Toronto.

SEITZ, S.T., 1972
Firearms, homicides and gun control effectiveness.
Law & Society Rev., **6**, 595–613.

SERENY, G., 1972
The case of Mary Bell.
London: Eyre Methuen.

STOBART, R.M., 1972
Serious assaults on police.
Police J., **45**, 108–26.

UNITED STATES OF AMERICA, 1972
Law enforcement officers killed in the line of duty.
FBI Law Enforcement Bulletin, March 1972, 3–7.

WENK, E.A., AND EMRICH, R.L., 1972
Assaultive youth: an exploratory study of the assaultive experience and assaultive potential of California youth authority wards.
J. Res. Crime & Delinq., **9**, 171–96.

ZIMRING, F.E., 1972
The medium is the message: firearm caliber as a determinant of death from assault.
J. Legal Studies, **1**, 97–123.

AMERICAN CRIMINAL LAW REVIEW, 1973
The victim in a forcible rape case: a feminist view, **11**, 335–54.

BLOCK, R., AND ZIMRING, F.E., 1973
Homicide in Chicago, 1965–1970.
J. Res. Crime & Delinq., **10**, 1–12.

BROWN, R.H., FOX, E.S., AND HUBBARD, E.L., 1973
Medical and legal aspects of the battered child syndrome.
Chicago-Kent Law Rev., **50**, 45–84.

COHEN, S., 1973
Property destruction, motives and meanings.

in C. Ward (ed.), *Vandalism.*
London: Architectural Press, 25–53.

Cohen, S., 1973
Campaigning against vandalism, in C. Ward (ed.), *Vandalism.*
London: Architectural Press, 215–57.

Harding, R.W., and Fahey, R.P., 1973
Killings by Chicago police, 1969–70: an empirical study.
Southern Calif. Law Rev., **46,** 284–315.

Maisch, H., 1973
Incest.
London: Andre Deutsch.

Mattick, H.W., 1973
The prosaic sources of prison violence.
Aust. & N.Z. J. Criminol., **6,** 12–20.

Rooth, G., 1973
Exhibitionism, sexual violence and paedophilia.
Brit. J. Psychiat., **122,** 705–10.

Scott, P.D., 1973
Parents who kill their children.
Medicine Science and the Law, **13,** 120–6.

Soothill, K.L., and Pope, P.J., 1973
Arson: a twenty-year cohort study.
Medicine Science and the Law, **13,** 127–38.

Tinklenberg, J.R., 1973
Alcohol and violence, in P.G. Bourne and R. Fox (eds.), *Alcoholism: Progress in research and treatment.*
New York: Academic Press, 195–210.

West, D.J., and Farrington, D.P., 1973
Who becomes delinquent?
London: Heinemann, 168–85.

Aromaa, K., 1974
Victimisation to violence: a Gallup Survey.
Internat. J. Criminol. & Penol., **2,** 333–56.

Aromaa, K., 1974
Our violence.
Scandinavian Studies in Criminology, **5.**
London: Martin Robertson, 35–46.

Berkowitz, L., Parke, R.O., Leyens, J.P., and West, S.G., 1974
Reactions of juvenile delinquents to 'justified' and 'less justified' movie violence.
J. Res Crime. & Delinq., **11,** 16–24.

Debuyst, C.H., 1974
Etiology of violence, in *Violence in society. Collected Studies in Criminological Resarch,* **11.** Strasbourg:
Council of Europe.

Evans, A.E., 1974
Report on aircraft hijacking in the United States: law and practice.
Criminal Law Bulletin, **10,** 589–604.

Helfer, R.E., and Kempe, C.H. (eds.), 1974
The battered child.
Chicago: Univ. Chicago Press.

Hogan, B., 1974
The killing ground: 1964–73.
Crim. Law Review, 1974, 387–401.

Horowitz, R., and Schwartz, G., 1974
Honor, normative ambiguity and gang violence.
Amer. Sociol. Rev., **39,** 238–51.

Jefferson, T., and Clarke, J., 1974
Down these mean streets: the meaning of mugging.
Howard J., **14,** 37–52.

McClintock, F.H., 1974
Phenomenological and contextual analysis of criminal violence, in *Violence in society. Collected Studies in Criminological Research,* **11.**
Strasbourg: Council of Europe, 125–76.

Robert, P., et al., 1974
Images du viol collectif et reconstruction d'objet.
Deviance et contrôle social, **15.**
Paris: Service d'Etudes Pénales et Criminologiques Bibliothèque.

Selosse, J., 1974
Statistical aspects of violent crime, in *Violence in society. Collected Studies in Criminological Research,* **11.**
Strasbourg: Council of Europe, 8–60.

5 Civil disorders and lawlessness

1 Their background and manifestations

DETROIT URBAN LEAGUE, N.D.
Riot participant study.

SANDBURG, C., 1919
The Chicago race riots, July 1919.
New York: Harcourt, Brace.

CHICAGO COMMISSION ON RACE RELATIONS, 1922
The Negro in Chicago.
Chicago: Univ. Chicago Press.

NEW YORK, CITY OF, 1935
Report of Mayor La Guardia's Commission on the Harlem riot of March 19, 1935.
Reprinted, New York: Arno Press and New York Times (1969).

GRIMSHAW, A.D., 1959
A study in social violence: urban race riots in the United States.
Unpublished Ph.D. dissertation, Univ. Pennsylvania.

HAYDEN, T., 1964
The New York riots: a factual report.
Facts, 15 Sept. 1964; reprinted in A.M. Rose and C.B. Rose (eds.), *Minority problems.*
New York: Harper & Sons, 1965

RUDWICK, E.M., 1964
Race riot at East St Louis, July 2, 1917.
Carbondale: Southern Illinois Univ. Press.

SHAPIRO, F.C., AND SULLIVAN, J.W., 1964
Race riots in New York 1964
New York: Thomas Y. Crowell Co.

UNITED STATES OF AMERICA, 1964
Report to the President on the riots in seven eastern cities and two western seaside resorts in the summer of 1964.
Washington, D.C.: Federal Bureau of Investigation, U.S. Dept. of Justice.

CLARKE, K.B., 1965
The wonder is there have been so few riots.
New York Times Magazine, 5 Sept. 1965.

GRIMSHAW, A.D., 1965.
Changing patterns of racial violence in the United States.
Notre Dame Lawyer, **40**, 534–48.

HAYDEN, T., 1965
Los Angeles riot participant study (juvenile offenders).
Los Angeles Probation Dept., Research Report No. 26, November 1965.

NOTRE DAME LAWYER, 1965
Violence in the streets (a symposium of articles). **40**, 497–557.

BERSON, L.E., 1966
Case study of a riot: the Philadelphia story.
American Jewish Committee.
New York: Institute of Human Relations Press.

BUGGS, J.A., 1966
Report from Los Angeles.
J. Intergroup Relations, **5**(1).

COHEN, J., AND MURPHY, W.S., 1966
Burn, baby, burn! The Los Angeles race riot, August 1965.
London: Victor Gollancz.

CRUMP, S., 1966
Black riot in Los Angeles: the story of the Watts tragedy.
Los Angeles: Trans-Anglo Books.

INSTITUTE OF GOVERNMENT AND PUBLIC AFFAIRS, 1966
Los Angeles riot study.
Los Angeles Inst. of Government and Public Affairs, Univ. Calif., unpublished.

MALCOLM X, 1966
The autobiography of Malcolm X.
New York: Grove Press.

RANSFORD, H.E., 1966
Negro participation in civil rights activity and violence.

Los Angeles: Univ. California, unpublished dissertation.

STAHL, D., SUSSMANN, F.B., AND BLOOMFIELD, N.J., 1966
The community and racial crises.
New York: Practising Law Institute.

EARLE, H.H., 1967
Police-community relations: crisis in our time.
Springfield, Ill.: C.C. Thomas, 128–35.

HAYDEN, T., 1967
Rebellion in Newark. Official violence and ghetto response.
New York: Vintage Books.

HAYDEN, T., 1967
Violence in the ghetto (symposium of articles).
Nation, 14 August 1967.

JUSTICE, B., 1967
Assessing potentials for racial violence, in S.A. Yefsky (ed.), *Law enforcement, science and technology.*
Washington, D.C.: Thompson Book Co., 709–16.

LOS ANGELES POLICE DEPARTMENT, 1967
Seven days in August.
Police Chief, **34**(4), 26–32.

MURPHY, R.J., AND WATSON, J.M., 1967
The strucure of discontent: the relationship between social structure, grievance, and support for the Los Angeles riot.
Los Angeles Riot Study MR-92.

SURACE, S.J., AND SEEMAN, M., 1967
Some correlates of civil rights activism.
Social Forces, **46,** 197–207.

UNITED COMMUNITY SERVICES, 1967
Anatomy of a riot.
Michigan: Research Dept. Grand Rapids and Kent County.

UNITED STATES OF AMERICA, 1967
The challenge of crime in a free society.
Report of the President's Commission on Law Enforcement and Administration of Justice, Washington, D.C. 37–8.

UNITED STATES OF AMERICA, 1967
Task force report: crime and its impact—an assessment.
Washington, D.C.: President's Commission on Law Enforcement and Administration of Justice, 116–22.

WASKOW, A.I., 1967
From race riot to sit-in, 1919 and the 1960's. *A study in the connections between conflict and violence.*
New York: Anchor Books, Doubleday & Co.

BLOOMBAUM, M., 1968
The conditions underlying race riots as portrayed by multidimensional scalogram analysis: a re-analysis of Lieberson and Silverman's data.
Amer. Sociol. Rev., **33,** 76–91.

BOWEN, D.R., AND MASOTTI, L.H., 1968
Civil violence: a theoretical overview, in L.H. Masotti and D.R. Bowen (eds.), *Riots and rebellion: civil violence in the urban community.*
Beverly Hills, Calif.: Sage Publications, 11–31.

CATALDO, E.F., JOHNSON, R.M., AND KELLSTADT, L.A., 1968
Social strain and urban violence, in L.H. Masotti and D.R. Bowen (eds.), *Riots and rebellion: civil violence in the urban community.*
Beverly Hill, Calif.: Sage Publications, 285–98.

COLUMBIA UNIVERSITY, 1968
Crisis at Columbia.
Report of the Fact Finding Commission appointed to investigate the disturbances at Columbia University in April and May 1968 (Cox Commission Report).
New York: Vantage Books.

COUCH, C.J., 1968
Collective behavior: an examination of some stereotypes.
Social Problems, **15,** 310–22.

GILBERT, B.W., 1968
Ten blocks from the White House, anatomy of the Washington riots of 1968.
London: Pall Mall Press.

GITTELL, M., AND KRUPP, S., 1968
A model of discrimination and tensions, in L.H. Masotti and D.R. Bowen (eds.), *Riots and rebellion: civil violence in the urban community.*
Beverly Hills, Calif: Sage Publications, 69–83.

GRIMSHAW, A.D., 1968
Three views of urban violence: civil disturbance, racial revolt, class assault, in

L.H. Masotti and D.R. Bowen (eds.), *Riots and rebellion: civil violence in the urban community.*
Beverly Hills, Calif.: Sage Publications, 103–19.

JUSTICE, B., 1968
Detection of potential community violence.
Final report to Office of Law Enforcement Assistance, U.S. Dept. of Justice.
LEAA dissemination document: Grant 207 (S.044), Washington, D.C., 1–59.

LANG, K., AND LANG, G.E., 1968
Racial disturbances as collective protest, in L.H. Masotti and D.R. Bowen (eds.), *Riots and rebellion: civil violence in the urban community.*
Beverly Hills, Calif.: Sage Publications, 121–30.

MATTICK, H.W., 1968
The form and content of recent riots.
Univ. Chicago Law Rev., **35,** 660.

NEW JERSEY, STATE OF, 1968
Report for action.
Trenton, N.J.: Governor's Select Committee on Civil Disorder in the State of New Jersey.

OBERSCHALL, A., 1968
The Los Angeles riot of August 1965.
Social Problems, **15,** 322–41.

QUARANTELLI, E.L., AND DYNES, R.R., 1968
Looting in civil disorders: an index of social change, in L.H. Masotti and D.R. Bowen (eds.), *Riots and rebellion: civil violence in the urban community.*
Beverly Hills, Calif.: Sage Publications, 131–41.

RANSFORD, H.E., 1968
Isolation, powerlessness, and violence: a study of attitudes and participation in the Watts riot.
Amer. J. Sociol., **73,** 581–91.

REYNOLDS, H.W. JR., 1968
Black power, community power, and jobs, in L.H. Masotti and L.R. Bowen (eds.), *Riots and rebellion: violence in the urban community.*
Beverly Hills, Calif.: Sage Publications, 237–59.

SCHULMAN, J., 1968
Ghetto-area residence, political alienation, and riot orientation, in L.H. Masotti and D.R. Bowen (eds.), *Riots and rebellion: civil violence in the urban community.*
Beverly Hills, Calif.: Sage Publications, 261–84.

SCHWARTZ, D.C., 1968
On the ecology of political violence: 'The long hot summer' as a hypothesis.
Amer. Behavioral Scientist, **11,** 24–8.

SEALE, B., 1968
Seize the time. The story of the Black Panther Party and Huey P. Newton.
London: Hutchinson.

UNITED STATES OF AMERICA, 1968
Report of the National Advisory Commission on Civil Disorders
(Kerner Report), Washington, D.C. (and New York: Bantam Books) Summary, Parts I, II, Ch. 15 and Recommendations for National Action.

UNITED STATES OF AMERICA. SENATE, 1968
Hearings before the Permanent Sub-committee on Investigations of the Senate Committee on Government Operations: Riots, civil and criminal disorders, 90th Congress, 1st session (Part 1).

WALKER, D., 1968
Rights in conflict. The violent confrontation of demonstrators and police in the parks and streets of Chicago during the week of the Democratic National Convention of 1968.
A report submitted to the National Commission on the Causes and Prevention of Violence.
New York: Bantam Books.

WILSON, J.Q. (ED.), 1968
The metropolitan enigma: inquiries into the nature and dimensions of America's 'Urban Crisis'.
Cambridge, Mass.: Harvard Univ. Press, 238–308.

WOLFGANG, M.E., 1968
Violence, U.S.A.: riots and crime.
Crime & Delinq., **14,** 289–305.

BENEWICK, R., 1969
Political violence and public order. A study of British fascism.
London: Allen Lane, Penguin Press, 193–262.

BOSKIN, J., 1969
Urban racial violence in the twentieth century.
Beverly Hills, Calif.: Glencoe Press.

CALIFORNIA, STATE OF, 1969
Mass violence in America.
The Los Angeles riots. Governor's Commission on the Los Angeles Riots.
New York: Arno Press & The New York Times.

CANTOR, N.F., 1969
The age of protest. Dissent and rebellion in the twentieth century.
London: George Allen & Unwin, 225–328.

COMER, J.P., 1969
The dynamics of black and white violence, in H.D. Graham and T.R. Gurr (eds.), *Violence in America: historical and comparative perspectives,* Vol. 2.
A report to the National Commission on the Causes and Prevention of Violence, Washington, D.C., 341–54.

DENVER LAW JOURNAL, 1969
Symposium on riots and the law. **46,** 1–171.

JANOWITZ, M., 1969
Patterns of collective racial violence, in H.D. Graham and T.R. Gurr (eds.), *Violence in America: historical and comparative perspectives,* Vol. 2.
A report to the National Commission on the Causes and Prevention of Violence, Washington, D.C., 317–39.

JONES, C.O., AND HOPPE, L.D., 1969
Urban crisis in America. The remarkable Ribicoff hearings.
Washington, D.C.: Washington National Press, 66–97.

LACHMAN, S.J., AND WATERS, T.F., 1969
Psychological profile of riot arrestees.
Psychol. Reports, **24,** 171–81.

MASOTTI, L.H., AND CORSI, J.R., 1969
Shoot-out in Cleveland: black militants and the police, July 23, 1968.
A report to the National Commission on the Causes and Prevention of Violence, Washington, D.C.

MASOTTI, L.H., SEMINATORE, K.F., HADDEN, J.K., AND CORSI, J.R., 1969
A time to burn? An evaluation of the present crisis in race relations.
Chicago: Rand McNally & Co.

MEIER, A., AND RUDWICK, E., 1969
Black violence in the 20th century: a study in rhetoric and retaliation, in H.D. Graham and T.R. Gurr (eds.), *Violence in America: historical and comparative perspectives,* Vol. 2.
A report to the National Commission on the Causes and Prevention of Violence, Washington, D.C. 307–16.

NORTHERN IRELAND, GOVERNMENT OF, 1969
Disturbances in Northern Ireland.
Report of the Commission appointed by the Governor of Northern Ireland, (Chairman, Lord Cameron), Cmd. 532.

NORTHERN IRELAND, GOVERNMENT OF, 1969
Report of the Advisory Committee on Police in Northern Ireland.
(Chairman, Lord Hunt). Cmd 535.

OPPENHEIMER, M., 1969
The urban guerilla.
Chicago: Quadrangle Books.

ORRICK, W.H.JR., 1969
Shut it down! A college in crisis: San Francisco State College, October 1968–April 1969.
A report to the National Commission on the Causes and Prevention of Violence, Washington, D.C.

SKOLNICK, J.H., 1969
The politics of protest: violent aspects of protest and confrontation.
A report to the National Commission on the Causes and Prevention of Violence, Washington, D.C., 3–96, 97–135, 251–7.

UNITED STATES OF AMERICA. SENATE, 1969
Staff study of campus riots and disorders—October 1967–*May* 1969.
Washington, D.C.: Permanent subcommittee on Investigations of the Committee on Government Operations.

UNITED STATES OF AMERICA, 1969
Miami Report. A report of the Miami Study team on Civil Disturbances in Miami, Florida during the week of August 5, 1968.
National Commission on the Causes and Prevention of Violence, Washington, D.C.

UNITED STATES OF AMERICA, 1969
Rights in concord: the response to the counter-inaugural protest activities in

Washington, D.C. January 18–20, 1969.
Task Force on Law and Law Enforcement.
National Commission on the Causes and Prevention of Violence, Washington, D.C.

WALTER, E.V., 1969
Terror and resistance. A study of political violence.
New York: Oxford Univ. Press.

WANDERER, J.J., 1969
An index of riot severity and some correlates.
Amer. J. Sociol., **74,** 500–5.

WARREN, D.I., 1969
Neighborhood structure and riot behavior in Detroit: some exploratory findings.
Social Problems, **16,** 464–84.

WILSON, F.T., 1969
Federal aid in domestic disturbances 1787–1903.
New York: Arno Press and The New York Times.

CALVERT, P., 1970
A study of revolution.
Oxford: Clarendon Press.

COHEN, N., 1970
The Los Angeles riots. A socio-psychological study.
New York: Praeger Publishers.

DYNES, R., AND QUARANTELLI, E.L., 1970
Organization as victim in mass civil disturbances.
Issues in Criminol., **5,** 181–93.

DYNES, R., AND QUARANTELLI, E.L., 1970
What looting in civil disturbances really means, in J.F. Short Jr. (ed.), *Modern criminals.*
Chicago: Aldine Publishing Co., 177–92.

FEIERABEND, I.K., AND NESVOLD, B., WITH FEIERABEND, R.L., 1970
Political coerciveness and turmoil, a cross-national inquiry.
Law & Society Rev., **5,** 93–118.

FERDINAND, T.N. AND LUCHTERHAND E.G., 1970
Inter-city youth, the police, the juvenile court and justice.
Social Problems, **17,** 510–27.

GESCHWENDER, J.A., AND SINGER, B.D., 1970
Deprivation and the Detroit riot.
Social Problems, **17,** 457–63.

GURR, T.R., 1970
Why men rebel.
Princeton, N.J.: Princeton Univ. Press.

HALLORAN, J.D., ELLIOTT, P., AND MURDOCK, G., 1970
Demonstrations and communication: a case study.
Harmondsworth: Penguin Books, 85–237.

HASTINGS, M., 1970
Ulster 1969: the fight for civil rights in Northern Ireland.
London: Victor Gollancz.

JOURNAL OF SOCIAL ISSUES, 1970.
Special issue on ghetto riots. **26.**

KAPSIS, R., SAUNDERS, B., AND SMITH, J. *et al.*, 1970
The reconstruction of a riot: a case study of community tension and civil disorder.
Massachusetts: Brandeis Univ.

SINGER, B.D., OSBORN, R.W., AND GESCHWENDER, J.A., 1970
Black rioters: a study of social factors and communication in the Detroit riot.
Lexington, Mass.: D.C. Heath and Co.

UNITED STATES OF AMERICA, 1970
Report of the President's Commission on Campus Unrest.
Washington, D.C., 17–116, 233–465.

JEFFRIES, V., TURNER, R.H., AND MORRIS, R.T., 1971
The public perception of the Watts riot as social protest.
Amer. Sociol. Rev., **36,** 443–51.

JOHNSON, P.B., AND SEARS, D.O., 1971
Black invisibility, the press, and the Los Angeles riot.
Amer. J. Sociol., **76,** 698–721.

MCPHAIL, C., 1971
Civil disorder participation: a critical examination of recent research.
Amer. Sociol. Rev., **36,** 1058–73.

PLATT, A. (ED.), 1971
The politics of riot commissions 1917–1970: a collection of official reports and critical essays.
New York: Macmillan.

SPILERMAN, S., 1971
The causes of racial disturbances: tests of an explanation.
Amer. Sociol. Rev., **36,** 427–42.

Abudu, M.J.G., Raine, W.J., Burbeck, S.L., and Davison, K.K., 1972
Black ghetto violence: a case study inquiry into the spatial pattern of four Los Angeles riot event-types.
Social Problems, **19,** 408–26.

Banton, M., 1972
Race and public order in an American city.
Police Journal, **45,** 198–213.

Berk, R., and Aldrich, H.E., 1972
Patterns of vandalism during civil disorders as an indicator of selection of targets.
Amer. Sociol. Rev., **37,** 533–47.

Firestone, J.M., 1972
Theory of the riot process.
Amer. Behavioral Scientist, **15,** 859–82.

Lyons, H.A., 1972
Riots and rioters in Belfast: a demographic analysis of 1,674 arrestees in a two-year period.
Econ. & Soc. Rev., **3,** 605–14.

Moinat, S.M., Raine, W.J., Burbeck, S.L., and Davison, K.K., 1972
Black Ghetto residents as rioters.
J. Soc. Issues., **28,** 45–62.

Northern Ireland, Government of, 1972
Violence and civil disturbances in Northern Ireland in 1969.
Report of Tribunal of Inquiry, Vols. 1, 2 and Appendices, Cmd. 566.

Adamek, R.J., and Lewis, J.M., 1973
Social control, violence and radicalization: the Kent State case.
Social Forces, **51,** 342–47.

Hadden, T., and Hillyard, P., 1973
Justice in Northern Ireland: a study in social confidence.
London: Cobden Trust.

Loohi, A.Q., and Tilly, C., 1973
Urbanization, crime, and collective violence in 19th-century France.
Amer. J. Sociol., **79,** 296–318.

Betz, M., 1974
Riots and welfare: are they related?
Social Problems, **21,** 345–55.

2 Their control

[*See also Section* 6(4) *on uses and abuses of police power.*]

Detroit Urban League, n.d.
Riot participant study.

Towler, J.E., 1964
The police role in racial conflicts.
Springfield, Ill.: C.C. Thomas.

United States of America, 1964
Report to the President on the riots in seven eastern cities and two western seaside resorts in the summer of 1964.
Washington, D.C.: Federal Bureau of Investigation, U.S. Dept. of Justice.

Leary, H.R., 1965
The role of the police in riotous demonstrations.
Notre Dame Lawyer, **50,** 499–507.

Sagalyn, A., 1965
The preservation of law and order: a fundamental function of government.
Notre Dame Lawyer, **40,** 549–51.

Berson, L.E., 1966
Case study of a riot: the Philadelphia story.
American Jewish Committee.
New York: Institute of Human Relations Press.

California, State of, 1966
Military support of law enforcement during civil disturbances.
Sacramento, California National Guard.
Mimeo.

CRUMP, S., 1966
Black riot in Los Angeles: the story of the Watts tragedy.
Los Angeles: Trans-Anglo Books.

LAW IN TRANSITION QUARTERLY, 1966
Symposium on Watts 1965, **3**, 174–96.

LOHMAN, J.D., AND MISNER, G.E., 1966
Field Surveys IV: *The police and the community*, Vol. 1.
Washington, D.C.: President's Commission on Law Enforcement and Administration of Justice, 98–106, 120–31.

LOHMAN, J.D., AND MISNER, G.E., 1966
Field Surveys IV: *The police and the community*, Vol. 2.
Washington, D.C.: President's Commission on Law Enforcement and Administration of Justice, 159–67.

STAHL, D., SUSSMAN, F.B., AND BLOOMFIELD, N.J., 1966
The community and racial crises.
New York: Practising Law Institute.

WATSON, N.A., 1966
Police-community relations.
Washington, D.C.: Research and Development Division, Int. Assn. of Chiefs of Police, 19–38.

AMERICAN BAR FOUNDATION, 1967
Firearms and legislative regulation.
Research contribution no. 6, Chicago, Ill.

BLACK, D.J., AND REISS, A.J.JR., 1967
Patterns of behavior in police and citizen transactions, in Field Surveys III: *Studies in crime and law enforcement in major metropolitan areas*, Vol. 2.
Washington, D.C.: President's Commission on Law Enforcement and Administration of Justice, 41–67.

CHAPMAN, S.G., 1967
Police firearms use policy.
A document submitted to the President's Commission on Law Enforcement and Administration of Justice, Washington, D.C. Mimeo.

COATES, J.F., 1967
Non-lethal weapons for domestic law enforcement officers, in S.A. Yefsky (ed.), *Law enforcement science and technology.*
Washington, D.C.: Thompson Book Co., 787–95.

EARLE, H.H., 1967
Police-community relations. Crisis in our time.
Springfield, Ill.: C.C. Thomas, 128–35.

PARNAS, R.I., 1967
Police response to the domestic disturbance.
Wisconsin Law Rev., 1967, 914–60.

GOURLEY, G.D., 1967
Effective police organisation and management.
A document submitted to the President's Commission on Law Enforcement and Administration of Justice, Washington, D.C., Vol. 3, 871–98.

LEA, E., 1967
Survey and inventory of current police weaponry, in S.A. Yefsky (ed.), *Law enforcement, science and technology.*
Washington, D.C.: Thompson Book Co., 783–86.

MOMBOISSE, R.M., 1967
Riots, revolts and insurrections.
Springfield, Ill.: C.C. Thomas

MORRIS, R.T., AND JEFFRIES, V., 1968
Violence next door.
Social Forces, **46**, 352–58.

SILVER, A., 1967
The demand for order in civil society: a review of some themes in the history of urban crime, police, and riot, in D.J. Bordua (ed.), *The police.*
New York: John Wiley & Sons, 1–24.

TERRIS, B.J., 1967
The role of the police.
Annals Amer. Acad. Pol. & Soc. Sci., **374**, 58–69.

WESTON, P.B., 1967
New concepts in police weapons systems, in S.A. Yefsky (ed.), *Law enforcement, science and technology.*
Washington, D.C.: Thompson Book Co., 797–802.

WILSON, O.W., 1967
Civil disturbances and the rule of law.
J. Crim. Law, Criminol. & Pol. Sci., **58**, 155–59.

BALTIMORE COMMITTEE ON THE ADMINISTRATION OF JUSTICE UNDER EMERGENCY CONDITIONS, 1968.
Report. Mimeo.

COLUMBIA LAW REVIEW, 1968
Compensation for victims of urban riots, **68,** 57–84.

COLUMBIA LAW REVIEW, 1968
Riot control: the constitutional limits of search, arrest and fair trial procedure, **68,** 85–115.

EDWARDS, G., 1968
The police on the urban frontier. A guide to community understanding.
New York: Institute of Human Relations Press, 38–90.

GOLDSTEIN, H., 1968
Police response to urban crisis.
Public Admin. Rev., **28,** 393.

HARVARD LAW REVIEW, 1968
Municipal liability for riot damage. **81,** 653–56.

HARVARD LAW REVIEW, 1968
Riot control and the use of federal troops. **81,** 638–52.

HARVARD LAW REVIEW, 1968
Riot control and the Fourth Amendment. **81,** 625–37.

JANOWITZ, M., 1968
Social control of escalated riots.
Chicago: Univ. of Chicago Center for Policy Study.

KRUG, A.S., 1968
Does firearm registration work? A statistical analysis of New York State and New York City crime data.
Riverside, Conn.: National Shooting Sports Foundation.

KUHN, R.S., 1968
Jury discrimination: the next phase.
Sourthern Calif. Law Rev., **41,** 235–328.

LINCOLN, J.H., 1968
The anatomy of a riot: a Detroit judge's report.
New York: McGraw-Hill, 21–47.

LOHMAN, J.D., 1968
Law enforement and the police, in L.H. Masotti and D.R. Bowen (eds.), *Riots and rebellion: civil violence in the urban community.*
Beverly Hills, Calif.: Sage Publications, 359–72.

MCGEE, H.W. JR., 1968
Arrests in civil disturbances: reflections on the use of deadly force in riots.
Rutgers Law Rev., **22,** 716–32.

MARYLAND CRIME INVESTIGATING COMMISSION, 1968
A report of the Baltimore civil disturbance of April 1968.
(623 Edmondson Avenue, Baltimore, Maryland).

MOMBOISSE, R.M., 1968–69.
Riot prevention and survival.
Chicago-Kent Law Rev., **45,** 143–56.

NEW JERSEY, STATE OF, 1968
Report for action, of the Governor's Select Commission on Civil Disorder in the State of New Jersey.
Trenton, N.J., February 1968.

NEW YORK LAW FORUM, 1968
Riots and municipal liability. **14,** 824–82.

PLATT, A., AND DUNKLE, S., 1968
The administration of justice in crisis: Chicago, April, 1968.
Chicago: Center for Studies in Criminal Justice, Univ. Chicago.

STAPLES, E.L., AND CLAYTON, R.T., 1968
A preliminary cost analysis of firearms control programs.
Prepared for National Commission on the Causes and Prevention of Violence.
Silver Springs, Md.: Research Associates.

YALE LAW JOURNAL, 1968
Riot insurance, **77,** 541–58.

APPLEGATE, R., 1969
Riot control—material and techniques.
Harrisburg, Pa.: Stackpole Books.

BOUMA, D.H., 1969
Kids and cops. A study in mutual hostility.
Grand Rapids, Mich.: William B. Eerdmans Publishing Co., 89–116.

CALCIA, R.M., AND WEINTRAUB, C.L., 1969
Bail and preventive detention during riots: a proposal.
Brooklyn Law Rev., **35,** 417–32.

CAMPBELL, J.S., STANG, D.P., AND SAHID, J.R., 1969
Law and order reconsidered, **10.**
A staff report of the Task Force on Law and Law Enforcement to the National Commission on the Causes and Prevention of Violence.
Washington, D.C.: 309–32, 333–63, 411–26, 427–67, 527–49.

CLENDENDEN, C.C., 1969
The national guard as a law-enforcement engency in the twentieth century, in R. Higham (ed.), *Bayonets in the streets—the use of troops in civil disturbances.*
Univ. Press of Kansas, 85–111.

DENVER LAW JOURNAL, 1969
Symposium on riots and the law. **46,** 1–171.

DOBROVIR, W.A., 1969
Justice in time of crisis.
A staff report to the District of Columbia committee on the administration of justice under emergency conditions.
Washington, D.C.

DODDS, R.H., AND DEMPSEY, R.R., 1969
Civil disorders: the impact of mass arrests on the criminal justice system.
Brooklyn Law Rev., **35,** 355–93.

GEORGE WASHINGTON LAW REVIEW, 1969
The response of the Washington D.C. community and its criminal justice system to the April 1968 riot. **37,** 862–1008.

GOLDSCHLAG, R., KREITZMAN, R.J., AND ZIEGLER, L.D., 1969
Legislation and riots: interaction.
Brooklyn Law Rev., **35,** 472–85.

GRIMSHAW, A.D., 1969
Actions of police and the military in American race riots, in A.D. Grimshaw (ed.), *Racial violence in the United States.*
Chicago, Ill.: Aldine Publishing Co., 269–87.

HOWARD LAW JOURNAL, 1969
The small businessman and riots: his remedies with or without insurance. **15,** 252–64.

INDIK, B.P., AND SMITH, G.M., 1969
Resolution of conflict through collective bargainings: an alternative to violence?
George Washington Law Rev., **37,** 848–61.

JEFFRIES, V., AND RANSFORD, H.E., 1969
Interracial social contact and middle-class white reactions to the Watts riot.
Social Problems, **16,** 312–24.

JUSTICE, B., 1969
Detection of potential community violence.
Final report to Office of Law Enforcement Assistance, U.S. Dept of Justice.
LEAA dissemination document—Grant 207 (S.044).
Washington, D.C., v–xiii, 60–76.

KNOPF, T.A., 1969
Youth patrols: an experiment in community participation (Approaches to the Study of Violence).
Brandeis Univ., Lemberg Center for the Study of Violence.

LEFKOWITZ, L.J., 1969
Municipal liability for damage caused by riot.
Brooklyn Law Rev., **35,** 412–16.

LINCOLN, J.H., 1969
The juvenile court during a riot.
Fed. Probation, **33**(3), 32–6.

LOCKE, H.G., 1969
The Detroit riot of 1967.
Detroit: Wayne State Univ. Press.

MASOTTI, L.H., AND CORSI, J.R., 1969
Shoot-out in Cleveland: black militants and the police, July 23, 1968.
A report to the National Commission on the Causes and Prevention of Violence, Washington, D.C., 61–83.

NEWTON, G.D., AND ZIMRING, F.E., 1969
Firearms and violence in American life.
A report to the National Commission on the Causes and Prevention of Violence, Washington, D.C., 55–60, 79–138.

SKOLNICK, J.H., 1969
The politics of protest: violent aspects of protest and confrontation.
A report to the National Commission on the Causes and Prevention of Violence, Washington, D.C., 139–60, 183–248, 257–64.

SOLOVE, R.S., AND SYRACUSE, V.J., 1969
Insurance in riot-prone areas.
Brooklyn Law Rev., **35,** 458–71.

UNITED STATES OF AMERICA, 1969
Commission statement on firearms and violence, by Dr. Milton S. Eisenhower, Chairman, National Commission on the Causes and Prevention of Violence, July 28, Washington, D.C.

UNIVERSITY OF CHICAGO LAW REVIEW, 1969
Criminal justice '*in extremis*'.
Administration of justice during the April 1968 Chicago disorder. **36,** 455–613.

WILLIAMS, T.A., 1969
The army in civil disturbances: a professional dilemma? in R. Higham (ed.), *Bayonets in the streets—the use of troops in civil disturbances.*
Univ. Press of Kansas, 157–83.

WRIGHT, P.B., 1969
The effect of federal firearms control on civil disorder.
Brooklyn Law Rev., **35,** 433–57.

DANIELS, D.N., ET AL, 1970
The gun law controversy. Issues, arguments, and speculations concerning firearms legislation, in D.N. Daniels, M.F. Gilula and F.M. Ochberg (eds.), *Violence and the struggle for existence.*
Boston: Little, Brown & Co., 257–89.

DOBROVIR, W.A., 1970
Preventive detention: the lesson of civil disorders.
Villanova Law Rev., **15,** 313–30.

GILLIN, J.C., AND OCHBERG, F.M., 1970
Firearms control and violence, in D.N. Daniels, M.F. Gilula and F.M. Ochberg (eds.), *Violence and the struggle for existence.*
Boston: Little, Brown & Co., 241–55.

GINSBERG, G.S., AND STARKMAN, G.L., 1970
Civil disturbances, mass processing and misdemeanants: rights, remedies and realities.
J. Crim. Law, Criminol. & Pol. Sci., **61,** 39–50.

KITCH, T.D., 1970
Police perception of riot activity.
J. Res. Crime & Delinq., **7,** 120–56.

KRUG, A.S., 1970
Firearms registration costs vs. benefits. A survey of state law enforcement agencies on firearms registration.
Riverside, Conn.: National Shooting Sports Foundation, 61–81.

UNITED STATES OF AMERICA, 1970
Report of the President's Commission on Campus Unrest.
Washington, D.C.: 117–83.

WILLIAMS, D.G.T., 1970
Protest and public order.
Cambridge Law J., **28,** 96–121.

ENGDAHL, D.E., 1971
Soldiers, riots and revolution: the law and history of military troops in civil disorders.
Iowa Law Rev., **57,** 1–73.

FELD, B.C., 1971
Police violence and protest.
Minnesota Law Rev., **55,** 731–78.

LEWIS, J.M., 1971
Review essay: the telling of Kent State.
Social Problems, **19,** 267–79.

UNITED KINGDOM, 1971
Report of the enquiry into allegations against the security forces of physical brutality in Northern Ireland arising out of events on the 9th August 1971 (Chairman, Sir Edmund Compton), London, Cmnd. 4823.

DASH, S., 1972
Justice denied. A challenge to Lord Widgery's report on 'Bloody Sunday'.
The Defence and Education Fund of the International League for the Rights of Man in Association with the National Council for Civil Liberties.
London: N.C.C.L.

UNITED KINGDOM, 1972
Report of the Committee of Privy Counsellors appointed to consider authorised procedures for the interrogation of persons suspected of terrorism. (Chairman, Lord Parker), London, Cmnd. 4901.

UNITED KINGDOM, 1972
Report of the Tribunal appointed to enquire into the events on Sunday Jan. 30, 1972, *which led to loss of life in connection with the procession in Londonderry on that day.* (The Widgery Tribunal), London, (H.L. 101, H.C. 220).

WARANOFF, N.B., 1972
Federal judicial control of the National Guard.
Boston Univ. Law Rev., **52,** 1–31.

Adamek, R.J., and Lewis, J.M., 1973
Social control violence and radicalization: the Kent State case.
Social Forces, **51**, 342–47.

McGovern, E.T., 1973
Internment and detention without trial in the light of the European convention on human rights, in J.W. Bridge, D. Lasok, D.L. Parrott and R.O. Plender (eds.), *Fundamental rights.*
London: Sweet & Maxwell, 219–31.

Wald, M.S., 1974
May Day revisited.
Crim. Law Bulletin, **10**, Part I, 377–435, Part II, 516–43.

6 The police

1 Some historical references

RADZINOWICZ, L., 1956–1968
A history of English criminal law.
London: Stevens, Vol. 2, 235–427; Vol. 3, 1–8, 417–76; Vol. 4, 158–251.

SMITH, B., 1960
Police systems in the United States. 2nd rev. ed.
New York: Harper & Row.

UNITED KINGDOM, 1962
Royal Commission on the Police 1962. Final Report.
London: Cmnd. 1728, 9–20.

MARSHALL, G., 1965
Police and government.
London: Methuen & Co., 58–104.

CRITCHLEY, T.A., 1967
A history of police in England and Wales 1900–1966.
London: Constable & Co., 267–322.

LANE, R., 1967
Policing the city.
Cambridge, Mass.: Harvard Univ. Press.

SILVER, A., 1967
The demand for order in civil society: a review of some themes in the history of urban crime, police, and riot, in D.J. Bordua (ed.) *The police: six sociological essays.*
New York: John Wiley & Sons, 1–24.

COLQUHOUN, P., 1969
A treatise on the police of the metropolis.
Reprinted from 7th London edition, 1806.
Montclair, N.J.: Patterson Smith.

FOSDICK, R.B., 1969
European police systems: the purpose and function of the police.
Montclair, N.J.: Patterson Smith, 3–37.

SMITH, B., 1969
The state police: organization and administration.
Montclair, N.J.: Patterson Smith.

RICHARDSON, J.F., 1970
The New York police, 1620–1900.
New York: Oxford Univ. Press.

SAVAGE, E.H., 1971
Police records and recollections.
Reprinted from 1873 edition.
Montclair, N.J.: Patterson Smith.

BOPP, W.J., AND SCHULTZ, D.O., 1972
A short history of American law enforcement.
Springfield, Ill.: C.C. Thomas.

COUNTRYMAN, V., 1973
The history of the FBI: democracy's development of a secret police, in P. Watters and S. Gillers (eds.), *Investigating the FBI: a tough fair look at the powerful bureau, its present and its future.*
New York: Doubleday & Co., 33–63.

WILCOX, A.F., 1974
Police 1964–1973.
Crim. Law Rev., 1974, 144–57.

2 Organization and role

RADZINOWICZ, L., 1956
A history of English criminal law and its administration from 1750. Vol. 2.
London: Stevens & Sons Ltd., 349–78.

WESTLEY, W.A., 1956
Secrecy and the police.
Social Forces, **34**, 254–7.

KEPHART, W.M., 1957
Racial factors and urban law enforcement.
Philadelphia: Univ. Pennsylvania Press.

TOCH, H.H., AND SCHULTE, R., 1961
Readiness to perceive violence as a result of police training.
Brit. J. Psychol., **52,** 389–93.

STINCHCOMBE, A.L., 1963
Institutions of privacy in the determination of police administrative practice.
Amer. J. Sociol., **69,** 150–60.

WILSON, J.Q., 1963
The police and their problems: a theory.
Public Policy, **12,** 189–216.

CUMMING, E., CUMMING, I., AND EDELL, L., 1964
Policeman as philosopher, guide and friend.
Social Problems, **12,** 276–86.

WHITAKER, B., 1964
The police.
London: Eyre & Spottiswoode, 110–67.

WILSON, J.Q, 1964
Generational and ethnic differences among career police officers.
Amer. J. Sociol., **69,** 522–8.

BORDUA, D.J., AND REISS, A.J., JR., 1966
Command, control, and charisma: reflections on police bureaucracy.
Amer. J. Sociol., **72,** 68–76.

PREISS, J.J., AND EHRLICH, H.J., 1966
An examination of role theory: the case of the state police.
Lincoln: Nebraska Univ. Press, 6–37.

SKOLNICK, J.H., 1966
Justice without trial: law enforcement in democratic society.
New York: John Wiley & Sons, 42–70, 230–45.

BITTNER, E., 1967
Police discretion in emergency apprehension of mentally ill persons.
Social Problems, **14,** 278–92.

BLOOM, J.N., AND CARROLL, P., 1967
Police effectiveness measurement—myth or reality? in S.A. Yefsky (ed.), *Law enforcement, science and technology.*
Washington, D.C.: Thompson Book Co., 619–24.

CLAYTON, T., 1967
The protectors, the inside story of Britain's private security forces.
London: Oldbourne.

DANIELSON, W.F., 1967
Police compensation.
A document submitted to the President's Commission on Law Enforcement and Administration of Justice, Washington, D.C. 34–53.

HAMILTON, P., 1967
Espionage and subversion in an industrial society.
London: Hutchinson.

LOHMAN, J.D., AND MISNER, G.E., 1967
Field Surveys IV: *The police and the community.*
Washington, D.C.: President's Commission on Law Enforcement and Administration of Justice, Vol. 1, 17–39; Vol. 2, 28–60.

MCNAMARA, J.H., 1967
Uncertainties in police work: the relevance of police recruits' backgrounds and training, in D.J. Bordua (ed.), *The police: six sociological essays.*
New York: John Wiley & Sons, 163–252.

MYREN, R.A., 1967
The role of the police.
A document submitted to the President's Commission on Law Enforcement and Administration of Justice, Washington, D.C.

NIEDERHOFFER, A., 1967
Behind the shield.
New York: Doubleday & Co., 11–151, 187–242.

REISS, A.J. JR., 1967
Career orientations, job satisfaction, and the assessment of law enforcement problems by police officers, in Field Surveys III:
Studies in crime and law enforcement in major metropolitan areas. Vol. 2(2).
Washington, D.C.: President's Commission on Law Enforcement and Administration of Justice.

REISS, A.J. JR., AND BORDUA, D.J., 1967
Environment and organization: a perspective on the police, in D.J. Bordua (ed.), *The police: six sociological essays.*
New York: John Wiley & Sons, 25–55.

United States of America, 1967
The challenge of crime in a free society.
Report of the President's Commission on Law Enforcement and Administration of Justice, Washington, D.C. 91–123, 245–71.

United States of America, 1967
Task force report: the police.
Washington, D.C.: President's Commission on Law Enforcement and Administration of Justice, 1–62, 68–112, 120–43.

Weldon, J.F., and Ledee, R., 1967
High-rise policing techniques, in S.A. Yefsky (ed.), *Law enforcement science and and technology.*
Washington, D.C.: Thompson Book Co., 755–61.

Wenninger, E.P., and Clark, J.P., 1967
A theoretical orientation for police studies, in M.W. Klein (ed.), *Juvenile gangs in context.*
Englewood Cliffs, N.J.: Prentice-Hall, 161–72.

Baehr, M.E., Furcon, F.E., and Froemel, E.C., 1968
Psychological assessment of patrolman qualifications in relation to field performance.
Report submitted to Office of Law Enforcement Assistance, United States Department of Justice, Washington, D.C. 223–39.

Bordua, D.J., and Reiss, A.J.Jr., 1968
Law enforcement, in P.F. Lazarsfeld, W.H. Sewell and H. Wilensky (eds.), *The uses of sociology.*
London: Weidenfeld & Nicolson, 275–303.

Cain, M.E., 1968
Role conflict among police juvenile liaison officers.
Brit. J. Criminol., **8,** 366–82.

Cressey, D.R., and Elgesem, E., 1968
The police and the administration of justice.
Scandinavian Studies in Criminology, **2.**
London: Tavistock, 53–72.

Currer-Briggs, N., 1968
Security: attitudes and techniques for management.
London: Hutchinson.

Oliver, E., and Wilson, J., 1968
Practical security in commerce and industry.
London: Gower Press.

Smith, A.B., Locke, B., and Walker, W.F., 1968
Authoritarianism in police college students and non-police college students.
J. Crim. Law, Criminol. & Pol. Sci., **59,** 440–3.

Stoddard, E.R., 1968
The informal 'code' of police deviancy: a group approach to 'blue-coat crime'.
J. Crim. Law, Criminol. & Pol. Sci., **59,** 201–13.

Wilson, J.Q., 1968
Varieties of police behavior: the management of law and order in eight communities.
Cambridge, Mass.: Harvard Univ. Press, 16–82, 140–226.

Boston University Law Review, 1969
Race as a basis for police duty assignments.
49, 590–608.

Gardiner, J.A., 1969
Traffic and the police: variations in law-enforcement policy.
Cambridge, Mass.: Harvard Univ. Press.

Gottesman, J., 1969
Personality patterns of urban police applicants as measured by the MMPI.
Stevens Institute of Technology, Hoboken, N.J., Mimeo., 129–39.

New York City Police Department, 1969
Project report submitted to the New York city police department and the law enforcement assistance administration United States Department of Justice.
Police training and performance study.
New York: New York City Police Department, 1–115.

Watson, N.A., and Sterling, J.W., 1969
Police and their opinions.
Washington, D.C.: International Association of Chiefs of Police, 1–36, 105–24.

Bittner, E., 1970
The function of the police in modern society: a review of background factors, current practices, and possible role models.
Chevy Chase, Maryland: National Institute of Mental Health, Center for Studies of Crime and Delinquency.

Clark, R., 1970
Crime in America: observations on its nature, causes, prevention and control.
New York: Simon & Schuster, 132–88.

Ford Foundation, 1970
A more effective arm.
A report on a police development fund, newly established by the Ford Foundation.

Mark, R., 1970
A police point of view. Thoughts from a psychological ghetto.
Medico-legal J., **38,** 4–14.

Niederhoffer, A., and Blumberg, A.S., 1970
The ambivalent force: perspectives on the police.
Waltham, Mass.: Ginn & Company, 1–147.

Nimmer, R., 1970
The public drunk: formalizing the police role as a social help agency.
Georgetown Law J., **58,** 1089–116.

O'Leary, V., and Newman, D.J., 1970
Conflict resolution in criminal justice.
J. Res. Crime & Delinq., **7,** 99–119.

Saunders, C.B., 1970
Upgrading the American police. Education and training for better law enforcement.
Washington, D.C.: Brookings Institution.

Smith, A.B., Locke, B., and Fenster, A., 1970
Authoritarianism in policemen who are college graduates and non-college police.
J. Crim. Law, Criminol. & Pol. Sci. **61,** 313–15.

United States of America, 1970
Training police as specialists in family crisis intervention.
L.E.A.A., National Institute of Law Enforcement and Criminal Justice, U.S Dept. of Justice, Washington, D.C.

Webster, J.A., 1970
Police task and time study.
J. Crim. Law, Criminol. & Pol. Sci., **61,** 94–100.

Banton, M. (ed.), 1971
The sociology of the police.
Police J., **44,** 227–43.

Berman, D.R., 1971
Law and order on campus: an analysis of the role and problems of the security police.
J. Urban Law., **49,** 513–31.

Bopp, W.J., 1971
The police rebellion. A quest for blue power.
Springfield, Ill.: C.C. Thomas.

Burpo, J.H., 1971
The police labor movement, problems and perspectives.
Springfield Ill.: C.C. Thomas.

Cain M. 1971
On the beat: interactions and relations in rural and urban police forces, in S. Cohen (ed.), *Images of deviance*
Harmondsworth: Penguin Books, 62–97.

Ellcott, J.F., and Sardino, T.J., 1971
The time required to commit crime.
Police, **16**(4), 26–9.

Hahn, H., 1971
A profile of urban police.
Law & Contemporary Problems, **36,** 449–66.

Hahn, H. (ed.), 1971
Police in urban society.
Beverly Hills, Calif.: Sage Publications.

Juris, H.A., 1971
The implications of police unionism.
Law & Society Rev., (Special police issue), **6,** 231–45.

Kakalik, J.S., and Wildhorn, S., 1971
Private police in the U.S.: findings and recommendations. (Vols. I & II).
Santa Monica, Calif.: Rand Corporation.

Lind, R.C., and Lipsky, J.P., 1971
The measurement of police output: conceptual issues and alternative approaches.
Law & Contemporary Problems, **36,** 566–88.

Manning, P.K., 1971
The police: mandate, strategies, and appearances, in J.D. Douglas (ed.), *Crime and justice in American society.*
New York: Bobbs-Merrill Co., 149–93.

Newberg, H.B., 1971
Building local citizen alliances to reduce crime and create a fairer and more effective criminal justice system.
J. Urban Law., **49,** 443–83.

Reiss, A.J.Jr., 1971
The police and the public.
New Haven & London: Yale Univ. Press.

ROKEACH, M., MILLER, M.G., AND SNYDER, J.A., 1971
The value gap between police and policed.
J. Social Issues, **27**, 155–71.

SAN FRANCISCO COMMITTEE ON CRIME, 1971
A report on the San Francisco police department. Parts I and II.
Berkeley, Calif.: Western Star Press.

SCOTT, T.M., AND MCPHERSON, M., 1971
The development of the private sector of the criminal justice system.
Law & Society Rev., (Special police issue), **6**, 267–88.

TROJANOWICZ, R.C., 1971
The policeman's occupational personality.
J. Crim. Law, Criminol. & Pol. Sci., **62**, 551–9.

VANDALL, F.J., 1971
Training to meet the police function.
Wisconsin Law Rev., 1971, 547–75.

WILSON, P.R., AND CHAPPELL, D., 1971
The effects of police withdrawal from traffic control: a comparative study.
J. Crim. Law, Criminol. & Pol. Sci., **61**, 567–72.

AMERICAN BAR ASSOCIATION, 1972
Standards relating to *The Urban police function.* Tentative draft, March 1972, A.B.A. Project on Standards for Criminal Justice, New York.

BALCH, R.W., 1972
The police personality: fact or fiction?
J. Crim. Law, Criminol. & Pol. Sci., **63**, 106–19.

BANTON, M., 1972
Labour-management relations in an American police department.
Police J., **45**, 302–11.

CHAPPELL, D., AND WILSON, P.R., 1972
Police in Australia, in D. Chappell and P.R. Wilson (eds.), *The Australian Criminal Justice System.*
Sydney: Butterworths, 245–60.

COHEN, B., 1972
The police internal system of justice in New York City.
J. Crim. Law, Criminol. & Pol. Sci., **63**, 54–67.

STEADMAN, R.F. (ED.), 1972
The police and the community.
Baltimore: Johns Hopkins Univ. Press.

UNIVERSITY OF PENNSYLVANIA LAW REVIEW, 1972
Legal controls on neighbourhood defense organisations. **120**, 952–82.

VOTEY, H.L., AND PHILLIPS, L., 1972
Police effectiveness and the production function for law enforcement.
J. Legal Studies, **1**, 423–36.

WILES, P., AND MCCLINTOCK, F.H., (EDS.) 1972
The security industry in the United Kingdom.
(Papers presented to the Cropwood Round-Table Conference).
Cambridge: Institute of Criminology.

CAIN, M.E., 1973
Society and the policeman's role.
London: Routledge & Kegan Paul.

COBERN, M., 1973
Some manpower aspects of the criminal justice system.
Crime & Delinq., **19**, 187–99.

COHEN, B., AND CHAIKEN, J.M., 1973
Police background characteristics and performance.
Lexington, Mass.: D.C. Heath & Co.

DANZIG, R., 1973
Towards the creation of a complementary, decentralised system of criminal justice.
Stanford Law Rev., **26**, 1–54.

JURIS, H.A., AND FEUILLE, P., 1973
Police unionism: power and impact in public sector bargaining.
Lexington, Mass.: D.C. Heath

MARTIN, J.P., AND WILLIAMS, A., 1973
The application of modern techniques of resource allocation in the field of crime problems.
Strasbourg: Council of Europe.

RICHMAN, J., 1973
Police auxiliaries—traffic wardens, some sociological aspects.
Police J., **46**, 135–49.

RUBENSTEIN, J., 1973
City police. New York: Farrar, Straus & Giroux.

TURNER, W.W., 1973
The FBI and other police forces, in P. Watters and S. Gillers (eds.), *Investigating the FBI: a tough fair look at the powerful bureau, its present and its future.*
New York: Doubleday & Co., 113–39.

WILSON, J.Q., 1973
Emerging patterns in American police administration.
Police J., **46,** 155–66.

BECKER, T.M., 1974
The place of private police in society: an area of research for the social sciences.
Social Problems, **21,** 438–53.

MARTIN, J.P., 1974
The scope of police manpower studies, in R.G. Hood (ed.), *Crime, criminology and public policy: essays in honour of Sir Leon Radzinowicz.*
London: Heinemann.

UNITED STATES OF AMERICA, 1974
Police.
National Advisory Commission on Criminal Justice Standards and Codes. Washington, D.C.

UNIVERSITY OF TORONTO, 1974
Private policing and security in Canada: a workshop.
Report of the Proceedings, Centre of Criminology, University of Toronto.

WILCOX, A.F., 1974
Police 1964–1973. *Crim. Law Rev.*, 1974, 144–57.

3 Community relations

MYRDAL, G., 1944
An American dilemma: the Negro problem and modern democracy.
New York: Harper & Brothers, 3rd ed., Vol. 1, 535–46.

GOURLEY, G.D., 1954
Police public relations.
Annals Amer. Acad. Pol. & Soc. Sci., **291,** 135–42.

UNITED KINGDOM, 1960
Interim Report of the Royal Commission on the Police.
London: Cmnd. 1222, 99–121.

MORTON-WILLIAMS, R., 1962
The relations between the police and the public.
Appendix IV to the Minutes of Evidence to the Royal Commission on the Police, London.

BANTON, M., 1964
The policeman in the community.
London: Tavistock.

BRENNAN, J.J., AND OLMSTED, D.W., 1965
Police work with delinquents: analysis of a training program.
Social Science Research Bureau, Michigan State Univ. 83–6.

CLARK, J.P., 1965
Isolation of the police: a comparison of the British and American situations.
J. Crim. Law, Criminol. & Pol. Sci., **56,** 307–19.

UNITED STATES OF AMERICA, 1966
Report of the President's Commission on Crime in the District of Columbia, Washington, D.C., 203–17.

WATSON, N.A., 1966
Police-community relations.
Washington, D.C.: International Association of Chiefs of Police, 99–115, 149–63.

BLACK, D.J., AND REISS, A.J.JR., 1967
Patterns of behavior in police and citizen transactions, in Field Surveys III: *Studies in crime and law enforcement in major metropolitan areas.* Vol. 2(1).
Washington, D.C.: President's Commission on Law Enforcement and Administration of Justice.

LOHMAN, J.D., AND MISNER, G.E., 1967
Field Surveys IV: *The police and the community*, Vol. 1.
Washington, D.C.: President's Commission on Law Enforcement and Administration of Justice, 40–131, 148–66; Vol. 2, 61–195, 289–316.

TERRIS, B.J., 1967
The role of the police.
Annals Amer. Acad. Pol. & Soc. Sci., **374**, 58–69.

UNITED STATES OF AMERICA, 1967
Field Surveys V: *A national survey of police and community relations.*
Washington, D.C.: President's Commission on Law Enforcement and Administration of Justice, 1–362.

UNITED STATES OF AMERICA, 1967
Task force report: the police.
Washington, D.C.: President's Commission on Law Enforcement and Administration of Justice, 144–207.

WERTHMAN, C., AND PILIAVIN, I., 1967
Gang members and the police, in D.J. Bordua (ed.),
The police: six sociological essays.
New York: John Wiley & Sons, 56–98.

BORDUA, D.J., 1968
Comments on police—community relations.
Connecticut Law Rev., **1**, 306–31.

MACK, J.A., 1968
Police juvenile liaison—practice and evaluation.
Univ. of Glasgow School of Social Study.

POLICE COMMUNITY RELATIONS, 1968
A survey among New York City patrolmen.
A study for the New York City Police Department and Vera Inst. of Justice.
High Wycombe: University Microfilms.

ALEX, N., 1969
Black in blue. A study of the Negro policeman.
New York: Appleton-Century-Crofts.

BAYLEY, D.H., AND MENDELSOHN, H., 1969
Minorities and the police: confrontation in America.
New York: Free Press.

BOUMA, D.H., 1969
Kids and cops: a study in mutual hostility.
Grand Rapids, Mich.: William B. Eerdmans Publishing Co.

CHAPPELL, D., AND WILSON, P.R., 1969
The police and the public in Australia and New Zealand.
St Lucia, Queensland: Univ. of Queensland Press, 37–77, 100–38.

MORRIS, A., 1969
What is the role of the community in the development of police systems?
Correctional Research, **19**, 1–21.

WATSON, N.A., AND STERLING, J.W., 1969
Police and their opinions.
Washington, D.C.: International Association of Chiefs of Police, 52–104.

CLARKE, C.F.O., 1970
Police/community relations.
Ditchley Paper No. 30, Enstone, Oxford: Ditchley Foundation.

COURTIS, M.C., 1970
Attitudes to crime and the police in Toronto: a report on some survey findings.
Centre of Criminology, University of Toronto, 50–142.

HUDSON, J.R., 1970
Police-citizen encounters that lead to citizen complaints.
Social Problems, **18**, 179–93.

JOHN, A., 1970
Race in the inner city. A report from Handsworth, Birmingham.
London: Runnymede Trust, 21–3.

KITCH, T.D., 1970
Police perception of riot activity.
J. Res. Crime & Delinq., **7**, 120–56.

LAMBERT, J.R., 1970
Race relations: the role of the police, in S. Zubaida (ed.),
Explorations in sociology—race and racialism.
London: Tavistock Publications, 73–97.

NATIONAL OPINION POLLS, MARKET RESEARCH LTD., 1970.
Report on attitudes towards crime, violence, and permissiveness in society.
76/86 Strand, London, W.C.2. Mimeo, 21–4.

NIEDERHOFFER, A., AND BLUMBERG, A.S., 1970
The ambivalent force: perspectives on the police.
Waltham, Mass.: Ginn & Company, 184–238

ROSE, G., AND HAMILTON, R.A., 1970
Effects of a juvenile liaison scheme.
Brit. J. Criminol., **10**, 2–20.

UNITED STATES OF AMERICA, 1970
Training police specialists in family crisis intervention.
L.E.A.A., National Institute of Law Enforcement and Criminal Justice, U.S. Dept. of Justice, Washington, D.C.

BLOCK, R.L., 1971
Fear of crime and fear of the police.
Social Problems, **19**, 91–101.

BORDUA, D.J., AND TIFFT, L.L., 1971
Citizen interviews, organizational feedback, and police-community relations decisions.
Law & Society Rev., (Special police issue), **6**, 155–82.

COFFEY, A., ELDEFONSO, E., AND HARTINGER, W., 1971
Human relations: law enforcement in a changing community.
Englewood Cliffs, N.J.: Prentice-Hall, 67–99.

CONKLIN, J.E., 1971
Criminal environment and support for the law.
Law & Society Rev., (Special police issue), **6**, 247–65.

GUREVITCH, M., DANET, B., AND SCHWARTZ, G., 1971
The image of the police in Israel.
Law & Society Rev., **5**, 367–88.

HAHN, H., 1971
Ghetto assessments of police protection and authority.
Law & Society Rev., (Special police issue), **6**, 183–94.

HAHN, H., 1971
Profile of urban police.
Law & Contemporary Problems, **36**, 449–66.

JOHNSON, D., AND GREGORY, R.J., 1971
Police-community relations in the United States: a review of recent literature and projects.
J. Crim. Law, Criminol. & Pol. Sci., **62**, 94–103.

MARX, G.T., AND ARCHER, D., 1971
Citizen involvement in the law enforcement process. The case of community police patrols.
Amer. Behavioral Scientist, **15**, 52–72.

NEWBERG, H.B., 1971
Building local citizen alliances to reduce crime and create a fairer and more effective criminal justice system.
J. Urban Law, **49**, 443–83.

REISS, A.J.JR., 1971
The police and the public.
New Haven & London: Yale Univ. Press.

VANDALL, F.J., 1971
Training to meet the police function.
Wisconsin Law Rev., 1971, 547–75.

WILSON, P.R., AND CHAPPELL, D., 1971
The law and order issue and police-public relations.
Aust. & N.Z.J. Criminol., **4**, 112–16.

AMERICAN BAR ASSOCIATION, 1972
Standards relating to *The Urban Police Function.*
Tentative draft, March 1972, A.B.A. Project on Standards for Criminal Justice, New York.

BANTON, M., 1972
Race and public order in an American city.
Police J., **45**, 198–213.

CHAPPELL, D., AND WILSON, P.R., 1972
The Australian police and public re-visited, in D. Chappell and P.R. Wilson (eds.), *The Australian Criminal Justice System.*
Sydney: Butterworths, 317–23.

DEAR, G.J., 1972
Coloured immigrant communities and the police.
Police J., **45**, 128–50.

GOLDNER, N.S., AND KOENIG, R., 1972
White middle-class attitudes toward an urban policemen's union.
Crime & Delinq., **18**, 168–75.

HUSEMAN, R.C., AND MCCURLEY, S.H., 1972
Police attitudes toward communication with the public.
Police Chief, **39**(12), 68–73.

PERRY, D.C., AND SORNOFF, P., 1972
Street level administration and the law:

the problem of police-community relations.
Crim. Law Bull., **8,** 43–61.

SHAW, M., AND WILLIAMSON, W., 1972
Public attitudes to the police.
Criminologist, **7**(26), 18–33.

STEADMAN, R.F. (ED.), 1972
The police and the community.
Baltimore: Johns Hopkins Univ. Press.

STOBART, B.J., 1967
Serious assaults on police.
Police J., **45,** 108–26.

UNITED KINGDOM, 1972
Select committee on race relations and immigration, Session 1971–72.
Police/Immigrant relations, Vol. 1. *Report;* Vols. 2 & 3, *Evidence*, 22–4, 40–6, 210–16, 229–41, 426–32, 618–39, 716–35, 749–59, 765–71, 786–98, 836–46. London.

UNITED STATES OF AMERICA, 1972
Law enforcement officers killed in the line of duty.
FBI Law Enforcement Bulletin, March 1972, 3–7.

WALKER, D. *et al*, 1972
Contact and support: an empirical assessment of public attitudes toward the police and the courts.
North Carolina Law Rev., **51,** 45–79.

FURSTENBERG, F.F. JR., AND WELLFORD C.F. 1973
Calling the police: the evaluation of police service.
Law & Society Rev. **7,** 393–406.

GABOR, I.R., AND LOW, C., 1973
The police role in the community.
Criminology, **4,** 383–314.

HAWKINS, R.O., 1973
Who called the cops?: decisions to report criminal victimisation.
Law & Society Rev., **7,** 427–44.

JACKSON, B., 1973
The police and the rest of us, a review essay.
Crim. Law Bull., **9,** 461–33.

NORRIS, D.F., 1973
Police-community relations: a program that failed.
Lexington, Mass.: Lexington Books.

RADELET, L.A., 1973
The police and the community.
Beverly Hills, Calif.: Glencoe Press.

SMITH, P.E., AND HAWKINS, R.O., 1973
Victimisation, types of citizen-police contacts, and attitudes towards the police.
Law & Society Rev., **8,** 135–52.

CRESSEY, D.R., 1974
Law, order and the motorist, in R.G. Hood (ed.), *Crime, criminology and public policy: essays in honour of Sir Leon Radzinowicz.*
London: Heinemann, 213–34.

4 Uses and abuses of power

[*See also Section* 1(4) *for references on police discretion to prosecute; Section* 5(2) *on control of civil disorder; Section* 14(2) *for reference on police records in relation to the status of offenders.*]

HALL, J., 1953
Police and law in a democratic society.
Indiana Law J., **28,** 133–77.

WESTLEY, W.A., 1953
Violence and the police.
Amer. J. Sociol., **56,** 34–41.

WESTLEY, W.A., 1956
Secrecy and the police.
Social Forces, **34,** 254–57.

UNITED KINGDOM, 1960
Interim report of the Royal Commission on the police.
London: Cmnd. 1222, 122–39.

BARRETT, E.L., 1962
Police practices and the law: from arrest to release or charge.
Calif. Law Rev., **50,** 11–55.

ROBIN, G.D., 1963
Justifiable homicide by police officers.
J. Crim. Law, Criminol. & Pol. Sci., **54,** 225–31.

HARVARD LAW REVIEW, 1964
The administration of complaints by civilians against the police. **77,** 499–519.

PACKER, H.L., 1964
Two models of the criminal process.
Univ. Penn. Law Rev., **113,** 1–68.

WHITAKER, B., 1964
The police.
London: Eyre & Spottiswoode, 168–93.

GRIGG, M., 1965
The Challenor case.
Harmondsworth: Penguin Books.

LAFAVE W.R., 1965
Improving police performance through the exclusionary rule—Part I: current police and local court practices.
Missouri Law Rev., **30,** 391–458; Part II: defining the norms and training the police, *ibid.*, 566–610.

LAFAVE, W.R., 1965
Arrest: the decision to take a suspect into custody.
Boston: Little, Brown & Co., 153–67, 379–406, 490–525.

O'HIGGINS, P., AND AUBREY, M., 1965
The Challenor Report.
Crim. Law Rev., 1965, 633–47.

GROSS, Z., AND REITMAN, A., 1966
Police power and citizen's rights: the case for an independent police review board.
New York: American Civil Liberties Union.

NEWMAN, D.J., 1966
Conviction: the determination of guilt or innocence without trial.
Boston: Little, Brown & Co., 188–96.

PACKER, H.L., 1966
The courts, the police and the rest of us, and comments by Kuh, Souris, Inbau, Broderick, English, Wilson, Desmond and Craig.
J. Crim. Law, Criminol. & Pol. Sci., **57,** 238–311.

SKOLNICK, J.H., 1966
Justice without trial: law enforcement in democratic society.
New York: John Wiley & Sons, 1–22, 71–245.

UNITED STATES OF AMERICA, 1966
Report of the President's Commission on Crime in the District of Columbia.
Washington, D.C., 217–23.

WATSON, N.A., 1966
Police-community relations.
Washington, D.C.: International Association of Chiefs of Police, 87–97.

BLACK, D.J., AND REISS, A.J.JR., 1967
Field Surveys III: *Studies in crime and law enforcement in major metropolitan areas.*
Vol. 2.
Washington, D.C.: President's Commission on Law Enforcement and Administration of Justice, 1–139.

CHAPMAN, S.G., 1967
Police firearms use policy.
A document submitted to the President's Commission on Law Enforcement and Administration of Justice, Washington, D.C. Mimeo.

GOURLEY, G.D., 1967
Effective police organization and management.
A document submitted to the President's Commission on Law Enforcement and Administration of Justice, Washington, D.C. Mimeo. Vol. 2, 330–77; Vol. 3, 871–98.

HESS, A.G., AND POOLE, F.L., 1967
Abuse of the record of arrest not leading to conviction.
Crime & Delinq., **13,** 494–505.

LOHMAN, J.D., AND MISNER, G.E., 1967
Field Surveys IV: *The police and the community*, Vol. 1.
Washington, D.C.: President's Commission on Law Enforcement and Administration of Justice, 132–47, 167–75; Vol. 2, 195–284.

SEEBURGER, R.H., AND STANTON WETTICK, R.JR., 1967
Miranda in Pittsburgh: a statistical study.
Univ. Pittsburgh Law Rev., **29,** 1–26.

SKOLNICK, J.H., AND WOODWORTH, J.R., 1967
Bureaucracy, information, and social control: a study of a morals detail, in D.J. Bordua (ed.), *The police: six sociological essays.*
New York: John Wiley & Sons, 99–136.

UNITED STATES OF AMERICA, 1967
Report on police field procedures.
A document submitted by the Police Procedures Advisory Group to the President's Commission on Law Enforcement and Administration of Justice.
Washington, D.C., Mimeo, Section II.

UNITED STATES OF AMERICA, 1967.
Task force report: the police.
Washington, D.C.: President's Commission on Law Enforcement and Administration of Justice, 208–19.

WESTIN, A.F., 1967
Privacy and freedom.
London: Bodley Head, 67–168, 365–99.

WILSON, J.Q., 1967
Police morale, reform, and citizen respect: the Chicago case, in D.J. Bordua (ed.), *The police: six sociological essays.*
New York: John Wiley & Sons, 137–62.

ADELSON, L., HUNTINGTON III, R.W., AND REAY, D.T., 1968
'A prisoner is dead'. A survey of 91 sudden and unexpected deaths which occurred while the defendant was in either police custody or penal detention.
Police (Sept.–Oct. 1968), 49–58.

BLACK, A.D., 1968
The people and the police.
New York: McGraw-Hill, 69–229.

BLACK, D.J., 1968
Police encounters and social organization: an observation study.
Unpublished Ph.D. dissertation, Dept. of Sociology, Univ. of Michigan.

CARDARELLI, A.P., 1968
An analysis of police killed by criminal action: 1961–1963.
J. Crim. Law, Criminol. & Pol. Sci., **59,** 447–53.

DRIVER, E.D., 1968
Confessions and the social psychology of coercion.
Harvard Law Rev., **82,** 42–61.

NIEDERHOFFER, A., 1968
Restraint of the force: a recurrent problem.
Connecticut Law Rev., **1,** 288–305.

REISS, A. J. JR., 1968
How common is police brutality?
Trans-action, **5**(8), July-August., 10–19, and in L. Radzinowicz and M.E. Wolfgang (eds., 1971), *Crime and justice*, Vol. 2, *The criminal in the arms of the law.*
New York: Basic Books, 293–308.

ROSSI, P.H. ET AL, 1968
Between white and black, the faces of American institutions in the ghetto, in *Supplemental studies for the Kerner Report.*
Washington, D.C., National Advisory Commission on Civil Disorders, 103–14.

RUMMEL, B., 1968
The right of law enforcement officers to use deadly force to effect an arrest.
New York Law Forum, **14,** 749–62.

SILVING, H., 1968
On 'police brutality'.
Revista juridica de la Universidad de Puerto Rico, **37,** 279–317.

WILSON, J.Q., 1968
Varieties of police behavior: the management of law and order in eight communities.
Cambridge, Mass.: Harvard Univ. Press, 83–139, 227–77.

ABBOTT, D.W., GOLD, L.H., AND ROGOWSKY, E.T., 1969
Police, politics and race. The New York City referendum on civilian review.
Cambridge, Mass.: Harvard Univ. Press.

BAYLEY, D.H., AND MENDELSOHN, H., 1969
Minorities and the police: confrontation in America.
New York: Free Press, 109–42.

CHEVIGNY, P., 1969
Police power: police abuses in New York City.
New York: Pantheon Books, 236–75.

COON, C., AND HARRIS, R., 1969
The release report on drug offenders and the law.
London: Sphere Books, 11–26.

HOFFMAN, W.E., 1969
Wiretapping, confessions, and physical evidence under the United States supreme

court and statutes.
New England Law Rev., **5,** 17–49.

INSTITUTE OF MODERN LEGAL THOUGHT, 1969
Law enforcement: the matter of redress.
A report by the American Civil Liberties Union of Southern California, Los Angeles.

MILLER, F.W., 1969
Prosecution. The decision to charge a suspect with a crime.
Boston: Little, Brown & Co.

REMINGTON, F.J., 1969
Review of *Discretionary justice: a preliminary inquiry*, by K.C. Davis.
U. Chicago Law Rev., **36,** 884–902.

RUBIN, A.B., AND MILLER, B.R., 1969
The law enforcement officer's use of deadly force: two approaches.
Amer. Crim. Law Quart., **8,** 27–40.

VIRGINIA LAW REVIEW, 1969
Grievance response mechanisms for police misconduct, **55,** 909–57.

ZEITZ, L., MEDALIE, R.J., AND ALEXANDER, P., 1969
Anomie, powerlessness, and police interrogation.
J. Crim. Law, Criminol. & Pol. Sci., **60,** 314–22.

AVINS, A., 1970
Equal protection against unnecessary police violence and the original understanding of the 14th amendment.
Buffalo Law Rev., **19,** 599–608.

BITTNER, E., 1970.
The functions of the police in modern society: a review of background factors, current practices, and possible role models.
Chevy Chase, Maryland: Nat. Inst. of Mental Health, Center for Studies of Crime and Delinquency.

BLACK, D.J., AND REISS, A.J., 1970
Police control of juveniles.
Amer. Sociol. Rev., **35,** 63–77.

CARRINGTON, F., 1970
Speaking for the police.
J. Crim. Law, Criminol. & Pol. Sci., **61,** 244–79.

CHAPMAN, B., 1970
Police state.
London: Pall Mall Press.

CHEVIGNY, P.G., 1970?
Police complainers. A handbook.
New York: American Civil Liberties Union.

CLARK R. 1970
Crime in America: observations on its nature causes prevention and control.
New York: Simon and Schuster, 132–88.

COLUMBIA JOURNAL OF LAW AND SOCIAL PROBLEMS, 1970.
Protection of the accused at police lineups.
6, 345–73.

CORNELL LAW REVIEW, 1970.
Eavesdropping at the government's discretion—first amendment implications of the national security eavesdropping power.
56, 161–70.

DURAND, A.L., 1970
The right to resist an unlawful arrest.
Louisiana Law Rev., **31,** 120–30.

FRANKLIN, C., 1970
The third degree.
London: Robert Hale, 75–136.

GOODERSON, R.N., 1970
The interrogation of suspects.
Canadian Bar Review, **48,** 270–307.

HARDING, R.W., 1970
Legality of killings by Australian police.
J. Res. Crime & Delinq., **7,** 177–87.

HAWKINS, G., AND WARD, P., 1970
Armed and disarmed police: police firearms policy and levels of violence.
J. Res. Crime & Delinq., **7,** 188–97.

HEIDENHEIMER, A.J., (ED.), 1970.
Political corruption: readings in comparative analysis.
New York: Holt, Rinehart & Winston, 167–78.

JOURNAL OF CRIMINAL LAW, CRIMINOLOGY AND POLICE SCIENCE, 1970
Police infiltration of dissident groups. **61,** 181–94.

MATTHEWS, A.R.JR., 1970.
Observations on police policy and procedures

for emergency detention of the mentally ill.
J. Crim. Law, Criminol. & Pol. Sci., **61,** 283–95.

MAYHALL, V.R.JR., 1970
Use of deadly force in the arrest process.
Louisiana Law Rev., **31,** 131–48.

NIEDERHOFFER, A., AND BLUMBERG, A.S., 1970
The ambivalent force: perspectives on the police.
Waltham, Mass.: Ginn & Company, 148–83, 239–338.

PEPINSKY, H.E., 1970
A theory of police reaction to Miranda v. Arizona.
Crime & Delinq., **16,** 379–92.

SAGARIN, E., AND MACNAMARA, D.E.J., 1970
The problem of entrapment.
Crime & Delinq., **16,** 363–78.

UNIVERSITY OF PENNSYLVANIA LAW REVIEW, 1970
Police bulletins and private searches. **119,** 163–73.

WESTLEY, WA., 1970
Violence and the police: a sociological study of law, custom and morality.
London: MIT Press.

WILLIAM AND MARY LAW REVIEW, 1970
Justifiable use of deadly force by the police: a statutory survey. **12,** 67–85.

YALE LAW JOURNAL, 1970
Announcement in police entries. **80,** 139–75.

ABRAMS, N., 1971
Internal policy: guiding the exercise of prosecutorial discretion.
UCLA Law Rev., **19,** 1–58.

AMERICAN BAR ASSOCIATION, 1971
Standards relating to electronic surveillance.
Proposed final draft and supplement, New York.

AMERICAN UNIVERSITY LAW REVIEW, THE, 1971
The new 'no-knock' provision and its effect on the authority of the police to break and enter. **20,** 467–81.

BURNS, H.JR., 1971
Tampering with the myths.
Can. J. Corrections, **13,** 122–32.

CAPLAN, G.M., 1971
The case for rule-making by law enforcement agencies.
Law & Contemp. Problems, **36,** 500–14.

CHAMBLISS, W.J., 1971
Vice, corruption, bureaucracy and power.
Wisconsin Law Rev., 1971, 1150–73.

CHAMBLISS, W.J., AND SEIDMAN, R.B., 1971
Law, order, and power.
Reading, Mass.: Addison-Wesley Publishing Co., 271–394.

CLEMENTS, J.M., 1971
Repression: beyond the rhetoric.
Issues in Criminol., **6,** 1–31.

CORNELL LAW REVIEW, 1971
Discrimination on the basis of arrest records.
56, 470–88.

DAVIS, S.M., 1971
Justice for the juvenile: the decision to arrest and due process.
Duke Law J., 1971, 913–37.

DUKE LAW JOURNAL, 1971
Socio-legal aspects of racially motivated police misconduct, 1971, 751–83.

FELD, B.C., 1971
Police violence and protest.
Minnesota Law Rev., **55,** 731–78.

GEORGETOWN LAW JOURNAL, 1971
Police perjury in narcotics 'dropsy' cases: a new credibility gap. **60,** 507–23.

GRAHAM, F.P., 1971
Police eavesdropping: law enforcement revolution.
Crim. Law Bull., **7,** 445–71.

HALPERN, W.I., AND GORDON, A., 1971
Drugs and the youthful police informer.
Amer. J. Psychiat., **128,** 649–51.

HUDSON, J.R., 1971
Police review boards and police accountability.
Law & Contemp. Problems, **36,** 515–38.

LEVINE, J.P., 1971
Implementing legal policies through operant conditioning: the case of police practices.
Law & Society Rev., (Special police issue), **6,** 195–222.

LIVERMORE, J.M., 1971
Policing.
Minnesota Law Rev., **55,** 649–729.

MILNER, N.A., 1971
The court and local law enforcement—the impact of Miranda.
Beverly Hills, Calif.: Sage Publications, 13–80, 188–232.

MILNER, N.A., 1971
Supreme court effectiveness and the police organisation.
Law & Contemp. Problems, **36,** 467–87.

POLLITT, D.H., 1971
Survey of recent decisions by the North Carolina supreme court in the area of criminal procedure.
North Carolina Law Rev., **49,** 262–90.

SAFER, J.D., 1971
Deadly weapons in the hands of the police officers, on duty and off duty.
J. Urban Law, **49,** 565–79.

STARK, R., 1971
Police riots, collective violence and law enforcement.
Belmont, Calif.: Wadsworth Pub. Co.

TIEGER, J.H., 1971
Police discretion and discriminatory enforcement.
Duke Law J., 1971, 717–50.

UNIVERSITY OF CHICAGO LAW REVIEW, 1971
Private police forces: legal powers and limitations. **38,** 555–82.

UNIVERSITY OF CHICAGO LAW REVIEW, 1971
Retention and dissemination of arrest records: judicial response. **38,** 850–74.

UVILLER, H.R., 1971
The judge at the cop's elbow.
Columbia Law Rev., **71,** 707–22.

VILLANOVA LAW REVIEW, 1971
Discriminatory hiring practices due to arrest records—private remedies. **17,** 110–29.

WEINER, N.L., AND WILLIE, C.V., 1971
Decisons by juvenile officers.
Amer. J. Sociol., **77,** 199–210.

WILBERDING, M.F., 1971
'Miranda-type warnings for consent searches?'.
North Dakota Law Rev., **47,** 281–86.

WILSON, J.V., AND ALPRIN, G.M., 1971
Controlling police conduct: alternatives to the exclusionary rule.
Law & Contemp. Problems, **36,** 488–99.

AMERICAN BAR ASSOCIATION, 1972
Standards relating to the urban police function.
Tentative draft, March 1972, A.B.A. Project on Standards for Criminal Justice, New York.

CHEVIGNY, P., 1972
Cops and rebels: a study of provocation.
New York: Random House, 277–307.

COFFEE, J.C., 1972
Privacy versus *parens patriae:* the role of police records in the sentencing and surveillance of juveniles.
Cornell Law Rev., **57,** 571–620.

COHEN, B., 1972
The police internal system of justice in New York City.
J. Crim. Law, Criminol. & Pol. Sci., **63,** 54–67.

COLUMBIA LAW REVIEW, 1972
Judicial review of military surveillance of civilians: big brother wears modern army green. **72,** 1009–47.

COLUMBIA HUMAN RIGHTS LAW REVIEW, 1972
Juvenile police record-keeping. **4,** 461–84.

COLUMBIA HUMAN RIGHTS LAW REVIEW, 1972
Police surveillance of political dissidents. **4,** 101–41.

COLUMBIA HUMAN RIGHTS LAW REVIEW, 1972
Police use of remote camera systems for surveillance of public streets. **4,** 143–202.

CRAY, E., 1972
The enemy in the streets: police malpractices in America.
New York: Anchor Books.

DEMPSEY, L.J., 1972
The Knapp commission and you.
Police Chiefs, **39**(11), 20–29 and 40(1), 2–36.

HOTIS, J.B., 1972
The Miranda warning during a street encounter.
FBA Law Enforcement Bulletin, Part I (February) 12–14 & Part II (March) 12–15.

HUDSON, J.R., 1972
Organizational aspects of internal and external review of the police.
J. Crim. Law, Criminol. & Pol. Sci., **63**, 427–33.

HUMPHRY, D., 1972
Police power and black people.
London: Panther Books.

JOURNAL OF URBAN LAW, 1972
Field interrogations: court rule and police response. **49**, 767–93.

KNAPP, W., 1972
Report of the Commission to investigate allegations of police corruption and the city's anti-corruption procedures.
(The Knapp Commission Report on Police Corruption).
New York: George Braziller.

KNOOHUISEN, R., FAHEY, R.P., AND PALMER, D.J., 1972
The police and their use of fatal force in Chicago.
Evanston, Ill.: Chicago Law Enforcement Study Group.

MCGOWAN, C., 1972
Rule-making and the police.
Michigan Law Rev., **70**, 659–94.

MOODY, L.A., 1972
Extending the shield of the First Amendment to the outspoken policeman.
Crim. Law Bull., **8**, 171–205.

NEW YORK, CITY OF, 1972
Corruption control manual.
(Issued by Police Commissioner Patrick V. Murphy).
Unpublished. Mimeo.

PRICE, B.R., 1972
Police corruption. An analysis.
Criminology, **10**, 161–76.

UNITED KINGDOM, 1972
Evidence (general). Eleventh Report of the Criminal Law Revision Committee.
London: Cmnd. 4991, 5–16.

UNIVERSITY OF ILLINOIS LAW FORUM, 1972
Police power in Illinois: the regulation of private conduct, 1972, 158–76.

WILCOX, A.F., 1972
The use of discretion in enforcing the law.
Medico-Legal J., **40**, 3–17.

ZANDER, M., 1972
Access to a solicitor in the police station.
Crim. Law Rev., 1972, 342–50.

BARKER, T., AND ROEBUCK, J., 1973
An empirical typology of police corruption: a study in organisational deviance.
Springfield, Ill.: C.C. Thomas.

BOSTON UNIVERSITY LAW REVIEW, 1973
Procedural due process in the context of informal administrative action: the requirements for notice, hearing and prospective standards relating to police selective enforcement practice. **53**, 1038–70.

COOK, F.J., 1973
Organized crime: the strange reluctance, in P. Watters and S. Gillers (eds.), *Investigating the FBI: a tough fair look at the powerful bureau, its present and its future.*
New York: Doubleday & Co., 140–66.

DICKINSON LAW REVIEW, 1973
Justifiable use of deadly force in law enforcement. **78**, 115–35.

DOLAN, T.J., 1973
The case for double jeopardy: black and poor.
Internat. J. Criminol. & Penol., **1**, 129–50.

DONNER, F., 1973
Political informers, in P. Watters and S. Gillers (eds.), *Investigating the FBI: a tough fair look at the powerful bureau, its present and its future.*
New York: Doubleday & Co., 338–68.

EMERSON, T.I., 1973
The FBI as a political police, in P. Watters and S. Gillers (eds.), *Investigating the FBI: a tough fair look at the bureau, its present and its future.*
New York: Doubleday & Co., 239–54.

FORDHAM LAW REVIEW, 1973
Neighborhood patrols and the law: citizens' response to urban crime. **41**, 973–90.

HANSEN, D.A., 1973
Police ethics.
Springfield, Ill.: C.C. Thomas.

HARDING, R.W., AND FAHEY, R.P., 1973
Killings by Chicago police, 1969–70: an empirical study.
Southern Calif. Law Rev., **46,** 284–315.

IOWA LAW REVIEW, 1973
Administrative control of police discretion.
58, 892–973.

JACKSON, B., 1973
The police and the rest of us, a review essay.
Crim. Law Bull., **9,** 416–33.

KOCH, J.V., AND GRUPP, S.E., 1973
Police and illicit drug markets: some economic considerations.
Brit. J. Addict., **68,** 351–62.

LEIGH, L.H., 1973
Prolegomenon to a study of police powers in England and Wales.
Notre Dame Lawyer, **48,** 861–80.

NAVAKSY, V., AND LEWIN, N., 1973
Electronic surveillance, in P. Watters and S. Gillers (eds.), *Investigating the FBI: a tough fair look at the powerful bureau, its present and its future.*
New York: Doubleday & Co., 297–337.

PARSONS, J.C., 1973
A candid analysis of police corruption.
Police Chief, **40**(3), 20–2, 67.

ROCK, P., 1973
Deviant behaviour.
London: Hutchinson, 172–203.

RUCHELMAN, L. (ED), 1973
Who rules of police?
New York: New York Univ. Press.

RULE, J., 1973
Private lives and public surveillance.
London: Allen Lane 44–96.

SIEDEL, G.J., 1973
Injunctive relief for police misconduct in the United States.
J. Urban Law, **50,** 681–99.

WITT, J.W., 1973
Non-coercive interrogation and the administration of criminal justice: the impact of Miranda on police effectuality.
J. Crim. Law & Criminol., **64,** 320–32.

BALDWIN, J., AND MCCONVILLE, M.J., 1974
The acquittal rate of professional criminals: a critical note.
Modern Law Rev., **37,** 439–43 and M. Zander, (1974) A reply, *Modern Law Rev.*, **37,** 444–49.

COWAN, P., EGLESON, N., AND HENTOFF, N., 1974
State secrets: police surveillance in America.
New York: Holt Rinehart & Winston.

GREENAWALT, K., 1974
Perspectives on the right to silence, in R.G. Hood (ed.), *Crime, criminology and public policy: essays in honour of Sir Leon Radzinowicz.*
London: Heinemann, 235–68.

KELLER, R.L., 1974
Police riots: collective violence and law enforcement.
Issues in Criminol., **9,** 147–51.

LEIGH, L.H., 1974
Powers of arrest in relation to vagrancy and related offences.
Crim. Law Rev., 1974, 157–65.

PENNSYLVANIA, COMMONWEALTH OF, 1974
Report on police corruption and the quality of law enforcement in Pennsylvania.
Crime Commission, Commonwealth of Pennsylvania.

ROEBUCK, J.B., AND BARKER, P., 1974
A typology of police corruption.
Social Problems, **21,** 423–37.

SHERMAN, L.W., 1974
Police corruption, a sociological perspective.
New York: Doubleday (Anchor Books).

UNITED KINGDOM, 1974
The handling of complaints against the police: a report. (Chairman, A.D. Gordon-Brown).
London: Home Office, Cmnd. 5582

WILLIAMS, D.G.T., 1974
Prosecution, discretion and the accountability of the police, in R.G. Hood (ed.), *Crime, criminology and public policy: essays in honour of Sir Leon Radzinowicz.*
London: Heinemann, 161–95.

ZANDER, M., 1974
Acquittal rates and not guilty pleas: what do the statistics mean?
Crim. Law Rev., 1974, 401–8.

7 Penal sanctions

1 Aims and scope of penal sanctions

STEPHEN, J.F., 1883
A history of the criminal law of England. Vol. II,
London: Macmillan, 75–93.

DURKHEIM, E., 1893
The division of labour in society.
Glencoe, Ill.: Free Press, 1933, 70–110.

SALEILLES, R., 1913
The individualisation of punishment.
Boston: Little, Brown & Co., 220–313.

FERRI, E., 1921
Preliminary project for an Italian penal code, etc. (trans. E. Betts).
Rome: Ministry of Justice, 181–95, 222–5, 229–40, 268–74.

RUSCHE, G., AND KIRCHHEIMER, O., 1939
Punishment and the social structure.
New York: Columbia Univ. Press.

HALL, J., 1947
General principles of criminal law. 2nd ed.
Indianapolis: Bobbs-Merrill, 600–21.

GLUECK, S., 1952
Principles of a rational penal code, in S. Glueck (ed.), *Crime and correction: selected papers.*
Cambridge, Mass.: Addison-Wesley Press, 72–101.

HARNO, A.J., 1955
Crime and punishment.
J. Crim. Law, Criminol. & Pol. Sci., **45,** 520–3.

AUBERT, V., AND MESSINGER, S.L., 1958
The criminal and the sick.
Inquiry, **1,** 137–60.

HART, H.M., 1958
The aims of the criminal law.
Law & Contemp. Problems, **23,** 401–41.

WILLIAMS, G., 1958
The sanctity of life and the criminal law.
London: Faber.

REDMOUNT, R.S., 1959
Some basic considerations regarding penal policy.
J. Crim. Law, Criminol. & Pol. Sci., **49,** 426–43.

CRIMINAL LAW REVIEW, 1961
Special issue on criminal law and public opinion. 1961, 345–432.

MORRIS, H., (ED.), 1961
Freedom and responsibility: readings in philosophy and law.
California: Stanford Univ. Press, 500–27, 546–7.

SILVING, H., 1961
Rule of law in criminal justice, in G.O.W. Mueller (ed.), *Essays in criminal science.*
London: Sweet & Maxwell, 77–154.

UNITED KINGDOM, 1961
Report of the Inter-Departmental Committee on the business of the criminal courts.
London: Home Office, Cmnd. 1289, 76–85.

CHURCH OF ENGLAND BOARD FOR SOCIAL RESPONSIBILITY, 1963
Punishment.
London: Church Information Office.

HART, H.L.A., 1963
Law, liberty and morality.
London: Oxford Univ. Press.

HEATH, J., 1963
Eighteenth century penal theory.
London: Oxford Univ. Press.

SCHWARTZ, L.B., 1963
Morals offences and the Model Penal Code.
Columbia Law Rev., **63,** 669–86.

WOOTTON, B., 1963
Crime and the criminal law.
London: Stevens, 32–57.

ALLEN, F.A., 1964
The borderland of criminal justice.
Chicago: Univ. Chicago Press.

MORRIS, N., AND HOWARD, C., 1964
Studies in criminal law.
Oxford: Clarendon Press, 154–77.

THOMAS, D.A., 1964
Theories of punishment in the Court of Criminal Appeal.
Mod. Law Rev., **27,** 546–67.

TOBY, J., 1964
Is punishment necessary?
J. Crim. Law, Criminol. & Pol. Sci., **55,** 332–37.

ANCEL, M., 1965
Social defence.
London: Routledge & Kegan Paul, 9–26, 71–87, 191–221.

BALL, H.V., AND FRIEDMAN, L.M., 1965
The use of criminal sanctions in the enforcement of economic legislation: a sociological view.
Stanford Law Rev., **17,** 197–223.

DEVLIN, P., 1965
The enforcement of morals.
London: Oxford Univ. Press.

GINSBERG, M., 1965
On justice in society.
London: Heinemann, 163–91.

PLAYFAIR, G., AND SINGTON, D., 1965
Crime: punishment and cure.
London: Secker & Warburg, 13–94, 156–89.

SCHUR, E.M., 1965
Crimes without victims.
Englewood Cliffs, N.J.: Prentice-Hall, 1–10.

SZASZ, T.S., 1965
Psychiatric justice.
New York: Macmillan.

DWORKIN, R., 1966
Lord Devlin and the enforcement of morals.
Yale Law J., **75,** 986–1005.

EDWARDS, J.Ll.J., 1966
Automatism and social defence.
Crim. Law Quart., **8,** 258–89.

MUELLER, G.O.W., 1966
Punishment, corrections and the law.
Nebraska Law Rev., **45,** 58–98.

RADZINOWICZ, L., 1966
Ideology and crime.
London: Heinemann.

ROGERS, C.H., 1966
Police control of obscene literature.
J. Crim. Law, Criminol. & Pol. Sci., **57,** 430–82.

GERBER, R.J., AND MCANANY, P.D., 1967
Punishment: current survey of philosophy and the law.
St Louis Univ. Law J., **11,** 491–535.

HART, H.L.A., 1967
Social solidarity and the enforcement of morality.
Univ. Chicago Law Rev., **35,** 1–13.

KADISH, S.H., 1967
The crisis of overcriminalisation.
Annals Amer. Acad. Pol. & Soc. Sci., **374,** 157–78.

SKOLNICK, J.H., 1967
Coercion to virtue: a sociological discussion of the enforcement of morals.
A document submitted to the President's Commission on Law Enforcement and Administration of Justice, Washington, D.C. Mimeo.

CHRISTIE, N., 1968
Changes in penal values.
Scandinavian Studies in Criminology, **2.**
London: Tavistock.

GOLDSTEIN, J., 1968
Psychoanalysis and jurisprudence.
Yale Law J., **77,** 1053–77.

GUSFIELD, J.S., 1968
On legislating morals; the symbolic process of designating deviance.
Calif. Law Rev., **56,** 54–73.

HART, H.L.A., 1968
Punishment and responsibility: essays in the philosophy of law.
Oxford: Clarendon Press, 1–27, 210–37.

MOBERLEY, SIR W., 1968
The ethics of punishment.
London: Faber.

WALKER, N., 1968
Crime and punishment in Britain.
Rev. ed. Edinburgh: Univ. Press, 124–44.

ACTON, H.B., (ED.), 1969
The philosophy of punishment.
London: Macmillan.

HONDERICH, T., 1969
Punishment, the supposed justifications.
London: Hutchinson.

PACKER, H.L., 1969
The limits of the criminal sanction.
California: Stanford Univ. Press.

PODGÓRECKI, A., 1969
Laws and morals in theory and operation.
Polish Sociolog. Bulletin, **1,** 26–38.

REMINGTON, F.J., 1969
Review of *Discretionary justice: a preliminary inquiry* by K.C. Davis.
Univ. Chicago Law Rev., **36,** 884–902.

WALKER, N., 1969
Sentencing in a rational society.
London: Allen Lane, Penguin Press, 1–42.

BURCHELL, E.M., AND HUNT, P.M.A., 1970
South African criminal law and procedure, I.
South Africa: Juta & Co., 67–80.

DAVIES, J.C., 1970
The politics of pollution.
New York: Pegasus.

FRIEDMAN, L., 1970
Political power and legal legitimacy: a short history of political trials.
Antioch Rev., **30,** 157–70.

GRIFFITHS, J., 1970
Ideology in criminal procedure, *or* a trend 'model' of the criminal process.
Yale Law J., **79,** 359–417.

JACOB B.R., 1970
Reparation or restitution by the criminal offender to his victim: applicability of an ancient concept in the modern correctional process.
J. Crim. Law, Criminol. & Pol. Sci., **61,** 152–67.

LASTER, R.E., 1970
Criminal restitution: a survey of its past history and an analysis of its present usefulness
Univ. Richmond Law Rev., **5,** 71–98.

MCGONAGLE, J.J.JR., 1970
Emergency detention acts: peacetime suspension of civil rights—with a postscript on the recent Canadian crisis.
Catholic U. Law Rev., **20,** 203–36.

STANMEYER, W.A., 1970
The jurisprudence of radical change: Herbert Marcuse's 'great refusal' vs. political due process.
St. John's Law Rev., **45,** 1–38.

AMERICAN FRIENDS SERVICE COMMITTEE, 1971
Struggle for justice.
New York: Hill & Wang.

ANTTILA, I., 1971
Conservative and radical criminal policy in the Nordic countries, in *Scandinavian Studies in Criminology*, **3.**
Oslo: Universitetsforlaget, 9–21.

DOLESCHAL, E., 1971
Victimless crime.
Crime & Delinq. Lit., **3,** 254–69.

DWORKIN, G., 1971
Paternalism, in R.A. Wasserstrom (ED.), *Morality and the law.*
Belmont, Calif.: Wadsworth Publ. Co., 107–26.

EHRENZWEIG, A., 1971
Psychoanalytic jurisprudence.
Dobbs Ferry, N.Y.: Oceana Publishers.

GOULD, L.C., AND NAMENWIRTH, J.Z., 1971
Contrary objectives: crime control and the rehabilitation of criminals, in J.D. Douglas (ed.), *Crime and justice in American society.*
New York: Bobbs-Merrill Co., 237–67.

GREENAWALT, K., 1971
Criminal law and population control.
Vanderbilt Law Rev., **24,** 465–523.

GRUPP, S.E. (ED.), 1971
Theories of punishment.
Bloomington, Ind.: Indiana University Press.

HADDEN, T., 1971
Contract, tort and crime: the forms of legal thought.
Law Quart. Rev., **87,** 240–60.

HOGARTH, J., 1971
Sentencing as a human process.
Univ. Toronto Press, 68–93.

PACIFIC LAW JOURNAL, 1971
Sexual freedom for consenting adults—why not? **2,** 206–25.

UNIVERSITY OF ILLINOIS LAW FORUM, 1971
Symposium, privacy and the law, 1971, 137–78.

ANTTILA, I., 1972
Punishment versus treatment—is there a third alternative?
Abstracts on Criminology and Penology, **12**, 287–90.

BARNES, H.E., 1972
The story of punishment, a record of man's inhumanity to man.
2nd ed. revised.
Montclair, N.J.: Patterson Smith.

DERSHOWITZ, A.M., 1972.
Wiretaps and national security.
Commentary, **53**(1), 56–61.

DURANT, M., THOMAS, M., AND WILCOCK, H.D., 1972
Crime, criminals and the law.
London: Office of Population Censuses and Surveys, Social Survey Division, 174–211.

EZORSKY, G. (ED.), 1972
Philosophical perspectives on punishment.
Albany: State Univ. of New York Press.

FORCE, R., 1972
Decriminalisation of Breach of the Peace Statute: a nonpenal approach to order maintenance.
Tulane Law Rev., **46**, 367–493.

GEIS, G., 1972
Not the law's business? An examination of homosexuality, abortion, prostitution, narcotics and gambling in the United States.
Crime and Delinquency Issues.
A monograph series. Washington, D.C.

GERBER, R.J., AND MCANANY, P.D. (EDS.), 1972
Contemporary punishment: views, explanations, and justifications.
Notre Dame, Ind.: Univ. Notre Dame Press.

HAKMAN, N., 1972
Political trials in the legal order: a political scientist's perspective.
J. Public Law., **21**, 73–126.

JUNKER, J.M., 1972
Criminalisation and criminogenesis.
UCLA Law Rev., **19**, 697–714.

KADISH, S.H., 1972
More on overcriminalisation: a reply to Professor Junker.
UCLA Law Rev., **19**, 719–22.

REVUE DE DROIT PÉNAL ET DE CRIMINOLOGIE, 1972
Les Frontières de la répression, Congrès international de criminologie organisé du 15 au 18 mars 1972. 1–350.

SEYMOUR, W.N.JR., 1972
Major surgery for the criminal courts?
Brooklyn Law Rev., **38**, 571–85.

SKOLNICK, J.H., 1972
Criminalisation and criminogenesis: a reply to Professor Junker.
U.C.L.A. Law Rev., **19**, 715–18.

SPAETH, Hon. E.B.JR., 1972
A response to 'Struggle for Justice'.
Prison J., **52**(1), 4–32.

UNITED KINGDOM, 1972
Report of the Departmental Committee on Section 2 of the Official Secrets Act 1911 (Chairman, Lord Franks), **1.**
London: Cmnd. 5104, 46–65.

UNITED KINGDOM, 1972
The penalties for homicide.
Report by the Committee appointed by the Secretary of State for Scotland and the Lord Advocate, Scottish Home and Health Department, Edinburgh: Cmnd. 5137.

UNITED STATES OF AMERICA, 1972
Supreme Court of the United States.
Furman v. Georgia, 69–5003, 29 June 1972.

WHEELER, M.E., 1972
Towards a theory of limited punishment: an examination of the Eighth amendment.
Stanford Law Rev., **24**, 838–73

BAGLEY, C., 1973
Social policy and the prevention of suicidal behaviour.
Brit. J. Social Wk., **3**, 473–95.

BLUMSTEIN, A., AND COHEN, J., 1973
A theory of the stability of punishment.
J. Crim. Law & Criminol., **64**, 198–207.

HERMANN, D.H.J., 1973
The evil Christ crucified: the ritual function of punishment.
Wayne Law Rev., **19**, 1409–55.

KAUPEN, W., 1973
Public opinion of the law in a democratic society, in A. Podgórecki, W. Kaupen, J. Van Houtte, P. Vinke and B. Kutchinsky.

Knowledge and opinion about law.
London: Martin Robertson, 43–64.

MacCormick, N., 1973
Justice according to Rawls.
Law Quart. Rev., **89**, 355, 393–417.

Morris, N., 1973
The future of imprisonment.
Aust. & N.Z. J. Criminol., **6**, 200–13.

Murphy, J.G., 1973
Marxism and retribution.
Philosophy & Public Affairs, **2**, 217.

Podgórecki, A., 1973
Public opinion on law, in A. Podgórecki, W. Kaupen, J. Van Houtte, P. Vinke and B. Kutchinsky, *Knowledge and opinion about law.*
London: Martin Robertson, 65–100.

Rock, P., 1973
Deviant behaviour.
London: Hutchinson, 122–71.

Smith, J.C., and Hogan, B., 1973
Criminal law. 3rd edition.
London: Butterworth, 3–16.

United Kingdom, 1973
Penalty for murder. Twelfth Report, Criminal Law Revision Committee.
London: Cmnd. 5184.

Van Houtte, J., and Vinke, P., 1973
Attitudes governing the acceptance of legislation among various social groups, in A. Podgórecki, W. Kaupen, J. Van Houtte, P. Vinke and B. Kutchinsky, *Knowledge and opinion about law.*
London: Martin Robertson, 13–42.

Votey, H.L., Jr., and Phillips, L., 1973
Social goals and appropriate policy for corrections: an economic appraisal.
J. Crim. Justice, **1**, 219–40.

Albany Law Review, 1974
Control of incohate crime—New York anti-loitering statute declared unconstitutional. **38**, 363–85.

Ancel, M., 1974
The relationship between criminology and 'politique criminelle', in R.G. Hood (ed.), *Crime, criminology and public policy: essays in honour of Sir Leon Radzinowicz.*
London: Heinemann 269–280.

Bayles M.D. 1974
Criminal paternalism in J.R. Pennock and J.W. Chapman (eds.), *The limits of law, Nomos*, **15**,
New York: Lieber-Atherton, 174–88.

Christie, N., 1964
Utility and social values in court decisions in punishment, in R.G. Hood (ed), *Crime, criminology and public policy: essays in honour of Sir Leon Radzinowicz.*
London: Heinemann, 281–296.

Finer, J.J., and Grant, P.H., 1974
Regulation and prohibition of sensual performances under non obscenity statutes.
Crim. Law Bull., **10**, 717–36.

Hood, R., 1974
Tolerance and the tariff: some reflections in fixing the time prisoners serve in custody.
London: National Association for the Care and Resettlement of Offenders, Papers and Reprints, No. 11.

Mäkelä, K., 1974
The societal tasks of the penal system.
Scandinavian Studies in Criminology, **5**.
London: Martin Robertson, 47–65.

Podgórecki, A., 1974
Jurisprudence empirically tested, in R.G. Hood (ed.), *Crime, criminology and public policy: essays in honour of Sir Leon Radzinowicz*,
London: Heinemann, 297–517.

Schafer, S., 1974
The political criminal: the problem of morality and crime.
New Jersey: Free Press.

Southern California Law Review, 1974
Asexual reproduction and genetic engineering: a constitutional assessment of the technology of cloning. **47**, 476–584.

Tittle, C.R., 1974
Prisons and rehabilitation: the inevitability of disfavor.
Social Problems, **21**, 385–95.

West, D.J., 1974
Thoughts on sex law reform, in R.G. Hood (ed.), *Crime, criminology and public policy: essays in honour of Sir Leon Radzinowicz.*
London: Heinemann, 469–87.

2 The problem of conflicting values in the implementation of penal sanctions

[See also Section 12 on new experiments in the treatment of offenders; Section 13 on parole selection and indeterminate sentences; Section 14 for references bearing on the status of prisoners.]

FERRI, E., 1921
Preliminary project for an Italian penal code, (trans. E. Betts).
Rome: Ministry of Justice, 181–95, 222–5, 229–40, 268–74.

BURGESS, E.W., BRUCE, A.A., HARNO, A.J., AND LANDESCO, J., 1928
The workings of the indeterminate sentence law and the parole system in Illinois.
Chicago, Ill.: Parole Board.

HARVARD LAW REVIEW, 1937
Indeterminate sentence laws—the adolescence of peno-correctional legislation.
50, 677–87.

MICHAEL, J., AND WECHSLER, H., 1940
Criminal law and its administration.
Chicago: Foundation Press, 983–1053.

MANNHEIM, H., 1946
Criminal justice and social reconstruction.
London: Kegan Paul, 219–37.

RUCK, S.K. (ED.), 1951
Paterson on prisons; collected papers of Sir A. Paterson.
London: F. Muller, 52–66.

GLUECK, S., 1952
Significant transformation in the administration of criminal justice, in S. Glueck (ed.), *Crime and correction: selected papers.*
Cambridge, Mass.: Addison-Wesley Press, 27–53.

UNITED NATIONS, 1954
The indeterminate sentence.
New York: Department of Social Affairs, ST/SOA/SD2.

MICHAEL, J., AND WECHSLER, H., 1956
1956 *supplement to Michael & Wechsler, Criminal law and its administration.*
Chicago: Foundation Press, 246–61.

TAPPAN, P.W., 1957
Young adults under the Youth Authority.
J. Crim. Law, Criminol. & Pol. Sci., **47,** 629–46.

GLUECK, S., 1958
Predictive devices and the individualization of justice.
Law & Contemp. Problems, **23,** 461–76.

GUTTMACHER, M.S., 1958
The psychiatric approach to crime and correction.
Law & Contemp. Problems, **23,** 633–49.

HAKEEM, M., 1958
A critique for the psychiatric approach to crime and correction.
Law & Contemp. Problems, **23,** 650–82.

HEYNER, N., 1958
Sentencing by an administrative board. *Law & Contemp. Problems*, **23,** 477–94

TAPPAN, P.W., 1958
Sentencing under the Model Penal Code.
Law & Contemp. Problems, **23,** 528–43

LITTLE, A., 1960
The indeterminate sentence.
Brit. J. Delinq., **10,** 217–19.

TAPPAN, P.W., 1960
Crime, justice and correction.
New York: McGraw-Hill, 455–75.

SILVING, H., 1961
'Rule of law' in criminal justice, in G.O.W. Mueller (ed.), *Essays in criminal science.*
London: Sweet and Maxwell, 77–154.

UNITED KINGDOM, 1963
Preventive detention (Report of the Advisory Council on the Treatment of Offenders).
London: Home Office, 23–9.

HALL WILLIAMS, J.E., 1964
Alternatives to definite sentences.
Law Quart. Rev., **80,** 41–62.

NEWMAN, C.L., 1964
Sourcebook on probation, parole and pardons.
Illinois: C.C. Thomas, 194–229.

CHRISTIE, N., 1965
Temperance boards and interinstitutional dilemmas: a case study of a welfare law.
Social Problems, **12,** 415–28.

GOULD, D.B., AND HURWITZ, I.L., 1965
Out of tune with the times: the Massachusetts SDP statute.
Boston Univ. Law Rev., **45,** 391–410.

HADDEN, T., 1965
A plea for punishment.
Cambridge Law J., 1965, 117–36.

MURRAH, A.P., AND RUBIN, S., 1965
Penal reform and the Model Sentencing Act.
Columbia Law Rev., **65,** 1167–79.

RUBIN, S., 1965
Psychiatry and criminal law.
New York: Oceana Publications, 88–201.

STERNBERG, D., 1965
Legal frontiers in prison group psychotherapy.
J. Crim. Law, Criminol. & Pol. Sci., **56,** 446–49.

BARKIN, E.N., 1966
The emergence of correctional law and the awareness of the rights of the convicted.
Nebraska Law Rev., **45,** 669–89.

LOPEZ-REY, M., 1966
Release and provisional release of sentenced prisoners.
Brit. J. Criminol., **6,** 236–68.

HALLECK, S., 1968
American psychiatry and the criminal.
Int. J. Psychiat., **6,** 185–208.

RITTS, R.E., 1968
A physician's view of informed consent in human experimentation.
Fordham Law Rev., **36,** 631–38.

SKOLNICK, J.H., 1968
Coercion to virtue: the enforcement of morals.
Southern Calif. Law Rev., **41,** 588–641.

BROOKS, A.D., 1969
Marijuana and the constitution: individual liberties and puritan virtues, in J.R. Wittenborn, H. Brill, J.P. Smith and S.A. Wittenborn (eds.), *Drugs and youth: Proceedings of the Rutgers symposium on drug abuse.*
Springfield, Ill.: C.C. Thomas, 280–98.

BUCHER, B., 1969
Some ethical issues in the therapeutic use of punishment, in R.D. Rubin and C.M. Franks (eds.), *Advances in behavior therapy, 1968.*
New York: Academic Press, 59–72.

DAVIS, K.C., 1969
Discretionary justice. A preliminary inquiry.
Baton Rouge: Louisiana State University Press, 215–33.

GRANUCCI, A.F., 1969
'Nor cruel and unusual punishments inflicted': the original meaning.
Calif. Law Rev., **57,** 839–65.

GREENAWALT, K., 1969
'Uncontrollable' actions and the eighth amendment: implications of Powell v. Texas.
Columbia Law Rev., **69,** 927–79.

KATZ, A., 1969
Dangerousness: a theoretical reconstruction of the criminal law.
Buffalo Law Rev., **19,** 1–33.

MORRIS, G.H., 1969
'Criminality' and the right to treatment.
Univ. Chicago Law Rev., **36,** 784–801.

PIRSIG, M.E., 1969
The constitutional validity of confining disruptive delinquents in penal institutions.
Minnesota Law Rev., **54,** 101–45.

ROBITSCHER, J., 1969
The right of society to protect its members, in J.R. Wittenborn, H. Brill, J.P. Smith and S.A. Wittenborn (eds.), *Drugs and youth: Proceedings of the Rutgers symposium on drug abuse.*
Springfield, Ill.: C.C. Thomas, 299–311.

SCHWITZGEBEL, R.K., 1969
Issues in the use of an electronic rehabilitation system with chronic recidivists.
Law & Society Rev., **3,** 597–615.

STEIN, P.M., 1969
Imprisonment for nonpayment of fines and costs: a new look at the law and the constitution.
Vanderbilt Law Rev., **22,** 611–44.

WESTEN, D.A., 1969
Fines, imprisonment, and the poor: 'thirty dollars or thirty days'.
Calif. Law Rev., **57,** 778–821.

AMERICAN SERIES OF FOREIGN PENAL CODES, 1970
The Greenland criminal code.
New Jersey: Fred B. Rothman & Co., 1–12.

BLUMBERG, A.S. (ED.), 1970
The scales of justice.
Chicago: Aldine Publishing Co., 1–29.

CORRECTIONAL ASSOCIATION OF NEW YORK, 1970
Recommendations to the 1970 Legislature.
New York: Mimeo.

GRIFFITHS, J., 1970
Ideology in criminal procedure or a third 'model' of the criminal process.
Yale Law J., **79,** 359–417.

FRIED, C., 1970
An anatomy of values: problems of personal and social choice.
Cambridge, Mass.: Harvard Univ. Press, 116–52.

HARVARD LAW REVIEW, 1970
Requiring a criminal defendant to submit to a government psychiatric examination: an invasion of the privilege against self-incrimination, **83,** 648–71.

JUSTICE, 1970
Privacy and the law.
A report by Justice.
London: Stevens & Sons, 27–41.

MEADOR, C.K., 1970
The mind of the physician, or why lawyers have trouble with doctors.
Albama Law Rev., **22,** 495–502.

MEADOR, D.J., 1970
The mind of the lawyer, or why doctors should not have trouble with lawyers.
Albama Law Rev., **22,** 503–12.

NEW YORK LAW FORUM, 1970
The XYY syndrome: a challenge to our system of criminal responsibility. **16,** 232–62.

NATIONAL OPINION POLLS, MARKET RESEARCH LTD., 1970
Report on attitudes towards crime, violence, and permissiveness in society.
London: Mimeo. 12–20.

SCHWENDINGER H. AND SCHWENDINGER, J. 1970
Defenders of order or guardians of human rights?
Issues in Criminol., **5,** 123–57.

SOLURSH, L.P., AND SOLURSH, M.J., 1970
Illusinogenic drugs. Their effects on criminal responsibility.
Toronto: Canadian Mental Health Association.

TAPP, J.L., AND LEVINE, F.J., 1970
Persuasion to virtue: a preliminary statement.
Law & Society Rev., **4,** 565–82.

TINGLER, R.A., 1970
Unconstitutional punishment.
Crim. Law Bulletin., **6,** 311–29.

UNIVERSITY OF PENNSYLVANIA LAW REVIEW, 1970
Equal protection and prison-to-hospital transfers:
United States ex rel. Schuster v. Herold. **118,** 410–23.

AMERICAN FRIENDS SERVICE COMMITTEE, 1971
Struggle for justice, a report on crime and punishment in America.
New York: Hill and Wang, 34–47, 83–123.

BLACK, C.L.JR., 1971
The crisis in capital punishment.
Maryland Law Rev., **31,** 289–311.

COLUMBIA LAW REVIEW, 1971
Fining the indigent. **71,** 1281–1308.

DUFFEE, D., AND O'LEARY, V., 1971
Models of correction: an entry in the Packer-Griffiths debate.
Crim. Law Bull., **7,** 329–52.

IOWA LAW REVIEW, 1971
Punishment of narcotic addicts for possession: a cruel but usual punishment. **56,** 578–97.

KITTRIE, N.N., 1971
The right to be different.
Baltimore, Md.: Johns Hopkins Press, 1–49, 340–410.

MILTON, J.R.L., AND FULLER, N.M., 1971
South African criminal law and procedure. III.
South Africa: Juta & Co., 104–37, 329–43.

MODERN LAW REVIEW, 1971
Immigration and the criminal courts, **34,** 135–48.

ROCKEFELLER, W., 1971
Executive clemency and the Death Penalty.
Catholic Univ. Law Rev., **21,** 94–102.

UNIVERSITY OF ILLINOIS LAW FORUM, 1971
Pretrial psychiatric examinations and the privilege against self-incrimination, 1971, 232–56.

VIGH, J., 1971
Grouping of recidivists and the indefinite term of imprisonment.
Annales Universitatis Scientiarum Budapestinensis de Rolando Eötvös nominatae, **13,** 159–79.

VUKOWICH, W.T., 1971
The dawning of the brave new world—legal, ethical ,and social issues of eugenics.
Univ. Illinois Law Forum, 1971, 189–231.

WALLACH, A., AND RUBIN, L., 1971
The premenstrual syndrome and criminal responsibility.
UCLA Law Rev., **19,** 210–312.

ALBANY LAW REVIEW, 1972
Legal aspects of euthanasia. **36,** 674–97.

ENNIS, B.J., 1972
Prisoners of psychiatry: mental patients, psychiatrists and the law.
New York: Harcourt Brace.

FINGARETTE, H., 1972
The meaning of criminal insanity.
Berkeley, Los Angeles: Univ. of California Press, 53–120.

HARVARD LAW REVIEW, 1972
Cruel and unusual punishments, the death penalty. **86,** 76–85.

HIRST, P.Q., 1972
Marx and Engels on crime, law and morality.
Economy & Society, **1,** 28–56.

IOWA LAW REVIEW, 1972
Mental suffering under sentence of death: a cruel and unusual punishment, **57,** 814–33.

LEROY, D.H., 1972
The potential criminal liability of human sex clinics and their patients.
St Louis Univ. Law J., **16,** 586–603.

MILLER, H.S., 1972
The lawyer's hang-up: due process versus the real issue.
Amer. Crim. Law Rev., **11,** 197–215.

PRETTYMAN, E.B., JR., 1972
The indeterminate sentence and the right to treatment.
Amer. Crim. Law Rev., **11,** 7–37.

SCHWITZGEBEL, R.K., 1972
Limitations on the coercive treatment of offenders.
Crim. Law Bull., **8,** 267–320.

SHAPIRO, M.H., 1972
The uses of behavior control technologies: a response.
Issues in Criminol., **7,** 55–93.

SPAETH, HON. E.B.JR., 1972
A response to 'Struggle for Justice'.
Prison J., **52**(1), 4–32.

SPECE, R.G. JR., 1972
Conditioning and other technologies used to 'treat?' 'rehabilitate?' 'demolish?' prisoners and mental patients.
Southern Calif. Law Rev., **45,** 616–81.

UNITED STATES OF AMERICA, 1972
Supreme Court of the United States.
Furman v. Georgia, 69–5003, 29 June 1972.

VERSELE, S.C., GOFFIN, R., TSAMADOU, C.H.R., LEGROS, P., AND VAN HAECHT, A., 1972–3
Justice pénale et opinion publique.
Bruxelles: l'Université de Bruxelles.

WESTIN, A.F., AND BAKER, M.A., 1972
Databanks in a free society, computers, record-keeping and privacy.
New York: Quadrangle Books, 47–64, 241–79.

WEXLER, D.B., 1972
Therapeutic justice.
Minnesota Law Rev., **57,** 289–338.

WHEELER, M.E., 1972
Towards a theory of limited punishment: an examination of the eight amendment.
Stanford Law Rev., **24,** 838–73.

ZIMRING, F.E., 1972
The medium is the message: firearm caliber as a determinant of death from assault.
J. Legal Studies, **1,** 97–123.

ALBANY LAW REVIEW, 1973
The death penalty—the alternatives left after Furman v. Georgia. **37,** 344–64.

CHANDLER, J.A., AND ROSE, S.F., 1973
The constitutional dilemma of a person predisposed to criminal behavior.
Vanderbilt Law Rev., **26,** 69–103.

DERSHOWITZ, A.M., 1973
Preventive confinement: a suggested framework for constitutional analysis.
Texas Law Rev., **51,** 1277–1324.

EHRHARDT, C.W., HUBBART, P.A., LEVINSON, L.H., SMILEY, W.McK.JR., AND WILLS, T.A., 1973
The future of capital punishment in Florida: analysis and recommendations.
J. Crim. Law & Criminol., **64,** 2–21.

FLEW, A., 1973
Crime or disease?
London: Macmillan.

JOURNAL OF CRIMINAL LAW AND CRIMINOLOGY, 1973
Capital punishment after Furman, **64**(3), 281–89.

MELTSNER, M., 1973
Cruel and unusual: the supreme court and capital punishment.
New York: Random House, 266–316.

MILLER, W.B., 1973
Ideology and criminal justice policy: some current issues.
J. Crim. Law & Criminol., **64,** 141–62.

MITFORD, J., 1973
Kind and usual punishment, the prison business.
New York: Alfred A. Knopf, 79–168.

MORRIS, N., 1973
The future of imprisonment.
Aust. & N.Z.J. Criminol., **6,** 200–13.

MURPHY, J.G., 1973
Marxism and retribution.
Philosophy & Public Affairs, **2,** 217.

PERROTT, D.L., 1973
The logic of fundamental rights, in J.W. Bridge, D. Lasok, D.L. Perrott and R.O. Plender (eds.), *Fundamental rights.*
London: Sweet & Maxwell, 1–14.

REASONS, C.E., 1973
The politicizing of crime, the criminal and the criminologist.
J. Crim. Law & Criminol., **64,** 471–77.

RENN, D.E., 1973
The right to treatment and the juvenile.
Crime & Delinq., **19,** 477–84.

SCHUR, E.M., 1973
Radical nonintervention: rethinking the delinquency problem.
Englewood Cliffs, N.J.: Prentice-Hall, 3–114.

SOUTHERN CALIFORNIA LAW REVIEW, 1973
Drug control of school children: the child's right to choose. **46,** 585–616.

WILLIAMS, G., 1973
Euthanasia.
Medical-Legal J., **41,** 14–34.

ALLEN, F.A., 1974
The crime of politics, political dimensions of criminal justice.
Cambridge, Mass.: Harvard Univ. Press.

AMOS, W.E., 1974
The philosophy of corrections: revisited.
Fed. Probation, **38**(1), 43–6.

BARRISH, I.J., 1974
Ethical issues and answers to behavior modification.
Corrective & Social Psychiat., **20**(2), 30–7.

BUCHHOLZ, E., HARTMANN, R., LEKSCHAS, J., AND STILLER, G., 1974
Socialist criminology: theoretical and methodological foundations.
Lexington, Mass.: Saxon House, 201–44.

COHEN, S., 1974
A futuristic scenario for the prison system, in F. Basaglia (ed.), *The Crimes of peace.*
Turin: Einaudi.

FLOUD, J., 1974
Sociology and the theory of responsibility: 'social background' as an excuse for crime, in R. Fletcher (ed.), *The Science of society and unity of mankind, a memorial volume for Morris Ginsberg.*
London: Heinemann, 204–221.

DERSHOWITZ, A., 1974
Toward a jurisprudence of 'harm prevention', in J.R. Pennock and J.W. Chapman (eds.), *The limits of Law, Nomos,* **15.**
New York: Lieber-Atherton, 135–58, (and comment by M.P. Golding, 168–73 and S.L. Wasby, Beyond Dershowitz: limits in attempting to secure change, 159–67).

ECKHOFF, T., 1974
Justice. Its determinants in social interaction.
Rotterdam Univ. Press. 167–201.

MIDGLEY, J., 1974
Public opinion and the death penalty in South Africa.
Brit. J. Criminol., **14,** 345–58.

MORRIS, N., 1974
The future of imprisonment.
Chicago: Univ. Chicago Press, 28–84.

OPTON, E.M., 1974
Psychiatric violence against prisoners: when therapy is punishment.
Mississippi Law J., **45,** 605–44.

REGAN, D.H., 1974
Justifications for paternalism, in J.R. Pennock and J.W. Chapman (eds.), *The limits of Law, Nomos,* **15.**
New York: Lieber-Atherton, 189–210.

BURT, R.A., 1975
Why we should keep prisoners from the doctors.
The Hastings Center Report, **5**(1), 25–34.

ROTHMAN, D.J., 1975
Behavior modification in total institutions.
The Hastings Center Report, **5**(1), 17–24.

WILKINS, L.T., 1975
Putting 'treatment' on trial.
The Hastings Center Report, **5**(1), 35–48.

3 Problems posed by special categories of offender

(*a*) *Psychopaths, sexual and dangerous offenders*

MYERSON, A., AYER, J.B., PUTNAM, T., KEELER, C.E., AND ALEXANDER, L., 1936
Eugenical sterilization: a re-orientation of the problem.
A report by a Committee of the American Neurological Association.
New York: Macmillan, 1–68, 177–83.

SUTHERLAND, E.H., 1950
The sexual psychopath law.
J. Crim. Law, Criminol. & Pol. Sci., **40,** 543–54 (and K. Schuessler (ed.), (1973), *Edwin H. Sutherland, on analysing crime.*
Chicago: Univ. of Chicago Press, 185–99).

TAPPAN, P.W., 1950
The habitual sex offender.
Report and recommendations of the New Jersey Commission on the Habitual Sex Offender, as formulated by P.W. Tappan.
New Jersey.

TAPPAN, P.W., 1951
Sentencing for sex criminals.
J. Crim. Law, Criminol. & Pol. Sci., **42,** 332–37.

UNITED KINGDOM, 1953
Report of the Royal Commission on Capital Punishment, 1949–1953.
London: Cmnd. 8932, 226–31 (paras 644–57).

GIBBENS, T.C.N., POND, D.A., AND STAFFORD-CLARK, D., 1955
A follow-up study of criminal psycopaths.
Brit. J. Delinq., **6,** 126–36.

GUTTMACHER, M.S., 1955
Principal difficulties with the present criteria of responsibility and possible alternatives, in *Model Penal Code, Tentative Draft No.* 4, 170–81; and correspondence with H. Wechser, 182–92, Philadelphia: American Law Institute.

TAPPAN, P.W., 1955
Some myths about the sex offender.
Fed. Probation, **19**(2), 7–12.

LE MAIRE, L., 1956
Danish experiences regarding the castration of sexual offenders.
J. Crim. Law, Criminol. & Pol. Sci., **47**, 294–310.

BREMER, J., 1959
Asexualization. A follow-up study of 244 cases.
New York: Macmillan, 1–36, 189–281, 301–22.

GOULD, J., 1959
The psychiatry of major crime.
J. Mental Science., **3**, 303–51.

WOOTTON, B., 1959
Social science and social pathology.
London: Allen & Unwin, 203–67.

GOLDSTEIN, J., AND KATZ, J., 1960
Dangerousness and mental illness. Some observations on the decision to release persons acquitted by reason of insanity.
Yale Law J., **70**, 225–39.

SCOTT, P.D., 1960
The treatment of psychopaths.
Brit. Med. J., **1**, 1641–5.

STÜRUP, G.K., 1960
Sex offences: the Scandinavian experience.
Law & Contemp. Problems, **25**, 361–75.

GUTTMACHER, M.S., 1963
Dangerous offenders.
Crime & Delinq., **9**, 381–90.

HALL, J., 1963
The purposes of a system for the administration of criminal justice.
Lecture delivered at Georgetown Univ. Law Center, 9 Oct. 1963. Mimeo.

HALLER, M.H., 1963
Eugenics: hereditarian attitudes in American thought.
New Brunswick, N.J.: Rutgers Univ. Press.

LEVASSEUR, G., 1963
Abnormal offenders, in C. Andersen *et al.*, *Mentally abnormal offenders*, 59–82.
Seminar organized at Bellagio, April 21–25, 1963, by the Association internationale de pénal, Fondation internationale pénale et pénitentiaire, Société internationale de criminologie, Société internationale de défense sociale.

TAYLOR, F.H., 1963
The treatment of delinquent psychopaths.
Howard J., **11**, 84–92.

WEST, D.J., 1963
The habitual prisoner.
London: Macmillan, 20–33, 60–75.

FOX, R., 1964
Sin, crime and the psychopath.
Medico-legal problems of psychopathic personality.
Modern Law Rev., **27**, 190–98.

BLIGH, R., 1965
Sterilization and mental retardation.
Amer. Bar Assn J., **51**, 1059–63.

BOWMAN, K.M., AND ENGLE, B., 1965
Sexual psychopath laws, in R. Slovenko (ed.), *Sexual behavior and the law.*
Illinois: C.C. Thomas, 757–78.

CONRAD, J.P., 1965
Crime and its correction.
London: Tavistock, 212–36.

CRAFT, M., 1965
Ten studies into psychopathic personality.
Bristol: John Wright & Sons, 7–32.

DAVIDSON, H.A., 1965
Forensic psychiatry, (psychiatric glossary for lawyers) 2nd ed.
New York: Ronald Press Co., 401–24.

GEBHARD, P.H., GAGNON, J.H., POMEROY, W.B., AND CHRISTENSON, C.V., 1965
Sex offenders.
New York: Harper & Row, 693–875.

GOULD, D.B., AND HURWITZ, I.L., 1965
Out of tune with the times: the Massachusetts SDP statute.
Boston Univ. Law Rev., **45**, 391–410.

GRAY, K.G., AND MOHR, J.W., 1965
Follow-up of male sexual offenders, in R. Slovenko (ed.), *Sexual behavior and the law.*
Illinois: C.C. Thomas, 742–56.

ORNO, A.M., 1965
Social, psychological and surgical treatment for sexual and chronic criminals.
Canad. J. Corrections, **7**, 415–22.

CRAFT, M. (ED.), 1966
Psychopathic disorders.
Oxford: Pergamon Press, 1–81, 105–226.

NASATIR, M., DEZZANI, D., AND SILBERT, M., 1966
Atascadero: ramifications of a maximum security treatment institution.
Issues in Criminology, **2**, 29–46.

PLOSCOWE, M., 1966
Sex offences in the new penal law.
Brooklyn Law Rev., **32**, 274–86.

ROCHE, M.R., 1966
The plight of the sexual psychopath: a legislative blunder and judicial acquiescence.
Notre Dame Lawyer, **41**, 527–56.

CRAIG, R., 1967
Sexual psychopath legislation.
A document submitted to the President's Commission on Law Enforcement and Administration of Justice, Washington, D.C. Mimeo.

BURICK, L.T., 1968
An analysis of the Illinois Sexually Dangerous Persons Act.
J. Crim. Law, Criminol. & Pol. Sci., **59**, 254–66.

MORRIS, N., 1968
Psychiatry and the dangerous criminal.
Southern Calif. Law Rev., **41**, 514–47.

REUCK, A.V.S., DE, AND PORTER, R., 1968
The mentally abnormal offender.
A Ciba Foundation Symposium.
London: J. & A. Churchill.

RITTS, R.E., 1968
A physician's view of informed consent in human experimentation.
Fordham Law Rev., **36**, 631–38.

STÜRUP, G.K., 1968
Treating the 'untreatable' chronic criminals at Herstedvester.
Baltimore: Johns Hopkins Press.

WEST, D.J. (ED.), 1968
Psychopathic offenders.
University of Cambridge: Institute of Criminology.

BANCROFT, J., 1969
Aversion therapy of homosexuality: a pilot study of 10 cases.
Brit. J. Psychiat., **115**, 1417–31.

CANADA, 1969
Toward unity: criminal justice and corrections.
Report of the Canadian Committee on Corrections.
Ottawa: Queen's Printer, 241–71.

KATZ, A., 1969 AND 1972
Dangerousness: a theoretical reconstruction of the criminal law.
Buffalo Law Rev., Part I, **19**, 1–33; Part II, **21**, 603–40.

LOW, P.W., 1969
Special offender sentencing.
Amer. Crim. Law Quart., **8**, 70–104.

WEST, D.J., (ED) 1969
Criminological implications of chromosome abnormalities.
University of Cambridge: Institute of Criminology. 100–7.

EKBLOM, B., 1970
Acts of violence by patients in mental hospitals.
Uppsala: Svenska Bokforlaget, 110–25.

FIELD, L.H., AND WILLIAMS, M., 1970
The hormonal treatment of sexual offenders.
Med. Sci. and the Law, **10**, 27–34.

GREENLAND, C., 1970
The three special hospitals in England and patients with dangerous violent or criminal propensities.
Med. Sci. and the Law, Part I, **9**, 253–65; Part II, **10**, 93–103.

MADDOCKS, P.D., 1970
A five year follow-up of untreated psychopaths.
Brit. J. Psychiat., **116**, 511–15.

SCHREIBER, A.M., 1970
Indeterminate therapeutic incarceration of dangerous criminals: perspectives and problems.
Virginia Law Rev., **56**, 602–34.

THOMAS, D.A., 1970
Principles of sentencing. The sentencing policy of the Court of Appeal Criminal Division.
London: Heinemann, 257–80.

DERSHOWITZ, A.M., 1971
The law of dangerousness: some fictions about predictions.
J. Legal Ed., **23**, 24–47.

GREENLAND, C., 1971
Violence and dangerous behaviour associated with mental illness: prospects for prevention.
Canad. J. Corrections, **13**, 331–39.

JOURNAL OF LAW REFORM, 1971
Organised crime Control Act of 1970, Title X, dangerous special offender sentencing. **4**, 628–50.

KATKIN, D., 1971
Habitual offender laws: a reconsideration.
Buffalo Law Rev., **21**, 99–120.

KITTRIE, N.N., 1971
The right to be different.
Baltimore, Md.: Johns Hopkins Press, 50–101, 169–209, 297–339.

SMITH, C.E., 1971
Recognising and sentencing the exceptional and dangerous offender.
Fed. Probation, **35**(4), 3–12.

TENNANT, T.G., 1971
The dangerous offender.
Brit. J. Hosp. Med., **6**, 269–74.

BERLIN, A., 1972
Treatment for the violent offender.
Crime & Delinq. Lit., **4**, 101–15.

CROWLEY, B., 1972
Maryland's defective delinquent law, nightmarish prelude to 1984.
Corrective Psychiatry, **18**, 15–20.

HIRSCH, A. VON, 1972
Prediction of criminal conduct and preventive confinement of convicted persons.
Buffalo Law Rev., **21**, 717–58.

KOZOL, H.L., BOUCHER, R.J., AND GAROFALO, R.F., 1972
The diagnosis and treatment of dangerousness.
Crime & Delinq., **18**, 371–92.

LE VINE, W.R., AND BORNSTEIN, P.E., 1972
Is the sociopath treatable? The contribution of psychiatry to a legal dilemma.
Washington Univ. Law Quart., 1972, 693–717.

WENK, E.A., AND EMRICH, R.L., 1972
Assaultive youth: an exploratory study of the assaultive experience and assaultive potential of California youth authority wards.
J. Res. Crime & Delinq., **9**, 171–96.

DERSHOWITZ, A.M., 1973.
Preventive confinement: a suggested framework for constitutional analysis.
Texas Law Rev., **51**, 1277–1324.

MCGRATH, P.G., 1973
The mentally abnormal offender.
Medico-Legal J., **41**, 4–13.

SIDLEY, N.T., AND STOLARZ, F.J., 1973
A proposed 'Dangerous Sex Offender' Law.
Amer. J. Psychiat., **130**, 765–68.

WALKER, N., AND MCCABE, S., 1973
Crime and insanity in England, Vol. II: *New solutions and new problems.*
Edinburgh Univ. Press, 82–245.

DERSHOWITZ, A., 1974
The origins of preventive confinement in Anglo-American law.
Univ. Cincinnati Law Rev., Part I, **43**, 1–60.

3 Problems posed by special categories of offender

(b) *Treatment of the mentally ill*

DEUTSCH, A., 1937
The mentally ill in America.
Columbia Univ. Press, 300–519.

MICHAEL, J., AND WECHSLER, J., 1940
Criminal law and its administration.
Chicago: Foundation Press, 1054–71.

GRAY, K.G., 1952
Hospital examination of adult offenders.
Amer. J. Psychiat., **108,** 625–27.

GUTTMACHER, M.S., 1955
Principal difficulties with the present criteria of responsibility and possible alternatives, in *Model Penal Code, Tentative Draft No.* 4, 170–81; and correspondence with H. Wechsler, 182–92.,
Philadelphia: American Law Institute.

WECHSLER, H., 1956
1956 *Supplement to Michael and Wechsler, Criminal law and its administration.*
Chicago: Foundation Press, 184–222, 246–61.

GUTTMACHER, M.S., 1958
The psychiatric approach to crime and correction.
Law & Contemp. Problems, **23,** 633–49.

HAKEEM, M., 1958
A critique of the psychiatric approach to crime and correction.
Law & Contemp. Problems, **23,** 650–82.

WECHSLER, H., 1959
Law, morals and psychiatry.
Address to the 37th Annual Meeting of the New York Society for Clinical Psychiatry. Jan. 15, 1959. Mimeo.

WOOTTON, B., 1959
Social science and social pathology.
London: Allen & Unwin, 203–67.

COMMITTEE ON PSYCHIATRY AND LAW, 1960
Report no. 45: *Confidentiality and privileged communication in the practice of psychiatry.*
New York: Group for the Advancement of Psychiatry.

GOLDSTEIN, J., AND KATZ, J., 1960
Dangerousness and mental illness. Some observations on the decision to release persons acquitted by reason of insanity.
Yale Law J., **70,** 225–39.

SCOTT, P.D., 1960
Assessing the offender for the courts: the role of the psychiatrist.
Brit. J. Criminol., **1,** 116–29.

LINDMAN, F.T., AND MCINTYRE, D.M., 1961
The mentally disabled and the law.
A report of the American Bar Foundation on the rights of the mentally ill.
Univ. Chicago Press, 183–91, 298–368.

MANNHEIM, H., 1961
The criminal law and mentally abnormal offenders.
Brit. J. Criminol., **1,** 203–20.

MESSINGER, E., AND APPELBERG, B., 1961
A quarter century of court psychiatry.
Crime & Delinq., **7,** 343–62.

CRIMINAL LAW QUARTERLY, 1962
Psychiatric treatment as an alternative to imprisonment. A seminar held at Hart House, Univ. of Toronto, June 1–2, 1961, **4,** 296–328.

UNITED STATES OF AMERICA, 1962
Mental illness and due process.
Report and recommendations etc. by the special committee.
New York: Cornell Univ. Press.

GOLDSTEIN, A.S., 1963
The psychiatrist and the legal process: the proposals for an impartial expert and for preventive detention.
Amer. J. Orthopsychiatry, **23,** 123–31.

GOLDSTEIN, J., AND KATZ, J., 1963
Abolish the insanity defense—why not?
Yale Law J., **72,** 853–76.

SCHEFF, T.J., 1964
The societal reaction to deviance: ascriptive elements in the psychiatric screening of mental patients in a midwestern state.
Social Problems, **11,** 401–13.

SZASZ, T.S., 1963
Law, liberty and psychiatry.
New York: Macmillan, 91–148.

WHITLOCK, F.A., 1963
Criminal responsibility and mental illness.
London: Butterworth & Co., 54–93.

WOOTTON, B., 1963
Crime and the criminal law.
London: Stevens, 58–90.

ZLATARIC, B., 1963
The legal status of abnormal offenders, in C. Andersen, *et al.*, *Mentally abnormal offenders,* 119–151. Seminar organized at

Bellagio, April 21–25, 1963, by the Association internationale de droit pénal, Fondation internationale pénale et pénitentiaire, Société internationale de criminologie, Société internationale de défense sociale.

COLUMBIA LAW REVIEW, 1965
District of Columbia hospitalization of the mentally ill act. **65,** 1062–74.

DAVIDSON, H.A., 1965
Forensic psychiatry, (psychiatric glossary for lawyers) 2nd ed.
New York: Ronald Press Co., 401–24.

JUDICIAL CONFERENCE OF THE DISTRICT OF COLUMBIA CIRCUIT 1964, 1965
Report of the Committee on problems connected with mental examination of the accused in criminal cases before trial.
Sidney S. Sachs, Chairman of the Committee, Washington, D.C.

RUBIN, S., 1965
Psychiatry and criminal law.
New York: Oceana Publications.

SZASZ, T.S., 1965
Psychiatric justice.
New York: Macmillan.

THOMAS, D.A., 1965
Sentencing the mentally disturbed offender.
Crim. Law Rev., 1965, 685–99.

HALL, J., 1966
Psychiatric criminology: is it a valid marriage? The legal view.
Presented at the annual meeting of the American Psychiatric Association, Atlantic City, N.J., May 10, 1966. Mimeo.

HARVARD LAW REVIEW, 1966
Civil commitment of the mentally ill: theories and procedures. **79,** 1288–98.

NASATIR, M., DEZZANI, D., AND SILBERT, M., 1966
Atascadero: ramifications of a maximum security treatment institution.
Issues in Criminology, **2,** 29–46.

PLATT, A., AND DIAMOND, B.L., 1966
The origins of the 'right' and 'wrong' test of criminal responsibility and its subsequent development in the United States: an historical survey.
Calif. Law Rev., **54,** 1227–60.

SMITH, C.E., 1966
Psychiatric approaches to the mentally ill federal offender.
Fed. Probation, **30**(2), 23–9.

UNITED STATES OF AMERICA, 1966
The mentally ill offender.
Report of the President's Commission on Crime in the District of Columbia, Washington, D.C., 530–61.

WALKER, N., 1966
Law, liability, culpability, in M. Craft (ed.), *Psychopathic disorders.*
Oxford: Pergamon Press, 32–55.

BROWN, B.S., AND COURTLESS, T.F., 1967
The mentally retarded offender.
Document submitted to the President's Commission on Law Enforcement and Administration of Justice, Washington, D.C. Mimeo.

GOLDSTEIN, A.S., 1967
The insanity defense.
New Haven: Yale Univ. Press, 211–26.

KATZ, J., GOLDSTEIN, J., AND DERSHOWITZ, A.M., 1967
Psychoanalysis, psychiatry and law.
New York: Free Press, 503–5.

LEWIS, A., 1967
The state of psychiatry. Essays and addresses.
London: Routledge & Kegan Paul, 179–94.

NORTH-WESTERN UNIVERSITY LAW REVIEW, 1967
New mental health codes: safeguards in compulsory commitment and release, **61,** 977–1010.

SHAH, S.A., 1967
The mentally disordered offender: a consideration of some aspects of the criminal-judicial-correctional process.
Document submitted to the President's Commission on Law Enforcement and Administration of Justice, Washington, D.C. Mimeo.

SIMON, R.J., 1967
The jury and the defense of insanity.
Boston: Little, Brown & Co., 120–9, 202–12.

WEIHOFEN, H., 1967
Capacity to appreciate 'wrongfulness' of

the 'criminality' under the A.L.I.-Model Penal Code test of mental responsibility. *J. Crim. Law, Criminol. & Pol. Sci.*, **58,** 27–31.

YALE LAW JOURNAL, 1967
Civil commitment of narcotic addicts. **76,** 1160–89.

ASSOCIATION OF THE BAR OF THE CITY OF NEW YORK, in co-operation with Fordham School of Law, 1968
Mental illness, due process and the criminal defendant.
A second report by the Special Committee on the Study of Commitment Procedures and the Law relating to Incompetents, Fordham Univ. Press, 1–138.

BRISCOE, O.V., 1968
The meaning of 'mentally ill person' in the Mental Health Act, 1958–1965 of New South Wales.
Aust. Law J., **42,** 207–15.

LEWIN, T.H., 1968
Disposition of the irresponsible: protection following commitment.
Michigan Law Rev., **66,** 721–36.

LIVERMORE, J.M., MALMQUIST, C.P., AND MEEHL, P.E., 1968
On the justifications for civil commitment.
Univ. Pennsylvania Law Rev., **117,** 75–96.

REUCK, A.V.S. DE, AND PORTER, R., 1968
The mentally abnormal offender.
A Ciba Foundation Symposium.
London: J. & A. Churchill.

WOOTTON, B., 1968
Review of Goldstein's The insanity defense.
Yale Law J., **77,** 1019–32.

BAZELON, D.L., 1969
Implementing the right to treatment.
Univ. Chicago Law Rev., **36,** 742–54.

GEORGETOWN LAW JOURNAL, 1969
A symposium: The right to treatment. **57,** 680–890.

JOBSON, K.B., 1969
Commitment and release of the mentally ill under criminal law.
Crim. Law Quart., **11,** 186–203.

KATZ, J., 1969
The right to treatment—an enchanting legal fiction? *Univ. Chicago Law Rev.*, **36,** 55–83.

MORROW, W.R., 1969
Escapes of psychiatric offenders.
J. Crim. Law, Criminol. & Pol. Sci., **60,** 464–71.

SCHEIDEMANDEL, P.L., AND KANNO, C.K., 1969
The mentally ill offender. A survey of treatment programs.
Baltimore, Md.: Garamond/Pridemark Press.

GREENLAND, C., 1970
Mental illness and civil liberty: a study of mental health review tribunals in England and Wales.
London: G. Bell & Sons.

THOMAS, D.A., 1970
Principles of sentencing. The sentencing policy of the Court of Appeal Criminal Division.
London: Heinemann, 257–80.

TWERSKI, A.D., 1970
Treating the untreatable—a critique of the proposed Pennsylvania right to treatment law.
Duquesne Law Rev., **9,** 220–29.

BRAKEL, S.J., AND ROCK, R.S., 1971
The mentally disabled and the law, (Rev. ed.).
Univ. Chicago Press.

KITTRIE, N.N., 1971
The right to be different.
Baltimore, Md.: Johns Hopkins Press, 50–101, 169–209, 297–339.

MORRIS, G.H., 1971
Mental illness and criminal commitment in Michigan.
J. Law Reform, **5,** 1–66.

PARTRIDGE, M., 1971
Psychiatry and the law.
Ditchley paper No. 40. Enstone, Oxfordshire: Ditchley Foundation.

CHAMBERS, D.L., 1972
Alternatives to civil commitment of the mentally ill: practical guides and constitutional imperatives.
Michigan Law Rev., **70,** 1107–1200.

CHERNOFF, P.A., AND SCHAFFER, W.G., 1972
Defending the mentally ill: ethical quicksand.
Amer. Crim. Law Rev., **10**, 505–32.

DRAKE, J., 1972
Enforcing the right to treatment: *Wyatt v. Stickney.*
Amer. Crim. Law Rev., **10**, 587–609.

ENNIS, B.J., 1972
Prisoners of psychiatry: mental patients, psychiatrists and the law.
New York: Harcourt Brace.

FINGARETTE, H., 1972
The meaning of criminal insanity.
Berkeley, Los Angeles: Univ. California Press, 53–120.

GOLTON, R.J., 1972
Role of defense counsel in the criminal commitment process.
Amer. Crim. Law Rev., **10**, 385–430.

GRAY, S.H., 1972
The insanity defense: historical development and contemporary relevance.
Amer. Crim. Law Rev., **10**, 559–86.

JOURNAL OF URBAN LAW, 1972
The disposition bearing: an alternative to the insanity defense. **49**, 711–32.

KAUFMAN, H., 1972
Evaluating competency: are Constitutional deprivations necessary?
Amer. Crim. Law Rev., **10**, 465–504.

KUMASAKA, Y., AND GUPTA, R.K., 1972
Lawyers and psychiatrists in the court: issues on civil commitment (with afterword by I. Brown).
Maryland Law Rev., **32**, 6–41.

LEFELT, S.L., 1972
Pretrial mental examinations: compelled cooperation and the Fifth Amendment.
Amer. Crim. Law Rev., **10**, 431–64.

PRINS, H.A., 1972
The 'abnormal' offender in the community.
Howard J. Penol. & Crime Prev., **13**, 220–33.

ROBITSCHER, J., 1972
The right to psychiatric treatment: a socio-legal approach to the plight of the state hospital patient.
Villanova Law Rev., **18**, 11–36.

SHADOAN, G., 1972
Raising the insanity defense: the practical side.
Amer. Crim. Law Rev., **10**, 533–58.

STONE, A.A., 1972
Psychoanalysis and jurisprudence: revisited.
Amer. Crim. Law Rev., **10**, 357–84.

SZASZ, T.S., 1972
The sane slave: social control and legal psychiatry.
Amer. Crim. Law Rev., **10**, 337–56.

AARVOLD, C., HILL, D., AND NEWTON, G.P., 1973
Report on the review of procedures for the discharge and supervision of psychiatric patients subject to special restrictions.
London: Cmnd. 5191.

LEAVY, M.R., 1973
The mentally ill criminal defendant.
Crim. Law Bulletin, **9**, 197–252.

NATIONAL COUNCIL FOR CIVIL LIBERTIES, 1973
The rights of the mentally abnormal offender.
The N.C.C.L. evidence to the Butler Committee, London: N.C.C.L.

WALKER, N., AND MCCABE, S., 1973
Crime and insanity in England. Vol. II: *New solutions and new problems.*
Edinburgh Univ. Press, 82–245.

WASHINGTON UNIVERSITY LAW QUARTERLY, 1973
Symposium: United States v Brawner, the insanity defense in the District of Columbia (articles by H. Weihofen, R.E. Schulman, R.C. Allen, D.D. Pugh, B.L. Diamond, J. Goldstein) 1973, 17–154.

PAYNE, C., MCCABE, S., AND WALKER, N., 1974
Predicting offender-patients' reconvictions.
Brit. J. Psychiat., **125**, 60–4.

8 Problems of sentencing

1 Plea bargaining

NEWMAN, D.J., 1966
Conviction. The determination of guilt or innocence without trial.
Boston: Little, Brown & Co., 76–111, 112–30, 166–72, 177–87.

ENKER, A., 1967
Perspectives on plea bargaining, in *Task force report: the courts.*
Washington, D.C.: President's Commission on Law Enforcement and Administration of Justice, 108–19.

ROSETT, A., 1967
The negotiated guilty plea.
Annals Amer. Acad. Pol. & Soc. Sci., **374,** 71–81.

UNITED STATES OF AMERICA, 1967
Task force report: the courts.
Washington, D.C.: President's Commission on Law Enforcement and Administration of Justice, 9–13.

ALSCHULER, A.W., 1968
The prosecutor's role in plea bargaining.
Univ. Chicago Law Rev., **36,** 50–112.

FOLBERG, H.J., 1968
The 'bargained for' guilty plea—an evaluation.
Crim. Law Bull., **4,** 201–12.

HARVARD LAW REVIEW, 1970
The unconstitutionality of plea bargaining.
83, 1387–1411.

NEWMAN, D.J., AND NEMOYER, E.C., 1970
Issues of propriety in negotiated justice.
Denver Law J., **47,** 367–407.

NEW YORK, STATE OF, 1970
Guilty plea bargaining, *Report of the New York State Joint Legislative Committee on Crime. Its causes, control and effect on society.*
Legislative document 1970, No. 6, 10–14.

THOMAS, P., 1970
Plea bargaining and the Turner case.
Crim. Law Rev., 1970, 559–66.

AMERICAN BAR ASSOCIATION, 1971
Project on standards for criminal justice: standards relating to the prosecution function and the defense function.
Approved draft 1971, New York, 35–6, 102–11.

BISHOP, A.N., 1971
Rights and responsibilities of the defendant pleading guilty.
J. Urban Law, **49,** 1–64.

CALIFORNIA LAW REVIEW, 1971
Judicial supervision over California plea bargaining: regulating the trade. **59,** 926–96.

DAVIS, A., 1971
Sentences for sale: a new look at plea bargaining in England and America.
Crim. Law Rev., 1971, 150–61 and 218–28.

JOURNAL OF LAW REFORM, 1971
Plea bargaining: a Model Court Rule. **4,** 487–516.

KLEIN, A.D., 1971
Plea bargaining.
Crim. Law Quart., **14,** 289–305.

KRAUS, K.A., 1971
Plea bargaining: a model court rule.
J. Law Reform, **4,** 487–516.

MCMENAMIN, B.B., 1971
Plea-bargaining in the military.
Amer. Crim. Law Rev., **10,** 93–105.

PURVES, R.F., 1971
That plea-bargaining business: some conclusions from research.
Crim. Law Rev., 1971, 470–75.

UNIVERSITY OF PENNSYLVANIA LAW REVIEW, 1971
Preplea discovery: guilty pleas and the

likelihood of convictions at trial. **119,** 527–35.

WHITE, W.S., 1971
A proposal for the reform of the plea bargaining process.
Univ. Penn. Law Rev., **119,** 439–65.

AMERICAN LAW INSTITUTE, 1972
A model code of pre-arraignment procedure.
Tentative Draft No. 5.
Philadelphia, Pa., 62–77.

ASSOCIATION OF THE BAR OF THE CITY OF NEW YORK, 1972
Plea bargaining in New York City.
Special committee on Legal Aid Inquiry, *Report* **VI,** 74–91.

BISHOP, A.N., 1972
Broken bargains.
J. Urban Law, **50,** 231–55.

FERGUSON, G.A., 1972
The role of the judge in plea bargaining.
Crim. Law Quart., **15,** 26–51.

HOFFMAN, W.E., 1972
Plea bargaining and the role of the judge.
Federal Rules Decisions, **53,** 500–7.

LAMBROS, T.D., 1972
Plea bargaining and the sentencing process.
Federal Rules Decisions, **53,** 509–23.

MINNESOTA LAW REVIEW, 1972
Plea bargaining—proposed amendments to Federal criminal Rule 11. **56,** 718–37.

YALE LAW JOURNAL, 1972
Restructuring the plea bargain. **82,** 286–312.

JOO SHIN, H., 1973
Do lesser pleas pay?: accommodations in the sentencing and parole processes.
J. Criminal Justice, **1,** 27–42.

NORTH CAROLINA LAW REVIEW, 1973
Enforcement of plea bargaining agreements. **51,** 602–10.

UNITED STATES OF AMERICA, 1973
The negotiated plea.
National Conference on Criminal Justice, U.S. Department of Justice, Washington, D.C. 37–64.

WEINREB, L.L., 1973
Leading constitutional cases on criminal justice.
Mineola, New York: Foundation Press, 526–33.

CALIFORNIA LAW REVIEW, 1974
The constitutionality of re-indicting successful plea-bargain appellants on the original, higher charges. **6,** 258–93.

KRESS, J.M., AND NEWMAN, D.J., 1974
Two perspectives on the Agnew plea bargain.
Crim. Law Bulletin, **10,** Kress 80–4, Newman 85–90.

MATHER, L.M., 1974
Some determinants of the method of case disposition: decision making by public defenders in Los Angeles.
Law & Society Rev., **8,** 187–216.

UNITED STATES OF AMERICA, 1974
Courts.

Report of the National Advisory Commission on Criminal Justice Standards and Goals, Washington, D.C. 42–65.

2 Sentencing practice

FRANKEL, E., 1940
The offender and the court.
J. Crim. Law, Criminol. & Pol. Sci., **31,** 448–56.

LANE, H.E., 1941
Illogical variations in sentences of felons committed to Massachusetts State Prison.
J. Crim. Law, Criminol. & Pol. Sci., **32,** 171–90.

GAUDET, F.J., 1949
The sentencing behavior of the judge, in V.C. Branham and S.B. Kutash (eds.), *Encyclopedia of criminology.*
New York: Philosophical Library, 449–61.

FLOOD, G.F., 1955
Sentencing function of the judge.
J. Crim. Law, Criminol. & Pol. Sci., **45,** 531–6.

DAVIS, G.F., 1956
Variations in sentencing.
Nat. Prob. & Parole Assn. J., **2,** 385–92.

NATIONAL PROBATION AND PAROLE ASSOCIATION JOURNAL, 1956
Special issue on sentencing, **2,** 305–92.

MANNHEIM, H., SPENCER, J.C., AND LYNCH, G., 1957
Magisterial policy in the London juvenile courts.
Brit. J. Delinq., **8,** 13–33, 119–38.

RADZINOWICZ, L. (ED.), 1957
Sexual offences.
London: Macmillan, 183–264.

AMERICAN BAR FOUNDATION, 1958
The Administration of criminal justice in the United States.
Chicago: A.B.F., Pilot project report, vol. III, 827–903; vol. V, 89–107.

BRANCALE, R., 1958
Diagnostic techniques in aid of sentencing.
Law & Contemp. Problems, **23,** 442–60.

MANNHEIM, H., 1958
Some aspects of judicial sentencing policy.
Yale Law J., **67,** 961–81.

BENNETT, J.V., 1961
Countdown for judicial sentencing.
Fed. Probation, **25**(3), 22–6.

BULLOCK, H.A., 1961
Significance of the racial factor in the length of prison sentences.
J. Crim. Law, Criminol. & Pol. Sci., **52,** 411–17.

GREEN, E., 1961
Judicial attitudes in sentencing.
London: Macmillan.

HALL WILLIAMS, J.E., 1961
The sentencing policy of the Court of Criminal Appeal.
Howard J., **10,** 201–11.

MCCLINTOCK, F.H., AND GIBSON, E., 1961
Robbery in London.
London: Macmillan, 73–85.

UNITED KINGDOM, 1961
Report of the Inter-Departmental Committee on the business of the Criminal Courts (Streatfeild Committee).
London: Home Office, Cmnd. 1289, 76–85.

FEDERAL RULES DECISIONS, 1962
Institutes on disparity. **30,** 449–54.

HOOD, R.G., 1962
Sentencing in magistrates' courts.
London: Stevens.

KADISH, S.H., 1962
Legal norm and discretion in the police and sentencing process.
Harvard Law Rev., **75,** 904–31.

NAGEL, S.S., 1962
Judicial backgrounds and criminal cases.
J. Crim. Law, Criminol. & Pol. Sci., **53,** 331–9.

UNITED STATES OF AMERICA, 1962
Seminar and institute on disparity of sentences for Sixth, Seventh and Eighth Judicial Councils (under the auspices of the Judicial Conference of the United States), Highland Park, Illinois, Oct. 12–13, 1961.
Federal Rules Decisions, **30,** 401–505.

WOLFGANG, M.E., KELLY, A., AND NOLDE, C., 1962
Comparisons of the executed and the commuted among admissions to death row.
J. Crim. Law, Criminol. & Pol. Sci., **53,** 301–11.

MCCLINTOCK, F.H., 1963
Crimes of violence.
London: Macmillan, 137–67.

GREEN, E., 1964
Inter- and intra-racial crime relative to sentencing.
J. Crim. Law, Criminol. & Pol. Sci., **55,** 348–58.

HOGARTH, J., 1964
Sentencing as a judicial function, in *Proceedings*, 4th Research Conference on Delinquency and Criminology, Montreal, 531–40.

PARSONS, J.B., 1964
The presentence investigation report must be preserved as a confidential document.
Fed. Probation, **28**(1), 3–7.

CROSS, R., 1965
Paradoxes in prison sentences.
Law Quart. Rev., **81,** 205–22.

LODGE, T.S., 1965
Sentencing research.

Thirteenth social defence colloquium, round table conference on some aspects of sentencing.
London, Mimeo.

SMITH, J.C., 1965
Sentencing in the superior English courts.
Thirteenth social defence colloquium, round table conference on some aspects of sentencing.
London, Mimeo.

SPARKS, R.F., 1965
Sentencing by magistrates: some facts of life, in P. Halmos (ed.), *Sociological studies in the British penal services.*
(Sociological Review, Monograph no. 9, Univ. of Keele), 71–86.

UNITED STATES OF AMERICA, 1965
The presentence investigation report.
Washington, D.C.: Administrative Office, U.S. Courts, Division of Probation. Publication No. 103.

WILKINS, L.T., AND CHANDLER, A., 1965
Confidence and competence in decision-making.
Brit. J. Criminol., **5,** 22–35.

CARTER, R.M., 1966
It is respectfully recommended . . .
Fed. Probation, 30(2), 38–42.

HOOD, R.G., 1966
A study of the effectiveness of pre-sentence investigations in reducing recidivism.
Brit. J. Criminol., **6,** 303–11 (and with I.R. Taylor) **8,** 1968, 431–4.

KRASNOW, E.G., 1966
Social investigation reports in the juvenile court.
Crime & Delinq., **12,** 151–64.

REED, J.P., AND KING, C.E., 1966
Factors in the decision-making of North Carolina probation officers.
J. Res. Crime & Delinq., **3,** 120–28.

UNITED STATES OF AMERICA, 1966
Report of the President's Commission on Crime in the District of Columbia.
Washington, D.C., 384–92.

BLUMBERG, A.S., 1967
Criminal justice.
Chicago: Quadrangle Books.

CARTER, R.M., 1967
The presentence report and the decision-making process.
J. Res. Crime & Delinq., **4,** 203–11.

CARTER, R.M., AND WILKINS, L.T., 1967
Some factors in sentencing policy.
J. Crim. Law, Criminol. & Pol. Sci., **58,** 503–14.

GREEN, E., 1967
The effect of the penalty imposed in the preceding case on sentences meted out in criminal cases, in S.A. Yefsky (ed.), *Law enforcement, science and technology.*
Washington, D.C.: Thompson Book Co., 965–74.

HOGARTH, J., 1967
Sentencing research—some problems of design.
Brit. J. Criminol., **7,** 84–93.

JACKSON, R.M., 1967
Enforcing the law.
London: Macmillan, 123–73.

NAGEL, S.S., 1967
Disparities in criminal procedure.
UCLA Law Rev., **14,** 1272–1305.

OVERBY, A.W. JR., 1967
Minority group discrimination in the administration of justice.
A document submitted to the President's Commission on Law Enforcement and Administration of Justice, Washington, D.C. Mimeo.

ROBIN, G.D., 1967
The corporate and judicial disposition of employee thieves.
Wisconsin Law Rev., 1967, 685–702.

THOMAS, D.A., 1967
Sentencing—the basic principles.
Crim. Law Rev., 1967, 455–65, 503–25.

UNITED STATES OF AMERICA, 1967
Task force report: corrections.
Washington, D.C.: President's Commission on Law Enforcement and Administration of Justice, 18–20.

UNITED STATES OF AMERICA, 1967
The challenge of crime in a free society.
Report of the President's Commission on

Law Enforcement and Administration of Justice, Washington, D.C., 127–30, 134–37, 141–42, 144–47, 154–57.

UNITED STATES OF AMERICA, 1967
Task force report: the courts.
Washington, D.C.: President's Commission on Law Enforcement and Administration of Justice, 14–26, 29–36.

ZAVATT, J.C., 1967
Sentencing procedures in the United States District Court for the Eastern District of New York.
Federal Rules Decisions, **41,** 469–93.

HARVARD LAW REVIEW, 1968
Procedural due process at judicial sentencing for felony, **81,** 821–46.

UNIVERSITY OF PENNSYLVANIA LAW REVIEW, 1968
Probation in Philadelphia.
Judicial decision and constitutional norms.
117, 323–55.

WHEELER, S. ET AL., 1968
Agents of delinquency control: a comparative analysis, in S. Wheeler (ed.), *Controlling delinquents.*
New York: John Wiley & Sons, 31–60.

DAWSON, R.O., 1969
Sentencing: the decision as to type, length and conditions of sentence.
Boston: Little, Brown & Co.

D'ESPOSITO, J.C. JR. 1969
Sentencing disparity: causes and cures.
J. Crim. Law, Criminol. & Pol. Sci., **60,** 182–94.

DIX, G.E., 1969
Judicial review of sentences: implications for individual disposition.
Law & the Social Order, 1969, 369–418.

LEWER, W.J., 1969
Disparity in sentencing: some observations.
Proceedings of the Institute of Criminology, Univ. of Sydney Faculty of Law, No. 1, 57–66.

NAGEL, S.S., 1969
The legal process from a behavioral perspective.
Homewood, Ill.: Dorsey Press, 81–112.

REMINGTON, F.J., 1969
Review of *Discretionary justice: a preliminary inquiry*, by K.C. Davis.
Univ. Chicago Law Rev., **36,** 884–902.

ROULSTON, R.P., AND WARD, P.G., 1969
The Sydney project on sentencing.
Proceedings of the Institute of Criminology, Univ. of Sydney Faculty of Law, No. 1, 81–127.

STEIN, P.M., 1969
Imprisonment for nonpayment of fines and costs: a new look at the law and the constitution.
Vanderbilt Law Rev., **22,** 611–44.

WALKER, N., 1969
Sentencing in a rational society.
London: Allen Lane, Penguin Press, 97–130, 148–73, 203–14.

WESTEN, D.A., 1969
Fines, imprisonment, and the poor: 'thirty dollars or thirty days'.
Calif. Law Rev., **57,** 778–821.

WOLFF, H.G., 1969
The relation between the courts and the National Parole Board.
Univ. Toronto Law Journal, **19,** 559–96.

ZEISEL, H., 1969
Methodological problems in studies of sentencing.
Law & Society Rev., **3,** 621–31.

DAVIES, M., 1970
Financial penalties and probation.
London: Home Office Research Studies, **5.**

HOOD, R., AND SPARKS, R., 1970
Key issues in criminology.
London: Weidenfield and Nicolson, 141–70.

HOSNER, C.T., 1970
Group procedures in sentencing: a decade of practice.
Fed. Probation, **34**(4), 18–25.

KATKIN, D., 1970
Presentence reports: an analysis of uses, limitations and civil liberties issues.
Minnesota Law Rev., **55,** 15–31.

SAMUELS, A., 1970
The fine: the principles.
Crim. Law Rev., 1970, 201–10, 268–72.

THOMAS, D.A., 1970
Establishing a factual basis for sentencing.
Crim. Law Rev., 1970, 80–90.

THOMAS, D.A., 1970
Principles of sentencing: the sentencing policy of the Court of Appeal Criminal Division.
London: Heinemann, 3–34, 313–45.

UNITED STATES OF AMERICA, 1970
National Commission on Reform of Federal Criminal Laws.
Working Papers, **2**, Washington, D.C., 1245–1335.

AMERICAN FRIENDS SERVICE COMMITTEE, 1971
Struggle for justice. A report on crime and punishment in America.
New York: Hill & Wang, 124–44.

BAKER, R.W., 1971
Sentencing felons to imprisonment under the Kansas criminal code: the need for a consistent sentencing policy.
Washburn Law Rev., **10**, 269–84.

BING, S., AND ROSENFELD, S.S., 1971
The quality of justice: in the lower criminal courts of metropolitan Boston.
Crim. Law Bull., **7**, 393–443, 604–32.

BLUMBERG, A.S., 1971
Criminal justice in America, in J.D. Douglas (ed.), *Crime and Justice in American society.*
New York: Bobbs-Merrill Co., 45–78.

BRAKEL, S.J., 1971
Diversion from the criminal process: informal discretion, motivation, and formalization.
Denver Law J., **48**, 211–38.

CHAMBLISS, W.J., AND SEIDMAN, R.B., 1971
Law, order, and power.
Reading, Mass.: Addison-Wesley Publishing Co., 447–72.

HICKEY, W.L., AND RUBIN, S., 1971
Suspended sentences and fines.
Crime & Delinq. Lit., **3**, 413–29.

HOGARTH, J., 1971
Sentencing as a human process.
Toronto: Univ. Toronto Press, 339–99.

HUNT, D.R., 1971
Sentencing in the military.
Amer. Crim. Law Rev., **10**, 107–24.

JUSTICE, 1971
The unrepresented defendant in magistrates' courts.
London: Stevens & Sons.

MATHIESON, D.A., AND WALKER, A.J., 1971
Social enquiry reports.
London: National Association of Probation Officers, Probation Papers No. 7.

MILESKI, M., 1971
Courtroom encounters: an observation study of a lower criminal court.
Law & Society Rev., **5**, 473–538.

MODERN LAW REVIEW, 1971
Immigration and the criminal courts. **34**, 135–48.

NORTHWESTERN UNIVERSITY LAW REVIEW, 1971
Sentencing and the exclusionary rule: deterrence and judicial integrity. **66**, 698–713.

REISS, A.J.JR., 1971
Research on administrative discretion and justice.
J. Legal Ed., **23**, 69–76.

SMITH, C.E., 1971
Recognising and sentencing the exceptional and dangerous offender.
Federal Probation, **36**(4), 3–12.

SPARKS, R.F., 1971
The use of suspended sentences.
Crim. Law Rev., 1971, 384–401.

WHITE, S., 1971
Homilies in sentencing.
Crim. Law Rev., 1971, 690–99.

CAMPBELL, R.B.JR., 1972
Sentencing: the use of psychiatric information and presentence reports.
Kentucky Law J., **60**, 285–321.

CHIRICOS, T.G., JACKSON, P.D., AND WALDO, G.P., 1972
Inequality in the imposition of a criminal label.
Social Problems, **19**, 553–72.

FORD, P., 1972
Advising sentencers. A study of recommendations made by probation officers to the courts.
Oxford: Basil Blackwell, 1–39.

HOOD, R.G., 1972
Sentencing the motoring offender.
London: Heinemann, 125–53.

LEVIN, M.A., 1972
Urban politics and judicial behavior.
J. Legal Studies, **1,** 193–221.

NAGEL, S., AND WEITZMAN, L.J., 1972
Double standard of American justice.
Trans-action, **9,** [March, 1972], 18–26.

NORTH CAROLINA LAW REVIEW, 1972
Probable cause and due process at sentencing.
50, 925–36.

OSGOODE HALL LAW JOURNAL, 1972
Sentencing as a human process by John Hogarth, an international review symposium. **10,** 233–80.

OTTE, G., 1972
Role theory and the judicial process: a critical analysis.
Saint Louis Univ. Law J., **16,** 420–36.

ROSETT, A., 1972
Discretion, severity and legality in cirminal justice.
Sourthern Calif. Law Rev., **46,** 12–50.

SINGER, R.G., 1972
Sending men to prison: constitutional aspects of the burden of proof and the doctrine of the least drastic alternative as applied to sentencing determination.
Cornell Law Rev., **58,** 51–89.

SOOTHILL, K.L., 1972
The suspended sentence for ex-prisoners.
Crim. Law Rev., 1972, 535–43.

WHITE, S., 1972
The effect of social inquiry reports on sentencing decisions.
Brit. J. Criminol., **12,** 230–49.

BOTTOMLEY, A.K., 1973
Decisions in the penal process.
London: Martin Robertson, 130–74.

COOK, B.B., 1973
Sentencing behavior of Federal judges: draft cases—1972.
Univ. Cincinnati Law Rev., **42,** 597–633, and M.E. Frankel, Comments of an independent variable sentencer, *ibid,* 667–71.

CRIME AND DELINQUENCY, 1973
The nondangerous offender should not be imprisoned: a policy statement by the Board of Directors, National Council on Crime and Delinquency. **19,** 449–56.

DANELSKI, D., 1973
Toward explanation of judicial behavior.
Univ. Cincinnati Law Rev., **42,** 659–66.

DAVIES, M., AND KNOPF, F., 1973
Social enquiry reports and the probation service.
London: Home Office Research Studies, **18.**

FRANKEL, M.E., 1973
Criminal sentences: law without order.
New York: Hill & Wang.

HANN, R.G., 1973
Decision making in the Canadian criminal court system: a systems analysis, Vol. II.
Research of the Center of Criminology, Univ. of Toronto, 415–62.

LITTLE, J.W., 1973
An empirical description of administration of justice in drunk driving cases.
Law & Society Rev., **7,** 473–92.

PLOTNIKOFF, J., 1973
A problem for law and social work: social enquiry reports on people pleading not guilty.
Brit. J. Social Wk., 3(2), 175–87.

SOFTLEY, B., 1973
A survey of fine enforcement.
London: Home Office Research Studies, **16.**

SPARKS, R.F., 1973
The enforcement of fines. The process from sentence to committal.
Brit. J. Criminol., **13,** 92–107.

TEMIN, C.E., 1973
Discriminatory sentencing of women offenders: the argument for E.R.A. in a nutshell.
Amer. Crim. Law Rev., **11,** 355–72.

UCLA LAW REVIEW, 1973
The prosecutor's role in Calfornia sentencing: advocate or informant. **20,** 1379–1407.

WASHINGTON LAW REVIEW, 1973
Discretion in felony sentencing—a study of influencing factors. **48,** 847–89.

WEINREB, L.L., 1973
Leading constitutional cases on criminal justice.
Mineola, New York: Foundation Press, 627–31.

WILSON, P.R., AND BROWN, J.W., 1973
Crime and the community.
Univ. of Queensland Press, 30–73.

BOWERS, W.J., 1974
Executions in America.
Lexington, Mass.: D.C. Heath & Co.

BRAUTIGAM, R.K., 1974
Criminal justice decision-making: an exploratory empirical study.
Howard J. Penol. & Crime Prev., **14,** 53–77.

CRIMINAL LAW REVIEW, 1974
Unsupported mothers and first prison sentence: an exercise in communication and involvement between a probation officer and a social worker. 1974, 415–19.

DAVIES, M., 1974
Social inquiry for the courts.
Brit. J. Criminol., **14,** 18–33.

FINCKENAUER, J.O., 1974
Theory and practice in sentencing the political criminal: a comment.
Crim. Law Bull., **10,** 737–48.

LEMON, N., 1974
Training, personality and attitude as determinants of magistrates' sentencing.
Brit. J. Criminol., **14,** 34–48.

SHEA, M., 1974
A study of the effect of the prosecutor's choice of charge on magistrates' sentencing behaviour.
Brit. J. Criminol., **14,** 269–72.

SINGER, R.G., AND HAND, R.C., 1974
Sentencing computation: laws and practices.
Crim. Law Bulletin, **10,** 318–47.

WOODS, G.D., 1974
Criminology and sentencing in the New South Wales Court of Criminal Appeal,
Crim. Law Rev., 1974, 409–14.

CROSS, R., 1975
The English sentencing system.
London: Butterworths, (2nd ed.), 130–74.

3 Sentencing structure, reform and legislative proposals

[*See also Section 12(2) for references on diversion from the criminal justice system.*]

GLUECK, S., 1952
Is a pre-sentence examination of the offender advisable? in S. Glueck (ed.), *Crime and correction: selected papers.*
Cambridge, Mass.: Addison-Wesley Press, 102–18.

CAMPBELL, W.J., 1954
Developing systematic sentencing procedures.
Fed. Probation, **18**(3), 3–9.

GLUECK, S., 1956
The sentencing problem.
Fed. Probation, **20**(4), 15–25.

MORRIS, A. (ED.), 1957
What's new in sentencing?
Correctional Research, **7,** United Prison Assn. of Massachusetts.

NATIONAL PROBATION AND PAROLE ASSOCIATION, Advisory Council of Judges, 1957
Guides for sentencing.
New York: Carnegie Press.

MANNHEIM, H., 1958
Comparative sentencing practice.
Law & Contemp. Problems, **23,** 577–82.

MANNHEIM, H., 1958
Some aspects of judicial sentencing policy.
Yale Law J., **67**, 961–81.

OHLIN, L.E., AND REMINGTON, F.J., 1958
Sentencing structure: its effect upon systems for the administration of criminal justice.
Law & Contemp. Problems, **23**, 495–507.

UNITED STATES OF AMERICA, HOUSE OF REPRESENTATIVES, 1958
85th Congress, 2nd Session, H.J. Res. 424 (Report No. 1946) Union Calendar No. 768.
Joint resolution, to improve the administration of justice by authorising the establishment of institutes and joint councils on sentencing for the development of objectives, standards, procedures and policies to be followed in the sentencing of persons convicted of offences against the United States.

CELLER, E., 1960
An expression of congressional interest in the Federal Sentencing Institute.
Fed. Probation, **24**(2), 3–6.

COLUMBIA LAW REVIEW, 1960
Statutory structures for sentencing felons to prison. **60**, 1134–72.

YALE LAW JOURNAL, 1960
Appellate review of primary sentencing decisions: a Connecticut case study. **69**, 1453–78.

DOYLE, R.F., 1961
A sentencing council in operation.
Fed. Probation, **25**(3), 27–30.

REMINGTON, F.J., 1961
The Highland Park Institute on sentencing disparity. Mimeo.

UNITED KINGDOM, 1961
Report of the Inter-Departmental Committee on the Business of the Criminal Courts
(Streatfeild Committee).
London: Home Office, Cmnd. 1289, 76–85.

WECHSLER, H., 1961
Sentencing, correction and the Model Penal Code.
U. Penn. Law Rev., **109**, 465–93.

AMERICAN LAW INSTITUTE, 1962
Model Penal Code.
Proposed official draft (May 4, 1962), Article 7, Authority of court in sentencing, 106–22; Tentative draft No. 2 (May 3, 1954), Article 7, 33–57; Tentative draft No. 4 (April 25, 1955), Article 7, 47–58.
Philadelphia, Pa.

FEDERAL PROBATION, 1962
Symposium on sentencing alternatives in the federal courts. **26**(6), 3–40.

FEDERAL RULES DECISIONS, 1962
Institutes on disparity. **30**, 449–54.

MUELLER, G.O.W., 1962
Penology on appeal: appellate review of legal but excessive sentences.
Vanderbilt Law Rev., **15**, 671–97.

NEW YORK, STATE OF, 1962
Chapter 547, An Act to amend the judiciary law, in relation to authorizing and directing the administrative board of the judicial conference to establish institutes of sentencing, prescribing the purposes thereof, and making an appropriation therefor, Sessions Laws of 1962.

PAULSEN, M.G., 1962
The problem of sentencing.
Number 10 of a series.
Joint Committee on Continuing Legal Education, Philadelphia, Pa.

REMINGTON, F.J., AND NEWMAN, D.J., 1962
The Highland Park Institute on sentencing disparity.
Fed. Probation, **26**(1), 3–9.

UNITED STATES OF AMERICA, 1962
Seminar and institute on disparity of sentences for Sixth, Seventh and Eighth Judicial Councils (under the auspices of the Judicial Conference of the United States), Highland Park, Illinois, Oct. 12–13, 1961.
Federal Rules Decisions, **30**, 401–505.

CALIFORNIA, STATE OF, 1963
Chapter 2075, An Act to add section 68508 to the Government Code, relating to judicial conferences concerning criminal matters, Sessions Laws of 1963.

CRIME AND DELINQUENCY, 1963
Symposium on Model Sentencing Act, **9**, (4).

FLOOD, G.F., 1963
The Model Sentencing Act—a higher level of penal law.
Crime & Delinq., **9**, 370–80.

NATIONAL COUNCIL ON CRIME AND DELINQUENCY, 1963
Model Sentencing Act.
New York: National Council on Crime and Delinquency, Advisory Council of Judges.

RUBIN, S., 1963
The law of criminal correction.
Minnesota: West Publishing Co., 74–108, 111–22, 128–33.

SMITH, T., 1963
The sentencing council and the problem of disproportionate sentences.
Fed. Probation, **27**(2), 5–9.

THOMAS, D.A., 1963
Sentencing—the case for reasoned decisions.
Crim. Law Rev., 1963, 243–53.

NEW YORK, STATE OF, 1964
Proposed New York Penal Law.
Appendix A, *Survey of the New York State sentencing structure as of* 1963, A, 33–56, 64–74.

MURRAH, A.P., AND RUBIN, S., 1965
Penal reform and the Model Sentencing Act.
Columbia Law Rev., **65**, 1167–79.

GLASER, D., COHEN, F., AND O'LEARY, V., 1966
The sentencing and parole process.
Washington, D.C.: U.S. Dept. of Health, Education & Welfare.

LEVIN, T., 1966
Toward a more enlightened sentencing procedure.
Nebraska Law Rev., **45**, 499–512.

MACLEOD, A.J., 1966
If a penologist was the sentencing judge.
Can. Bar J., **9**, 24–9.

UNITED STATES OF AMERICA, 1966
Report of the President's Commission on Crime in the District of Columbia.
Washington, D.C., 384–92.

YOUNGDAHL, L.W., 1966
Development and accomplishments of sentencing institutes in the federal judicial system.
Nebraska Law Rev., **45**, 513–19.

DEVITT, E.J., 1967
How can we effectively minimize unjustified disparity in federal criminal sentences?
Federal Rules Decisions, **41**, 249–56.

RUBIN, S., 1967
Federal sentencing problems and the Model Sentencing Act.
Federal Rules Decisions, **41**, 506–17.

UNITED STATES OF AMERICA, 1967
The challenge of crime in a free society.
Report of the President's Commission on Law Enforcement and Administration of Justice, Washington, D.C. 127–30, 134–7, 141–2, 144–7, 154–7.

ZAVATT, J.C., 1967
Sentencing procedures in the United States District Court for the Eastern District of New York.
Federal Rules Decisions, **41**, 469–93.

AMERICAN BAR ASSOCIATION, 1968
Standards relating to appellate review of sentences.
Project on minimum standards for criminal justice.
New York: A.B.A., 1–12.

AMERICAN BAR ASSOCIATION, 1968
Sentencing alternatives and procedures.
Project on minimum standards for criminal justice.
New York: A.B.A., 1–42, 200–31.

HARVARD LAW REVIEW, 1968
Procedural due process at judicial sentencing for felony. **81**, 821–46.

LOW, P.W., 1968
Memorandum on sentencing structure for the Federal Criminal Code, *National Commission on Reports of the Federal Criminal Law*, Sec. 3, 27–36. Mimeo. Univ. of Virginia, School of Law.

MIDDENDORF, W., 1968
Desirable developments in the administration of justice, in *Criminological aspects of road traffic offences.*
Collected Studies in Criminological Research, **2.**
Strasbourg: Council of Europe, 45–68.

WECHSLER, H., 1968
Codification of criminal law in the United States: the Model Penal Code.
Columbia Law Rev., **68**, 1450–56.

WEIGEL, S.A., 1968
Appellate revision of sentences: to make the punishment fit the crime.
Stanford Law Rev., **20,** 405–22.

BARRY, J.V.W., 1969
The courts and criminal punishments.
Wellington, N.Z.: Govt. Printing Office, 32–68.

LOW, P.W., 1969
Special offender sentencing.
Amer. Crim. Law Quart., **8,** 70–104.

REMINGTON, F.J., 1969
Review of *Discretionary Justice: a preliminary inquiry.* by K.C. Davis.
Univ. Chicago Law Rev., **36,** 884–902.

WALKER, N., 1969
Sentencing in a rational society.
London: Allen Lane, Penguin Press, 97–130, 148–73, 203–14.

AMERICAN BAR ASSOCIATION, 1970
Standards relating to criminal appeals.
Project on standards for criminal justice.
New York: A.B.A., 7–13.

AMERICAN BAR ASSOCIATION, 1970
Standards relating to probation.
Project on standards for criminal justice.
New York: A.B.A.

BERG, R.K., AND SAMUELS, R.L., 1970
Improving the administration of justice in traffic court.
DePaul Law Rev., **19,** 503–24.

CLARK, R., 1970
Crime in America: observations on its nature, causes, prevention and control.
New York: Simon & Schuster, 132–88.

PUGH, G.W., AND CARVER, M.H., 1970
Due process and sentencing: from *Mapp* to *Mempa* to *McGautha.*
Texas Law Rev., **49,** 25–49.

UNITED STATES OF AMERICA, 1970
Study draft of a new Federal Criminal Code.
Washington, D.C.: National Commission on Reform of Federal Criminal Laws, 267–309.

UNITED STATES OF AMERICA, 1970
Working Papers. **2.**
Washington, D.C.: National Commission on Reform of Federal Criminal Laws, 1245–1335.

AMERICAN FRIENDS SERVICE COMMITTEE, 1971
Struggle for justice. A report on crime and punishment in America.
New York: Hill & Wang, 124–44.

BURR, C.B., 1971
Appellate review as a means of controlling criminal sentencing discretion—a workable alternative?
Univ. Pittsburgh Law Rev., **33,** 1–27.

DAVIES, K.C., 1971
Discretionary justice.
J. Legal Ed., **23,** 56–62.

LOW, P.W., 1971
Reform of the sentencing process.
Cambridge Law J., 1971, 237–57.

NATIONAL COUNCIL ON CRIME AND DELINQUENCY, 1972
Model sentencing act, 2nd ed.
Crime & Delinq., **18,** 335–70.

PERCY, C., 1972
The federal corrections reorganization act: blueprint for a criminal justice system.
Amer. Crim. Law Rev., **11,** 65–96.

ROSETT, A., 1972
Discretion, severity and legality in criminal justice.
Southern Calif. Law Rev., **46,** 12–50.

RUBIN, S., 1972
Developments in correctional law.
Crime & Delinq., **18,** 213–28.

SAINT LOUIS UNIVERSITY LAW JOURNAL, 1972
Appelate review of sentences: a survey.
17, 221–62.

SPAETH, HON. E.B. JR., 1972
A response to 'Struggle for justice'.
Prison J., **52**(1), 4–32.

THOMAS, D.A., 1972
Increasing sentences on appeal—a re-examination.
Crim. Law Rev., 1972, 288–306.

AUSTRALIA (South Australia), 1973
Sentencing and corrections.
First Report of the Criminal Law and Penal

Methods Reform Committee of South Australia (Chairman Hon. Justice Mitchell). Adelaide: Government Printer, 5–134.

COLUMBIA LAW REVIEW 1973
Screening of criminal cases in the federal courts of appeal: practice and proposals.
73, 77–105.

FRANKEL, M.E., 1973
Criminal sentences: law without order.
New York: Hill & Wang.

IOWA LAW REVIEW, 1973
Equal protection applied to sentencing.
58, 596–617.

MOTLEY C.B., 1973
'Law and order' and the criminal justice system.
J. Crim. Law & Criminol., **64,** 259–69.

NATIONAL CONFERENCE ON CRIMINAL JUSTICE, 1973
Sentencing.
Washington, D.C., U.S., Department of Justice, C–100–31.

PALMER, L.I., 1973
A model of criminal dispositions: an alternative to official discretion in sentencing.
Georgetown Law J., **62,** 1–59.

DUBOSE, E.Z.JR., 1974
Criminal sentencing: point and counterpoint.
J. Crim. Law & Criminol., **65,** 122–28.

LAW REFORM COMMISSION OF CANADA, 1974
The principles of sentencing and dispositions, Working Paper No. 3 (March 1974), in *Can. J. Criminol. & Corrections*, (1975), **17,** (1).

LOW, P.W., 1974
Review of M.E. Frankel, *Criminal sentences, law without order.*
Harvard Law Review, **87,** 687–92.

MCGEE, R.A., 1974
A new look at sentencing.
Fed. Probation, **38,** Part I (2), 3–8; Part II, (3) 3–11.

ORLAND, L., AND TYLER, H.R.JR., 1974
Justice in sentencing.
Papers and proceedings of the Sentencing Institute for the First and Second Judicial Circuits. Mineola.
New York: Foundation Press.

SINGER, R.G., AND HAND, R.C., 1974
Sentencing computation: laws and practices.
Crim. Law Bulletin, **10,** 318–47.

THOMAS, D.A., 1974
The control of discretion in the administration of criminal justice and James, Lord Justice, A judicial note, in R.G. Hood (ed.), *Crime, criminology and public policy: essays in honour of Sir Leon Radzinowicz.*
London: Heinemann, 139–59.

THOMAS, D.A., 1974
Developments in sentencing.
Crim. Law Rev., 1974, 685–92.

UNITED STATES OF AMERICA, 1974
Courts.
Report of the National Advisory Commission on Criminal Justice Standards and Goals, Washington, D.C. 109–43.

WECHSLER, H., 1974
The model penal code and the codification of American criminal law, in R.G. Hood (ed.), *Crime, criminology and public policy: essays in honour of Sir Leon Radzinowicz.*
London: Heinemann, 419–68.

4 Bail-preventive detention

FREED, D.J., AND WALD, P.M., 1964
Bail in the United States: 1964.
Prepared as a working paper for the national conference on bail and criminal justice (Washington, D.C., May 27–29, 1964).

FOOTE, C., 1965
The coming constitutional crisis in bail.
Univ. Penn. Law Rev., **113,** 959–1185.

GOLDFARB, R., 1965
Ransom: a critique of the American bail system.
New York: Harper & Row.

SUFFET, F., 1966
Bail setting: a study of courtroom interaction.
Crime & Delinq., **12,** 318–31.

AMERICAN BAR ASSOCIATION, 1968
Standards relating to pretrial release.
Project on minimum standards for criminal justice.
New York: American Bar Association.

HICKEY, J.P., 1969
Preventive detention and the crime of being dangerous.
Georgetown Law J., **58,** 287–316.

MILLER, W.L., 1969
The bail reform act of 1966: the need for reform in 1969.
Catholic Univ. Amer. Law Rev., **19,** 24–49.

MITCHELL, J.M., 1969
Bail reform and the constitutionality of pretrial detention.
Virginia Law Rev., **55,** 1223, 1224, 1230–37.

ALLINGTON, T.B., 1970
Preventive detention of the accused before trial.
Univ. Kansas Law Rev., **19,** 109–24.

BOTTOMLEY, A.K., 1970
Prison before trial: a study of remand decisions in magistrates' courts.
London: Bell & Sons.

COGAN, N., 1970
The Pennsylvania bail provisions: the legality of preventive detention.
Temple Law Quart., **44,** 51–72.

MILLER, P.E., 1970
Preventive detention—a guide to the eradication of individual rights.
Harvard Law J., **16,** 1–18.

PRISON JOURNAL, THE, 1970
Special number on preventive detention, bail and the alternatives. **50,** (2).

TRIBE, L.H., 1970
An ounce of detention: preventive justice in the world of John Mitchell.
Virginia Law Rev., **56,** 371, 399–405.

WICE, P., AND SIMON, R.J., 1970
Pretrial release: a survey of alternative practices.
Fed. Probation, **34**(4), 60–3.

AMERICAN BAR FOUNDATION, 1971
Preventive detention: an empirical analysis.
Chicago, Illinois. (reprinted from *Harvard Civil Rights-Civil Liberties Law Review*, **6**(2), March 1971).

COLUMBIA JOURNAL OF LAW AND SOCIAL PROBLEMS, 1971
Pre-trial detention in the New York City jails. **7,** 350–80.

COLUMBIA LAW REVIEW, 1971.
Speedy trials and the second circuit rules regarding prompt disposition in criminal cases. **71,** 1059–76.

DAVIES, C., 1971
Pre-trial imprisonment: a Liverpool study.
Brit. J. Criminol., **11,** 32–48.

DERSCHOWITZ, A.M., 1971
The law of dangerousness: some fictions about predictions.
J. Legal Ed., **23** 24–47 (and comments by C. Foote and L.H. Frankel, 48–56).

HESS, F.D., 1971
Pretrial detention and the 1970 District of Columbia Crime Act—the next step in bail reform.
Brooklyn Law Rev., **37,** 277–322.

KING, M., 1971
Bail or custody.
London: The Cobden Trust.

URBAN RESEARCH CORPORATION, 1971
Preventive detention.
Chicago: Urban Research Corporation.

UVILLER, H.R., 1971
Bail, preventive detention and speedy trials.
Columbia J. Law & Social Problems, **8,** 1–32.

ZANDER, M., 1971
A study of bail/custody decisions in London magistrates' courts.
Crim. Law Rev., 1971, 191–211.

CALIFORNIA LAW REVIEW, 1972
Pretrial release under California Penal Code

Section 853.6: an examination of citation release. **60,** 1339–70.

Criminal Law Bulletin, 1972
The unconstitutional administration of bail: Bellamy v. The Judges of New York City. **8,** 439–513.

Hailsham, Lord, 1972
To bail or not to bail.
Magistrate, **28,** 21–4.

Meyer, H.M., 1972
Constitutionality of pretrial detention.
Georgetown Law J., **60,** 1139–94, 1382–1474.

Pacific Law Journal, 1972
Preventive detention in California: can some criminal defendants be detained prior to trial? **3,** 142–65.

University of Illinois Law Forum, 1972
The administration of Illinois bail provisions: an empirical study of four downstate Illinois counties, 1972, 341–87.

Wald, P.M., 1972
The right to bail revisited: a decade of promise without fulfillment, in S.S. Nagel (ed.), *The rights of the accused.*
Sage Criminal Justice System Annuals, **1.**
Beverly Hills, Calif.: Sage Publications, 175–205.

Bottomley, A.K., 1973
Decisions in the penal process.
London: Martin Robertson, 84–105.

Conklin, J.E., and Meagher, D., 1973
The percentage deposit bail system: an alternative to the professional bondsman.
J. Crim. Justice, **1,** 299–317.

Landes, W.M., 1973
The bail system: an economic approach.
J. Legal Studies, **25,** 79–105.

Weinreb, L.L., 1973
Leading constitutional cases on criminal justice.
Mineola, New York: Foundation Press, 509–11.

Wice, P.B., 1973
Bail and its reform: a national survey.
L.E.A.A., National Institute of Law Enforcement and Criminal Justices, U.S. Dept. of Justice, Washington, D.C.

Wice, P.B., 1973
Bail reform in American cities.
Crim. Law Bulletin, **9,** 770–97.

King, M., 1974
Bail reform: the working party and the ideal bail system.
Crim. Law Rev., 1974, 451–57.

United Kingdom, 1974
Bail procedures in magistrates' courts.
Report of the working party.
London: Home Office.

5 Jury decisions: a preliminary list

Kalven, H., and Zeisel, H., 1966
The American jury.
Boston: Little, Brown & Co., 55–81, 104–17.

Simon, R.J., 1967
The jury and the defense of insanity.
Boston: Little, Brown & Co., 98–119, 132–79.

Virginia Law Review, 1967
Jury sentencing in Virginia. **53,** 968–1001.

American Bar Association, 1968
Standards relating to trial by jury.
Project on minimum standards for criminal justice.
New York: A.B.A.

CORNISH, W.F., 1968
The jury.
London: Allen Lane, Penguin Press, 149–75, 252–75.

ZEISEL, H., 1968
Some data on juror attitudes towards capital punishment.
Univ. Chicago Printing Department.

DUTILE, F.N., 1969
Jury consideration of parole.
Catholic Univ. Amer. Law Rev., **18,** 308–34.

COLUMBIA SURVEY OF HUMAN RIGHTS LAW, 1970
The Federal Jury Selection Act of 1968: a critique. **2,** 52–90.

ERLANGER, H.S., 1970
Jury research in America, its past and future.
Law & Society Rev., **4,** 345–70.

YALE LAW JOURNAL, 1970
The case for black juries. **79,** 531–50.

SIMON, R.J., AND MAHAN, L., 1971
Quantifying burdens of proof: a view from the Bench, the jury and the classroom.
Law & Society Rev., **5,** 319–30.

KAIRYS, D., 1972
Juror selection: the law, a mathematical method of analyis, and a case study.
Amer. Crim. Law Rev., **10,** 771–806.

MCCABE, S., AND PURVES, R., 1972
By-passing the jury. A study of changes of plea and directed acquittals in higher courts.
Oxford: Basil Blackwell.

MCCABE, S., AND PURVES, R., 1972
The jury at work.
Oxford: Basil Blackwell.

SIMON, R.J., AND MARSHALL, P., 1972
The jury system, in S.S. Nagel (ed.), *The rights of the accused.*
Sage Criminal Justice System Annuals, **1.**
Beverly Hills, Calif.: Sage Publications, 209–33.

CRIMINAL LAW REVIEW, 1973
Juries and the rules of evidence: L.S.E. jury project, 1973, 208–23.

HADDEN, S.C., 1973
Social dimensions of jury decision making.
Internat. J. Criminol. & Penol., **1,** 269–77.

HESTER, R.K., AND SMITH, R.E., 1973
Effects of a mandatory death penalty on the decisions of simulated jurors as a function of heinousness of the crime.
J. Crim. Justice, **1,** 319–26.

IOWA LAW REVIEW, 1973
'Jury-mandering': Federal jury selection and the generation gap. **52,** 401–19.

MARK, R., 1973
Minority verdict: the 1973 *Dimbleby Lecture.*
London: British Broadcasting Corporation.

SHOEMAKER, D.J., SOUTH, D.R., AND LOWE, J., 1973
Facial stereotypes of deviants and judgments of guilt or innocence.
Social Forces, **51,** 427–33.

WHITE, W.S., 1973
The constitutional invalidity of convictions imposed by death-qualified juries.
Cornell Law Rev., **58,** 1176–1220.

BALDWIN, J., AND MCCONVILLE, M.J., 1974
The acquittal rate of professional criminals: a critical note.
Modern Law Rev., **37,** 439–43 and M. Zander [1974] A reply, *Modern Law Rev.*, **37,** 444–49.

MCCABE, S., 1974
Jury research in England and the United States.
Brit. J. Criminol., **14,** 276–79.

MCCABE, S., AND PURVES, R., 1974
The shadow jury at work: an account of a series of deliberations where 'shadow' juries were present during actual trials.
Oxford: Basil Blackwell.

ZANDER, M., 1974
Acquittal rates and not quilty pleas: what do the statistics mean?
Crim. Law Rev., 1974, 401–8.

ZEISEL, H., AND DIAMOND, S.S., 1974
'Convincing empirical evidence' on the six member jury.
Univ. Chicago Law Rev., **41,** 281–95.

WALKER, N., (ED.), 1975
The British jury system.
Univ. of Cambridge: Institute of Criminology.

6 Judges and magistrates—their background and attitudes : a preliminary list

SCHROEDER, T., 1918
The psychological study of judicial opinions.
Calif. Law Rev., **6,** 89–113.

WINICK, C., GERVER, I., AND BLUMBERG, A.S., 1961
The psychology of judges, in H. Toch (ed.), *Legal and criminal psychology.*
New York: Holt, Rinehart & Winston, 121–45.

WALTHER, R.H., AND MCCUNE, S.D., 1962 and 1965
Juvenile court judges in the United States.
Crime & Delinq., **8.** 121–31, and **11,** 384–93.

KLEIN, F.J., 1963
Judicial administration and the legal profession: a bibliography.
New York: Oceana Publications, 275–85.

NAGEL, S.S., 1963
Off the bench attitudes, in G.B. Schubert (ed.), *Judicial decision-making.*
New York: Free Press, 29–47.

GROSSMAN, J.B., 1965
Lawyers and judges: the ABA and the politics of judicial selection.
New York: John Wiley & Sons, 7–81.

MCCUNE, S.D., AND SKOLER, D.L., 1965
Juvenile court judges in the United States.
Crime & Delinq., **11,** 121–31.

KARLEN, D., 1966
Judicial education.
Am. Bar Assn. J., **52,** 1049–54.

MÄKELÄ, K., 1966
Public sense of justice and judicial practice.
Acta Sociologica, **10,** 42–67.

UNITED STATES OF AMERICA, 1967
Task force report: the courts.
Washington, D.C.: President's Commission on Law Enforcement and Administration of Justice, 65–72.

WOOD, A.L., 1967
Criminal lawyer.
New Haven, Conn.: College & Univ. Press.

DOWNING, R.G., 1970
Judicial ethics and the political role of the courts.
Law and Contemp. Problems, **35,** 94–107.

KARLEN, D., 1970
Judicial administration: the American experience.
Dobbs Ferry, New York: Oceana Publications, 25–58.

MILLER, A.S., 1970
Public confidence in the judiciary: some notes and reflections.
Law and Contemp. Problems, **35,** 69–93.

BRAITHWAITE, W.T., 1971
Who judges the judges?
Chicago: American Bar Foundation.

HOGARTH, J., 1971
Sentencing as a human process.
Univ. Toronto Press, 34–67.

AMERICAN BAR ASSOCIATION, 1972
Standards relating to the function of the Trial Judge.
Project on standards for criminal justice.
New York: A.B.A., 1–24.

CASPER, G., AND ZEISEL, H., 1972
Lay judges in the German criminal courts.
J. Legal Studies, **1,** 135–91.

HALL, D.J., 1972
Judicial removal for off-bench behavior: why?
J. Public Law, **21,** 127–49.

HENNESSY, M.T., 1972
Qualification of California justice court judges: a dual system.
Pacific Law J., **3,** 439–74.

HOOD, R.G., 1972
Sentencing the motoring offender.
London: Heinemann, 41–62.

JUSTICE, 1972
The judiciary.
The report of a Justice sub-committee.
London: Stevens & Sons.

HARVARD LAW REVIEW, 1973
Disqualification of judges and justices in the Federal Courts. **86,** 736–64.

KLEIN, F.J., AND WITZTUM, R.J., 1973
Judges—selection, conduct, censure, removal and involuntary retirement,

1972/73 *Annual Survey of American Law.*
New York Univ. School of Law, 717–48.

Wilson, R.J., 1973
British judges as political actors.
Internat. J. Criminol. & Penol., **1**, 197–215.

United States of America, 1974
Courts.
Report of the National Advisory Commission on Criminal Justice Standards and Goals, Washington, D.C., 145–59.

9 The court and the young offender

DUNHAM, H.W., 1958
The juvenile court: contradictory orientations in processing offenders.
Law & Contemp. Problems, **23**, 401–582.

NYQUIST, O., 1960
Juvenile justice.
London: Macmillan, 138–50, 219–43.

UNITED KINGDOM, 1960
Report of the Committee on Children and Young Persons (Ingleby Committee).
London: Home Office, Cmnd. 1191, 21–42.

WALTHER, R.H., AND MCCUNE, S.D., 1962 and 1965
Juvenile court judges in the United States.
Crime & Delinq., **8**, 121–131 and **11**, 384–93.

COHN, J., 1963
Criteria for the probation officer's recommendations to the juvenile court judge.
Crime & Delinq., **9**, 262–75.

LABOUR PARTY OF THE UNITED KINGDOM, 1964
Crime—a challenge to us all.
Report of the Labour Party's Study Group.

MATZA, D., 1964
Delinquency and drift.
New York: John Wiley & Sons, 101–51.

CHRISTIE, N., 1965
Temperance boards and interinstitutional dilemmas: a case study of a welfare law.
Social Problems, **12**, 415–28.

HARTUNG, F.E., 1965
Crime, law and society.
Wayne State Univ. Press, 219–44.

KETCHAM, O,W., 1965
Legal renaissance in the juvenile court.
North-Western Univ. Law Rev., **60**, 585–98.

PAULSEN, M.G., 1965
The juvenile court and the whole of the law.
Wayne Law Rev., **11**, 597–616.

SLOANE, H.W., 1965
The juvenile court: an uneasy partnership of law and social work.
J. Family Law, **5**, 170–89.

UNITED KINGDOM, 1965
The child, the family and the young offender.
London: Home Office, Cmnd. 2742, 3–14.

WESTBROOK, J.E., 1965
Mens rea in the juvenile court.
J. Family Law, **5**, 121–38.

BROWN, L.N., 1966
The legal background to the family court.
Brit. J. Criminol., **6**, 139–51.

CAVENAGH, W.E., 1966
What kind of court or committee?
Brit. J. Criminol., **6**, 123–38.

CHAITIN, M.R., AND DUNHAM, H.W., 1966
The juvenile court in its relationship to adult criminality: a replicated study.
Social Forces, **45**, 114–19.

DOWNEY, B.W.M., 1966
White Paper: 'The child, the family and the young offender'.
Modern Law Rev., **29**, 409–13.

GARLAND, N.M., 1966
Collateral attack on juvenile court delinquency decisions.
J. Crim. Law, Criminol. & Pol. Sci., **57**, 136–44.

KAHAN, B.J., 1966
'The child, the family and the young offender': revolutionary or evolutionary?
Brit. J. Criminol., **6**, 159–69.

KILBRANDON, THE HON. LORD, 1966
Children in trouble.
Brit. J. Criminol., **6**, 112–22.

KRASNOW, E.G., 1966
Social investigation reports in the juvenile court.
Crime & Delinq., **12**, 151–64.

PAULSEN, M.G., 1966
Juvenile courts, family courts and the poor man.
Calif. Law Rev., **54,** 694–716.

PAULSEN, M.G., 1966
Kent v. United States: the constitutional context of juvenile cases.
Supreme Ct. Rev. 1966, 167–92.

SCOTT, P.D., 1966
The child, the family and the young offender.
Brit. J. Criminol., **6,** 105–11.

UNITED STATES OF AMERICA, 1966
Standards for juvenile and family courts.
Washington, D.C.: Social and Rehabilitation Service, Children's Bureau, Department of Health, Education and Welfare.

WELCH, T.A., 1966
Delinquency proceedings—fundamental fairness for the accused in a quasi-criminal forum.
Minnesota Law Rev., **50,** 653–96.

WHEELER, S., AND COTTRELL, L.S. JR., 1966
Juvenile delinquency, its prevention and control.
New York: Russell Sage Foundation, 31–6.

WINTON, D., 1966
Family courts in Japan.
Brit. J. Criminol., **6,** 202–9.

COLUMBIA LAW REVIEW, 1967
Rights and rehabilitation in the juvenile courts. **67,** 281–341.

KETCHAM, O.W., AND PAULSEN, M.G., 1967
Cases and materials relating to juvenile courts.
Brooklyn: Foundation Press.

LEMERT, E.M., 1967
Legislating change in the juvenile court.
Wisconsin Law Rev., 1967, 421–48.

PAULSEN, M.G., 1967
Child abuse reporting laws: the shape of the legislation.
Columbia Law Rev., **67,** 1–49.

UNITED STATES OF AMERICA, 1967
The challenge of crime in a free society.
Report of the President's Commission on Law Enforcement and Administration of Justice, Washington, D.C., 79–81, 84–9.

UNITED STATES OF AMERICA, 1967
Task force report: corrections.
Washington, D.C.: President's Commission on Law Enforcement and Administration of Justice, 119–29.

UNITED STATES OF AMERICA, 1967
Task force report: juvenile delinquency and youth crime.
Washington, D.C.: President's Commission on Law Enforcement and Administration of Justice, 57–76, 77–83, 84–90, 91–105.

INDIANA LAW JOURNAL, 1968
Symposium on juvenile problems: *in re Gault* (87 Sup.Ct. 1428). **43,** 523–676.

PARKER, G., 1968
American child-saving. The climate of reform as reflected in the National Conference of Charities and Corrections, 1875–1900.
Univ. Toronto Law J., **18,** 371–93.

PAULSEN, M.G., 1968
The law and abused children, in R.E. Helfer and C.H. Kempe (eds.), *The battered child.*
Chicago: Univ. Chicago Press, 175–200.

UNITED KINGDOM, 1968
Children in trouble.
London: Home Office, Cmnd. 3601.

UNIVERSITY OF PITTSBURGH LAW REVIEW, 1968
Double jeopardy and due process in the juvenile courts. **29,** 756–66.

WOOTTON, B., 1968
The White Paper on children in trouble.
Crim. Law Rev., 1968, 465–77 (including a comment by D. Napley).

EMERSON, R.M., 1969
Judging delinquents. Context and process in juvenile court.
Chicago: Aldine Publishing Co., 3–80, 172–278.

FERSTER, E.Z., SNETHEN, E.N., AND COURTLESS, T.F., 1969
Juvenile detention: protection, prevention or punishment?
Fordham Law Rev., **38,** 161–96.

HOOD, R.G., AND SPARKS, R.F. (EDS.), 1969
Community homes and the approved schools system.
University of Cambridge: Institute of Criminology, 7–13.

KITTRIE, N.N., 1969
Can the right to treatment remedy the ills of the juvenile process?
Georgetown Law J., **57,** 848–85.

LEFSTEIN, N., STAPLETON, V., AND TEITELBAUM, L., 1969
In search of juvenile justice: *Gault* and its implementation.
Law & Society Rev., **3,** 491–562.

LEMERT, E.M., 1969
Records in the juvenile court, in S. Wheeler (ed.), *On record: files and dossiers in American life.*
New York: Russell Sage Foundation, 355–87.

NATIONAL COUNCIL ON CRIME AND DELINQUENCY, 1969
Model rules for juvenile courts.
New York, 61–88.

PLATT, A.M., 1969
The child savers: the invention of delinquency.
Univ. Chicago Press.

BOTTOMS, A.E., MCCLEAN, J.D., AND PATCHETT, K.W., 1970
Children, young persons and the courts—a survey of the new law.
Crim. Law Rev., 1970, 368–95.

BRISCOE, O.V., 1970
The juvenile court: Judge Jeffreys or Father Christmas?
Med. Sci and the Law, **10,** 149–57.

COHEN, J.H., 1970
The standard of proof in juvenile proceedings: *Gault* beyond a reasonable doubt.
Michigan Law Rev., **68,** 567–602.

FOX, S.J., 1970
Juvenile justice reform: an historical perspective.
Stanford Law Rev., **22,** 1187–1239

FOX, S.J., 1970
Prosecutors in the juvenile court: a statutory proposal.
Harvard J. Legislation, **8,** 33–53.

LAWTON, M.C., 1970–71
Juvenile proceedings: the new look.
American Univ. Law Rev., **20,** 342–72.

LEMERT, E.M., 1970
Social action and legal change: revolution within the juvenile court.
Chicago: Aldine Publishing Co.

MCMILLAN, T., AND MCMURTRY, D.L., 1970
The role of the defense lawyer in the juvenile court—advocate or social worker?
Saint Louis Univ. Law J., **14,** 561–603.

MILTON, M.M., 1970
Post-Gault: a new prospectus for the juvenile court.
New York Law Forum, **16,** 57–92.

MORRIS, N., AND HAWKINS, G., 1970
The honest politician's guide to crime control.
Univ. Chicago Press, 146–72.

ARNOLD, W.R., 1971
Race and ethnicity relative to other factors in juvenile court dispositions.
Amer. J. Sociol., **77,** 211–27.

CAYTON, C.E., 1971
Emerging patterns in the administration of juvenile justice.
J. Urban Law, **49,** 377–98.

DODD, L.R., 1971
Notes on the juvenile jury trial case—a regrettable 'policy decision'.
Louisiana Law Rev., **32,** 133–45.

DUFFEE, D., AND SIEGEL, L. J., 1971
The organization man: legal counsel in the juvenile court.
Crim. Law Bull., **7,** 544–53.

FERSTER, E.Z., COURTLESS, T.F., AND SNETHEN, E.N., 1971
The juvenile justice system: in search of the role of counsel.
Fordham Law Rev., **39,** 375–412.

FORE, F.L., AND MILLER, S., 1971
Juries for juveniles.
J. Family Law, **11,** 107–20.

FOX, R.G., AND SPENCER, M.J., 1971
The young offenders' bill: destigmatizing juvenile delinquency.
Crim. Law Quart., **14,** 172–219.

GOLD, S., 1971
Equal protection of juvenile girls in need of supervision in New York State.
New York Law Forum, **17,** 570–98.

HAWES, J.M., 1971
Children in urban society. Juvenile delinquency in nineteenth-century America.
New York: Oxford Univ. Press, 158–90, 223–62.

KITTRIE, N.N., 1971
The right to be different.
Baltimore, Md.: Johns Hopkins Press, 102–68.

LEMERT, E.M., 1971
Instead of court: diversion in juvenile justice.
Chevy Chase, Md.: National Institute of Mental Health, Center for Studies of Crime & Delinquency.

MACDONALD, J.A., 1971
A critique of Bill C–192—the young offender act.
Can. J. Corrections, **13**, 166–80.

MAY, D., 1971
Delinquency control and the treatment model: some implications of recent legislation.
Brit. J. Criminol., **11**, 359–70.

MICHIGAN LAW REVIEW, 1971
Juvenile courts—juveniles in delinquency proceedings are not constitutionally entitled to the right of trial by jury—McKeiver v. Pennsylvania. **70**, 171–94.

NATIONAL COUNCIL ON CRIME AND DELINQUENCY, 1971
Provision of counsel in juvenile courts.
New York: Advisory council of judges.

NORTH DAKOTA LAW REVIEW, 1971
Symposium: some theoretical and practical problems in formalizing the juvenile court procedure. **47**, 287–16.

SUSSMANN, F.B., AND MCGRATH, W.T., 1971
Brief on young offenders act Bill C–192.
Can. J. Corrections, **13**, 307–18.

UCLA LAW REVIEW, 1971
Juvenile delinquency laws: juvenile women and the double standard of morality. **19**, 313–42.

BROOKLYN LAW REVIEW, 1972
McKeiver v. Pennsylvania: a retreat in juvenile justice. **38**, 650–92.

COFFEE, J.C., 1972
Privacy versus *parens patriae:* the role of police records in the sentencing and surveillance of juveniles.
Cornell Law Rev., **57**, 571–620.

COLUMBIA HUMAN RIGHTS LAW REVIEW, 1972
Juvenile police record-keeping. **4**, 461–84.

DAVIS, S.M., 1972
The jurisdictional dilemma of the juvenile court.
North Carolina Law Rev., **51**, 195–231.

FERSTER, E.Z., AND COURTLESS, T.F., 1972
Pre-dispositional data, role of counsel and decisions in a juvenile court.
Law & Society Rev., **7**, 195–222.

FERSTER, E.Z., AND COURTLESS, T.F., 1972
Post-disposition treatment and recidivism in the juvenile court: towards justice for all.
J. Family Law, **11**, 683–709.

FREY, M.A., AND BUBANY C.P., 1972
Pre-adjudication review of the social record in juvenile court: a low-visibility obstacle to a fair process.
J. Family Law, **12**, 391–404.

HARRIS, B., 1972
Children's Act in trouble: an appreciation of the children and young persons Act 1969 in operation.
Crim. Law Rev., 1972, 670–84.

JAMES, C., 1972
Children's Act in trouble: further consideration.
Crim. Law Rev., 1972, 688–92.

JOURNAL OF FAMILY LAW, 1972
Juvenile right to counsel at a probation revocation hearing. **11**, 745–64.

KETCHAM, O.W., 1972
McKeiver v. Pennsylvania: the last word on juvenile court adjudications.
Cornell Law Rev., **57**, 561–70.

KLAPMUTS, N., 1972
Children's rights: the legal rights of minors in conflict with law or social custom.
Crime & Delinquency Lit. **4**, 449–77.

Langley, M.H., 1972
The juvenile court: the making of a delinquent.
Law & Society Rev., **7,** 273–98.

Langley, M.H., Graves, H.R., and Norris, B., 1972
The juvenile court and individualized treatment.
Crime & Delinq., **18,** 79–92.

Levine, H.A. Hon., 1972
The youthful offender under the New York criminal procedure law.
Albany Law Rev., **36,** 241–56.

McClean, J.D., 1972
Children's Act in trouble: another view.
Crim. Law Rev., 1972, 684–87.

McNulty, J.K., 1972
The right to be left alone.
Amer. Crim. Law Rev., **11,** 141–64.

Malmquist, C.P., 1972
Juvenile detention: right and adequacy of treatment issues.
Law & Society Rev., **7,** 159–93.

Mennell, R.M., 1972
Origins of the juvenile court: changing perspectives on the legal rights of juvenile delinquents.
Crime & Delinq., **18,** 68–78.

Morris, A.M., 1972
Children's hearings in Scotland.
Crim. Law Rev., 1972, 693–701.

Saint Louis University Law Journal, 1972
The administrative transfer of juveniles to adult penal institutions. **16,** 479–96.

Stanford Law Review, 1972
Juvenile court jurisdiction over 'immoral' youth in California. **24,** 568–86.

Stanford Law Review, 1972
Double jeopardy and the waiver of jurisdiction in California's juvenile courts. **24,** 874–902.

Alers, M.S., 1973
Transfer of jurisdiction from juvenile to criminal court.
Crime & Delinq., **19,** 519–27.

Bagley, C., 1973
The welfare of the child: an examination of judicial opinion about medical and social work evidence in adoption cases.
Brit. J. Social Wk., **3,** 79–90.

Boston University Law Review, 1973
Sentencing under the Federal Youth Corrections Act: the need for an explicit finding and a statement of reason. **53,** 1071–86.

Chase, E., 1973
Schemes and visions: a suggested revision of juvenile sentencing.
Texas Law Rev., **51,** 673–706.

Chused, R.H., 1973
The juvenile court process: a study of three New Jersey counties.
Rutgers Law Rev., **26,** 488–615.

Empey, L.T., 1973
Juvenile justice reform, in L.E. Ohlin (ed.), *Prisoners in America.*
Englewood Cliffs, N.J.: Prentice-Hall, 13–48.

Franklin, J., and Gibbons, D.C., 1973
New directions for juvenile courts, Probation Officers' views.
Crime & Delinq., **19,** 508–18.

Howlett, F.W., 1973
Is the YSB all it's cracked up to be?
Crime & Delinq., **19,** 485–92.

Keiter, R.B., 1973
Criminal or delinquent? A study of juvenile cases transferred to the criminal court.
Crime & Delinq., **19,** 528–38.

Mennel, R.M., 1973
Thorns and thistles: juvenile delinquents in the United States 1825–1940.
Hanover, New Hampshire: Univ. Press of New England, 124–57.

Renn, D.E., 1973
The right to treatment and the juvenile.
Crime & Delinq., **19,** 477–84.

Schultz, J.L., 1973
The cycle of juvenile court history.
Crime & Delinq., **19,** 457–76.

Susman, J., 1973
Juvenile justice: even-handed or many-handed? An empirical investigation

of decision processes in disposition hearings.
Crime & Delinq., **19**, 493–507.

THORNBERRY, T.P., 1973
Race, socioeconomic status and sentencing in the juvenile justice system.
J. Crim. Law & Criminol., **64**, 90–8.

UNITED STATES OF AMERICA, 1973
House of Representatives 93rd Congress, 1st Session, Part 2, *Street crime in America (corrections approaches)*, hearings before the Select Committee on Crime (statement by Jerome G. Miller), Washington, D.C., 649–74.

UNITED STATES OF AMERICA, 1973
New approaches to diversion and treatment of juvenile offenders.
L.E.A.A., National Institute of Law Enforcement and Criminal Justice, U.S. Dept. of Justice, Washington, D.C.

YALE LAW JOURNAL, 1973
Parens Patriae and statutory vagueness in the juvenile court. **82**, 745–71.

AMERICAN CRIMINAL LAW REVIEW, 1974
Juveniles and the law: a symposium. **12**, 1–178.

BOTTOMS, A.E., 1974
On the decriminalisation of the English juvenile courts, in R.G. Hood (ed.), *Crime, criminology and public policy: essays in honour of Sir Leon Radzinowicz.*
London: Heinemann, 319–45.

CRESSEY, D.R., AND MCDERMOTT, R.A., 1974
Diversion from the juvenile justice system.
L.E.A.A. National Institute of Law Enforcement and Criminal Justice, U.S. Dept. of Justice, Washington, D.C.

DAHL, T.S., 1974
The emergence of the Norwegian child welfare law.
Scandinavian Studies in Criminology, **5**.
London: Martin Robertson, 83–98.

FLACKETT, J.M., 1974
Juvenile offenders in the community, some recent experiences in the United States.
Howard J. Penol. & Crime Prev., **14**, 22–36.

GIBBS, L.E., 1974
The effects of juvenile legal procedures on juvenile offenders' self-attitudes.
J. Research Crime & Delinq., **11**, 51–5.

MORRIS, A.M., 1974
Scottish juvenile justice: a critique, in R.G. Hood (ed.), *Crime criminology and public policy: essays in honour of Sir Leon Radzinowicz.*
London: Heinemann, 347–74.

NOVAK, R.A., 1974
The incorrigible child under the new Pennsylvania Juvenile Act: an unsound, unsupportable, and unfortunate policy choice.
Univ. Pittsburgh Law Rev., **35**, 73–92.

SUSSMAN, A., 1974
Psychological testing and juvenile justice: an invalid judicial function.
Crim. Law Bull., **10**, 117–48.

10 Effectiveness of punishment and treatments

1 General deterrence

TARDE, G., 1912
Penal philosophy.
Boston: Little, Brown & Co., 473–83.

FERRI, E., 1917
Criminal sociology.
Boston: Little, Brown & Co., 209–41.

ANDENAES, J., 1952
General prevention—illusion or reality?
J. Crim. Law, Criminol. & Pol. Sci., **43,** 176–98.

UNITED KINGDOM, 1953
Report of the Royal Commission on Capital Punishment, 1949–1953.
London: Cmnd. 8932, 18–24; Appendix 6, 328–80.

BALL, J.C., 1955
The deterrence concept in criminal law.
J. Crim. Law, Criminol. & Pol. Sci., **46,** 347–54.

SELLIN, T., 1959
The death penalty.
Philadelphia, Pa.: American Law Institute, 69–79.

WILKINS, L.T., 1962
Criminology: an operational research approach, in A.T. Welford *et al.* (eds.), *Society: problems and methods of study.*
London: Routledge & Kegan Paul, 321–26.

NEW YORK, STATE OF, 1965
Special report on capital punishment.
Temporary Commission on revision of the penal law and criminal code, 30–40. Mimeo.

ANDENAES, J., 1966
The general preventive effects of punishment.
Univ. Penn. Law Rev., **114,** 949–83.

CHAMBLISS, W.J., 1966
The deterrent influence of punishment.
Crime & Delinq., **12,** 70–5.

GIBBS, J.P., 1966
Sanctions.
Social Problems, **14,** 147–59.

CHAMBLISS, W.J., 1967
Types of deviance and the effectiveness of legal sanctions.
Wisconsin Law Rev., 1967, 703–19.

CLASTER, D.S., 1967
Comparison of risk perception between delinquents and non-delinquents.
J. Crim. Law, Criminol. & Pol. Sci., **58,** 80–6.

SCHWARTZ, R.D., AND ORLEANS, S., 1967
On legal sanctions.
Univ. Chicago Law Rev., **34,** 274–300.

ANDENAES, J., 1968
Does punishment deter crime?
Crim. Law Quart., **11,** 76–93.

BECKER, G.S., 1968
Crime and punishment: an economic approach.
J. Pol. Econ., **76,** 169–217.

CALIFORNIA, STATE OF, 1968
Deterrent effects of criminal sanctions.
Progress Report of the Assembly Committee on Criminal Procedure. Sacramento.

CAMPBELL, D.T., AND ROSS, H.L., 1965
The Connecticut crackdown on speeding: time series data in quasi-experimental analysis.
Law & Society Rev., **3,** 33–53.

COHEN, J., AND PRESTON, B., 1968
Causes and prevention of road accidents.
London: Faber and Faber, 200–20.

SCHWARTZ, B., 1968
The effect in Philadelphia of Pennsylvania's increased penalties for rape and attempted rape.

J. Crim. Law, Criminol. & Pol. Sci., **59,** 509–15.

SHEPPARD, D., 1968
The 1967 drink and driving campaign—a survey among drivers.
Ministry of Transport: Road Research Laboratory.

UNITED STATES OF AMERICA. SENATE. 1968
A bill to abolish the death penalty under all laws of the United States and for other purposes.
Hearings before the Subcommittee on Criminal Laws and Procedures of the Committee on the Judiciary Washington, D.C.

ZIMRING, F., AND HAWKINS, G., 1968
Deterrence and marginal groups.
J. Res. Crime & Delinq., **5,** 100–14.

ASHWORTH, A.J., 1969
A short note on the English murder rate.
Crim. Law Rev., 1969, 645–54.

CHAMBLISS, W.J., 1969
Crime and the legal process.
New York: McGraw-Hill, 359–78.

CRAMPTON, R.C., 1969
Driver behavior and legal sanctions: a study of deterrence.
Michigan Law Rev., **67,** 421–54.

HAAG, E. VAN DEN, 1969
On deterrence and the death penalty.
J. Crim. Law, Criminol. & Pol. Sci., **60,** 141–47.

HAWKINS, G.J., 1969
Deterrence: the problematic postulate.
Proceedings of the Inst. Criminol., Univ. of Sydney Faculty of Law, No. 1, 38–56.

HAWKINS, G.J., 1969
Punishment and deterrence: the educative, moralising and habituative effects.
Wisconsin Law Rev., 550–65.

JENSEN, G.F., 1969
'Crime doesn't pay': correlates of a shared misunderstanding.
Social Problems, **17,** 189–201.

LUNDEN, W.A., 1969
Is there any penalty in the death penalty?
Ames, Iowa: Art Press.

TITTLE, C.R., 1969
Crime rates and legal sanctions.
Social Problems, **16,** 409–23.

WILLIAMS, G.P., 1969
1968—the first full year of the breathalyser: a regional analysis of official Home Office statistics. London: Christian Economic & Social Research Foundation.

BEDAU, H., 1970
The death penalty as a deterrent: argument and evidence.
Ethics, **82,** 205–17.

CHIRICOS, T.G., AND WALDO, G.P., 1970
Punishment and crime: an examination of some empirical evidence.
Social Problems, **18,** 200–17.

COHEN, B.L., 1970
Law without order. Capital punishment and the liberals.
New Rochelle, New York: Arlington House.

MCMAHON, J.P., 1970
Air hijacking: extradition as a deterrent.
Georgetown Law J., **58,** 1135–52.

ROSS, H.L., CAMPBELL, D.T., AND GLASS, G.V., 1970
Determining the social effects of a legal reform.
The British 'breathalyser' crackdown of 1967.
Amer. Behav. Scientist., **13,** 493–509.

TAPP, J.L., AND LEVINE, F.J., 1970
Persuasion to virtue: a preliminary statement.
Law & Society Rev., **4,** 565–82.

WALDO, G.P., AND HALL, E., 1970
Delinquency potential and attitudes toward the criminal justice system.
Social Forces, **49,** 291–98.

AMERICAN FRIENDS SERVICE COMMITTEE, 1971
Struggle for justice. A report on crime and punishment in America.
New York: Hill & Wang, 48–67.

ANDENAES, J., 1971
Deterrence and specific offenses.
Univ. Chicago Law Rev., **38,** 537–53.

ANDENAES, J., 1971
The moral or educative influence of criminal law.
J. Social Issues, **27,** 17–31.

BEDAU, H.A., 1971
The death penalty in America: review and forecast.
Fed. Probation, **35**, (1), 32–43.

BEDAU, H.A., 1971
Deterrence and the death penalty: a reconsideration.
J. Crim. Law, Criminol. & Pol. Sci., **61**, 539–48.

EDISON, M., 1971
The empirical assault on capital punishment.
J. Legal Ed., **23**, 2–15.

INBAU, F.E., AND CARRINGTON, F.G., 1971
There's more to crime control than the 'get tough' approach.
Annals Amer. Acad. Pol. & Soc. Sci., **397**, 28–39.

ZIMRING, F.E., 1971
Perspectives on deterrence.
Chevy Chase, Md.: National Institute of Mental Health, Centre for Studies of Crime and Delinquency.

ZIMRING, F.E., AND HAWKINS, G., 1971
The legal threat as an instrument of social change.
J. Social Issues, **27**, 33–48.

ANDERSON, D.C., AND WHITMAN, T.L., 1972
The control of behavior through law: theory and practice.
Notre Dame Lawyer, **47**, 815–52.

BOWERS, W.J., AND SALEM, R.G., 1972
Severity of formal sanctions as a repressive response to deviant behavior.
Law & Society Rev., **6**, 427–41.

BUIKHUISEN, W., 1972
General deterrence: research and theory.
Groningen Univ., Netherlands: Criminological Institute. Mimeo.

CHAPPELL, D., GEIS, G., AND HARDT, R., 1972
Exploration in deterrence and criminal justice.
Crim. Law Bull., **8**, 514–38.

DECKER, J.F., 1972
Curbside deterrence?
Criminol., **10**, 127–42.

EHRLICH, I., 1972
The deterrent effect of criminal law enforcement.
J. Legal Studies, **1**, 259–76.

FATTAH, E.A., 1972
A study of the deterrent effect of capital punishment with special reference to the Canadian situation.
Research Centre Report 2, Department of the Solicitor General Canada.
Ottawa: Information Canada.

KIKUTA, K., 1972
The system of capital punishment and public opinion, in *Reform of the Federal Criminal Laws.*
Hearing before the sub-committee on criminal laws and procedures of the Committee on the Judiciary United States Senate 92nd Congress, Part III, March 21, 1972, Washington, D.C., 2128–42.

LOGAN, C.G., 1972
General deterrent effects of imprisonment.
Social Forces, **51**, 64–73.

MCGRATH, W.T., 1972
The death penalty.
An official statement of policy, Canadian Criminology and Correction Association, Ottawa.

PHILLIPS, L., AND VOTEY, H.L.JR., 1972
An economic analysis of the deterrent effect of law enforcement on criminal activity.
J. Crim. Law, Criminol. & Pol. Sci., **63**, 330–42.

RADZINOWICZ, L., 1972
The criminal law explosion—can it be controlled?
Columbia J. Law & Social Problems, **9**, 88–130.

SALEM, R.G., AND BOWERS, W.J., 1972
Severity of formal sanctions as a deterrent to deviant behavior, in S. Krislov, *et al.* (eds.), *Compliance and the law.*
Beverly Hills, Calif.: Sage Publications, 313–32.

SCHLOSS, B., AND GIESBRECHT, N.A., 1972
Murder in Canada: a report on capital and non-capital murder statistics 1961–1970
Research report of the Centre of Criminology, Univ. of Toronto.

TEEVEN, J.J.JR., 1972
Deterrent effects of punishment: the Canadian case.
Can. J. Criminol. & Corrections, **14**, 68–82.

THORSELL, B.A., AND KLEMKE, L.W., 1972
The labelling process: reinforcement and deterrent?
Law & Society Rev., **6**, 393–403.

UNITED KINGDOM, 1972
The penalties for homicide.
Report by the Committee appointed by the Secretary of State for Scotland and the Lord Advocate.
Edinburgh: Scottish Home and Health Department, Cmnd. 5137.

UNITED STATES OF AMERICA, 1972
Supreme Court of the United States,
Furman v. Georgia, 69–5003, 29 June 1972

VERSELE, S.C., GOFFIN, R., TSAMADOU, C.H.R., LECROSS, P., AND VAN HAECHT, A., 1972–3
Justice pénale et opinion publique.
Bruxelles: l'Université de Bruxelles.

WALDO, G.P., AND CHIRICOS, T.G., 1972
Perceived penal sanctions and self-reported criminality: a neglected approach to deterrence research.
Social Problems, **19**, 522–40.

ANTUNES, G., AND HUNT, A.L., 1973
The impact of certainty and severity of punishment on levels of crime in American states: an extended analysis.
J. Crim. Law & Criminol., **64**, 486–93.

BEDAU, H.A., 1973
The Nixon administration and the deterrent effect of the death penalty.
Univ. Pittsburgh Law Rev., **34**, 557–66.

BREIT, W., AND ELZINGA, K.G., 1973
Antitrust penalties and attitudes towards risk: an economic analysis.
Harvard Law Rev., **86**, 693–735.

EHRHARDT, C.W., HUBBART, P.A., LEVINSON, L.H., SMILEY, W.McK.JR., and WILLS, T.A., 1973
The future of capital punishment in Florida: analysis and recommendations.
J. Crim. Law & Criminol., **64**, 2–21.

JAYEWARDENE, C.H.S., 1973
The death penalty and the safety of Canadian policemen.
Can. J. Criminol. & Corrections, **15**, 356–66.

JOURNAL OF CRIMINAL LAW AND CRIMINOLOGY, 1973
Capital punishment after Furman. **64**, 281–89.

KNEALE, A., 1973
Against birching: judicial corporal punishment in the Isle of Man.
London: National Council for Civil Liberties.

MORRISON, W.A., 1973
Criminal homicide and the death penalty in Canada: time for re-assessment and new directions: toward a typology of homicide.
Can. J .Criminol. & Corrections, **15**, 367–96.

ROBERTSON, L.S., RICH, R.F., AND ROSS, H.L., 1973
Jail sentences for driving while intoxicated in Chicago: a judicial policy that failed.
Law & Society Rev., **8**, 55–68.

ROSS, H.L., 1973
Law, science and accidents: the British Road Safety Act of 1967.
J. Legal Studies, **2**, 1–78.

ROTTENBERG, S. (ED.), 1973
The economics of crime and punishment: a conference sponsored by American Enterprise Institute for Public Policy Research. Part II, Does punishment deter? (papers by L. Phillips, C.R. Tittle. Comments on papers in seminar: G. Krohm, B. Klein, J.P. Gibbs).
Washington, D.C.: American Enterprise Institute for Public Policy Research, 65–116.

SULLIVAN, R.F., 1973
The economics of crime: an introduction to the literature.
Crime & Delinq., **19**, 138–49.

TITTLE, C.R., AND LOGAN, C.H., 1973
Sanctions and deviance: evidence and remaining questions.
Law & Society Rev., **7**, 371–92.

UNITED KINGDOM, 1973
Penalty for murder.
Criminal Law Revision Committee, twelfth report.
London: Cmnd. 5184.

UNITED NATIONS ECONOMIC AND SOCIAL COUNCIL, 1973
Capital punishment.
Report of the Secretary-General, 54th session, Agenda item 13, E/5242, 23 February 1973, New York.

WARD, P.G., AND MISNER, R.L., 1973
Methodological problems in determining the effects of severe penalties on road safety.
Aust. N.Z.J. Criminol., **6,** 240–45.

ZIMRING, F.E., AND HAWKINS, G.J., 1973
Deterrence: the legal threat in crime control.
Univ. Chicago Press.

ANDENAES, J., 1974
Punishment and deterrence.
Ann Arbor: Univ. Michigan Press.

OZENNE, T., 1974
The economics of bank robbery.
J. Legal Studies, **3,** 19–51.

TITTLE, C.R., AND ROWE, A.R., 1974
Certainty of arrest and crime rates: a further test of the deterrence hypothesis.
Social Forces, **52,** 455–62.

WELLFORD, C.F., 1974
Deterrence: issues and methodologies in the analysis of the impact of legal threat in crime control.
J. Crim. Law & Criminol., **65,** 117–22.

BAXTER, R., AND NUTTALL, C., 1975
Severe sentences: no deterrent to crime?
New Society, **31,** (639), 2 Jan., 11–13.

2 Follow-up and comparative studies of established sanctions

ZUCKERMAN, S.B., BARRON, A.J., AND WHITTIER, H.B., 1953
A follow-up study of Minnesota state reformatory inmates.
J. Crim. Law, Criminol. & Pol. Sci., **43,** 622–36.

ENGLAND, R.W., 1955
A study of post-probation recidivism among five hundred federal offenders.
Fed. Probation, **19** (3), 10–16.

GIBBENS, T.C.N., POND, D.A., AND STAFFORD-CLARK, D., 1955
A follow-up study of criminal psychopaths.
Brit. J. Delinq., **6,** 126–36.

MANNHEIM, H., AND WILKINS, L.T., 1955
Prediction methods in relation to borstal training.
London: H.M.S.O., 1–27.

MORRISON, R.L., 1955
Predictive research: a critical assessment of its practical applications.
Brit. J. Delinq., **6,** 99–115.

WILKINS, L.T., 1955
Some developments in prediction methodology in applied social research.
Brit. J. Sociol., **6,** 348–54.

CAMBRIDGE DEPARTMENT OF CRIMINAL SCIENCE, 1958
Results of probation.
London: Macmillan, 1–11, 26–36, 51–60.

SELLIN, T., 1958
Recidivism and maturation.
Nat. Prob. & Parole Assn. J., **4,** 241–50.

WILKINS, L.T., 1958
A small comparative study of the results of probation.
Brit. J. Delinq., **8,** 201–9.

BENSON, G., 1959
Prediction methods and young prisoners.
Brit. J. Delinq., **9,** 192–9.

GLUECK, S. AND GLUECK, E., 1959
Predicting delinquency and crime.
Cambridge, Mass.: Harvard Univ. Press, 61–87.

GRÜNHUT, M., 1960
After effects of punitive detention.
Brit. J. Delinq., **10,** 178–94.

CITIZENS' COMMITTEE ON CHILDREN OF NEW YORK, INC., 1961
Research and potential application of research in probation, parole, delinquency prediction.

Research Clinic, New York School of Social Work, Columbia University; summary by P. Lerman, 1–11.

Lopez-Rey, M., 1961
Some misconceptions in contemporary criminology, in G.O.W. Mueller (ed.), *Essays in criminal science.*
London: Stevens, 5–29.

McClintock, F.H., 1961
Attendance centres.
London: Macmillan, 1–11, 26–49, 80–99.

Gibbens, T.C.N., 1963
Psychiatric studies of borstal lads.
London: Oxford Univ. Press, Appendix A, 205–9.

Hammond, W.H., and Chayen, E., 1963
Persistent criminals.
London: H.M.S.O., 89–100.

Glaser, D., 1964
The effectiveness of a prison and parole system.
Indianapolis: Bobbs-Merrill Co., 13–85, 465–96.

Shoham, S., and Sandberg, M., 1964
Suspended sentences in Israel.
Crime & Delinq., **10,** 74–83.

Babst, D.V., and Mannering, J.W., 1965
Probation versus imprisonment for similar types of offenders.
J. Res. Crime & Delinq., **2,** 60–71.

Goodman, N., 1965
Manchester senior attendance centre.
Brit. J. Criminol., **5,** 275–88.

Hood, R.G., 1965
Borstal re-assessed.
London: Heinemann, 207–15.

Wilkins, L.T., 1965
Research in criminology: a critical notice.
Internat. Rev. Crim. Policy, **23,** 47–55.

Bailey, W.C., 1966
Correctional outcome: an evaluation of 100 reports.
J. Crim. Law, Criminol. & Pol. Sci., **57,** 153–60.

Banks, C., 1966
Borstal, prison and detention centres, in H.J. Klare (ed.), *Changing concepts of crime and its treatment.*
Oxford: Pergamon Press, 117–38.

Eichman, C.J., and Wainwright, L.L., 1966.
The impact of the Gideon decision upon crime and sentencing in Florida: a study of recidivism and sociocultural change.
Tallahassee: Florida Division of Corrections Monograph No. 2, 69–73.

Glaser, D., and O'Leary, V., 1966
Personal characteristics and parole outcome.
Washington, D.C.: U.S. Dept. of Health, Education & Welfare, Welfare Administration, Office of Juvenile Delinquency and Youth Development.

Grygier, T., 1966
The effect of social action: current prediction methods and two new models.
Brit. J. Criminol., **6,** 269–93.

Hall Williams, J.E., 1966
Evaluating penal methods.
Internat. Social Science J., **18,** 162–75.

Adams, S., 1967
Some findings from correctional caseload research.
Fed. Probation, **31** (4), 48–57.

Gottfredson, D.M., 1967
Assessment and prediction methods in crime and delinquency, in *Task force report: juvenile delinquency and youth crime.*
Washington, D.C.: President's Commission on Law Enforcement and Administration of Justice, 171–87.

Hood, R.G., 1967
Research on the effectiveness of punishments and treatments, in *Collected studies in criminological research*, **1.**
Strasbourg: Council of Europe, 73–113.

McEachern, A.W., and Taylor, E.M., 1967
The effects of probation.
University of Southern California: Youth Studies Center, Mimeo.

Pennsylvania, Commonwealth of, 1967
A 20-year study of convicted parole violators returned to prison from 1 June, 1946 to 30 June, 1966.
Pennsylvania Board of Control.

McClintock, F.H., and Avison, N.H., 1968
Crime in England and Wales.
London: Heinemann, 220–49.

SCARPITTI, F.R., AND STEPHENSON, R.M., 1968
A study of probation effectiveness.
J. Crim. Law, Criminol. & Pol. Sci., **59,** 361–69.

SPARKS, R.F., 1968
Types of treatment for types of offender, *Collected studies in criminological research,* **3.**
Strasbourg: Council of Europe, 129–69.

PLOWMAN, D.E.G., 1969
What are the outcomes of casework?
Social Work, **26** (1), 10–19.

SAAKE, R.D., 1969
California juvenile camps and recidivism. A follow-up study of wards released from juvenile camps in 1966
Sacramento: California Department of Justice, Division of Law Enforcement, Bureau of Criminal Statistics. Mimeo.

UNITED KINGDOM, 1969
The sentence of the court; a handbook for courts on the treatment of offenders. London: Home Office.

WOLFGANG, M.E., 1969
Present status of research aimed at statistical evaluation of treatment programs.
Annales Internat. de Criminol., **8,** 409–36.

ADAMS, S., 1970
A comparative study of recidivism rates in six correctional systems.
District of Columbia Department of Corrections, Research Report No. 21.

HOOD, R., AND SPARKS, R., 1970
Key issues in criminology.
London: Weidenfeld & Nicolson, 171–214.

MASSACHUSETTS, STATE OF, 1970
An analysis of recidivism among convicted murderers.
Massachusetts Department of Correction. Mimeo.

SPARKS, R.F., 1970
Research on the use and effectiveness of probation, parole and measures of after-care, in *Practical organisation of measures for the supervision and after-care of conditionally sentenced or conditionally released offenders.*
Strasbourg: Council of Europe, 249–73.

WHITELEY, S., 1970
The response of psychopaths to a therapeutic community.
Brit. J. Psychiat., **116,** 517–29.

ANCEL, M., 1971
Suspended sentence.
London: Heinemann, 61–4.

LEVIN, M.A., 1971
Policy, evaluation and recidivism.
Law & Society Rev., **6,** 17–46.

MARTIN, J.P., AND WEBSTER, D., 1971
The social consequences of conviction.
London: Heinemann, 74–223.

NEWTON, M., 1971
Reconviction after treatment at Grendon.
CP Report, Series B, No. 1.
London: Prison Department, Home Office.

SIMON, F.H., 1971
Prediction methods in criminology, including a prediction study of young men on probation.
London: Home Office Research Studies, **7.**

CARR-HILL, G.A., AND CARR-HILL, R.A., 1972
Reconviction as a process.
Brit. J. Criminol., **12,** 35–43.

DAVIES, J., AND GOODMAN, N., 1972
Girl offenders aged 17 to 20 years.
London: Home Office Research Studies, **14.**

HESKETH, J.L., AND HEWITT, P.J., 1972
100 probation breakdowns and the concept of failure.
Brit. J. Criminol., **12,** 390–99.

LEFERENZ, H., 1972
Investigations on the validity of prediction tables in the field of probation, in G. Kaiser and T. Wurtenberger (eds.), *Criminological research trends in Western Germany.*
Berlin: Springer-Verlag, 62–73.

LE VINE, W.R., AND BORNSTEIN, P.E., 1972
Is the sociopath treatable? The contribution of psychiatry to a legal dilemma.
Washington Univ. Law Quart., 1972, 693–717.

LOGAN, C.H., 1972
Evaluation research in crime and delinquency: a reappraisal.
J. Crim. Law, Criminol. & Pol. Sci., **63,** 378–89.

MOBERG, D.O., AND ERICSON, R.C., 1972
A new recidivism outcome index.
Fed. Probation, **36** (2), 50–7.

SCHAFFSTEIN, F., 1972
Research into the effectiveness of probation results, in G. Kaiser and T. Wurtenberger (eds.), *Criminological research trends in Western Germany*.
Berlin: Springer-Verlag, 74–88.

SPENCER, C., AND BERECOCHEA, J.E., 1972
Recidivism among women parolees: a long term survey.
Sacramento: California Department of Corrections, Research Report No. 47, 1–3, 54–61.

UUSITALO, P., 1972
Recidivism after release from closed and open penal institutions.
Brit. J. Criminol., **12,** 211–29.

VENEZIA, P.S., 1972
Unofficial probation; an evaluation of its effectiveness.
J. Res. Crime & Delinq., **9,** 148–70.

WENK, E.A., ROBISON, J.O., AND SMITH, G.W., 1972
Can violence be predicted?
Crime & Delinq., **18,** 393–402.

WOLFGANG, M.E., FIGLIO, R.M., AND SELLIN, T., 1972
Delinquency in a birth cohort.
Univ. Chicago Press, 65–105, 244–55.

BELKIN, J., BLUMSTEIN, A., AND GLASS, W., 1973
Recidivism as a feedback process: an analytical model and empirical validation.
J. Crim. Justice., **1,** 7–26.

BOTTOMS, A.E., 1973
The efficacy of the fine: the case for agnosticism.
Crim. Law Rev., 1973, 543–51.

FRIDAY, P.C., AND PETERSEN, D.M., 1973
Shock of imprisonment: comparative analysis of short-term incarceration as a treatment technique.
Can. J. Criminol. & Corrections, **15,** 281–91.

GRAY, W.J., 1973
The English prison medical service: its historical background and more recent developments, in *Medical care of prisoners and detainees*.
CIBA Foundation Symposium **16** (new series).
Amsterdam: Associated Book Publishers, 129–42.

SHOHAM, S., BEN-DAVID, S., AND SMILANSKY, J., 1973
Rehabilitation treatment in institutions for juvenile delinquents in Israel, in S. Shoham (ed), *Israel studies in criminology*, **2.**
Jerusalem: Jerusalem Academic Press, 230–41.

SLAIKEU, K.A., 1973
Evaluation studies on group treatment of juvenile and adult offenders in correctional institutions.
J. Res. Crime & Delinq., **10,** 87–100.

SOFTLY, P., 1973
A survey of fine enforcement.
London: Home Office Research Studies, **16.**

WARD, D.A., 1973
Evaluative research for corrections, in L.E. Ohlin (ed.), *Prisoners in America.*
Englewood Cliffs, N.J.: Prentice-Hall, 184–206.

WILLETT, T.C., 1973
Drivers after sentence.
London: Heinemann, 96–143.

BUIKHUISEN, W., AND HOEKSTRA, H.A., 1974
Factors related to recidivism.
Brit. J. Criminol., **14,** 63–9.

CLARKE, R.V.G., AND SINCLAIR, I., 1974
Towards more effective treatment evaluation, in *Methods of evaluation and planning in the field of crime. Collected studies in criminological research*, **12,** 58–87.
Strasbourg: Council of Europe.

MARTINSON, R., 1974
What works?—questions and answers about prison reform.
Public Interest, No. 35, 22–54.

MARTINSON, R., LIPTON, D., AND WILKS, J., 1974

The effectiveness of correctional treatment.
New York: Praeger.

PAYNE, C., MCCABE, S., AND WALKER, N., 1974
Predicting offender-patients' reconvictions,
Brit. J. Psychiat., **125,** 60–4.

ROSS, H.L., AND BLUMENTHAL, M., 1974
Sanctions for the drinking driver.
J. Legal Studies, **3,** 53–61.

WALLER, I., 1974
Men released from prison.
Univ. Toronto Press, 146–92.

11 Assessing the impact of imprisonment

1 Prison community and social structure

AMERICAN PRISON ASSOCIATION, 1953
Prison riots and disturbances.
New York: American Prison Association Committee on Riots.

MCCORKLE, LL.W., AND KORN, R., 1954
Resocialisation within walls.
Annals Amer. Acad. Pol. & Soc. Sci., **293,** 88–98.

MACCORMICK, A.H., 1954
Behind the prison riots.
Annals Amer. Acad. Pol. & Soc. Sci., **293,** 17–27.

SCHRAG, C., 1953
Leadership among prison inmates.
Amer. Sociol. Rev., **19,** 37–42.

CRESSEY, D.R., AND KRASSOWSKI, W., 1957–8
Inmate organisation and anomie in American prisons and Soviet labor camps.
Social Problems, **5,** 217–30.

CLEMMER, D., 1958
The prison community.
New York: Holt, Rinehart & Winston.

SYKES, G., 1958
The society of captives.
New York: Univ. Princeton Press.

CLOWARD, R.A. (ED.), 1960
Theoretical studies in the social organisation oj the prison.
New York: Social Science Research Council Pamphlet, **15.**

SCHRAG, C., 1960
The sociology of prison riots.
American Correctional Association, Proceedings of the Ninetieth Annual Congress of Correction, 136–46.

SYKES, G., AND MESSINGER, S.L., 1960
Inmate social system, in R.A. Cloward (ed.), *Theoretical studies in the social organisation of the prison.*
New York: Social Science Research Council Pamphlet, **15.**

CRESSEY, D.R. (ED.), 1961
The prison, studies in institutional organisation and change.
New York: Holt, Rinehart & Winston.

MORRISON, R.L., 1962
Research in penal institutions.
Prison Service J., **1,** 44–52.

POLSKY, H.W., 1962
Cottage six: the social system of delinquent boys in residential treatment.
New York: Russell Sage Foundation.

MORRIS, T.P., AND MORRIS, P.M., 1963
Pentonville: a sociological study of an English prison.
London: Routledge & Kegan Paul, 161–91, 207–302.

MOULEDOUS, J.C., 1963
Organizational goals and structural change: a study of the organization of a prison social system.
Social Forces, **41,** 283–90.

GLASER, D., 1964
The effectiveness of a prison and parole system.
Indianapolis: Bobbs-Merrill Co., 89–148, 504–13.

IRWIN, J., AND CRESSEY, D.R., 1964
Thieves, convicts and the inmate culture, in H.S. Becker (ed.), *The other side.*
Glencoe, Ill.: Free Press, 225–45.

DUNLOP, A.B., AND MCCABE, S., 1965
Young men in detention centres.
London: Routledge & Kegan Paul.

GIBBONS, D.C., 1965
Changing the lawbreaker.
Englewood Cliffs, N.J.: Prentice-Hall, 189–227.

MATHIESEN, T., 1965
Resistance to change in correctional institutions, in *Collected studies in criminological research*, **1.**
Strasbourg: Council of Europe, 157–70.

MATHIESEN, T., 1965
The defences of the weak. A sociological study of a Norwegian correctional institution.
London: Tavistock, 53–210.

MORRIS, P., 1965
Prisoners and their families.
London: Allen &Unwin, 214–27.

STREET, D., 1965
The inmate group in custodial and treatment settings.
Amer. Sociol. Rev., **30,** 40–55.

THURRELL, R.J., HALLECK, S.L., AND JOHNSON, A.F., 1965
Psychosis in prison.
J. Crim. Law, Criminol. & Pol. Sci., **56,** 271–76.

WARD, D.A., AND KASSEBAUM, G.G., 1965
Women's prison: sex and social structure.
Chicago: Aldine Publishing Co.

CALDWELL, W.F., 1966
Black Muslims behind bars.
Research Studies, **34,** 185–203.

GIALLOMBARDO, R., 1966
Society of women: a study of a women's prison.
New York: John Wiley & Sons.

MATHIESEN, T., 1966
The sociology of prisons: problems for future research.
Brit. J. Sociol., **17,** 360–79.

STREET, D., VINTER, R.D., AND PERROW, C., 1966
Organization for treatment. A comparative study of institutions for delinquents.
New York: Free Press.

BLOMBERG, D., 1967
Survey from the standpoint of sociological and cultural studies of the environment of the place of detention or treatment, in *The effectiveness of punishments and other measures of treatment.*
Strasbourg: Council of Europe, 157–88.

MORRIS, T., 1967
Research on the prison community, in *Collected studies in criminological research*, **1.**
Strasbourg: Council of Europe, 125–56.

WELLFORD, C., 1967
Factors associated with adoption of the inmate code: a study of normative socialization.
J. Crim. Law, Criminol. & Pol. Sci., **58,** 197–203.

BAUM, M., AND WHEELER, S., 1968
Becoming an inmate, in S. Wheeler (ed.), *Controlling delinquents.*
New York: John Wiley & Sons, 153–85.

BRENT, J.E., 1968
A preliminary report on intergroup conflict at a penitentiary between black Muslim inmates and non-Muslim Negro inmates from Washington, D.C.
Washington, D.C. Mimeo.

DAVIS, A.J., 1968
Report on sexual assaults in the Philadelphia prison system and sheriff's vans.
Trans-actions, **6** (2), 8–15.

NEW YORK TIMES, 1968
Arkansas prisons: a grisly record of death, inmates living a nightmare of fear.
New York: N.Y. Times, (28 March), 1 and 32.

STUDT, E., MESSINGER, S.L., AND WILSON, T.P., 1968
C-Unit—search for community in prison.
New York: Russell Sage Foundation, 273–88.

VOGELMAN, R.P., 1968
Prison restrictions—prisoner rights.
J. Crim. Law, Criminol. & Pol. Sci., **59,** 386–96.

WHEELER, S., 1969
Socialisation in correctional institutions, in D.A. Goslin (ed.), *Handbook of socialization theory and research.*
New York: Rand McNally & Co.

AMERICAN CORRECTIONAL ASSOCIATION, 1970

Causes, preventive measures, and methods of controlling riots and disturbances in correctional institutions (Chairman, W.D. Leeke), Washington, D.C.

BRODSKY, S.L., AND EGGLESTON, M.E. (EDS.), 1970
The military prison. Theory, research, and practice.
Carbondale, Ill.: Southern Illinois University Press, 131–80.

CORMIER, B.M., 1970
Therapeutic community in a prison setting.
Annales Internat. de Criminol., **9,** 419–41.

EDWARDS, A.R., 1970
Inmate adaptations and socialization in the prison.
Sociology, **4,** 213–25.

GARABEDIAN, P.G., 1970
The natural history of an inmate community in a maximum security prison.
J. Crim. Law, Criminol. & Pol. Sci., **61,** 78–85.

HOOD, R., AND SPARKS, R., 1970
Key issues in criminology.
London: Weidenfeld and Nicolson, 215–34.

IRWIN, J., 1970
The felon.
Englewood Cliffs, N.J.: Prentice-Hall, 36–85.

MANOCCHIO, A.J., AND DUNN, J., 1970
The time game. Two views of a prison.
Beverly Hills, Calif.: Sage Publications.

CALIFORNIA, STATE OF, 1971
Report to Governor Ronald Reagan on violence in California prisons.
Sacramento: Board of Corrections.

CRIMINAL LAW BULLETIN, 1971
Attica: a look at the causes and the future, **7,** 817–43.

FOX, V., 1971
Why prisoners riot.
Fed. Probation, **35** (1), 9–14.

JOHNSON, E., 1971
The homosexual in prison.
Soc. Theory & Practice, **1,** 83–95.

KASSEBAUM, G., WARD, D.A., AND WILNER, D.M., 1971
Prison treatment and parole survival—an empirical assessment
New York: John Wiley & Sons, 118–76.

LEEKE, W.D., 1971
Collective violence in correctional institutions.
Amer. J. Correction, **33** (3), 12–16.

MATHIESEN, T., 1971
Across the boundaries of organizations.
Berkeley, Calif.: Glendessary Press.

RENTERIA, R.A., AND HOLT, N., 1971
The anatomy of an escape.
Amer. J. Correction, **33** (1), 10–15.

ROTHMAN, D.J., 1971
The discovery of the asylum, social order and disorder in the New Republic.
Boston: Little, Brown & Co.

SCHWARTZ, B., 1971
Pre-institutional vs. situational influence in a correctional community.
J. Crim. Law, Criminol. & Pol. Sci., **62,** 532–42.

ALBANY LAW REVIEW, 1972
Sexual assaults and forced homosexual relationships in prison: cruel and unusual punishment. **36,** 428–38.

ATKINS, B., AND GLICK, H.R., (ED). 1972
Prisons, protest and politics.
Englewood Cliffs, N.J.: Prentice-Hall.

BADILLO, H., AND HAYNES, M., 1972
A bill of no rights: Attica and the American prison system.
New York: Outerbridge & Lazard.

BRIGGS, D., 1972
A 'penal approach': communities in prison, in S. Whiteley, D. Briggs and M. Turner (eds.), *Dealing with deviants.*
London: Hogarth Press, 95–171.

COHEN, S., AND TAYLOR, L., 1972
Psychological survival.
Harmondsworth: Penguin Books.

COOPER, B.D., AND PEARSON, J., 1972
'C' wing—Parkhurst.
Prison Service J., **8,** 3–5.

GALLER, M., AND MARQUESS, H.E., 1972
Soviet prison camp speech: a survivor's glossary.
Madison, Wis.: Univ. of Wisconsin Press, 11–56.

HEFFERNAN, E., 1972
Making it in prison, the square, the cool, and the life.
New York: John Wiley & Sons.

HOLT, N., AND MILLER, D., 1972
Exploration in inmate-family relationships.
Sacramento, California: Research Division, Department of Corrections, Research Report **46.**

NEW YORK, STATE OF, 1972
Attica.
Official report of Special Commission (Chairman, Robert B. McKay).
New York: Bantam Books.

OSWALD, R.G., 1972
Attica—my story.
New York: Doubleday & Co.

THOMAS, C.W., AND FOSTER, S.C., 1972
Prisonization in the inmate contraculture.
Social Problems, **20,** 229–39.

BANISTER, P.A., SMITH, F.V., HESKIN, K.J., AND BOLTON, N., 1973–1974
Psychological correlates of long term imprisonment.
Brit. J. Criminol., Part I, Cognitive variables **13,** 312–23; Part II, Personality variables, **13,** 323–30; Part III, Attitudinal variables, **14,** 150–57 ; Part IV, A longitudinal analysis. **16,** 38–47.

BRADSHAW, J., EMERSON, D., AND HAXBY, D., 1973
Reception to prison.
Brit. J. Social Wk., **2,** 323–35.

COUNCIL OF EUROPE, 1973
Aspects of the prison community.
Strasbourg: European Committee on Crime Problems, DPC/BCC/COOR (70).

HANEY, C., BANKS, C., AND ZIMBARDO, P., 1973
Interpersonal dynamics in a simulated prison.
Internat. J. Criminol. & Penol., **1,** 69–97.

MATTICK, H.W., 1973
The prosaic sources of prison violence.
Aust. & N.Z.J. Criminol., **6,** 12–20.

THOMAS, C.W., 1973
Prisonization or resocialization? A study of external factors associated with the impact of imprisonment.
J. Res. Crime & Delinq., **10,** 13–21.

UNITED STATES OF AMERICA. HOUSE OF REPRESENTATIVES, 1973
93rd Congress, 1st Session, Union Calendar No. 157, House Report No. 93–329,
Reform of our correctional systems, a report by The Select Committee on Crime, Washington, D.C.

WELLFORD, C.F., 1973
Contact and commitment in a correctional community.
Brit. J. Criminol., **13,** 108–20.

WILBANKS, W.L., 1973
The report of the Commission on Attica.
Fed. Probation, **37** (1), 3–7.

WRIGHT, E.O., 1973
The politics of punishment: a critical analysis of prisons in America.
New York: Harper & Row, 57–261.

AKERS, R.L., HAYNER, N.S., AND GRUNINGER, W., 1974
Homosexual and drug behavior in prison: a test of the functional and importation models of the inmate system.
Social Problems, **21,** 410–22.

BENNETT, L.A., 1974
The application of self-esteem measures in a correctional setting: II, Changes in self-esteem during incarceration.
J. Res. Crime & Delinq., **11,** 9–15.

CAIRD, R., 1974
A good and useful life.
London: Hart-Davis, MacGibbon, 134–88.

JACOBS, J.B., 1974
Street gangs behind bars.
Social Problems, **21,** 395–409.

MCVICAR, J., 1974
McVicar, by himself. (edited by G. Rees).
London: Hutchinson, 31–142.

SHAW, M., 1974
Social work in prison: an experiment in the use of extended contact with offenders.
London: Home Office Research Studies, **22,** 26–41, 90–104.

SUTHERLAND, E.H., AND CRESSEY, D.R., 1974
Criminology. (9th ed.),
Chicago: Lippincott, 521–58.

2 Correctional standards and organizational problems

WEBER, G.H., 1957
Conflict between professional and non-professional personnel in institutional delinquency treatment.
J. Crim. Law, Criminol. & Pol. Sci., **48**, 26–43.

LOPEZ-REY, M., 1958
Some considerations on the character and organisation of prison labor.
J. Crim. Law, Criminol. & Pol. Sci., **49**, 10–28.

JOHNSTON, N., 1961
Recent trends in correctional architecture.
Brit. J. Criminol., **1**, 317–38.

GILL, H.B., 1962
Correctional philosophy and architecture.
J. Crim. Law, Criminol. & Pol. Sci., **53**, 312–22.

COOPER, M.H., AND KING, R.D., 1965
Social and economic problems of prisoners' work, in P. Halmos (ed.), *Sociological studies in the British penal services.*
Keele: Sociol. Rev. Monograph No. 9, 145–73.

LOPEZ-REY, M., 1965
Administrative penology (England and Wales).
Brit. J. Criminol., **5**, 4–21.

MATHIESEN, T., 1965
Resistance to change in correctional institutions, in *Collected studies in criminological research*, **1.**
Strasbourg: Council of Europe, 157–70.

ROSE, A.G., 1965
Administrative consequences of penal objectives, in P. Halmos (ed.), *Sociological studies in the British penal services.*
Sociological Review monograph No. 9, 211–26.

AMERICAN CORRECTIONAL ASSOCIATION, 1966
Manual of correctional standards. 3rd ed.
New York: Amer. Correctional Assn., 313–86.

LEOPOLD, N., 1966
What is wrong with the prison system?
Nebraska Law Rev., **45**, 33–57.

NASATIR, M., DEZZANI, D., AND SILBERT, M., 1966
Atascadero: ramifications of a maximum security treatment institution.
Issues in Criminol., **2**, 29–46.

NATIONAL COUNCIL ON CRIME AND DELINQUENCY, 1966
Standard Act for state correctional services.
New York.

NEW YORK, STATE OF, 1966
County jails and penitentiaries in New York State.
New York State Commission of Investigation.

PICKERING, I.G., 1966
Problems of the long-term prisoner.
Medico-Legal J., **34**, 159–67.

UNITED KINGDOM, 1966
Report of the inquiry into prison escaped and security (Mountbatten Report).
London: Home Office, Cmnd. 3175, 53–91.

WENDELL, M., 1966
Multijurisdictional aspects of corrections.
Nebraska Law Rev., **45**, 520–41.

BREED, A.F., 1967
The significance of classification procedures to the field of correction.
A document submitted to the President's Commission on Law Enforcement and Administration of Justice, Washington, D.C. Mimeo.

CRIME AND DELINQUENCY, 1967
Special issue on: Correction in in the United States.
A survey for the President's Commission.
13, (1), whole issue.

FREEDMAN, M., AND PAPPAS, N., 1967
The training and employment of offenders.
A document submitted to the President's Commission on Law Enforcement and Administration of Justice, Washington, D.C.

MACCORMICK, A., 1967
Adult correctional institutions in the United States.
A document submitted to the President's Commission on Law Enforcement and

Administration of Justice, Washington, D.C. Mimeo., 9–20, 34–53.

McGee, R.A., and Reimer, E., 1967
The federal government's role in corrections.
A document submitted to the President's Commission on Law Enforcement and Administration of Justice, Washington, D.C. Mimeo.

United States of America, 1967
Task force report: corrections.
Washington, D.C.: President's Commission on Law Enforcement and Administration of Justice, 1–16, 20–2, 45–59, 72–81, 93–114, 141–9, 162–8, 177–84, 191–205, 209–15.

United Kingdom, 1967
Royal Commission on the Penal System in England and Wales.
Written evidence from government departments, miscellaneous bodies and individual witnesses.
London, **4,** 101–26 (evidence submitted by prisoners).

United States of America, 1967
The challenge of crime in a free society.
Report of the President's Commission on Law Enforcement and Administration of Justice, Washington, D.C. 159–65, 171–9.

Verborgen, L., 1967
Imprisonment and conjugal life. A proposal for legislation.
Hartwick Review, **3,** 67–78.

Cantor, B., and Adams, S., 1968
The cost of correcting youthful offenders.
District of Columbia Department of Corrections.
Research report No. 6. Mimeo.

United Kingdom, 1968
The regime for long-term prisoners in conditions of maximum security.
Report of the Advisory Council on the Penal System (Chairman, Leon Radzinowicz).
London: Home Office.

United States of America, 1968
Custodial Manual.
Federal Prison Service. Policy Statement 20,001A (rev.). Bureau of Prisons. Mimeo.

United States of America, 1968
Special Report: *The Delta prisons: punishment for profit.*
Southern Regional Council, Atlanta 3, Georgia. Mimeo.

University of Florida Law Review, 1968
Prisoners' gain time: incentive, deterrent or ritual response? **21,** 103–16.

Gallington, D.J., 1969
Prison disciplinary decisions.
J. Crim. Law, Criminol. & Pol. Sci., **60,** 152–64.

Seliger, S.G., 1969
Toward a realistic reorganization of the penitentiaries.
J. Crim. Law, Criminol. & Pol. Sci., **60,** 47–58.

United Kingdom, 1969
People in prison (England and Wales).
London: Cmnd. 4214.

American Correctional Association, 1970
Causes, preventive measures, and methods of controlling riots and disturbances in correctional institutions (Chairman, W.D. Leeke).
Washington, D.C.

American Law Institute, 1970
Model penal code.
Part III (Treatment and correction) and Part IV (Organization of correction).
Philadelphia: American Law Institute.

Clark, R., 1970
Crime in America.
New York: Simon and Schuster, 212–38.

Emery, F.E., 1970
Freedom and justice within walls: the Bristol prison experiment.
London: Tavistock, 1–20.

McCleery, R.H., 1970
Policy change in prison management, in A. Etzioni (ed.), *A sociological reader on complex organizations.* (2nd ed.)
London: Holt, Rinehart & Winston, 200–22.

Morris, N., and Hawkins, G., 1970
The honest politician's guide to crime control.
Univ. Chicago Press, 111–44.

PARKER, T., 1970
The frying-pan: a prison and its prisoners.
London: Hutchinson & Co.

SELLIN, T., 1970
The origin of the 'Pennsylvania system of prison discipline'.
Prison J., (special number on the rise and fall of Eastern Penitentiary 1829–1970), **50** (1), 13–21.

TEETERS, N.K., 1970
The passing of Cherry Hill: most famous prison in the world.
Prison J., (special number on the rise and fall of Eastern Penitentiary 1829–1970), **50** (1), 3–12.

CRIMINAL LAW BULLETIN, 1971
Attica: a look at the causes and the future.
7, 817–43.

DICKINSON LAW REVIEW, 1971
Punitive segregation in state prisons—the need for definite time limitations. **76,** 125–43.

FLYNN, E.E., AND MOYER, F.D., 1971
Corrections and architecture: a synthesis.
Prison J., **51,** 43–53.

GILBERT, A., 1971
Observations about recent correctional architecture.
Prison J., **51,** 7–14.

GLASER, D., 1971
Politicalization of prisoners: a new challenge to American penology.
Amer. J. of Correction, **33,** 6–9.

O'LEARY, V., AND DUFFEE, D., 1971
Correctional policy, a classification of goals designed for change.
Crime & Delinq., **17,** 373–86.

SPARKS, R.F., 1971
Local prisons: the crisis in the English penal system.
London: Heinemann, 89–104.

BRADSHAW, J., EMERSON, D., AND HAXBY, D., 1972
Reception to prison.
Brit. J. Social Work, **2,** 323–35.

DURANT, M., THOMAS, M., AND WILCOCK, H.D., 1972
Crime, criminals and the law.
London: Office of Population Censuses and Surveys, Social Survey Division, 68–115.

GARSON, G.D., 1972
Force versus restraint in prison riots.
Crime & Delinq., **18,** 411–21.

GARSON, G.D., 1972
The disruption of prison administration: an investigation of alternative theories of the relationship among administrators, reformers and involuntary social service clients.
Law & Society Rev., **6,** 531–61.

JEPSON, N.A., 1972
The value of prison?
Howard J. Penol. & Crime Prev., **13,** 234–45.

KUTAK, R.J., AND KLIPPERT, G.B., 1972
Prisons on the endangered list.
Amer. Crim. Law Rev., **11,** 165–96.

NEW YORK, STATE OF, 1972
Attica.
Official report of Special Commission (Chairman, Robert B. McKay).
New York: Bantam Books.

OSWALD, R.G., 1972
Attica—my story.
Garden City, New York: Doubleday & Co.

RICHMOND, M.S., 1972
Measuring the cost of correctional services.
Crime & Delinq., **18,** 243–52.

ROTHMAN, D.J., 1972
The invention of the penitentiary.
Crim. Law Bull., **8,** 555–86.

SCHWITZGEBEL, R.K., 1972
Development and legal regulation of coercive behavior modification techniques with offenders.
Rockville, Md.: N.I.M.H. Center for Studies of Crime and Delinquency.

TAGGART, R., 1972
The prison of unemployment: manpower programs for offenders.
Baltimore: Johns Hopkins Univ. Press.

THOMAS, J.E., 1972
The English prison officer since 1850.
London: Routledge & Kegan Paul, 181–231.

UNITED KINGDOM, 1972
The penalties for homicide.
Report by the Committee appointed by The Secretary of State for Scotland and the

Lord Advocate, Scottish Home and Health Department, Edinburgh, Cmnd. 5137.

UNITED STATES OF AMERICA, 1972
American prisons in turmoil, Parts I and II, Hearings before the Select Committee on Crime, House of Representatives, 92nd Congress, Washington, D.C.

WILLIAMS, V.L., AND FISH, M., 1972
Optimum prison size: cost behavior vs. rehabilitation goals.
Amer. J. of Correction, **34,** 14–19.

COUNCIL OF EUROPE, 1973
Aspects of the prison community.
Strasbourg: European Committee on Crime Problems, DPC/BCC/COOR (70).

HOPKINS, A., 1973
The prison strike: some general considerations and a case study.
Aust. & N.Z.J. Criminol., **6,** 32–46.

JOHNSTON, N., 1973
The human cage: a brief history of prison architecture.
New York: Walker & Co.

MARKLEY, C.W., 1973
Furlough programs and conjugal visiting in adult correctional institutions.
Fed. Probation, **37** (1), 19–26.

MATTICK, H.W., 1973
The prosaic sources of prison violence.
Aust. & N.Z.J. Criminol., **6,** 12–20.

MEUNIER, P.D., AND SCHWARTZ, H.D., 1973
Beyond Attica, prison reform in New York State, 1971–1973.
Cornell Law Rev., **58,** 924–1023.

MISNER, R.L., 1973
Prison discipline: the inherent conflicts.
Aust. & N.Z.J. Criminol., **6,** 21–31.

MORRIS, N., AND HAWKINS, G.M., 1973
Attica revisited: the prospect for prison reform.
Arizona Law Rev., **14,** 747–63.

MORRIS, T.P., 1973
Custodial treatment of offenders, Ditchley paper No. 45.
Enstone, Oxon: Ditchley Foundation.

SINGER, L.R., 1973
Women and the correctional process.
Amer. Crim. Law Rev., **11,** 295–308.

SINGER, N.M., 1973
Incentives and the use of prison labor.
Crime & Delinq., **19,** 200–11.

STOLLMACK, S., 1973
Predicting inmate populations from arrest, court disposition, and recidivism rates.
J. Res. Crime & Delinq., **10,** 141–62.

UNITED KINGDOM, 1973
Penalty for murder.
Criminal Law Revision Committee, Twelfth report.
London, Cmnd. 5184.

UNITED STATES OF AMERICA. HOUSE OF REPRESENTATIVES, 1973
93rd Congress, 1st Session, Union Calendar No. 157, House Report No. 93–329,
Reform of our correctional systems.
A report by the Select Committee on Crime, Washington, D.C.

WILBANKS, W.L., 1973
The report of the Commission on Attica.
Fed. Probation, **37** (1), 3–7.

COHEN, S., 1974
A futuristic scenario for the prison system, in F. Basaglia (ed.), *The crimes of peace.*
Turin: Einaudi.

COUNCIL OF EUROPE, 1974
Short-term treatment of adult offenders.
Strasbourg: Council of Europe.

LIPMAN, D.M., 1974
Mississippi's prison experience.
Mississippi Law J., **45,** 685–753.

MILLER, M.B., 1974
At hard labour: rediscovering the 19th century prison.
Issues in Criminol., **9,** 91–114.

STENDER, F., 1974
The 'closing' of O Wing at Soledad prison: reflections on the use of lock-up.
Mississippi Law J., **45,** 645–73.

12 New approaches to the treatment of offenders

[*See also Section 7(2) on problems of conflicting values; Section 14(1) on rights of prisoners.*]

1 Experimental studies

WEEKS, H.A., 1958
Youthful offenders at Highfields.
Univ. Michigan Press.

GRANT, J.D., AND GRANT, M.Q., 1959
A group dynamics approach to the treatment of non-conformists in the navy.
Annals Amer. Acad. Pol. & Soc. Sci., **322,** 126–35.

ADAMS, S., 1961
Interaction between individual interview therapy and treatment amenability in older youth authority wards, in *Inquiries concerning kinds of treatments for kinds of delinquents.*
Sacramento: California Board of Corrections, monograph No. 2. 27–44.

ADAMS, S., AND GRANT, M.Q., 1961
A demonstration project: an evaluation of community-located treatment for delinquents.
Sacramento: California Board of the Youth Authority, C.T.P. Research Report No. 1.

CALIFORNIA, STATE OF, 1961
Demonstration-treatment research projects.
Sacramento: California Department of Corrections, Research Report no. 1.

EMPEY, L.T., AND RABOW, J., 1961
The Provo experiment in delinquency rehabilitation.
Amer. Sociol. Rev., **26,** 679–96.

GRANT, M.Q., 1961
Interaction between kinds of treatments and kinds of delinquents, in *Inquiries concerning kinds of treatments for kinds of delinquents.*
Sacramento: California Board of Corrections, monograph No. 2, 5–14.

MCCLINTOCK, F.H., 1961
Attendance centres.
London: Macmillan, 1–11, 26–49.

BALL, A.C., 1963
Reducing state correctional costs, *in Saginaw Probation Demonstration Project.*
Michigan Crime and Delinquency Council, 1–4.

HAVEL, J., 1963
SIPU 4: the high base expectancy study.
Sacramento: California Department of Corrections, Research Reports No. 10 (and summary).

ELIAS, A., AND PILNICK, S., 1964
The Essexfields group rehabilitation project for youthful offenders, in *Correction in the community, alternatives to incarceration.*
Sacramento: California Board of Corrections, monograph No. 4, 51–7.

HEIM, R.B., 1964
Perceptions and reactions of prison inmates to two therapeutic communities.
Sacramento: Institute for the Study of Crime and Delinquency, Mimeo.

MILLER, D., 1964
Growth to freedom.
London: Tavistock, xi–61, 155–206.

WARREN, M.Q., 1964
An experiment in alternatives to incarceration for delinquent youth: recent findings in the community treatment project, in *Correction in the community, alternatives to incarceration.*
Sacramento: California Board of Corrections, Monograph No. 4, 39–50.

BERNTSEN, K., AND CHRISTIANSEN, K.O.,
A resocialisation experiment with short-term offenders, *Scandinavian Studies in Criminology*, **1.**
London: Tavistock, 35–54.

GLASER, D., 1965
Correctional research: an elusive paradise.
J. Res. Crime & Delinq., **2,** 1–11.

GLASER, D., 1965
New trends in research on the treatment of offenders and the prevention of crime in the United States.
Internat. Rev. Crim. Policy, **23,** 3–9.

MANDEL, N.G., AND PARSONAGE, W.H., 1965
An experiment in adult 'group-parole' supervision.
Crime & Delinq., **11,** 313–25.

CRAFT, M., 1966
The Balderton psychopathic unit, in M. Craft (ed.), *Psychopathic disorders.*
Oxford: Pergamon Press, 116–34.

HOOD, R.G., 1966
Homeless borstal boys.
Occasional Papers on Social Administration, No. 18.
London: G. Bell & Sons, 11–17, 26–43.

ADAMS, S., 1967
Some findings from correctional caseload research.
Fed. Probation, **31** (4), 48–57.

CALIFORNIA, STATE OF, AND THE NATIONAL INSTITUTE OF MENTAL HEALTH, 1967
The Community treatment project after 5 years.
Sacramento: California, Department of the Youth Authority. Mimeo.

EMPEY, L.T., 1967
Alternatives to incarceration.
Washington, D.C.: Department of Health, Education & Welfare, Office of Juvenile Delinquency and Youth Development.

EMPEY, L.T., 1967
The Provo experiment, in H. Gold and F.R. Scarpitti (eds.), *Combating social problems.*
New York: Holt, Rinehart & Winston, 371–404.

LOHMAN, J.D., WAHL, A., CARTER, R.M., AND LEWIS, S.P., 1967
The 'intensive supervision caseloads': a preliminary evaluation, in San Francisco Project, Research Report No. 11, School of Criminology, Univ. of California, 1–3, 25–37, 37–8.

WARD, D.A., 1967
Evaluations of correctional treatment: some implications of negative findings, in S.A. Yefsky (ed.), *Law enforcement, science and technology.*
Washington, D.C.: Thompson Book Co., 201–14.

WARREN, M.Q., 1967
Classification of offenders as an aid to efficient management and effective treatment.
A document submitted to the President's Commission on Law Enforcement and Administration of Justice, Washington, D.C. 22–39. Mimeo.

WARREN, M.Q., 1967
The community treatment project: history and prospects, in S.A. Yefsky (ed.), *Law enforcement, science and technology.*
Washington, D.C.: Thompson Book Co., 191–200.

SPARKS, R.F., 1968
Types of treatment for types of offenders, in *Collected studies in criminological research,* **3.**
Strasbourg: Council of Europe, 129–69.

STUDT, E., MESSINGER, S.L., AND WILSON, T.P., 1968
C-Unit—search for community in prison.
New York: Russell Sage Foundation, 273–88.

BANCROFT, J., 1969
Aversion therapy of homosexuality: a pilot study of 10 cases.
Brit. J. Psychiat., **115,** 1417–31.

BURKHART, W.R., 1969
The parole work unit programme: an evaluation report.
Brit. J. Criminol., **9,** 125–47.

KIRBY, B.C., 1969
Crofton House: an experiment with a county halfway house.
Fed. Probation, **33** (1), 53–58.

WILKINS, L.T., 1969
Evaluation of penal measures.
New York: Random House, 114–56.

WILKINS, L.T., AND GOTTFREDSON, D.M., 1969
Research, demonstration and social action.
Davis, Calif.: National Council on Crime and Delinquency, ix–xviii, 21–42. Mimeo.

AMERICAN BAR ASSOCIATION, 1970
Standards relating to probation.
Project on standards for criminal justice.
New York: A.B.A.

EMERY, F.E., 1970
Freedom and justice within walls: the Bristol Prison experiment.
London: Tavistock.

HARLOW, E., 1970
Intensive intervention: an alternative to institutionalisation.
Crime & Delinq. Literature, **2,** 3–46.

KNIGHT, D., 1970
The Marshall program. Assessment of a short-term institutional treatment program.
Part II Amenability to confrontive peer-group treatment.
Sacramento: California Department of the Youth Authority, Research report No. 59. 55–71.

PALMER, T., 1970
The Phase I, II and III experiments: developments and progress. California's community treatment project.
Sacramento: California Department of the Youth Authority, C.T.P. Research Report No. 10.

PARKER, T., 1970
The frying-pan: a prison and its prisoners.
London: Hutchinson & Co.

ROBERTS, C.F.JR., 1970
A final evaluation of the narcotic control program for youth authority parolees.
Sacramento: California Department of the Youth Authority, Research report no. 58, 69–83.

ROBISON, J., 1970
The California prison, parole and probation system. 'It's time to stop counting'.
A special report to the Assembly.
Technical supplement no. 2. State of California, Sacramento. Mimeo, 40–78.

UNITED STATES OF AMERICA, 1970
Differential treatment . . . a way to begin.
Washington, D.C.: Department of Justice, Bureau of Prisons.

WARREN, M.Q., 1970
The case for differential treatment of delinquents.
Can. J. Correct., **12,** 451–65.

WHITELEY, S., 1970
The response of psychopaths to a therapeutic community.
Brit. J. Psychiat., **116,** 517–29.

ADAMS, R., AND VETTER, H.J., 1971
Probation caseload size and recidivism rate.
Brit. J. Criminol., **11,** 390–93.

EMPEY, L.T., AND LUBECK, S.G., 1971
The Silverlake experiment—testing delinquency theory and community intervention.
Chicago, Ill.: Aldine Publishing Co., 3–21, 253–76, 299–311.

GARABEDIAN, P.G., 1971
Research and practice in planning correctional change.
Crime & Delinq., **17,** 41–56.

HOLT, N., 1971
Temporary prison release, California's prerelease furlough program.
Crime & Delinq., **17,** 414–30.

JESNESS, C.F., 1971
The Preston typology study—an experiment with differential treatment in an institution.
J. Res. Crime & Delinq., **8,** 38–52.

KASSEBAUM, G., WARD, D.A., AND WILNER, D.M., 1971
Prison treatment and parole survival—an empirical assessment.
New York: John Wiley & Sons, 207–324.

NEWTON, M., 1971
Reconviction after treatment at Grendon.
CP Report, Series B, No. 1.
London: Prison Dept., Home Office.

PALMER, T.B., 1971
California's community treatment program for delinquent adolescents.
J. Res. Crime & Delinq., **8,** 74–92.

ROBISON, J., 1971
The effectiveness of correctional programs.
Crime & Delinq., **17,** 67–80.

SADOFF, R.L., ROETHER, H.A., AND PETERS, J.J., 1971
Clinical measure of enforced group psychotherapy.
Amer. J. Psychiat., **128,** 224–7.

SEALY, A.P., AND BANKS, C., 1971
Social maturity, training, experience and

recidivism amongst British borstal boys.
Brit. J. Criminol., **11,** 245–64.

SETHNA, E.R., AND HARRINGTON, J.A., 1971
Evaluation of group psychotherapy.
Brit. J. Psychiat., **118,** 641–58.

SETHNA, E.R., AND HARRINGTON, J.A., 1971
A study of patients who lapsed from group psychotherapy.
Brit. J. Psychiat., **119,** 59–69.

UNITED KINGDOM, 1971
A Borstal typology study, by members of the Psychology Dept., H.M. Prison Wormwood Scrubs.
London: Home Office, Prison Department, 3–16.

WARREN, M.Q., 1971
Classification of offenders as an aid to efficient management and effective treatment.
J. Crim. Law, Criminol. & Pol. Sci., **62,** 239–58.

CLARKE, R.V.G., AND CORNISH, D.B., 1972
The controlled trial in institutional research—paradigm or pitfall for penal evaluators?
London: Home Office Research Studies, **15.**

EMPEY, L.T., AND ERICKSON, M.L., 1972
The Provo experiment: evaluating community control of delinquency.
Lexington, Mass.: D.C. Heath & Co.

HODGKIN, N., 1972
The new careers project at Vacaville: a Californian experiment.
Howard J. Penol. & Crime Prev., **13,** 184–211.

JESNESS, C.F., DERISI, W.J., MCCORMICK, P.M., AND WEDGE, R.F., 1972
The youth center research project.
A report to American Justice Institute in cooperation with California Youth Authority, Sacramento, Calif., 305–32.

RUTHERFORD, A., 1972
The California probation subsidy programme.
Brit. J. Criminol., **12,** 186–88.

SHIREMAN, C.H., MANN, K.B., LARSEN, C., AND YOUNG, T., 1972
Findings from experiments in treatment in the correctional institution.
Social Service Rev., **46,** 38–59.

WARREN, M.Q., 1972
Correctional treatment in community settings. A report of current research.
Rockville, Md.: National Institute of Mental Health.

BARON, R., FEENEY, F., AND THORNTON, W., 1973
Preventing delinquency through diversion: the Sacremento County 601 diversion project.
Fed. Probation, **37** (1), 13–18.

HUDSON, C.H., 1973
An experimental study of the differential effects of parole supervision for a group of adolescent boys and girls.
L.E.A.A. National Institute of Law Enforcement and Criminal Justice, U.S. Dept. of Justice, Washington, D.C.

PALMER, T., 1973
The Phase III experiment: progress to date.
Sacramento: California Department of the Youth Authority, C.T.P. Research Report No. 13.

WARD, D.A., 1973
Evaluative research for corrections in L.E. Ohlin (ed.), *Prisoners in America.*
Englewood Cliffs, N.J.: Prentice-Hall, 184–206.

WARREN, M.Q., 1973
All things being equal.
Crim. Law Bull., **9,** 473–90.

ADAMS, S., 1974
Evaluative research in corrections: status and prospects.
Fed. Probation, **38** (1), 14–21.

BARRISH, I.J., 1974
Ethical issues and answers to behavior modification.
Corrective & Soc. Psychiat., **20** (2), 30–7.

FOLKARD, M.S. ET AL, 1974
IMPACT. Intensive matched probation and after-care treatment, Vol. I, The design of the probation experiment and an interim evaluation.
London: Home Office Research Studies, **24.**

PALMER, T.B., 1974
The youth authority's community treatment project.
Fed. Probation, **38** (1), 3–14.

SHAW, M., 1974
Social work in prison: an experiment in the use of extended contact with offenders.
London: Home Office Research Studies, **22.**

2 Innovations in corrections

LE MAIRE, L., 1956
Danish experience regarding the castration of sexual offenders.
J. Crim. Law, Criminol. & Pol. Sci., **47,** 294–310.

WOLFGANG, M.E., 1959
Victim compensation in crimes of personal violence.
Minnesota Law Rev., **50,** 223–41.

RAPOPORT, R.N., 1960
Community as doctor.
London: Tavistock, 268–305.

SCHAFER, S., 1960
Restitution to victims of crime.
Chicago: Quadrangle Books, 15–114.

MORRISON, R.L., 1961
Group counselling in penal institutions.
Howard J., **10,** 279–97.

DE BERKER, P., 1962
Group counselling in prisons and borstals.
International Penal and Penitentiary Foundation, Report No. 3.

FENTON, N., 1962
An introduction to group counselling in correctional service.
New York: American Correctional Assn., 1–26.

MANLEY, H.A., AND SHERMAN, M.B., 1963
Summary of the half-way house in the correctional process, in *Proceedings of the 93rd Annual Congress of Correction of the American Correctional Assn.*
Washington, D.C. 311–15.

WAHL, A., AND GLASER, D., 1963
Pilot time study of the federal probation officer's job.
Fed. Probation, **27**(3), 20–5.

GLASER, D., 1964
The effectiveness of a prison and parole system.
Indianapolis: Bobbs-Merrill Co., 214–23.

SCHACHTER, S., AND LATANÉ, B., 1964
Crime, cognition and the autonomic nervous system, in D. Levine (ed.), *Nebraska Symposium on Motivation* 1964
Lincoln: Univ. Nebraska Press, 221–75.

BRITISH JOURNAL OF CRIMINOLOGY, 1965
Behavior and aversion therapy in the treatment of delinquency (Symposium by H. Gwynne Jones, M. Gelder and H.M. Holden). **5,** 355–87.

CONRAD, J.P., 1965
Crime and its correction.
Calif. Univ. Press, 172–304.

CRESSEY, D.R., 1965
Social psychological foundations for using criminals in the rehabilitation of criminals.
J. Res. Crime & Delinq., **2,** 49–59.

FENTON, N., 1965
A handbook on the use of group counselling in juvenile and youth correctional institutions.
Sacramento, Calif.: Institute for the Study of Crime and Delinquency, 103–19.

GIBBONS, D.C., 1965
Changing the lawbreaker.
Englewood Cliffs, N.J.: Prentice-Hall, 189–299.

GRANT, J.D., 1965
Delinquency treatment in an institutional setting, in H.C. Quay (ed.), *Juvenile*

delinquency research and theory.
Princeton: D. Van Nostrand Co., 263–97.

Lunden, W.A., 1965
Jobs for ex-cons. An analysis of employment policies and practices of 95 business firms in 16 midwestern cities.
Report prepared for the Iowa Board of Parole. Ames, Iowa. Mimeo.

Rachman, S., 1965
Current status of behavior therapy.
Arch. Gen. Psychiat., **13,** 418–23.

Alexander, M.E., 1966
Current concepts in corrections.
Fed. Probation, **30** (3), 3–8.

Alexander, M.E., 1966
Corrections in transition.
Nebraska Law Rev., **45,** 10–21.

Carter, Sir Walter, 1966
The work of the Criminal Injuries Compensation Board.
Medico-Legal J., **34,** 48–57.

Edwards, J.Ll.J., 1966
Compensation to victims of crimes of personal violence.
Fed. Probation, **20** (2), 3–10.

Kutner, L., 1966
Crime—torts: due process of compensation for crime victims.
Notre Dame Lawyer, **41,** 487–501.

Lopez-Rey, M., 1966
Release and provisional release of sentenced prisoners.
Brit. J. Criminol., **6,** 236–68.

Marks, I.M., and Gelder, M.G., 1966
Common ground between behavior therapy and psychodynamic methods.
Brit. J. Med. Psychol., **39,** 11–23.

Pilnick, S., Elias, A., and Clapp, N.W., 1966
The Essexfields concept: a new approach to the social treatment of juvenile delinquents.
J. Applied Behavioral Sci., **2,** 109–25.

Scarpitti, F.R., and Stephenson, R.M., 1966
The use of the small group in the rehabilitation of delinquents.
Fed. Probation, **30** (3), 45–50.

Taylor, F.H., 1966
The Henderson therapeutic community, in M. Craft (ed.), *Psychopathic disorders.*
New York: Pergamon Press, 105–15.

United Kingdom, 1966
Group work in prisons and borstals 1962–6.
London: Home Office, Prison Department.

University of Chicago Law Review, 1966
Compensation for victims of crime. **33,** 531–57.

Conrad, J.P., 1967
Trends in European corrections.
A document submitted to the President's Commission on Law Enforcement and Administration of Justice, Washington, D.C. Mimeo.

Council of Europe, 1967
Short-term methods of treatment for young offenders.
Strasbourg: Council of Europe, 1–23, 62–73.

Grupp, S.E., 1967
Work release and the misdemeanant, in H. Gold and F.R. Scarpitti (eds.), *Combating social problems: techniques of intervention.*
New York: Holt, Rinehart & Winston, 332–41.

Keve, P., 1967
Imaginative progress in probation and parole.
Univ. Minnesota Press.

Normandeau, A., 1967
Compensation d'Etat aux victimes de la criminalité.
Revue internationale de criminologie et de police technique, **21,** 183–92.

Samuels, A., 1967
Compensation for criminal injuries in Britain.
Univ. Toronto Law J., **17,** 20–50.

United States of America, 1967
The challenge of crime in a free society.
Report of the President's Commission on Law Enforcement and Administration of Justice, Washington, D.C. 170–9.

United States of America, 1967
Task force report: corrections.
Washington, D.C.: President's Commission

on Law Enforcement and Administration of Justice, 27–37, 38–44, 60–71, 130–41, 149–54, 155–61, 169–76, 184–90, 206–9.

VERBORGEN, L., 1967
Imprisonment and conjugal life, a proposal for legislation.
Hartwick Review, **3** (1), 67–78.

CRESSEY, D.R., 1968
Sources of resistance to the use of offenders and ex-offenders in the correctional process, in *Report of a seminar convened by the Joint Commission on Correctional Manpower and Training.*
Washington, D.C. 31–49.

ERIKSSON, T., 1968
The Swedish furlough system for prisons, in M.E. Wolfgang (ed.), *Crime and culture: essays in honor of Thorsten Sellin.*
New York: John Wiley & Sons, 417–27.

JOINT COMMISSION ON CORRECTIONAL MANPOWER AND TRAINING, 1968
The public looks at crime and corrections.
Washington, D.C.

MACLENNAN, B.W., AND FELSENFELD, N., 1968
Group counselling and psychotherapy with adolescents.
New York: Columbia Univ. Press, 51–84.

EMPEY, L. T., 1969
Contemporary programs for the convicted juvenile offenders: problems of theory, practice and research, in D.J. Mulvihill, M.M. Tumin and L.A. Curtis (eds.), *Crimes of violence*, **13.**
A staff report to the National Commission on the Causes and Prevention of Violence, Washington, D.C., Appendix 30, 1377–1426.

GALVIN, J.J., AND KARACKI, L., 1969
Manpower and training in correctional institutions.
Staff report.
Washington, D.C.: Joint Commission on Correctional Manpower and Training.

GARABEDIAN, P.G., 1969
Challenges for contemporary corrections.
Fed. Probation, **33** (1), 3–10.

GEIS, G., 1969
Compensation for victims of violent crime, in D.J. Mulvihill, M.M. Tumin and L.A. Curtis (eds.), *Crimes of violence*, **13.**
A staff report to the National Commission on the Causes and Prevention of Violence, Washington, D.C. Appendix 34, 1559–97.

GELDER, M.G., 1969
Behaviour therapy, in J.L. Crammer (ed.), *Practical treatment in psychiatry.*
Oxford: Blackwell, 39–58.

GRIFFITHS, W.A., 1969
The development of an after-care hostel.
Brit. J. Criminol., **9**, 312–44.

HOLT, N., AND RENTERIA, R., 1969
Prerelease program evaluation: some implications of negative findings.
Fed. Probation, **33** (2), 40–5.

HOPPER, C.B., 1969
Sex in prison. The Mississippi experiment with conjugal visiting.
Baton Rouge: Louisiana State Univ. Press.

JOINT COMMISSION ON CORRECTIONAL MANPOWER AND TRAINING, 1969
Volunteers look at corrections.
Report of a survey made by Louis Harris and Associates, Washington, D.C.

LONDON, P., 1969
Behaviour control, in D.J. Mulvihill, M.M. Tumin and L.A. Curtis (eds.), *Crimes of violence*, **13.**
A staff report to the National Commission on the Causes and Prevention of Violence, Washington, D.C., Appendix 29, 1359–1375.

MABRY, J.A., ET AL., 1969
A review of pre-release programs.
Criminal Justice Monograph, Vol. I, No. 2.
Huntsville, Texas: Institute of Contemp. Corrections & the Behavioral Sciences.

MONGER, M., 1969
The English probation hostel.
Probation Papers No. 6.
London: National Assn. of Probation Officers.

NELSON, E.K., JR., AND LOVELL, C.H., 1969
Developing correctional administrators.
Staff report.
Washington, D.C.: Joint Commission on Correctional Manpower and Training.

POWNALL, G.A., 1969
Employment problems of released prisoners.

Washington, D.C.: Manpower Administration, U.S. Dept. of Labor, 1–24.

RACHMAN, S., AND TEASDALE, J., 1969
Aversion therapy and behavior disorders: an analysis.
London: Routledge & Kegan Paul, 1–13, 29–38, 78–105.

SCHWITZGEBEL, R.K., 1969
Issues in the use of an electronic rehabilitation system with chronic recidivists.
Law & Society Rev., **3,** 597–615.

SELIGER, S.G., 1969
Towards a realistic reorganisation of the penitentiaries.
J. Crim. Law, Criminol. & Pol. Sci., **60,** 47–58.

SEYMOUR, J.A., 1969
Periodic detention in New Zealand.
Brit. J. Criminol. **9,** 182–87.

WELLS, J.M., 1969
Group counselling in prisons and borstals in England and Wales, 1958–1967.
A report to the Joseph Rowntree Memorial Trust. Mimeo.

CHOPPEN, V., 1970
The origins of the philosophy of detention centres.
Brit. J. Criminol., **10,** 158–68.

COOPER, W.D., 1970
Employers and employees in the work-release program in North Carolina.
Crime & Delinq., **16,** 427–33.

EMERY, F.E., 1970
Freedom and justice within walls. The Bristol Prison experiment.
London: Tavistock.

FIELD, L.H., AND WILLIAMS, M., 1970
The hormonal treatment of sexual offenders.
Med. Sci. and the Law, **10,** 27–34.

FLACKETT, J.M., AND FLACKETT, G., 1970
Criswell House: an alternative to institutional commitment for the juvenile offender.
Fed. Probation, **34** (4), 30–7.

GRYGIER, T., NEASE, B., AND ANDERSON, C.S., 1970
An exploratory study of halfway houses.
Crime & Delinq., **16,** 280–91.

HARE, R.D., 1970
Psychopathy: theory and research.
New York: John Wiley & Sons, 110–18.

INSTITUTE FOR THE STUDY OF CRIME AND DELINQUENCY, 1970
The non-prison. A rational correctional program.
St. Paul, Minn.: Bruce Publishing Co.

JOHNSON, E.H., 1970
Report on an innovation—state work—release programs.
Crime & Delinq., **16,** 417–26.

JOINT COMMISSION ON CORRECTIONAL MANPOWER AND TRAINING, 1970
Perspectives on correctional manpower and training.
Washington, D.C.

KELLER, O.J.JR., AND ALPER, B.S., 1970
Halfway houses: community-centered correction and treatment.
Lexington, Mass.: D.C. Heath and Co.

MARYLAND, LAW REVIEW, 1970
Criminal victim compensation in Maryland, **30,** 266–82.

MORRIS, A., 1970
The involvement of offenders in the prevention and correction of criminal behavior.
Correctional Research, **20,** 1–36.

MORRIS, N., AND HAWKINS, G., 1970
The honest politician's guide to crime control.
Univ. Chicago Press, 111–44.

ROBISON, J., 1970
The California prison, parole and probation system. 'It's time to stop counting.'
A special report to the Assembly, Technical Supplement, No. 2.
State of California, Sacramento, Mimeo.

SCHAFER, S., 1970
Compensation and restitution to victims of crime (2nd ed.).
Montclair, N.J.: Patterson Smith.

STEWART, E.I., AND MALFETTI, J.L., 1970
Rehabilitation of the drunken driver: a corrective course in Phoenix, Arizona, for persons convicted of driving under the influence of alcohol.
New York: Teachers College Press, 1–24.

STRATTA, E., 1970
The education of borstal boys. A study of their educational experiences prior to, and during, borstal training.
London: Routledge & Kegan Paul, 142–80.

SVERI, K., 1970
Sociological and criminological aspects of the organisation of corrections in a modern state in *Collected studies in criminological research*, **5.**
Strasbourg: Council of Europe, 59–82.

UNITED KINGDOM, 1970
Non-custodial and semi-custodial penalties.
Report of the Advisory Council on the Penal System (Chairman, Lady Wootton).
London: Home Office.

UNITED KINGDOM, 1970
Reparation by the offender.
Report of the Advisory Council on the Penal System (Chairman, Lord Justice Widgery).
London: Home Office.

VASOLI, R.H., AND FAHEY, F.J., 1970
Halfway house for reformatory releases.
Crime & Delinq., **16,** 292–304.

VERA INSTITUTE OF JUSTICE, 1970
The Manhattan court employment project.
Summary report on phase one: November 1, 1967 to October 3, 1969. U.S. Dept. of Labour. New York.

YATES, A.J., 1970
Behavior therapy.
New York: John Wiley & Sons, 3–74, 207–45.

ANCEL, M., 1971
Suspended sentence.
London: Heinemann.

BARR, H., 1971
Volunteers in prison after-care. The report of the teamwork associates pilot project.
London: George Allen & Unwin, 23–39, 124–54.

BRAKEL, S.J., 1971
Diversion from the criminal process: informal discretion, motivation and formalisation.
Denver Law J., **48,** 211–38.

DAVIES, M., AND SINCLAIR, I., 1971
Familes, hostels and delinquents: an attempt to assess cause and effect.
Brit. J. Criminol., **11,** 213–29.

DUNBAR, I., 1971
Long Lartin—the development of a concept.
Prison Service J., (3), 6–8.

GARABEDIAN, P.G., 1971
Research and practice in planning correctional change.
Crime & Delinq., **17,** 41–56.

LAMBORN, LEROY L., 1971
The methods of government compensation of victims of crime.
Univ. Illinois Law Forum, 1971, 655–81.

RADICAL ALTERNATIVES TO PRISON, 1971
London. Mimeo.

ROBISON, J.O., *et al.*, 1971
By the standard of his rehabilitation. Information decision, and outcome in terminations from parole: the implementation of Penal Code Section 2943.
Sacramento: California Department of Corrections, Research report No. 39.

SHAW, M., AND JARVIS, F.V., 1971
Casework with prisoners.
Probation, (17), 74–6.

SINCLAIR, I., 1971
Hostels for probationers.
London: Home Office Research Studies, **6.**

SINCLAIR, J., SILBERMAN, M., CHAPMAN, B., AND LEISSNER, A., 1971
Explorations in after-care.
London: Home Office Research Studies, **9.**

TROJANOWICZ, R.C., 1971
Inherent treatment characteristics in a halfway house for delinquent boys.
Fed. Probation, **35** (1), 18–26.

UNIVERSITY OF SAN FRANCISCO LAW REVIEW, 1971
Symposium: the purposes of corrections: directions for improvement. **6,** 1–102.

WILLS, W.D., 1971
Spare the child. The story of an experimental approved school.
Harmondsworth, Penguin Books.

AGRAS, W.S. (ED.), 1972
Behaviour modification principles and clinical applications.
Boston: Little, Brown & Co.

BELLASSAI, J.P., AND SEGAL, P.N., 1972
Addict diversion: an alternative approach for the criminal justice system.
Georgetown Law J., **60**, 667–710.

BERLIN, A., 1972
Treatment for the violent offender.
Crime & Delinq., **4**, 101–15.

BRAUTIGAM, R.K., 1972
Work-release: a case study and comment.
Prison J., **52** (2), 20–35.

BRIGGS, D.L., 1972
A transitional therapeutic community for young, violent offenders.
Howard J. of Penol. & Crime Prev., **13**, 171–83.

CARTER, R.M., 1972
The diversion of offenders.
Fed. Probation, **36** (4), 31–6.

FOGEL, D., GALAWAY, B., AND HUDSON, J., 1972
Restitution in criminal justice: Minnesota experiment.
Crim. Law Bull., **8**, 681–91.

GRIGGS, B.S., AND MCCUNE, G.R., 1972
Community-based correctional programs: a survey and analysis.
Fed. Probation, **36** (2), 7–13.

GUNN, J., 1972
Psychiatry and prisoners.
Prison Service J., **8**, 13–15.

JEW, C.C., CLANON, T.L., AND MATTOCKS, A.L., 1972
The effectiveness of group psychotherapy in a correctional institution.
Amer. J. Psychiat., **129**, 602–5.

MASSACHUSETTS CORRECTIONAL ASSOCIATION, 1972
Correctional reform: illusion and reality,
Correctional Research, **22**.

RISKIN, L.L., 1972
Removing impediments to employment of work-release prisoners.
Crim. Law Bull., **8**, 761–81.

TRASLER, G. ET AL., 1972
Specialised hostels for homeless offenders.
Internat. J. Offender Therapy and Comparative Criminol., **16**, 224–49.

TURNER, M., 1972
The need for hostel community, in S. Whiteley, D. Briggs and M. Turner (eds.),
Dealing with deviants.
Hogarth Press, 174–239.

WHITELEY, S., 1972
Medical attitudes to social deviance: moral insanity to psychopathic disorder, in S. Whiteley, D. Briggs and M. Turner (eds.),
Dealing with deviants.
London: Hogarth Press, 19–92.

AUSTRALIA (South Australia), 1973
Sentencing and corrections.
First Report of the Criminal Law and Penal Methods Reform Committee of South Australia (Chairman, Hon. Justice Mitchell).
Adelaide: Government Printer, 135–63.

BROOKS, J., 1973
Compensating victims of crime: the recommendations of program administrators.
Law & Society Rev., **7**, 445–71.

BROOKS, J., 1973
Crime compensation programs: an opinion survey of program administrators.
Criminology, **11**, 258–74.

EDELHERTZ, H., CHAPPELL, D., GEIS, G., SULTON, L.P., 1973
Public compensation of victims of crime: a survey of New York experience.
Crim. Law Bull., **9**, 5–47, 101–23.

GLASER, D., 1973
Correction of adult offenders in the community, in L.E. Ohlin (ed.), *Prisoners in America.*
Englewood Cliffs, N.J.: Prentice-Hall, 86–116.

GOLDFARB, R.L., AND SINGER, L.R., 1973
After conviction.
New York: Simon & Schuster, 527–674.

GUNN, J., 1973
Psychiatry and prisoners II, a retrospective

look at Wormwood Scrubs Psychiatric Unit.
Prison Service J., (10), 15–18.

HERSCHEL, D., 1973
The criminal Injuries Compensation Board, in Lord Lloyd of Hampstead, E.H. Schamell and H. Cohen (eds.), *Current legal problems*, 1973.
London: Stevens.

JOHNSON, E.H., AND KOTCH, K.E., 1973
Two factors in development of work release: size and location of prisons.
J. Criminal Justice, **1,** 43–50.

MARKLEY, C.W., 1973
Furlough programs and conjugal visiting in adult correctional institutions.
Fed. Probation, **37** (1), 19–26.

RACHMAN, S.J., 1973
The effects of psychological treatment, in H.J. Eysenck (ed.), *Handbook of abnormal psychology*.
London: Pitmans, 805–61.

ROOT, L.S., 1973
State work release programs: an analysis of operational politics.
Fed. Probation, **37** (4), 52–8.

SAMUELS, A., 1973
Criminal injuries compensation board.
Crim. Law Rev., 1973, 418–31.

STUMPHAUZER, J.S., (ED.), 1973
Behavior therapy with delinquents.
Springfield, Ill.: C.C. Thomas.

UCLA LAW REVIEW, 1973
Rehabilitation of the victims of crime: an eye-view. **21,** 317–70.

UNITED STATES OF AMERICA. HOUSE OF REPRESENTATIVES, 1973
93rd Congress, 1st Session, Part 2, *Street crime in America (corrections approaches)*, hearings before the Select Committee on Crime (statement by Jerome G. Miller).
Washington, D.C. 649–74.

UNITED STATES OF AMERICA, 1973
New approaches to diversion and treatment of juvenile offenders.
L.E.A.A., National Institute of Law Enforcement and Criminal Justice, U.S. Dept. of Justice, Washington, D.C.

VORENBERG, E.W., AND VORENBERG, J., 1973
Early diversion from the Criminal Justice System, in L.E. Ohlin (ed.), *Prisoners in America.*
Englewood Cliffs, N.J.: Prentice-Hall, 151–83.

VOTEY, H.L.JR., AND PHILLIPS, L., 1973
Social goals and appropriate policy for corrections: an economic appraisal.
J. Crim. Justice, **1,** 219–40.

WEIS, C.W., 1973
Diversion of the public inebriate from the criminal justice system.
L.E.A.A., National Institute of Law Enforcement and Criminal Justice, U.S. Dept. of Justice, Washington, D.C.

WENK, E.A., AND FRANK, C., 1973
Some progress in the evaluation of institutional programs.
Fed. Probation, **37** (3) 30–7.

BALCH, R.W., 1974
Deferred prosecution: the juvenilization of the criminal justice system.
Fed. Probation, **38** (2), 46–50.

BARRISH, I.J., 1974
Ethical issues and answers to behavior modification.
Corrective & Social Psychiat., **20** (2), 30–7.

CARTER, R.M., DIGHTMAN, C.R., AND KLEIN, M.W., 1974
The system rate approach to description and evaluation of criminal justice systems.
Criminology, **11,** 462–83.

CRESSEY, D.R., AND MCDERMOTT, R.A., 1974
Diversion from the juvenile justice system.
L.E.A.A., National Institute of Law Enforcement and Criminal Justice, U.S. Dept. of Justice, Washington, D.C.

EDELHERTZ, H., AND GEIS, G., 1974
Public compensation of victims of crime.
New York: Praeger.

FLACKETT, J.M., 1974
Juvenile offenders in the community: some recent experiences in the United States.
Howard J. Penol. & Crim. Prev., **14,** 22–36.

HALL, J., 1974
Penal institutions and behavior modification.
Probation J., **21** (2), 46–50.

HOOD, R., STEER, D., AND HAWKINS, K., 1974
Young adult offenders: comments on the Report of the Advisory Council on the Penal System.
Brit. J. Criminol., **14**, 388–403.

MONKMAN, G.S., 1974
Cost-benefit analysis, three applications to corrections—probation subsidy, diversion, employment.
Prepared by the Correctional Economics Center of the A.B.A. Commission on Correctional Facilities & Services, Washington, D.C.

MORRIS, N., 1974
The future of imprisonment.
Univ. Chicago Press, 9–27, 85–121.

NIMMER, R.T., 1974
Diversion, the search for alternative forms of prosecution.
Chicago: American Bar Foundation.

OHLIN, L.E., COATES, R.B., AND MILLER, A.D., 1974
Radical correctional reform: a case study of the Massachusetts Youth Correctional System.
Harvard Educational Review, **44**, 74–111.

OPTON, E.M., 1974
Psychiatric violence against prisoners: when therapy is punishment.
Mississippi Law J., **45**, 605–44.

RUSSELL, E.W., 1974
Special monograph supplement: The power of behavior control: a critique of behavior modification methods.
J. Clinical Psych., **30**, 111–36.

RUTHERFORD, A., 1974
The dissolution of the training schools in Massachusetts.
Columbus, Ohio: Academy for Contemporary Problems.

SCHAFER, S., 1974
Compensation of victims of criminal offences.
Crim. Law Bull., **10**, 605–36.

SHAPIRO, M.H., 1974
Legislating the control of behavior control: autonomy and the coercive use of organic therapies.
Southern Calif. Law Rev., **47**, 237–356.

SKOLER, D., 1974
Protecting the rights of defendants in pretrial intervention programs.
Crim. Law Bull., **10**, 473–92.

STANFORD LAW REVIEW, 1974
Diversion of drug offenders in California.
26, 923–44.

SULLIVAN, D.C., SEIGEL, L.J., AND CLEAR, T., 1974
The halfway house, ten years later: reappraisal of correctional innovation.
Can. J. Criminol. & Corrections, **16**, 188–97.

TEMPLE LAW QUARTERLY, 1974
An evaluation of the Home Furlough program in Pennsylvanian correctional institutions. **47**, 288–320.

UNITED KINGDOM, 1974
Young adult offenders.
Report of the Advisory Council on the Penal System (Chairman, Sir Kenneth Younger).
London: Home Office.

UNITED STATES OF AMERICA, 1974
Courts.
Report of the National Advisory Commission on Criminal Justice Standards and Goals.
Washington, D.C. 27–41.

YALE LAW JOURNAL, 1974
Pretrial diversion from the criminal process.
83, 827–54.

ZIMRING, F.E., 1974
Measuring the impact of pretrial diversion from the criminal justice system.
Univ. Chicago Law Rev., **41**, 224–41.

13 Parole

1 Selection: criteria and legal bases

[See also Section 7(2) for references relating to indeterminate sentences; Section 14(2) for references relating to prisoners' rights.]

OHLIN, L.E., 1951
Selection for parole.
New York: Russell Sage Foundation.

AMERICAN CORRECTIONAL ASSOCIATION, 1958
Proceedings of the 88th Annual Congress of Correction.
Workshop 9 on parole criteria.
Washington, D.C. 225–58.

HAYNER, N.S., 1958
Why do parole boards lag in the use of prediction scores?
Pacific Sociol. Rev., **1,** 73–6.

YALE LAW JOURNAL, 1962
Freedom and rehabilitation in parole revocation hearings. **72,** 368–82.

NATIONAL COUNCIL ON CRIME AND DELINQUENCY, 1963
Guides for parole selection.
Advisory Council on Parole.
New York: N.C.C.D.

NEW YORK UNIVERSITY LAW REVIEW, 1963
Parole: a critique of its legal foundations and conditions. **38,** 702–39.

SKLAR, R.B., 1964
Law and practice in probation and parole revocation hearings.
J. Crim. Law, Criminol. & Pol. Sci., **55,** 175–98.

BENJAMIN, F., 1966
Due process and revocation of conditional liberty.
Wayne Law Rev., **12,** 638–56.

DAWSON, R.O., 1966
The decision to grant or deny parole: a study of parole criteria in law and practice.
Washington Univ. Law Quart., **3,** 243–303.

GOTTFREDSON, D.M., AND BALLARD, K.B.JR., 1966
Differences in parole decisions associated with decision-makers.
J. Res. Crime & Delinq., **3,** 112–19.

UNITED STATES OF AMERICA, 1967
Task force report: corrections.
Washington, D.C.: President's Commission on Law Enforcement and Administration of Justice, 60–71.

BASSETT, J., 1969
Discretionary power and procedural rights in the granting and revoking of probation.
J. Crim. Law, Criminol. & Pol. Sci., **60,** 479–93.

POWERS, E., 1969
Parole eligibility of prisoners serving a life sentence.
Boston, Mass.: Massachusetts Correctional Association. Mimeo.

SAMUELS, A., 1969
Parole: a critique.
Crim. Law Rev., 1969, 456–64.

WHITE, W.S., 1969
The fourth amendment rights of parolees and probationers.
Univ. Pittsburgh Law Rev., **31,** 167–203

WOLFF, H.G., 1969
The relation between the courts and the National Parole Board.
Univ. Toronto Law J., **19,** 559–96.

COHEN, W.M., 1970
Due process, equal protection and state parole revocation proceedings.
Colorado Law Rev., **42,** 197–230.

NEWMAN, D.J., 1970
Legal model for parole: future developments, in America Correctional Association *Proceedings of the One Hundredth Annual Congress of Correction.*
Washington, D.C., 294–307.

PETERSON, R.M., 1970
The future and the paroling authority. Discretionary power and procedural rights in the revocation of parole.
Chicago, Ill.: Mimeo.

TAKAGI, P.T., 1970
The role of the inmate in the prerelease process, in R.M. Carter and L.T. Wilkins (eds.), *Probation and parole.*
New York: John Wiley & Sons, 206–14.

UNITED STATES OF AMERICA, 1970
Study draft of a new Federal Criminal Code.
Washington, D.C.: National Commission on Reform of Federal Criminal Laws, 296–301.

DYKE, J.V., 1971
Parole revocation hearings in California: the right to counsel.
California Law Rev., **59,** 1215–59.

GAYLIN, W., 1971
No exit. The turf of the federal parole board is a landscape of illogic.
Harper's Magazine, Nov. 1971, 86–94.

HAWKINS, K.O., 1971
Parole selection: the American experience.
Unpublished dissertation for the degree of Doctor of Philosophy at University of Cambridge, 250–350.

HOUSTON LAW REVIEW, 1971
The emerging right to counsel at parole revocation hearings. **9,** 290–304.

ROBISON, J.O., *et al.*, 1971
By the standard of his rehabilitation. Information decision, and outcome in terminations from parole: the implementation of Penal Code Section 2943.
Sacramento: California Department of Corrections, Research Report No. 39.

UNITED STATES OF AMERICA, 1971
Rules of the United States Board of Parole.
With statutes and directives.
Washington, D.C.: Department of Justice.

UNIVERSITY OF PENNSYLVANIA LAW REVIEW, 1971
The parole system. **120,** 282–377.

WASHINGTON UNIVERSITY LAW QUARTERLY, 1971
Rights to counsel at parole release hearings—*Menechino v. Oswald*, 430 *F.2d* 403 (2*d. Cir.* 1970), 1971, 502–12.

BUFFALO LAW REVIEW, 1972
Prisons on trial: a symposium on the changing law of corrections. **21,** 643–985.

GEORGE WASHINGTON LAW REVIEW, 1972
Legal representation at parole revocation: proposed resolution of a developing judicial conflict. **40,** 778–96.

HAWKINS, K.O., 1972
Some consequences of a parole system for prison management, in D.J. West (ed.), *The future of parole.*
London: Duckworth, 96–115.

HOFFMAN, P.B., 1972
Paroling policy feedback.
J. Res. Crim. & Delinq., **9,** 117–33.

JAMES, L., 1972
Prisoners' perceptions of parole.
University of Toronto, Centre of Criminology, 178–94.

JOBSON, K., 1972
Fair procedure in parole.
Univ. Toronto Law J., **22,** 267–303.

NEWMAN, D.J., 1972
Court intervention in the parole process.
Albany Law Rev., **36,** 257–304.

O'LEARY, V., 1972
Issues and trends in parole administration in the United States.
Amer. Crim. Law Rev., **11,** 97–140.

O'LEARY, V., AND NUFFIELD, J., 1972
Parole decision-making characteristics:

report of a National Survey.
Crim. Law Bull., **8,** 651–80.

PARKER, W., 1972
Parole (origins, development, current practices and statutes).
Corrections Parole MDT Project, Resource Document No. 1. College Park, Md.
American Correctional Association, 190–206.

PARSONS-LEWIS, H.S., 1972
Parole release decisions.
California Law Rev., **60,** 1518–56.

PRESERVATION OF THE RIGHTS OF PRISONERS, 1972
Statement of Intent (Issued by R.P. Pooley, 96 Victoria Avenue, Hull, Yorkshire).

SHEA, F., 1972
Parole philosophy in England and America, in D.J. West (ed.), *The future of parole.*
London: Duckworth, 66–95.

UCLA LAW REVIEW, 1972
Parole holds: their effect on the rights of the parolee and the operation of the parole system. **19,** 759–803.

WALLER, J.I., 1972
Parole for the ex-prisoner: carrot, stick or illusion? in D.J. West (ed.), *The future of parole.*
London: Duckworth, 116–34.

AUSTRALIA (South Australia), 1973
Sentencing and corrections.
First Report of the Criminal Law and Penal Methods Reform Committee of South Australia (Chairman, Hon. Justice Mitchell).
Adelaide: Government Printer, 42–51.

BOTTOMLEY, A.K., 1973
Parole decisions in a long-term closed prison.
Brit. J. Criminol., **13,** 26–40.

CANADA, 1973
Report of the task force on release of inmates (Chairman, J.K. Hugessen).
Office of Solicitor General, Ottawa: Information Canada.

CANADIAN CRIMINOLOGY AND CORRECTIONS ASSOCIATION, 1973
The parole system in Canada.
Can. J. Criminol. & Corrections, **15,** 144–69.

GIRGENTI, R., 1973
Judicial application of procedural due process in parole release and revocation.
Amer. Crim. Law Rev., **11,** 1017–43.

HAWKINS, K., 1973
Parole procedure: an alternative approach.
Brit. J. Criminol., **13,** 6–25.

HOFFMAN, P.B., AND GOLDSTEIN, H.M., 1973
Do experience tables matter?
J. Crim. Law & Criminol., **64,** 339–47.

NUTTALL, C., 1973
Parole selection.
Brit. J. Criminol., **13,** 41–5.

SHIN, H. JOO, 1973
Do lesser pleas pay? Accommodations in the sentencing and parole processes.
J. Crim. Justice., **1,** 27–42.

BANISTER, P.A., HESKIN, K.J., BOLTON, N., AND SMITH, F.V., 1974
A study of variables related to the selection of long-term prisoners for parole.
Brit. J. Criminol., **14,** 359–68.

BORRIE, G.J., 1974
The prisoner's status in parole decision-making, in D.A. Thomas (ed.), *Parole, its implications for the criminal justice and penal systems.*
Cambridge: Institute of Criminology, 18–29.

CITIZENS' INQUIRY ON PAROLE AND CRIMINAL JUSTICE, INC., 1974
Report on New York parole.
New York: Mimeo, 1–45, 256–298.

DEGOSTIN, L.K., AND HOFFMAN, P.B., 1974
Administrative review of parole decisions.
Fed. Probation, **38** (2), 24–8.

FISHER, H., 1974
Parole and parole revocation procedures after Morrisey and Gagnon. *J. Crim. Law & Criminol.*, **65,** 46–61.

HOFFMAN, P.B., 1974
Mandatory release: a measure of Type II error.
Criminology, **11,** 541–54.

HOOD, R., 1974
Some fundamental dilemmas of the English parole system and a suggestion for an alternative structure, in D.A. Thomas (ed.),

Parole: its implications for the penal and criminal justice systems.
Cambridge: Institute of Criminology.

HOOD, R., 1974
Tolerance and the tariff: some reflections on fixing the time prisoners serve in custody.
London: National Association for the Care and Resettlement of Offenders, Papers and Reprints, No. 11.

HOOD, R., STEER, D., AND HAWKINS, K., 1974
Young adult offenders: comments on the Report of the Advisory Council on the Penal System.
Brit. J. Criminol., **14**, 388–43.

MCGEE, R.A., 1974
A new look at sentencing.
Fed. Probation, **38**, Part I, (2), 3–8; Part II, (3), 3–11.

2 Parole outcome

[*See also Section 10(2) on follow-up studies in general.*]

SCHUESSLER, K.F., 1954
Parole prediction: its history and status.
J. Crim. Law, Criminol. & Pol. Sci., **45**, 425–31.

MANNHEIM, H., AND WILKINS, L.T., 1955
Prediction methods in relation to borstal training.
London, 1–27.

MORRISON, R.L., 1955
Predictive research: a critical assessment of its practical applications.
Brit. J. Delinq., **6**, 99–115.

WILKINS, L.T., 1955
Some developments in prediction methodology in applied social research.
Brit. J. Sociol., **6**, 348–54.

HAYNER, N.S., 1958
Why do parole boards lag in the use of prediction scores?
Pacific Sociol. Rev., **1**, 73–6.

GLUECK, S. AND GLUECK, E., 1959
Predicting delinquency and crime.
Cambridge, Mass.: Harvard Univ. Press, 61–87.

CITIZENS' COMMITTEE ON CHILDREN OF NEW YORK, INC., 1961
Research and potential application of research in probation, parole, delinquency prediction.
Research Clinic, New York School of Social Work, Columbia University.
Summary by P. Lerman, 1–11.

LOPEZ-REY, M., 1961
Some misconceptions in contemporary criminology, in G.O.W. Mueller (ed.), *Essays in criminal science.*
London: Stevens, 5–29.

CRIME AND DELINQUENCY, 1962
Symposium on prediction tables, **8**, 209–81.

EVJEN, V.H., 1962
Current thinking on parole prediction tables.
Crime & Delinq., **8**, 215–38.

GLASER, D., 1964
The effectiveness of a prison and parole system.
Indianapolis: Bobbs-Merrill Co., 289–310.

MARTINSON, R.M., KASSEBAUM, G.G., AND WARD, D.A., 1964
A critique of research in parole.
Fed. Probation, **28** (3), 34–8.

GLASER, D., AND O'LEARY, V., 1966
Personal characteristics and parole outcome.
Washington, D.C.: Department of Health, Education and Welfare.

GOTTFREDSON, D.M., BALLARD, K.B., JR., AND O'LEARY, V., 1966
Uniform parole reports: a feasibility study.
J. Res. Crime & Delinq., **3**, 97–111.

GRYGIER, T., 1966
The effect of social action: current prediction methods and two new models.
Bri. J. Criminol., **6,** 269–93.

GOTTFREDSON, D.M., 1967
Assessment and prediction methods in crime and delinquency, in *Task force report: juvenile delinquency and youth crime.*
Washington, D.C.: President's Commission on Law Enforcement and Administration of Justice, 171–87.

UNITED STATES OF AMERICA, 1967
Task force report: corrections.
Washington, D.C.: President's Commission on Law Enforcement and Administration of Justice, 60–71.

BROWN, B.S., MARKMAN, E.M., AND DU PONT, R.L., 1969
Evaluation of institutional and community experiences by successful and unsuccessful paroles.
Washington, D.C.: District of Columbia, Department of Corrections, Research Report No. 19.

JAMAN, D.R., AND DICKOVER, R.M., 1969
A study of parole outcome as a function of time served.
Sacramento: California Department of Corrections, Research Report No. 35.

KNIGHT, D., 1969
The Marshall program. Part 1: Parole outcome and background characteristics.
Sacramento: California Department of the Youth Authority, Research Report No. 56.

TAKAGI, P.T., AND ROBISON, J., 1969
The parole violator: an organizational reject.
J. Res. Crime & Delinq., **6,** 78–86.

ROBERTS, C.F., JR., 1970
A final evaluation of the narcotic control program for youth authority parolees.
Sacramento: California Department of the Youth Authority, Research Report No. 58, 69–83.

ROBISON, J., 1970
The California prison, parole and probation system. 'It's time to stop counting'.
A special report to the Assembly.
Technical supplement No. 2. State of California, Sacramento. Mimeo, 40–78.

ROBISON, J., AND TAKAGI, P.T., 1970
The parole violator as an organization reject, in R.M. Carter and L.T. Wilkins (eds.), *Probation and parole.*
New York: John Wiley & Sons, 233–54.

SPARKS, R.F., 1970
Research on the use and effectiveness of probation, parole and measures of after-care, in *Practical organization of measures for the supervision and after-care of conditionally sentenced or conditionally released offenders.*
Strasbourg: Council of Europe, 249–73.

BABST, D.V., INCIARDI, J.A., AND JAMAN, D.R., 1971
The uses of configural analysis in parole prediction research.
Can. J. Corrections, **13,** 200–8.

GRYGIER, T., BLUM, F., AND POREBSKI, O.R., 1971
Decision and outcome: studies in parole prediction.
Can. J. Corrections, **13,** 133–46.

KASSEBAUM, G., WARD, D.A., AND WILNER, D.M., 1971
Prison treatment and parole survival—an empirical assessment.
New York: John Wiley & Sons, 207–324.

UNIVERSITY OF PENNSYLVANIA LAW REVIEW, 1971
The parole system. **120,** 282–377.

BABST, D.V., AND CHAMBERS, C.D., 1972
New dimensions for parole expectancy research.
Criminology, **10,** 353–65.

BABST, D.V., KOVAL, M., AND NEITHERCUTT, M.G., 1972
Relationship of time served to parole outcome for different classifications of burglars based on males paroled in fifty jurisdictions in 1968 and 1969.
J. Res. Crime & Delinq., **9,** 99–116.

HOLT, N., AND MILLER, D., 1972
Explorations in inmate-family relationships.
Sacramento: California Department of Corrections, Research Report No. 46.

JAMAN, D.R., DICKOVER, R.M., AND BENNETT, L.A., 1972
Parole outcome as a function of time served.
Brit. J. Criminol., **12,** 5–34.

JAMES, L., 1972
Prisoners' perceptions of parole.
University of Toronto, Centre of Criminology, 178–94.

NEITHERCUTT, M.G., 1972
Parole violation patterns and commitment
J. Res. Crime & Delinq., **9**, 87–98.

O'LEARY, V., AND GLASER, D., 1972
The assessment of risk in parole decision making, in D.J. West (ed.), *The future of parole.*
London: Duckworth, 135–98.

HUDSON, C.H., 1973
An experimental study of the differential effects of parole supervision for a group of adolescent boys and girls.
L.E.A.A., National Institute of Law Enforcement and Criminal Justice, U.S. Dept. of Justice, Washington, D.C.

WALLER, I., 1974
Conditional and unconditional discharge from prison: effects and effectiveness.
Fed. Probation, **38** (2), 9–14.

WALLER, I., 1974
Men released from prison.
Univ. Toronto Press, 46–214.

14 Status and rights of offenders

1 Rights in prison

[*See also Section 7(2) for references on conflicting values in the implementation of sanctions; Section 12 on experimental studies and innovations in corrections.*]

BRITISH JOURNAL OF CRIMINOLOGY, 1965
Behaviour and aversion therapy in the treatment of delinquency (Symposium by H. Gwynn Jones, M. Gelder and H.M. Holden), **5,** 355–87.

CALDWELL, W.F., 1966
Black muslims behind bars.
Research Studies, **34,** 185–203.

BRENT, J.E., 1968
A preliminary report on intergroup conflict at a penitentiary between black muslim inmates and non-muslim negro inmates from Washington, D.C.
Washington, D.C. Mimeo.

PRISON JOURNAL, THE, 1968
Special number of rights of prisoners in confinement in the United States. **48** (1).

VOGELMAN, R.P., 1968
Prison restrictions—prisoner rights.
J. Crim. Law, Criminol. & Pol. Sci., **59,** 386–96.

BAZELON D.L., 1969
Implementing the right to treatment.
Univ. Chicago Law Rev., **36,** 742–54.

BUCHER, B., 1969
Some ethical issues in the therapeutic use of punishment, in R.D. Rubin and C.M. Franks (eds.), *Advances in behavior therapy,* 1968
New York: Academic Press, 59–72.

BURRIS, D.S. (ED.), 1969
The right to treatment.
New York: Springer Publishing Co.

COHEN, F., 1969
The legal challenge to corrections: implications for manpower and training.
Maryland: American Correctional Association, 64–87.

HIRSCHKOP, P.J., AND MILLEMANN, M.A., 1969
The unconstitutionality of prison life.
Virginia Law Rev., **55,** 795–839.

HOPPER, C.B., 1969
Conjugal and family visitation in Mississippi, in *Proceedings of the 99th Annual Congress of Correction of the American Correctional Association.*
Washington, D.C. 254–61.

JABLONSKI, J.A., 1969
Resolving civil problems of correctional inmates.
Wisconsin Law Rev., 574–86.

KATZ, J., 1969
The right to treatment—an enchanting legal fiction?
Univ. Chicago Law Rev., **36,** 755–83.

MARTIN, R.L., 1969
Administrative fairness in corrections.
Wisconsin Law Rev., 1969, 587–601.

MORRIS, G.H., 1969
'Criminality' and the right to treatment.
Univ. Chicago Law Rev., **36,** 784–801.

SCHWITZGEBEL, R.K., 1969
Issues in the use of an electronic rehabilitation system with chronic recidivists (with Commentary by B. Beck).
Law & Society Rev., **3,** 611–15.

WHITE, W.S., 1969
The fourth amendment rights of parolees and probationers.
Univ. Pittsburgh Law Rev., **31,** 167–203.

WILSON, L.E., 1969
Conjugal visiting and family participation in California, in *Proceedings of the 99th Annual Congress & Correction of the American Correctional Association.*
Washington, D.C. 261–64.

ALI, B.E.D., 1970
A pilot study on standard minimum rules. The standard minimum rules for the treatment of prisoners in the light of recent developments in the correctional field.
International prisoners aid association. Fourth United Nations Congress on the prevention of crime and the treatment of offenders, Kyoto.

AMERICAN UNIVERSITY LAW REVIEW, THE, 1970–71.
Prisoners' rights and equal protection. **20,** 482–89.

GOLDFARB, R.L., AND SINGER, L.R., 1970
Redressing prisoners' grievances.
George Washington Law Rev., **39,** 175–320.

HOSEY, P., 1970
Prison censorship of attorney-client mail.
Baylor Law Rev., **22,** 623–31.

ICHIDA, W.W., 1970
Prisoners' rights: access to courts.
Colorado Law Rev., **42,** 275–304.

JACOB, B.R., 1970
Prison discipline and inmate rights.
Harvard Civil Rights, Civil Liberties Law Rev., **5,** 227–77.

JOHNSON, B.M., 1970
Prisoners' rights: restrictions on religious practices.
Colorado Law Rev., **42,** 387.

KRAFT, L., 1970
Prison disciplinary practices and procedures: is due process provided?
North Dakota Law Rev., **47,** 9–76.

MAYHEW, S.J., 1970
Prisoners' rights: personal security.
Colorado Law Rev., **42,** 305–86.

NATIONAL SHERIFFS' ASSOCIATION, 1970
Manual on jail administration. A handbook designed to ease the difficult task of a jail administrator.
Washington, D.C.

SINGER, R., 1970
Bringing the constitution to prison: substantive due process and the eighth amendment.
Univ. Cincinnati Law Rev., **39,** 650–84.

SINGER, R.G., 1970
Censorship of prisoners' mail and the constitution.
Amer. Bar Assoc. J., **56,** 1051–5.

TINGLER, R.A., 1970
Unconstitutional punishment.
Crim. Law Bull., **6,** 311–29.

TWERSKI, A.D., 1970
Treating the untreatable—a critique of the proposed Pennsylvania right to treatment law.
Duquesne Law Rev., **9,** 220–9.

AMERICAN FRIENDS SERVICE COMMITTEE, 1971
Struggle for justice. A report on crime and punishment in America.
New York: Hill & Wang, 154–73.

CALIFORNIA, STATE OF, 1971
Report to Governor Ronald Reagan on violence in California prisons.
Sacramento: California Board of Corrections.

FLINT, D.P., 1971
Justice through litigation: 1929–1970.
Prison J., **51** (2), 15–36.

GLASER, D., 1971
Politicalization of prisoners: a new challenge to American penology.
Amer. J. Correction, **33** (6), 6–9.

JOHNS, D.R., 1971
Alternatives to conjugal visiting.
Fed. Probation, **35** (1), 45–51.

JOURNAL OF CRIMINAL LAW, CRIMINOLOGY AND POLICE SCIENCE, 1971
Prisoner correspondence: an appraisal of the judicial refusal to abolish banishment as a form of punishment. **62,** 40–55.

LOUISIANA LAW REVIEW, 1971
Penal institutions and the Eighth Amendment—a broadened conception of cruel and unusual punishment. **31,** 395–404.

MILLEMANN, M.A., 1971
Prison disciplinary hearings and

procedural due process—the requirement of a full administrative hearing.
Maryland Law Rev., **31,** 27–59.

Pacific Law Journal, 1971
Restoration of rights to felons in California. **2,** 718–36.

Pacific Law Journal, 1971
The sovereign should be liable for the wrongful injury of prisoners. **2,** 697–717.

Radical Alternatives to Prison, 1971
The case for radical alternatives to prison.
10 Newgate St., London, E.C.1. Mimeo.

Sanders, R.C., Kerper, H.B., Killinger, G.G., and Watkins, J.C., 1971
Prisoners' first amendment rights within the institution.
Huntsville, Texas: Institute of Contemporary Corrections and the Behavioral Sciences, Criminal Justice Monograph, **3,** (3).

Singer, L.R., McArthur, V.A., and Schuman, A.M., 1971
The center for correctional justice—a way to resolve prisoners' grievances?
Prison J., **51** (2), 37–42.

Singer, R.G., 1971
Confining solitary confinement: constitutional argument for a 'new penology'.
Iowa Law Rev., **56,** 1251–96.

Singer, R.G., 1971
Prison conditions: an unconstitutional road-block to rehabilitation.
Catholic Univ. Law Rev., **20,** 365–93.

Southern California Law Review, 1971
Courts, corrections and Eighth Amendment: encouraging prison reform by releasing inmates. **44,** 1060–91.

Turner, W.B., 1971
Establishing the rule of law in prisons: a manual for prisoners' rights litigation.
Stanford Law Rev., **23,** 473–518.

University of Chicago Law Review, 1971
The role of the Eighth Amendment in prison reform. **38,** 647–64.

Villanova Law Review, 1971
Prisoners' rights and the correctional scheme: the legal controversy and problems of implementation: a symposium. **16,** 1029–1118.

Virginia Law Review, 1971
Decency and fairness: an emergency judicial role in prison reform. **57,** 841–84.

Yale Law Review, 1971
Prison mail censorship and the First Amendment. **61,** 87–111.

Albany Law Review, 1972
Sexual assaults and forced homosexual relationships in prison: cruel and unusual punishment. **36,** 428–38.

Atkins, B.M., and Glick, H.R. (eds.), 1972
Prisons, protest and politics.
Englewood Cliffs, N.J.: Prentice-Hall.

Buffalo Law Review, 1972
Prisons on trial: a symposium on the changing law of corrections. **21,** 643–985.

Cornell Law Review, 1972
The constitutional status of solitary confinement. **57,** 476–89.

Dawson, R.O., 1972
The sentencing and correctional process, in S.S. Nagel (ed.), *The rights of the accused. Law and Action,* Vol. 1, Sage Criminal Justice System Annuals, Beverly Hills, Calif.: Sage Publications, 259–80.

Dickinson Law Review, 1972
Judicial recognition of prisoners' constitutional rights to send and receive mail. **76,** 775–98.

Drake, J., 1972
Enforcing the right to treatment: Wyatt v. Stickney.
Amer. Crim. Law Rev., **10,** 587–609.

Durant, M., Thomas, M., and Wilcock, H.D., 1972
Crime, criminals and the law.
London: Office of Population, Censuses and Surveys, Social Survey Division, 68–115.

Edwards, G., 1972
Penitentiaries produce no penitants.
J. Crim. Law, Criminol. & Pol. Sci., **63,** 154–61.

FOX, B.M., 1972
The First Amendment rights of prisoners.
J. Crim. Law, Criminol. & Pol. Sci., **63,** 162–84.

HARVARD CENTER FOR CRIMINAL JUSTICE, 1972
Judicial intervention in prison discipline.
J. Crim. Law, Criminol. & Pol. Sci., **63,** 200–28.

HIRSCHKOP, P.J., CRISMAN, N., AND MILLEMANN, M.A., 1972
Litigating an affirmative prisoners' rights action.
Amer. Crim. Law Rev., **11,** 39–64.

HOLLEN, C.R., 1972
Emerging prisoners' rights.
Ohio State Law J., **33,** 1–79.

HOPPER, C.B., 1972
Sex in prison. The Mississippi experiment with conjugal visiting.
Baton Rouge: Louisiana State Univ. Press.

NATIONAL COUNCIL ON CRIME AND DELINQUENCY, 1972
A model act for the protection of rights of prisoners.
Crime & Delinq., **18,** 1–14.

PACIFIC LAW JOURNAL, 1972
The penal ombudsman: a step towards penal reform. **3,** 166–89.

PEPPER, C., 1972
Judicial activism and prison reform.
Catholic Univ. of America Law Rev., **22,** 96–107.

PRACTISING LAW INSTITUTE, 1972
Prisoners rights (2 volumes).
New York.

SCHWARTZ, B., 1972
Deprivation of privacy as a 'functional prerequisite': the case of the prison.
J. Crim. Law, Criminol. & Pol. Sci., **63,** 229–39.

SCHWITZGEBEL, R.K., 1972
Development and legal regulation of coercive behavior modification techniques with offenders.
Rockville, Md.: N.I.M.H. Center for Studies of Crime and Delinquency.

SINGER, R.G., 1972
Prisoners as wards of the court—a nonconstitutional path to assure correctional reform by the courts.
Univ. Cincinatti Law Rev., **41,** 769–806.

SIRICO, L.J., 1972
Prisoner classification and administrative decision making.
Texas Law Rev., **50,** 1229–54.

SOUTH CAROLINA, STATE OF, 1972
The emerging rights of the confined.
The Correctional Development Foundation Inc., Columbia S.C.: Department of Corrections.

SOUTHERN CALIFORNIA LAW REVIEW, 1972
Conditioning and other technologies used to 'treat'? 'rehabilitate?' 'demolish?' prisoners and mental patients. **45,** 616–81.

SOUTHERN CALIFORNIA LAW REVIEW, 1972
Duress and the prison escape: a new use for an old defence. **45,** 1062–82.

STRAIGHT, M., 1972
A prisoner-press interview right.
Amer. Crim. Law Rev., **11,** 273–89.

TIBBLES, L., 1972
Ombudsmen for American prisons.
North Dakota Law Rev., **48,** 383–441.

VERMA, H.L., HUETTNER, D.A., AND NEUHARD, J.R., 1972
Escaped prisoners: a statistical analysis of their constitutional right to a jury trial.
J. Urban Law, **50,** 199–208.

WARD, D.A., 1972
Inmate rights and prison reform in Sweden and Denmark.
J. Crim. Law, Criminol. & Poll Sci., **63,** 240–55.

WISCONSIN LAW REVIEW, 1972
Solitary confinement—punishment within the letter of the law, or psychological torture? 1972, 223–37.

YALE LAW JOURNAL, 1972
Bargaining in correctional institutions: restructuring the relation between the inmate and the prison authority. **81,** 726–57.

ZALMAN, M., 1972
Prisoners' rights to medical care.
J. Crim. Law, Criminol. & Pol. Sci., **63,** 185–99.

ARKANSAS LAW REVIEW, 1973
Procedural due process for intraprison disciplinary hearings: an Arkansas analysis. **27,** 44–64.

CHICAGO-KENT LAW REVIEW, 1973
Due process at in-prison disciplinary proceedings. **50,** 498–509.

ENGLISH, P., 1973
Prisoners' rights: quis custodiet ipsos custodes? in J.W. Bridge, D. Lasok, D.L. Perrott and R.O. Plender (eds.), *Fundamental rights.*
London: Sweet & Maxwell, 201–18.

FITCH, W.A., AND TEPPER, J., 1973
Structuring correctional decision making: a traditional proposal.
Catholic Univ. Law Rev., **22,** 774–806.

GOLDFARB, R.L., AND SINGER, L.R., 1973
After conviction.
New York: Simon & Schuster, 359–526.

HERMAN, M.G., AND HAFT, M.G. (EDS.), 1973
Prisoners' rights sourcebook.
New York: Clark Boardman Co.

HOPKINS, A., 1973
The prison strike: some general considerations and a case study.
Aust. & N.Z. J. Criminol., **6,** 32–46.

JUSTICE, W.W., 1973
Prisoners' litigation in the federal courts.
Texas Law Rev., **51,** 707–20.

KAUFMAN, I.R., 1973
Prison: the judge's dilemma.
Fordham Law Rev., **41,** 495–516.

KLEIN, M., 1973
Problems arising from biological experimentation in prisons, in A. Storr (ed.), *Medical care of prisoners and detainees*, Ciba Foundation Symposium **16.**

Amsterdam: Associated Scientific Publishers, 37–49, 65–78.

MCGOVERN, E.T., 1973
Internment and detention without trial in the light of the European convention on human rights, in J.W. Bridge, D. Lasok, D.L. Perrott and R.O. Plender (eds.), *Fundamental rights.*
London: Sweet & Maxwell, 219–31.

MARKLEY, C.W., 1973
Furlough programs and conjugal visiting in adult correctional institutions.
Fed. Probation, **37** (1), 19–26.

MILLEMANN, M.A., 1973
Protected inmate liberties: a case for judicial responsibility.
Oregon Law Rev., **53,** 29–55.

MISNER, R.L., 1973
Prison discipline: the inherent conflicts.
Aust. & N.Z. J. Criminol., **6,** 21–31.

MITFORD, J., 1973
Kind and usual punishment, the prison business.
New York: Alfred H. Kopf, 79–168, 228–97.

MURPHY, G.F., 1973
The courts look at prisoners' rights. A review.
Criminology, **4,** 441–59.

NEW YORK LAW FORUM, 1973
Prisoners have a right to receive correspondence from attorney regarding establishment of prisoner's union. **18,** 1016–24.

NOTRE DAME LAWYER, 1973
Eighth Amendment rights of prisoners: adequate medical care and protection from the violence of fellow inmates. **49,** 454–69.

O'LEARY, V., *et al.*, 1973
Peaceful resolution of prison conflict.
Hackensack, N.J.: National Council on Crime and Delinquency.

PALMER, J.W., 1973
Constitutional rights of prisoners.
Cincinatti: W.H. Anderson Co.

RUBIN, S., 1973
Law and the penal system.
Can. J. Criminol. & Corrections, **15,** 59–73.

RUDOVSKY, D., 1973
The rights of prisoners: the basic ACLU guide to a prisoner's rights.
An American Civil Liberties Union handbook
New York: Avon Books.

SINGER, L.R., AND KEATING, J.M., JR., 1973
The courts and the prisons: a crisis of confrontation.
Crim. Law Bull., **9,** 337–57.

SOUTHERN CALIFORNIA LAW REVIEW, 1973
Granting workmen's compensation benefits to prison inmates. **46,** 1223–62.

TEXAS LAW REVIEW, 1973
State prisoners' suits: proper forum, choice remedy, and effect of judgment. **51,** 1364–1410.

UCLA LAW REVIEW, 1973
Judicial intervention in corrections: the California experience—an empirical study. **20,** 452–580.

UNITED STATES OF AMERICA, 1973
Corrections.
Washington, D.C. National Conference on Criminal Justice, Department of Justice, Document C–23–75.

WASHINGTON UNIVERSITY LAW QUARTERLY, 1973
Symposium: A model act for the protection of rights of prisoners. 1973, 551–646.

WICK, W.D., 1973
Procedural due process in prison disciplinary hearings: the case for specific constitutional requirements.
South Dakota Law Rev., **18,** 309–26.

WRIGHT, E.O., 1973
The politics of punishment: a critical analysis of prisons in America.
New York: Harper & Row, 262–346.

BARRISH, I.J., 1974
Ethical issues and answers to behavior modification.
Corrective & Social Psychiat., **20** (2), 30–7.

CARDARELLI, A.P., AND FINKELSTEIN, M.M., 1974
Correctional administrators assess the adequacy and impact of prison legal services programs in the United States.
J. Crim. Law & Criminol., **65,** 91–102.

COHEN, S., 1974
A futuristic scenario for the prison system, in F. Basaglia (ed.), *The crimes of peace.*
Turin: Einaudi.

CROMWELL, P.F., JR., 1974
A vote for the jail ombudsman.
Fed. Probation, **38** (1), 54–6.

FISHER, H., 1974
Parole and probation revocation procedures after Morrissey and Gagnon.
J. Crim. Law & Criminol., **65,** 46–61.

FORDHAM LAW REVIEW, 1974
The evolving right of due process at prison disciplinary hearings. **42,** 878–89.

HALL, J., 1974
Penal institutions and behaviour modification.
Probation J., **21,** 46–50.

JACKSON, M., 1974
Justice behind the walls—a study of the disciplinary process in a Canadian penitentiary
Osgoode Hall Law J., **12,** 1–103.

MATHIESEN, T., 1974
The politics of abolition:
Scandinavian Studies in Criminology, **4.**
London: Martin Robertson.

OPTON, E.M., 1974
Psychiatric violence against prisoners: when therapy is punishment.
Mississippi Law J., **45,** 605–44.

PRICE, R.R., 1974
Bringing the rule of law to corrections.
Can. J. Criminol. & Corrections, **16,** 209–55.

RUSSELL, E.W., 1974
Special monograph supplement. The power of behavior control: a critique of behavior modification methods.
J. Clinical Psych., **30,** 111–36.

SHAPIRO, M.H., 1974
Legislating the control of behavior control: autonomy and the coercive use of organic therapies.
Southern Calif. Law Rev., **47,** 237–356.

SILBERT, J.D., AND SUSSMAN, A.N., 1974
The rights of juveniles confined in training schools and the experience of a training school ombudsman.
Brooklyn Law Rev., **40,** 605–33.

UNIVERSITY OF CINCINATTI LAW REVIEW, 1974
Prison discipline and the Eighth Amendment: a psychological perspective. **43,** 101–32.

VIRGINIA LAW REVIEW, 1974
Procedural due process in the involuntary institutional transfer of prisoners. **60,** 333–62.

2 Other rights, in relation to police, courts, employment, etc.

[*See also Section 6(4) on use and abuse of police powers; Section 13(1) on parole selection.*]

HESS, A.G., AND POOLE, F.L., 1967
Abuse of the record of arrest not leading to conviction.
Crime & Delinq., **13,** 494–505.

ALLEN, F.A., 1969
Small crimes and large problems: some constitutional dimensions, in *Mass production justice and the constitutional ideal.*
Papers presented and proceedings of a conference on 'Problems associated with misdemeanor'.
Charlottesville, Va.: Michie Co., 74–96.

CANADA, 1969
Toward unity: criminal justice and corrections.
Report of the Canadian Committee on Corrections.
Ottawa: Queen's Printer, 407–12.

HARVARD LAW REVIEW, 1970
Requiring a criminal defendant to submit to a government psychiatric examination: an invasion of the privilege against self-incrimination. **83,** 648–71.

JOURNAL OF CRIMINAL LAW, CRIMINOLOGY AND POLICE SCIENCE, 1970
The convict's right to a speedy trial. **61,** 352–66.

KOGON, B., AND LOUGHERY, D.L., JR., 1970
Sealing and expungement of criminal records—the big lie.
J. Crim. Law, Criminol. & Pol. Sci., **61,** 378–92.

PATERSON, A., 1970
A report on legal aid as a social service.
London: Cobden Trust, 27–43.

PORTNOY, B.M., 1970
Employment of former criminals.
Cornell Law Rev., **55,** 306–20.

VANDERBILT LAW REVIEW, 1970
The collateral consequences of a criminal conviction.
Special project. **23,** 929–1241.

CORNELL LAW REVIEW, 1971
Discrimination on the basis of arrest record. **56,** 470–88.

CRIME AND DELINQUENCY, 1971
Preventive detention. A policy statement. **17,** 1–8.

COHEN, N.P., AND RIVKIN, D.H., 1971
Civil disabilities: the forgotten punishment.
Fed. Probation, **35** (2), 19–25.

DAUBER, E., 1971
Reforming the detainer system: a case study.
Crim. Law Bull., **7,** 669–717.

MUKAI, C., 1971
Prisoners' clothing during trial.
Cleveland State Law Rev., **20,** 391–400.

SIMMON, R., 1971
Rights of probationers—specifically considering revocation of probation: does the Miranda Warning apply?
Baylor Law Rev., **23,** 431–44.

UNIVERSITY OF CHICAGO LAW REVIEW, 1971
Retention and dissemination of arrest records: judicial response. **38,** 850–74.

URBAN RESEARCH CORPORATION, 1971
Preventive detention.
Chicago: Urban Research Corporation.

VILLANOVA LAW REVIEW, 1971
Discriminatory hiring practices due to arrest records—private remedies. **17,** 110–29.

WEXLER, D.B., AND HERSHEY, R.A., 1971
Criminal detainers in a nutshell.
Crim. Law Bull., **7,** 753–76.

JUSTICE, 1972
Living it down.
Report of a committee set up by the Howard League for Penal Reform and NACRO, under the chairmanship of Lord Gardiner.
London: Stevens.

KARABIAN, W.J., 1972
Record of arrest: the indelible stain.
Pacific Law J., **3,** 20–36.

NAGEL, S.S., (ED.), 1972
The rights of the accused. Law and Action, Vol. 1. Sage Criminal Justice System Annuals.
Beverly Hills, Calif.: Sage Publications.

NATIONAL COUNCIL FOR CIVIL LIBERTIES, 1972
The rights of suspects.
A re-examination of the Judges' Rules, and a commentary on the Report of the Criminal Law Revision Committee 'Evidence (General)'.
London: N.C.C.L.

SAINT LOUIS UNIVERSITY LAW JOURNAL, 1972
Police records of arrest: a brief for the right to remove them from police files. **17,** 263–78.

STEELE, W.W., 1972
A suggested legislative device for dealing with abuses of criminal records.
J. Law Reform, **6,** 32–57.

UCLA LAW REVIEW, 1972
Maintenance and dissemination of criminal records: a legislative proposal. **19,** 654–89.

WAGNER, A., 1972
Sentence credit for 'dead' time.
Crim. Law Bull., **8,** 393–417.

WESTIN, A.F., AND BAKER, M.A., 1972
Databanks in a free society: computers, record-keeping and privacy.
New York: Quadrangle Books, 47–64, 241–79.

ZANDER, M., 1972
Legal advice and criminal appeals: a survey of prisoners, prisons and lawyers.
Crim. Law Rev., 1972 132–73.

GOLDFARB, R.L., AND SINGER, L.R., 1973
After conviction.
New York: Simon & Schuster, 316–58.

HASKEL, P.B., 1973
The arrest record and New York City public hiring: an evaluation.
Columbia J. Law & Social Problems, **9,** 442–94.

MCNAMARA, R.M., AND STARR, J.R., 1973
Confidentiality of narcotic addict treatment records: a legal and statistical analysis.
Columbia Law Rev., **73,** 1579–1612.

MELTSNER, M., CAPLAN, M., AND LANE, W.C., 1973
An act to promote the rehabilitation of criminal offenders in the State of New York.
Syracuse Law Rev., **24,** 885–923.

NATIONAL COUNCIL FOR CIVIL LIBERTIES, 1973
The rights of the mentally abnormal offender.
The N.C.C.L. evidence to the Butler Committee.
London: N.C.C.L.

PARKER, C.F., 1973
A right to know the reasons for a decision of a magistrates' court? in J.W. Bridge, D. Lasok, D.L. Perrott and R.O. Plender (eds.), *Fundamental rights.*
London: Sweet & Maxwell, 189–200.

BOSHIER, R., AND JOHNSON, D., 1974
Does conviction affect employment opportunities?
Brit. J. Criminol., **14,** 264–68.

SENNA, J.J., 1974
Right to counsel at adult probation revocation hearings—a survey and analysis of current law: a comment.
Crim. Law Bull., **10,** 228–38.

SKOLER, D., 1974
Protecting the rights of defendants in pretrial intervention programs.
Crim. Law Bulletin, **10,** 473–92.

SOOTHILL, K., 1974
The prisoner's release: a study of the employment of ex-prisoners.
London: George Allen & Unwin.

WALLER, I., 1974
Men released from prison.
Univ. Toronto Press, 74–104.

YALE LAW JOURNAL, 1974
The need to reform ex-felon disenfranchisement laws. **83,** 580–601.

15 Manipulation of environment: the problem of prevention

1 Delinquency prevention programmes

(a) *Some aspects of poverty and community action*

[*See also Section 2(1) on economic conditions and crime.*]

NELSON, E.K., 1963
Experimentation by the Youth Studies Center in a community education program, in *Proceedings of the 93rd Annual Congress of Correction of the American Correctional Association.*
Washington, D.C. 265–72.

HARLEM YOUTH OPPORTUNITIES UNLIMITED INC., 1964
Youth in the Ghetto.
New York.

CLOWARD, R.A., 1965
The war on poverty. Are the poor left out?
Nation, 2 August 1965, 55–60.

COSER, L.A., 1965
The sociology of poverty. To the memory of Georg Simmel.
Social Problems, **13**, 140–48.

FISHMAN, L. (ED.), 1966
Poverty and affluence.
Yale Univ. Press, 99–123, 182–229.

MEISSNER, H.H. (ED.),
Poverty in the affluent society
New York: Harper & Row.

MILLER, S.W., AND REIN, M., 1966
Poverty, inequality, and policy, in H.S. Becker (ed.), *Social problems: a modern approach.*
New York: John Wiley & Sons, 426–516.

BECK, B.M., 1967
Bedbugs, stench, dampness, and immorality: a review essay on recent literature about poverty.
Social Problems, **15**, 101–14.

BLUMENTHAL, R., 1967
Community action: the organs of a government program.
Senior thesis, Harvard College.

BRAGER, G.E., AND PURCELL, F.P., (EDS.), 1967
Community action against poverty. Readings from the mobilization experience.
New Haven, Conn.: College & Univ. Press.

MARRIS, P., AND REIN, M., 1967
Dilemmas of social reform. Poverty and community action in the United States.
London: Routledge & Kegan Paul.

PERLMAN, R., AND JONES, D., 1967
Neighborhood service centers.
Washington, D.C.: U.S. Dept. of Health, Education and Welfare.

ROACH, J.L., AND GURSSLIN, O.R., 1967
An evaluation of the concept 'culture of poverty'.
Social Forces, **45**, 383–92.

WALD, P.M., 1967
Poverty and criminal justice, in *Task force report: the courts.*
Washington, D.C.: President's Commission on Law Enforcement and Administration of Justice, 139–51.

GANS, H.J., 1968
Urban poverty and social planning, in P.F. Lazarsfeld, W.H. Sewell and H.L. Wilensky (eds.),
The uses of sociology.
London: Weidenfeld & Nicolson, 437–76.

GROSSER, C.F., 1968
Helping youth. A study of six community organisation programs.
Washington, D.C.: U.S. Dept. of Health, Education and Welfare.

MILLER, W., 1968
The elimination of the American lower class as a national policy: a critique of the ideology of the poverty movement of the 1960's, in D.P. Moynihan (ed.), *On understanding poverty. Perspectives from the social sciences.*
New York: Basic Books, 260–315.

MOYNIHAN, D.P., 1968
The professors and the poor, in D.P. Moynihan (ed.), *On understanding poverty. Perspectives from the social sciences.*
New York: Basic Books, 3–35.

KRAMER, R.M., 1969
Participation of the poor: comparative community case studies in the war on poverty.
Englewood Cliffs, N.J.: Prentice-Hall, 1–21, 239–59.

LEVINE, R.A., 1969
Evaluating the war on poverty, in J.L. Sundquist (ed.), *Perspectives on poverty II. On fighting poverty.*
New York: Basic Books, 188–216.

MOYNIHAN, D.P., 1969
Maximum feasible misunderstanding: community action in the war on poverty.
New York: Free Press.

MOYNIHAN, D.P., 1969
Toward a national urban policy, in *Violent crime. The challenge to our cities.*
The Report of the National Commission on the Causes and Prevention of Violence.
New York: George Braziller, 1–30.

ROBIN, G.D., 1969
Anti-poverty programs and delinquency.
J. Crim. Law, Criminol. & Pol. Sci., **60,** 323–51.

SUNDQUIST, J.L. (ED.), 1969
The end of the experiment? in J.L. Sundquist (ed.), *Perspectives on poverty II. On fighting poverty.*
New York: Basic Books, 235–51.

CLARK, K.B., AND HOPKINS, J., 1970
A relevant war against poverty. A study of community action programs and observable social change.
New York: Harper & Row, 59–204.

COATES, K., AND SILBURN, R., 1970
Poverty: the forgotten Englishmen.
Harmondsworth: Penguin Books, 43–156.

DORSEN, N., 1970
The role of the lawyer in America's ghetto society.
Texas Law Rev., **49,** 50–68.

LEVINE, R.A., 1970
The poor ye need not have with you. Lessons from the war on poverty.
Cambridge, Mass.: M.I.T. Press, 91–189.

TOWNSEND, P., 1970
Measures and explanations of poverty in high income and low income countries: the problems of operationalizing the concepts of development, class and poverty, in P. Townsend (ed.), *The concept of poverty.*
London: Heinemann, 1–45.

JEFFERY, C.R., 1971
Crime prevention through environmental design.
Beverly Hills, Calif.: Sage Publications, 130–225.

MATZA, D., 1971
Poverty and disrepute, in R.K. Merton and R. Nisbet (eds.), *Contemporary social problems,* (3rd ed.),
New York: Harcourt Brace Jovanovich, 601–56.

NEWBERG, H.B., 1971
Building local citizen alliances to reduce crime and create a fairer and more effective criminal justice system.
J. Urban Law, **49,** 443–83.

1 Delinquency prevention programmes

(*b*) *Delinquency and crime prevention programmes*

Power, E., and Witmer, H., 1951
An experiment in the prevention of delinquency.
New York: Columbia Univ. Press.

Witmer, H.L., and Tufts, E., 1954
The effectiveness of delinquency prevention programs.
Washington, D.C.: Children's Bureau, Publication No. 350.

Maccoby, E.E., Johnson, J.P., and Church, R., 1958
Community integration and the social control of juvenile delinquency.
J. Social Issues, **14**, 38–51.

Miller, W.B., 1958
Inter-institutional conflict as a major impediment to delinquency prevention.
Human Organization, **17**, 20–3.

Annals of the American Academy of Political and Social Science, 1959
Special number on *Prevention of juvenile delinquency*. **322**, (March 1959).

McKay, H.D., 1960
Differential association and crime prevention: problems of utilization.
Social Problems, **8**, 25–37.

Middendorff, W., 1960
New forms of juvenile delinquency: their origin, prevention and treatment.
Second U.N. Congress on prevention of crime and the treatment of offenders.
New York: U.N. Document A/*Conf.*/17/6.

United Nations, 1960
Special police services for the prevention of juvenile delinquency.
Second U.N. Conference on the Prevention of Crime and the Treatment of Offenders.
New York: U.N. Document A/CONF, 17/20, 18–23.

United States of America, 1960
Community programs and projects for the prevention of juvenile delinquency.
Juvenile Delinquency, Facts and Facets, No. 14.
Washington, D.C.: Department of Health, Education and Welfare.

Martin, J.M., 1961
Three approaches to delinquency prevention: a critique.
Crime & Delinq., **7**, 16–24.

Mobilization for Youth Inc., 1961
A proposal for the prevention and control of delinquency by expanding opportunities.
(9 December 1961; 2nd ed. August 1962).
New York: Mimeo.

Nelson, E.K., 1961
Community approaches to the prevention of crime and delinquency—some research leads.
Working Paper 4.
Los Angeles: Youth Studies Center, Univ. of S. Calif.

Radzinowicz, L., 1961
In search of criminology.
London: Heinemann, 141–48.

United States of America, 1961
Establishing the President's Committee on Juvenile Delinquency and Youth Crime.
Executive Order 10940, 11 May 1961, Press Release. Mimeo.
Counter-Attack on Delinquency.
The program of the Federal Government to stimulate communities to develop rational answers to a growing crisis (8 August 1963).
Washington, D.C. Mimeo.

United States of America, 1961
Public Law 87–274. An Act to provide federal assistance for projects which will demonstrate or develop techniques and practices leading to a solution of the Nation's juvenile delinquency control problem:
75 STAT.572, 87th Congress, S.279, 22 September 1961, Washington, D.C.
Conditions governing demonstration and training project grant awards under Public Law 87–274 (the Juvenile Delinquency and Youth Offenses Control Act of 1961) (rev. October 1962).
Washington, D.C.: Mimeograph issued by Dept. of Health, Education and Welfare.
The federal delinquency program objectives and juvenile delinquency and youth crime, and the Juvenile Delinquency and Youth

Offenses Control Act of 1961 (Public Law 87–274) (November 1962).
Washington, D.C.: Mimeograph issued by Dept. of Justice, Dept. of Health, Education and Welfare, Dept. of Labor.
Review of training program policy for fiscal year 1964 (August 1963). Mimeographed draft, Washington, D.C.
Policy guides to the presentation of proposals for funding under Public Law 87–274 (5 September 1963). Washington, D.C.: Mimeograph issued by Dept. of Health, Education and Welfare. *Summaries of training projects funded under P.L.* 87–274, prepared by the President's Committee on Juvenile Delinquency and Youth Crime (September 1963).
Washington, D.C., Mimeo.

MILLER, W.B., 1962
The impact of a 'total community' delinquency control project.
Social Problems, **10,** 168–91.

CLIFFORD, W., 1963
The evaluation of methods used for the prevention and treatment of juvenile delinquency in Africa south of the Sahara.
Internat. Rev. Crim. Policy, **21,** 17–31.

CLOWARD, R.A., 1963
The prevention of delinquent subcultures: issues and problems, in W.R. Carriker (ed.), *Role of the school of juvenile delinquency*.
A research symposium sponsored by U.S. Office of Education & Phi Delta Kappa (Cooperative Research monograph, 10).
Washington, D.C.: U.S. Dept. of Health, Education and Welfare and Office of Education, 69–84.

KAHN, A.J., 1963
Planning community services for children in trouble.
New York: Columbia Univ. Press, 45–113, 477–523.

MACK, J.A., 1963
Police juvenile liaison schemes.
Brit. J. Criminol., **3,** 361–75.

MORRISON, R.L., 1963
The effectiveness of current programmes for the prevention of juvenile delinquency.
Strasbourg: Council of Europe.

UNITED NATIONS, 1963
The evaluation of methods in the prevention of juvenile delinquency—European seminar.
Internat. Rev. Crim. Policy, **21,** 9–16.

WATTENBERG, W.W., AND BUFE, N., 1963
The effectiveness of police youth bureau officers.
J. Crim. Law, Criminol. & Pol. Sci., **54,** 470–75.

WITMER, H.L., 1963
A brief guide to the evaluation of measures for the prevention of juvenile delinquency.
Internat. Rev. Crim. Policy, **21,** 55–61.

NEW YORK CITY YOUTH BOARD, 1964
Reaching the teenage addict: a study of street club work with a group of adolescent users.
New York.

PIVEN, F., 1964
Conceptual themes in the evolution of MFY.
Prepared for the training institute program on Urban Community Development Projects: selected aspects of the mobilization for youth experience, April 27–May 1, 1964.
New York: Mimeo.

SWEDEN, 1964
Action against juvenile delinquency.
A proposal for experimental activities in a Swedish town.
Stockholm: Ministry of Justice.

REID, W., 1964
Interagency co-ordination in delinquency prevention and control.
Social Service Rev., **38,** 418–28.

BECK, B.M., 1965
Innovations in combating juvenile delinquency.
Children, **12,** 69–74.

INTERNATIONAL CHILD WELFARE REVIEW, 1965
Prevention of juvenile delinquency—evaluation of different types of action.
19, 5–39.

RADZINOWICZ, L., 1965
The need for criminology.
London: Heinemann, 28–33.

RHODES, W.C., 1965
Delinquency and community action, in

H.C. Quay (ed.), *Juvenile delinquency research and theory.*
Princeton: D. Van Nostrand Co., 209–62.

ROSENFELD, E., 1965
Social research and social action in prevention of juvenile delinquency, in A.W. Gouldner and S.M. Miller (eds.), *Applied sociology: opportunities and problems.*
New York: Free Press, 367–80.

UNITED NATIONS, 1964
The young adult offender. A review of current practices and programmes in prevention and treatment.
New York: Department of Economic and Social Affairs, 30–51.

YABLONSKY, L., 1965
Experiences with the criminal community, in A.W. Gouldner and S.M. Miller (eds.), *Applied sociology: opportunities and problems.*
New York: Free Press, 55–73.

KLEIN, M.W., 1966
A structural approach to gang intervention: the Lincoln Heights project.
Univ. of Southern California, Youth Studies Center. Mimeo.

LENTZ, W.P., 1966
Social status and attitudes toward delinquency control.
J. Res. Crime & Delinq., **3**, 147–54.

SPERGEL, I., 1966
Street gang work. Theory and practice.
Mass.: Addison-Wesley Pub. Co., 120–46.

UNITED STATES OF AMERICA, 1966
Report of the President's Commission on Crime in the District of Columbia.
Washington, D.C. 733–92.

WHEELER, S., AND COTTRELL, L.S.JR., 1966
Juvenile delinquency, its prevention and control.
New York: Russell Sage Foundation, 5–27.

ADAMS, S., 1967
A cost approach to the assessment of gang rehabilitation techniques.
J. Res. Crime & Delinq., **4**, 166–82.

AMOS, W.E., AND WELLFORD, C.F. (EDS.), 1967
Delinquency prevention.
Englewood Cliffs, N.J.: Prentice-Hall, 51–248.

BERLEMAN, W.C., AND STEINBURN, T.W., 1967
The execution and evaluating of a delinquency prevention program.
Social Problems, **14**, 413–23.

BIBB, M., 1967
Gang related services of mobilization for youth, in M. Klein (ed.), *Juvenile gangs in context.*
Englewood Cliffs, N.J.: Prentice-Hall, 175–210.

CHRISTIE, N., 1967
Research into methods of crime prevention.
Collected studies in criminological research, **1.**
Strasbourg: Council of Europe, 55–71.

HYMAN, M., 1967
Urban development for crime prevention, in S.A. Yefsky (ed.), *Law enforcement, science and technology.*
Washington, D.C.: Thompson Book Co., 57–61.

SKOLER, D.L., 1967
Federal assistance in developing the technology of criminal justice, in S.A. Yefsky (ed.), *Law enforcement, science and technology.*
Washington, D.C.: Thompson Book Co., 47–56.

UNITED STATES OF AMERICA, 1967
The challenge of crime in a free society.
Report of the President's Commission on Law Enforcement and Administration of Justice, Washington, D.C., 58–79, 81–4, 57–103, 279–91.

UNITED STATES OF AMERICA, 1967
Task force report: juvenile delinquency and youth crime.
Washington, D.C.: President's Commission on Law Enforcement and Administration of Justice.
(Reports by J.P. Fitzpatrick, B.M. AND D.B. Beck, K. Polk, V.M. Burns & L.W. Stern, S. Wheeler, *et al.*), 317–428.

UNITED STATES OF AMERICA, 1967
Task force report: the police.
Washington, D.C.: President's Commission on Law Enforcement and Administration of Justice, 221–28.

CLINE, H., FREEMAN, H.E., and WHEELER, S., 1968
The anaysis and evaluation of detached-worker programs, in S. Wheeler (ed.), *Controlling delinquents.* New York: John Wiley & Sons, 287–307.

GLUECK, S. and GLUECK, E., 1968
Delinquents and non-delinquents in perspective.
Cambridge, Mass.: Harvard Univ. Press, 182–201.

HUNTER, E.F., 1968
Reduction of delinquency through expansion of opportunity—a preliminary analysis.
(Research Report No. 33).
Los Angeles: Probation Dept., Office of Research and Standards.

KAHN, A.J., 1968
From delinquency treatment to community development, in P.F. Lazarsfeld, W.H. Sewell and H.L. Wilensky (eds.), *The uses of sociology.*
London: Weidenfeld & Nicolson, 477–505.

KANTOR, D., AND BENNETT, W.I., 1968
Orientations of street-corner workers and their effect on gangs, in S. Wheeler (ed.), *Controlling delinquents.*
New York: John Wiley & Sons, 271–86.

MILLER, W.B., BAUM, R.C., AND McNEIL, R., 1968
Delinquency prevention and organizational relations, in S. Wheeler (ed.), *Controlling delinquents.*
New York: John Wiley & Sons, 61–100.

LINDSAY, J., 1969
The City.
London: Bodley Head, 164–88.

MOYNIHAN, D.P., 1969
Maximum feasible misunderstanding: community action in the war on poverty.
New York: Free Press.

ROBIN, G.D., 1969
Anti-poverty programs and delinquency.
J. Crim. Law, Criminol. & Pol. Sci., **60,** 323–31.

SPERGEL, I.A., 1969
Community problem solving: the delinquency example.
Univ. Chicago Press, 281–313.

WEISSMAN, H.H., (ED.), 1969
Justice and the law in the mobilization for youth experience.
New York: Association Press.

WILKINS, L.T., AND GOTTFREDSON, D.M., 1969
Research, demonstration and social action.
Davis, Calif.: National Council on Crime and Delinquency, 179–194. Mimeo.

HACKLER, J.C., AND LINDEN, E., 1970
The response of adults to delinquency prevention programs: the race factor.
J. Res. Crime & Delinq., **7,** 31–45.

GRANT, J.D., 1971
Delinquency prevention through participation in social change.
Crim. Law Bull., **7,** 530–43.

POLK, K., 1971
Delinquency prevention and the youth service bureau.
Crim. Law Bull., **7,** 490–511.

POSTON, R.W., 1971
The gang and the establishment.
New York: Harper & Row.

TAYLOR, M., 1971
Study of the juvenile liaison scheme in West Ham, 1961–1965.
London: Home Office Research Studies, **8.**

CALIFORNIA LAW REVIEW, 1972
California's predelinquency statute: a case study and suggested alternatives. **60,** 1163–95.

COUNCIL OF EUROPE, 1972
The role of the school in the prevention of juvenile delinquency.
Strasbourg: Council of Europe.

DOLESCHAL, E., 1972
Criminal justice programs in model cities.
Crime & Delinq. Lit., **4,** 292–328.

NEWMAN, O. 1972
Defensible space: crime prevention through urban design.
New York: Macmillan, 1–50, 187–208.

SMITH, C., FARRANT, M.R., AND MARCHANT, H.J., 1972
The Wincroft Youth Project. A social-work programme in a slum area.
London: Tavistock, 3–44, 205–67.

Baron, R., Feeney, F., and Thornton, W., 1973
Preventing delinquency through diversion: the Sacramento County 601 diversion project.
Fed. Probation, **37** (1), 13–18.

Schuessler, K. F. (ed.), 1973
Edwin H. Sutherland: on analysing crime.
Univ. Chicago Press, 131–40.

United States of America, 1973
Community crime prevention.
Washington, D.C.: National Advisory Commission on Criminal Justice Standards and Goals.

2 Identification and prediction of potential criminality

Glueck, S. and Glueck, E., 1960
Unraveling juvenile delinquency.
Cambridge, Mass.: Harvard Univ. Press, 13–18, 27–39, 257–71.

Reiss, A.J., Jr., 1951
Unraveling juvenile delinquency, II. An appraisal of the research methods.
Amer. J. Sociol., **57,** 115–20.

Glueck, E.T., 1956
Spotting potential delinquents: can it be done?
Fed. Probation, **20** (3), 7–13.

Glueck, S. and Glueck, E., 1959
Predicting delinquency and crime.
Cambridge, Mass.: Harvard Univ. Press, 1–17, 23–32.

Glaser, D., 1960
Differential association and criminological prediction.
Social Problems, **8,** 6–14.

Glueck, S., 1960
Ten years of unraveling juvenile delinquency.
J. Crim. Law, Criminol. & Pol. Sci., **51,** 283–308.

Keniston, K. 1960
Entangling juvenile delinquency.
Commentary (June 1960).

United States of America, 1960
Identifying potential delinquents.
Washington, D.C.: Children's Bureau.

Bordua D.J. 1961
Prediction and selection of delinquents.
Washington, D.C.: U.S. Children's Bureau, Dept. of Health, Education and Welfare.

Craig, M.M., and Glick, S.J., 1963
Ten year's experience with the Glueck social prediction table.
Crime & Delinq., **9,** 249–61.

Glueck, E.T., 1963
Towards further improving the identification of delinquents.
J. Crim. Law, Criminol. & Pol. Sci., **54,** 178–80.

Prigmore, C.S., 1963
Rate reliability on the Glueck scale for the prediction of juvenile delinquency.
J. Crim. Law, Criminol. & Pol. Sci., **54,** 30–41.

Voss, H.L., 1963
The predictive efficiency of the Glueck social prediction table.
J. Crim. Law, Criminol. & Pol. Sci., **54,** 421–30.

Glueck, S. and Glueck, E., 1964
Potential juvenile delinquents can be identified: what next?
Brit. J. Criminol., **4,** 215–25.

Briggs, P.F., and Wirt, R.D., 1965
Prediction, in H.C. Quay (ed.), *Juvenile delinquency research and theory.*
Princeton: D. Van Nostrand Co., 170–208.

KAHN, A.J., 1965
The case of the premature claims.
Crime & Delinq., **11,** 217–28.

MOLOF, M.J., 1965
Prediction of future assaultive behavior among youthful offenders.
Sacramento: California Department of the Youth Authority, Research report No. 41.

POWER, M.J., 1965
An attempt to identify at first appearance before the courts those at risk of becoming persistent juvenile offenders.
Proceedings of the Royal Society of Medicine, **58,** 12–13.

TOBY, J., 1965
An evaluation of early identification and intensive treatment programs for predelinquents.
Social Problems, **13,** 160–75.

GLUECK, E.T., 1966
A more discriminative instrument for the identification of potential delinquents at school entrance.
J. Crim. Law, Criminol. & Pol. Sci., **57,** 27–30.

GLUECK, E.T., 1966
Identification of potential delinquents at 2–3 years of age.
Excerpta criminologica, **6,** 309–14.

ROBINS, L.N., 1966
Deviant children grown up.
Baltimore: Williams & Wilkins Co., 135–58.

WHEELER, S., AND COTTRELL, L.S.JR., 1966
Juvenile delinquency, its prevention and control.
New York: Russell Sage Foundation, 22–7.

GOTTFREDSON, D.M., 1967
Assessment and prediction methods in crime and delinquency, in *Task force report: juvenile delinquency.*
Washington, D.C.: President's Commission on Law Enforcement and Administration of Justice, 171–87.

HIRSCHI, T., AND SELVIN, H.C., 1967
Delinquency research. An appraisal of analytical methods.
New York: Free Press, 235–56.

POWER, M.J., SCHOENBERG, E., AND ALDERSON, M.R., 1967
Identifying persistent juvenile offenders. The use of predictive methods in social work.
London: National Institute for social work training. Mimeo.

ROSE, G., 1967
Early identification of delinquents.
Brit. J. Criminol., **7,** 6–35.

WARD, P.G., 1967
Validating prediction scales. The case of the false technique.
Brit. J. Criminol., **7,** 36–44.

WELLFORD, C.F., 1967
The prediction of delinquency, in W.E. Amos and C.F. Wellford (eds.), *Delinquency prevention.*
New Jersey: Prentice-Hall, 22–36.

WILKINS, L.T., 1967
Prediction methods: a survey of the field from the standpoint of facts and figures, in *The effectiveness of punishment and other measures of treatment.*
Strasbourg: Council of Europe, 62–9.

POLLOCK, C.B., 1968
Early case findings as a means of prevention of child abuse, in R.E. Helfer and C.H. Kempe (eds.), *The battered child.*
Chicago: Univ. Chicago Press, 149–71.

STANFIELD, R.E., AND MAHER, B., 1968
Clinical and actuarial predictions of juvenile delinquency, in S. Wheeler (ed.), *Controlling delinquents.*
New York: John Wiley & Sons, 245–70.

UNKOVIC, C.M., AND DUCSAY, W.J., 1969
An application of configurational analysis to the recidivism of juvenile delinquent behavior.
J. Crim. Law, Criminol. & Pol. Sci., **60,** 340–44.

LABRIE, R.A., 1970
Verification of the Glueck prediction table by mathematical statistics following a computerized procedure of discriminant function analysis.
J. Crim. Law, Criminol. & Pol. Sci., **61,** 229–34.

SIMON, F.H., 1971
Prediction methods in criminology. Including a

Prediction study of young men on probation.
London: Home Office Research Studies, **7**. 3–15, 30–57, 137–58.

VENEZIA, P.S., 1971
Delinquency prediction: a critique and a suggestion.
J. Res. Crime & Delinq., **8**, 108–17.

BLUMENTHAL, M.D., KAHN, R.L., ANDREWS, F.M., AND HEAD, K.B., 1972
Justifying violence: attitudes of American men.
Ann Arbor, Mich.: Institute for Social Research, Univ. of Michigan, 211–41.

DOOTJES, I., 1972
Predicting juvenile delinquency.
Aust. & N.Z.J. Criminol., **5**, 157–71.

WEST, D.J., AND FARRINGTON, D.P., 1973
Who becomes delinquent?
London: Heinemann, 128–50, 186–201.

GLUECK, S., AND GLUECK, E., 1974
Of delinquency and crime: a panorama of years of search and research.
Springfield, Ill.: C.C. Thomas, 177–224.

16 Crime commissions: a comparison of their methods and recommendations

POUND, R., AND FRANKFURTER, F. (EDS.), 1922
Criminal justice in Cleveland.
Ohio: Cleveland Foundation.

FRANKFURTER, F., 1927
Progress report of Harvard survey of crime and law in Boston. Mimeo.

NEW YORK, STATE OF, 1927–1932
Report of the Crime Commission. 5 vols.
Albany, New York.

ILLINOIS ASSOCIATION FOR CRIMINAL JUSTICE, 1929
The Illinois crime survey.
Chicago: Blakely Printing Co.

BETTMAN, A., 1931
Criminal justice surveys analysis, in *National Commission on Law Observance and Enforcement.*
Washington, D.C. 39–221.

UNITED STATES OF AMERICA, 1931
Report of the National Commission on Law Observance and Enforcement.
(Wickersham Commission).
Washington, D.C. Vols. 1–6.

MICHAEL, J., AND ADLER, M.J., 1933
Crime, law and social science.
New York: Harcourt, Brace & Co.

RUML, B., LLEWELLYN, K.N., AND MCKEON, R., 1934
Crime, law and social science: a symposium.
Columbia Law Rev., **34**, 273–309.

AMERICAN BAR FOUNDATION, 1955
The administration of criminal justice in the United States.
Chicago, 1–17.

SHERRY, A.H., 1955
The administration of criminal justice in the United States: plan for a survey to be conducted under the auspices of the American Bar Foundation.
Chicago: Amer. Bar Foundation, 1–24, 73–100, 107–83.

COHEN, A., LINDESMITH, A., AND SCHUESSLER, K. F. (EDS.), 1956
The Sutherland papers.
Bloomington: Indiana Univ. Press, 229–46.

REMINGTON, F.J., 1960
Criminal justice research.
J. Crim. Law, Criminol. & Pol. Sci., **51**, 7–18.

RADZINOWICZ, L., 1961
In search of criminology.
London: Heinemann, 114–66.

ROSE, A.G., 1961
The struggle for penal reform.
London: Stevens, 263–85.

CHRISTIE, N., 1965
Research trends in the Scandinavian countries.
Internat. Rev. Crim. Policy, **23**, 19–23.

RADZINOWICZ, L., 1965
The need for criminology and a proposal for an Institute of Criminology.
London: Heinemann.

GLUECK, S., 1966
Interdisciplinary institutes and academies of criminal justice, in R. Slovenko (ed.), *Crime, law and corrections.*
Springfield, Ill.: C.C. Thomas, 552–64.

UNITED STATES OF AMERICA, 1966
Report of the Presidents' Commission on Crime in the District of Columbia.
Washington, D.C.

GIBBONS, D.C., 1967
A review of 'The challenge of crime in a free society. By the President's Commission on Law Enforcement and Administration of Justice'.
Can. J. of Corrections, **9**, 347–54.

McINTYRE, D.M. JR. (ED.), 1967
Law enforcement in the metropolis: a working paper on the criminal law system in Detroit.
Chicago: American Bar Foundation.

SKOLER, D.L., 1967
Federal assistance in developing the technology of criminal justice, in S.A. Yefsky (ed.), *Law enforcement, science and technology.*
Washington, D.C.: Thompson Book Co., 47–56.

UNITED STATES OF AMERICA, 1967
The challenge of crime in a free society.
Report of the President's Commission on Law Enforcement and Administration of Justice, Washington, D.C., 273–91; and supporting document: *Implementation,* by the Organization for Social and Technical Innovation, 111–40.

UNITED STATES OF AMERICA, 1967
President's task force on crime.
Report of a Committee to the President nder the Chairmanship of James Q. Wilson, Dec. 15, 1967.
Washington, D.C.

UNIVERSITY OF TORONTO, CRIMINOLOGICAL CENTER, 1967
Proceedings.
First Conference of Directors of North American Criminological Institutes. Mimeo.

BLUMSTEIN, A., 1968
A national program of research, development, test and evaluation on law enforcement and criminal justice.
Prepared for Law Enforcement Assistance Administration, U.S. Dept. of Justice, by the Institute for Defence Analyses, Arlington, Virginia.

NEW JERSEY, STATE OF, 1968
A survey of crime control and prevention in New Jersey.
Commission to study the Cause and Prevention of Crime in New Jersey.
Trenton, N.J.

NEW YORK, STATE OF, 1968
Preliminary report of the Governor's Special Committee on Criminal Offenders.
New York.

SILVER, I., 1968
The President's Crime Commission revisited.
New York Univ. Law Rev., **43,** 916–66.

UNITED STATES OF AMERICA, 1968
Report of the National Advisory Commission on Civil Disorders.
(Kerner Report).
Washington, D.C. and New York: Bantam Books.

WALKER, D., 1968
Rights in conflict.
A report submitted to the National Commission on the Causes and Prevention of Violence.
New York: Bantam Books.

LIPSKY, M., AND OLSON, D.J., 1969
Riot commission politics.
Trans-action, **6** (9), 9–21.

MASSACHUSETTS, COMMONWEALTH OF, 1969
A summary of the comprehensive criminal justice plan for crime prevention and control
Committee on Law Enforcement and Administration of Criminal Justice. Boston.

MUELLER, G.O.W., 1969
Crime, Law and the scholars.
London: Heinemann, 95–108, 165–75.

UNITED STATES OF AMERICA, 1969
Report of the National Commission on the Causes and Prevention of Violence (plus all supporting documents).
Washington, D.C.

CLARK, K.B., AND HOPKINS, J., 1970
A relevant war against poverty: a study of community action programs and observable social change.
New York: Harper & Row Publishers, 59–204.

UNITED STATES OF AMERICA, 1970
The role of the federal agencies in the crime and delinquency field.
Washington, D.C.: NIMH, Dept. Health, Education and Welfare.

CALIFORNIA, STATE OF, 1971
California correctional system study: final report.
3 vols.: *The System; Institutions; Field Services.*

Sacramento: Board of Corrections, Human Relations Agency.

PLATT, A. (ED.), 1971
The politics of riot commissions 1917–1970: a collection of official reports and critical essays.
New York: Macmillan.

DICKINSON LAW REVIEW, 1972
Pennsylvania crime commission . . . heroes or heavies? **77,** 47–72.

ERICKSON, W.H., 1972
The standards of criminal justice in a nutshell.
Louisiana Law Rev., **32,** 369–407.

LAWYERS' COMMITTEE FOR CIVIL RIGHTS UNDER LAW, 1972
Law and disorder III, State and federal performance under Title 1 *of the Omnibus Crime Control and Safe Streets Act* 1968.
Washington, D.C.: Lawyers' Committee for Civil Rights under Law.

UNITED STATES OF AMERICA, 1972
An inventory of surveys of the public on crime, justice and related topics.
L.E.A.A., National Institute of Law Enforcement and Criminal Justice, U.S. Department of Justice, Washington, D.C.

BLAWIE, M.J., AND BLAWIE, J.L., 1973
The other cease fires: wind down of the domestic wars; cause for concern about the relationship between crime control and local government structures.
J. Urban Law., **50,** 545–629.

CAPLAN, G., 1973
Reflections on the nationalisation of crime, 1964–1968.
Law & Social Order, 1973, 583–635.

CAPLAN, G.M., 1973
Concern and choice: the selection of program priorities in criminal justice system.
J. of Criminal Justice, **1,** 289–98.

GALLIHER, J.F., AND MCCARTNEY, J.L., 1973
The influence of funding agencies on juvenile delinquency research.
Social Problems, **21,** 77–90.

JACKSON, B., 1973
The police and the rest of us, a review essay.
Crim. Law Bull., **9,** 416–33.

RIST, R.C., 1973
Policy, politics, and social research: a study in the relationship of federal commissions and social science.
Social Problems, **21,** 113–28.

UNITED STATES OF AMERICA, 1973
Reports to the National Advisory Commission on Criminal Justice Standards and Goals: *A National Strategy to Reduce Crime; Criminal Justice System; Police, Courts, Corrections; Community Crime Prevention; Proceedings of the National Conference on Criminal Justice.*, Washington. D.C.

AMERICAN BAR ASSOCIATION, 1974
Standards relating to the administration of criminal justice.
Project on minimum standards for Criminal Justice.
New York: A.B.A.

AMERICAN CRIMINAL LAW REVIEW, 1974 AND 1975
Special issue, a symposium: The American Bar Association Standards relating to the administration of criminal justice. **12,** Part I, 251–377, Part II, 415–503.

FARRAR, J.H., 1974
Law reform and the Law Commission.
London: Sweet & Maxwell.

HOOD, R.G., 1974
Criminology and penal change: a case study of the nature and impact of some recent advice to governments, in R.G. Hood (ed.), *Crime, criminology and public policy: essays in honour of Sir Leon Radzinowicz.*
London: Heinemann, 375–417.

PENNSYLVANIA, COMMONWEALTH OF, 1974
Report on police corruption and the quality of law enforcement in Pennsylvania.
Pennsylvania Crime Commission.

17 Some international comparative references

GAROFALO, R., 1914
Outline of principles suggested as a basis for an international penal code, in *Criminology*.
Boston: Little, Brown & Co., 404–16.

RADZINOWICZ, L., 1948
International collaboration in criminal science, in L. Radzinowicz and J.W.C. Turner (eds.), *The modern approach to criminal law*.
London: Macmillan, 467–97.

TEETERS, N.G., 1949
Deliberations of the International Penal and Penitentiary Congresses.
Philadelphia: Temple Univ. Bookstore.

UNITED NATIONS, 1958
Standard minimum rules for the treatment of prisoners and related recommendations.
New York: Dept of Economic and Social Affairs.

LOPEZ-REY, M., 1960
United Nations activities in the prevention of crime and the treatment of offenders.
Amer. J. Corrections, **22,** 4–6, 18–20.

SCHAFER, S., 1960
Restitution to victims of crime.
Chicago: Quadrangle Books, 15–114.

UNITED NATIONS, 1960
New forms of juvenile delinquency: their origin, prevention and treatment, by W. Middendorff.
Second U.N. Congress on the prevention of crime and the treatment of offenders.
New York: U.N. Document A/CONF./17/6.

GINSBURGS, G., AND MASON, G., 1961
Soviet criminal law reform, in G.O.W. Mueller (ed.), *Essays in criminal science*.
London: Sweet & Maxwell, 409–44.

HAYNER, N.S., 1962
Correctional systems and national values.
Brit. J. Criminol., **3,** 163–75.

SHARGORODSKII, M.D., 1962
The causes and prevention of crime.
Soviet Sociology, **3** (1), 23–39.

UNITED NATIONS, 1963
The evaluation of methods in the prevention of juvenile delinquency—European seminar.
Internat. Rev. Crim. Policy, **21,** 9–6.

EATON, J.W., 1964
Prisons in Israel: a study of policy innovations.
Univ. Pittsburgh Press.

ELTON-MAYO, Mrs P., 1964
Probation and after-care in certain European countries.
Report presented to the European Committee on Crime Problems.
Strasbourg: Council of Europe.

LABOUR PARTY OF THE UNITED KINGDOM, 1964
Crime—a challenge to us all.
Report of the Labour Party's Study Group.

LIN, F.S., 1964
Communist China's emerging fundamentals of criminal law.
Amer. J. Comparative Law, **13,** 80–93.

LOPEZ-REY, M., 1964
Analytical penology, in M. Lopez-Rey and C. Germain (eds.), *Studies in penology: in memory of Sir Lionel Fox.*
The Hague: Martinus Nijhoff, 138–83.

SELLIN, T., 1964
Lionel Fox and the IPPC, in M. Lopez-Rey and C. Germain (eds.), *Studies in Penology, in memory of Sir Lionel Fox.*
The Hague: Martinus Nijhoff, 194–207.

CHRISTIE, N., 1965
Research trends in the Scandinavian countries.
Internat. Rev. Crim. Policy, **23,** 19–23.

CLIFFORD, W., 1965
Problems in criminological research in Africa south of the Sahara.
Internat. Rev. Crim. Policy, **23,** 11–18.

KARPETS, I.I., 1965
Quelques problèmes de méthodologie en droit pénal et dans les recherches criminologiques.
Annuaires de L'URSS, 1965, 191–200.

NAGEL, W.H., 1965
International collaboration in the field of criminology, in *Le droit pénal international: recueil d'études en hommage a J.M. van Bemmelen.*
Leiden: E.J. Brill, 193–222.

PATRICK, C.H., 1965
The status of capital punishment: a world perspective.
J. Crim. Law, Criminol. & Pol. Sci., **56,** 397–411.

SWEDEN, 1965
The penal code of Sweden (trans. by Thorsten Sellin).
Stockholm: Ministry of Justice.

UNITED NATIONS, 1965
Capital punishment.
New York, ST/SOA/SD/9.

UNITED NATIONS, 1965
The young adult offender. A review of current practices and programmes in prevention and treatment.
New York: Department of Economic and Social Affairs.

BERMAN, H.J., 1966
Introduction and analysis, in H.J. Berman and J.W. Spindler (translators), *Soviet criminal law and procedure.*
Russian Research Center Studies, **50,** Cambridge, Mass.: Harvard Univ. Press, 1–139.

CRIMINAL LAW QUARTERLY, 1966
The 1965 white paper on crime by the Government of Japan. **9,** 9–15.

KARPETS, I.I., 1966
The nature and causes of crime in the USSR.
Soviet Law and Government, **5** (1), 52–60.

LOVELAND, F., 1966
International concern with crime and corrections.
Nebraska Law Rev., **45,** 717–27.

SHOHAM, S., 1966
Crime and social deviation.
Chicago: Henry Regnery Co., 128–65.

TAO, L.S., 1966
The criminal law of Communist China.
Cornell Law Rev., **52,** 43–68.

LENG, S.C., 1967
Justice in communist China: a survey of the judicial system of the Chinese People's Republic.
New York: Oceana Publications.

UNITED NATIONS, 1967
Capital punishment developments, 1961–65.
New York: Department of Economic and Social Affairs.

WOLFGANG, M.E., 1967
International criminal statistics: a proposal.
J. Crim. Law, Criminol. & Pol. Sci., **58,** 65–9.

AMERICAN BAR ASSOCIATION, 1968
The criminal process and the rule of law, in *A contrast between the legal systems in the United States and the Soviet Union.*
Baltimore, Md.: Port City Press, 105–228.

BAVCON, E., VODOPIVEC, K. AND UDERMAN, B., 1968
Individualizacija kazni i praksi nasih sodisc.
Ljubljana. Mimeo.
English summary 'Individualization of penal sanctions in the practice of our courts', 165–90.

COHEN, J.A., 1968
The criminal process in the People's Republic of China, 1949–1963.
Cambridge, Mass.: Harvard Univ. Press.

NEW ZEALAND, 1968
Crime in New Zealand.
Department of Justice, Wellington, New Zealand: R.E. Owen, Government Printer, 9–19, 397–407.

PETERS, A.A.G., 1968
Comparative survey of juvenile delinquency in Asia and the Far East.
United Nations, Asian and Far East Institute, Tokyo, Japan.

ALI, B.E.D., 1969
Treatment of prisoners in nine nations.
A pilot study on standard minimum rules.
Criminologica, **7** (3), 2–18.

BOLDYREV, Y., 1969
The study and prevention of juvenile delinquency.
Soviet Rev., (May), 20–7.

CANADA, 1969
Toward unity: criminal justice and corrections.
Report of the Committee on Corrections.
Research, planning and advisory committees.
Ottawa: Queen's Printer. 423–32.

GHOSH, S.K., 1969
The law of preventive detention in India.
Bombay: N.M. Tripathi Private Ltd.

HAZARD, J.N., 1969
Communists and their law. A search for the common core of the legal systems of the Marxian socialist states.
Chicago: Univ. Chicago Press 417–79.

HOLLANDER, P., 1969
A converging social problem: juvenile delinquency in the Soviet Union and the United States.
Brit. J. Criminol., **9**, 148–66.

LUBMAN, S., 1969
Form and function in the Chinese criminal process.
Columbia Law Rev., **69**, 535–75.

MILNER, A. (ED.), 1969
African penal systems.
London: Routledge & Kegan Paul.

PARKER, G., 1969
Reform of the criminal justice system—a Canadian view 'Law and order'.
Boston Univ. Law Rev., **49**, 552–83.

PRICE, E.T., 1969
The correction of adult offenders with special reference to South Australia.
Australian J. Soc. Issues, **4**, 57–77.

UNITED KINGDOM, 1969
People in prison (England and Wales).
London: Cmnd. 4214.

BURTON-BRADLEY, B.G., 1970
Psychiatry and the law in the developing country with special reference to the Territory of Papua and New Guinea.
Technical paper No. 164.
New Caledonia: South Pacific Commission. Mimeo.

COUNCIL OF EUROPE, 1970
Current trends in criminological research, in *Collected studies in criminological research*, **6.**
Strasbourg: Council of Europe, 149–371.

GIBBONS, D.C., 1970
Delinquent behavior.
Englewood Cliffs, N.J.: Prentice-Hall, 204–20.

GÖPPINGER, H., AND WITTER, H. (EDS.), 1970
Vorträge bei der XV Tagung der Gesellschaft fur die gesamte Kriminologie vom 2, bis 5, October 1969 in Saarbrücken, (Reports on Criminological Research in several countries).
Kriminologische Gegenwartsfragen, **9**, 1–91.
Stuttgart: Ferdinand Enke Verlag.

JAPAN, 1970
The trends of juvenile delinquency and procedures for handling delinquents in Japan.
Ministry of Justice.

JAPAN, 1970
Statistical data of criminality in Japan.
Ministry of Justice.

KOSHI, G.M., 1970
The Japanese legal advisor. Crimes and punishments.
Tokyo, Japan: Charles E. Tuttle Co., 241–382.

SEYMOUR, J.A., 1970
The penal system: a developing pattern.
Aust. & N.Z.J. Criminol., **3**, 166–84.

TANNER, R.E.S., 1970
Homicide in Uganda 1964.
Crime in East Africa.
Uppsala: Scandinavian Institute of African Studies.

TANNER, R.E.S., 1970
Three studies in East African criminology.
Crime in East Africa.
Uppsala: Scandinavian Institute of African Studies.

TANNER, R.E.S., 1970
The witch murders in Sukumaland—a sociological commentary.
Crime in East Africa, **4.**
Uppsala: Scandinavian Institute of African Studies.

UNITED NATIONS, 1970
Working papers prepared by the Secretariat for the fourth United Nations congress on the prevention of crime and the treatment of offenders.
(Kyoto, Japan, 17–26 August 1970), on *Standard Minimum Rules for the Treatment of Prisoners; public participation in crime prevention; organisation of research; social defence policy in relation to development planning.*
New York: U.N. Documents A/Conf. 43/1; A/Conf. 43/2; A/Conf. 43/3; A/Conf. 43/4.

UNITED STATES OF AMERICA, 1970
Administration of justice in a changing society.
A report on developments in the United States—1965 to 1970.
Prepared for the fourth United Nations Congress on the prevention of crime and treatment of offenders. Kyoto, Japan. Mimeo.

YANAGIMOTO, M., 1970
Some features of the Japanese prison system.
Brit. J. Criminol., **10,** 209–24.

ANNALES INTERNATIONALES DE CRIMINOLOGIE, 1971
Reports from the XXth International Course in Criminology on non-institutional treatment of offenders. **10,** 7–34.

ANTTILA, I., 1971
Conservative and radical criminal policy in the Nordic countries, in *Scandinavian studies in criminology*, **3.**
Oslo: Universitetsforlaget, 9–21.

BOEHRINGER, G.H., 1971
Aspects of penal policy in Africa, with special reference to Tanzania.
J. African Law, **15,** 182–212.

BRNČIĆ, J., AND POPOVIC, V., 1971
Implementation of the standard minimum rules for the treatment of prisoners in Yugoslavia.
Internat. Rev. Crim. Policy, **29,** 32–9.

CANADA, 1971
The cost of crime and crime control.
Analysis of the work of the Second International Symposium in Comparative Criminology.
Department of Solicitor General.
Ottawa: Information Canada.

CANADIAN JOURNAL OF CORRECTIONS, 1971
The prison report of the Canadian committee of corrections. **13,** 52–9.

CHRISTIE, N., 1971
Scandinavian criminology facing the 1970's, in *Scandinavian studies in criminology* **3.**
Oslo: Universitetsforlaget, 121–49.

COUNT-VAN MANEN, G., 1971
A deviant case of deviance: Singapore.
Law & Society Rev., **5,** 389–406.

KARPETS, I.I., 1971
The concept of recidivism in the Soviet Criminal Law, in *Les Problèmes du recidivisme.*
XVIII International Course in Criminology, Institute of Criminology, Belgrade, 239–50.

KARPETS, I.I., 1971
Criminological research in recidivism in USSR its in the prevention of recidivist criminality, in *Les Problèmes du recidivisme.*
XVIII International Course in Criminology, Institute of Criminology, Belgrade, 251–62.

KUDRIAVTSEV, V.N., 1971
Relationship between theory and practice in organizing action to combat criminality in the Union of Soviet Socialist Republics.
Internat. Rev. Crim. Policy, **29,** 3–10.

LEKSCHAS, J., 1971
On some aspects of criminality in socialist society.
Law and Legislation in the German Democratic Republic, **1,** 16–24.

MATHEWS, A.S., 1971
Law, order and liberty in South Africa.
Berkeley: Univ. California Press.

NATIONAL INSTITUTE OF MENTAL HEALTH, 1971
Crime and delinquency research in selected European countries.
Center for Studies of Crime and Delinquency, Rockville, Maryland.

PLAWSKI, S., 1971
Le récidivisme et les mesures de sa repression dans le droit pénal polonais, in *Les Problèmes du recidivisme.*
XVIII International Course in Criminology, Institute of Criminology, Belgrade, 278–90.

RADZINOWICZ, L., 1971
Some current problems and future prospects of international collaboration in penal matters, in *Saertryk af Festskrift til Folketingets Ombudsman Professor, Dr. Jur. Stephan Hurwitz.*
Kobenhavn: Juristforbundets Forlag.

ROBERT, P., 1971
Operational research in the system of criminal justice, in *Collected studies in criminological research*, **8**, 51–135.
Strasbourg: Council of Europe.

STEYN, J.H., 1971
Public participation in the prevention of crime.
South African Law J., **88**, 210–26.

SWEDEN, 1971
Kriminalvarden 1970 (The correctional system 1970).
National Correctional Administration, Stockholm.

UNITED NATIONS, ASIAN AND FAR EAST INSTITUTE, 1971
Report for 1970 *and resource material series no.* 1.
Tokyo, Japan, 39–157.

UNITED STATES OF AMERICA, 1971
Program and project plan for fiscal year 1971.
L.E.A.A., National Institute of Law Enforcement and Criminal Justice, U.S. Dept. of Justice, Washington, D.C.

VERMES, M., 1971
Le récidivisme et les mesures de la repression dans le droit pénal Hongrois, in *Les Problèmes du recidivisme.*
XVIII International Course in Criminology, Institute of Criminology, Belgrade, 263–77.

VIGH, J., 1971
Grouping of recidivists and the indefinite term of imprisonment.
Annales Univ. Scient. Budapest, **13**, 159–79.

VODOPIVEC, K., 1971
Some results of research in recidivism, conducted at the Institute of Criminology, Faculty of Law, University of Ljubljana, in *Les Problèmes du recidivisme.*
XVIII International Course in Criminology, Institute of Criminology, Belgrade, 294–316.

ALPER, B.S., AND BOREN, J.F., 1972
Crime: international agenda.
Lexington, Mass.: D.C. Heath.

BILES, D., 1972
Australian prisons and their use, in D. Chappell and P. Wilson (eds.), *The Australian criminal justice system,*
Sydney: Butterworths, 623–55.

CHAPPELL, D., AND WILSON, P. R., 1972
The Australian police and public re-visited, in D. Chappell and P. Wilson (eds.), *The Australian criminal justice system.*
Sydney: Butterworths, 317–23.

CHAPPELL, D., AND WILSON, P.R., 1972
Police in Australia, in D. Chappell and P. Wilson (eds.), *The Australian criminal justice system.*
Sydney: Butterworths, 245–60.

CLIFFORD, W., 1972
An introduction to African criminology.
East Africa. Oxford Univ. Press.

CONNOR, W.D., 1972
Deviance in Soviet society. Crime, delinquency, and alcoholism.
New York: Columbia Univ. Press.

CONNOR, W.D., 1972
The Soviet criminal correctional system: change and stability.
Law & Society Rev., **6**, 367–91.

COUNCIL OF EUROPE, 1972
International exchange of information on current criminological research projects in member states.
(Published annually).
Strasbourg: Council of Europe.

FRANCIS, R.D., 1972
Migration and crime, in D. Chappell and P. Wilson (eds.), *The Australian criminal justice system.*
Sydney: Butterworths, 201–22.

JOHNSTON, S.W., 1972
Criminal homicide rates, in D. Chappell and P. Wilson (eds.), *The Australian criminal justice system.*
Sydney: Butterworths, 31–47.

KAISER, G., AND WURTENBERGER, T. (EDS.), 1972
Criminological research trends in Western Germany.
Berlin: Springer-Verlag.

LABUSCHAGNE, J.J., 1972
Crime in South Africa.
Crime, Punishment and Correction, **2,** 6–17.

LETHBRIDGE, H.J., 1972
Penal policy and crime rates: comments on the Hong Kong experience.
Hong Kong Law J., **2,** 54–68.

MARNELL, G., 1972
Comparative correctional systems: United States and Sweden.
Crim. Law Bull., **8,** 748–60.

RADZINOWICZ, L., 1972
The criminal law explosion—can it be controlled?
Columbia J. Law & Social Problems, **9,** 88–130.

SHEA, E., 1972
Parole philosophy in England and America, in D.J. West (ed.), *The future of parole.*
London: Duckworth & Co., 66–95.

TOLLEMACHE, R., 1972
Alternatives to prison in Holland.
Social Work Today, **4** (4), 13–16.

UNITED NATIONS, 1972
Crime prevention and control.
Note by the Secretary-General, Twenty-seventh session, Agenda item 53, A/8844, 19 October 1972.
New York: General Assembly.

WARD, P., AND WOODS, G., 1972
Law and order in Australia.
Sydney: Angus & Robertson.

BUFFARD, S., 1973
Le froid pénitentiaire: l'impossible réforme des prisons.
Paris: Éditions du Seuil.

CANADA, 1973
The criminal in Canadian society: a perspective on corrections. Paper prepared in anticipation of the Federal-Provincial Conference on Corrections, Department of Solicitor General.
Ottawa: Information Canada.

CLIFFORD, W., 1973
Development and crime.
Justice of the Peace, **137,** 244–6, 259–62, 276–8.

CLINARD, M.B., AND ABBOTT, D.J., 1973
Crime in developing countries.
New York: John Wiley & Sons.

CONNOR, W.D., 1973
Criminal homicide, U.S.S.R./U.S.A.: reflections on Soviet data in a comparative framework.
J. Crim. Law & Criminol., **64,** 111–17.

GUREVITCH, M., DANET, B., AND SCHWARTZ, G., 1973
The image of the police in Israel, in S. Shoham (ed.), *Israel studies in criminology*, **2,** 171–96. Jerusalem: Jerusalem Academic Press, and in *Law and Society Rev.*, **5,** 367–88.

JOHNSON, E.H., 1973
Finland's penal colonies: the forbearant model and community-based corrections.
J. Crim. Justice, **1,** 327–38.

JOURNAL OF THE INTERNATIONAL COMMITTEE FOR THE DEFENCE OF HUMAN RIGHTS IN THE U.S.S.R., 1973
Human rights in the U.S.S.R. (No. 2–3), Feb.–March 1973.

LOPEZ-REY, M., 1973
The role of the United Nations Congresses on the prevention of crime and the treatment of offenders.
Fed. Probation, **37** (3), 24–9.

MOSELEY, L.G., 1973
Finnish labour colonies.
Howard J. Penol. & Crime Prev., **13,** 317–30.

DEL OLMO, R., 1973
Sentencing practices in Caracas: Venezuela's penal courts.
Internat. J. Criminol. & Penol., **1**, 47–54.

PEPINSKY, H.E., 1973
The people v. the principle of legality in the people's republic of China.
J. Crim. Justice, **1**, 51–60.

RUO-WANG, B., AND CHELMINSKI, R., 1973
Prisoner of Mao.
New York: Coward, McCann & Geohegan.

SHOHAM, S., BEN-DAVID, S., AND SMILANSKY, J., 1973
Rehabilitation treatment in institutions for Juvenile delinquents in Israel, in S. Shoham jed.), *Israel studies in criminology*, **2**, 230–41.
Jerusalem: Jerusalem Academic Press.

TOLLEMACHE, R., 1973
Crisis agencies and the treatment of offenders in the Netherlands.
Howard J. Penol. & Crime Prev., **13**, 297–317.

TOMIC-MALIC, M., 1973
Probation in France: its operation and results.
Internat. J. Criminol. & Penol., **1**, 279–88.

UNITED NATIONS, 1973
Capital punishment.
Report of the Secretary-General, 54th session, Agenda item 13, E/5242, 23 February 1973.
New York: Economic and Social Council.

UNITED NATIONS, 1973
Report of the Secretary-General of the meeting of the working group of experts on the standard minimum rules for the treatment of prisoners, held at United Nations headquarters, from 25 to 29 September 1972.
Committee on Crime Prevention, E/AC.57/8.
New York: Economic and Social Council.

WILSON, P.R., AND BROWN, J.W., 1973
Crime and the community.
Univ. Queensland Press.

ANTTILA, I., 1974
The foundation of co-operation in European criminological research: Sir Leon Radzinowicz and the Criminological Scientific Council at the Council of Europe, in R.G. Hood (ed.), *Crime, criminology and public policy: essays in honour of Sir Leon Radzinowicz.*
London: Heinemann, 25–32.

BUCHOLZ, E., HARTMANN, R., LEKSCHAS, J., AND STILLER, G., 1794
Socialist Criminology: theoretical and methodical foundations.
Farnborough, Hants.: Saxon House, D.C. Heath & Co.

ESBJÖRNSSON, E., 1974
International criminality in Sweden.
Scandinavian studies in criminology, **5**.
London: Martin Robertson, 11–23.

HAUGE, R., AND WOLF, P., 1974
Criminal violence in three Scandinavian countries.
Scandinavian studies in criminology, **5**.
London: Martin Robertson, 25–33.

JESCHECK, H-H., 1974
Modern criminal policy in the Federal Republic of Germany and the German Democratic Republic, in R.G. Hood (ed.), *Crime, criminology and public policy: essays in honour of Sir Leon Radzinowicz.*
London Heinemann, 509–25.

LOPEZ-REY, M., 1974
United Nations social defence policy and the problem of crime, in R.G. Hood (ed.), *Crime, criminology and public policy: essays in honour of Sir Leon Radzinowicz.*
London: Heinemann, 489–508.

MARNELL, G., 1974
Penal reform: a Swedish viewpoint.
Howard J. Penol. & Crime Prev., **14**, 8–21.

MIDGLEY, J., 1974
Public opinion and the death penalty in South Africa.
Brit. J. Criminol., **14**, 345–58.

NIXON, A.J., 1974
A child's guide to crime: new perspectives on criminology.
Sydney: Angus & Robertson, 50–78.

SOLOMAN, P.H., 1974
Soviet criminology—its demise and rebirth 1928–1963, in R.G. Hood (ed.), *Crime, criminology and public policy: essays in honour of Sir Leon Radzinowicz.*
London: Heinemann, 571–93.

STEYN, J.H., 1974
The punishment scene in South Africa—developments over the past decade and prospects for reform, in R.G. Hood (ed.), *Crime, criminology and public policy: essays in honour of Sir Leon Radzinowicz.*
London: Heinemann, 527–70.

UNITED KINGDOM, 1974
Young adult offenders.
Report of the Advisory Council on the Penal System (Chairman, Sir Kenneth Younger).
London: Home Office.

WALLER, I., AND CHAN, J., 1974
Prison use: a Canadian and international comparison.
Crim. Law Quart., **17**, 47–71.

UNITED KINGDOM, 1975
Summary of research within the Unit and of Research supported by Grant.
London: Home Office Research Unit.
Mimeo.

See also:

Acts and Proceedings of various Regional and International organisations, such as:
Amnesty
Benelux Penitentiary Commission
International Association of Criminal Law
International Commission of Jurists
International Penal and Penitentiary Foundation
International Society of Criminology
International Society of Social Defence
International Union of Child Welfare
Interpol (International Criminal Police Organisation)
Nordic Association of Criminal Lawyers
Scandinavian Research Council of Criminology

18 Bibliographies

AMERICAN LAW INSTITUTE
Annual report.
Bibliographies with reference to codification and revision of criminal law.
Philadelphia; A.L.I.

YALE LAW LIBRARY, N.D.
Abortion—selected recent writings.
A bibliography. Mimeo.

YALE LAW LIBRARY, N.D.
Student protest—selected writings.
A bibliography. Mimeo.

KLEIN, F.J., 1963
Judicial administration and the legal profession: an annotated bibliography.
Published for the American Judicature Society and the Institute of Judicial Administration.
New York: Oceana Publications.

TOMPKINS, D.C., 1963
The offender—a bibliography.
Berkeley, Calif.: Institute of Governmental Studies, Univ. of California.

TOMPKINS, D.C., 1964
Probation since World War II—a bibliography.
Berkeley, Calif.: Institute of Governmental Studies, Univ. of California.

BERG, P.S.D., AND TYLER, R.R., 1965
A bibliography on aggressive and violent behaviour (1930–60).
Sacramento: California Department of Corrections, Research report No. 17.

SEYMOUR, J.A., 1965
Family courts and councils: a select bibliography with special reference to the White Paper 'The child, the family and the young offender'.
(Cmnd. 2742). Bibliographical Series No. 2.
Cambridge: Institute of Criminology.

HAWKINS, K., 1966
Deprivation of liberty as a means of treating juvenile delinquency in Great Britain 1940–1965.
Bibliographical Series No. 1.
Cambridge: Institute of Criminology.

INSTITUTE OF JUDICIAL ADMINISTRATION, 1966
Minimum standards for criminal justice project, selected bibliography.
New York: The Institute of Judicial Administration.

JORDY, S.P., 1966
International bibliography of studies on alcohol,
Vol. 1. References 1901–1950.
New Brunswick, N.J.: Rutgers Centre of Alcohol Studies.

MILLER, M.G., 1966
A bibliography in police and community relations.
The National Center on Police and Community Relations, Michigan State Univ. Mimeo.

NATIONAL CENTER ON POLICE AND COMMUNITY RELATIONS, 1966
A bibliography on police and community relations. compiled by Martin G. Miller.
The National Center on Police and Community Relations, Michigan State Univ. Mimeo.

TOMPKINS, D.C., 1966
Juvenile gangs and street groups—a bibliography.
Berkeley, Calif.: Institute of Governmental Studies, Univ. of California.

CALIFORNIA STATE LIBRARY, 1967
Compensation for victims of crime: a selective bibliography.
Sacramento, Calif.: California State Library, Law Library.

HEWITT, W.H., 1967
A bibliography of police administration, public safety and criminology (to July 1, 1965).
Springfield, Ill.: C.C. Thomas.

Institute of Judicial Administration, 1967
Minimum standards for criminal justice project, selected bibliography.
Supplement I.
New York: The Institute of Judicial Administration.

Rawlin, J.W., and Laughlin, P.L., 1967
Selected references on LSD and related hallucinogens.
Edwardsville, Ill.: Center for the Study of Crime, Delinquency and Correction, Southern Illinois Univ. Mimeo.

Sells, H.F., 1967
Drug dependence. A bibliography.
Fortworth, Texas: Texas Christian Univ. Press.

Smith, S.C., 1967
Selected writings on recidivism: a bibliography.
Yale Law Library.

Tompkins, D.C., 1967
White collar crime—a bibliography.
Berkeley, Calif.: Institute of Government Studies, Univ. of California.

United States of America, 1967
The challenge of crime in a free society.
Report of the President's Commission on Law Enforcement and Administration of Justice, Washington, D.C. 211–31, 302–3.

American Judicature Society, 1968
Report No. 1. *The jury process. A bibliography.*
Chicago.

American Judicature Society, 1968
Report No. 4. *News media and the administration of justice. A bibliography.*
Chicago.

Becker, H.K., and Felkenes, G.T., 1968
Law enforcement: a selected bibliography.
Metuchen, N.J.: Scarecrow Press.

Court, J., and Thomson, L., 1968
Battered child syndrome: a bibliography.
London: NSPCC.

Dahl, R.C., and Bolden, C.E., 1968
The American judge. A bibliography.
Virginia: Coiner Publications.

Geis, G. (ed.), 1968
White-collar criminal: the offender in business and the professions.
New York: Atherton Press, 433–38.

International Police Association, 1968
International bibliography of selected police literature.
M. & W. Publications (Liverpool) Ltd., 19a Ashley Place, London S.W.1.

Kavaler, F., 1968
A commentary and annotated bibliography on the relationship between narcotics addiction and criminality.
Municipal Ref. Library, **62,** 45–76.

Kwan, V.H.Y., and Rajeswaran, P., 1968
Recent additions to a bibliography on cannabis. *J. Forensic Sciences*, **13,** 279–89.

New York, State of, 1968
Annotated bibliography of literature on narcotic addiction.
Narcotic Addiction Control Commission, New York State. Mimeo.

Northwestern University, Transportation Center Library 1968
Police administration: a bibliography.
Evanston, Ill.: Northwestern Univ. Traffic Institute.

United States of America, 1968
Annotated bibliography of literature on narcotic addiction.
New York: Narcotic Addiction Control Commission and Washington, D.C.: U.S. Dept. of Justice, Federal Bureau of Prisons.

University of Chicago, The Law School, 1968
A selected international bibliography on capital punishment.
Centre for studies in Criminal Justice, Univ. Chicago.

West, D.J., 1968
Homosexuality.
London: Duckworth & Co., 274–301.

American Judicature Society, 1969
Report No. 28. *Sentencing patterns and problems: an annotated bibliography.*
Chicago.

CALIFORNIA STATE LIBRARY, 1969
Riots and demonstrations—a selected bibliography.
Sacramento. Mimeo.

MEYER, J.K., 1969
Bibliography on the urban crisis.
Chevy Chase, Md.: National Institute of Mental Health.

NATIONAL COUNCIL ON CRIME AND DELINQUENCY, 1969
Parole in foreign countries. Bibliography. New York.

SOLOMAN, P.H. JR., 1969
Soviet criminology: a selective bibliography.
Bibliographical Series No. 4.
Cambridge: Institute of Criminology.

UNITED NATIONS, 1969
List of documents and publications of the United Nations and the specialised agencies on the prevention of crime and the treatment of offenders.
List No. 6 (69–46427). New York.

WEISSMAN, H.H. (ED.), 1969
Justice and the law in the mobilization for youth experience.
New York: Association Press, 205–13.

YALE LAW LIBRARY, 1969
Selected writings on artificial insemination. Bibliography. Mimeo.

YALE LAW LIBRARY, 1969
Bail—selected writings. A bibliography. Mimeo.

YALE LAW LIBRARY, 1969
Criminal law and criminal procedure (1959–1969) *—selected writings. A bibliography.* Mimeo.

YALE LAW LIBRARY, 1969
Drugs and the law—selected writings. A bibliography. Mimeo.

ABORTION LAW REFORM ASSOCIATION, 1970
Reading list. Mimeo. Wheathamsptead, Herts.

CARTER, A., HOGGETT, D., AND ROBERTS, A., 1970
Non-violent action: a selected bibliography.
London: Housmans.

CHAMBLISS, W.J., AND SEIDMAN, R.B., 1970
Sociology of the law :a research bibliography.
Berkeley, Calif.: Glendessary Press.

DIAS, R.W.M., 1970
A bibliography of jurisprudence. (2nd ed.).
London: Butterworths.

DOLLEN, C., 1970
Abortion in context: a select bibliography.
Metuchen, N.J.: Scarecrow Press.

FERRACUTI, F., AND GIANNINI, M.C., 1970
Manpower and training in the field of social defence. A commentary and bibliography.
Rome: United Nations Social Defence Research Institute.

GARSSE, Y., VAN, 1970
Genocide, crimes against humanity and war crimes. A bibliography.
Sint Niklaas Waas, Belgium: Studiecentrum voor Kriminologie en Gerechtelijke Gneeskunde, **1.**

HEWITT, W.H., AND NEWMAN, C.L., 1970
Police–community relations. An anthology and bibliography.
Mineola, New York: Foundation Press.

HOMOSEXUAL INFORMATION CENTER, 1970
A selected bibliography on homosexuality.
(4th ed.).
Holywood, Calif.

LEWIS, J., 1970
Selected titles in criminology and corrections.
Carbondale Ill.: Center for the Study of Crime, Delinquency and Corrections.
Mimeo.

LINDBY, K., 1970
Some economics of crime and crime control, A bibliography.
Montreal: International Centre for Comparative Criminology.

SINGER, R.G., 1970
Prisoner's legal rights: a bibliography.
Cincinnati, Ohio: College of Law, Univ. of Cincinnati.

TOMPKINS, D.C., 1970
Poverty in the United States during the sixties. A bilbiography.
Berkeley, Calif.: Institute of Governmental Studies, Univ. of California.

TOMPKINS, D.C., 1970
Administration of criminal justice 1949–1956*— a selected bibliography.*
Montclair, N.J.: Patterson Smith.

YALE LAW LIBRARY, 1970
The contempt process—selected writings. Bibliography. Mimeo.

YALE LAW LIBRARY, 1970
Judges—appointment and removal—selected writings. A bilbiography. Mimeo.

YALE LAW LIBRARY, 1970
The right to privacy—selected writings of the last decade (1958–1968). *A bibliography*. Mimeo.

CALIFORNIA, STATE OF (1971?)
A bibliography of Community Treatment Project publications.
Sacramento: Department of the Youth Authority. Mimeo.

GRAD, F.P., GOLDBERG, A.L., AND SHAPIRO, B.A., 1971
Alcoholism and the law.
Dobbs Ferry, N.Y.: Oceana Publications, 159–69.

HAWKINS, K., 1971
Parole. A select bibliography with especial reference to American experience.
Bibliographical Series No. 3 (2nd ed.).
Cambridge: Institute of Criminology.

HOWARD, D.L., 1971
The education of offenders. A bibliography.
Institute of Criminology Library, University of Cambridge.

MINISTERODI GRAZIA E GIUSTIZIA, 1971
La droga: aspetti sociologici e criminologici. A bibliography 1950–1970.
Rome: Tipografia delle Mantellate.

SPENCER, M.J., 1971
Shoplifting: a bibliography.
Centre of Criminology, Univ. of Toronto. Mimeo.

TOMPKINS, D.C., 1971
Sentencing the offender. A bibliography.
Berkeley, Calif.: Institute of Governmental Studies, Univ. of California.

UNITED NATIONS, 1971
Bibliography on capital punishment.
Doc/UNSDRI/1971/4.
Rome: Social Defence Research Institute. Mimeo.

YALE LAW LIBRARY, 1971
Homosexuals and the law—selected writings.
A bibliography. Mimeo.

YALE LAW LIBRARY, 1971
War crimes. A bibliography. No.7, Vol. 14, March 1971, U.S.: Yale University.

AMERICAN CRIMINAL LAW REVIEW, 1972
Bibliography of the Grand Jury. **10,** 867–78.

AMERICAN CRIMINAL LAW REVIEW, 1972
A bibliography of law and psychiatry. **10,** 619–34.

AMERICAN CRIMINAL LAW REVIEW, 1972
Bibliography on sentencing and corrections. **11,** 217–26.

HICKEY, W., 1972
Modern correctional design.
Crime & Delinq. Lit., **4,** 116–36.

KAISER, G., AND WURTENBERGER, T. (EDS.), 1972
Criminological research trends in Western Germany.
Berlin: Springer-Verlag, 133–66.

LYONS, D.B., 1972
Capital punishment: a selected bibliography.
Crim. Law Bull., **8,** 783–802.

NATIONAL CHILDREN'S BUREAU, 1972
Intermediate treatment: a bibliography.
Booklist, **26.** London.

POLICE COLLEGE, 1972
The police of England and Wales. A bibliography.
Bramshill House, Hartley Witney, England.

TOMPKINS, D.C., 1972
The prison and the prisoner, public policy bibliographies: **1.**
Berkeley, Calif.: Institute of Governmental Studies, Univ. of California.

UNITED STATES OF AMERICA, 1972
An inventory of surveys of the public on crime, justice and related topics.
L.E.A.A., National Institute of Law Enforcement and Criminal Justice, U.S. Department of Justice. Washington, D.C.

WEINBERG, M., AND BELL, A.P., 1972
Homosexuality: an annotated bibliography.
New York: Harper & Row.

YALE LAW LIBRARY, 1972
Lie detection. A bibliography.

AMERICAN CRIMINAL LAW REVIEW, 1973
Bibliography on white collar crime. **11,** 1011–13.

CANADA, 1973
Final report of the Commission of Inquiry into the non-medical use of drugs. (Le Dain Commission).
References and selected bibliography on drugs and their effects, 482–558, 765–77, 811–31.

CHLOROS, A.G. (ED.), 1973
A bibliographical guide to the law of the United Kingdom, the Channel Islands and the Isle of Man, (2nd ed.).
London: Institute of Advanced Legal Studies, Univ. of London.

COMPREHENSIVE DISSERTATION INDEX 1861–1972, 1973
Prepared by Xerox University Microfilms, Volumes **17** & **27,** see relevant headings: crime, delinquency, police, prisons, punishment, etc.
Michigan: Xerox Corporation.

COUNCIL OF EUROPE, 1973
The application of modern techniques of resource allocation in the field of crime problems.
Bibliography, 84–107. European Committee on crime problems. Strasbourg.

INSTITUTE OF ADVANCED LEGAL STUDIES, 1973
List of official committees, commission and other bodies concerned with the reform of the law, No. 7.
London: Institute of Advanced Legal Studies, Univ. of London.

TOMPKINS, D.C., 1973
Court organization and administration.
Berkeley, Calif.: Institute of Government Studies, Univ. of California.

TOMPKINS, D.C., AND BUSHER, W.H., 1973
Furlough from prison. Public policy bibliographies, **5.** Berkeley, Calif.: Institute of Governmental Studies, Univ. of California.

UNITED STATES OF AMERICA, 1973
Selected references on the abused and battered child (revised).
Washington, D.C.: National Institute of Mental Health. Department of Health, Education and Welfare Publication No. (HMS) 73–9034.

UNITED STATES OF AMERICA, 1973
Police.
Report of the National Advisory Commission on Criminal Justice Standards and Goals, Washington, D.C. 617–38.

AMERICAN BAR ASSOCIATION, 1974
The economics of crime and corrections—bibliography.
Prepared by the Correctional Economic Center of the A.B.A. Commission on Correctional Facilities and Services, Washington, D.C.

AMERICAN CRIMINAL LAW REVIEW, 1974
Bibliography: juvenile justice system. **12,** 179–89.

JEFFRIES, F., 1974
Private policing: a bibliography.
Centre of criminology, University of Toronto.

UNITED STATES OF AMERICA, 1974
Courts.
Report of the National Advisory Commission on Criminal Justice Standards and Goals. Bibliography: 323–37, Washington, D.C.

WEST, D.J., WILES, P., AND STANWOOD, C., 1974
Research on violence: some suggestions together with a bibliography (Bibliographical Series No. 6).
Cambridge: Institute of Criminology.

WRIGHT, M. (ED.), 1974
Use of criminological literature.
London: Butterworth.

19 Selected Textbooks and Readings

1 Selected textbooks

Elliott, M.A., 1952
Crime in modern society.
New York: Harper & Bros.

Vold, G.B., 1958
Theoretical criminology.
New York: Oxford Univ. Press.

Barnes, H.E. and Teeters, N.K., 1959
New horizons in criminology.
Englewood Cliffs, N.J.: Prentice-Hall.
3rd ed.

Korn, R.R. and McCorkle, Ll.W., 1959
Criminology and penology.
New York: Holt, Rinchart & Winston.

Cavan, R.S., 1962
Criminology.
New York: Thomas Y. Cromwell Co.
3rd ed.

Taft, D.R. and England, R.W., 1964
Criminology. New York: Macmillan.

Mannheim, H., 1965
Comparative criminology.
2 vols., London: Routledge & Kegan Paul.

Radzinowicz, L., 1966
Ideology and crime.
New York: Columbia University Press and London: Heinemann.

Reckless, W.C., 1967
The crime problem.
New York: Appleton-Century-Crofts.
4th ed.

West, D.J., 1967
The young offender.
London: Duckworth (also in a Penguin paperback edition).

Clinard, M.B., 1968
Sociology of deviant behaviour.
New York: Holt, Rinehart & Winston.
3rd ed.

Walker, N., 1968
Crime and punishment in Britain.
Edinburgh: Univ. Press.

Cavan, R.S., 1969
Juvenile delinquency.
Philadelphia: Lippincott Co. 2nd ed.

McClean, J.D. and Wood, J.C., 1969
Criminal justice and the treatment of offenders.
London: Sweet & Maxwell

Bloch, H.A. and Geis, G., 1970
Man, crime and society.
New York: Random House 2nd ed.

Hall Williams, J.E., 1970
The English penal system in transition.
London: Butterworths.

Haskell, M.R. and Yablonsky, L., 1970
Crime and delinquency.
Chicago: Rand, McNally

Hood, R.G. and Sparks, R.F., 1970
Key issues in criminology.
London: Weindenfeld & Nicolson.

Knudten, R.D., 1970
Crime in a complex society: an introduction to criminology.
Homewood, Ill.: Dorsey Press

Morris, N., and Hawkins, G., 1970
The honest politician's guide to crime control.
University Chicago Press.

Quinney, R., 1970
The problem of crime.
New York: Dodd, Mead & Co.

QUINNEY, R., 1970
The social reality of crime.
Boston: Little, Brown & Co.

WILDEMAN, J., 1970
Teaching criminology, a guide to the social reality of crime by Richard Quinney.
Boston: Little, Brown & Co.

BOX, S., 1971
Deviance, reality and society.
New York: Holt, Rinehart and Winston.

GLASER, D., 1971
Social deviance.
Chicago: Markham.

PHILLIPSON, M., 1971
Sociological aspects of crime and delinquency.
London: Routledge & Kegan Paul.

GLASER, D., 1972
Adult crime and social policy.
Englewood Cliffs, N.J.: Prentice-Hall.

BOTTOMLEY, A.K., 1973
Decisions in the penal process.
London: Martin Robertson.

GIBBONS, D.C., 1973
Society, crime and criminal careers.
Englewood Cliffs, N.J.: Prentice-Hall. 2nd ed.

PRINS, H.A., 1973
Criminal behaviour: an introduction to its study and treatment.
London: Pitman.

RECKLESS, W.C., 1973
American criminology: new directions.
New York: Appleton-Century Crofts.

ROCK, P., 1973
Deviant behaviour.
London: Hutchinson.

TAYLOR, I., WALTON, P. AND YOUNG, J., 1973
The new criminology. For a social theory of deviance.
London: Routledge & Kegan Paul.

TAYLOR, L., 1973
Deviance and society.
London: Nelson.

TROJANOWICZ, R.C., 1973
Juvenile delinquency: concepts and control.
Englewood Cliffs, N.J.: Prentice-Hall.

DAVIES, M., 1974
Prisoners of society, attitudes and after-care.
London: Routledge & Kegan Paul.

GLASER, D. (ED.), 1974
Handbook of criminology.
Chicago: Rand McNally.

JOHNSON, E.H., 1974
Crime, correction and society.
Homewood, Ill.: Dorsey Press. 3rd ed.

NETTLER, G., 1974
Explaining crime.
New York: McGraw-Hill.

SUTHERLAND, E.H. AND CRESSEY, D.R., 1974
Principles of criminology.
Philadelphia Lippincott Co. 9th ed.

HALL WILLIAMS, J.E., 1975
Changing prisons.
London: Peter Owen.

MAYS, J.B., 1975
Crime and its treatment.
London: Longman. 2nd ed.

2 Readings

VEDDER, C.B., KOENIGS, S. AND CLARK, R.E. (EDS.), 1953
Criminology, a book of readings.
New York: Dryden Press.

DRESSLER, D. (ED.), 1964
Readings in criminology and penology.
New York: Columbia Univ. Press.

GOLD, H. AND SCARPITTI, F.R. (EDS), 1967
Combating social problems.
New York: Holt, Rinehart & Winston.

WOLFGANG, M.E., (ED.), 1967
Studies in homicide.
New York: Harper and Row.

DINITZ, S. AND RECKLESS, W.C. (EDS.), 1968
Critical issues in the study of crime.
Boston: Little, Brown and Co.

GEIS, G. (ED.), 1968
White-collar criminal.
New York: Atherton Press.

HAZELRIGG, L.E. (ED.), 1968
Prison within society: a reader in penology.
New York: Doubleday.

KNUDTEN, R.D., (ED.), 1968
Criminological controversies.
New York: Appleton-Century-Crofts.

LEFTON, M., SKIPPER, J.K. AND MCCAGHY, C.H., (EDS.), 1968
Approaches to deviance: theories, concepts and research findings.
New York: Appleton-Century-Crofts.

MINNIS, M.S. AND CARTWRIGHT, W.J. (EDS.), 1968
Sociological perspectives: readings in deviant behavior and social problems.
Dubuque, Ill.: Wm. C. Brown Book.

SHORT, J.F. (ED.), 1968
Gang delinquency and delinquent subcultures.
New York: Harper and Row.

STRATTON, J.R. AND TERRY, R.M. (EDS.), 1968
Prevention of delinquency: problems and programs.
New York: Macmillan.

WINSLOW, R.W. (ED.), 1968
Crime in a free society and *Juvenile delinquency in a free society.*
Selections from the President's Commission on Law Enforcement and Administration of Justice, California: Dickenson.

CAVAN, R.S. (ED.), 1969
Readings in juvenile delinquency,
Philadelphia: Lippincott and Co. 2nd ed.

CRESSEY, D.R. AND WARD, D.A. (EDS.), 1969
Delinquency, crime and social process.
New York: Harper and Row

DINITZ, S., DYNES, R.R. AND CLARKE, A.C. (EDS.), 1969
Deviance—studies in the process of stigmatization and societal reaction.
New York: Oxford Univ. Press

KORN, R.R. (ED.), 1969
Juvenile delinquency.
New York: Thomas Y. Cromwell Co.

QUINNEY, R. (ED.), 1969
Crime and justice in society.
Boston: Little, Brown & Co.

RUSHING, W.A. (ED.), 1969
Deviant behavior and social process.
Chicago: Rand McNally.

SYKES, G.M. AND DRABEK, T.E. (EDS.), 1969
Law and the lawless: a reader in criminology.
New York: Random House.

ARNOLD, D.O. (ED.), 1970
The society of subcultures.
Berkeley: The Glendessary Press.

BARSANI, C.A. (EDS.), 1970
Crime and delinquency: a reader.
New York: Macmillan.

CARTER, R.M. AND WILKINS, L.T. (ED.), 1970
Probation and parole: selected readings.
New York: John Wiley & Sons.

COHEN, B.J. (ED.), 1970
Crime in America.
Itasca, Ill.: F.E. Peacock.

DOUGLAS, J.D. (ED.), 1970
Observations of deviance.
New York: Random House.

DOUGLAS, J.D. (ED.), 1970
Deviance and respectability, the social construction of moral meanings.
New York: Basic Books.

GARABEDIAN, P.G. AND GIBBONS, D.C. (EDS.), 1970
Becoming delinquent: young offenders and the correctional system.
Chicago: Aldine.

GUENTHER, A.L. (ED.), 1970
Criminal behavior and social systems: contributions of American sociology.
Chicago: Rand McNally.

HUGHES, H.M. (ED.), 1970
Delinquents and criminals: their social world.
Boston: Allyn and Bacon.

JOHNSTON, N., SAVITZ, L. AND WOLFGANG, M.E., (EDS.), 1970
The sociology of punishment and correction.
New York: John Wiley & Sons 2nd ed.

KNUDTEN, R.D. (ED.), 1970
Crime, criminology, and contemporary society.
Homewood, Ill.: The Dorsey Press.

TEELE, J.E. (ED.), 1970
Juvenile delinquency: a reader.
Itasca, Ill.: F.E. Peacock.

VOSS, H.L. (ED), 1970
Society, delinquency and delinquent behaviour.
Boston: Little Brown & Co.

WOLFGANG, M.E., SAVITZ, L. AND JOHNSTON, N. (EDS.), 1970
The sociology of crime and delinquency.
New York: John Wiley & Sons. 2nd ed.

CRESSEY, D.R. (ED.), 1971
Crime and criminal justice.
Chicago: Quadrangle Books.

DOUGLAS, J.D. (ED.), 1971
Crime and justice in American society.
New York: Bobbs Merrill Co.

GRUPP, S.E. (ED.), 1971
Theories of punishment.
Bloomington, Ind.: Indiana Univ. Press.

MacNAMARA, D. AND SAGARIN, E. (EDS.), 1971
Perspectives on correction.
New York: Thomas Y. Cromwell Co.

RADZINOWICZ, L. AND WOLFGANG, M.E. (EDS.), 1971
Crime and justice (3 volumes): I *The criminal in society.* II *The criminal in the arms of the law.* III *The criminal in confinement.*
New York: Basic Books (2nd ed. due 1976).

DOUGLAS, J.D. (ED.), 1972
Research on deviance.
New York: Random House.

FILSTEAD, W.J. (ED.), 1972
Introduction to deviance: readings in the process of making deviants.
Chicago: Markham.

GERBER, R.J. AND McANANY, P.D., (EDS.), 1972
Contemporary punishment: views, explanations, and justifications.
Notre Dame, Ind.: Univ. Notre Dame Press.

GIALLOMBARDO, R. (ED.), 1972
Juvenile delinquency: a book of readings.
New York: John Wiley & Sons. 2nd ed.

MAYS, J.B. (ED.), 1972
Juvenile delinquency, the family and the social group: a reader.
London: Longman.

PALMER, S. AND LINSKY, A. (EDS.), 1972
Rebellion and retreat: readings in the form and processes of deviance.
Columbus, Ohio: Bobbs Merrill Co.

REED, J.P. AND BAALI, F. (ED.), 1972
Faces of delinquency.
Englewood Cliffs N.J.: Prentice-Hall.

RESNIK, H.L.P. AND WOLFGANG, M.E. (ED.), 1972
Sexual behaviors: social, clinical and legal aspects.
Boston: Little Brown & Co.

SCOTT, R.A. AND DOUGLAS, J.D. (EDS.), 1972
Theoretical perspectives on deviance.
New York: Basic Books.

SHORT, J.F. AND WOLFGANG, M.E. (EDS.), 1972
Collective violence.
Chicago: Aldine.

SYLVESTER, S.F., (ED.), 1972
The heritage of modern criminology.
Cambridge, Mass.: Schenkman.

TOBIAS, J.J. (ED.), 1972
Nineteenth-century crime, prevention and punishment.
Newton Abbot: David and Charles.

BAILEY, R.V. AND YOUNG, J. (EDS.), 1973
Contemporary social problems in Britain,
Farnborough, Hants: Saxon House.

CLINARD, M.B. AND QUINNEY, R. (EDS.), 1973
Criminal behavior systems.
New York: Holt, Rinehart & Winston 2nd ed.

COHEN, S. AND YOUNG, J. (EDS.), 1973
The manufacture of news: social problems, deviance and the mass media.
London: Constable.

CONKLIN, J.E. (ED.), 1973
The crime establishment: organised crime and American society.
Englewood Cliffs, N.J.,: Prentice-Hall.

DENISOFF, R.S. AND McCAGHY, C.H. (EDS.), 1973
Deviance, conflict and criminality.
Chicago: Rand McNally.

HERMANN, M.G. AND HAFT, M.G. (EDS.), 1973
Prisoners rights sourcebook: theory, litigation, practice.
New York: Clarke Boardman.

KILLINGER, G.G. AND CROMWELL, P.F. (EDS.), 1973
Penology: the evolution of corrections in America.
St. Paul, Minn.: West Publishing Co.

LYLE, W.H. AND HORNER, T.W. (EDS.), 1973
Behavioural science and modern penology: a book of readings.
Springfield, Ill.: C.C. Thomas.

ORLAND, L. (ED.), 1973
Justice, punishment, treatment: the correctional process.
New York: Free Press.

RUBINGTON, E. AND WEINBERG, M.S. (EDS.), 1973
Deviance—the interactionist perspective.
New York: Macmillan. 2nd ed.

WEINBERG, M.S. AND RUBINGTON, E. (EDS.), 1973
The study of social problems, five perspectives.
New York: Oxford Univ. Press.

BRYANT, C.D. (ED.), 1974
Deviant behaviour: occupational and organizational bases.
Chicago: Rand McNally.

ELDEFONSO, E. (ED.), 1974
Issues in corrections: a book of readings.
Beverly Hills: Glencoe Press.

RIEDEL, M. AND THORNBERRY, T.P. (EDS.), 1974
Crime and delinquency: dimensions of deviance.
New York: Praeger.

CARSON, W.G. AND WILES, P. (EDS.), 1975
The sociology of crime and delinquency in Britain.
London: Martin Robertson & Co., 2 vols. (2nd ed. of vol. 1).

HENSHEL, R.L. AND SILVERMAN, R. (EDS.), 1975
Perception in criminology.
New York: Columbia Univ. Press.

MAYS, J.B. (ED.), 1975
The social treatment of young offenders: a reader.
London: Longman.

STEFFENSMEIER, D.J. AND TERRY, R.M. (EDS.), 1975
Examining deviance experimentally: selected readings.
Port Washington: Alfred Publishing Co.

SUPPLEMENT

[Up to February 1976]

Contents of Supplement

I Dimensions of crime and the problem of measurement

1 Criminal statistics and the amount of crime

[*See also Section 3 for references on various types of crime, Section 4 on violence and 5 on civil disorders and lawlessness.*]

UNITED STATES OF AMERICA, 1972
The economic impact of crimes against business
Preliminary Staff Report.
U.S. Dept. of Commerce, Washington, D.C.

HOFFMAN-BUSTAMANTE, D., 1973
The nature of female criminality.
Issues in Criminol., **8,** 117–36.

ERSKINE, H., 1974
The polls: fear of violence and crime.
Public Opinion Quart., **38,** 131–45.

GRABOSKY, P.N., 1974
Patterns of criminality in New South Wales, 1788–1973.
Aust. & N.Z. J. Criminol., **7,** 215–29.

WEIS, K., AND MILAKOVICH, M., 1974
Who's afraid of crime?: or: how to finance a decreasing rate of increase, in S.F. Sylvester, Jr., and E. Sagarin (eds.), *Politics and crime.*
New York: Praeger, 31–42.

BANKS, C., MALONEY, E., AND WILLCOCK, H.D., 1975
Public attitudes to crime and the penal system.
Brit. J. Criminol., **15,** 228–40.

BARNETT, A., KLEITMAN, D.J., AND LARSON, R.C., 1975
On urban homicide: a statistical analysis.
J. Crim. Justice, **3,** 85–110.

BRAITHWAITE, J., 1975
Population growth and crime.
Aust. & N.Z. J. Criminol., **8,** 57–61.

CONKLIN, J.E., 1975
The impact of crime.
New York: Macmillan, 1–49, 73–104.

GIBSON, E., 1975
Homicide in England and Wales, 1967–1971.
London: Home Office Research Studies, **31.**

SIMON, R.J., 1975
Contemporary woman and crime.
National Institute of Mental Health, Washington, D.C.

WADSWORTH, M.E.J., 1975
Delinquency in a national sample of children
Brit. J. Criminol., **15,** 167–74.

INTERNATIONAL CRIMINAL POLICE REVIEW, 1976
Crime in France as revealed by Police statistics for 1973.
Nos. 294 & 295. (Jan.–Feb.).

SIMON, R.J., 1976
American women and crime.
Annals Amer. Acad. Pol. & Soc. Sci., **423,** 31–46.

2 Criminal statistics: limitations and possible improvements

BLUMSTEIN, A., 1974
Seriousness weights in an index of crime.
Amer. Sociol. Rev., **39,** 854–64.

RIEDEL, M., 9174
The effect of perceived circumstances on judgments of offense seriousness, in T.P.

Thornberry and E. Sagarin (eds.), *Images of crime: offenders and victims.*
New York: Praeger, 113–22.

ROSSI, P.H., WAITE, E., BOSE, C.E., AND BERK, R.E., 1974
The seriousness of crimes: normative structure and individual differences.
Amer. Social. Rev., **39**, 224–37.

SMITH, D.M., 1974
Crime rates as territorial social indicators: the case of the United States.
University of London, Dept. of Geography, Occasional Papers No. 1, Mimeo.

BANKS, C., AND SAPSFORD, R.J., 1975
Homicide, in *Homicide: control and authority in institution; uniform model for individual dossiers in clinical criminology.*
4th Int. Seminar in Comp. Clinical Criminol. Montreal: Univ. of Montreal, 50–78.

BRIDGES, G.S., AND LISAGOR, N.S., 1975
Scaling seriousness: an evaluation of magnitude and category scaling techniques.
J. Crim. Law & Criminol., **66**, 215–21.

FIGLIO, R.M., 1975
The seriousness of offenses: an evaluation by offenders and nonoffenders.
J. Crim. Law & Criminol., **66**, 189–200.

LESIEUR, H.R., AND LEHMAN, P.M., 1975
Remeasuring delinquency: a replication and critique.
Brit. J. Criminol., **15**, 69–80.

MALTZ, M.D., 1975
Crime statistics: a mathematical perspective.
J. Crim. Justice, **3**, 177–93.

PEASE, K., IRESON, J., AND THORPE, J., 1975
Modified crime indices for eight countries.
J. Crim. Law & Criminol., **66**, 209–14.

RIEDEL, M., 1975
Perceived circumstances, inferences of intent and judgements of offense seriousness.
J. Crim. Law & Criminol., **66**, 201–8.

SKOGAN, W.G., 1975
Measurement problems in official and survey crime rates.
J. Crim. Justice, **3**, 17–31.

WELLFORD, C.F., AND WIATROWSKI, M., 1975
On the measurement of delinquency.
J. Crim. Law & Criminol., **66**, 175–88.

3 The dark figure: hidden crime, its nature and extent

REISS, A.J., 1973
Surveys of self-reported delicts.
Yale University: Mimeo.

KROHN, M., WALDO, G.P., AND CHIRICOS, T.G., 1974
Self-reported delinquency: a comparison of structured interviews and self-administered checklists.
J. Crim. Law & Criminol., **65**, 545–53.

THORNBERRY, T.P., AND FIGLIO, R.M., 1974
Victimization and criminal behaviour in a birth cohort, in T.P. Thornberry and E. Sagarin (eds.), *Images of crime: offenders and victims.*
New York: Preager, 102–12.

BELSON, W.A., 1975
Juvenile theft: the causal factors.
London: Harper & Row, 69–104.

BIDERMAN, A.D., 1975
Victimology and victimization surveys, in I. Drapkin and E. Viano (eds.), *Victimology: a new focus. Vol. 3. Crimes, victims and justice.*
Lexington, Mass.: Heath Lexington Books, 153–69.

BYTHEWAY, B., 1975
The statistical association between social class and self-reported delinquency.
Int. J. Criminol. & Penol., **3,** 243–51.

HOLMSTROM, L.L., AND BURGESS, W., 1975
Rape: the victim and the criminal justice system.
Int. J. Criminol. & Penol., **3,** 101–10.

HOWARD, M.K., 1975
Police reports and victimization survey results: an empirical study.
Criminol., **12,** 433–46.

MALTZ, M.D., 1975
Crime statistics: a mathematical perspective.
J. Crim. Justice, **3,** 177–93.

REYNOLDS, P.D., AND BLYTH, D.A., 1975
Sources of variation affecting the relationship between police and survey-based estimates of crime rates, in I. Drapkin and E. Viano (eds.), *Victimology: a new focus. Vol. 3. Crimes, victims and justice.*
Lexington, Mass.: Heath Lexington Books, 201–25.

SKOGAN, W.G., 1975
Measurement problems in official and survey crime rates.
J. Crim. Justice, **3,** 17–31.

UNITED STATES OF AMERICA, 1975
Crime in eight American cities. Advance Report.
L.E.A.A., National Institute of Law Enforcement and Criminal Justice, U.S. Dept. of Justice, Washington, D.C.

UNITED STATES OF AMERICA, 1975
Criminal victimization in the United States, 1973 Advance Report, 1.
L.E.A.A., National Criminal Justice Information and Statistics Service, U.S. Dept. of Justice, Washington, D.C.

UNITED STATES OF AMERICA, 1975
Criminal victimization surveys in 13 American cities.
L.E.A.A., National Criminal Justice Information and Statistics Service, U.S. Dept. of Justice, Washington, D.C.

MANN, F., FRIEDMAN, C.J., AND FRIEDMAN, A.S., 1976
Characteristics of self-reported violent offenders versus court identified violent offenders.
Int. J. Criminol. & Penol., **4,** 69–87.

4 Police and court discretion: their impact on criminal statistics

[*See also Section 2(1) for references on labelling; Section 4(4) for references on police discretion to prosecute; and Section 12(2) for references on diversion from the criminal justice system.*]

BIENVENUE, R.M., AND LATIF, A.H., 1974
Arrests, disposition and recidivism: a comparison of Indians and whites.
Can. J. Criminol. & Corrections, **16,** 105–16.

NEUBAUER, D.W., 1974
After the arrest: the charging decision in Prairie City.
Law & Soc. Rev., **8,** 495–517.

SEIDMAN, D., AND COUZENS, M., 1964
Getting the crime rate down: political pressure and crime reporting.
Law & Soc. Rev., **8,** 457–93.

SIEGEL, L.J., SULLIVAN, D.C., AND GREENE, J.R., 1974
Decision games applied to police decision making: an exploratory study of information usage.
J. Crim. Justice, **2,** 131–46.

WALKER, N., 1974
Caution: some thoughts on the penal involvement rate, in L. Blom-Cooper (ed.), *Progress in penal reform.*
Oxford: Clarendon Press, 221–37.

BRITT, D.W., AND TITTLE, C.R., 1975
Crime rates and police behavior: a test of two hypotheses.
Social Forces, **54,** 441–51.

BURKE, P.J., AND TURK, A.T., 1975
Factors affecting postarrest dispositions: a model for analysis.
Social Problems, **22,** 313–32.

DEFLEUR, L.B., 1975
Biasing influences on doing arrest records: implications for deviance research.
Amer. Sociol. Rev., **40,** 88–103.

GARRETT, M., AND SHORT, J.F., JR., 1975
Social class and delinquency: predictions and outcomes of police-juvenile encounters.
Social Problems, **22,** 368–83.

HALL, D.J., 1975
The role of the victim in the prosecution and disposition of a criminal case.
Vanderbilt Law Rev., **28,** 931–85.

HOWARD, M.K., 1975
Police reports and victimization survey results: an empirical study.
Criminol., **12,** 433–46.

MCCABE, S., 1975
The police and the citizen. London:
Home Office Res. Unit Bulletin, **2,** 1–4.

REYNOLDS, P.D., AND BLYTH, D.A., 1975
Sources of variation affecting the relationship between police and survey-based estimates of crime rates, in I. Drapkin and E. Viano (eds.), *Victimology: a new focus, Vol.* 3, *Crimes, victims and justice.*
Lexington, Mass.: Heath Lexington Books, 201–25.

BOTTOMLEY, A.K., AND COLEMAN, C.A., 1976
Criminal statistics: the police role in the discovery and detection of crime.
Int. J. Criminol. & Penol., **4,** 33–58.

2 Crime in its social setting

1 Economic conditions

[*See also Section 15* (1a) *for references on poverty.*]

QUINNEY, R., 1973
Crime control in capitalist society: a critical philosophy of legal order.
Issues in Criminol., **8,** 75–99.

BOSHIER, R., AND HAWES, R., 1974
The work behaviour of offenders and non-offenders.
Aust. & N.Z. J. Criminol., **7,** 173–8.

UNITED NATIONS SOCIAL DEFENCE RESEARCH INSTITUTE, 1974
Economic crisis and crime: interim report and materials.
Rome: UNSDRI.

VOTEY, H.L., JR., AND PHILLIPS, L., 1974
The control of criminal activity: an economic analysis, in D. Glaser (ed.), *Handbook of Criminology.*
Chicago: Rand McNally, 1055–93.

CHIRICOS, T.G., AND WALDO, G.P., 1975
Socioeconomic status and criminal sentencing: an empirical assessment of a conflict proposition.
Amer. Sociol. Rev., **40,** 753–72.

DENISOFF, R.S., AND MCQUARIE, D., 1975
Crime control in capitalist society: a reply to Quinney.
Issues in Criminol., **10,** 109–19.

CHESTER, C.R., 1976
Perceived relative deprivation as a cause of property crime.
Crime & Delinq., **22,** 17–30.

GORDON, D.M., 1976
Class and the economics of crime, in W.J. Chambliss, and M. Mankoff (eds.), *Whose law? What order?: a conflict approach to criminology.*
New York: John Wiley & Sons, 193–214.

2 Crime and social class

[*See also Section 1(3) and 1(4) for references on the dark figure and police discretion in relation to the social class of official and hidden delinquents.*]

DAVIES, L., AND CUNNINGHAM, D., 1974
The criminal and social aspects of families with a multiplicity of problems.
Aust. & N.Z. J. Criminol., **7,** 197–213.

JARVIS, G.K., AND MESSINGER, H.B., 1974
Social and economic correlates of juvenile delinquency rates: a Canadian case.
Can. J. Criminol. & Corrections, **16,** 361–72.

MILLER, F.J.W., COURT, S.D.M., KNOX, E.G., AND BRANDON, S., 1974
The school years in Newcastle upon Tyne 1952–62.
London: Oxford Univ. Press, 203–11.

BYTHEWAY, B., 1975
The statistical association between social class and self-reported delinquency.
Int. J. Criminol. & Penol., **3,** 243–51.

GARRETT, M., AND SHORT, J.F., Jr., 1975
Social class and delinquency: predictions and outcomes of police-juvenile encounters.
Social Problems, **22,** 368–83.

MCKISSACK, I.J., 1975
Early socialisation: the baseline in delinquency research.
Int. J. Criminol. & Penol., **3,** 43–51.

WILSON, H., 1975
Juvenile delinquency, parental criminality and social handicap.
Brit. J. Criminol., **15**, 241–50.

GORDON, D.M., 1976
Class and the economics of crime, in W.J. Chambliss and M. Mankoff (eds.), *Whose law? What order?: a conflict approach to criminology.*
New York: John Wiley & Sons, 193–214.

3 Social disorganization and the ecological school

CHILTON, R., AND DUSSICH, J.P.J., 1974
Methodological issues in delinquency research: some alternative analyses of geographically distributed data.
Social Forces, **53**, 73–82.

GILLIS, A.R., 1974
Population density and social pathology: the case of building type, social allowance and juvenile delinquency.
Social Forces, **53**, 306–14

BALDWIN, J., 1975
British areal studies of crime: an assessment.
Brit. J. Criminol., **15**, 211–27.

BRANTINGHAM, P.J., AND BRANTINGHAM, P.L., 1975
The spatial patterning of burglary.
Howard J. of Penol. & Crime Prev., **14**, 11–23.

PEARSON, G., 1975
The deviant imagination: psychiatry, social work and social change.
London: Macmillan, 143–76.

VINSON, T., AND HOMEL, R., 1975
Crime and disadvantage: the coincidence of medical and social problems in an Austrialian city.
Brit. J. Criminol., **15**, 21–31.

SNODGRASS, J., 1967
Clifford R. Shaw and Henry D. McKay: Chicago criminologists.
Brit. J. Criminol., **16**, 1–19.

4 Differential association

BELSON, W.A., 1975
Juvenile theft: the causal factors.
London: Harper & Row, 209–242, 281–300.

KNIGHT, B.J., AND WEST, D.J., 1975
Temporary and continuing delinquency.
Brit. J. Criminol., **15**, 43–50.

5 Frustrations in opportunity and anomie

[*See also Section 3(2) for references relating to studies of gangs.*]

(a) *Theories and concepts*

CLARKE, M., 1974
On the concept of 'sub-culture'.
Brit. J. Sociol., **25**, 428–41.

MARKS, S., 1974
Durkheim's theory of anomie.
Amer. J. Sociol., **80**, 329–63.

YOUNG, J., 1974
New directions in sub-cultural theory, in J. Rex (ed.), *Approaches to sociology. An introduction to major trends in British sociology.*
London: Routledge & Kegan Paul, 160–86.

POPE, W., 1975
Concepts and explanatory structure in Durkheim's theory of suicide.
Brit. J. Sociol., **26**, 417–34.

CHESTER, C.R., 1976
Perceived relative deprivation as a cause of property crime.
Crime & Delinq., **22**, 17–30.

5 Frustrations in opportunity and anomie

[*See also Section 3(2) for references relating to studies of gangs.*]

(*b*) *Empirical studies*

QUICKER, J.C., 1974
The effect of goal discrepancy on delinquency.
Social Problems, **22**, 76–86.

BELSON, W.A., 1975
Juvenile theft: the causal factors.
London: Harper & Row, 363–411.

BREZNITZ, T., 1975
Juvenile delinquents' perceptions of own and others' commitment to delinquency.
J. Res. Crime & Delinq., **12**, 124–32.

DATESMAN, S.K., SCARPITTI, F.R., AND STEPHENSON, R.M., 1975
Female delinquency: an applicaton of self and opportunity theories.
J. Res. Crime & Delinq., **12**, 107–23.

6 Racial and cultural schisms

[*See also Section 5(1) for references relating to racial clashes in civil disorders.*]

BANTON, M., 1974
Policing a divided society.
Police J., **47**, 304–21.

BERGER, A.S., AND SIMON, W., 1974
Black families and the Moynihan Report: a research evaluation.
Social Problems, **22**, 145–61.

BIENVENUE, R.M., AND LATIF, A.H., 1974
Arrests, disposition and recidivism: a comparison of Indians and whites.
Can. J. Criminol. & Corrections, **16**, 105–16.

CARROLL, L., 1974
Hacks, blacks and cons: race relations in a maximum security prison.
Lexington, Mass.: Heath Lexington Books.

DAVIS, J.A., 1974
Justification for no obligation: views of black males toward crime and the criminal law.
Issues in Criminol., **9**, 69–87.

MORRIS, F.L., 1974
Black political consciousness in Northern state prisons, in H. Jacob (ed.), *The potential for reform of criminal justice.*
Sage Criminal Justice System Annuals, **3**, Beverly Hills, Calif.: Sage Publications, 291–329.

TRUJILLO, L.D., 1974
"La Evolución del 'Bandido' al 'Pachuco' ": a critical examination and evaluation of criminological literature on Chicanos.
Issues in Criminol., **9**, 43–67.

BATTA, I.D., MCCULLOCH, J.W., AND SMITH, N.J, 1975
A study of juvenile delinquency amongst Asians and half-Asians.
A comparative study of a Northern town, based on official statistics
Brit. J. Criminol., **15,** 32–42

COUNCIL OF EUROPE, 1975
Aspects of criminality among immigrant workers
Report of the European Committee on Crime Problems.
Strasbourg.

HALL, E.L., AND SIMKUS, A.A., 1975
Inequality in the types of sentences received by native Americans and whites.
Criminol., **13,** 199–222.

DAVIS, J.A., 1976
Blacks, crime, and American culture.
Annals Amer. Acad. Pol. & Soc. Sci., **423,** 89–98.

7 Deviance: social functions, labelling and interaction

[*See also Section 1(4) for references on Police Discretion to Prosecute. Section 7(1) for references relating to aims of penal sanctions. Section 10(1) for references on the general preventive effects of penal sanctions.*]

DELMATER, J., 1968
On the nature of deviance.
Social Forces, **46,** 445–55.

GAYLIN, W., 1970
In the service of their country: war resisters in prison.
New York: Grosset & Dunlop, 266–318.

DOMINICK, J.R., 1973
Crime and law enforcement on prime-time television.
Public Opinion Quart., **37,** 241–50.

AGETON, S.S., AND ELLIOTT, D.S., 1974
The effects of legal processing on delinquent orientations.
Social Problems, **22,** 87–100.

BALDWIN, J., 1974
The role of victim in certain property offences.
Crim. Law Rev., 1974, 353–8.

CARLEN, P., 1974
Remedial routines for the maintenance of control in magistrates' courts.
Brit. J. Law & Soc., **1,** 101–17.

CHAMBLISS, W.J., 1974
The state, the law and the definition of behavior as criminal or delinquent, in D. Glaser (ed.), *Handbook of criminology*.
Chicago: Rand McNally, 7–43.

COULTER, J., 1974
What's wrong with the new criminology?
Sociol. Rev., **22,** 119–35.

DAMER, S., 1974
Wine alley: the sociology of a dreadful enclosure.
Sociol. Rev., **22,** 221–48.

DENZIN, N.K., 1974
The methodological implicaions of symbolic interactionism for the study of deviance.
Brit. J. Sociol., **25,** 269–82.

EMERSON, R.M., 1974
Role determinants in juvenile court, in D. Glaser (ed.), *Handbook of criminology.*
Chicago: Rand McNally, 621–50.

ERICSON, R.V., 1974
British criminology: a new subject or old politics?
Can. J. Criminol. & Corrections, **16,** 352–60.

GALLIHER, J.F., AND MCCARTNEY, J.L., 1974
The influence of funding agencies on juvenile delinquency research.
Social Problems, **21,** 77–90.

HEPWORTH, M., AND TURNER, B.S., 1974
Confessing to murder: critical notes on the sociology of motivation.
Brit. J. Law. & Soc., **1,** 31–49.

LANDAU, S.F., 1974
The offender's perception of the victim, in I. Drapkin and E. Viano (eds.), *Victimology: a new focus. Vol. 1. Theoretical issues in victimology.*
Lexington, Mass.: Heath Lexington Books, 137–54.

MAHONEY, A.R., 1974
The effecting of labeling upon youths in the juvenile justice system: a review of the evidence.
Law & Soc. Rev., **8**, 583–614.

MEADE, A.C., 1974
The labeling approach to delinquency: state of the theory as a function of method.
Social Forces, **53**, 83–91.

NEWMAN, G.R., 1974
The effects of stereotypes upon perceptions of deviance.
Aust. & N.Z. J. Criminol., **7**, 135–43.

REED, J.P., AND REED, R.S., 1974
Status, images, and consequences: once a criminal always a criminal, in T.P. Thornberry and E. Sagarin (eds.), *Images of crime: offenders and victims.*
New York: Praeger, 123–34.

ROGERS, J.W., AND BUFFALO, M.D., 1974
Fighting back: nine modes of adaptation to a deviant label.
Social Problems, **22**, 101–18.

SCHUR, E., 1974
The trend toward decriminalization: some sociological observations, in S.F. Sylvester, Jr., and E. Sagarin (eds.), *Politics and crime.*
New York: Praeger, 108–18.

SKOLNICK, J.H., 1974
Perspectives on law and order, in S.F. Sylvester, Jr., and E. Sagarin (eds.), *Politics and crime.*
New York: Praeger, 6–16.

SPITZER, S., 1974
Labeling and deviant identity: a proposal for conceptual refinement and systematic research, in T.P. Thornberry and E. Sagarin (eds.), *Images of crime: offenders and victims.*
New York: Praeger, 57–66.

SYKES, G.M., 1974
The rise of critical criminology.
J. Crim. Law & Criminol., **65**, 206–13.

WALKER, N., 1974
Explaining misbehaviour.
Cambridge Univ. Press.

WERKENTIN, F., HOFFERBERT, M., AND BAURMANN, M,. 1974
Criminology as police science, or: "How old is the new criminology?"
Crime & Social Justice, **2**, 24–41.

WILKINSON, K., 1974
The broken family and juvenile delinquency: scientific explantion or ideology?
Social Problems, **21**, 721–39.

YOUNG, J., 1974
New directions in sub-cultural theory, in J. Rex (ed.), *Approaches to sociology: an introduction to major trends in British sociology.*
London: Routledge & Kegan Paul, 160–86.

BEYLEVELD, D., AND WILES, P., 1975
Man and method in David Matza's "Becoming deviant."
Brit. J. Criminol., **15**, 111–27.

CHIBNALL, S., 1975
The crime reporter: a study in the production of commercial knowledge.
Sociol., **9**, 49–66.

CONKLIN, J.E., 1975
The impact of crime.
New York: Macmillan, 50–72, 154–84.

ERICSON, R.V., 1975
Criminal reactions: the labelling perspective.
Farnborough, Hants.: Saxon House.

ERICSON, R.V., 1975
Responsibility, moral relativity, and response ability: some implications of deviance theory for criminal justice.
Univ. Toronto Law J., **25**, 23–41.

ERICSON, R.V., 1975
Young offenders and their social work.
Farnborough, Hants.: Saxon House, 125–215.

GROVE, W.R., AND CHAUNCEY, R.L., 1975
Replies to T.J. Scheff "The labelling theory of mental illness" and rejoinder from Scheff.
Amer. Sociol. Rev., **40**, 232–57.

HARRIS, A., 1975
Imprisonment and the expected value of

criminal choice: a specification and test of aspects of the labeling perspective.
Amer. Sociol. Rev., **40,** 71–87.

HEPWORTH, M., 1975
Blackmail: publicity and secrecy in everyday life.
London: Routledge & Kegan Paul.

HOLBORN, J., 1975
Some male offender's problems: II. casework with short-term prisoners.
London: Home Office Research Studies, **28,** 67–78.

KNIGHT, B.J., AND WEST, D.J., 1975
Temporary and continuing delinquency.
Brit. J. Criminol., **15,** 43–50.

MACMILLAN, J., 1975
Deviant drivers.
Farnborough, Hants.: Saxon House, 121–202.

MANNING, P.K., 1975
Deviance and dogma: some comments on the labelling perspective.
Brit. J. Criminol., **15,** 1–20.

MARZOTTO, M., PLATT, T., AND SNARE, A., 1975
A reply to Turk.
Crime & Social Justice, **4,** 43–5.

NEWMAN, G.R., 1975
A theory of deviance removal.
Brit. J. Sociol., **26,** 203–17.

NEWTON, C.H., AND SHELDEN, R.G., 1975
The delinquent label and its effects on future behaviour: an empirical test of Lemert's levels of deviance.
Int. J. Criminol. & Penol., **3,** 229–41.

NEWTON, C.H., SHELDEN, R.G., AND JENKINS, S., 1975
The homogenization process within the juvenile justice system.
Int. J. Criminol., & Penol., **3,** 213–27.

ORCUTT, J.D., 1975
Deviance as a situated phenomenon: variations in the social interpretation of marijuana and alcohol use.
Social Problems, **22,** 346–56.

PEARSON, G., 1975
The deviant imagination: psychiatry, social work and social change.
London: Macmillan.

RAFKY, D.M., AND SEALEY, R.W., 1975
The adolescent and the law: a survey.
Crime & Delinq., **21,** 131–8.

ROSENBLUM, K.E., 1975
Female deviance and the female sex role: a preliminary investigation.
Brit. J. Sociol., **26,** 169–85.

ROTENBERG, M., 1975
Self-labelling theory: preliminary findings among mental patients.
Brit. J. Criminol., **15,** 360–75.

SANDERS, C.R., 1975
Caught in the con games: the young, white drug user's contact with the legal system.
Law & Soc. Rev., **9,** 197–217.

SCIMECCA, J.A., 1975
The implications of the sociology of C. Wright Mills for modern criminological theory.
Int. J. Criminol. & Penol., **3,** 145–53.

SEPPILLI, T., AND ABBOZZO, G.G., 1975
The state of research into social control and deviance in Italy in the post-war period (1945–1973), in H. Bianchi, M. Simondi and I. Taylor (eds.), *Deviance and control in Europe: papers from the European group for the study of deviance and social control.*
London: John Wiley & Sons, 35–50.

SILVERMAN, R.A., 1975
Victim-offender relationships in face-to-face delinquent acts.
Social Problems, **22,** 383–93.

SPITZER, S., 1975
Punishment and social organisation: a study of Durkheim's theory of penal evolution.
Law & Soc. Rev., **9,** 613–35.

SZABO, D., 1975
Comparative criminology.
J. Crim. Law & Criminol., **66,** 366–79.

THOMPSON, E.P., 1975
The crime of anonymity, in D. Hay, P. Linebaugh and E.P. Thompson (eds.), *Albion's fatal tree: crime and society in eighteenth-century England.*
London: Allen Lane, 255–344.

TITTLE, C.R., 1975
Deterrents or labeling?
Social Forces, **53**, 399–410.

TURK, A.T., 1975
Prospects and pitfalls for radical criminology: a critical response to Platt.
Crime & Social Justice, **4**, 41–2.

VODOPIVEC, K., 1975
On the distance to reality.
Int. J. Criminol. & Penol., **3**, 309–22.

WELLFORD, C., 1975
Labelling theory and criminology: an assessment.
Social Problems, **22**, 322–45.

WHITE, G.F., 1975
Public responses to hypothetical crimes: effect of offender and victim status and seriousness of the offenses on punitive reactions.
Social Forces, **53**, 411–19.

WHITE, S., 1975
Criminological theory and deviance theory: review article.
Aust. & N.Z. J. Criminol., **8**, 47–56.

CHAMBLISS, W.J., 1976
Functional and conflict theories of crime: the heritage of Emile Durkheim and Karl Marx, in W.J. Chambliss and M. Mankoff (eds.), *Whose law? What order?: a conflict approach to criminology.*
New York: John Wiley & Sons, 1–28.

FISHMAN, G., 1976
The paradoxical effect of labelling.
Int. J. Criminol. & Penol., **4**, 1–7.

MANKOFF, M., 1976
Societal reaction and career deviance: a critical analysis, in W.J. Chambliss and M. Mankoff (eds.), *Whose law? What order?: a conflict approach to criminology.*
New York: John Wiley & Sons, 240–56.

3 Some categories of crime and criminals

1 Problems of classification

GLASER, D., 1974
The classification of offenses and offenders, in D. Glaser (ed.), *Handbook of criminology*.
Chicago: Rand McNally, 45–83.

GORECKI, J., 1974
Crime causation theories: failures and perspectives.
Brit. J. Sociol., **25**, 461–77.

GIBBONS, D.C., 1975
Offender typologies—two decades later.
Brit. J. Criminol., **15**, 140–56.

KRIEFMAN, S., 1975
Driving while disqualified.
London: Home Office Research Studies, **27**, 52–62, 117–23.

WERNER, E., 1975
Psychological and ethnic correlates of interpersonal maturity among delinquents.
Brit. J. Criminol., **15**, 51–68.

2 Delinquent subcultures and youth gangs

See also Section 2(5) for references on studies of frustrations in opportunity perceived by gang members.]

SHORT, J.F., JR., 1974
Collective behaviour, crime and delinquency, in D. Glaser (ed.), *Handbook of Criminology*.
Chicago: Rand McNally, 403–49.

CARMICHAEL, B.G., 1975
Youth crime in urban communities: a descriptive analysis of street hustlers and their crimes.
Crime & Delinq., **21**, 139–48.

CHAMBLISS, W.J., 1976
The saints and the roughnecks, in W.J. Chambliss and M. Mankoff (eds.), *Whose law? What order?: a conflict approach in criminology*.
New York: John Wiley & Sons, 148–61.

3 Professional and organised crime

UNITED STATES OF AMERICA, SENATE, 1972
Effects of organised criminal activity on interstate and foreign commerce.
Hearings before the Committee on Commerce, 92nd Congress, 1st Session, Washington, D.C.

MILNER, C., AND MILNER, R., 1973
Black players: the secret world of black pimps.
London: Michael Joseph.

OVERLY, D.H., AND SCHELL, T.H., 1973
New effectiveness measures for organized crime control efforts: development and evaluation.
L.E.A.A. National Institute of Law Enforcement and Criminal Justice, U.S. Dept. of Justice, Washington, D.C.

CHAPPELL, D., AND WALSH, M., 1974
"No questions asked": a consideration of the crime of criminal receiving.
Crime & Delinq., **20**, 157–68.

DAVID, P.R. (ED.), 1974
The world of the burglar.
Albuquerque: Univ. of New Mexico Press.

EHRENWERTH, D.H., 1974
The effect of the new Pennsylvania crimes codes on organised crime: too little but not too late.
Duquesne Law Rev., **12,** 812–48.

EINSTADTER, W.J., 1974
Contingencies and risk in criminalization: on becoming a systematic robber, in T.P. Thornberry and E. Sagarin (eds.), *Images of crime: offenders and victims.*
New York: Praeger, 15–24.

HESS, H., 1974
Mafia and Mafiosi: the structure of power.
Farnborough, Hants.: Saxon House.

HOMER, F.D., 1974
Guns and garlic: myths and realities of organized crime.
West Lafayette, Indiana: Purdue Univ. Press.

INCIARDI, J.A., 1974
Vocational crime, in D. Glaser (ed.), *Handbook of criminology.*
Chicago: Rand McNally, 299–401.

KLOCKARS, C.B., 1974
The professional fence.
New York: The Free Press.

MAURER, D.W., 1974
The American confidence man.
Springfield, Ill.: C.C. Thomas.

TOBIAS, J.J., 1974
Prince offences: the life and crimes of Ikey Solomons.
London: Vallentine, Mitchell.

UNITED STATES OF AMERICA, SENATE, 1974
Criminal redistribution (fencing) of goods stolen from legitimate business activities and their effect on commerce.
Part 3, U.S. Senate. 93rd Congress, 2nd Session, Washington, D.C.

VASOLI, R.H., AND TERZOLA, D.A., 1974
Sutherland's professional thief.
Criminol., **12,** 131–54.

WALSH, M., AND CHAPPELL, D., 1974
Operational parameters in the stolen property system.
J. Crim. Justice, **2,** 113–29.

BRANTINGHAM, P.J., AND BRANTINGHAM, P.L., 1975
The spatial patterning of burglary.
Howard J. of Penol. & Crime. Prev., **14,** 11–23.

MCINTOSH, M., 1975
The organisation of crime.
London: Macmillan.

MIDDLEMAS, K., 1975
The double market: art theft and art thieves.
Farnborough, Hants.: Saxon House, 49–96.

PACE, D.F., AND STYLES, J.C., 1975
Organised crime: concepts and control.
Englewood Cliffs, N.J.: Prentice Hall, Appendix B, Organised Crime Control Act of 1970, 247–95.

SMITH, D.C., Jr., 1975
The Mafia mystique
London: Hutchinson.

UNIVERSITY OF PENNSYLVANIA LAW REVIEW, 1975
Organised crime and the infiltration of legitimate business: civil remedies for 'criminal activity'.
124, 192–222.

4 Drug abuse

(*a*) *Sources, forms and incidence*

TART, C.T., 1971
On being stoned: a psychological study oj marijuana intoxication.
Palo Alto, Calif.: Science & Behavior Books.

MITCHESON, M., AND HARTNOLL, R., 1973
Attitudes of young people towards drug use, in *Expert group on drugs in modern society:*

community reactions to drug use by young people.
New York: United Nations, 67–98.

CHAMBERS, C.D., 1974
Narcotic addiction and crime: an empirical review, in J.A. Inciardi and C.D. Chambers (eds), *Drugs and the criminal justice system.*
Sage Criminal Justice System Annuals, **2,**
Beverly Hills, Calif.: Sage Publications, 125–42.

GLATT, M.M., 1974
Drugs, society and man: a guide to addiction and its treatment.
Lancaster, England: Medical & Technical Publ., Co., 121–213.

GOULD, L.C., 1974
Crime and the addict: beyond commonsense, in J.A. Inciardi and C.D. Chambers (eds,), *Drugs and the criminal justice system.*
Sage Criminal Justice System Annuals, **2,**
Beverly Hills, Calif.: Sage Publications, 57–75.

INCIARDI, J.A., 1974
Drugs, drug-taking and drug-seeking: notations on the dynamics of myth, change, and reality, in J.A. Inciardi and C.D. Chambers (eds.), *Drugs and the criminal justice system.*
Sage Criminal Justice System Annuals, **2,**
Beverly Hills, Calif.: Sage Publications, 203–20.

JUDSON, H.F., 1974
Heroin addiction in Britain.
New York: Harcourt Brace Jovanovich, 3–62.

MCAULIFFE, W.E., AND GORDON, R.A., 1974
A test of Lindsmith's theory of addiction: the frequency of euphoria among long-term addicts.
Amer. J. Sociol., **79,** 795–840.

MORGAN, H.W., (ED.), 1974
Yesterday's addicts: American society and drug abuse 1865–1920.
Norman: Univ. of Oklahoma Press, 3–34.

CONNELL, P.H., AND DORN, N., (EDS.), 1975
Cannabis and man: psychological and clinical aspects and patterns of use.
Edinburgh: Churchill Livingstone.

DEFLEUR, L.B., 1975
Biasing influences on drug arrest records: implications for deviance research.
Amer. Sociol. Rev., **40,** 88–103.

DUNCAN, D.F., 1975
Marijuana and heroin: a study of initiation of drug use by heroin addicts.
Brit. J. Addict., **70,** 192–7.

GRUPP, S.E., AND BRIDGES, C.K., 1975
Criminal record characteristics of California and Illinois adult marijuana arrestees.
Aust. & N.Z. J. Criminol., **8,** 25–35.

JOHNSON, B.D., 1975
Interpreting official British statistics on addiction.
Internat. J. Addict., **10,** 557–87,
and in *Bulletin on Narcotics*, **27**(1), 49–66.

KAPLAN, J., 1975
A primer on heroin.
Stanford Law Rev., **27,** 801–26.

MOTT, J., 1975
The criminal histories of male non-medical opiate users in the United Kingdom.
Bulletin on Narcotics, **27**(4), 41–8.

MOTT, J., 1975
Drug misuse and crime, in *The importance of narcotics in relation to criminality.*
Collected Studies in Criminological Research, **13,**
Strasbourg, 67–98.

ORCUTT, J.D., 1975
Deviance as a situated phenomenon: variations in the social interpretation of marijuana and alcohol use.
Social Problems, **22,** 346–56.

PLANT, M.A., 1975
Drugtakers in an English town
London: Tavistock.

STEPHENS, R.C., AND ELLIS, R.D., 1975
Narcotic addicts and crime: analysis of recent trends.
Criminol., **12,** 474–88.

TEFF, H., 1975
Drugs, society and the law.
Farnborough, Hants.: Saxon House, 47–73, 199–204.

MOTT, J., 1976
The epidemiology of self-reported drug misuse in the United Kingdom.
Bulletin on Narcotics, **28**(1), 43–54.

4 Drug abuse

(b) Legal and treatment aspects

GOLDENBERG, I.I., AND KEATINGE, E., 1973
Businessmen and therapists: prejudices against employment, in L.R.S. Simmons and M.B. Gold (eds.), *Discrimination and the addict: notes toward a general theory of addict rehabilitation.* International Yearbook of Drug Addiction and Society, **1**,
Beverly Hills, Calif.: Sage Publications, 123–46.

UNITED NATIONS, 1973
Expert group on drugs in modern society: community reactions to drug use by young people.
New York.

CHAMBERS, C.D., AND INCIARDI, J.A., 1974
Forecasts for the future: where we are and where we are going, in J.A. Inciardi and C.D. Chambers (eds.), *Drugs and the criminal justice system.*
Sage Criminal Justice System Annuals, **2**,
Beverly Hills, Calif.: Sage Publications, 221–30.

COATES, R.B., AND MILLER, A.D., 1974
Patrolmen and addicts: a study of police perception and police citizen interaction.
J. Police Sci. & Admin., **2**, 308–21.

CRIME AND DELINQUENCY, 1974
Drug addiction: a medical, not a law enforcement, problem. A policy statement.
Board of Directors, National Council on Crime and Delinquency, **20**, 4–9.

GALLIHER, J.F., MCCARTNEY, J.L., AND BAUM, B.E., 1974
Nebraska's marijuana law: a case of unexpected legislative innovation.
Law & Soc. Rev., **8**, 441–55.

GLASER, D., 1974
Interlocking dualities in drug use, drug control, and crime, in J.A. Inciardi and C.D. Chambers (eds.), *Drugs and the criminal justice system.*
Sage Criminal Justice System Annuals, **2**,
Beverly Hills, Calif.: Sage Publications, 39–56.

GLATT, M.M., 1974
Drugs, society and man: a guide to addiction and its treatment.
Lancaster, England: Medical & Technical Publ. Co., Ltd., 217–318.

JUDSON, H.F., 1974
Heroin addiction in Britain.
New York: Harcourt Brace Jovanovich, 63–164.

KING, R., 1974
"The American system": legal sanctions to repress drug abuse, in J. A. Inciardi and C.D. Chambers (eds.), *Drugs and the criminal justice system.*
Sage Criminal Justice System Annuals **2**,
Beverly Hills, Calif.: Sage Publication, 17–37.

MCGLOTHLIN, W.H., AND TUBBUSH, V.C., 1974
Costs, benefits, and potential for alternative approaches to opiate addiction control, in J.A. Inciardi and C.D. Chambers (eds.), *Drugs and the criminal justice system.*
Sage Criminal Justice System Annuals, **2**,
Beverly Hills, Calif.: Sage Publications, 77–124.

NEW YORK UNIVERSITY LAW REVIEW, 1974
Employment discrimination against rehabilitated drug addicts.
49, 67–86.

PETERSEN, D.M., 1974
Some reflections on compulsory treatment of addiction, in J.A. Inciardi and C.D. Chambers (eds.), *Drugs and the criminal justice system.*
Sage Criminal Justice System Annuals, **2,** Beverly Hills, Calif.: Sage Publications, 143–69

SIMMONS, L.R.S., AND SAID, A.A., (EDS.), 1974
Drugs, politics, and diplomacy: the international connection.
Beverly Hills, Calif.: Sage Publications.

WALD, P.M., 1974
Alcohol, drugs and criminal responsibility.
Georgetown Law J., **63,** 69–86.

WILMARTH, S.S., AND GOLDSTEIN, A., 1974
Therapeutic effectiveness of methadone maintenance programs in the management of drug dependence of morphine type in the U.S.A.
Geneva: World Health Organization.

ZAHN, M.A., AND WILSON, R.A., 1974
Who do they trust?: teenagers' evaluations of drugs information sources, in T.P. Thornberry and E. Sagarin (eds.), *Images of crime: offenders and victims.*
New York: Praeger, 935–46.

BAILEY, W.C., 1975
Addicts on parole: short-term and long-term prognosis.
Internat., J. Addict., **10,** 417–31.

BRUUN, K., PAN, L., AND REXED, I., 1975
The gentlemen's club: international control of drugs and alcohol.
Univ. of Chicago Press.

CORNELL LAW REVIEW, 1975
Drug abuse, law abuse and the eighth amendment: New York's 1973 drug legislation and the prohibition against cruel and unusual punishment.
60, 638–69.

FINGARETTE, H., 1975
Addiction and criminal responsibility.
Yale Law J., **84,** 413–44.

GOLDFARB, R., 1975
Jails: the ultimate ghetto.
New York: Anchor Press/Doubleday, 113–92.

HOTCHEN, J.S., 1975
Drug misuse and the law: the regulations.
London: Macmillan-Winthrop.

KAPLAN, J., 1975
A primer on heroin.
Stanford Law Rev., **27,** 801–26.

MCCABE, O.L., KURLAND, A.A., AND SULLIVAN, D., 1975
Paroled narcotic addicts in a verified abstinence program: results of a five-year study.
Internat. J. Addict., **10,** 211–28.

MELOTTE, C., 1975
A rehabilitation hostel for drug users: one year's admissions.
Brit. J. Criminol., **15,** 376–85.

SANDERS, C.R., 1975
Caught in the con game: the young, white drug user's contact with the legal system.
Law & Soc. Rev., **9,** 197–217.

SZASZ, T., 1975
Ceremonial chemistry: the ritual prosecution of drugs, addicts and pushers.
London: Routledge & Kegan Paul.

TEFF, H., 1975
Drugs, society and the law.
Farnborough, Hants.: Saxon House, 1–46, 75–197

UNIVERSITY OF CHICAGO LAW REVIEW, 1975
The rights of prisoners to medical care and the implications for drug dependent prisoners and pre-trial detainees.
42, 705–32.

BERNTSEN, K., 1976
Treatment of drug addicts: a six years' experiment.
Bulletin on Narcotics, **28**(1), 9–24.

GRAHAM, J. M., 1976
Amphetamine politics on Capitol Hill, in W.J. Chambliss and M. Mankoff (eds.), *Whose law? What order?: a conflict approach to criminology.*
New York: John Wiley & Sons, 107–22.

5 Drunkenness

(a) Sources, forms and incidence

MALIKIN, D., 1973
Social disability: alcoholism, drug addiction, crime and social disadvantage.
London: Univ. of London Press, 8–30, 40–65.

DAMER, S., 1974
Wine alley: the sociology of a dreadful enclosure.
Sociol. Rev., **22**, 221–48.

GLATT, M.M., 1974
Drugs, society and man: a guide to addiction and its treatment.
Lancaster, England: Medical & Technical Publ. Co., 47–93.

PITTMAN, D.J., 1974
Drugs, addiction and crime, in D. Glaser (ed.), *Handbook of criminology.*
Chicago: Rand McNally, 217–32.

ORCUTT, J.D., 1975
Deviance as a situated phenomenon: variations in the social interpretation of marijuana and alcohol use.
Social Problems, **22**, 346–56.

5 Drunkenness

(b) *Legal and treatment aspects*

GUSFIELD, J.R., 1962
Symbolic crusade: status, politics and the American temperance movement
Urbana: Univ. Illinois Press.

BLUMBERG, L., SHIPLEY, T.E., JR., AND SHANDLER, I.W., 1973
Skid row and its alternatives.
Philadelphia: Temple Univ. Press.

GLATT, M.M., 1974
Drugs, society and man: a guide to addiction and its treatment.
Lancaster, England: Medical & Technical Publ. Co., 217–318.

PITTMAN, D.J., 1974
Decriminalization of the public drunkenness offense: an internaional overview, in S.F. Sylvester, Jr., and E. Sagarin (eds.), *Politics and crime.*
New York: Praeger, 127–36.

WALD, P.M., 1974
Alcohol, drugs and criminal responsibility.
Georgetown Law J., **63**, 69–86.

BRUUN, K., PAN, L., AND REXED, I., 1975
The gentlemen's club: international control of drugs and alcohol.
Univ. of Chicago Press, 165–80.

GOLDFARB, R., 1975
Jails: the ultimate ghetto.
New York: Anchor Press/Doubleday, 193–285.

ROSS, H.L., 1975
The Scandinavian myth: the effectiveness of drinking-and-driving legislation in Sweden and Norway.
J. Legal Studies, **4**, 285–310.

WILLIAMS, A.F., RICH, R.F., ZADOR, P.L., AND ROBERTSON, L.S., 1975
The legal minimum drinking age and fatal motor vehicle crashes.
J. Legal Studies, **4**, 219–39.

6 White collar crime

(*a*) *Empirical studies*

MYRDAL, G., 1968
Asian drama: an inquiry into the poverty of nations.
Harmondsworth; Penguin Books, **2**, 937–58.

GEIS, G., 1974
Avocational crime, in D. Glaser (ed.), *Handbook of criminology.*
Chicago: Rand McNally, 273–98.

PEPINSKY, H.E., 1974
From white collar crime to exploitation: redefinition of a field.
J. Crim. Law & Criminol., **65**, 225–53.

6 White collar crime

(*b*) *The concept challenged*

ROBIN, G.D., 1974
White-collar crime and employee theft.
Crime & Delinq., **20**, 251–62.

SHOEMAKER, D.J., AND SOUTH, D.R., 1974
White-collar crime, in C.D. Bryant (ed.), *Deviant behavior: occupational and organizational bases.*
Chicago: Rand McNally, 189–200.

BRILOFF, A., 1975
"We often paint fakes" (Sypmosium on accounting and the federal securities laws).
Vanderbilt Law Rev., **28**, 165–200.

REED, J.P., AND REED, R.S., 1975
"Doctor, lawyer, Indian chief": old rhymes and new on white collar crime.
Int. J. Criminol. & Penol., **3**, 279–93.

6 White collar crime

(*c*) *Attempts at control*

BREIT, W., AND ELZINGA, K.G., 1974
The instruments of antitrust enforcement.
Emory Law J., **12**, 943–61.

FINCKENAUER, J.O., 1974
Theory and practice in sentencing the political criminal: a comment.
Crim. Law Bull., **10**, 737–48.

Hare, D.M., 1974
The need for new anti-corruption laws in local government.
Public Law, 1974, 146–74.

Rubin, S., 1974
Rethinking state antitrust enforcement.
Univ. Florida Law Rev., **26,** 653–757.

Briloff, A., 1975
"We often paint fakes" (Symposium on accounting and the federal securities laws).
Vanderbilt Law Rev., **28,** 165–200.

Kauper, T.E., 1975
Department of justice: antitrust perspective (in a symposium on antitrust in times of economic, technological and sociological crisis).
Univ. Pittsburgh Law Rev., **36,** 667–75.

Pečar, J., 1975
White collar crime and social control.
Int. J. Criminol. & Penol., **3,** 183–99.

Thomforde, F.H., Jr., 1975
Patterns of disparity in SEC administrative sanctioning practice.
Tennessee Law Rev., **42,** 465–525

Vaughan, D., and Carlo, G., 1975
The appliance repairman: a study of victim-responsiveness and fraud.
J. Res. Crime & Delinq., **12,** 153–61.

7 Abortion: criminological and legal aspects: a preliminary list

[*See also Section 6*(1) *on scope of penal sanctions.*]

Hindell, K., and Simms, M., 1971
Abortion law reformed.
London: Peter Owen.

Journal of Family Law, 1973–74
A proposed statute for implementing the abortion decisions.
13, 332–65.

Delgado, R., and Keyes, J.D., 1974
Parental preferences and selective abortion: a commentary on Roe v. Wade, Doe v. Bolton, and the shape of things to come.
Washington Univ. Law Quart., 1974, 203–26.

Dellapenna, J.W., 1974
Nor piety nor wit: the Supreme Court on abortion.
Columbia Human Rights Law Rev., **6,** 379–413.

Friedman, J.M., 1974
Legal implications of amniocentesis.
Univ. Pennsylvania Law Rev., **123,** 92–156.

Journal of Urban Law, 1974
The case of abortion.
52, 277–338.

Lee, L.T., and Paxman, J.M., 1974
Pregnancy and abortion in adolescence: a comparative legal survey and proposals for reform.
Columbia Human Rights Law Rev., **6,** 307–55.

Sarvis, B., and Rodman, H., 1974
The abortion controversy.
New York: Columbia Univ. Press, 2nd ed.

Vieira, N., 1974
Roe and Doe: substantive due process and the right to abortion.
Hastings Law J., **25,** 867–79.

Destro, R.A., 1975
Abortion and the constitution: the need for a life-protective amendment.
Calif. Law Rev., **63,** 1250–1351.

Cavadino, P., 1976
Illegal abortions and the Abortion Act 1967.
Brit. J. Criminol., **16,** 63–7.

8 Homosexuality: criminological and legal aspects: a preliminary list

[*See also Section 6*(1) *on scope of penal sanctions; Section 11*(1) *for references on homosexuality in penal institutions.*]

UNITED KINGDOM, 1957
Report of the committee on homosexual offences and prostitution.
(Chairman, Sir John Wolfenden).
London: Cmnd. 247, 7–77.

WESTWOOD, G., 1960
A minority: a report on the life of the male homosexual in Britain.
London: Longmans.

HOOKER, E., 1965
Male homosexuals and their 'worlds', in J. Marmor (ed.), *Sexual inversion: the multiple roots of homosexuality.*
New York: Basic Books, 83–107.

SCHOFIELD, M., 1965
Sociological aspects of homosexuality: a comparative study of three types of homosexuals.
London: Longmans.

SZASZ, T., 1965
Legal and moral aspects of homosexuality, in J. Marmor (ed.), *Sexual inversion: the multiple roots of homosexuality.*
New York: Basic Books, 124–39.

GINSBURG, K.N., 1967
The 'meat rack': a study of male prostitution.
Amer. J. Psychotherapy, **21**, 170–85.

HOFFMAN, M., 1968
The gay world.
New York: Basic Books, 43–63, 79–99.

KARLEN, A., 1971
Sexuality and homosexuality.
New York: W.W. Norton.

WILLIAMS, C.J., AND WEINBERG, M.S., 1971
Homosexuals in the military: a study of less than honorable discharge.
New York: Harper & Row.

ALBANY LAW REVIEW, 1973
Homosexuality and the law—a right to be different.
38, 84–104.

AMERICAN JOURNAL OF PSYCHIATRY, 1973
A symposium. Should homosexuality be in the APA nomenclature?
130, 1207–1216.

HARRIS, B., 1973
The dilly boys.
London: Groom Helm.

HEYDON, J.D., 1973
The problem of entrapment.
Camb. Law J., **32**, 268–86.

SAGHIR, M.T., AND ROBINS, E., 1973
Male and female homosexuality: a comprehensive investigation.
Baltimore: Williams & Wilkins.

AKERS, R.L., HAYNER, N.S., AND GRUNINGER, W., 1974
Homosexual and drug behavior in prison: a test of the functional and importation models of the inmate system.
Social Problems, **21**, 410–22.

BANCROFT, J., 1974
Deviant sexual behaviour: modification and assessment.
London: Oxford Univ. Press, 52–156, 206–26.

GAGNON, J.H., 1974
Sexual conduct and crime, in D. Glaser (ed.), *Handbook of criminology.*
Chicago: Rand McNally, 254–59.

GREEN, R., 1974
Sexual identity conflict.
London: Duckworth.

GREY, A., 1974
Homosexuality: some social and legal aspects, in J.A. Loraine (ed.), *Understanding homosexuality: its biological and psychological bases.*
Lancaster, England: Medical & Technical Publ. Co., 141–57.

MICHIGAN LAW REVIEW, 1974
The constitutionality of laws forbidding private homosexual conduct.
72, 1613–37.

VIANO, E.C., 1974
Sexual deviance and law enforcement: dilemmas of police policy regarding victimless crimes of sexual deviation, in R.L. Akers and E. Sagarin (eds.), *Crime prevention and social control.*
New York: Praeger, 107–17.

WEISS, C., AND FRIAR, D.J., 1974
Terror in the prison: homosexual rape and why society condones it.
New York: Bobbs Merrill.

WILLIAMS, V.L., AND FISH, M., 1974
Convicts, codes and contraband: the prison life of men and women.
Cambridge, Mass.: Ballinger, 58–71, 101–20.

DAVIES, C., 1975
Permissive Britain.
London: Pitman, 93–139.

NATIONAL COUNCIL FOR CIVIL LIBERTIES, 1975
Homosexuality and the teaching profession.
London: N.C.C.L. Report No. 8.

SAGARIN, E., AND MACNAMARA, D.E.J., 1975
The homosexual as a crime victim.
Int. J. Criminal & Penol., **3,** 13–25.

STURGESS, B., 1975
No offence—the case for homosexual equality at law.
London: Campaign for Homosexual Equality, Scottish Minorities Group and Union for Sexual Freedom in Ireland.

WILLICK, D.H., GEHLKER, G., AND WATTS, A.McF., 1975
Social class as a factor affecting judicial disposition: defendants charged with criminal homosexual acts.
Criminol., **13,** 13–25.

WOLFE, R.W., AND MARINO, D.R., 1975
A program of behavior treatment for incarcerated pedophiles.
Amer. Crim. Law Rev., **13,** 69–83.

9 Pornography: criminological and legal aspects: a preliminary list

[*See also Section 6(1) on scope of penal sanctions.*]

CANADA, 1973
Criminal law: obscenity, A study paper prepared for the prohibited and regulated conduct project of the Law Reform Commission of Canada.
Ottowa: Information Canada.

ALBANY LAW REVIEW, 1974
Obscenity: a step forward by a step back?
38, 764–97.

BURNETT, A.L., 1974
Obscenity: search and seizure and the first amendment.
Denver Law J., **51,** 41–74.

HARDY, J., 1974
Miller v. California and *Paris Adult Theatre I v. Staton*: the obscenity doctrine reformulated.
Columbia Human Rights Law Rev., **6,** 219–37.

HUNSAKER, D.M., 1974
The 1973 obscenity-pornography decisions: analysis, impact and legislative alternatives.
San Diego Law Rev., **11,** 906–56.

MCGAFFEY, R., 1974
A realistic look at expert witnesses in obscenity cases.
Northwestern Law Rev., **69,** 218–32.

NEEF, M., AND NAGEL, S., 1974
Judicial behavior in pornography cases.
J. Urban Law, **52,** 1–23.

RICHARDS, D.A.J., 1974
Free speech and obscenity law: toward a moral theory of the first amendment.
Univ. Penn. Law Rev., **123,** 45–91.

HARVARD LAW REVIEW, 1975
Community standards, class actions, and obscenity under Miller v. California.
88, 1838–74.

KASSNER, H.S., 1975
Obscenity leads to perversion.
New York Law Forum, **20,** 551–68.

LARSEN, O.N., 1975
The commission on obscenity and pornography: from function and failure, in M. Komarovsky (ed.), *Sociology and public policy: the case of Presidential Commissions.* New York: Elsevier, 9–41.

4 Violence against the person

1 Historical, cultural and biological influences

[*See also Section 5 for references on civil disorder and lawlessness.*]

BRITISH BROADCASTING CORPORATION, 1972
Violence on television: programme content and viewer perception.
A BBC audience research department report.
London.

DILLON, W.S., 1972
Anthropological perspectives on violence, in G. Usdin (ed.), *Perspectives on violence.*
New York: Brunner/Mazel, 71–107.

UNITED STATES OF AMERICA, 1972
Television and growing up: the impact of televised violence.
Report to the Surgeon General United States Public Health Service. From the Surgeon General's Scientific Advisory Committee on Television and Social Behavior.
Supporting technical reports on *Television and Social Behavior*, Vol. 1. Media content and control. Vol. 2. Television and social learning. Vol. 3. Television and adolescent aggressiveness. Vol. 4. Television in day-to-day life: patterns of use. Vol. 5. Television's effects: further explorations.
Washington, D.C.

FROMM, E., 1973
The anatomy of human destructiveness.
London: Jonathan Cape.

BOYDELL, C.L., 1974
Public opinion toward legal sanctions for crimes of violence.
J. Crim. Law & Criminol., **65,** 113–6.

ERLANGER, H.S., 1974
The empirical status of the subculture of violence thesis.
Social Problems, **22,** 280–92.

LOFTIN, C., AND HILL, R.H., 1974
Regional subculture and homicide: an examination of the Gastil-Hackney thesis.
Amer. Sociol. Rev., **39,** 714–24.

STANFORD LAW REVIEW, 1974
The regulation of televised violence.
26, 1291–325.

VAN DEN BERGHE, P.L., 1974
Bringing beasts back in: toward a biosocial theory of aggression.
Amer. Sociol. Rev., **39,** 777–88.

BROWN, R.M., 1975
Strain of violence: historical studies of American violence and vigilantism.
New York: Oxford Univ. Press.

GOLDSTEIN, J.H., 1975
Aggression and crimes of violence.
New York: Oxford Univ. Press.

JAYEWARDENE, C.H., 1975
Violence among the Eskimos.
Can. J. of Criminol. & Corrections, **17,** 307–14.

LANDAU, S.F., 1975
Pathologies among homicide offenders: some cultural profiles. *Brit. J. Criminol.*, **15,** 157–66.

MAGURA, S., 1975
Is there a sub-culture of violence?
Comment on Ball-Rokeach (A.S.R. **38,** 736–49), and rejoinder by S.J. Ball-Rokeach.
Amer. Sociol. Rev., **40,** 831–8.

SHORT, J.F., JR., 1975
The national commission on the causes and prevention of violence: reflections on the contributions of sociology and sociologists,

in M. Komarovsky (ed.), *Sociology and public policy: the case of presidential commissions.*
New York: Elsevier, 61–91.

SMITH, S.M., 1975
The battered child syndrome.
London: Butterworths, 3–20.

2 Individual acts

BRITISH BROADCASTING CORPORATION, 1972
Violence on television: programme content and viewer perception.
A BBC audience research department report.
London.

HAWKINS, G.J., (ED.). 1972
Armed robbery: proceedings of the Institute of Criminology seminar No. 2.
Sydney: Univ. of Sydney.

MENZIES, E.S., 1972
The effects of repeated exposure to televised violence upon attitudes towards violence among youthful offenders.
FCI research reports, Vol. 4, No. 5.
Tallahassee, Florida: Federal Correctional Institution.

PALMER, S., 1972
The violent society.
New Haven, Conn.: College & Univ. Press, 13–90.

CURTIS, L.A., 1973
Criminal violence: inquiries into national patterns and behavior.
Ann Arbor, Mich.: Univ. Microfilms.

JOURNAL OF URBAN LAW, 1973
Shooting to kill the handgun: time to martyr another American "hero."
51, 491–542.

AGOPIAN, M.W., CHAPPELL, D., AND GEIS, G., 1974
Interracial rape in a North American city: an analysis of 63 cases, in T.P. Thornberry and E. Sagarin (eds.), *Images of crime: offenders and victims.*
New York: Praeger, 91–101.

BLOM-COOPER, L., 1974
Criminal homicide in contemporary Britain.
Bedford College, London: Mimeo.

ELLIS, D., GRASMICK, H.G., AND GILMAN, B., 1974
Violence in prisons: a sociological analysis.
Amer. J. Sociol., **80,** 16–43.

ERSKINE, H., 1974
The polls: control of crime and violence.
Public Opinion Quart., **38,** 490–502.

ERSKINE, H., 1974
The polls: politics and law and order.
Public Opinion Quart., **38,** 623–34.

FERRACUTI, F., AND NEWMAN, G., 1974
Assaultive offenses in D. Glaser (ed.), *Handbook of criminology.*
Chicago: Rand McNally, 175–207.

GAGNON, J.H., 1974
Sexual conduct and crime, in D. Glaser (ed.), *Handbook of criminology.*
Chicago: Rand McNally, 253–72.

GLASER, D., AND ZEIGLER, M., 1974
Use of the death penalty v. outrage at murder.
Crime & Delinq., **20,** 333–8.

GREENBERG, B.S., 1974
British children and televised violence.
Public Opinion Quart. **38,** 531–47.

HEPWORTH, M., AND TURNER, B.S., 1974
Confessing to murder: critical notes on the sociology of motivation.
Brit. J. Law & Soc., **1,** 31–49.

LANDAU, S.F., DRAPKIN, I., AND ARAD, S., 1974
Homicide victims and offenders: an Israeli study.
J. Crim. Law & Criminol., **65,** 390–6.

MINTZ, B., 1974
Forcible rape: causes and participants, (review of M. Amir, "Patterns of forcible rape").
Stanford Law Rev., **26,** 981–8.

MUSHANGA, T.M., 1974
Criminal homicide in Uganda: a sociological study of violent deaths in Ankole, Kigezi and Toro districts of Western Uganda.
Kampala: East African Literature Bureau.

PLOTKIN, R., 1974
Surviving justice: prisoners' rights to be free from physical assault.
Cleveland State Law Rev., **23,** 387–422.

ROSENBLATT, E., AND GREENLAND, C., 1974
Female crimes of violence.
Can. J. Criminol. & Corrections, **16,** 173–80.

SMITH, S.M., HANSON, R., AND NOBLE, S., 1974
Social aspects of the battered baby syndrome.
Brit. J. Psychiat., **125,** 568–82.

SUSSMAN, A., 1974
Reporting child abuse: a review of the literature.
Family Law Court., **8,** 245–313.

TAKAGI, P., 1974
A garrison state in "democratic society."
Crime & Social Justice, **1,** 27–33.

VINSON, T., 1974
Homicides and serious assaults in New South Wales.
Anglo-American Law Rev., **3,** 29–36.

VIRKKUNEN, M., 1974
Alcohol as a factor precipitating aggression and conflict behaviour leading to homicide.
Br. J. Addict., **69,** 149–54.

WEISS, J.A., 1974
A reply to advocates of gun-control law.
J. Urban Law, **52,** 577–89.

BANKS, C., AND SAPSFORD, R.J., 1975
Homicide, in *Homicide, control and authority in institution: uniform model for individual dossiers in clinical criminology.*
4th Int. Seminar in Comp. Clinical Criminol.
Montreal: Univ. of Montreal, 50–78.

BARTHOLOMEW, A.A., MILTE, K.L., AND GALBALLY, F., 1975
Sexual murder: psychopathology and psychiatric jurisprudential considerations.
Aust. & N.Z. J. Criminol., **8,** 143–52.

BIDNA, H., 1975
Effects of increased security on prison violence.
J. Crim. Justice, **3,** 33–45.

BROWNMILLER, S., 1975
Against our will: men, women and rape.
London: Secker & Warburg.

COHEN, M.L., GAROFALO, R., BOUCHER, R., AND SEGHORN, T., 1975
The psychology of rapists, in S.A. Pasternack (ed.), *Violence and victims.*
New York: Spectrum, 113–40.

DEL OLMO, R., 1975
Limitations for the prevention of violence: the Latin American reality and its criminological theory.
Crime & Social Justice, **3,** 21–9.

DIAMOND, B.L., 1975
Murder and the death penalty: a case report.
Amer. J. Orthopsychiat., **45,** 712–22.

GAYFORD, J., 1975
Wife battering: a preliminary survey of 100 cases.
Brit. Med. J., **1,** 194–97.

GIBSON, E., 1975
Homicide in England and Wales 1967–1971.
London: Home Office Research Studies, **31.**

HARTNAGEL, T.F., TEEVEN, J.J., JR., AND MCINTYRE, J.J., 1975
Television violence and violent behavior.
Social Forces, **54,** 341–51.

HURT, M., 1975
Child abuse and neglect: a report on the status of the research.
Washington, D.C.: U.S. Dept. of Health, Education and Welfare.

INDEPENDENT BROADCASTING AUTHORITY, 1975
The portrayal of violence on television.
Second Interim Report of Working Party.
London.

KOBLER, A.L., 1975
Figures (and perhaps some facts) on police killing of civilians in the United States, 1965–1969.
J. Social Issues, **31**(1), 185–91.

KOBLER, A.L., 1975
Police homicide in a democracy.
J. Social Issues, **31**(1), 163–84.

LION, J.R., 1975
Developing a violence clinic, in S.A. Pasternack (ed.), *Violence and victims.*
New York: Spectrum, 71–88.

MICHALOWSKI, R.J., JR., 1975
Violence on the road: the crime of vehicular homicide.
J. Res. Crime & Delinq., **12**, 30–43.

SMITH, S.M., 1975
The battered child syndrome.
London: Butterworths.

STURGESS, J., 1975
Non-accidental injury to children under the age of 17. London: *Home Office Res. Unit Bull.*, **2**, 36–8.

UNITED KINGDOM, 1975
Report of the advisory group on the law of rape.
London: Cmnd. 6352.

UNITED KINGDOM, 1975
Report of the Select Committee on violence in marriage.
Vol. 2. *Report, Minutes of Evidence and Appendices.*
London.

VIRKKUNEN, M., 1975
Victim-precipitated pedophilia offences.
Brit. J. Criminol., **15**, 175–80.

WISCONSIN LAW REVIEW, 1975
Violence in professional sports.
1975, 771–90.

ZIMRING, F.E., 1975
Firearms and federal law: the gun control act of 1968.
J. Legal Studies, **4**, 133–98.

BAILEY, W.C., 1976
Use of the death penalty v. outrage at murder: some additional evidence and considerations.
Crime & Delinq., **22**, 31–9.

GLASER, D., 1976
A response to Bailey: more evidence on capital punishment as correlate of tolerance for murder.
Crime & Delinq., **22**, 40–3.

GUNN, J., AND GRISTWOOD, J., 1976
Twenty-seven robbers.
Brit. J. Criminol., **16**, 56–62.

MANN, F., FRIEDMAN, C.J., AND FRIEDMAN, A.S., 1976
Characteristics of self-reported violent offenders versus court identified violent offenders.
Int. J. Criminol. & Penol., **4**, 69–87.

5 Civil disorders and lawlessness

1 Their background and manifestations

PALMER, S., 1972
The violent society.
New Haven, Conn.: College & Univ. Press, 151–74.

CRAMER, R., 1974
Comment on M. Betz, "Riots and welfare: are they related?" and reply by Betz.
Social Problems, **22**, 304–7, 307–10.

DREW, P., 1974
Domestic political violence: some problems of measurement.
Sociol. Rev., **22**, 5–25.

QUINAULT, R., AND STEVENSON, J., (EDS)., 1974
Popular protest and public order: six studies in British history 1790–1920.
London: Allen & Unwin.

STARK, M.A.J., RAINE, W.J., BURBECK, S.L., AND DAVISON, K.K., 1974
Some empirical patterns in a riot process.
Amer. Sociol. Rev., **39**, 865–76.

BOYLE, K., HADDEN, T., AND HILLYARD, P., 1975
Law and state: the case of Northern Ireland.
London: Martin Robertson, 6–36.

DEANE-DRUMMOND, A., 1975
Riot control.
London: Thornton Cox, 7–48, 86–97.

LINEBAUGH, P., 1975
The Tyburn riot against the surgeons, in D. Hay, P. Linebaugh and E.P. Thompson (eds.), *Albion's fatal tree: crime and society in eighteenth-century England.*
London: Allen Lane, 65–117.

MILTE, K., 1975
Terrorism and international order.
Aust. & N.Z. J. Criminol., **8**, 101–11.

2 Their control

[*See also Section 6(4) on uses and abuses of police power.*]

AMNESTY INTERNATIONAL, 1972
Report of an enquiry into allegations of ill-treatment in Northern Ireland.
London: Amnesty International.

PALMER, S., 1972
The violent society.
New Haven, Conn.: College & Univ. Press, 175–95.

BALBUS, I.D., 1973
The dialectics of legal repression: black rebels before the American criminal courts.
New York: Russell Sage Foundation.

VANDALL, F.J., 1973
Riot prevention: police training for the street gathering.
J. Urban Law, **51**, 49–78.

YOUNG, R., AND ADAMS, J., 1974
The case for detention.
London: Bow Group Publications.

BOYLE, K., HADDEN, T., AND HILLYARD, P., 1975
Law and state: the case of Northern Ireland.
London: Martin Robertson, 37–185.

BRITISH INSTITUTE OF HUMAN RIGHTS, THE, 1975
Minimum standards of treatment.
Chichester, Sussex: Barry Rose, 35–86.

CLUTTERBUCK, R., 1975
Living with terrorism.
London: Faber & Faber.

DEANE-DRUMMOND, A., 1975
Riot control.
London: Thornton Cox, 49–85, 98–134.

PYE, A.K., AND LOWELL, C.H., 1975
The criminal process during civil disorders.
Duke Law J., 1975, 581–690.

STREET, H., 1975
The prevention of terrorism (temporary provisions) Act 1974.
Crim. Law Rev., 1975, 192–9.

UNITED KINGDOM, 1975
Report of a committee to consider, in the context of civil liberties and human rights, measures to deal with terrorism in Northern Ireland.
(Chairman, Lord Gardiner).
London: Cmnd. 5847.

6 The police

1 Some historical references

O'Connor, D., 1974
The modern approach to the police function.
Aust. & N.Z. J. Criminol., **7,** 69–86.

Richardson, J.F., 1974
Urban police in the United States.
Port Washington, N.Y.: Kennikat Press.

Keeton, G.W., 1975
Keeping the peace.
Chichester, Sussex: Barry Rose.

Moss, G.L., (ed.), 1975
Police forces in history.
Beverly Hills, Calif.: Sage Publications.

Parks, E.L., 1976
From constabulary to police society: implications for social control, in W.J. Chambliss and M. Mankoff (eds.), *Whose law? What order?: a conflict approach to criminology.*
New York: John Wiley & Sons, 129–47.

2 Organization and role

Jeffries, F., (ed)., 1973
Private policing and security in Canada: a workshop.
Toronto: Centre of Criminology, Univ. of Toronto.

Kelly, R.M., and West, G., 1973
The racial transition of a police force: a profile of white and black policemen in Washington, D.C., in J.R. Snibbe and H.M. Snibbe (eds.), *The urban policeman in transition a psychological and sociological review.*
Springfield, Ill.: C.C. Thomas, 354–81.

Lefkowitz, J., 1973
Attitudes of police toward their job, in J.R. Snibbe and H.M. Snibbe (eds.), *The urban policeman in transition: a psychological and sociological review.*
Springfield, Ill.: C.C. Thomas, 203–32.

Olson, B.T., 1973
Police opinions of work: an exploratory study, in J.R. Snibbe and H.M. Snibbe (eds.), *The urban policeman in transition: a psychological and sociological review.*
Springfield, Ill.: C.C. Thomas, 233–49.

Reese, C.D., 1973
Police academy training and its effects on racial prejudice.
J. Police Sci. & Admin., **1,** 257–68.

Snibbe, H.M., Azen, S.P., Montgomery, H.R., and Marsh, S.H., 1973
Predicting job performance of law enforcement officers: a ten and twenty-years study, in J.R. Snibbe and H.M. Snibbe (eds.), *The urban policeman in transition: a psychological and sociological review.*
Springfield, Ill.: C.C. Thomas, 101–116.

Walther, R.H., McCune, S.D., and Trojanowicz, R.C., 1973
The contrasting occupational cultures of policemen and social workers, in J.R. Snibbe and H.M. Snibbe (eds.), *The urban policeman in transition: a psychological and sociological review.*
Springfield, Ill.: C.C. Thomas, 261–80.

BANTON, M., 1974
Policing a divided society.
Police J., **47,** 304–21.

CARTER, R.L., 1974
Theft in the market.
London: Institute of Economic Affairs.

CLARK, J.P., AND SYKES, R.E., 1974
Some determinants of police organization and practice in a modern industrial democracy in D. Glaser (ed.), *Handbook of criminology.*
Chicago: Rand McNally, 455–94.

COHEN, B., 1974
Police background characteristics and performance: findings, in R.L. Akers and E. Sagarin (eds.), *Crime prevention and social control.*
New York: Preager, 67–76.

FRIEDLANDER, C.P., AND MITCHELL, E., 1974
The police: servants or masters?
London: Hart-Davis, 72–80.

GIFFORD, J.P., 1974
Professionalizing police labor relations: the New York City Police Department's response to unionization.
J. Police Sci. & Admin., **2,** 94–106.

HALPERN, S.C. 1974.
Police employee organization and accountability procedures in three cities: some reflections on police policy-making.
Law & Soc. Rev., **8,** 561–82.

KELLING, G.L., ET AL., 1974
The Kansas City preventive patrol experiment: a summary report.
Washington, D.C.: The police Foundation.

KROES, W.H., MARGOLIS, B.L., AND HURRELL, J.J., 1974
Job stress in policemen.
J. Police Sci. & Admin., **2,** 45–55.

MACNAMARA, D.E.J., AND RIEDEL, M. (EDS.), 1974
Police: perspectives, problems, prospects.
New York: Praeger.

PLEHWE, R., 1974
Police and government: the Commissioner of Police for the Metropolis.
Public Law, 1974, 316–35.

SMITH, D.C., AND OSTROM, E., 1974
The effects of training and education on police attitudes and performance: a preliminary analysis, in H. Jacob (ed.), *The potential for reform of criminal justice.*
Sage Criminal Justice System Annuals, **3,** Beverly Hills, Calif.: Sage Publications, 45–81.

SWIMMER, G., 1974
The relationship of police and crime: some methodological and empirical results.
Criminol., **12,** 293–314.

TIFET, L.L., 1974
The 'Cop Personality' reconsidered.
J. Police Sci. & Admin., **2,** 266–78.

TREGER, H., THOMSON, D., AND JAECK, G.S., 1974
A police-social work team model: some preliminary findings and implications for system change.
Crime & Delinq., **20,** 281–90.

VAN MAANEN, J., 1974
Working the street: a development view of police behavior, in H. Jacob (ed.), *The potential for reform of criminal justice.*
Sage Criminal Justice System Annuals, **3,** Beverly Hills, Calif.: Sage Publications, 83–100.

WEINER, N.L., 1974
The effect of education on police attitudes.
J. Crim. Justice, **2,** 317–28.

GROSMAN, B.A., 1975
Police command: decisions and discretion.
Toronto: Macmillan of Canada, 1–76, 111–32.

LEFKOWITZ, J., 1975
Psychological attributes of policemen: a review of research and opinion.
J. Social Issues, **31,** (1), 3–26.

McCABE, S., 1975
The police and the citizen.
London: *Home Office Res. Unit. Bull.*, **2,** 1–4.

MANCKE, J.B., 1975
Removal, suspension or demotion of a municipal police officer: a review and analysis.
Dickinson Law Rev., **79,** 380–400.

PUNCH, M., 1975
Research and the police, in J. Brown and G. Howes (eds.), *The Police and the community*. Farnborough, Hants.: Saxon House, 83–93.

RAFKY, D.M., 1975
Racial discriminaion in urban police departments.
Crime & Delinq., **21**, 233–42.

TEAHAN, J.E.,
A longitudinal study of attitude shifts among black and white police officers.
J. Social Issues, **31**(1), 47–56.

TOCH, H., GRANT, J.D., AND GALVIN, R.T., 1975
Agents of change: a study in police reform.
New York: John Wiley & Sons.

3 Community relations

CARTE, G.E., 1973
Changes in public attitudes toward the police: a comparison of 1938 and 1971 surveys.
J. Police Sci. & Admin., **1**, 182–200.

CRAWFORD, T.J., 1973
Police overperception of ghetto hostility.
J. Police Sci. & Admin., **1**, 168–74.

EISENBERG, T., 1973
Project pace: an attempt to reduce police community conflict, in J.R. Snibbe and H.M. Snibbe (eds.), *The urban policeman in transition: a psychological and sociological review.*
Springfield, Ill.: C.C. Thomas, 139–67.

RAFKY, D.M., 1973
Police race attitudes and labelling.
J. Police Sci. & Admin., **1**, 65–86.

REESE, C.D., 1973
Police academy training and its effects on racial prejudice.
J. Police Sci. & Admin., **1**, 257–68.

WALLACH, I.A., AND JACKSON, C.C., 1973
Perception of the police in a black community in J.R. Snibbe and H.M. Snibbe (eds.), *The urban policeman in transition: a psychological and sociological review.*
Springfield, Ill.: C.C. Thomas, 382–403.

WILLIAMS, M.E., 1973
The Portsmouth police story: successful blueprint for police-community relations.
New York: Exposition Press, 78–129.

FINK, J., AND SEALY, L.G., 1974
The community and the police-conflict or cooperation?
New York: John Wiley & Sons.

KLYMAN, F.I., AND KRUCKENBERG, J., 1974
A methodology for assessing citizen perceptions of police.
J. Crim. Justice, **2**, 219–33.

WILEY, M.G., AND HUDIK, T.L., 1974
Police-citizen encounters: a field test of exchange theory.
Social Problems, **22**, 119–27.

BELSON, W.A., 1975
The public and the police: an extended summary of the aims, methods and findings of a three part enquiry into the relations between the London public and its metropolitan police force.
London: Harper & Row.

BOGGS, S.L., AND GALLIHER, J.F., 1975
Evaluating the police: a comparison of black street and household respondents.
Social Problems, **22**, 393–406.

CHAPPELL, D., AND MEYER, J.C., JR., 1975
Cross-cultural differences in police attitudes: an exploration in comparative research.
Aust. & N.Z. J. Criminol., **8**, 5–13.

KELLY, R.M., 1975
Generalizations from an OEO experiment in Washington, D.C. (with comment by R. Shellow and reply by R.M. Kelly).
J. Social Issues, **31**(1), 57–98.

WILSON, J.Q., 1975
Thinking about crime.
New York: Basic Books, 81–124.

4 Uses and abuses of power

[*See also Section 1(4) for references on police discretion to prosecute; Section 5(2) on control of civil disorder; Section 14(2) for reference on police records in relation to the status of offenders.*]

AMNESTY INTERNATIONAL, 1972
Report of an enquiry into allegations of ill-treatment in Northern Ireland.
London: Amnesty International.

AMNESTY INTERNATIONAL, 1973
Report on torture.
London: Duckworth.

LEVY, R.J., 1973
A method for identification of the high-risk police applicant, in J.R. Snibbe and H.M. Snibbe (eds.), *The urban policeman in transition: a psychological and sociological review.*
Springfield, Ill.: C.C. Thomas, 25–52.

WILKINS, R., AND CLARK, R., 1973
Search and destroy: a report by the commission of inquiry into the black panthers and the police.
New York: Metropolitan Applied Research Center.

AMSTERDAM, A.G., 1974
Perspective on the fourth amendment.
Minnesota Law Rev., **58,** 349–477.

BEIGEL, H., 1974
The investigation and prosecution of police corruption.
J. Crim. Law & Criminol., **65,** 135–56.

BITTNER, E., 1974
Florence Nightingale in pursuit of Willie Sutton, in H. Jacob (ed.), *The potential for reform of criminal justice.*
Sage Criminal Justice System Annuals, **3,** Beverly Hills, Calif.: Sage Publications, 17–44.

CRIME AND DELINQUENCY, 1974
Official corruption. A position statement. Law Enforcement Council, National Council on Crime and Delinquency.
20, 15–19.

DAVIS, K.C., 1974
An approach to legal control of the police.
Texas Law Rev., **52,** 703–25.

GANDARA, D., 1974
Admissibility of confessions in federal prosecutions: implementation of section 3501 by law enforcement officials and the courts.
Georgetown Law J., **63,** 305–21.

HAGAN, J., 1974
Parameters of criminal prosecution: an application of path analysis to a problem of criminal justice.
J. Crim. Law & Criminol., **65,** 536–44.

HALPERN, S.C., 1974
Police association and department leaders: the politics of co-optation.
Lexington, Mass.: Heath Lexington Books, 1–9, 87–104.

HALPERN, S.C., 1974
Police employee organisations and accountability procedures in three cities: some reflections on police policy-making.
Law & Soc. Rev., **8,** 561–82.

ISRAEL, J.H., 1974
Legislative regulation of searches and seizures: the Michigan proposals.
Michigan Law Rev., **73,** 222–316.

KAPLAN, J., 1974
The limits of the exclusionary rule.
Stanford Law Rev., **26,** 1027–55.

LUNDMAN, R.J., 1974
Routine police arrest practices: a commonweal perspective.
Social Problems, **22,** 127–41.

MACNAMARA, D.E.J., AND RIEDEL, M., (EDS.), 1974
Police: perspectives, problems, prospects.
New York: Praeger.

NAKELL, B., 1974
Search of the person incident to a traffic arrest: a comment on Robinson and Gustafson.
Crim. Law Bull., **10,** 827–41.

NEUBAUER, D.W., 1974.
Confessions in Prairie city: some causes and effects.
J. Crim. Law & Criminol., **65**, 103–12.

NORTHWESTERN UNIVERSITY LAW REVIEW, 1974
On the limitations of empirical evaluations of the exclusionary rule: a critique of the Spiotto research and United States v. Calandon.
69, 740–78.

QUINN, J., 1974
The effect of police rule-making on the scope of fourth amendment rights.
J. Urban Law, **52**, 25–54.

REISS, A.J., JR., 1974
Citizen access to criminal justice.
Brit. J. Law & Soc., **1**, 31–49.

SEVILLA, C.M., 1974
The exclusionary rule and police perjury.
San Diego Law Rev., **11**, 839–79.

SIEGEL, L.J., SULLIVAN, D.C., AND GREENE, J.R., 1974
Decision games applied to police decision making: an exploratory study of information usage.
J. Crim. Justice, **2**, 131–46.

SWAN, L.A., 1974
The politics of identification: a perspective of police accountability.
Crime & Delinq., **20**, 119–28.

TAKAGI, P., 1974
A garrison state in 'democratic society'.
Crime & Social Justice, **1**, 27–33.

WISCONSIN LAW REVIEW, 1974
Police accountability in Wisconsin.
1974, 1131–66.

ZANDER, M., 1974
Are too many professional criminals avoiding conviction?: a study in Britain's two busiest courts.
Modern Law Rev., **37**, 28–61.

AMERICAN LAW INSTITUTE, 1975
A model code of pre-arraignment procedure: complete text and commentary.
Philadelphia: The American Law Institute.

BOX, S. AND RUSSELL, K., 1975
The politics of discreditability: disarming complaints against the police.
Sociol. Rev., **23**, 315–46.

CENTER FOR RESEARCH ON CRIMINAL JUSTICE, 1975
The iron fist and the velvet glove: an analysis of the U.S. police.
Berkeley, Calif.: Center for Research on Criminal Justice.

DEFLEUR, L.B., 1975
Biasing influences on drug arrest records: implications for deviance research.
Amer. Sociol. Rev., **40**, 88–103.

GOLDSTEIN, J., 1975
For Harold Lasswell: some reflections on human dignity, entrapment, informed consent and the plea bargain.
Yale Law J., **84**, 683–703.

GORECKI, J., 1975
Miranda and beyond: the fifth amendment reconsidered.
Univ. Illinois Law Forum, 1975, 295–312.

GROSMAN, B.A., 1975
Police command. Decisons and discretion.
Toronto: Macmillan of Canada, 77–109, 133–48.

HARDING, R.W., 1975
Changing patterns in the use of lethal force by police in Australia.
Aust. & N.Z. J. Criminol., **8**, 125–36.

KOBLER, A.L., 1975
Figures (and perhaps some facts) on police killing of civilians in the United States, 1965–1969.
J. Social Issues, **31**(1), 185–91.

KOBLER, A.L., 1975
Police homicide in a democracy.
J. Social Issues, **31**(1), 163–84.

LEIGH, L.H., 1975
Police powers in England and Wales.
London: Butterworths, 219–37.

LIDSTONE, K.W., 1975
A policeman's duty not to take liberties.
Crim. Law Rev., 1975, 617–28.

POLICE JOURNAL, 1975
Police corruption: psychological and organisational factors.
A symposium.
48, 21–54.

THEIS, W., 1975
'Good faith' as a defense to suits for police deprivations of individual rights.
Minnesota Law Rev., **59,** 991–1026.

UNIVERSITY OF MIAMI LAW REVIEW, 1975
Aspects of police search and seizure without warrant in England and the United States.
29, 491–558.

ROBERTSON, G., 1976
Reluctant Judas: the life and death of the the special branch informer, Kenneth Lennon.
London: Temple Smith, 167–215.

7 Penal sanctions

1 Aims and scope of penal sanctions

KLEINIG, J., 1973
Punishment and desert.
The Hague: Martinus Nijhoff.

MAESTRO, M., 1973
Cesare Beccaria and the origins of penal reform.
Philadelphia: Temple Univ. Press, 3–45, 125–60.

BOSTON UNIVERSITY LAW REVIEW, 1974
The Supreme Judicial Court and the death penalty: the effects of judicial choice on legislative options.
54, 158–85.

ECKHOFF, T., 1974
Justice: its determinants in social interaction.
Rotterdam Univ. Press, 167–200.

GERBER, R.J., 1974.
A death penalty we can live with.
Notre Dame Lawyer, **50,** 251–72.

MIERS, D.R., 1974
Victim participation in criminal behaviour.
Anglo-American Law Rev., **3,** 86–97.

SCHULHOFER, S., 1974
Harm and punishment: a critique of emphasis on the results of conduct in the criminal law.
Univ. Penn. Law Rev., **122,** 1497–607.

SCHUR, E.M., AND BEDAU, H.A., 1974
Victimless crimes: two sides of a controversy.
Englewood Cliffs, N.J.: Prentice-Hall.

STANFORD LAW REVIEW, 1974
Roe and *Paris:* does privacy have a principle?
26, 1161–89.

UNITED KINGDOM, 1974
Working party on vagrancy and street offences: working paper.
London: Home Office.

VIDMAR, N., AND ELLSWORTH, P., 1974
Public opinion and the death penalty.
Stanford Law Rev., **26,** 1245–70.

BANKS, C., MALONEY, E., AND WILLCOCK, H.D., 1975
Public attitudes to crime and the penal system.
Brit. J. Criminol., **15,** 228–40.

BLOCK, M.K., AND LIND, R.C., 1975
Crime and punishment reconsidered.
J. Legal Studies, **4,** 241–7.

BRAZIER, R., 1975
Reform of sexual offences.
Crim. Law Rev., 1975, 421–9.

BUFFALO LAW REVIEW, 1975
The eighth amendment, Beccaria, and the enlightenment: an historical justification for Weems v. United States excessive punishment doctrine.
24, 783–838.

CARD, R., 1975
Sexual relations with minors.
Crim. Law Rev., 1975, 370–80.

CLEVELAND STATE LAW REVIEW, 1975
Rape reform legislation: is it the solution?
24, 463–503.

ERICSON, R.V., 1975
Responsibility, moral relativity, and response ability: some implications of deviance theory for criminal justice.
Univ. Toronto Law J., **25,** 23–41.

GREY, A., 1975
Sexual Law Reform Society, working party report.
Crim. Law Rev., 1975, 323–35.

HARRIS, M.K., 1975
Disquisition on the need for a new model for criminal sanctioning systems.
W. Virginia Law Rev., **77**, 263–326.

LEIGH, L., 1975
Vagrancy, morality and decency.
Crim. Law Rev., 1975, 381–90, 413–20.

MÄKELÄ, K., 1975
The societal tasks of the system of penal law, in H. Bianchi, M. Simondi and I. Taylor (eds.), *Deviance and control in Europe: papers from the European group for the study of deviance and social control.*
London: John Wiley & Sons, 157–74.

NEWMAN, G., 1975
Theories of punishment reconsidered: rationalisations for removal.
Int. J. Criminol. & Penol., **3**, 163–82.

RYAN, H.R.S., 1975
Principles of sentencing and disposition: comment on the working paper of the Law Reform Commission of Canada.
Ottowa Law Rev., **7**, 270–80.

SPITZER, S., 1975
Punishment and social organisation: a study of Durkheim's theory of penal evolution.
Law & Soc. Rev., **9**, 613–35.

STURGESS, B., 1975
No offence: the case for homosexual equality at law.
London: Campaign for Homosexual Equality, Scottish Minorities Group and Union for Sexual Freedom in Ireland.

VAN DEN HAAG, E., 1975
Punishing criminals: concerning a very old and painful question.
New York: Basic Books.

HIRSCH, A. VON, 1976
Doing justice: the choice of punishments.
Report of the Committee for the Study of Incarceration.
New York: Hill & Wang, xxi–94.

KENNEDY, M.C., 1976
Beyond incrimination: some neglected facets of the theory of punishment, in W.J. Chambliss and M. Mankoff (eds.), *Whose law? What order?: a conflict approach to criminology.*
New York: John Wiley & Sons, 34–65.

2 The problem of conflicting values in the implementation of penal sanctions

[*See also Section 12 on new experiments in the treatment of offenders; Section 13 on parole selection and indeterminate sentences; Section 14 for references bearing on the status of prisoners.*]

GAYLIN, W., 1970
In the service of their country: war resisters in prison.
New York: Grosset & Dunlop, 266–318.

BISHOP, N., 1974
Aspects of European penal systems, in L. Blom-Cooper (ed.), *Progress in penal reform.*
Oxford: Clarendon Press, 83–100.

CARGAN, L., AND COATES, M.A., 1974
The indeterminate sentence and judicial bias.
Crime & Delinq., **20**, 145–65.

CONRAD, J.P., 1974
Winners and losers: a perspective on penal change, in L. Blom-Cooper (ed.), *Progress in penal reform.*
Oxford: Clarendon Press, 196–208.

DERSHOWITZ, A.M., 1974
Indeterminate confinement: letting the therapy fit the harm.
Univ. Penn. Law Rev., **123**, 297–339.

HARVARD LAW REVIEW, 1974
Discretion and the constitutionality of the new death penalty statute.
87, 1690–719.

HASTINGS LAW JOJURNAL, 1974
California's cruelty criteria: evaluating sentences after in Re Lynch.
25, 636–56.

HAWKINS, G., 1974
The ideology of imprisonment in L. Blom-Cooper (ed.), *Progress in penal reform.* Oxford: Clarendon Press, 101–15.

IRWIN, J., 1974
Adaption to being corrected: corrections from the convict's perspective, in D. Glaser (ed.), *Handbook of criminology.*
Chicago: Rand McNally, 971–93.

JOURNAL OF URBAN LAW, 1974
Behaviour modification and other legal imbroglios of human experimentation.
52, 155–7.

KLEIN, M.W., 1974
Labeling, deterrence, and recidivism: a study of police dispositions of juvenile offenders.
Social Problems, **22,** 292–303.

MOYA, C.B., AND ACHTENBERG, R., 1974
Behavior modification: legal limitations on methods and goals.
Notre Dame Lawyer, **50,** 230–50.

REDER, M.W., 1974
Citizen rights and the cost of law enforcement.
J. Legal Studies, **3,** 435–55.

SOUTHERN CALIFORNIA LAW REVIEW, 1974
Guilt by physiology: the constitutionality of tests to determine predisposition to violent behavior.
48, 489–507.

STEIN, P., AND SHAND, J., 1974
Legal values in Western Society
Edinburgh: Edinburgh Univ. Press, 59–83.

TITTLE, C.R., 1974
Prisons and rehabilitation: the inevitability of disfavor.
Social Problems, **21,** 385–95.

ALLEN, F.A., 1975
The judicial quest for penal justice: the Warren court and the criminal cases.
Univ. Illinois Law Forum, 1975, 518–42.

ANTTILA, I., 1975
Probation and parole: social control or social service?
Int. J. Criminol. & Penol., **3,** 79–84.

BUFFALO LAW REVIEW, 1975
The eighth amendment, Beccaria, and the enlightenment: an historical justification for the Weems v. United States excessive punishment doctrine.
24, 783–838.

COFFEE, J.C., JR., 1975
The future of sentencing reform: emerging legal issues in the individualisation of justice.
Michigan Law Rev., **73,** 1362–462.

CONRAD, J.P., 1975
We should never have promised a hospital.
Fed. Probation, **39**(4), 3–9.

CORNELL LAW REVIEW, 1975
Drug abuse, law abuse and the eighth amendment: New York's 1973 drug legislation and the prohibition against cruel and unusual punishment.
60, 638–69.

GAYLIN, W., AND BLATTE, H., 1975
Behavior modification in prisons.
Amer. Crim. Law Rev., **13,** 11–35.

GOBERT, J.G., 1975
Psychosurgery, conditioning, and the prisoner's right to refuse 'rehabilitation'.
Virginia Law Rev., **61,** 155–96.

GOLDBERGER, D., 1975
Court challenges to prison behavior modification programs: a case history.
Amer. Crim. Law Rev., **13,** 37–68.

GREENAWALT, K., 1975
Discretion and judicial decision: the elusive quest for the fetters that bind judges.
Columbia Law Rev., **75,** 359–99.

HARRIS, M.K., 1975
Disquisition on the need for a new model for criminal sanctioning systems.
W. Virginia Law Rev., **77,** 263–326.

HOOD, R., 1975
The case against executive control over time in custody: a rejoinder to Professor Walker's criticisms.
Crim. Law Rev., 1975, 545–52.

INDIANA LAW JOURNAL, 1975
Pretrial diversion from the criminal process: some constitutional considerations.
50, 783–807.

LERMAN, P., 1975
Community treatment and social control: a critical analysis of juvenile correctional policy.
Univ. Chicago Press, 78–104, 204–25.

MULLAN, D.J., 1975
Fairness: the new natural justice?
Univ. Toronto Law J., **25,** 281–316.

PARLOUR, R.R., 1975
Behavioral techniques for sociopathic clients.
Fed. Probation, **39**(1), 3–11.

REASONS, C.E., AND KAPLAN, R.L., 1975
Tear down the walls?: some functions of prisons.
Crime & Delinq., **21,** 360–72.

SKINNER, B.F., 1975
The ethics of helping people.
Crim. Law Bull., **11,** 623–36.

SZASZ, T.S., 1975
The control of conduct: authority vs. autonomy.
Crim. Law Bull., **11,** 617–22.

WALKER, N., 1975
Release by executive decision: a defence.
Crim. Law Rev., 1975, 540–4.

WEXLER, D.B., 1975
Behavior modification and other behavior change procedures: the emerging law and the proposed Florida guidelines.
Crim. Law Bull., **11,** 600–16.

WEXLER, S., 1975
Discretion: the unacknowledged side of law.
Univ. Toronto Law J., **25,** 120–82.

BOTTOMS, A.E., AND MCCLEAN, J.D., 1976
Defendants in the criminal process.
London: Routledge & Kegan Paul, 226–42.

PARSLOE, P., 1976
Social work and the justice model.
Brit. J. Social Wk. **6,** 71–89.

3 Problems posed by special categories of offender

(a) *Psychopaths, sexual and dangerous offenders*

DERSHOWITZ, A., 1974
The origins of preventive confinement in Anglo-American law.
Part II, the American experience.
Cincinnati Law Rev., **43,** 781–846.

DIAMOND, B.L., 1974
The psychiatric prediction of dangerousness.
Univ. Penn. Law Rev., **123,** 439–52.

ENNIS, B.J., AND LITWACK, T.R., 1974
Psychiatry and the presumption of expertise: flipping coins in the courtroom.
Calif. Law Rev., **62,** 693–752.

FLEMING, J.G., AND MAXIMOV, B., 1974
The patient or his victim: the therapist's dilemma.
Calif. Law Rev., **62,** 1025–68.

GARNEY, F.L., 1974
The indeterminate sentence at Patuxent.
Crime & Delinq., **21,** 135–43.

JOURNAL OF URBAN LAW, 1974
Behavior modification and other legal imbroglios of human experimentation.
52, 155–75.

MORRIS, N., 1974
The future of imprisonment.
Univ. Chicago Press, 62–73.

PIPERNO, A., 1974
Indefinite commitment in a mental hospital for the criminally insane: two models of administration of mental health.
J. Crim. Law & Criminol., **65,** 520–7.

SHAH, S.A., 1974
Some interactions of law and mental health in the handling of social deviance.

Catholic Univ. Amer. Law Rev., **23,** 674–719.

Southern California Law Review, 1974
Guilt by physiology: the constitutionality of tests to determine predisposition to violent behavior.
48, 489–507.

Steadman, H.J., and Cocozza, J.J., 1974
Careers of the criminally insane: excessive social control of deviance.
Lexington, Mass.: Heath Lexington Books.

Wexler, D.B., 1974
Of rights and reinforcers.
San Diego Law Rev., **11,** 957–71.

Bleechmore, J.F., 1975
Towards a rational theory of criminal responsibility: the psychopathic offender, Part 1.
Melbourne Univ. Law Rev., **10,** 19–46.

Gilman, D., 1975
Sentencing-imprisonment consequences (comment on New York parole report).
Crim. Law Bull., **11,** 318–26.

Gilman, D., 1975
The sanction of imprisonment: for whom, for what, and how.
Crime & Delinq., **21,** 337–47.

Greenberg, D.F., 1975
The incapacitative effects of imprisonment: some estimates.
Law & Soc. Rev., **9,** 541–80.

Kozol, K., 1975
The diagnosis of dangerousness, in S.A. Pasternack (ed.), *Violence and victims.*
New York: Spectrum, 3–13.

Monahan, J., 1975
The prediction of violence, in D. Chappell and J. Monahan (eds.), *Violence and criminal justice.*
Lexington, Mass.: Heath Lexington Books, 15–31.

Monahan, J., and Cummings, L., 1975
Social policy implications of the inability to predict violence.
J. Social Issues, **31**(2), 153–64.

Quinsey, V.L., Warneford, A., Pruesse, M. and Link, N., 1975
Released Oak Ridge patients: a follow-up study of review board discharges.
Brit. J. Criminol., **15,** 264–70.

Rubin, B., 1975
Prediction of dangerousness in mentally ill criminals, in S.A. Pasternack (ed.), *Violence and victims.*
New York: Spectrum, 15–40.

Scottish Home and Health Department, 1975
Crime and the prevention of crime.
A memorandum by the Scottish Council on Crime.
Edinburgh, H.M.S.O., 50–69.

Serber, M., Hiller, C., Keith, C., and Taylor, J., 1975
Behavior modification in maximum security settings: one hospital's experience.
Amer. Crim. Law Rev., **13,** 85–99.

Steadman, H.J., and Braff, J., 1975
Crimes of violence and incompetency diversion.
J. Crim. Law & Criminol., **66,** 73–8.

United Kingdom, 1975
Report of the Committee on Mentally Abnormal Offenders (Butler Report).
London: Cmnd. 6244, 56–100, 112–20, 176–84, 266–85, 291–302.

Canada, 1976
The Criminal process and mental disorder.
Law Reform Commission of Canada, working paper, 14 (1975), in *Can. J. Criminol. & Corrections*, **18**(1).

Monahan, J., and Geis, G., 1976
Controlling "dangerous" people.
Annals Amer. Acad. Pol. & Soc. Sci., **423,** 142–51.

3 Problems posed by special categories of offender

(b) *Treatment of the mentally ill*

ECKERMAN, W.C., 1972
A nationwide survey of mental health and correctional institutions for adult mentally disordered offenders.
Center for Studies in Crime and Delinquency. Rockville, Maryland: National Institute of Mental Health.

JACOBSON, D., CRAVEN, W., AND KUSHNER, S., 1973
A study of police referral of allegedly mentally ill persons to a psychiatric unit, in J.R. Snibbe and H.M. Snibbe (eds.), *The urban policeman in transition: a psychological and sociological review.*
Springfield, Ill.: C.C. Thomas, 533–51.

ANNAS, G.J., AND GLANTZ, L.H., 1974
Psychosurgery: the law's response.
Boston Univ. Law Rev., **54,** 249–67.

BOSTON UNIVERSITY LAW REVIEW, 1974
Kaimowitz v. Department of Mental Health: a right to be free from experimental psychosurgery?
54, 301–39.

BURT, R.A., 1974
Of mad dogs and scientists: the perils of the "criminal-insane."
Univ. Penn. Law Rev., **123,** 258–96.

CATHOLIC UNIVERSITY OF AMERICA LAW REVIEW, 1974
The right against treatment: behavior modification and the involuntarily committed
23, 774–87.

ENNIS, B.J., AND LITWACK, T.R., 1974
Psychiatry and the presumption of expertise: flipping coins in the courtroom.
Calif. Law Rev., **62,** 693–752.

GRAZIA, E. DE., 1974
Diversion from the criminal process: the 'mental health' experiment.
Connecticut Law Rev., **6,** 432–528.

JOURNAL OF URBAN LAW, 1974
Behavior modification and other legal imbroglios of human experimentation.
52, 155–75.

MORRIS, G.H., 1974
Institutionalising the rights of mental patients: committing the legislature.
Calif. Law Rev., **62,** 957–1024.

REISNER, R., AND SEMMEL, H., 1974
Abolishing the insanity defence: a look at the proposed Federal Criminal Code Reform Act in the light of Swedish experience.
Calif. Law Rev., **62,** 753–88.

SCHWITZGEBEL, R.K., 1974
The right to effective mental treatment.
Calif. Law Rev., **62,** 936–56.

SHAH, S.A., 1974
Some interactions of law and mental health in the handling of social deviance.
Catholic Univ. Amer. Law. Rev., **23,** 674–719.

STEADMAN, H.J., AND BRAFF, J., 1974
Effects of incompetency determinations on subsequent criminal processing: implications for due process.
Catholic Univ. Amer. Law Rev., **23,** 754–68.

UNIVERSITY OF CHICAGO LAW REVIEW, 1974
Commitment and release standards and procedure: uniform treatment for the mentally ill.
41, 825–40.

WALES, H.W., 1974
The rise, the fall, and the resurrection of the medical model.
Georgetown Law J., **63,** 87–105.

YALE LAW JOURNAL, 1974
Mental illness: a suspect classification.
83, 1237–70.

AMNESTY INTERNATIONAL, 1975
Prisoners of conscience in the USSR: their treatment and conditions.
London: Amnesty International, 101–44.

FRIEDMAN, P.R., 1975
Legal regulation of applied behavior analysis in mental institutions and prisons.
Arizona Law Rev., **17,** 39–104.
and commentaries by I. Goldiamond, R. Clemons and D.B. Wexler, 105–43.

HARVARD JOURNAL ON LEGISLATION, 1975
Beyond the "cuckoo's nest": proposal for federal regulation of psychosurgery.
12, 610–67.

HOFFMAN, P.B., AND DUNN, R.C., 1975
Beyond *Rouse* and *Wyatt:* an administrative-law model for expanding and implementing the mental patient's right to treatment.
Virgina Law Rev., **61,** 297–339.

LION, J.R., 1975
Developing a violence clinic, in S.A. Pasternack (ed.), *Violence and victims.*
New York: Spectrum, 71–88.

SALUTIN, L., 1975
Psychiatric involvement in the criminal process.
Can. J. Criminol. & Corrections, **17,** 236–49.

UNITED KINGDOM, 1975
Report of the Committee on Mentally Abnormal Offenders (Butler Report).
London: Cmnd. 6244.

YALE LAW JOURNAL, 1975
The *Wyatt* case: implementation of a judicial decree ordering institutional change.
84, 1338–79.

CANADA, 1976
The criminal process and mental disorder.
Law Reform Commission of Canada, Working Paper, 14 (1975) in *Can. J. Criminol. & Corrections,* **18**(1).

JACOB, J., 1976
The right of the mental patient to his psychosis.
Modern Law Rev., **39,** 17–42.

8 Problems of sentencing

1 Plea bargaining

CASPER, J.D., 1972
American criminal justice: the defendant's perspective.
Englewood Cliffs, N.J.: Prentice-Hall, 77–99.

KATZ, L., LITWIN, L., AND BAMBERGER, R., 1972
Justice is the crime: pretrial delay in felony cases.
Cleveland: Press of Case Western Reserve Univ., 193–215.

ARCURI, A.F., 1973
Police perceptions of plea bargaining: a preliminary inquiry.
J. Police Sci. & Admin., **1,** 93–101.

BORMAN, P.D., 1974
The chilled right to appeal from a plea bargain conviction: a due process cure.
Northwestern Univ. Law Rev., **69,** 663–715.

BUFFALO LAW REVIEW, 1974
The plea bargain in historical perspective.
23, 499–527.

DE PAUL LAW REVIEW, 1974
Guilty pleas in Illinois—the enigma of substantial compliance.
24, 42–99.

GEORGETOWN LAW JOURNAL, 1974
Judicial discretion to reject negotiated pleas.
63, 241–55.

HASTINGS LAW JOURNAL, 1974
Convictions of unincluded lesser offenses: informal amendments and plea bargains.
25, 1075–104.

JOURNAL OF CRIMINAL LAW AND CRIMINOLOGY, 1974
Bargaining mishaps—the possibility of collaterally attacking the resultant plea of guilty.
J. Crim. Law & Criminol., **65,** 171–80.

MATHER, L.M., 1974
The outsider in the courtroom: an alternative role for defense, in H. Jacob (ed.), *The potential for reform of criminal justice.*
Sage Criminal Justice System Annuals, **3,**
Beverly Hills, Calif.: Sage Publications, 263–89.

NIMMER, R.T., 1974
Judicial reform: informal processes and competing effects, in H. Jacob (ed.), *The potential for reform of criminal justice.*
Sage Criminal Justice System Annuals, **3.**
Beverly Hills, Calif.: Sage Publications, 207–34.

ALSCHULER, A.W., 1975
The defence attorney's role in plea bargaining.
Yale Law J., **84,** 1179–314.

AMERICAN LAW INSTITUTE, 1975
A model code of pre-arraignment procedure: complete text and reporter's commentary.
Philadelphia: The American Law Institute 608–25.

FINKELSTEIN, M., 1975
A statistical analysis of guilty plea practices in the federal courts.
Harvard Law Rev., **89,** 293–315.

FOGEL, D., 1975
'. . . *We are the living proof* . . .' *The justice model for corrections.*
(Appendix on plea bargaining from 'The Michigan public speaks out on crime.' Market opinion research, April 1975).
Cincinnati: W.H. Anderson Co., 299–300.

GOLDSTEIN, J., 1975
For Harold Lasswell: some reflections on human dignity, entrapment, informed consent and the plea bargain.
Yale Law J., **84,** 683–703.

HEUMANN, M., 1975
A note on plea bargaining and case pressure.
Law & Soc. Rev., **9,** 515–28.

IOWA LAW REVIEW, 1975
The elimination of plea bargaining in Black Hawk County: a cause study.
60, 1053–71.

KUH, R.H., 1975
Plea bargaining: guidelines for the Manhattan District Attorney's office.
Crim. Law Bull., **11,** 48–61.

NOTRE DAME LAWYER, 1975
'Upping the ante' against the defendant who successfully attacks his guilty plea: double jeopardy and due processs implications.
50, 857–79.

BOTTOMS, A.E., AND MCCLEAN, J.D., 1976
Defendants in the criminal process.
London: Routledge & Kegan Paul, 104–34.

2 Sentencing practice

ALTAHR-CEDERBERG, N., AND HAMMOND, W.H., 1974
Study of the extent to which a recommendation on sanction in presentence enquiry is followed by the court when deciding on the case, in *Sentencing*. Report by the sub-committee of the European committee on crime problems.
Strasbourg: Council of Europe, 49–60.

BARBER, R., 1974
Judge and jury attitudes to rape.
Aust. & N.Z. J. Criminol., **7,** 157–72.

BOYDELL, C.L., 1974
Public opinion toward legal sanctions for crimes of violence. *J. Crim. Law & Criminol.*, **65,** 113–6.

BUFFALO LAW REVIEW, 1974
Judicial activity and public attitude: a quantitative study of selective service sentencing in the Vietnam war period.
23, 465–98.

CAPLAN, A., AND LEBLANC, M., 1974
Sophisticated methodology versus good methodology: a methodological critique of 'Sentencing as a Human Process', by John Hogarth.
Can. J. Criminol. & Corrections, **16,** 77–93.

CARGAN, L., AND COATES, M.A., 1974
The indeterminate sentence and judicial bias.
Crime & Delinq., **20,** 145–56.

CARLEN, P., 1974
Remedial routines for the maintenance of control in magistrates' courts.
Brit. J. Law & Soc., **1,** 101–17.

COUNCIL OF EUROPE, 1974
Sentencing. Report by the sub-committee of the European committee on crime problems.
Strasbourg.

ERSKINE, H., 1974
The polls, politics and law and order,
Public Opinion Quart., **38,** 623–34.

GAYLIN, W., 1974
Partial justice: a study of bias in sentencing.
New York: Alfred A. Knopf.

HAGAN, J., 1974
Extra-legal attributes and criminal sentencing: an assessment of a sociological viewpoint.
Law & Soc. Rev., **8,** 357–83.

HAMMOND, W.H., 1974
Statistics relating to sentencing, in *Sentencing*. Report by the sub-committee of the European committee on crime problems.
Strasbourg: Council of Europe, 43–47.

JONES, M., 1974
Justice and journalism: a study of the influence of newspaper reporting upon the administration of justice by magistrates.
Chichester, Sussex: Barry Rose, 133–68.

PERRY, F.G., 1974
Information for the court: a new look at social inquiry reports.
Cambridge: Institute of Criminology, 1–32, 67–103.

ASHWORTH, A.J., 1975
Sentencing in provocation cases.
Crim. Law Rev., 1975, 553–63.

BOSHIER, R., AND RAE, C., 1975
Punishing criminals: a study of the relationship between conservatism and punitiveness.
Aust. & N.Z. J. Criminol., **8**, 37–45.

CARLEN, P., 1975
Magistrates' courts: a game theoretic analysis.
Sociol. Rev., **23**, 347–79.

CHIRICOS, T.G., AND WALDO, G.P., 1975
Socioeconomic status and criminal sentencing: an empirical assessment of a conflict proposition.
Amer. Sociol. Rev., **40**, 753–72.

DAUNTON-FEAR, M.W., 1975
Social enquiry reports: comprehensive and reliable?
Brit. J. Criminol., **15**, 128–39.

EVANS, W., AND GILBERT, F.S., JR., 1975
The sentencing process: better methods are available.
Fed. Probation, **39**(4), 35–9.

FALLON, P., 1975
Crown court practice: sentences
London: Butterworths.

HAGAN, J., 1975
Law, order and sentencing: a study of attitude in action.
Sociometry, **38**, 374–84.

HALL, E.L., AND SIMKUS, A.A., 1975
Inequality in the types of sentences received by native Americans and whites.
Criminol., **13**, 199–222.

JOURNAL OF CRIMINAL LAW AND CRIMINOLOGY, 1975
Proposed changes in presentence investigation report procedures.
J. Crim. Law & Criminol., **66**, 57–67.

KUH, R.H., 1975
Sentencing: guidelines for the Manhattan District Attorney's office.
Crim. Law Bull., **11**, 62–6.

LEVIN, M.A., 1975
Delay in five criminal courts.
J. Legal Studies, **4**, 83–131.

PETERSEN, D.M., AND FRIDAY, P.C. 1975
Early release from incarceration: race as a factor in the use of "shock probation."
J. Crim. Law & Criminol., **66**, 79–87.

PRINS, H., 1975
Psychiatric services and the magistrates' and juvenile courts. An analysis of the views of probation officers and magistrates.
Brit. J. Criminol., **15**, 315–32.

ROBIN, G.D., 1975
Judicial resistance to sentencing accountability
Crime & Delinq., **21**, 201–12.

TIFFANY, L.P., AVICHAI, Y., AND PETERS, G.W., 1975
A statistical analysis of sentencing in federal courts: defendants convicted after trial, 1967–1968.
J. Legal Studies, **4**, 369–90.

WALKER, N., 1975
Curiosities of criminal justice.
Police J., **48**, 6–19.

WILLICK, D.H., GEHLKER, G., AND WATTS, A.McF., 1975
Social class as a factor affecting judicial disposition: defendants charged with criminal homosexual acts.
Criminol., **13**, 57–77.

WOLFGANG, M.E., AND RIEDEL, M., 1975
Rape, race, and the death penalty in Georgia.
Amer. J. Orthopsychiat., **45**, 658–68.

YALE LAW JOURNAL, 1975
Parole release decision making and the sentencing process. **84**, 810–902.

CARLEN, P., 1976
The staging of magistrates' justice.
Brit. J. Criminol., **16**, 48–55.

3 Sentencing structure, reform and legislative proposals

[*See also Section 12(2) for references on Diversion from the criminal justice system.*]

BERKOWITZ, M.C., 1974
The constitutional requirement for a written statement of reasons and facts in support of the sentencing decision: a due process proposal.
Iowa Law Rev., **60**, 205–28.

BLOM-COOPER, L., 1974
The constitutional framework of the English penal system, and Sentencing structure: a paradigm for the future, in L. Blom-Cooper (ed.), *Progress in penal reform.*
Oxford: Clarendon Press, 25–34, 174–81.

COUNCIL OF EUROPE, 1974
Sentencing. Report by the sub-committee of the European committee on crime problems.
Strasbourg.

HASTINGS LAW JOURNAL, 1974
California's cruelty criteria: evaluating sentences after in Re Lynch.
25, 636–56.

JAMES, SIR A., 1974
The sentencing process: present practice and future policy, in L. Blom-Cooper (ed.), *Progress in penal reform.*
Oxford: Clarendon Press, 165–73.

KUTAK, R.J., AND GOTTSCHALK, J.M., 1974
In search of a rational sentence: a return to a concept of appellate review.
Nebraska Law Rev., **53**, 463–520.

MARYLAND LAW REVIEW, 1974
Toward a probable cause standard in sentencing: *Nickens v. State.* **34**, 133–53.

UNITED STATES OF AMERICA, DIVISION OF PROBATION, 1974
The selective presentence investigation report.
Fed. Probation, **38**(4), 47–54.

BUFFALO LAW REVIEW, 1975
The eighth amendment, Beccaria, and the enlightenment: an historical justification for the Weems v. United States excessive punishment doctrine.
24, 783–838.

CANADA, 1975
Imprisonment and release.
Law Reform Commission of Canada, working paper No. 11, (1975), in, *Can. J. Criminol. & Corrections*, **17**(4), 5–31.

CANADA, 1975
The principles of sentencing and dispositions.
Law Reform Commission of Canada, working paper No. 3, (March 1974), in, *Can J. Criminol. & Corrections*, **17**(1).

CARAWAY, W.L., 1975
Sentencing reform in multiple offense cases: judicial and legislative avenues.
Connecticut Law Rev., **7**, 257–86.

COFFEE, J.C., JR., 1975
The future of sentencing reform: emerging legal issues in the individualization of justice.
Michigan Law Rev., **73**, 1362–462.

CONNOLLY, P.K., 1975
The possibility of a prison sentence is a necessity.
Crime & Delinq., **21**, 356–9.

CRIME AND DELINQUENCY, 1975
The nondangerous offender should not be imprisoned. A policy statement.
Board of Directors, National Council on Crime and Delinquency.
21, 315–22.

GILMAN, D., 1975
The sanction of imprisonment: for whom, for what, and how.
Crime & Delinq., **21**, 337–47.

HOFFMANN, P.B., AND DEGOSTIN, L.K., 1975
An argument for self-imposed explicit judicial sentencing standards.
J. Crim. Justice, **3**, 195–206.

IMLAY, C.H., AND REID, E.L., 1975
The probation officer, sentencing, and the winds of change.
Fed. Probation, **39**(4), 9–17.

O'LEARY, V., GOTTFREDSON, M., AND GELMAN, A., 1975
Contemporary sentencing proposals.
Crim. Law Bull., **11**, 555–86.

ROBIN, G.D., 1975
Judicial resistance to sentencing accountability.
Crime & Delinq., **21**, 201–12.

HIRSCH, A. VON, 1976
Doing justice: the choice of punishments.
Report of the Committee for the Study of Incarceration.
New York: Hill & Wang, 95–179.

4 Bail-preventive detention

KATZ, L., LITWIN, L., AND BAMBERGER, R., 1972
Justice is the crime: pretrial delay in felony cases.
Cleveland: Press of Case Western Reserve Univ., 137–75.

SCOLLIN, J.A., 1972
The bail reform act: an analysis of amendments to the criminal code related to bail and arrest.
Toronto: Carswell, 3–14.

CROMWELL, P.F., JR., AND RIOS, O.G., 1974
Bond supervision: implementing the Federal Bail Reform Act.
Fed. Probation, **38**(4), 30–34.

GOTTFREDSON, M.R., 1974
An empirical analysis of pre-trial release decisions.
J. Crim. Justice, **2**, 287–303.

HASTINGS LAW JOURNAL, 1974
Bail as a matter of right, in Re Underwood.
26, 559–87.

HILL, A.K.R., 1974
The constitutional controversy of a juvenile's right to bail in juvenile preadjudication proceedings.
Hastings Constitutional Law Quart., **1**, 215–33.

LANDES, W.M., 1974
Legality and reality: some evidence on criminal procedure.
J. Legal Studies, **3**, 287–337.

SNOUFFER, WC., 1974
An article of faith abolishes bail in Oregon.
Oregon Law Rev., **53**, 273–337.

WRIGHT, M., 1974
Bail: recognition of the need for reform.
Crim. Law Rev., 1974, 457–61.

BOTTOMLEY, K., AND DELL, S., 1975
Bail procedure in magistrates' courts (critical notes).
Brit. J. Criminol., **15**, 81–7.

DILL, F., 1975
Discretion, exchange and social control: bail bondsmen in criminal courts.
Law & Soc. Rev., **9**, 639–74.

LEWIS, D., AND HUGHMAN, P., 1975
Just how just?
London: Secker & Warburg, 39–64,

SIMON, F., AND WILSON, S., 1975
Field Wing bail hostel: the first nine months.
London: Home Office Research Studies, **30.**

BOTTOMS, A.E., AND MCCLEAN, J.D., 1976
Defendants in the criminal process.
London: Routledge & Kegan Paul, 188–225.

5 Jury decisions: a preliminary list

SEALY, A.P., AND CORNISH, W.R., 1973
Jurors and their verdicts.
Modern Law Rev., **36,** 496–508.

SUE, S., SMITH, R.E., AND CALDWELL, C., 1973
Effects of inadmissible evidence on the decisions of simulated jurors: a moral dilemma.
J. Applied Social Psychol., **4,** 345–53.

CINCINNATI LAW REVIEW, 1974
Smaller juries and non-unanimity: analysis and proposed revision of the Ohio jury system.
43, 583–609.

DE CANI, J.S., 1974
Statistical evidence in jury discrimination cases.
J. Crim. Law & Criminol., **65,** 234–8.

SPERLICH, P.W., AND JASPOVICE, M., 1974
Grand juries, grand jurors and the constitution.
Hastings Constitutional Law Quart., **1,** 63–95.

YALE LAW JOURNAL, 1974
Towards principles of jury equity.
83, 1023–54.

ZANDER, M., 1974
Are too many professional criminals avoiding conviction?: a study in Britain's two busiest courts.
Modern Law Rev., **37,** 28–61.

BERMANT, G., AND JACOUBOVITCH, M.D., 1975
Fish out of water: a brief overview of social and psychological concerns about videotaped trials.
Hastings Law J., **26,** 999–1011.

BERMANT, G., CHAPPELL, D., CROCKETT, G.T., JACOUBOVITCH, M.D., AND MCGUIRE, M., 1975
Juror responses to prerecorded videotape trial representations in California and Ohio.
Hastings Law J., **26,** 975–98.

BUFFALO LAW REVIEW, 1975
Attica, jury pools and the intent requirement of the equal protection clause.
24, 347–68.

CHEVIGNY, P.G., 1975
The Attica cases: a successful jury challenge in a northern city.
Crim. Law Bull., **11,** 157–72.

CONNECTICUT LAW REVIEW, 1975
Taylor v. Louisiana: the jury cross section crosses the state line.
7, 508–28.

FRIED, M., KAPLAN, K.J., AND KLEIN, K.W., 1975
Juror selection: an analysis of voir dire, in R.J. Simon (ed.), *The jury system in America: a critical overview.*
Sage Criminal Justice System Annuals, **4,** Beverly Hills, Calif.: Sage Publications, 49–66.

JOINER, C.W., 1975
Perspectives on the function and value of the jury in America: from the bench, in R.J. Simon (ed.), *The jury system in America: a critical overview.*
Sage Criminal Justice System Annuals, **4,** Beverly Hills, Calif.: Sage Publications, 145–57.

JOURNAL OF CRIMINAL LAW AND CRIMINOLOGY, 1975
The exclusion of young adults from juries: a threat to jury impartiality.
66, 150–64.

KENNEBECK, E., 1975
Perspectives on the function and value of the jury in America: from the jury box, in R.J. Simon (ed.), *The jury system in America: a critical overview.*
Sage Criminal Justice System Annuals, **4,** Beverly Hills, Calif.: Sage Publications, 235–50.

KESSLER, J.B., 1975
The social psychology of jury deliberations, in R.J. Simon (ed.), *The jury system in America: a critical overview.*
Sage Criminal Justice System Annuals, **4,** Beverly Hills, Calif.: Sage Publications, 69–93.

LEMPERT, R.O., 1975
Uncovering "nondiscernible" differences: empirical research and the jury-size cases.
Michigan Law Rev., **73,** 644–708.

PADAWER-SINGER, A.M., AND BARTON, A.H., 1975
The impact of pretrial publicity on jurors' verdicts, in R.J. Simon (ed.), *The jury system in America: a critical overview.*
Sage Criminal Justice System Annuals, **4,** Beverly Hills, Calif.: Sage Publications, 125–39.

STEPHAN, C., 1975
Selective characteristics of jurors and litigants: their influences on juries' verdicts, in R.J. Simon (ed.), *The jury system in America: a critical overview.*
Sage Criminal Justice System Annuals, **4,** Beverly Hills, Calif.: Sage Publications, 97–121.

VAN DYKE, J.M., 1975
Jury service is a fundamental right.
Hastings Constitutional Law Quart., **2,** 27–31.

VIRGINIA LAW REVIEW, 1975
Judges' nonverbal behavior in jury trials: a threat to judicial impartiality.
61, 1266–98.

GORDON, G., AND BARBER, D., 1976
Members of the jury
London: Wildwood House.

6 Judges and magistrates—their background and attitudes: a preliminary list

UNITED STATES OF AMERICA, SENATE, 1958
Legislative history of the United States circuit courts of appeals and the judges who served during the period 1801 *through March* 1958.
Committee on the Judiciary, 85th Congress, Second Session, Washington, D.C.

BLAUSTEIN, A.P., AND MERSKY, R.M., 1969
The statistics on the supreme court, in L. Friedman and F.L. Israel (eds.), *The justices of the United States Supreme Court* 1789–1969.
New York: Chelsea House & Bokwer, 3187–265.

CASPER, J.D., 1972
American criminal justice: the defendant's perspective.
Englewood Cliffs, N.J.: Prentice-Hall, 135–44.

CHASE, H.W., 1972
Federal judges: the appointing process.
Minneapolis: Univ. of Minnesota Press.

JACOB, H., 1973
Urban justice: law and order in American cities.
Englewood Cliffs, N.J.: Prentice-Hall, 64–79.

MORRISON, F.L., 1973
Courts and the political process in England.
Beverly Hills, Calif.: Sage Publications, 70–91.

BARBER, R., 1974
Judge and jury attitudes to rape.
Aust. & N.Z. J. Criminol., **7,** 157–72.

GAYLIN, W., 1974
Partial justice: a study of bias in sentencing.
New York: Alfred A. Knopf, 44–162.

HAWKER, G., 1974
Magistrates in the crown court: report of a survey.
Institute of Judicial Administration, Univ. of Birmingham. Mimeo.

HAZARD, G.C., 1974
Justice courts in Oregon (an introduction, plus report of the study).
Oregon Law Rev., **53,** 407–56.

LONG, L., 1974
Innovation in urban criminal misdemeanor courts, in H. Jacob (ed.), *The potential for reform of criminal justice.*
Sage Criminal Justice System Annuals, **3,** Beverly Hills, Calif.: Sage Publications, 173–206.

MARYLAND LAW REVIEW, 1974
Discipline of judges in Maryland.
34, 612–33.

PATERSON, A.A., 1974
The infirm judge.
Brit. J. Law & Soc., **1,** 31–49.

PATERSON, A.A., 1974
Judges: a political elite?
Brit. J. Law & Soc., **1,** 118–35.

SEIDMAN, R.B., AND CHAMBLISS, W.J., 1974
Appeals from criminal convictions, in D. Glaser (ed.), *Handbook of criminology.*
Chicago: Rand McNally, 651–57.

BALDWIN, J., 1975
The compulsory training of the magistracy.
Crim. Law Rev., 1975, 634–43.

CADY, F.C., AND COE, G.E., 1975
Education of judicial personnel: coals to Newcastle?
Connecticut Law Rev., **7,** 423–77.

PARKER, C.F., 1975
The status and functions of lay magistrates in the crown court.
Crim. Law Rev., 1975, 492–504.

9 The court and the young offender

Reifen, D., 1972
The juvenile court in a changing society: young offenders in Israel.
London: Weidenfeld & Nicolson, 85–141.

Stapleton, W.V., and Teitelbaum, L.E., 1972
In defense of youth: a study of the role of counsel in American juvenile courts.
New York: Russell Sage Foundation.

Katz, B.F., 1973–74
Juveniles committed to penal institutions: do they have the right to a jury trial?
J. Family Law, **13**, 675–712.

Schultz, J.L., and Pickerel, P., 1973
Developments in juvenile justice.
1972/1973 Annual Survey of American Law, 629–53.

Berlins, M., and Wansell, G., 1974
Caught in the act: children, society, and the law.
Harmondsworth.: Penguin Books, 77–124.

Davis, S.M., 1974
Rights of juveniles: the juvenile justice system.
New York: Mark Boardman.

Emerson, R.M., 1974
Role determinants in juvenile court, in D. Glaser (ed.), *Handbook of criminology.*
Chicago: Rand McNally, 621–50.

Erickson, P.G., 1974
The defence lawyer's role in juvenile court: an empirical investigation into judges' and social workers' points of view.
Univ. Toronto Law J., **24**, 126–48.

Fox, S.J., 1974
Philosophy and the principles of punishment in the juvenile court.
Family Law Quart., **8**, 373–84.

Hill, A.K.R., 1974
The constitutional controversy of a juvenile's right to bail in juvenile preadjudication proceedings.
Hastings Constitutional Law Quart., **1**, 215–33.

Jones, M., 1974
Justice and journalism: a study of the influence of newspaper reporting upon the administration of justice by magistrates.
Chichester, Sussex: Barry Rose, 122–32.

Levin, M.M., and Sarri, R.C., 1974
Juvenile delinquency: a study of juvenile codes in the U.S.
Ann Arbor, Michigan: National Assessment of Juvenile Corrections, Univ. of Michigan.

Mahoney, A.R., 1974
The effect of labeling upon youths in the juvenile justice system: a review of the evidence.
Law & Soc. Rev., **8**, 583–614.

Notre Dame Laywer, 1974
Judicial recognition and implementation of a right to treatment for institutionalised juveniles.
49, 1051–63.

Rutherford, A., 1974
Facts and fantasies concerning developments in Massachusetts.
Prison J., **54**, 12–22.

Sharma, V.D., 1974
The criminal responsibility of children in England.
Anglo-American Law Rev., **3**, 157–83.

Silbert, J.D., and Sussman, A., 1974
Rights of juveniles confined in training schools.
Crime & Delinq., **20**, 373–88.

VIRGINIA LAW REVIEW, 1974
Limits on punishment and entitlement to rehabilitative treatment of institutionalised juveniles: *Nelson v. Heyne*.
60, 864–83.

VIRGINIA LAW REVIEW, 1974
Review of improper juvenile transfer hearings.
50, 818–39.

ALBANY LAW REVIEW, 1975
Juvenile justice: alternative answers.
40, 179–98.

AREEN, J., 1975
Intervention between parent and child: a reappraisal of the State's role in child neglect and abuse cases.
Georgetown Law J., **63,** 887–937.

BRUCE, N., 1975
Children's hearings: a retrospect (with a commentary by P.D. Scott and a rejoinder).
Brit. J. Criminol., **15,** 333–47.

CONSERVATIVE LAYWERS, SOCIETY OF, 1975
Apprentices in crime: a study of the workings of the Children and Young Persons Act., 1969.
London: Conservative Central Office.

CRIME AND DELINQEUNCY, 1975
Jurisdiction over status offenses should be removed from the juvenile court. A policy statement.
Board of Directors, National Council on Crime and Delinquency.
21, 97–9.

ERICKSON, P., 1975
Legalistic and traditional role expectations for defence counsel in juvenile court.
Can. J. Criminol. & Corrections, **17,** 78–93.

FORD, D., 1975
Children, courts, and caring: a study of the Children and Young Persons Act, 1969.
London: Constable, 11–88.

KRAUS, J., 1975
Decision process in children's court and the social background report.
J. Res. Crime & Delinq., **12,** 17–29.

MARON, A.W., 1975
Constitutional problems of diversion of juvenile delinquents.
Notre Dame Lawyer, **51,** 22–47.

MIDGLEY, J., 1975
Children on trial: a study of juvenile justice.
Cape Town: National Institute for Crime Prevention and the Rehabilitation of Offenders.

NEWTON, C.H., SHELDEN, R.G., AND JENKINS, S., 1975
The homogenization process within the juvenile justice system.
Int. J. Criminol. & Penol., **3,** 213–27

PRINS, H., 1975
Psychiatric services and the magistrates' and juvenile courts. An analysis of the views of probation officers and magistrates.
Brit. J. Criminol., **15,** 315–32.

SCHAEFER, J.L., 1975
The federal youth corrections Act: the purposes and uses of vacating the conviction.
Fed. Probation **39**(3), 31–8.

SYRACUSE LAW REVIEW, 1975
Due process for juveniles facing strict-security confinement.
26, 1017–49.

THOMAS, C.W., AND FITCH, W.A., 1975
An inquiry into the association between respondent's personal characteristics and juvenile court dispositions.
William & Mary Law Rev., **17,** 61–83.

THOMAS, C.W., AND SIEVERDES, C.M., 1975
Juvenile court intake: an analysis of discretionary decision-making.
Criminol., **12,** 413–32.

UNITED KINGDOM, 1975
The Children and Young Persons Act, 1969
Eleventh Report from the Expenditure Committee, House of Commons, Session 1974–75.

London: Vol. **I**. Report. Vol. **II**. Minutes of Evidence and Appendices.

WALD, M., 1975
State intervention on behalf of 'neglected' children: a search for realistic standards.
Stanford Law Rev., **27,** 985–1040.

WHITEBREAD, C.H., AND BATEY, R., 1975
Juvenile double jeopardy.
Georgetown Law J., **63,** 857–85.

GANDY, J.M., 1976
Canada's juvenile justice system: proposed new legislation.
Brit. J. Criminol., **16,** 68–72.

10 Effectiveness of punishment and treatments

1 General deterrence

WILLCOCK, H.D., 1968
Deterrents and incentives to crime among boys and young men aged 15–21 years.
London: Office of Population Censuses and Surveys, Social Survey Division.

ANTUNES, G., AND HUNT, A.L., 1973
The deterrent impact of criminal sanctions: some implications for criminal justice policy.
J. Urban Law, **51,** 145–61.

FATTAH, E.A., 1973
The deterrent effect of capital punishment: the Canadian experience, in E. Sagarin and D.E.J. MacNamara (eds.), *Corrections: problems of punishment and rehabilitation.*
New York: Praeger, 106–14.

BAILEY, W.C., 1974
Murder and the death penalty.
J. Crim. Law & Criminol., **65,** 416–23.

BANKSTON, W.B., AND CRAMER, J.A., 1974
Toward a macro-sociological interpretation of general deterrence.
Criminol., **12,** 251–80.

GERBER, R.J., 1974
A death penalty we can live with.
Notre Dame Lawyer, **50,** 251–72.

GLASER, D., AND ZEIGLER, M., 1974
Use of the death penalty v. outrage at murder.
Crime & Delinq., **20,** 333–8.

GRUPP, S.E., 1974
Deterrence and the marijuana smoker, in R.L. Akers and E. Sagarin (eds.), *Crime prevention and social control.*
New York: Praeger, 39–50.

HENSHEL, R.L., 1974
Deterrence and knowledge of sanctions, in R.L. Akers and E. Sagarin (eds.), *Crime prevention and social control.*
New York: Praeger, 51–64.

MACKENNA, SIR B., 1974
General deterrence, in L. Blom-Cooper (ed.), *Progress in penal reform.*
Oxford: Clarendon Press, 182–95.

SCHULHOFER, S., 1974
Harm and punishment: a critique of emphasis on the results of conduct in the criminal law.
Univ. Penn. Law Rev., **122,** 1497–607.

ANDENAES, J., 1975
General prevention revisited: research and policy implications.
J. Crim. Law & Criminol., **66,** 338–65.

BAILEY, W.C., 1975
Murder and capital punishment: some further evidence.
Amer. J. Orthopsychiat., **45,** 669–88.

BELSON, W.A., 1975
Juvenile theft: the causal factors.
London: Harper & Row, 105–44.

BLOCK, M.K., AND LIND, R.C., 1975
An economic analysis of crimes punishable by imprisonment.
J. Legal Studies, **4,** 479–92.

FRIEDMAN, L.M., 1975
The legal system: a social science perspective.
New York: Russell Sage Foundation, 67–104.

GEERKEN, M.R., AND COVE, W.R., 1975
Deterrence: some theoretical considerations.
Law & Soc. Rev., **9,** 497–513.

GIBBS, J.P., 1975
Crime, punishment and deterrence.
New York: Elsevier.

PASSELL, P., 1975
The deterrent effect of the death penalty: a statistical test.
Stanford Law Rev., **28,** 61–80.

PHILLIPS, L., AND VOTEY, H.L., JR., 1975
Crime control in California.
J. Legal Studies, **4,** 327–49.

ROBINSON, C.D., 1975
Social implications of driver disqualification: reality and road traffic laws.
Aust. & N.Z. J. Criminol., **8,** 169–75.

ROSS, H.L., 1975
The Scandinavian myth: the effectiveness of drinking-and-driving legislation in Sweden and Norway.
J. Legal Studies, **4,** 285–310.

SHINNAR, S., AND SHINNAR, R., 1975
The effects of the criminal justice system on the control of crime: a quantitative approach.
Law & Soc. Rev., **9,** 581–611.

SWEDEN, NATIONAL COUNCIL FOR CRIME PREVENTION, 1975
General deterrence—a conference on current research and standpoints.
Stockholm.

WHITE, S., 1975
Deterrence and criminal appeals: the effect of the Criminal Appeal Act 1966.
Modern Law Rev., **38,** 369–96.

WILSON, J.Q., 1975
Thinking about crime.
New York: Basic Books, 162–82.

ZIMRING, F.E., 1975
Firearms and federal law: the gun control act of 1968.
J. Legal Studies, **4,** 133–98.

BAILEY, W.C., 1976
Use of the death penalty v. outrage at murder: some additional evidence and considerations.
Crime & Delinq., **22,** 31–9.

GLASER, D., 1976
A response to Bailey: more evidence on capital punishment as correlate of tolerance for murder.
Crime & Delinq., **22,** 40–3.

2 Follow-up and comparative studies of established sanctions

GLASER, D., 1973
Routinizing evaluation: getting feedback on effectiveness of crime and delinquency programs.
Rockville, Maryland: National Institute of Mental Health.

LEWIS, M.V., 1973
Prison education and rehabilitation: illusion or reality? A case study of an experimental program.
Institute for Research on Human Resources, Pennsylvania State Univ. 91–107.

CLARKE, S.H., 1974
Getting 'em out of circulation: does incarceration of juvenile offenders reduce crime?
J. Crim. Law & Criminol., **65,** 528–35.

JEFFERY, R., AND WOOLPERT, S., 1974
Work furlough as an alternative to incarceration: an assessment of its effects on recidivism and social cost.
J. Crim. Law & Criminol., **65,** 405–15.

KLEIN, M.W., 1974
Labeling, deterrence, and recidivism: a study of police dispositions of juvenile offenders.
Social Problems, **22,** 292–303.

KRAUS, J., 1974
The deterrent effect of fines and probation on male juvenile offenders.
Aust. & N.Z. J. Criminol., **7,** 231–40.

SCHWITZGEBEL, R.K., 1974
The right to effective mental treatment.
Calif. Law Rev., **62,** 936–56.

TITTLE, C.R., 1974
Prisons and rehabilitation: the inevitability of disfavor.
Social Problems, **21,** 385–95.

ADAMS, S., 1975
Evaluative research in corrections: a practical guide.
L.E.A.A., National Institute of Law Enforcement and Criminal Justice, U.S. Dept. of Justice, Washington, D.C.

CORNISH, D.B., AND CLARKE, R.V.G., 1975
Residential treatment and its effects on delinquency.
London: Home Office Research Studies, **32.**

ERICSON, R.V., 1975
Young offenders and their social work.
Farnborough, Hants.: Saxon House, 125–215.

GLASER, D., 1975
Achieving better questions: a half century's progress in correctional research.
Fed. Probation, **39**(3), 3–9.

GREENBERG, D.F., 1975
The incapacitative effects of imprisonment: some estimates.
Law & Soc. Rev., **9,** 541–80.

McWILLIAMS, W., 1975
Sentencing and recidivism: an analysis by personality type.
Brit. J. Social Wk., **5,** 311–24.

MILLHAM, S., BULLOCK, R., AND CHERRETT, P., 1975
After grace-teeth. A comparative study of the residential experience of boys in approved schools.
London: Human Context Books, Chaucer Publ. Co., 202–298.

PALMER, T., 1975
Martinson revisited.
J. Res. Crime & Delinq., **12,** 133–52.

VIANO, E.C., 1975
Growing up in an affluent society: delinquency and recidivism in suburban America.
J. Crim. Justice, **3,** 223–35.

BRODY, S.R., 1976
The effectiveness of sentencing—a review of the literature.
London: Home Office Research Studies, **35.**

11 Assessing the impact of imprisonment

1 Prison community and social structure

Gaylin, W., 1970
In the service of their country: war resisters in prison.
New York: Grosset & Dunlop.

Haney, C., Banks, C., and Zimbardo, P., 1973
A study of prisoners and guards in a simulated prison.
Naval Research Rev., **26**(1), 1–17.

Ingraham, B.L., 1973
Will legal relief for inmates prevent violence in correctional institutions?, in United States of America, *Prevention of violence in correctional institutions.* Criminal Justice Monograph.
L.E.A.A., National Institute of Law Enforcement and Criminal Justice, U.S. Dept. of Justice, Washington, D.C., 33–49.

Brody, S.A., 1974
The political prisoner syndrome: latest problem of the American penal system.
Crime & Delinq., **20**, 97–106.

Carroll, L., 1974
Hacks, blacks and cons: race relations in a maximum security prison.
Lexington, Mass.: Heath Lexington Books.

Cochrane, R., 1974
The impact of a training school experience on the value systems of young offenders.
Brit. J. Criminol., **14**, 336–44.

Desroches, F., 1974
The April 1971 Kingston penitentiary riot.
Can. J. Criminol. & Corrections, **16**, 317–31.

Desroches, F., 1974
Patterns in prison riots.
Can. J. Criminol. & Corrections, **16**, 332–51.

Dunlop, A.B., 1974
The approved school experience: an account of boys' experiences of training under differing regimes of approved schools, with an attempt to evaluate the effectiveness of that training.
London: Home Office Research Studies, **25**, 23–86.

Ellis, D., Grasmick, H.G., and Gilman, B., 1974
Violence in prisons: a sociological analysis.
Amer. J. Sociol., **80**, 16–43.

Giallombardo, R., 1974
The social world of imprisoned girls: a comparative study of institutions for juvenile delinquents.
New York: John Wiley & Sons, 30–54, 145–266.

Gill, O., 1974
Residential treatment for young offenders: the boys' perspectives.
Brit. J. Criminol., **14**, 318–35.

Ibrahim, A.I., 1974
Deviant sexual behaviour in men's prisons.
Crime & Delinq., **20**, 38–44.

James, L., 1974
Influence in the prison environment.
Univ. of Toronto: Centre of Criminology. Mimeo.

Moran, R., 1974
Advertisements of self: the search for identity amongst inmates, in T.P. Thornberry and E. Sagarin (eds.), *Images of crime: offenders and victims.*
New York: Praeger, 67–78.

Morris, F.L., 1974
Black political consciousness in Northern State prisons, in H. Jacob (ed.), *The potential for reform of criminal justice.*

Sage Criminal Justice System Annuals, **3**, Beverly Hills, Calif.: Sage Publications, 291–329.

WEISS, C., AND FRIAR, D.J., 1974
Terror in the prisons: homosexual rape and why society condones it.
New York: Bobbs-Merrill.

WILLIAMS, V.L., AND FISH, M., 1974
Convicts, codes and contraband: the prison life of men and women.
Cambridge, Mass.: Ballinger.

BIDNA, H., 1975
Effects of increased security on prison violence.
J. Crim. Justice, **3**, 33–45.

CLARKE, R.V.G., AND MARTIN, D.N., 1975
A study of absconding and its implications for the residential treatment of delinquents, in J. Tizard, I. Sinclair and R.V.G. Clarke (eds.), *Varieties of residential experience.*
London: Routledge & Kegan Paul, 249–74.

CULBERTSON, R.G., 1975
The effect of institutionalization on the delinquent inmate's self concept.
J. Crim. Law & Criminol., **66**, 88–93.

CURCIONE, N.R., 1975
Social relations among inmate addicts.
J. Res. Crime & Delinq., **12**, 61–74.

DAWSON, S., 1975
Power and influences in prison workshops, in P. Abell (ed.), *Organisations as bargaining and influence systems.*
London: Heinemann, 151–86.

DENFIELD, D., AND HOPKINS, A., 1975
Racial-ethnic identification in prisons: "right on from the inside."
Int. J. Criminol. & Penol., **3**, 355–66.

ERICSON, R.V., 1975
Young offenders and their social work.
Farnborough, Hants.: Saxon House, 27–123.

FOGEL, D., 1975
'*. . . We are the living proof . . .' The justice model for corrections.*
Cincinatti: W.H. Anderson Co., 70–109.

FOSTER, T.W., 1975
Make-believe families: a response of women and girls to the deprivation of imprisonment.
Int. J. Criminol. & Penol., **3**, 71–8.

GUENTHER, A.L., 1975
Compensations in a total institution: the forms and functions of contraband.
Crime & Delinq., **21**, 243–54.

HOLBORN, J., 1975
Some male offenders' problems: II. Casework with short-term prisoners.
London: Home Office Research Studies, **28**, 79–127.

JACOBS, J.B., AND RETSKY, H.G., 1975
Prison guard.
Urban Life & Culture, **4**(1).

MILLHAM, S., BULLOCK, R., AND CHERRETT, P., 1975
After grace-teeth. A comparative study of the residential experience of boys in approved schools.
London: Human Context Books, Chaucer Publ. Co.

MORRIS, P., AND BEVERLY, F., 1975
On licence. A study of parole.
London: John Wiley & Sons, 24–74.

REASONS, C.E., AND KAPLAN, R.L., 1975
Tear down the walls?: some functions of prisons.
Crime & Delinq., **21**, 360–72.

THOMAS, C.W., AND POOLE, E.D., 1975
The consequences of incompatible goal structures in correctional settings.
Int. J. Criminol. & Penol., **3**, 27–42.

TROYER, J.G., AND FREASE, D.E., 1975
Attitude change in a Western Canadian penitentiary.
Can. J. Criminol. & Corrections, **17**, 250–62.

CHANG, D.H., AND ZASTROW, C.H., 1976
Inmates' and security guards' perceptions of themselves and of each other: a comparative study.
Int. J. Criminol. & Penol., **4**, 89–98.

HAWKINS, G., 1976
The prison: policy and practice.
Univ. Chicago Press, 56–107.

2 Correctional standards and organizational problems

BAGDIKIAN, B.H., AND DASH, L., 1972
The shame of the prisons.
New York: Pocket Books.

CAIRD, R., 1974
A good and useful life. Imprisonment in Britain today.
London: Hart-Davis, MacGibbon, 109–88.

ECKERMAN, W.C., 1972
A nationwide survey of mental health and correctional institutions for adult mentally disordered offenders.
Center for Studies of Crime and Delinquency.
Rockville, Maryland: National Institute of Mental Health.

INTERNATIONAL PENAL AND PENITENTIARY FOUNDATION, 1973
Communication and democratisation in the penitentiary field.
Proceedings of the Fourth Meeting of Heads of Prison Administrations, Oxford, 23–29 September, 1973.
London: IPPF, 21–49, 64–92.

NAGEL, W.G., 1973
The new red barn: a critical look at the modern American prison.
New York: Walker & Co.,

AMERICAN BAR ASSOCIATION, 1974
Survey and handbook on state standards and inspection legislation for jails and juvenile detention facilities.
Statewide jail standards and inspection systems project.
Washington, D.C.: A.B.A.

CARR, R., RT. HON., 1974
Violent and dangerous men in British prisons. Abridged version of a statement by the Home Secretary, May 11, 1973.
Internat. J. Offender Therapy, **18,** 192–5.

COUNCIL OF EUROPE, 1974
Group and community work with the offenders.
Strasbourg.

GIALLOMBARDO, R., 1974
The social world of imprisoned girls: a comparative study of institutons for juvenile delinquents.
New York: John Wiley & Sons, 55–144.

GIFIS, S.H., 1974
Decision making in a prison community.
Wisconsin Law Rev., 1974, 349–427.

KEVE, P.W., 1974
Prison life and human worth.
Minneapolis: Univ. of Minnesota Press, 15–76, 128–64.

MCLACHLAN, N., 1974
Penal reform and penal history, in L. Blom-Cooper (ed.), *Progress in penal reform.*
Oxford: Clarendon Press, 1–24.

MATTICK, H.W., 1974
The contemporary jails of the United States: an unknown and neglected area of justice, in D. Glaser (ed.), *Handbook of criminology.*
Chicago: Rand McNally, 777–848.

OHLIN, L.E., 1974
Organizational reform in correctional agencies, in D. Glaser (ed.), *Handbook of criminology.*
Chicago: Rand McNally, 995–1020.

PLOTKIN, R., 1974
Surviving justice: prisoners' rights to be free from physical assault.
Cleveland State Law Rev., **23,** 387–422.

SHOVER, N., 1974
"Experts" and diagnosis in correctional agencies.
Crime & Delinq., **20,** 347–58.

SKOLER, D., AND LOEWENSTEIN, R., 1974
Minorities in correction.
Crime & Delinq., **20,** 339–46.

THOMAS, J.E., 1974
Policy and administration in penal establishments, in L. Blom-Cooper (ed.), *Progress in penal reform.*
Oxford: Clarendon Press, 54–67.

VIGOD, Z.L., 1974
A prison therapeutic community and its decision-making structure.
Can. J. Criminol. & Corrections, **16**, 411–20.

WAYSON, B.L., 1974
Prison administration in a time of change, in D. Glaser (ed), *Handbook of criminology*.
Chicago: Rand McNally, 849–63.

BANKS, C., MAYHEW, P., AND SAPSFORD, R.J., 1975
Absconding from open prisons.
London: Home Office Research Studies, **26.**

BIDNA, H., 1975
Effects of increased security on prison violence.
J. Crim. Justice, **3**, 33–45.

BUNDY, M.L., AND HARMON, K.R., 1975
National prison directory—organisational profiles of prison reform groups in the United States.
College Park Maryland: Urban Information Interpreters.

DI GENNARO, G., ET AL, 1975
Prison architecture an international survey of representative closed institutions and analysis of current trends in prison design.
UNSDRI, United Nation's Social Defence Research Institute.
London: Architectural Press.

FOGEL, D., 1975
"... *We are the living proof* ..." *The justice model for corrections.*
Cincinnati: W.H. Anderson Co., 1–68, 260–88.

FOUCAULT, M., 1975
Surveiller et punir: naissance de la prison.
Paris: Gallimard.

GOLDFARB, R., 1975
Jails: the ultimate ghetto.
New York: Anchor Press/Doubleday, 1–112.

GOLDSMITH, S.B., 1975
Prison health: travesty of justice.
New York: Prodist.

JEPSON, N., 1975
Administration: staff structure and training today, in S. McConville (ed.), *The use of imprisonment.*
London: Routledge & Kegan Paul, 17–31.

JUSTICE, THE HOWARD LEAGUE FOR PENAL REFORM, THE NATIONAL ASSOCIATION FOR THE CARE AND RESETTLEMENT OF OFFENDERS, 1975
Boards of visitors of penal institutions.
Report of the committee (Chairman, Lord Jellicoe).
Chichester and London: Barry Rose.

MCCONVILLE, S., 1975
Boards of visitors of penal institutions: a note.
Brit. J. Criminol., **15**, 391–4.

MCCONVILLE, S., 1975
Future prospects of imprisonment in Britain, in S. McConville (ed.), *The use of imprisonment.*
London: Routledge & Kegan Paul, 107–25.

MURPHY, B.C., 1975
Foundations of scientific corrections classification and programming: structured applications of the *law of effect* and *differential association* to legal and illegal earnings.
Can. J. Criminol. & Corrections, **17**, 154–64.

SMITH, R.R., 1975
A survey of good time policies and practices in American correctional agencies.
J. Crim. Justice, **3**, 237–41.

SOUTHERTON, P., 1975
The story of a prison.
Reading: Osprey Publishing, 43–108.

STEELE, E.H., AND JACOBS, J.B., 1975
A theory of prison systems.
Crime & Delinq., **21**, 149–62.

TAKAGI, P., 1975
Walnut Street jail: a penal reform to centralize the powers of state.
Fed. Probation, **39**(4), 18–26.

THOMAS, J.E., 1975
Special units in prisons, in K. Jones (ed.), *Yearbook of social policy in Britain*, 1974.
London: Routledge & Kegan Paul, 89–100.

UNITED STATES OF AMERICA, 1975
Census of state correctional facilities, 1974.
Advance report.
National Prisoner Statistics Special Report, L.E.A.A., National Criminal Justice Information & Statistical Service, U.S. Dept of Justice, Washington, D.C.

CLARKSON, F., AND DAUNCEY, R.M., 1976
Management by objectives in Borstal.
Prison Service J., **No. 21**, 2–6.

HAWKINS, G., 1976
The prison: policy and practice.
Univ. Chicago Press, 1–55, 108–32, 160–85.

12 New approaches to the treatment of offenders

1 Experimental studies

[*See also Section 7(2) on problems of conflicting values; Section 14(1) on rights of prisoners.*]

CORMIER, B.M., AND ANGLIKER, C.C.J., 1973
A therapeutic community for persistent offenders, in E. Sagarin and D.E.J. MacNamara (eds.), *Corrections: problems of punishment and rehabilitation.*
New York: Praeger, 96–105.

GLASER, D., 1973
Routinizing evaluation: getting feedback on effectiveness of crime and delinquency programs.
Rockville, Maryland: National Institute of Mental Health, 55–83.

UNITED STATES OF AMERICA, 1973
Evaluation in criminal justice programs: guidelines and examples.
L.E.A.A., National Institute of Law Enforcement and Criminal Justice, U.S. Dept of Justice, Washington, D.C.

ADAMS, S., 1974
Measurement of effectiveness and efficiency in corrections, in D. Glaser (ed.), *Handbook of criminology.*
Chicago: Rand McNally, 1021–49.

COATES, R.B., OHLIN, L.E., AND MILLER, A.D., 1974
The Massachusetts experiment: closing of institutions, in *Differential diagnosis and prognosis of the state of dangerousness and treatment of juvenile delinquency.*
3rd Int. Seminar in Comp. Clinical Criminol.
Montreal: Univ. of Montreal, 167–208.

DUNLOP, A.B., 1974
The approved school experience: an account of boy's experiences of training under differing regimes of approved schools, with an attempt to evaluate the effectiveness of thet training.
London: Home Office Research Studies, **25,** 5–22, 87–106.

WILMARTH, S.S., AND GOLDSTEIN, A., 1974
Therapeutic effectiveness of methadone maintenance programs in the management of drug dependence of morphine type in the U.S.A.
Geneva: World Health Organization.

ADAMS, S., 1975
Evaluative research in corrections: a practical guide.
L.E.A.A., National Institute of Law Enforcement and Criminal Justice, U.S. Dept. of Justice, Washington, D.C., 60–73.

JESNESS, C.F., 1975
The impact of behavior modification and transactional analysis on institution social climate.
J. Res. Crime & Dellq., **12,** 79–81.

KÜHLHORN, E., 1975
Non-institutional treatment: a preliminary evaluation of the Sundsvall experiment.
Stockholm: The National Swedish Council for Crime Prevention.

LEENHOUTS, K.J., 1975
Volunteers in probation: not just a band-aid

story, in C.R. Dodge (ed.), *A nation without prisons.*
Lexington, Mass.: Heath Lexington Books, 133–45.

LERMAN, P., 1975
Community treatment and social control. A critical analysis of juvenile correctional policy.
Univ. Chicago Press.

MARTINSON, R., AND WILKS, J.A., 1975
A static-descriptive model of field supervision.
Criminol., **13,** 3–20.

SIMMONS, R.J., (ED.), 1975
M-2 (man-to-man) job therapy, in C.R. Dodge (ed.), *A nation without prisons.*
Lexington, Mass.: Heath Lexington Books, 171–95.

2 Innovations in corrections

FRIDAY, P.C., AND PETERSEN, D.M., 1973
Shock of imprisonment: short-term incarceration as a treatment technique, in E. Sagarin and D.E.J. MacNamara (eds.), *Corrections: problems of punishment and rehabilitation.*
New York: Praeger, 61–69.

ALBANY LAW REVIEW, 1974
Project: temporary release in New York State correctional facilities.
38, 691–763.

BURDMAN, M., 1974
Ethnic self-help groups in prison and on parole.
Crime & Delinq., **20,** 107–118.

COUNCIL OF EUROPE, 1974
New trends in the treatment of young offenders.
Strasbourg.

DAVIES, M., 1974
Prisoners of society: attitudes and after-care.
London: Routledge & Kegan Paul, 151–71.

DURHAM, E.L., 1974
St. Leonard's House: a model in the use of ex-offenders in the administration of correction.
Crime & Delinq., **20,** 269–80.

ERSKINE, H., 1974
The polls: control of crime and violence.
Public Opinion Quart., **38,** 490–502.

ERSKINE, H., 1974
The polls: politics and law and order.
Public Opinion Quart., **38,** 623–34.

GEIS, G., AND EDELHERTZ, H., 1974
California's new crime victim compensation statute.
San Diego Law Rev., **11,** 880–905.

GRAZIA, E. DE, 1974
Diversion from the criminal process: the 'mental health' experiment.
Connecticut Law Rev., **6,** 432–528.

HOLLAND, J.G., 1974
Behavior modification for prisoners, patients and other people as a prescription for the planned society.
Prison J., **54,** 23–37.

JEFFERY, R., AND WOOLPERT, S., 1974
Work furlough as an alternative to incarceration: an assessment of its effects on recidivism and social cost.
J. Crim. Law & Criminol., **65,** 405–15.

LAWS, D.R., 1974
The failure of a token economy.
Fed. Probation, **38**(3), 33–8.

MILAN, M.A., AND MCKEE, J.M., 1974
Behavior modification: principles and applications in corrections, in D. Glaser (ed.), *Handbook of criminology.*
Chicago: Rand McNally, 745–76.

MOYA, C.B., AND ACHTENBERG, R., 1974
Behavior modification: legal limitations on methods and goals.
Notre Dame Lawyer, **50,** 230–50.

RUTHERFORD, A., 1974
Facts and fantasies concerning developments in Massachusetts.
Prison J. **54,** 12–22.

SCHOENBACH, B., AND LIPTON, D., 1974
Special proposal: an alliance of state and industry for the rehabilitation of our correctional system.
Albany Law Rev., **39,** 5–13.

SCOTT, J.E., AND BENNETT, P.A., 1974
Ex-offenders as parole officers: an evaluation of the parole officer aide program in Ohio.
Columbus, Ohio: Ohio State Univ., 1–7, 98–103.

SMITH, R.R., MCKEE, J.M., AND MILAN, M.A., 1974
Study-release policies of American correctional agencies: a survey.
J. Crim. Justice, **2,** 357–63.

SOOTHILL, K., 1974
The prisoner's release: a study of the employment of ex-prisoners.
London: Allen & Unwin.

STANFORD LAW REVIEW, 1974
Aversion therapy: its limited potential for use in the correctional setting.
26, 1327–41.

UNITED STATES OF AMERICA, 1974
Pre-trial intervention: a program evaluation of nine manpower-based pre-trial intervention projects developed under the manpower administration.
National Technical Information Service, Springfield, Virginia.

WALKER, N., 1974
Caution: some thoughts on the penal involvement rate, in L. Blom-Cooper (ed.), *Progress in penal reform.*
Oxford: Clarendon Press, 221–37.

WEXLER, D.B., 1974
Of rights and reinforcers.
San Diego Law Rev., **11,** 957–71.

ALFORD, J.G., 1975
Accelerated rehabilitative disposition: the newest facet of the criminal justice system (the Allegheny County program).
Duquesne Law Rev., **13,** 499–519.

ANTTILA, I., 1975
Probation and parole: social control or social service?
Int. J. Criminol. & Penol., **3,** 79–84.

AYLLON, T., 1975
Behavior modification in institutional settings.
Arizona Law Rev., **17,** 3–18.
And commentaries by E.M. Opron, Jr., J. Gotkin and J. G. Perpich, 20–38.

BEHA, J.A., 1975
Halfway houses in adult corrections: the law, practice and results.
Crim. Law Bull., **11,** 434–77.

BRIGGS, D., 1975
In place of prison.
London: Temple Smith, 107–40.

BROOKS, J., 1975
How well are criminal injury compensation programs performing?
Crime & Delinq., **21,** 50–6.

CANADA, 1975
Diversion.
Law Reform Commission of Canada, working paper 7 (Jan. 1975), in, *Can. J. Criminol. & Corrections,* **17**(3).

CANADA, 1975
Restitution and compensation. Fines.
Law Reform Commission of Canada, working papers 5 & 6 (October 1974), in, *Can. J. Criminol. & Corrections,* **17**(2).

CLEVELAND STATE LAW REVIEW, 1975
Behavior modification: winners in the game of life?
24, 422–62.

CONNOLLY, P.K., 1975
The possibility of a prison sentence is a necessity.
Crime & Delinq., **21,** 356–9.

COUNCIL OF EUROPE, 1975
Compensation for victims of crime.
Strasbourg: DPC/CEPC.XXIX(75)10.

CRIME AND DELINQUENCY, 1975
The nondangerous offender should not be imprisoned. A policy statement. Board of Directors, National Council on Crime and Delinquency.
21, 315–22.

DICKIE, J., 1975
New careers project in Bristol.
Prison Service J., **No. 18,** 7–10.

DWORKIN, G., 1975
Rehabilitation of Offenders Act 1974.
Modern Law Rev., **38,** 429–35.

EVJEN, V.H., 1975
The federal probation system: the struggle to achieve it and its first 25 years.
Fed. Probation, **39**(2), 3–15.

GAYLIN, W., AND BLATTE, H., 1975
Behavior modification in prisons.
Amer. Crim. Law Rev., **13,** 11–35.

GILMAN, D., 1975
The sanction of imprisonment: for whom, for what, and how.
Crime & Delinq., **21,** 337–47.

GOBERT, J.G., 1975
Psychosurgery, conditioning, and the prisoner's right to refuse 'rehabilitation.'
Virginia Law Rev., **61,** 155–96.

HALL, P., LAND, H., PARKER, R., AND WEBB, A., 1975
Detention centres: the experiment which could not fail, in P. Hall, H. Land, R. Parker and A. Webb, *Change, choice and conflict in social policy.*
London: Heinemann, 311–70.

HALL WILLIAMS, J.E., 1975
Changing prisons.
London: Peter Owen, 43–109.

HAWKINS, K., 1975
Alternatives to imprisonment, in S. McConville (ed), *The use of imprisonment.*
London: Routledge & Kegan Paul, 67–87.

HUDSON, J., GALAWAY, B., HENSCHEL, W., LINDGREN, J., AND PENTON, J., 1975
Diversion programming in criminal justice: the case of Minnesota.
Fed. Probation, **39**(2), 11–19.

INDIANA LAW JOURNAL, 1975
Pretrial diversion from the criminal process: some constitutional considerations.
50, 783–807.

JOHNSON, E.H., AND HERREMAN, J., 1975
Work release in Belgium: tolerance and the urban job market.
Int. J. Criminol. & Penol., **3,** 367–80.

LERMAN, P., 1975
Community treatment and social control. A critical analysis of juvenile correctional policy.
Univ. Chicago Press, 107–225.

MARON, A.W., 1975
Constitutional problems of diversion of juvenile delinquents.
Notre Dame Lawyer, **51,** 22–47.

MEEKER, B.S., 1975
The federal probation system: the second 25 years.
Fed. Probation, **39**(2), 16–25.

MEYER, P.B., 1975
Medical experimentation on prisoners: some economic considerations.
Washington, D.C.: Correctional Economics Center, American Bar Assn.

MORRIS, T., 1975
Prison—or community care?
Ditchley J., **2**(2), 35–53.

MULLEN, J., 1975
The dilemma of diversion. Resource materials on adult pre-trial intervention programs.
L.E.A.A., National Institute of Law Enforcement and Criminal Justice, U.S. Dept. of Justice, Washington, D.C.

NELSON, C.W., 1975
Cost-benefit analysis and alternatives to incarceration.
Fed. Probation, **39**(4), 45–50.

OHLIN, L.E., COATES, R.B., AND MILLER, A.D., 1975
Evaluating the reform of youth correction in Massachusetts.
J. Res. Crime & Delinq., **12,** 3–16.

PALMER, J.W., 1975
Pre-arrest diversion: the night prosecutor's program in Columbus, Ohio.
Crime & Delinq., **21,** 100–8.

PARLOUR, R.R., 1975
Behavioral techniques for sociopathic clients.
Fed. Probation, **39**(1), 3–11.

PEASE, K., DURKIN, P., EARNSHAW, I., PAYNE, D., AND THORPE, J., 1975
Community service orders.
London: Home Office Research Studies, **29.**

PETERSEN, D.M., AND FRIDAY, P.C., 1975
Early release from incarceration: race as a factor in the use of 'shock probation.'
J. Crim. Law & Criminol., **66,** 79–87.

REASONS, C.E., AND KAPLAN, R.L., 1975
Tear down the walls?: some functions of prisons.
Crime & Delinq., **21,** 360–72.

RECTOR, M.G., 1975
The extravagance of imprisonment.
Crime & Delinq., **21,** 323–30.

RUTHERFORD, R.B., 1975
Establishing behavioral contracts with delinquent adolescents.
Fed. Probation. **39**(2), 28–32.

SACKS, M.J., 1975
Making work release work: convincing the employer.
Crime & Delinq., **21,** 255–65.

SCHUELER–SPRINGORUM, H., 1975
A critical comparison of the British detention centres and the German 'Jugendarrest' system.
Int. J. Criminol. & Penol., **3,** 201–11.

THORNSTEDT, H., 1975
The day-fine system in Sweden.
Crim. Law Rev., 1975, 307–12.

TRASLER, G., 1975
In defence of 'young adult offenders.'
Howard J. Penol. & Crime Prev., **14,** 3–11.

UNITED KINGDOM, 1975
The Children and Young Persons Act., 1969
Eleventh Report from the Expenditure Committee, House of Commons, Session 1974–75.
London: Vol. **1.** Report, paras., 104–67.

WEXLER, D.B., 1975
Behavior modification and other behavior change procedures: the emerging law and the proposed Florida guidelines.
Crim. Law Bull., **11,** 600–16.

WHITLAM, M.R., AND RUTHERFORD, A., 1975
Taylor House: two views.
1. An experiment in Borstal hostels.
2. An example of penal tokenism.
Howard J. Penol. & Crime Prev., **14,** 43–49.

MORRIS, T., 1976
Offenders in the community.
Ditchley J., **3**(1), 38–57.

RYAN, M., 1976
Radical Alternatives to Prison.
Pol. Quart., **47,** 71–81.

13 Parole

1 Selection: criteria and legal bases

[See also Section 7(2) for references relating to indeterminate sentences; Section 14(2) for references relating to prisoners' rights.]

GAYLIN, W., 1970
In the service of their country: war resisters in prison.
New York: Grosset & Dunlop, 319–44.

INCIARDI, J.A., 1973
Parole prediction: a fifty year fantasy, in E. Sagarin and D.E.J. MacNamara (eds.), *Corrections: problems of punishment and rehabilitation.*
New York: Praeger, 125–33

DUKE LAW JOURNAL, 1974
Procedural protection at parole release hearings: the need for reform.
1974, 1119–63.

FISHER, H.R., 1974
Probation and parole revocation: the anomaly of divergent procedures.
Fed. Probation. **38**(3), 23–9.

GOTTFREDSON, D.M., WILKINS, L.T., HOFFMAN, P.B., AND SINGER, S.M., 1974
The utilisation of experience in parole decision-making. Summary report.
L.E.A.A., National Institute of Law Enforcement and Criminal Justice, U.S. Dept. of Justice, Washington, D.C.

HASTINGS LAW JOURNAL, 1974
The impossible dream?: due process guarantee for California parolees and probationers.
25, 602–35.

HOFFMAN, P.B., AND BECK, J.L., 1974
Parole decision-making: a salient factor score.
J. Crim. Justice, **2**, 195–206.

HOFFMAN, P.B., AND DEGOSTIN, L.K., 1974
Parole decision-making: structuring discretion.
Fed. Probation, **38**(4), 7–15.

JAMES, L., 1974
Influence in the prison environment.
Univ. of Toronto: Centre of Criminology, 45–75, 83–92.

O'LEARY, V., 1974
Parole administration, in D. Glaser (ed.), *Handbook of criminology.*
Chicago: Rand McNally, 909–48.

PRICE, R.R., 1974
Bringing the rule of law to corrections.
Can. J. Criminol. & Corrections, **16**, 209–55.

SCOTT, J.E., 1974
The use of discretion in determining the the severity of punishment for incarcerated offenders.
J. Crim. Law & Criminol., **65**, 214–24.

STANFORD LAW REVIEW, 1974
California department of corrections and adult authority decision making procedures for male felons.
26, 1353–82.

TOBRINGER, M.O., AND COHEN, H., 1974
How much process is 'due'? Parolees and prisoners.
Hastings Law J., **25**, 801–11.

VANDERBILT LAW REVIEW, 1974
Parole release—Federal Circuits conflict on applicability of Due Process and Administrative Procedure Act to parole release decisions.
27, 1257–77.

BECK, J.L., 1975
The effect of representation at parole hearings.
Criminol., **13,** 114–17.

BENNETT, L.A., AND ZIEGLER, M., 1975
Early discharge: a suggested approach to increased efficiency in parole.
Fed. Probation, **39**(3), 27–30.

BUFFALO LAW REVIEW, 1975
The prisoner's right to a statement of reasons for parole denial: silence is not always golden.
4, 567–94.

CALIFORNIA LAW REVIEW, 1975
California Supreme Court 1973–74: Prison Law.
63, 266–301.

CANADA, 1975
Imprisonment and release.
Law Reform Commission of Canada, working paper, 11 (1975), in, *Can. J. Criminol. & Corrections*, **17**(4), 33–46.

CITIZENS' INQUIRY ON PAROLE AND CRIMINAL JUSTICE, INC., 1975
Prison without walls. Report on New York parole.
(Chairman, Ramsey Clark).
New York: Praeger.

CRIMINAL LAW BULLETIN, 1975
Report on New York parole: a summary, by Citizens' Inquiry on Parole and Criminal Justice, Inc.
11, 273–303.

FOGEL, D., 1975
'... *We are the living proof* ...' *The justice model for corrections.*
Cincinnati: W.H. Anderson Co., 236–60. 289–95, 307–11.

GILMAN, D., 1975
The sanction of imprisonment: for whom, for what, and how.
Crime & Delinq., **21,** 337–47.

GILMAN, D., 1975.
Sentencing-imprisonment consequences (comment on New York parole report).
Crim. Law Bull., **11,** 318–26.

GOTTFREDSON, D.M., HOFFMAN, P.B., SIGLER, M.H., AND WILKINS, L.T., 1975
Making paroling policy explicit.
Crime & Delinq., **21,** 34–44.

GREENBERG, D.F., 1975
The incapacitative effects of imprisonment: some estimates.
Law & Soc. Rev., **9,** 541–80.

HALL WILLIAMS, J.E., 1975
Natural justice and parole.
Crim. Law Rev., **1975,** 82–91, 215–23.

HAWKINS, K., 1975
An 'efficient, just and credible parole system.'
Brit. J. Criminol., **15,** 284–8.

HOOD, R., 1975
The case against executive control over time in custody: a rejoinder to Professor Walker's criticisms.
Crim. Law Rev., 1975, 545–52.

LEE, N., AND ZUCKERMAN, D.H., 1975
Representing parole violators (comments on New York parole report).
Crim. Law Bull. **11,** 327–34.

MORRIS, P., AND BEVERLY, F., 1975
On licence. A study of parole.
London: John Wiley & Sons, 1–23, 79–92.

MOSELEY, W.H., AND GEROULD, M.H., 1975
Sex and parole: a comparison of male and female parolees.
J. Crim. Justice, **3,** 47–57.

O'LEARY, V., 1975
Parole theory and outcomes re-examined (comment on New York parole report).
Crim. Law Bull., **11,** 304–17.

PETERSEN, D.M., AND FRIDAY, P.C., 1975
Early release from incarceration: race as a factor in the use of 'shock probation.'
J. Crim. Law & Criminol., **66,** 79–87.

RUDENSTINE, D., 1975
The rehabilitation and risk assessment goals of parole theory: a reply to Professor Vincent O'leary.
Crim. Law Bull., **11,** 488–97.

SCOTT, J.E., AND SNIDER, P.J., 1975
Perceptual effects of penal institutions on the severity of punishment.
Int. J. Criminol. & Penol., **3,** 53–62.

SIGLER, M.H., 1975
Abolish parole?
Fed. Probation, **39**(2), 42–8.

TRASLER, G., 1975
In defence of 'young adult offenders.'
Howard J. Penol. & Crime Prev., **14,** 3–11.

WALKER, N., 1975
Release by executive decision: a defence.
Crim. Law Rev., 1975, 540–4.

YALE LAW JOURNAL, 1975
Parole release decision making and the sentencing process.
84, 810–902.

2 Parole outcome

[*See also Section 10(2) on follow-up studies in general.*]

ERICKSON, R.J., CROW, W.J., ZURCHER, L.A., AND CONNETT, A.V., 1973
Paroled but not free.
New York: Behavioral Publications.

DAVIES, M., 1974
Prisoners of society: attitudes and after-care.
London: Routledge & Kegan Paul, 62–104.

JUNG, J., 1974
The parole supervisor's perception of the parolee's situation.
Can. J. Criminol. & Corrections, **16,** 272–81.

SAMPSON, A., 1974
Post-prison success prediction.
Criminol., **12,** 155–73.

BAILEY, W.C., 1975
Addicts on parole: short-term and long-term prognosis.
Internat. J. Addict., **10,** 317–31.

GREENBERG, D.F., 1975
The incapacitative effects of imprisonment: some estimates.
Law & Soc. Rev., **9,** 541–80.

MCCABE, O.L., KURLAND, A.A., AND SULLIVAN, D., 1975
Paroled narcotic addicts in a verified abstinence program: results of a five-year study.
Internat. J. Addict., **10,** 211–28.

MORRIS, P., AND BEVERLY, F., 1975
On licence. A study of parole.
London: John Wiley & Sons, 93–166.

O'LEARY, V., 1975
Parole theory and outcomes re-examined (comment on New York parole report).
Crim. Law Bull., **11,** 304–17.

14 Status and rights of offenders

1 Rights in prison

[*See also Section 7(2) for references on conflicting values in the implementation of sanctions; Section 12 on experimental studies and innovations in corrections.*]

INGRAHAM, B.L., 1973
Will legal relief for inmates prevent violence in correctional institutions?, in United States of America, *Prevention of violence in correctional institutions*, Criminal Justice Monograph.
L.E.A.A., National Institute of Law Enforcement and Criminal Justice, U.S. Dept. of Justice, Washington, D.C., 33–49.

INTERNATIONAL PENAL AND PENITENTIARY FOUNDATION, 1973
Communication and democratisation in the penitentiary field. Proceedings of the Fourth Meeting of Heads of Prison Administrations, Oxford, 23–29 September, 1973
London: IPPF, 21–49, 64–92.

KRANTZ, S., BELL, R.A., GRANT, J., AND MARGRUDER, M., 1973
Prisoners' rights and responsibilities: model rules and regulations.
St. Paul, Minn.: West Publ. Co.

STRATTON, B., 1973
Who guards the guards?
North London Group of PROP, 339a Finchley Road, London N.W.3.

AMERICAN BAR ASSOCIATION, 1974
Survey and handbook on state standards and inspection legislation for jails and juvenile detention facilities.
Statewide Jail Standards and Inspection Systems Project.
Washington, D.C., A.B.A.

ANNAS, G.J., AND GLANTZ, L.H., 1974
Psychosurgery: the law's response.
Boston Univ, Law Rev., **54,** 249–67.

ARIZONA LAW REVIEW, 1974
A remedy for discrimination against women prisoners.
16, 974–1000.

AUSTRALIAN AND NEW ZEALAND JOURNAL OF CRIMINOLOGY, 1974
Standard minimum rules for the treatment of prisoners. (United Nations Rules reprinted.)
7, 110–7.

BOSTON UNIVERSITY LAW REVIEW, 1973
Discipline in jails: the due process rights of pretrial detainees.
54, 796–827.

BOSTON UNIVERSITY LAW REVIEW, 1974
Freedom of speech and of the press: prison regulation limiting press access to prisoners held unconstitutional.
54, 670–88.

DWYER, P., AND BOTEIN, M., 1974
The right to rehabilitation for prisoners—judicial reform of the correctional process.
New York Law Forum, **20,** 273–311.

FISHER, H.R., 1974
Probation and parole revocation: the anomaly of divergent procedures.
Fed. Probation, **38**(3), 23–9.

FITZGERALD, M., 1974
'*Control Units*': *imprisonment* 1974.
London: PROP, 339a Finchley Road, London N.W.3.

GIFIS, S.H., 1974
Decision making in a prison community.
Wisconsin Law Rev., 1974, 349–427.

HASTINGS LAW JOURNAL, 1974
The impossible dream? Due process guarantees for California parolees and probationers.
25, 602–35.

HUFF, C.R., 1974
Unionization behind the walls.
Criminol., **12,** 175–93.

INDIANA LAW JOURNAL, 1974
A prisoner's right to a protective transfer from State to Federal prison.
50, 143–53.

INTERNATIONAL REVIEW OF CRIMINAL POLICY, 1974
Meeting of a group of experts on the standard minimum rules for the treatment of prisoners. New York, 25–29 September. 1972.
31, 84–90.

LESNICK, H., 1974
Grievance procedures in Federal prisons: practices and proposals.
Univ. Penn. Law Rev., **123,** 1–44.

MCARTHUR, V., 1974
Inmate grievance mechanisms: a survey of 209 American prisons.
Fed. Probation, **38**(4), 41–7.

MICHIGAN LAW REVIEW, 1974
Conjugal visitation rights and the appropriate standard of judicial review for prison regulations.
73, 398–423.

MORRIS, G.H., 1974
Institutionalizing the rights of mental patients: committing the legislature.
Calif. Law Rev., **62,** 957–1024.

MOYA, C.B., AND ACHTENBERG, R., 1974
Behavior modification: legal limitation on methods and goals.
Notre Dame Lawyer, **50,** 230–50.

NOTRE DAME LAWYER, 1974
Judicial recognition and implementation of a right to treatment for institutionalized juveniles.
49, 1051–63.

PLOTKIN, R., 1974
Surviving justice: prisoners' rights to be free from physical assault.
Cleveland State Law Rev., **23,** 387–422.

REASONS, C., 1974
Racism, prisons, and prisoners' rights.
Issues in Criminol., **9,** 3–20.

SCHWITZGEBEL, R.K., 1974
The right to effective mental treatment.
Calif. Law Rev., **62,** 936–56.

SOUTHERN CALIFORNIA LAW REVIEW, 1974
Guilt by physiology: the constitutionality of tests to determine predisposition to violent behavior.
48, 489–507.

STENDER, F., 1974
The 'closing' of O Wing at Soledad prison: reflections on the use of lock-up.
Mississippi Law J., **45,** 645–73.

TOBRINGER, M.O., AND COHEN, H., 1974
How much process is 'due'? Parolees and prisoners.
Hastings Law J., **25,** 801–11.

VIRGINIA LAW REVIEW, 1974
Limits on punishment and entitlement to rehabilitative treatment of institutionalized juveniles: *Nelson v. Heyne.*
60, 864–83.

VIRGINIA LAW REVIEW, 1974
Review of improper juvenile transfer hearings.
60, 818–39.

WEISSMAN, A.B., 1974
The discriminatory application of penal laws by state judicial and quasi-judicial officers: playing the shell game of rights and remedies.
Northwestern Univ. Law Rev., **69,** 489–554.

ALBANY LAW REVIEW, 1975
Non-therapeutic prison research: an analysis of potential legal remedies.
39, 799–825.

AMNESTY INTERNATIONAL, 1975
Prisoners of conscience in the USSR: their treatment and conditions.
London: Amnesty International.

British Institute of Human Rights, The 1975
Minimum standards of treatment.
Chichester, Sussex: Barry Rose.

Buffalo Law Review, 1975
The prisoner's right to a statement of reasons for parole denial: silence is not always golden.
24, 567–94.

Clark, L.D., and Parker, G.M., 1975
The labor law problems of the prisoner.
Rutgers Law Rev., **28,** 840–60.

Cleveland State Law Review, 1975
Behavior modification: winners in the game of life? **24,** 422–62.

Criminal Law Bulletin, 1975
The United Nations Standard Minimum Rules for the treatment of prisoners.
11, 637–46.

Dickinson Law Review, 1975
Prisoner mail censorship regulations subject to first amendment review.
Procunier v. Martinez 416 U.S. 396 (1974).
79, 352–65.

Donzelot, J., 1975
The prison movement in France, in H. Bianchi, M. Simondi and I. Taylor (eds.), *Deviance and control in Europe: papers from the European group for the study of deviance and social control.*
London: John Wiley & Sons, 109–14.

Duke Law Journal, 1974
Procedural protection at parole release hearings: the need for reform.
1974, 1119–63.

Fogel, D., 1975
'... *We are the living proof ...' The justice model for corrections.*
Cincinnati: W.H. Anderson Co., 112–77, 204–36, 296–8.

Fitzgerald, M., 1975
The British prisoners' movement: its aims and methods, in H. Bianchi, M. Simondi and I. Taylor (eds.), *Deviance and control in Europe: papers from the European group for the study of deviance and social control.*
London: John Wiley & Sons, 97–107.

Fordham Law Review, 1975
Habeas corpus challenges to prison discipline.
43, 963–88.

Friedman, P.R., 1975
Legal regulation of applied behavior analysis in mental institutions and prisons.
Arizona Law Rev., **17,** 39–104.
And commentaries by I. Goldiamond, R. Clemons and D.B. Wexler, 105–43.

Gardner, M.R., 1975
The defense of necessity and the right to escape from prison—a step towards incarceration free from sexual assault.
S. Calif. Law Rev., **49,** 110–52.

Gaylin, W., and Blatte, H., 1975
Behavior modification in prisons.
Amer. Crim. Law Rev., **13,** 11–35.

Gilman, D., 1975
Developments in correctional law.
Crime & Delinq., **21,** 163–73.

Gobert, J.G., 1975
Psychosurgery, conditioning, and the prisoner's right to refuse 'rehabilitation.'
Virginia Law Rev., **61,** 155–96.

Goldberger, D., 1975
Court challenges to prison behavior modification programs: a case study.
Amer. Crim. Law Rev., **13,** 37–68.

Goldfarb, R., 1975
Jails: the ultimate ghetto.
New York: Anchor Press/Doubleday, 345–415.

Goldsmith, S.B., 1975
Prison health: travesty of justice.
New York: Prodist.

Guenther, P., 1975
Enfranchisement for prisoners: a look at present laws and practices.
Can. J. Criminol. & Corrections, **17,** 206–14.

Hall Williams, J.E., 1975
Natural justice and parole.
Crim. Law Rev., 1975, 82–91, 215–23.

HASTINGS LAW JOURNAL, 1975
The fourteenth amendment and prisons: a new look at due process for prisoners.
26, 1277–98.

JUSTICE, THE HOWARD LEAGUE FOR PENAL REFORM, THE NATIONAL ASSOCIATION FOR THE CARE AND RESETTLEMENT OF OFFENDERS, 1975
Boards of visitors of penal institutions.
Report of the committee (Chairman, Lord Jellicoe).
Chichester and London: Barry Rose, 69–75, 83–4.

KEATING, J.M., JR., AND KOLZE, R.C., 1975
An inmate grievance mechanism: from design to practice.
Fed. Probation, **39**(3), 42–6.

LEE, N., AND ZUCKERMAN, D.H., 1975
Representing parole violators (comment on New York parole report).
Crim. Law Bull., **11,** 327–34.

MCCORMACK, W., 1975
The expansion of federal question jurisdiction and the prisoner complaint case load.
Wisconsin Law Rev., 1975, 523–51.

MATHIESEN, T., AND RØINE, W., 1975
The prison movement in Scandinavia, in H. Bianchi, M. Simondi and I. Taylor (eds.), *Deviance and control in Europe: papers from the European group for the study of deviance and social control.*
London: John Wiley & Sons, 85–95.

MEYER, P.B., 1975
Medical experimentation on prisoners: some economic considerations.
Washington, D.C.: Correctional Economics Center, American Bar Assn.

NORTHWESTERN UNIVERSITY LAW REVIEW, 1975
A giant step backwards: the Supreme Court speaks out on prisoners' first amendment rights.
70, 352–71.

PLOTKIN, R., 1975
Recent developments in the law of prisoners' rights.
Crim. Law Bull., **11,** 405–33.

RAUTY, R., 1975
Introductory note to the prison revolts in Italy (1973), in H. Bianchi, M. Simondi and I. Taylor (eds.), *Deviance and control in Europe: papers from the European group for the study of deviance and social control.*
London: John Wiley & Sons, 115–24.

RUBIN, S., (ED.), 1975
A model act to provide for minimum standards for the protection of rights of prisoners. In *United States Prison Law. Vol.* 2 491–500.
New York: Oceana Publications.

SERBER, M., HILLER, C., KEITH, C., AND TAYLOR, J., 1975
Behavior modification in maximum security settings: one hospital's experience.
Amer. Crim. Law Rev., **13,** 85–99.

SULLIVAN, D.C., AND TIFFT, L.L., 1975
Court intervention in correction: roots of resistance and problems of compliance.
Crime & Delinq., **21,** 213–22.

UNIVERSITY OF CHICAGO LAW REVIEW, 1975
The rights of prisoners to medical care and the implications for drug-dependent prisoners.
42, 705–32.

WEXLER, D.B., 1975
Behavior modification and other behavior change procedures: the emerging law and the proposed Florida guidelines.
Crim. Law Bull., **11,** 600–16.

WOLFE, R.W., AND MARINO, D.R., 1975
A program of behavior treatment for incarcerated pedophiles.
Amer. Crim. Law Rev., **13,** 69–83.

ZELLICK, G., 1975
Prisoners and the law, in S. McConville (ed.), *The use of imprisonment.*
London: Routledge & Kegan Paul, 1–16.

BOYLE, C., 1976
Confidentiality in correctional institutions.
Can. J. Criminol. & Corrections, **18,** 26–41.

HAWKINS, G., 1976
The prison: policy and practice.
Univ. Chicago Press, 133–49.

2 Other rights, in relation to police, courts, employment, etc.

[*See also Section 6*(4) *on use and abuse of policies powers; Section 13*(1) *on parole selection.*]

SHAPIRO, D., 1973
Federal habeas corpus: a study in Massachusetts.
Harvard Law Rev., **87**, 321–72.

NEW YORK UNIVERSITY LAW REVIEW, 1974
Employment discrimination against rehabilitated drug addicts.
49, 67–86.

ALABAMA LAW REVIEW, 1975
The loss of rights upon criminal conviction in Alabama.
27, 126–54.

ATKINS, B.M., AND BOYLE, E.W., 1975
Prisoners' perceptions of their constitutional rights: a client's view of the world of criminal justice.
Emory Law J., **24**, 67–91.

CONNECTICUT LAW REVIEW, 1975
The scope of the indigent federal prisoner's right to a trial transcript—McCollom v. United States, 511 F. 2d 1116 (9th Cir. 1974).
7, 479–507.

HASTINGS LAW JOURNAL, 1975
The revolving door: the effect of employment discrimination against ex-prisoners.
26, 1403–33.

INDIANA LAW JOURNAL, 1975
Pretrial diversion from the criminal process: some constitutional considerations.
50, 783–807.

KLINE, T., 1975
Ex-convict civil disabilities: an analysis of Bergansky v. State of New York Liquor Authority.
Crim. Law Bull., **11**, 29–47.

LENIHAN, K.J., 1975
The financial condition of released prisoners.
Crime & Delinq., **21**, 266–81.

LERMAN, P., 1975
Community treatment and social control. A critical analysis of juvenile correctional policy.
Univ. Chicago Press, 78–104, 204–25.

15 Manipulation of environment: the problem of prevention

1 Delinquency prevention programmes

(b) *Delinquency and crime prevention programmes*

MALTZ, M.D., 1972
Evaluation of crime control programs.
L.E.A.A., National Institute of Law Enforcement and Criminal Justice, U.S. Dept. of Justice, Washington, D.C.

RECKLESS, W.C., AND DINITZ, S., 1972
The prevention of juvenile delinquency: an experiment.
Columbus, Ohio: Ohio State Univ. Press, 42–163.

UNITED STATES OF AMERICA, 1973
Deterrence of crime in and around residences.
Criminal Justice Monograph.
L.E.A.A., National Institute of Law Enforcement and Criminal Justice, U.S. Dept. of Justice, Washington, D.C.

UNITED STATES OF AMERICA, 1973
Research on street crime control.
Criminal Justice Monograph.
L.E.A.A., National Institute of Law Enforcement and Criminal Justice, U.S. Dept. of Justice, Washington, D.C.

BALDWIN, J., 1974
The role of victim in certain property offences.
Crim. Law Rev., 1974, 353–8.

CARTER, R.L., 1974
Theft in the market.
London: The Institute of Economic Affairs.

EMPEY, L.T., 1974
Crime prevention: the fugitive utopia, in D. Glaser (ed.), *Handbook of criminology.*
Chicago: Rand McNally, 1095–123.

ERSKINE, H., 1974
The polls: control of crime and violence.
Public Opinion Quart., **38**, 490–502.

KELLING, G.L., ET AL, 1974
The Kansas City preventive patrol experiment: a summary report.
Washington, D.C.: The Police Foundation.

KNIGHTS, D., GOLDSTEIN, R., AND GUTIERREZ, J., 1974
Organising for youth development and delinquency prevention—youth development/delinquency research project—a second year report.
Sacramento, Calif.: California Youth Authority.

RICCIO, L.J., 1974
Direct deterrence—an analysis of the effectiveness of police patrol and other crime prevention technologies.
J. Crim. Justice, **2**, 207–17.

CONKLIN, J.E., 1975
The impact of crime.
New York: Macmillan, 105–53, 185–247.

UNITED KINGDOM, 1975
Protection against vandalism.
Report by a Working Party of the Home Office Standing Committee on Crime Prevention.
London.

MAYHEW, P., CLARKE, R.V.G., STURMAN, A., AND HOUGH, J.M., 1976
Crime as opportunity.
London: Home Office Research Studies, **34.**

SNODGRASS, J., 1976
Clifford R. Shaw and Henry D. McKay: Chicago criminologists.
Brit. J. Criminol., **16**, 1–19.

2 Identification and prediction of potential criminality

MILLER, F.J.W., COURT, S.D.M., KNOX, E.G., AND BRANSON, S., 1974
The school years in Newcastle upon Tyne 1952–62.
London: Oxford Univ. Press, 203–11.

WEIS, K., 1974
The Glueck social prediction table—an unfulfilled promise.
J. Crim. Law & Criminol., **65**, 397–404.

16 Crime commissions: a comparison of their methods and recommendations

ALLEN, H.E., 1973
The task force model as a vehicle for correctional change: liability or asset? in E. Sagarin and D.E.J. MacNamara (eds.), *Corrections: problems of punishment and rehabilitation.*
New York: Praeger, 80–87.

EMMER, G.P., 1973
The management of change in L.E.A.A.'s impact program, in United States of America, *The change process in criminal justice.* Criminal Justice Monograph.
L.E.A.A., National Institute of Law Enforcement and Criminal Justice, U.S. Dept. of Justice, Washington, D.C., 18–35.

LARSEN, O.N., 1975
The commission on obscenity and pornography: form, function and failure, in M. Komarovsky (ed.), *Sociology and public policy: the case of Presidential commissions.*
New York: Elsevier, 9–41.

LAZARSFELD, P.L., AND JAECKEL, M., 1975
The use of sociology by Presidential commissions, in Mr. Komarovsky (ed.), *Sociology and public policy: the case of Presidential commissions.*
New York: Elsevier, 117–42.

MCLAUCHLAN, G., 1975
L.E.A.A.: A case study in the development of the social industrial complex.
Crime & Social Justice, **4**, 15–23.

MERTON, R.K., 1975
Social knowledge and public policy. Sociological perspectives on four Presidential commissions, in M. Komarovsky (ed.), *Sociology and public policy: the case of Presidental commissions.*
New York: Elsevier, 153–77.

MILAKOVICH, M.E., AND WEIS, K., 1975
Politics and measures of success in the war on crime.
Crime & Delinq., **21**, 1–10.

OHLIN, L.E., 1975
Report on the President's commission on law enforcement and administration of justice, in M. Komarovsky (ed.), *Sociology and public policy: the case of Presidential commissions.*
New York: Elsevier, 93–115.

SHORT, J.F., JR., 1975.
The national commission on the causes and prevention of violence: reflections on the contributions of sociology and sociologists, in M. Komarovsky (ed.), *Sociology and public policy: the case of Presidential commissions.*
New York: Elsevier, 61–91.

WILSON, J.Q., 1975
Thinking about crime.
New York: Basic Books, 43–77.

WRIGHT, M., 1975
Tactics of reform, in S. McConville (ed.), *The use of imprisonment.*
London: Routledge & Kegan Paul, 88–106.

17 Some international comparative references

MYRDAL, G., 1968
Asian drama. An inquiry into the povery of nations.
Harmondsworth: Penguin Books, **2,** 937–58.

FERRACUTI, F., LAZZARI, R., AND WOLFGANG, M.E., (EDS.), 1970
La violenza in Sardegna.
Rome: Mario Bulzoni.

EVENSEN, A., 1972
Social defence in Norway.
Oslo: Ministry of Social Affairs.

REIFEN, D., 1972
The juvenile court in a changing society: young offenders in Israel.
London: Weidenfeld & Nicolson.

SHARPLES, K.S., 1972
The legal framework of judicial sentencing policy.
Amsterdam: University Press, 157–338.

SLATTERY, B., 1972
A handbook on sentencing: with particular reference to Tanzania.
Nairobi: East African Literature Bureau.

AMNESTY INTERNATIONAL, 1973
Report on torture.
London: Duckworth.

CLIFFORD, W., 1973
Development and crime.
Chichester, Sussex: Barry Rose.

SMITH, G., 1973
Popular participation in the administration of justice in the Soviet Union: comrades' courts and the Brezhnev regime.
Indiana Law J., **49,** 238–52.

SOLZHENITSYN, A., 1973
The Gulag Archipelago.
Glasgow: Collins and Harvill Press.

BISHOP, N., 1974
Aspects of European penal systems, in L. Blom-Cooper (ed), *Progress in penal reform.*
Oxford: Clarendon Press, 83–100.

BEKAERT, H., 1974
Les fluctuations de la criminalité en Belgique.
Bruxelles: Centre National de Criminologie.

CLIFFORD, W., 1974
An introduction to African criminology.
Nairobi: Oxford Univ. Press.

HASSON, U., AND SEBBA, L., 1974
Compensation to victims of crime: a comparative study in I. Drapkin and E. Viano (eds.), *Victimology: a new focus. Vol. 2, society's reaction to victimization.*
Lexington, Mass.: Heath Lexington Books, 103–20.

HEIJDER, A., 1974
The recent trend towards reducing the prison population in the Netherlands.
Internat. J. Offender Therapy, **18,** 233–40.

INTERNATIONAL REVIEW OF CRIMINAL POLICY, 1974
Capital punishment: report of the Secretary-General.
31, 91–101.

UNITED NATIONS SOCIAL DEFENCE RESEARCH INSTITUTE, 1974
Recent contributions to Soviet criminology.
Rome: UNSDRI.

VASSALLI, G., 1974
The reform of the Italian penal code.
Wayne Law Rev., **20,** 1031–69.

WILSON, A., 1974
New approaches in the handling of juvenile delinquents in Scotland: a) recent developments in social work.
Internat. J. Offender Therapy, **18,** 247–59.

AMNESTY INTERNATIONAL, 1975
Prisoners of conscience in the USSR: their treatment and conditions.
London: Amnesty International.

CLIFFORD, W., 1975
New dimensions in criminality—national and transnational.
Aust. & N.Z. J. Criminol., **8**, 67–85.

COUNCIL OF EUROPE, 1975
Compensation for victims of crime.
Strasbourg: DPC/CEPC XXIX (75) 10.

CRIMINAL LAW BULLETIN, 1975
The United Nations standard minimum rules for the treatment of prisoners.
11, 637–46.

DONZELOT, J., 1975
The prison movement in France, in H. Bianchi, M. Simondi and I. Taylor (eds.), *Deviance and control in Europe: papers from the European group for the study of deviance and social control.*
London: John Wiley & Sons, 109–14.

JOHNSTONE, S.W., 1975
Problems in the enforcement of world criminal law.
Aust. & N.Z. J. Criminol., **8**, 87–100.

LØNBERG, A., 1975
The penal system of Denmark.
Copenhagen Ministry of Justice.

MATHIESEN, T., AND RØINE, W., 1975
The prison movement in Scandinavia, in H. Bianchi, M. Simondi and I. Taylor (eds.), *Deviance and control in Europe: papers from the European group for the study of deviance and social control.*
London: John Wiley & Sons, 85–95.

MIDGLEY, J., 1975
Children on trial: a study of juvenile justice.
Cape Town: National Institute for Crime Prevention and the Rehabilitation of Offenders.

OSBOROUGH, N., 1975
Borstal in Ireland.
Dublin: Institute of Public Administration.

PEASE, K., IRESON, J., AND THORPE, J., 1975
Modified crime indices for eight countries.
J. Crim. Law & Criminol., **66**, 209–14.

RAUTY, R., 1975
Introductory note to the prison revolts in Italy (1973), in H. Bianchi, M. Simondi and I. Taylor (eds). *Deviance and control in Europe: papers from the European group for the study of deviance and social control.*
London: John Wiley & Sons, 115–24.

SCOTTISH HOME AND HEALTH DEPARTMENT, 1975
Crime and the prevention of crime.
A memorandum by the Scottish Council on Crime.
Edinburgh: H.M.S.O.

SCHUELER-SPRINGORUM, H., 1975
A critical comparison of the British detention centres and the German 'Jugandarrest' system.
Int. J. Criminol. & Penol., **3**, 201–11.

SCHUMANN, K.F., 1975
Approaching crime and deviance: a note on contributions by scientists, officials of social control and social activists during the last five years in West Germany, in H. Bianchi, M. Simondi and I. Taylor (eds.), *Deviance and control in Europe: papers from the European group for the study of deviance and social control.*
London: John Wiley & Sons, 59–76.

SEPPILLI, T., AND ABBOZZO, G.G., 1975
The state of research into social control and deviance in Italy in the post-war period (1945–1973), in H. Bianchi, M. Simondi and I. Taylor (eds.), *Deviance and social control in Europe: papers from the European group for the study of deviance and social control.*
London: John Wiley & Sons, 35–50.

SILVERMAN, R.A., AND JEEVAN, J.J., JR., (EDS.), 1975
Crime in Canadian society.
Toronto: Butterworths.

SOLZHENITSYN, A., 1975
The Gulag Archipelago (2)
London: Collins and Harvill Press.

STANG DAHL, T., 1975
The state of criminology in Norway: a short report, in H. Bianchi, M. Simondi and I. Taylor (eds.), *Deviance and control in Europe: papers from the European group for the study of deviance and social control.*
London: John Wiley & Sons, 77–81.

GANDY, J.M., 1976
Canada's juvenile justice system: proposed new legislation.
Brit. J. Criminol., **16**, 68–72.

LOPEZ-REY, M., 1976
United Nations policy in crime problems, the problems of crime and the problem of criminology.
Int. J. Criminol. & Penol., **4**, 59–67.

18 Bibliographies

PARKER, W., 1971
Homosexuality: a selective bibliography of over 3000 items.
Metuchen, N.Y.,: The Scarecrow Press.

BANCROFT, J., 1974
Bibliography, in *Deviant sexual behaviour; modification and assessment.*
London: Oxford Univ. Press, 168–252.

CHAPPELL, D., GEIS, G., AND FOGARTY, F., 1974
Forcible rape: bibliography.
J. Crim. Law & Criminol., **65,** 248–63.

COUNCIL OF EUROPE, 1974
Select bibliography in *Group and community work with the offenders.*
Strasbourg, 111–25.

GOYER-MICHAUD, F., 1974
The adult female offender: a selected bibliography.
Criminal Justice & Behavior, **1,** 340–56.

PFEIL, H.P., VON, 1974
Juvenile rights since 1967: an annotated, bibliography of selected articles and books.
South Hackensack, N.J.: Fred B. Rothman.

PROSTANO, E.T., AND PICCIRILLO, M.L., 1974
Law enforcement: a selective bibliography.
Littleton, Colo: Libraries Unlimited.

AMERICAN CRIMINAL LAW REVIEW, 1975
Bibliography on behavior modification in prisons.
13, 101–13.

FOGARTY, F., 1975
Violence and criminal justice: a bibliography 1969–1974, in D. Chappell and J. Monahan (eds.), *Violence and criminal justice.*
Lexington, Mass.: Heath Lexington Books, 113–41.

TESLIK, W.R., 1975
Prosecutorial discretion—the decision to charge—an annotated bibliography.
National Institute of Law Enforcement and Criminal Justice, Washington, D.C.

WOLFGANG, M.E., FIGLIO, R.M., AND THORNBERRY, T.P., 1975
Criminology index: research and theory in criminology in the United States, 1945–1972.
New York: Elsevier, 2 vols.

MARCUS, M., (ED), 1976
Criminal Justice bibliography.
Georgia State Univ.: School of Urban Life. 2nd ed.

19 Selected textbooks and readings

1 Selected textbooks

WINSLOW, R.W., 1970
Society in transition. A social approach to deviancy.
New York: The Free Press.

COOK, J.G., 1972
Constitutional rights of the accused: pre-trial rights.
Rochester: Lawyers Cooperative, Bancroft-Whitney.

KAPLAN, J., 1973
Criminal justice: introductory cases and materials.
Mineola: Foundation Press.

RUBIN, S., 1973
The law of criminal correction.
St. Paul, Minn.: West Publishing Co. 2nd ed.

COOK, J.G., 1974
Contsitutional rights of the accused: trial rights.
Rochester: Lawyers Cooperative, Bancroft-Whitney.

KASSEBAUM, G., 1974
Delinquency and social policy.
Englewood Cliffs, N.J.: Prentice-Hall.

NEWMAN, D.J., 1974
Introduction to criminal justice.
Philadelphia: J.B. Lippincott.

BLANCHARD, R.E., 1975
Introduction to the administration of justice.
New York: John Wiley & Sons.

CARTER, R.M., MCGEE, R.A., AND NELSON, E.K., 1975
Corrections in America.
Philadelphia: J.B. Lippincott.

CAVAN, R.S., AND FERDINAND, T.N., 1975
Juvenile delinquency.
Philadelphia: J.B. Lippincott, 3rd ed.

DINITZ, S., DYNES, R.R., AND CLARKE, A.C., 1975
Deviance, Studies in definition, management and treatment.
New York: Oxford Univ. Press. 2nd ed.

RICH, V., 1975
Law and the administration of justice.
New York: John Wiley & Sons.

RUBIN, S., (ED.), 1975
United States prison law. Vols. 1 & 2.
New York: Oceana Publications.

GIBBONS, D.C., 1976
Delinquent behavior.
Englewood Cliffs, N.J.: Prentice-Hall. 2nd ed.

SCHAFER, S., 1976
Introduction to criminology.
Reston, Virginia: Reston Publ. Co.

2 Readings

WINSLOW, R.W., (ED), 1972
The emergence of deviant minorities: social problems and social change.
San Ramon, Calif.: Consensus Publ.

CROMWELL, P.F., JR., AND KEEFER, G., (EDS.), 1973
Police-community relations.
St. Paul, Minn.: West Publishing Co.

CURRAN, J.T., FOWLER, A., AND WARD, R.H., (EDS.), 1973
Police and law enforcement, 1972.
New York: AMS Press.

McCUEN, G.E., (ED)., 1973
America's prisons: correctional institutions or universities of crime.
Anoka: Minn.: Greenhaven Press.

BECKER, G.S., AND LANDES, W.M., (EDS.), 1974
Essays in the economics of crime and punishment.
New York: Columbia Univ. Press.

MESSINGER, S.L., HALLECK, S., LERMAN, P., MORRIS, N., MURPHY, P.V., AND WOLFGANG, M.E., (EDS.), 1974
The Aldine crime and justice annual, 1973
Chicago: Aldine.

PLATT, A., AND COOPER, L., (EDS.), 1974
Policing America.
Englewood Cliffs, N.J.: Prentice-Hall.

QUINNEY, R., (ED.), 1974
Criminal justice in America: a critical understanding.
Boston: Little, Brown & Co.

AKERS, R.L., AND HAWKINS, R., (EDS.),
Law and control in society.
Englewood Cliffs, N.J.: Prentice-Hall.

CAVAN, R.S., (ED.), 1975
Readings in juvenile delinquency.
Philadelphia: J.B. Lippincott.

CHAMBLISS, W.J., (ED.), 1975
Criminal law in action.
Santa Barbara, Calif.: Hamilton.

DAVIS, F.J., AND STIVERS, R., (EDS.), 1975
The collective definition of deviance.
New York: The Free Press.

SKOLNICK, J., AND GRAY, T., (EDS.), 1975
Police in America.
Boston: Little, Brown & Co.

CHAMBLISS, W.J., AND MANKOFF, M., (EDS.), 1976
Whose law? What order?: a conflict approach to criminology.
New York: John Wiley & Sons.

Index